DATA STRUCTURES
USING MODULA-2

DATA STRUCTURES USING MODULA-2

WILLIAM C. JONES, JR.
Central Connecticut State University

WILEY
JOHN WILEY & SONS
New York   Chichester   Brisbane   Toronto   Singapore

Library of Congress Cataloging-in-Publication Data:

Jones, William C. (William Charles), 1944–
   Data structures using Modula-2.

   Bibliography: p. 601
   Includes index.
   1. Modula-2 (Computer program language) 2. Data
structures (Computer science) I. Title.

QA76.73.M63J66 1988   005.7'3   88-5736
ISBN 0-471-60497-6

Printed in the United States of America

10 9 8 7 6 5 4 3 2 1

VAX 780 is a trademark of Digital Equipment Corporation.
Logitech is a trademark of Logitech, Inc.

Dedicated to my daughter, Catherine Anne Jones

HUG O' WAR

I will not play at tug o' war.
I'd rather play at hug o' war,
Where everyone hugs
Instead of tugs,
Where everyone giggles
And rolls on the rug,
Where everyone kisses,
And everyone grins,
And everyone cuddles,
And everyone wins.

—copyright 1983 by Shel Silverstein

PREFACE

For the Student

Niklaus Wirth developed Modula-2 about 10 years after he developed Pascal. Part of his goal was to improve on Pascal. It is easier to avoid certain kinds of programming errors in Modula-2 than in Pascal; Modula-2 also has certain features that make advanced forms of programming easier. These features make Modula-2 much more suitable than Pascal for presenting the subject matter of this book. Ada is just as suitable, but it is a more complicated language than is Modula-2. Thus all the programs in this book are presented in Modula-2.

The central purposes of this book are to help you understand (1) several fundamental data structures and data types, (2) various useful algorithms, and (3) the distinction between an abstract data type (what it can do) and its implementation (how it does it). Modula-2 is merely the vehicle for accomplishing this. It is reasonable for a person to study the material in this book without writing any programs in Modula-2; in particular, Pascal, C, or Ada can be used for writing programs (since they all support recursion, among other features). But if you will be programming in Modula-2 and have not used it before, you will need to study Chapter 1 carefully. Otherwise, you may skim or skip Chapter 1.

Chapter 2 introduces the concept of an abstract data type and gives several examples. It also introduces three important language tools used frequently in this book—library modules, pointers, and recursion.

The remaining chapters cover the standard topics of a data structures and algorithms course. The last few sections in most chapters are starred, which means that they may be skipped or postponed without loss of continuity. This does *not* mean that all of them are less important. As much material as possible was put in starred sections, even what many instructors would consider essential, in order to provide instructors with maximum flexibility in the ordering of topics.

You already know how to write programs. This text will help you learn how to develop much longer, more complicated programs by concentrating on the kinds of relations information values have to one another, independently of the actual coding. Abstraction and modularization are key tools in managing a large programming project. You will also learn to compare several algorithms for efficiency in terms of execution time, space requirements, and amount of programming effort.

For the Instructor

This book covers all the topics recommended by the Association for Computing Machinery for the CS2 course, plus sufficient additional material for the CS7 course. For instance, material on address computations, though peripheral to the main subject of data structures, is recommended for CS2. Extra material is included to allow you a high degree of flexibility in the choice of topics.

The maximum flexibility in sequencing of topics has been incorporated in this text. After you cover the first part of each of Chapters 2 through 5 (the unstarred sections), the rest of the chapters can be covered in any order, except that a few of their later sections (clearly indicated) refer to earlier starred sections. Starred sections can be postponed or deleted as desired. Moreover, the first few sections of Chapter 6 can be covered directly after the unstarred part of Chapter 2, and any one or more of the first few sections of Chapter 7 can be covered after the unstarred part of Chapter 3.

Students who have previously learned to program in Modula-2 can skip Chapter 1. Its purpose is to provide sufficient material so that students who have learned to program in another language need nothing additional other than a short reference manual for the particular Modula-2 compiler they will be using. I assume that most of these students learned Pascal; but the Pascal material is clearly marked so it can be bypassed. This chapter should be valuable in classes where most students have had Modula-2 but in which there are several transfer students who learned Pascal.

Chapter 2 introduces abstract data types with examples. Library modules and recursion are discussed in detail. Pointers to dynamic variables are used only in opaque type declarations and for speeding up execution of array algorithms. This means that, by the time students see NIL and linked lists in Chapter 4, they should be reasonably comfortable with pointers. Some examples of information-handling modules are given—for student records, for excessively big cardinals, and for strings of characters. These modules have some fundamental procedures in common, but of course the names of the modules differ. In most of the book, I assume that imports are coming from InfoADT, although they could as easily come from BigCardADT or LineADT.

Chapter 3 presents several library modules: StackADT, QueueADT, ListADT, TableADT, and DictiADT (the last-named for tables that allow processing values in order). These modules, which import from InfoADT (Section 2.3) or its equivalent, get the student off to an early start in thinking in terms of modularity. The modules are designed to be realistic and flexible, which means that they are more complex than "toy" modules for strictly demonstration purposes. I compensate by beginning with very simple (and often slow-executing) array implementations; the similarities among these first implementations of the modules make it easier to keep it all straight. Later chapters introduce faster implementations.

The approach taken here has a benefit that may not at first be apparent: When a student writes a programming project with a main module that imports from the list-handler ListADT and the information-handler InfoADT, and the student sees that ListADT can easily be replaced by any of the ones written for earlier projects or the ones on the diskette available to instructors, and that InfoADT can similarly be replaced, that student has a concrete concept of modularity and well-defined interfaces. In addition, the student has a useful program development device—first write and debug any one of the three modules as a replacement for the corresponding module in a previous project; then repeat for the other two modules, thereby completely replacing the previous program.

Chapter 4 presents linked lists as an important method of implementing stacks, queues, lists, and tables. No new abstract data types are introduced, but many implementations and applications are presented. Methods of algorithm development are treated more thoroughly here.

Chapter 5 presents binary trees; although recursion has been used frequently before, it occurs in almost every section of Chapter 5. The library module BinADT describes the abstract data-type binary trees. Binary trees are also used for efficient implementations of ListADT, TableADT, and DictiADT. General trees are described abstractly in TreeADT.

Chapter 6 concentrates on sorting algorithms. Chapter 7 presents a number of larger applications, ending with a large program that can be the basis for some larger programming projects; it shows applications of various library modules and reinforces the student's understanding of recursion. I feel that students on this level should study a large program in detail; this one should be accessible and highly profitable. Chapter 8 presents additional abstract data types—graphs, sparse arrays, strings, sets, and generalized lists.

An important pedagogical principle for this material is that students learn by doing, not by reading. That is why almost every section has short exercises—more than 270 with the answers in the back of the book and some 270 more unanswered exercises (marked NA) suitable for homework assignments. These exercises give students a valuable method of testing their understanding of the material; most of the answered exercises can be completed in less than 5 minutes each. Another aid to learning by doing is the partial development of many library modules. Instead of describing them informally, the key type declarations are given and one or two procedures are coded. The student then has a base from which to work. In general, abstractions are supported by plenty of concrete examples, and a high level of mathematical sophistication is not presumed; I feel that this course is the place to begin developing it.

Some texts do an excellent job of presenting abstract data types but omit much of the standard material on data structures and algorithms. Some texts cover the standard topics well, but only partially in the context of abstract data types. I believe that I have avoided both errors in this text.

Additional Features

- Heavy emphasis is placed on the use of *recursion* (where it arises naturally) and *Boolean expressions*. The latter topic is particularly important for computer science majors. Some of the applications do double duty as introductory material on computability and automata, to lay a foundation for later courses.
- *Examples are written with great care* for nomenclature and modularization. Abbreviations are greatly restricted. I almost never use one-character identifiers other than K for a cardinal and P for a pointer, and those only over a short range of statements. Few procedures have as many as 10 Modula-2 statements. Indentation principles are strictly followed.
- Each chapter begins with an *overview* and ends with a *Chapter Review* followed by a *Practice Test* of six to nine short programming problems with answers.
- At the end of each chapter are a dozen or more *Programming Problems* that can be assigned for lab work.
- All programs have been *compiled and run* using the VAX and Logitech Modula-2 compilers.
- An *Instructor's Manual* is available free to instructors who adopt the book. This manual contains solutions to most of the NA exercises and some of the programming problems, as well as notes on subtle points raised by the text.
- A *diskette containing all modules in the text* is available free to instructors who adopt the book. Examples in the book that are parts of modules are rearranged to form compile-and-run modules that can be used for demonstration purposes or in conjunction with programming assignments, a total of 70 compilable modules.

ACKNOWLEDGMENTS

I would like to thank the following reviewers for their many helpful suggestions:

Prof. Siam Ural
Department of Computer Science
University of California-Santa Barbara

Prof. David Poplanski
Department of Mathematics and Computer Science
Michigan Technological University

Prof. Clifford L. Pelletier
Department of Mathematics and Computer Science
Central Connecticut State University

Prof. John P. Grillo
Bentley College

Prof. Ronald White
Jacksonville State University

Prof. Stephen Longo
Department of Computer Science
La Salle College

Dr. Ronald Dutton
Department of Computer Science
University of Central Florida

BRIEF CONTENTS

CONTENTS

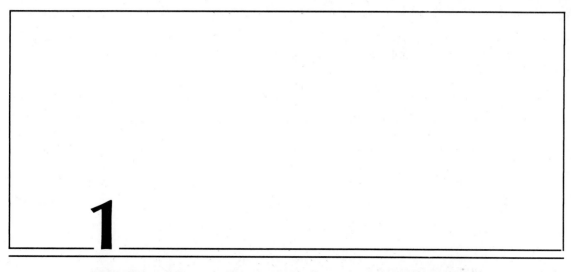

1
ELEMENTARY MODULA-2

This chapter presents the elements of Modula-2 for students who have done little or no programming in Modula-2, although I assume that you have successfully completed and profited from a first course in programming. The programming language you learned could have been PL/1, Pascal, Ada, Modula-2, C, or one of the higher-level forms of FORTRAN or BASIC. If it was Modula-2, you could go directly to Chapter 2; but it might be best to review the subsections on programming style in Sections 1.3, 1.6, and 1.7, and the subsection on address calculations in Section 1.9. If it was another language, you should have already seen almost all the concepts that I describe in this chapter; just the syntax should be different. Topics in this chapter include arrays and records.

Actually, the syntax will not be all that much different from what you are used to. If you will not be writing programs in Modula-2, you should be able to skim this chapter in 1 or 2 hours for a reading ability in Modula-2.

Modula-2 was developed as an improvement on Pascal. Almost all the aspects of Pascal that did not need fixing have been left as they were. Thus Modula-2 looks more like Pascal than any of the other languages just mentioned.

1.1 INTRODUCTION TO MODULA-2; REAL AND CARDINAL TYPES

Two numeric types, REAL and CARDINAL, are discussed in this section; the other simple types defined in Modula-2 are introduced later in this chapter. I will start by telling you just enough about Modula-2 so that you can understand the

1

following sample program reasonably well. After you read it through, I will explain each aspect of it thoroughly.

Just ignore for now the four lines at the top of Example 1.1A. The next few lines tell you that this program computes the total cost, with sales tax, of a number of items purchased in a store. SalesTaxRate stands for the constant 0.075 throughout this program. NumberPurchased is a CARDINAL variable, which means you can store a *nonnegative* integer value in it. A WriteLn statement causes an end-of-output-line action, also known as a carriage return. The FLOAT function converts the integer value in NumberPurchased to a REAL number (i.e.,

EXAMPLE 1.1A _____

```
MODULE Taxing;
FROM InOut     IMPORT ReadCard, WriteCard,
                      WriteString, WriteLn;
FROM RealInOut IMPORT ReadReal, WriteReal;
    (* Accept from the user a number of items purchased and
       the amount paid per item; then report the total cost
       including sales tax. *)
    (* Written by William C. Jones, September, 19-- *)

CONST
    SalesTaxRate = 0.075;
VAR
    CostPerItem, CostWithoutTax, SalesTax : REAL;
    NumberPurchased : CARDINAL;
BEGIN

(* accept from the user the number of items and the cost of
   each item *)
    WriteString ('This is a little calculator program.');
    WriteString ('  How many items did you buy? ');
    ReadCard (NumberPurchased);
    WriteLn;
    WriteString ('How much did you pay for each one? ');
    ReadReal (CostPerItem);
    WriteLn;

(* compute net cost and sales tax *)
    CostWithoutTax := FLOAT (NumberPurchased)
                        * CostPerItem;
    SalesTax := CostWithoutTax * SalesTaxRate;

(* report the total cost including sales tax *)
    WriteString (" The total cost of ");
    WriteCard (NumberPurchased, 1);
    WriteString (" items including tax is ");
    WriteReal (CostWithoutTax + SalesTax, 1);
    WriteLn;

END Taxing.
```

a number with a decimal point) so it can be multiplied by another REAL number and the result stored in the REAL variable CostWithoutTax. The 1 in the Write-Card and WriteReal statements of Example 1.1A prevents extra blanks from being printed in front of the numbers.

Constant-identifiers

The sample program declares five names that are used to identify the constants and variables; they are called **constant-identifiers** and **variable-identifiers**, respectively. The two lines beginning CONST declare SalesTaxRate as the name for the real number 0.075. The value of SalesTaxRate cannot be changed within the program, as indicated by the word **CONST**. These two lines form the **constant section** of this program. A **constant** is any expression whose value can be computed by the compiler at that point in the compilation without evaluating any function. Thus the following constant section would also be legal:

```
CONST    ScreenCharacters = 80 * 25;
         AllBut50 = ScreenCharacters - 50;
```

Variable-identifiers

The two lines beginning **VAR** declare CostPerItem, CostWithoutTax, and Sales-Tax as variable-identifiers—the names for three **REAL** variables. REAL number values always have decimal points. You can only assign a REAL value to a REAL variable; you cannot assign an integer value.

The second line after VAR declares NumberPurchased as the identifier of a **CARDINAL** variable. CARDINAL is the name for nonnegative integers (up to a certain limit, typically 65535 on 16-bit microcomputers). The three lines beginning VAR are called the **VAR section** of the program; they declare all variables used in this program.

Variables in Modula-2 are not initialized to zero or to any other value by the code produced by the compiler; a variable declaration merely reserves space for the value and associates a name with that space. Until a statement is executed that assigns a value to the variable, its value is **indeterminate** (vulgarly known as "garbage").

Some languages do not require you to declare your variables—the type is determined by the name of the variable. The disadvantage of declaring variables is that you waste a minute of your time doing so. The advantage of being required to declare your variables is that sometimes you save hours of your time debugging a program because the compiler tells you that you have a spelling error.

REAL and CARDINAL Expressions

Modula-2 does not allow you to mix CARDINAL and REAL types in an expression. The reason is simple: Almost all implementations of Modula-2 use different methods of representing the two kinds of values in the computer's memory. However, the built-in function **FLOAT** can be used to convert the value of a CARDINAL expression to the corresponding REAL value. There is also a built-in function **TRUNC** that can be used to convert the value of a REAL expression to the corresponding CARDINAL value, dropping the fractional part if any; so TRUNC(2.8) = 2. For example, the following **assignment statement** would be legal in our sample program (the := is called the **assignment symbol**):

```
NumberPurchased := TRUNC (CostPerItem);
```

If you have this statement in your program, you have to be sure that the value of CostPerItem is in the allowable range for CARDINAL values (typically 0 to 65535) at the time of execution of this statement, otherwise the program will terminate abruptly. The two built-in functions FLOAT and TRUNC allow you to mix REAL and CARDINAL values in an expression as long as you explicitly make the conversion from one form to the other.

Input and Output Procedures

In Modula-2, as in Pascal, we use the term **read** to mean "accept input from the user or other outside source (such as a floppy disk file)." Some other languages use the word INPUT or GET. When you refer to the current value of a variable, as in IF X = 3 THEN..., do not call that "reading" the value of X; you could call it "inspecting" or "looking at" the value of X instead. Similarly, we use the term **write** to mean "report information to the user or other outside destination (such as a floppy disk file)." Some other languages use PRINT or PUT.

Input and output are more disciplined in Modula-2 than in most other general-purpose computer languages. For instance, the sample program reads a REAL value into a REAL variable named CostPerItem, so it uses the statement **ReadReal**(CostPerItem). To read a CARDINAL value into a CARDINAL variable named NumberPurchased, it uses the statement **ReadCard**(NumberPurchased). ReadReal(NumberPurchased) cannot be used, since NumberPurchased is not a REAL variable.

A **procedure** is a sequence of statements that can be executed by using the name of the procedure in a statement. ReadReal and ReadCard are names of procedures; thus they are called **procedure-identifiers**. Each of these two procedure statements must have exactly one **parameter** (the variable within the parentheses). If you want to read two REAL values, one into X and another into Y, you have to use the two statements ReadReal(X); ReadReal(Y). *Note:* The character following a numeric value obtained by the ReadReal or ReadCard procedure must be a blank, tab, or end-of-line. You should not have any characters between the last number on a line and the end-of-line.

Similarly, there is a different procedure for each different output situation. **WriteLn** is used to write an end-of-line indicator, such as is produced by pressing the RETURN key on a keyboard; WriteLn has no parameters. **WriteString** is used to write one string of characters, as in WriteString('hello'). This string is delimited by apostrophes (that is, marked at the beginning and end); but that is allowed only if the string does not contain apostrophes. If you wish, you may delimit the string by quote marks, but only if the string does not contain quote marks. For example, WriteString("hello") means exactly the same as WriteString('hello'). But in WriteString("can't") and WriteString(' "Hi" '), the delimiters cannot be changed.

WriteCard is used to write one CARDINAL value. It has two parameters: The first parameter is the CARDINAL expression whose value is to be written, and the second parameter is a CARDINAL expression that tells the minimum number of characters to write (using leading blanks if needed). For example, if N is a CARDINAL variable whose current value is 5137, WriteCard(N, 7) would print three blanks followed by the four characters of 5137 and WriteCard(N, 5) would print only one blank before the four characters of 5137. In no case is the printed value of the number chopped off to make it fit the number of characters specified; WriteCard(N, 1) would write the four characters of 5137 with no leading blanks, just as WriteCard(N, 4) would.

WriteReal is used to write one REAL value; otherwise it behaves like Write-Card. For example, if the current value of SalesTax is 21.13, WriteReal(SalesTax, 7) would print two leading blanks followed by 21.13, but WriteReal(SalesTax, 1) would print just the five characters of 21.13. Some implementations of Modula-2 may, however, use exponential form for the WriteReal procedure; the language does not prescribe the exact form of printed reals.

Comments and Program Structure

Comments (known as remarks in some languages) begin with the two-character combination (* and end with *). Comments can be nested; for example, (* this is a (* comment inside another *) comment *). It is good programming style to give a short description of the purpose of the program in a comment heading, as well as tell the author of the program and the date when it was written.

Each program must have a name; the program in Example 1.1A is named Taxing. This requires that the first line of the sample program be MODULE Taxing and the last line be END Taxing. The statements that prescribe the action to be taken by the program follow the word BEGIN. You can put a semicolon at the end of every statement in Modula-2; the semicolon is optional except when it separates a statement from the next one. In particular, the last semicolon in Example 1.1A is optional, since END is not a statement.

Compilation Units

In Modula-2, a group of related procedures can be collected in one file and compiled separately from the programs that use those procedures. This is of great advantage when the procedures are generally useful. Such a collection of procedures is called a **library module**. A library module can also declare constants and variables; such declarations are normally used to make it convenient to use the procedures in the library module.

A library module is actually compiled in two parts: The **definition module** describes the objects that are declared in the library module; the **implementation module** gives the details of their implementations. The primary difference between them is that the definition module contains just the heading of the procedures; the statements of the procedure are in the implementation module. Thus there are three different kinds of **compilation units** in Modula-2: One kind is the ordinary **program module**, which we normally just call a **program**; the others are the definition module and the implementation module.

InOut is a library module that contains procedures and other declarations for handling input and output. Modula-2 does not have input-output procedures built-in the way they are in most other general-purpose computer languages; you have to **import** the input-output procedures from library modules. Procedures for input and output of reals are in a separate module named RealInOut. The two lines beginning FROM InOut in Example 1.1A form the first **import section**; it allows the program to use the four procedures named there. The second import section allows the program to use the ReadReal and WriteReal procedures. Both these library modules export other identifiers, but I have imported only the ones used in the sample program.

Almost every implementation of Modula-2 will have the InOut and RealInOut modules as described in this book, possibly with some minor differences; for example, some implementations put the declarations for reals in InOut, so there is no separate RealInOut module. The ReadReal procedure typically accepts as input numerals that do not contain decimal points and makes the conversion appropriately.

The final WriteLn in the sample program is necessary because many implementations of Modula-2 do not write the material on a line of text until a WriteLn command (or the equivalent) is issued, except when there is a prompt for input (as with the second and third statements in the sample program). If you omit the final WriteLn, the whole line that tells the results will fail to appear on the screen. Since it is good programming style to code so that the program works the same on all implementations of the language, you should include a final WriteLn in each program.

Some implementations of Modula-2 may put an upper limit on the length of a single line. Thus failure to use WriteLn (or the equivalent) before the 133rd character is printed on a line (or 81st or 255th for some implementations) may cause the program to **crash** (terminate execution prematurely) or to lose some of the output.

Warnings

The following reviews the differences that are most likely to foul up people who are fresh to Modula-2 from another language.

- ☐ You cannot use = for an assignment; use := instead. On the other hand, you cannot use := in a constant declaration; use = instead.
- ☐ When you write :=, do not put a blank between the colon and the equal.
- ☐ Variables are not initialized to zero, just to "garbage."
- ☐ REALs and CARDINALs cannot be combined using an operator; use FLOAT and TRUNC as needed. For example, 7.5 + 100 is illegal.
- ☐ Do not forget the second parameter (usually 1) in WriteReal or WriteCard.
- ☐ You cannot have apostrophes between apostrophes, not even doubled ones as in Pascal (similarly for quote marks).
- ☐ You cannot use input-output procedures without importing them.

Check Your Understanding

1. Rewrite the following program segment to accomplish what the programmer apparently intended.

```
CONST
    PhraseToBeTyped := 'Winter isn''t far away.';
VAR
    N, M : CARDINAL
    X, Y : REAL
BEGIN
    X = 1.3 - M;
    N = 47.0;
    WriteReal (4.72 * 3);
```

2. Write the body of a Modula-2 program to accept two CARDINALs as input and write their product.

3. (NA) Write a Modula-2 program to accept three REALs as input: miles traveled, hours for the trip, and gallons of gas used. Write the miles per gallon and the miles per hour for the trip.

Note: The answers to all Check Your Understanding exercises are in the back of the book except those marked **NA** (which means "no answer"). I think you will do a lot better with this material if you work all exercises not marked NA and check your answer in the back after each one. Your instructor may want to assign the NA exercises for homework.

1.2 TOKENS, SYNTAX, SEMANTICS, AND EBNF

This section reviews some technical definitions and concepts and covers the notation known as Extended Backus-Naur Formalism, which is a way of describing language constructs.

Tokens

A compiler breaks up a Modula-2 program into semantic units (units of meaning) called **tokens**. Tokens can be divided into three categories: word tokens, literals, and special symbols. The **special symbols** include the comma, the left and right parentheses, and the multiplication operator. Most special symbols have one character, but some have two (such as the assignment symbol :=).

Literals are tokens that indicate a constant directly; they include numeric literals (which always begin with a digit or a negative sign) and string literals (which either begin and end with an apostrophe or else begin and end with a quote mark). The ending apostrophe must be on the same line of the program as the beginning one (similarly for quote marks). Numeric literals include **exponential notation**, such as 2.7E4 (for 27000) and 2.7E−4 (for 0.00027); that is, the part after the E tells the power of 10 to be multiplied by the part before the E. One kind of token that Modula-2 does not have is a statement number; Modula-2 has no GOTO statement.

Word tokens in a program can be divided into four categories: reserved words, built-in identifiers, import identifiers, and internally declared identifiers. **Reserved words** are certain words whose meaning is fixed by the language; the reserved words in Example 1.1A are MODULE, FROM, IMPORT, CONST, VAR, BEGIN, and END.

Built-in identifiers are names of objects that are defined by the language; their meaning can be changed by the programmer under certain circumstances, but this is not recommended. The built-in identifiers in the sample program are REAL, CARDINAL, and FLOAT.

Import identifiers are declared by a programmer in another module; the import identifiers in Example 1.1A are the eight mentioned in the three lines of the import sections. **Internally declared identifiers** are declared by the programmer within the module under discussion; the internally declared identifiers in this sample program are SalesTaxRate and the four variable-identifiers.

An identifier is allowed to include digits as well as letters; but its first character (which may be its only character) must be a letter. Most Modula-2 compilers allow very long identifiers, up to 132 or 255 characters; however, they may ignore any characters past the tenth one (or thirty-first or whatever).

Often an identifier is made up of several English words. An identifier must be clearly recognizable by the compiler as denoting a single object, so spaces are not allowed within identifiers. Some languages make an identifier easier to read by allowing special separators within identifiers, as in sales_tax (PL/1) or sales.tax

(BASIC) or sales-tax (COBOL). This sort of thing is not allowed in standard Modula-2; so I capitalize the first letter of English words that appear in the middle of identifiers (as in SalesTax). This makes such "compound identifiers" more easily recognizable, and I strongly recommend the practice to you.

Capitalization and Spacing

The compiler must be able to tell where one token ends and another one begins. This is easy except when a word token is directly followed by a token that begins with letters or digits. So the rule is that two consecutive tokens that begin with letters or digits must be separated by spacing. **Spacing** consists of blanks and ends-of-lines, and perhaps tabs and form-feeds (which cause a start-a-new-page effect), depending on the implementation you are using. Spacing is optional between other kinds of tokens, but I strongly recommend that you use it liberally to improve readability. After all, that is why they make the space bar the easiest key on the keyboard to hit.

Modula-2 is **case-sensitive**, which means that it distinguishes between uppercase and lowercase letters in identifiers. For example, BEGIN, Begin, and begin are considered to be three different words in Modula-2; BEGIN is a reserved word, but Begin and begin are merely identifiers. All reserved words and built-in identifiers in Modula-2 are capitalized.

The only kind of token that can contain a blank is a string literal (as shown in the WriteString statements of Example 1.1A).

Syntax Diagrams

You should be familiar with syntax diagrams as a way of telling what constructs are legal in a computer language. To illustrate, Figure 1 is the syntax diagram of a **statement sequence**, which often occurs in Modula-2 programs. In plain English, a statement sequence is a sequence of one or more statements with semicolons to separate them.

In the syntax diagrams in this book, phrases in lowercase indicate a class of things that can also be defined. Arrows are used to show the order in which things are put together to form the language element being defined. Punctuation (such as the semicolon) and words entirely in uppercase indicate precisely the token written. As another example, the syntax diagram for a normal Modula-2 program module is shown in Figure 2 (I will discuss a "block" shortly).

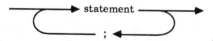

FIGURE 1. *Syntax diagram for a statement sequence.*

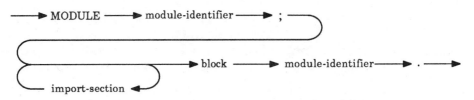

FIGURE 2. Syntax diagram for a program module.

EBNF Notation

The rules for constructing a Modula-2 program module can be specified using
extended Backus-Naur formalism (EBNF), which is much easier to type than a
syntax diagram. The EBNF definitions for a statement sequence and a program
module, logically equivalent to the syntax diagrams just shown, are as follows. If
you have any trouble understanding them, refer back to the syntax diagrams for a
translation.

$ statement-sequence = statement { ";" statement } .
$ program-module = MODULE module-identifier ";"
                 { import-section } block module-identifier "." .

In this symbolism, things within quotes (such as the semicolon and the period) or
entirely capitalized (such as the word MODULE) indicate that particular token.
Words entirely in lowercase and hyphens describe language elements that are
defined elsewhere. The beginning of the definition is indicated by a dollar sign
and the end by a period (not within quotes). The division between the phrase
being defined and its definition is an equals symbol.

There is one other kind of symbol used in the EBNF definition that I have not
yet discussed: the **braces** (vulgarly known as "wavy" parentheses). They indicate
that the material inside them can occur zero or more times. Thus the definition
of a statement-sequence says that you can get by with just one statement; you
can have as many more as you like, as long as you put a semicolon before each
additional one. The definition of a program module says that you can put as many
import sections as you like in your program-module, or even none at all, as long
as they come before the block of the program module.

A **block** has three parts: a number of declaration sections, an action section,
and then the word END. Figure 3 displays the syntax diagram for a block. The
EBNF for a block presents the same information in a different way, namely,

$ block = { declaration } [BEGIN statement-sequence] END .

This definition says that you can have as many declarations as you like (such as
CONST and VAR sections), or even none at all (though this is quite rare). You
may also, if you like, specify some action that the program is to take when it is

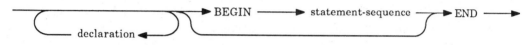

FIGURE 3. *Syntax diagram for a block.*

executed; this is done with BEGIN followed by a statement sequence. You would almost always have an action section, but technically it is optional; that is the meaning of the **brackets** in the EBNF notation (brackets are vulgarly known as "square" parentheses). In general, the material in brackets in a EBNF definition is to appear one time or not at all, at your option. At the very end of a block, you put the word END.

You have only seen two kinds of declaration so far, a CONST section and a VAR section. The EBNF for a CONST section is:

$ const-section = CONST { constant-declaration ";" } .

$ constant-declaration = new-identifier "=" const-expression .

I use "new-identifier" to mean an identifier that has not been declared in any other way for the block to which the CONST section belongs.

A **type-denoter** is any word or phrase that denotes a type from which the values of a variable can be chosen. The only type-denoters you have seen so far are the type-identifiers CARDINAL and REAL. The EBNF for a VAR section is:

$ var-section = VAR { variable-declaration ";" } .

$ variable-declaration = new-identifier { "," new-identifier } ":" type-denoter .

There is one other kind of EBNF notation: A vertical bar is used to indicate that any one of several alternatives is allowed for a given construct. The bar can be read as "OR." For example, a **compilation unit** is EITHER a program module OR a definition module OR an implementation module; this is expressed in EBNF notation as:

$ compilation-unit = program-module | definition-module
                          | implementation-module .

The Empty Statement

Perhaps you noticed that the one sample program you have seen so far appears to violate the definitions just given. That is, the definition of a statement sequence does not allow a semicolon after the last statement in the sequence. There is, however, a real advantage in allowing a semicolon after every statement: It makes it easier for the programmer to delete or add statements in the sequence later without causing a syntax error. So Modula-2 allows a statement to consist of no tokens at all; this **empty statement** is a useful fiction to give people a choice on whether to use the "terminating semicolon." Thus BEGIN WriteLn; END actually has two statements in the statement sequence: a procedure statement (calling the WriteLn procedure) and an empty statement (between the semicolon and the word END).

Warnings

The following are a few aspects of Modula-2 that are likely to cause you difficulty when you first start programming in Modula-2.

- [ ] When you start a string literal with an apostrophe, the ending apostrophe must be on the same line with the beginning apostrophe (similarly for quote marks).
- [ ] You cannot use underscores or periods within identifiers.
- [ ] You must capitalize all reserved words and built-in identifiers. And, when you declare an identifier with certain letters capitalized, you must write all uses of that identifier with the same capitalization.

Check Your Understanding

1. Write out your best guess for the EBNF definition of an import section, based on the one sample program you have seen.

2. Write out an EBNF definition for each of the two kinds of nonempty statements that appear in Example 1.1A. Use the terms "expression," "variable-designator," and "procedure-designator" in your EBNF definitions without defining them.

3. (NA) The paragraph following the EBNF definition for a block gives the meaning of the definition in ordinary English. Write a similar paragraph for a var-section.

4. (NA) Same directions as in Exercise 3, but for a variable-declaration.

1.3 FUNDAMENTAL CONTROL STATEMENTS; BOOLEAN TYPE

This section discusses the most commonly used control statements in Modula-2: WHILE, IF, FOR, and REPEAT. Most of these statements require the use of BOOLEAN expressions and variables, which are also discussed in this section. The following examples illustrate the syntax of WHILE and IF statements in Modula-2:

```
ReadReal (X);              IF X > 0 THEN
WHILE X > 0 DO                 WriteString ('It is positive');
    WriteReal (X, 1);      ELSE
    ReadReal (X);              WriteString ("It's too small");
END;                       END;
```

The WHILE statement tests whether the value of X is positive. Each time the test yields a TRUE result, the two statements between DO and END are executed and the test repeated. When the test yields a FALSE result (i.e., the value of X is not positive), execution of the WHILE statement is terminated.

The IF statement also tests whether the value of X is positive. If it is, the phrase "It is positive" is printed; if the value of X is not positive, the phrase "It's too small" is printed. There is a more general form of the IF statement that is quite often useful; an example is:

```
IF X > 0 THEN
    WriteString ('It is positive');
ELSIF X = 0 THEN
    WriteString ('It is zero');
ELSE
    WriteString ('It is negative');
END;
```

The ELSE clause is optional; if used, it must come after all ELSIF clauses. ELSIF clauses can be used as many times as desired. The syntax diagrams for the WHILE and IF statements are shown in Figure 4. Example 1.3A illustrates the use of these statements in a program (the operator # means "not equal").

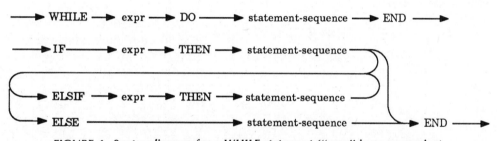

FIGURE 4. Syntax diagram for a WHILE statement ("expr" is an expression).

EXAMPLE 1.3A _____

```
MODULE SentinelValue;
FROM InOut     IMPORT WriteString, WriteLn;
FROM RealInOut IMPORT ReadReal, WriteReal;
     (* Read bank transactions and tell what % are checks *)
     (* Written by William C. Jones, May 19-- *)

VAR
    CheckCount  : CARDINAL; (* Number of negatives so far*)
    TotalCount  : CARDINAL; (* Number of values so far   *)
    Transaction : REAL;     (* Most recently read value  *)
BEGIN

(* give description of program to user *)
    WriteString ('This program tells what percentage of ');
    WriteString ('transactions are checks (negative).');
    WriteLn;
    WriteString ('Enter transactions to be processed.  ');
    WriteString ('When done, enter 0.');
    WriteLn;

(* read transactions and compute the counts *)
    CheckCount := 0;
    TotalCount := 0;
    ReadReal (Transaction);
    WHILE Transaction # 0.0 DO
        IF Transaction < 0.0 THEN
            CheckCount := CheckCount + 1;
        END;
        TotalCount := TotalCount + 1;
        ReadReal (Transaction);
    END;

(* print the results *)
    WriteString ('The percentage of checks entered was ');
    WriteReal (100.0 * FLOAT (CheckCount) /
                        FLOAT (TotalCount), 1);
    WriteLn;

END SentinelValue.
```

The FOR Statement

The following segments of program code illustrate the FOR statement. The one on the left prints all the integers from 50 up to 200, inclusive. The one on the right prints all the multiples of 25 from 1000 down to 100, inclusive.

```
FOR K := 50 TO 200 DO      FOR Count := 1000 TO 100 BY -25 DO
    WriteCard (K, 5);          WriteCard (Count, 1);
END;                           WriteString (', ');
                           END;
```

The FOR statement has a number of restrictions on how it can be used. You can only use a simple variable-identifier as the **control variable** (such as, K in the first FOR statement and Count in the second FOR statement). The body of the loop cannot change the value of the control variable; the FOR statement itself takes care of that. Most importantly, you cannot count on the value of K being 200 when the first FOR statement terminates; it might be 201 or some entirely unrelated value. In general, the value of the control variable is indeterminate after a FOR statement is executed.

The BY clause in a FOR statement tells by how much the value of the control variable is to be changed on each iteration of the loop; this quantity is called the **BY value**. If the BY clause is missing, 1 is added to the control variable on each iteration (in other words, the BY value **defaults** to 1). The expression in the BY clause must be a constant integer expression; in particular, no variables or functions can be used in the expression, although operators can be used. However, any expression of the same type as the control variable is allowed before and after TO.

If Limit is a variable with the value 6, then FOR K := 8 TO Limit DO Write-Card(Limit, 1); END does not write anything at all, nor does it crash the program. Since the BY value is 1 (by default) and the initial value of K is already above the final value, the body of the loop is not executed. Similarly, FOR K := 3 TO Limit BY −1 does not cause any iterations when Limit is 6.

The REPEAT Statement

The following two program segments have exactly the same effect when the program user enters at least one nonzero number. Either segment computes the product of a list of numbers read in until a **sentinel value** of 0 is seen.

```
Product := 1.0;                      Product := 1.0;
ReadReal (Value);                    ReadReal (Value);
REPEAT                               WHILE Value # 0.0 DO
    Product := Product * Value;          Product := Product * Value;
    ReadReal (Value);                    ReadReal (Value);
UNTIL Value = 0.0;                   END;
```

There are only two differences between the REPEAT and WHILE statements (other than the syntax): In WHILE, the condition is checked *before* the loop is executed; in REPEAT, the condition is not checked until *after* the loop executes once. After the given condition is checked, the statement sequence subordinate to WHILE is executed when the condition was found to be TRUE; the statement sequence subordinate to REPEAT is executed when the condition is found to be FALSE.

The IF, WHILE, REPEAT, and FOR statements are called **control statements**, since they control the order in which statements are executed. In the absence of a control statement, statements are executed in the order in which they are written. Modula-2 has several other control statements, which are discussed later in this chapter.

Boolean Expressions

The expression that follows WHILE, UNTIL, IF or ELSIF must be a **Boolean expression**, that is, an expression that has one of the two values **TRUE** or **FALSE**. Another name for a Boolean expression is a **condition**. One way of forming a condition is to place a **relational operator** between two expressions of the same type. The seven relational operators that can be used in that way are <, <=, >, >=, =, <>, and #. <> is an alternative to # for the "not equal" operation; most Modula-2 compilers allow the use of <>. Note that greater-equal is expressed by >=, not by =>. Similarly, less-equal is expressed by <=, not by =<. No blank is allowed between the two characters of >= or <= or <>.

A condition can be formed by putting **NOT** in front of a condition; this reverses the sense of the condition (evaluating as TRUE if the condition was FALSE, as FALSE if the condition was TRUE). A condition can also be formed by using AND or OR to combine two conditions.

Assume that B and C are both conditions. Then the condition B **AND** C is TRUE only if B is TRUE and also C is TRUE; the condition is FALSE if B is FALSE or if B is TRUE and C is FALSE. The condition B **OR** C is FALSE only if B is FALSE and also C is FALSE; the condition is TRUE if B is TRUE or if B is FALSE and C is TRUE. *Note:* Many implementations of Modula-2 allow ~ in place of NOT, and all allow & in place of AND.

This definition of AND is different from the one used in certain other computer languages, notoriously Pascal. To see the difference, consider a statement that begins IF (X # 0.0) AND (Y/X > 4.0) THEN.... This is apparently an attempt to be sure that we do not divide by zero. Such a statement is silly in Pascal; if X is zero, a Pascal compiler will (probably) go ahead and compute Y/X > 4.0 in any case, since that is the way the language is supposed to work. The definition of AND in Modula-2 says that, if X # 0.0 is FALSE, the condition after AND is not to be evaluated. This is called **partial evaluation** or **short-circuiting**. Partial evaluation also is used for conditions formed with OR; that is, in evaluating B OR C, if the processor finds that B is TRUE, it does not evaluate C.

Boolean Variables

Since there are Boolean expressions in Modula-2, it follows that there should be Boolean variables. That is, there are variables to which you can assign the value TRUE or the value FALSE or any expression that has one of those two values. TRUE and FALSE are constant-identifiers (since they are the names of constants). For example, if you declare SeenALittleOne as a variable of type **BOOLEAN**, you can execute the statement SeenALittleOne := TRUE, since TRUE is a Boolean value. You can also execute the statement SeenALittleOne := (Max<Lower-

Limit), since the expression in parentheses is either TRUE or FALSE at that point in the execution of the program. Note the analogy with N := (Max+Lower-Limit) (assuming that N, Max, and LowerLimit identify CARDINAL variables). The former is just as valid as the latter, since < and + are both operators that yield values.

Boolean variables are often used within IF...THEN or WHILE...DO. For instance, you might want to find out whether a sequence of numbers contains a number larger than 100. If the sequence is terminated by a sentinel value of 0, you could use the following coding:

```
REPEAT
    ReadCard (Value);
    BigNumberSeen := Value > 100;
UNTIL BigNumberSeen OR (Value = 0);
IF BigNumberSeen THEN
    WriteString ('There was a big number.');
END;
```

PROGRAMMING STYLE

The three kinds of looping statements just described allow the programmer a good deal of flexibility. Good programming style dictates that REPEAT should be used if the statement sequence is to be executed at least once in all possible situations, otherwise WHILE should be used, with two exceptions: If the number of iterations can be expressed easily, a FOR statement should normally be used. And certain rare situations dictate that a LOOP statement (described later in this chapter) should be used.

In Example 1.3A, TotalCount must be initialized to 0 before the statement that adds 1 to it is executed; otherwise you would be adding 1 to an indeterminate value. By contrast, Transaction is not initialized to 0 before the ReadReal statement is executed, since ReadReal does not require that the variable already have a value. Similarly, Example 1.1A did not initialize SalesTax to 0 before executing the statement SalesTax := CostWithoutTax * SalesTaxRate—you do not have to have a value in a variable before an assignment is made to that variable. The two kinds of initialization just described are **extraneous initializations**, since they might as well have not been made. Extraneous statements are poor programming style.

The pattern of indentation used in the programs in this book is carefully planned to make the overall structure of the program and of the statement part of the program as clear as possible to someone who reads the program:

☐ The words MODULE, FROM, EXPORT, PROCEDURE, TYPE, CONST, VAR, and BEGIN are in the far left margin, together with the END that matches that BEGIN (we discuss EXPORT, PROCEDURE, and TYPE later). All other material is indented at least four blanks from that.

☐ For statements that contain statement sequences, END, ELSE, ELSIF, and UNTIL are aligned with the first word of their statements, and the entire subordinate statement sequence is indented four blanks.

☐ Each statement starts on a new line, aligned with the other statements in its statement sequence.

Syntax for the Fundamental Control Statements

The syntax of the fundamental kinds of control statements in Modula-2 is given by the following EBNF definitions. The > in place of = means that what follows is only a partial definition of the language element mentioned at the left. In other words, the following EBNF says that a statement is defined to be any one of a number of different things, only four of which are listed here.

```
$ statement > WHILE expression DO statement-sequence END
            | REPEAT statement-sequence UNTIL expression
            | FOR variable-identifier ":=" expression TO expression
                [ BY const-expression ] DO statement-sequence END
            | IF expression THEN statement-sequence
                { ELSIF expression THEN statement-sequence }
                [ ELSE statement-sequence ] END .
```

Warnings

The following is a review of some aspects of Modula-2 that may cause trouble to people who are used to programming in other languages.

☐ Write ELSIF as all one word without an interior E.

☐ Put an END to every IF, WHILE, and FOR, even if it has only one statement in its statement sequence. BEGIN is not part of any statement.

☐ Never assign a new value to the control variable inside the statement sequence of a FOR statement. If you feel the FOR statement should have such an assignment, write the loop as a WHILE or REPEAT statement instead.

☐ A Boolean expression formed with a relational operator (=, >, etc.) must be within parentheses if it is an operand of AND, OR, or NOT.

Check Your Understanding

1. Write a program segment that uses a FOR statement to print the multiples of 6 from 30 to 98, inclusive.

2. What change should be made in Example 1.3A to use a REPEAT statement, if you assume that at least one nonzero integer will be entered?

3. Write each of these two statements as a single assignment statement:

```
IF (X > 5) AND (U <= 7) THEN     IF X > 5 THEN
    Condition := TRUE;               Condition := TRUE;
ELSE                             ELSE
    Condition := FALSE;              Condition := TimeToStop;
END;                             END;
```

4. (NA) Modify Example 1.3A so it asks the user of the program for the number of transactions to be entered, then reads that many transactions and reports what percentage of them were negative.

5. (NA) Modify Example 1.3A to also report the total of the values of the checks entered.

1.4 EXTERNAL FILES

In this section, I discuss how you can read from or write to a file that is stored on a device external to main memory, such as a floppy disk or hard disk. Then you can write material using your program editor and have a program read it.

File Input and Output

READ statements (such as ReadReal and ReadCard) take input from the current **input channel**, which is the keyboard by default. **WRITE statements** (such as WriteReal, WriteCard, and WriteLn) send output to the current **output channel**, which defaults to the screen. It is often desirable to change one or both of these channels to be a file stored on a floppy disk or other medium; the InOut library module makes it easy to do this.

OpenInput and **CloseInput** are two procedures that can be imported from InOut. With most implementations of Modula-2, when you execute the statement OpenInput(''), the system asks the user for the name of the external file from which the information is to be read. Then, if there is such a file, it becomes the input channel. This means that every use of ReadReal, ReadCard, or any other input procedure imported from InOut or RealInOut refers to that external file instead of to the keyboard. This continues until the statement CloseInput is executed, at which point the input channel becomes the keyboard again.

For instance, in Example 1.3A, the numbers can be read from a floppy disk file instead of from the keyboard. All you need to do is put OpenInput('') as the first statement, CloseInput as the last statement, and add those two procedure-identifiers to the list of identifiers imported from InOut.

The analogous situation holds for output. **OpenOutput('')** causes the system to ask the user for the name of the floppy disk file (or whatever file) to which the information is to be written. All output generated by WriteReal, WriteCard, WriteLn, or any other output procedure in InOut or RealInOut goes to that external file instead of to the user's screen. This continues until **CloseOutput** is executed, at which point the output channel switches back to the user's screen.

The two open statements can have any reasonable string of characters inside the parentheses rather than the **null string** shown (the string with no characters in it). The effect differs from one implementation to another. For some implementations, the string names the default file, that is, the file to open if the user simply presses return when asked for the name of a file. For other implementations, the string names the default file extension.

The next sample program imports a Boolean variable **Done** from the library module InOut. Each execution of a READ statement should cause Done to be set to TRUE or FALSE. Done is assigned TRUE if the READ statement was executed ("done") without problems, otherwise Done is assigned FALSE. Done is tested to find out whether the end of the file has been reached or the file requested by OpenInput exists. The program (Example 1.4A) should not crash if ReadCard encounters a letter instead of a digit or encounters the end of the file. *Caution:* Some implementations may crash the program for some failures of attempts to read.

When the user of the program is entering values at the keyboard, the program can test Done to see if end-of-file has occurred. The signal that the user gives to indicate that he or she is finished entering values might be a CTRL/Z or CTRL/D or something else, depending on the implementation.

Check Your Understanding

1. What changes should be made in Example 1.3A so that the answers are written to an external file rather than to the screen?

2. Write a statement sequence that reads REALs from a file until end-of-file is reached and then tells the user the sum of those REALs.

3. (NA) Write a program in Modula-2 that reads 20 CARDINALs from the keyboard and writes all the ones above 1000 to an external file.

4. (NA) Write a program in Modula-2 that reads CARDINALs from a file until end-of-file is reached and then tells the user the smallest one that was seen.

EXAMPLE 1.4A _____

```
MODULE FindLargest;
FROM InOut IMPORT ReadCard, WriteCard, WriteString,
                WriteLn, Done, OpenInput, CloseInput,
                OpenOutput, CloseOutput;
    (* Find largest of one or more cardinals read from the
       input file and print the result to the output file.
       Also say if none were below a specified LowerLimit *)
    (* Written by William C. Jones, September 19-- *)

CONST
    LowerLimit = 100;
VAR
    Largest,                  (* Largest number seen so far *)
    Value : CARDINAL;         (* Most recently read number  *)
    SeenALittleOne : BOOLEAN;  (* Seen a little one yet? *)
BEGIN

(* tell the user the purpose of the program *)
    WriteString ('This program finds the largest of some');
    WriteString (' nonnegative integers.');
    WriteLn;

(* read the input file and do computations *)
    OpenInput ('');
    ReadCard (Largest);
    SeenALittleOne :=  Largest < LowerLimit;
    ReadCard (Value);
    WHILE Done DO
        IF Value > Largest THEN
            Largest := Value;
        ELSIF Value < LowerLimit THEN
            SeenALittleOne := TRUE;
        END;
        ReadCard (Value);
    END;
    CloseInput;

(* write the answers to the output file *)
    OpenOutput ('');
    WriteString ('The largest of the numbers entered is ');
    WriteCard (Largest, 1);
    IF NOT SeenALittleOne THEN
        WriteString ('; none were less than ');
        WriteCard (LowerLimit, 1);
    END;
    WriteLn;
    CloseOutput;

END FindLargest.
```

1.5   INTEGER TYPE; OPERATORS AND EXPRESSIONS

In this section, you will learn about the INTEGER type and how it compares with the CARDINAL type. Also, I describe all the integer operators used in Modula-2; DIV and MOD might be new to you.

INTEGER Type

Another built-in type-identifier in Modula-2 is **INTEGER**, which includes both negative and positive integers, as well as 0. For microcomputers, it is typical to have the range of values for INTEGER be from −32767 to 32767, inclusive, and the range for CARDINAL be from 0 to 65535, inclusive. This is because 65535 is the largest 16-digit integer in base 2 (the **binary system**), and usually 16 **bits** (*B*inary dig*ITS*) of storage space are used for storing integers. To store positive and negative integers in such a storage location, one bit has to be used for the sign, which leaves only 15 bits for the digits; 32767 is the largest 15-digit integer in base 2.

ReadInt and **WriteInt** can be imported from InOut; they are analogous to ReadCard and WriteCard. In particular, WriteInt has a second parameter that tells the minimum number of characters to use in printing the value.

INTEGER and CARDINAL are two different types. You cannot add an INTEGER expression to a CARDINAL expression, just as you cannot add a REAL expression to a CARDINAL expression. For example, if Int is declared as an INTEGER variable and Card is declared as a CARDINAL variable, then both Int := Int+Card and Card := Int−Card are illegal.

You have seen the built-in FLOAT and TRUNC functions, used to convert between CARDINAL and REAL values. You can use the type-identifiers INTEGER and CARDINAL as built-in functions to transfer between CARDINAL and INTEGER values. With Int and Card declared as before, Int := Int + INTEGER(Card) and Card := CARDINAL(Int)−Card would be used to avoid any difficulty with trying to combine two different types of objects in the same expression.

Modula-2 does have one situation in which strict type-checking is relaxed; this is the only such situation other than for subranges, described later in this chapter. It is legal to *assign* an INTEGER value to a CARDINAL variable or vice versa. With Int and Card declared as before, Int := Card and Card := Int are legal. However, a run-time crash occurs if Card := Int is executed when Int is negative, or if Int := Card is executed when Card is too large. Also, Int := Card−1 will cause a crash when Card has the value 0, since the expression is of CARDINAL type and a CARDINAL expression cannot have the value −1. If you are worried about this happening, you can prevent it by using Int := INTEGER(Card)−1. In summary, INTEGER and CARDINAL types are **assignment-compatible** but not operator-compatible.

Numeric Operators

Five operators can be used to combine two CARDINAL expressions to obtain a new CARDINAL expression. They are + (addition), − (subtraction), ∗ (multiplication), DIV (quotient from division), and MOD (remainder from division). DIV and MOD might be new to you, so I present a few examples:

20 DIV 7 = 2, the quotient	20 MOD 7 = 6, the remainder
23 DIV 5 = 4, the quotient	23 MOD 5 = 3, the remainder
16 DIV 4 = 4, the quotient	16 MOD 4 = 0, the remainder
0 DIV 3 = 0, the quotient	0 MOD 3 = 0, the remainder

The second operand of DIV or MOD cannot be zero, since it does not make sense to divide by zero. Some implementations of Modula-2 do not allow 0 to be the first operand of MOD. The same five operators are used to combine two INTEGER expressions to obtain a new INTEGER expression, with the same meaning. The first operand of MOD must be nonnegative.

For REAL expressions, only +, −, ∗, and / can be used to obtain a REAL expression from two REAL expressions. / means ordinary division; it causes a crash of the program if the second operand is zero.

The program segment in Example 1.5A computes the least common multiple (LCM) of two positive integers, assuming that some of the variables are of INTEGER type and others are of CARDINAL type. Note carefully the type conversions. In the FOR clause, Factor must be assigned a CARDINAL value, so First is converted. Two of the three variables in the IF condition are INTEGER, so the third one (Factor) is converted to INTEGER. No conversion is needed for assignments of INTEGERs to CARDINALs or vice versa, so LCM could be of either INTEGER or CARDINAL type.

The ODD and ABS Functions

Two useful built-in functions are ODD and ABS. **ODD**(X) accepts any INTEGER or CARDINAL expression and returns a value of either TRUE or FALSE, depend-

EXAMPLE 1.5A _____

```
(* Find the least common multiple of First and Second,
   which are INTEGER variables.  Factor is a CARDINAL
   variable.  LCM can be either INTEGER or CARDINAL.   *)

  FOR Factor := CARDINAL (First) TO 1 BY -1 DO
      IF INTEGER (Factor) * Second MOD First = 0 THEN
         LCM := Factor * CARDINAL (Second);
      END;
  END;
```

ing on whether the value of the expression is odd or not. **ABS(X)** accepts any numeric expression and returns the absolute value of X; the type of the returned value is the same as that of the given expression.

Precedence of Operators

In algebra you learned that the expression A+B*C is evaluated by first multiplying B by C and then adding the result to A. However, (A+B)*C is evaluated by first adding B to A and then multiplying the result by C. A−B+C is evaluated by first subtracting B from A and then adding C to that result. These evaluations are familiar applications of the three **rules of precedence**:

1. An operator of higher precedence is evaluated before one of lower precedence.
2. Operators of equal precedence are evaluated from left to right.
3. The two preceding rules of precedence can be overridden by the appropriate use of parentheses.

The operator of highest precedence is NOT (and its equivalent ~ when available). Next come the multiplication-like operators: * / DIV MOD AND &. Next come the addition-like operators: + − OR. Of lowest precedence are the **relational operators** such as <= and #. Note that AND takes precedence over OR, and that parentheses are required around an expression using a relational operator when that expression is an operand of AND or OR. Figure 5 shows the precedences graphically.

Warnings

The following aspects of Modula-2 may cause you some trouble in the first few programs you write.

- ☐ Do not combine INTEGER and CARDINAL expressions in the same expression without using explicit transfer functions.
- ☐ Do not use MOD with a negative first operand.
- ☐ Watch out for an expression of the form Card−1 where Card is a CARDINAL variable that can have the value 0 (and similar situations).

Check Your Understanding

1. If A is 16, B is 3, and C is 5, find the values of the following:
   (a) A * B MOD C (b) A * B DIV C (c) A MOD B DIV C

2. In Example 1.5A, what would be the effect of replacing the line beginning FOR by: FOR Factor := 1 TO CARDINAL(First) DO?

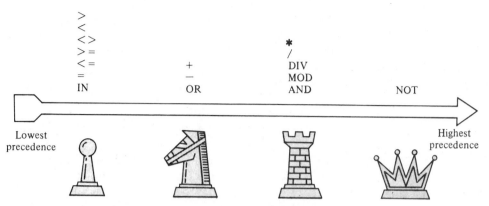

FIGURE 5. *Precedence of operators in Modula-2.*

3. (NA) Rewrite the FOR statement in Example 1.5A as a WHILE statement that increases Factor on each iteration and finds the correct answer sooner.

4. (NA) Write a program to find the greatest common divisor of two input numbers. *Hint:* What is the product of the greatest common divisor with the least common multiple? If you do not know, experiment to find out.

1.6 PROCEDURES AND PARAMETERS

The purpose of a procedure is to accomplish a single well-defined task. It is a good idea to avoid having very long procedures, since that makes it harder for the reader of the program to comprehend the procedure as a whole. I normally aim for three to seven statements in a procedure, and I very rarely have more than 10. I find that having more than 10 usually makes a procedure too difficult to comprehend easily. In connection with this, note that the statement part of the programs earlier in this chapter were divided into short algorithmic units of at most 10 statements, each with a well-defined task described by the comment heading the unit.

Statement and Function Procedures

The vocabulary of Modula-2 distinguishes two kinds of procedures: A **statement procedure** is called by using the procedure-identifier as a statement (together with any parameters). A **function procedure** is called by using the procedure-identifier in an expression to be evaluated (together with any parameters). The parameters listed in the procedure call are its **actual parameters**; the parameters listed in the procedure heading and used in the statements of the procedure are called the **formal parameters** of the procedure.

The statement procedure in the next example is named GetInput. It has two formal parameters named First and Second, both of type INTEGER. Since both are **VAR parameters** (indicated by the *VAR* in the parentheses of the procedure heading), the corresponding actual parameters must be VARiables of type INTE-GER. The actual parameters happen to have the same names, but that is not required; the correspondence of parameters is by position in the parameter lists, not by name. For instance, the first actual parameter of any procedure call is associated with the first formal parameter in the procedure heading regardless of the names used. The main point about VAR parameters is that the formal parameter is an *alias* for the actual parameter throughout execution of the procedure; that is, any reference to the formal parameter is in fact a reference to the actual parameter.

In Example 1.6A, LCM is the name of the function procedure. LCM has two formal parameters named First and Second, both of type CARDINAL. Both are **value parameters** (indicated by the lack of VAR before either of their names). This means that the actual parameters must be expressions whose *VALUE* is to be assigned to the formal parameters just before execution of the statements of the procedure. The use of CARDINAL parameters for LCM instead of INTEGER allows First∗Second to be a larger value and probably permits the program to execute faster.

A function procedure differs from a statement procedure in four respects:

1. The last part of the heading (": CARDINAL" in this case) tells the **result type**, the kind of value that will be returned to the statement that **activated** (called) the function procedure.
2. Execution of a function procedure must terminate by executing a RETURN statement. The RETURN statement must include an expression to tell the value to be returned to the calling statement. That expression must be of a type that can be assigned to a variable of the given result type.
3. A function procedure is activated by being used in an expression rather than by being used as a statement.
4. Parentheses are required in a function heading and in each use of a function identifier, even if it does not have any formal parameters.

If a declaration of an identifier is between the second word of a procedure heading and the END of that procedure, we say the declaration of that identifier is **contained by** that procedure. If the declaration of an identifier is not *contained by* any procedure, we say that declaration is **global** to the program. Otherwise, the declaration is said to be **local** to the procedure that **closest contains** that declaration. The program in Example 1.6A has six locally declared identifiers:

☐ GetInput declares First and Second as identifiers of VAR parameters.

EXAMPLE 1.6A _____

```
MODULE FindLeastCommonMultiple;
FROM InOut IMPORT WriteString, WriteLn, Done,
                  WriteInt, ReadInt;
    (* Print the least common multiple of any two
       nonzero integers supplied by the user *)
    (* Written by William C. Jones, May 19-- *)
(***********************************************************)

PROCEDURE  GetInput (VAR First, Second : INTEGER);
    (* Get two nonzero integer values from the user *)
BEGIN

    REPEAT
        WriteString ('Enter a nonzero integer: ');
        ReadInt (First);
        WriteLn;
        WriteString ('Enter another: ');
        ReadInt (Second);
        WriteLn;
    UNTIL Done AND (First # 0) AND (Second # 0);

END GetInput;
(***********************************************************)

PROCEDURE LCM (First, Second : CARDINAL) : CARDINAL;
    (* Find the least common multiple of First and Second*)
VAR
    K, Result : CARDINAL;
BEGIN

    FOR K := First TO 1 BY -1 DO
        IF K * Second MOD First = 0 THEN
            Result := K * Second;
        END;
    END;
    RETURN Result;

END LCM;
(***********************************************************)

VAR
    First, Second : INTEGER;  (* the input from the user *)

BEGIN           (* program *)

    GetInput (First, Second);
    WriteString ('Their least common multiple is ');
    WriteInt (LCM (ABS (First), ABS (Second)), 1);
    WriteLn;

END FindLeastCommonMultiple.
```

☐ LCM declares First and Second as identifiers of VALUE parameters.

☐ LCM declares K and Result as identifiers of local variables.

Thus there are three different declarations of the identifier First in this program, only one of which is global.

➤ PROGRAMMING STYLE

Quite honestly, the LCM function is not written in the best of style, because I wanted to illustrate some things about functions. For one thing, the statement part of the function could be written as follows:

```
FOR K := 1 TO First DO    (* UNTIL RETURN *)
    IF K * Second MOD First = 0 THEN
        RETURN K * Second;
    END;
END;
```

This is a shorter and simpler way to compute the least common multiple. Note that I put a comment that makes it clear to the reader that this FOR statement may not execute for all values of K. It is good style to indicate when the reader's expectations may be disappointed. Some people may argue that it is not proper to RETURN from within a FOR statement, since a FOR statement promises the reader that it will execute the number of times indicated by its heading. By that logic, there should be no RETURN from within a WHILE statement either, since a WHILE statement promises the reader that it will execute until the condition given in its heading becomes true. So some instructors feel that it is bad programming style to have a RETURN statement inside any looping statement. *Reminder:* The most important promise that a FOR statement makes is that it is not an infinite loop (since the language makes it illegal to change the value of the control variable inside the loop).

Comments describing the task performed by a procedure, program, or other algorithmic unit are essential in helping someone understand your coding, unless you can be sure that the someone has ready access to external documentation. Since most procedures in this book are explained in the accompanying text (the external documentation), some of them have less such documentation that they would in a stand-alone context. For the same reason, the description of itself that a program displays for the user is also skimpier in this book than it would be in a stand-alone program. Your programs should have comment descriptions for most (if not all) procedures; procedures should rarely be more than 10 statements long.

It is of utmost importance that the nature of the value stored in each variable be easily understood by the reader of the coding. The most effective means of doing this is the choice of the identifier of the variable; self-documenting names such as LargestSeenSoFar leave no one in doubt. This is often impractical when the variable is used more than three or four times or when the nature is not easily described in 10 to 20 characters; in such cases, a **table of identifiers** (as illustrated in the VAR section of Example 1.4A) describing the function of each variable is valuable. *Exception:* If a variable is only used over a very short span of statements, such as the variable K in Example 1.6A, the coding itself is usually enough to make its function clear. *Exception to the exception:* Do not have more than one or two such variable identifiers, or it becomes confusing anyway. Also, it is a good idea to use a consistent notation; for instance, I habitually use K for a local integer variable, usually one that goes in steps of 1.

VALUE Parameters versus VAR Parameters

Note that a CARDINAL value is the actual parameter of the WriteInt procedure in Example 1.6A. This is legal, since the formal parameter of WriteInt is an INTEGER value parameter, and you can assign a CARDINAL value to an INTEGER variable. A VALUE parameter is just like a local variable of the procedure with one difference: Its value is initialized to the value of the actual parameter, which must therefore be an expression. By contrast, invoking a procedure with a VAR parameter does not create a local variable for the VAR parameter; instead, the storage location assigned to the actual parameter is used. Therefore, the actual parameter of a formal VAR parameter must be a variable of exactly the same type.

The global variable First is an actual parameter of both procedures in Example 1.6A. When GetInput causes a change in its formal VAR parameter named First, that causes a change in the global variable First, since they both refer to the same storage location. But if you were to insert a statement in the LCM procedure that changed its formal VALUE parameter named First, that would have no effect on the global variable First; the two are distinct variables.

It is illegal to have the control variable of a FOR statement be an actual VAR parameter, a formal parameter, or an imported variable. As a general rule, you should always declare the control variable local to the procedure that closest contains it. In fact, any variable used in a program should be declared as locally as the logic of the program allows.

As a general rule, when a procedure is called for the purpose of assigning a value to a variable, the variable should be passed as a VAR parameter; otherwise it should not. An exception arises when the variable requires a large amount of storage, as for large arrays—execution is faster if such variables are passed as VAR parameters, even if they are not changed by the procedure. Figure 6 diagrams these principles.

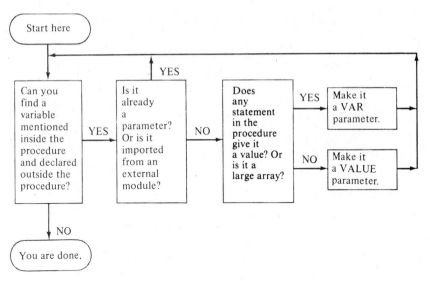

FIGURE 6. *Contrasting VAR and VALUE parameters.*

Order of Declarations

In Modula-2, CONST, VAR, TYPE, and PROCEDURE declarations can come in any order, as long as all declarations are defined before they are used in other declarations. There are even two exceptions to that: One applies to pointers (which I discuss later), and the other is that a *statement* can refer to an identifier that is declared later in the program. As a rule, declarations and initializations should occur as close to the point in the program where they are used as possible; so the global variables in this program and most others in this book are declared just before the body of the program.

This freedom of order has its price, of course; a compiler must make at least two passes through the program before it can finish compilation, first for the declarations and then again for the statements. Some compilers (such as Borland's) restrict the programmer to declaring all identifiers used in a statement before the statement occurs, so the compiler can work faster.

The free-ordering property of Modula-2 can be used to solve two problems that occur when programming in Pascal. One problem is that there should be a way to guarantee that a global variable is not changed by a call to a procedure except when that global variable is passed as a VAR parameter. This avoidance of **side effects** is one of the most important precepts of programming style. For instance, if Example 1.6A declared a global variable named Ersa, how would you tell that it is not changed by the call to the function LCM? Only by reading the body of the function. The problem does not arise for the global variable First; any reference to First within the function will be taken as a reference to the local value parameter

First rather than to the global variable First, since a local declaration of an identifier "masks out" a global declaration.

The second problem is that it is more natural for the reader of a program to see the body of the program first, followed by the procedures that the body of the program calls. This is not possible in Pascal, and technically not possible in Modula-2, although it is normal in languages such as FORTRAN, BASIC, C, and PL/1. But since a Modula-2 procedure can be called by a statement that is placed either before or after that procedure heading, you can accomplish the same thing by replacing the statements in the body of the program by the one statement PerformTask and then adding a new first procedure to Example 1.6A as follows:

```
PROCEDURE PerformTask;
VAR
     First, Second : INTEGER;       (* the input from the user *)
BEGIN
     (* move all statements from the body of the program to here *)
END PerformTask;
```

There are no global variables as a result of these changes; therefore, it is impossible for a procedure to have side effects. You will see an illustration of this format in Example 1.7B. People who come to Modula-2 from FORTRAN, BASIC, C, or PL/1 will probably choose to use this style of programming or its equivalent; people who come to Modula-2 from Pascal will probably do things the way they are used to.

Another reason for explicitly stating the **interface** (means of communication with the outside world) in the parameter list of a procedure is that it makes it much more likely that the procedure can be "lifted" from the program and moved to another program that can use it profitably. This is called the **Don't reinvent the wheel** principle.

The RETURN Statement

A RETURN statement is allowed within any procedure, whether statement or function procedure. If the procedure closest containing the RETURN statement is a function procedure, an expression *must* follow the word RETURN; if a statement procedure closest contains it, the word RETURN *cannot* be followed by an expression.

The effect of executing a RETURN statement is to immediately terminate execution of the procedure closest containing it; if it is a function procedure, the expression is returned to the calling statement to be used in an expression there. The returned expression must be assignable to a variable of the result type of the function; so it is legal for a CARDINAL function to return an INTEGER value and vice versa.

EXAMPLE 1.6B _____

```
PROCEDURE PrintIntegers;
    (*  The input consists of one or more INTEGERs
        separated by CARDINALs.  Print all such integers.
        Thus the syntax of the input is:
              integer  {  cardinal  integer  }              *)
VAR
    Value : INTEGER;      (* input value to be written   *)
    Junk  : CARDINAL;     (* input value to be discarded *)
BEGIN
    ReadInt (Value);
    WHILE Done DO
        WriteInt (Value, 6);
        ReadCard (Junk);
        IF NOT Done THEN
            RETURN;
        END;
        ReadInt (Value);
    END;
END PrintIntegers;
```

Notice that the procedure in Example 1.6B does not have parameters. This is perfectly legal. The procedure does not mention any globally defined variables, so the side-effects style rule does not require that it have parameters. Notice also that it is necessary to have a cardinal variable into which a cardinal number is read, but the value of that cardinal number is not germane to the task to be performed. Many people make a habit of naming such a variable "Junk," to inform the reader of the program that the value is not important.

Warnings

The following are some aspects of Modula-2 that give some people trouble:

- [ ] Do not omit the word VAR from the description of a formal parameter when the calling statement "expects" the procedure to affect that parameter.
- [ ] The heading of a function procedure, and each instance of a function call, must have parentheses, even if the function has no parameters.

Check Your Understanding

1. List all the global identifiers declared as procedures or variables in Example 1.6A.

2. Write a function that reads integers until a zero is seen and then tells how many integers were greater than 50.

3. What is the effect of omitting VAR in the parameter list for GetInput in Example 1.6A?

4. What is the effect of inserting VAR in the parameter list for LCM in Example 1.6A?

5. (NA) Write a function that reads 20 integers and then tells how many of those integers were greater than 50.

6. (NA) Write a statement procedure that accepts three real numbers as parameters and writes the largest of the three.

7. (NA) Write a function that accepts three integers as parameters and tells how many are odd numbers.

1.7 ARRAYS; TYPE SECTIONS

This section presents the syntax and semantics of Modula-2 as they apply to arrays, which require that you use a type of variable for which there is no built-in type already defined. The type-denoter for an array variable is therefore a phrase. A type declaration can be used to declare an identifier to stand for that phrase; this has certain advantages.

Definitions for Arrays

An **array** is a structure that contains several variables of the same type, each of which can be accessed independently of the others. You can refer to an individual component in the array by using an index. For example, if X is declared as AR-RAY [1..20] OF REAL, then X contains 20 REAL variables; X[3] refers to the third REAL variable, whose index is 3.

Array components in a program commonly are used with a variable as the index. Typically, X[K] is referenced where K takes on various values. For instance, Example 1.7A is a function procedure that tells whether a given array of REAL variables contains a negative number. The algorithm consists of looking at all the components, one after the other. If you see a component with a negative number

EXAMPLE 1.7A _____

```
PROCEDURE HasNegs (GivenArray : ARRAY OF REAL) : BOOLEAN;
    (* Tell whether the GivenArray contains a negative *)
VAR
    K : CARDINAL;
BEGIN
    FOR K := 0 TO HIGH (GivenArray) DO
        IF GivenArray [K] < 0.0 THEN
            RETURN TRUE;
        END;
    END;
    RETURN FALSE;
END HasNegs;
```

in it, you return a value of TRUE as the result of the function. If, on the other hand, you get all the way to the end without having seen any negatives at all, you return the value FALSE.

Open-array Parameters

The parameter of Example 1.7A is described as ARRAY OF REAL. This phrase is not an actual type, since it does not tell how much storage space to allot for the parameter; we call the phrase ARRAY OF REAL the **formal type** of the parameter. This kind of formal parameter is called an **open-array parameter**; any array of REAL variables can be the actual parameter.

We often need to know the minimum and maximum values for the indices of an array parameter. In Modula-2, when the formal type is ARRAY OF something, the lowest index of the formal parameter is 0, regardless of what it is for the actual parameter, and the built-in CARDINAL function HIGH tells the highest index counting up from 0. For instance, the variable X: ARRAY [1..20] OF REAL can be an actual parameter of the HasNegs function, in which case GivenArray[0] is X[1], GivenArray[19] is X[20], and HIGH(GivenArray) is 19. If the variable Edgar: ARRAY [10..35] OF REAL is the actual parameter, GivenArray is indexed from 0 to 25, HIGH(GivenArray)=25, and GivenArray[3] is actually Edgar.

Type Declarations

Sometimes you have a need to refer to an array type in more than one place in the program. In such a case, Modula-2 requires you to declare an identifier to stand for that array type and to use the identifier to refer to that type. For example, assume you declare X: ARRAY [0..10] OF INTEGER in one place in your program, and you declare Y: ARRAY [0..10] OF INTEGER in another place in your program. If you want X and Y to be the same type, you have made a mistake; you cannot execute X := Y. You should instead have declarations like the following:

```
TYPE    LotsOfNumbers = ARRAY [0..10] OF INTEGER;
VAR     X : LotsOfNumbers;
    (* Later in the program *)
        Y : LotsOfNumbers ...
```

Now X and Y are the same type. Two variables are considered the same type if and only if the specified type is the same **type-identifier** or they are declared in the same identifier-list.

When you specify in a type declaration the lowest and highest indices allowed for an array, you must use a constant expression. This means you can use arithmetic operators, but you cannot use function calls or variables.

A Telepathy Experiment

The next example demonstrates the use of a TYPE section and contains another illustration of the use of an open-array parameter. As a consequence, the two procedure headings show inconsistency in style.

For this example, the task to be performed is to make a report on the results of some tests for telepathy. One experiment consists of a person shuffling a deck of 100 cards, each card containing one of the numbers from 1 to 5. Then the person turns over one card, rings a bell, thinks hard about the card, and records the number. The person repeats this for each of the 100 cards. A second person in the

EXAMPLE 1.7B _____

```
MODULE Telepathy;
FROM InOut IMPORT WriteString, WriteLn,   Done,
                  ReadCard,     WriteCard,
                  OpenInput,    CloseInput;
    (* Report on the results of some experiments.  The
       data from one experiment consists of an ID number
       followed by Size values representing the first set
       of responses followed by Size values representing
       the second set of responses.  For each experiment,
       report the number of matches between the two sets.*)
    (* Written by William C. Jones, May 19-- *)

CONST
    Size = 100;
TYPE
    LotsOfNumbers = ARRAY [0 .. Size - 1] OF CARDINAL;
(*******************************************************)

PROCEDURE PerformTask;
VAR
    IDNumber : CARDINAL;
    Sender, Receiver : LotsOfNumbers;
BEGIN
    ReadCard (IDNumber);
    WHILE Done DO
        WriteString ('The ID number of this run is ');
        WriteCard (IDNumber, 1);
        WriteLn;

        ReadTwoArrays (Sender, Receiver);
        WriteString ('   The number of matches is ');
        WriteCard (NumberOfMatches (Sender, Receiver), 1);
        WriteLn;

        ReadCard (IDNumber);
    END;
END PerformTask;
(*******************************************************)

(* continued on next page *)
```

```
(* EXAMPLE 1.7B continued *)


PROCEDURE ReadTwoArrays
          (VAR Sender, Receiver : LotsOfNumbers);
    (* Read Size numbers into Sender, then into Receiver *)
VAR
    K : CARDINAL;
BEGIN
    FOR K := 0 TO Size - 1 DO
        ReadCard (Sender [K]);
    END;
    FOR K := 0 TO Size - 1 DO
        ReadCard (Receiver [K]);
    END;
END ReadTwoArrays;
(*******************************************************)

PROCEDURE NumberOfMatches
    (VAR Sender, Receiver : ARRAY OF CARDINAL) : CARDINAL;
    (* Compute and report the number of cases where Sender
        and Receiver have equal-valued components *)
VAR
    Count, K : CARDINAL;
BEGIN
    Count := 0;
    FOR K := 0 TO HIGH (Sender) DO
        IF Sender [K] = Receiver [K] THEN
            Count := Count + 1;
        END;
    END;
    RETURN Count;
END NumberOfMatches;
(*******************************************************)

BEGIN          (* program *)

    WriteString ('This program reports statistics on ');
    WriteString ('the results of telepathy experiments.');
    WriteLn;

    OpenInput ('');
    PerformTask;
    CloseInput;

END Telepathy.
```

next room hears the bell, tries to read the first person's mind, and records the number "received."

For this program, the input file contains an unknown number of groups of 201 nonnegative integers. Each group consists of an identification number followed by the list of 100 numbers recorded by the "sender" followed by a list of the 100 numbers recorded by the "receiver." The program in Example 1.7B is to report, for each group of 201 numbers, the identification number and the number of matches.

⮕ PROGRAMMING STYLE

The two parameters of the NumberOfMatches procedure are VAR parameters even though the procedure does not change them. The reason is that making them value parameters would waste considerable time and storage space. It would cause a new copy of the arrays to be made and their values copied from the actual parameters to the formal parameters. This waste is saved by making the parameters VAR parameters. It would be a good idea to make the parameter in Example 1.7A a VAR parameter also.

As a general rule, a function procedure should not change the value of any of its parameters. A VALUE parameter should be used (instead of VAR) for any simple parameter (INTEGER, REAL, CHAR, etc.) whose value is not changed by the procedure.

The primary purpose of good programming style is to make the program as clear and readable as possible. Some important points of style are as follows; the first two are the most important ones:

☐ **Declare each variable as locally as possible.**

☐ **Any variable declared outside a procedure and mentioned inside the procedure should be a parameter of that procedure.**

☐ Put spacing between each two consecutive tokens in the program, except when one of them is punctuation (comma, period, semicolon, parentheses, brackets, or the ".." symbol). In particular, it is easier to read an expression when there are spaces around + and *.

☐ Use visual dividers before each procedure heading (either a dark line in comment symbols or several blank lines or both).

☐ Do not use abbreviations unless they are at least as clear as the spelled-out word, as in NumWords or MaxLength.

Multidimensional Arrays

Modula-2 allows much more flexibility in array declarations that do many other general-purpose programming languages. It is legal to declare an array of any type that is known to the compiler at that point. If you want to declare a two-dimensional array of REALs, you simply declare an array of one-dimensional arrays of REALs. For example, assume you make the following declaration:

```
VAR  X : ARRAY [1..10] OF ARRAY [100..200] OF REAL;
```

Then X is an array of 10 objects, each of which is an array of 101 REAL variables. X[1] is the first array of 101 REAL variables, two of which are denoted X[1][117] and X[1][200]. X[7] is the seventh array of 101 REAL variables, two of which are denoted X[7][100] and X[7][139].

There is a "shorthand" form of declaring and referring to arrays of arrays: X[7,139] means the same thing as X[7][139], and similarly for other combinations. Moreover, the following declaration for X is equivalent to the one just given:

```
VAR X : ARRAY [1..10] , [100..200] OF REAL;
```

Elements of Matrix Handling

A two-dimensional array is called a **matrix**. Consider the following declarations for 5-by-5 matrices:

```
CONST   Size = 5;
        Zero = 0.0;
TYPE    Numeric = REAL;
        Matrix = ARRAY [1..Size], [1..Size] OF Numeric;
```

The name Numeric is used instead of REAL, and Zero is used instead of 0.0, so that any program developed using these declarations can be easily switched from working with REAL values to working with INTEGER or CARDINAL values if you want. Figure 7 shows a matrix with Size 5. A matrix M can have all components in use initialized to zero using the following coding:

```
FOR Row := 1 TO Size DO
    FOR Col := 1 TO Size DO
        M [Row, Col] := Zero;
    END;
END;
```

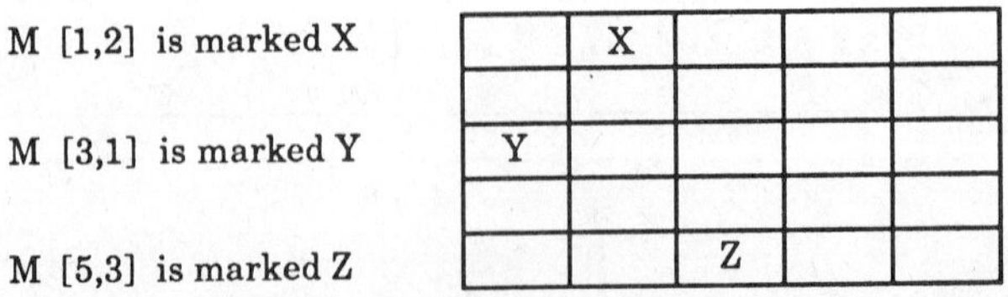

M [1,2] is marked X

M [3,1] is marked Y

M [5,3] is marked Z

FIGURE 7. A matrix M with size = 5 (thus a 5-by-5 matrix).

You can make Result the sum of two matrices B and C using the following coding:

```
FOR Row := 1 TO Size DO
    FOR Col := 1 TO Size DO
        Result [Row, Col] := B [Row, Col] + C [Row, Col];
    END;
END;
```

You can compute the sum of the values on the diagonal of a given matrix M using the following coding:

```
Sum := Zero;
FOR K := 1 TO Size DO
    Sum := Sum + M [K, K];
END;
```

For a program that is to work with 8-by-8 matrices, you only need declare Size as 8 instead of 5. A difficulty with this kind of declaration occurs when the program is to work with matrices of several different sizes (perhaps some 5-by-5 and others 8-by-8) and when the size of the matrix is not known in advance. Section 2.2 shows a way to eliminate this problem.

Syntax

Modula-2 allows many different kinds of type-denoters. An **ordinal-type** is a type for which the system associates an integer with each value in the type. For instance, [10..20] denotes an ordinal type. The following EBNF notation describes all the kinds of type-denoters we have discussed so far ("type-identifier" means an identifier that has previously been declared in a TYPE section):

$ ordinal-type > "[" const-expression ".." const-expression "]"
       | INTEGER | CARDINAL | BOOLEAN .
$ type-denoter > ARRAY ordinal-type { "," ordinal-type } OF type-denoter
       | ordinal-type | REAL | type-identifier .

Reminder: I use the > symbol instead of = in EBNF definitions to indicate that there are other possibilities besides the ones listed. Thus > indicates a partial definition.

The parentheses in a procedure heading describe the formal parameters of the procedure. The parentheses must contain a number of **formal-parameter sections** with semicolons separating them from each other. A formal-parameter section is defined by the following EBNF notation:

$ formal-type > [ARRAY OF] type-identifier .
$ formal-parameter-section = [VAR] new-identifier
                            { "," new-identifier } ":" formal-type .

A means of referring to a variable in a program is called a **variable-designator**. You have now seen two kinds of variable-designator, which can be described as:

$ variable-designator > variable-identifier { selector } .
$ selector > "[" expression { "," expression } "]" .

Warnings

The following can cause difficulty to people who are new to Modula-2.

☐ Do not have the value of an index of an array be larger than the largest value specified in the declaration of the array, nor smaller than the smallest value specified. This can cause the program to crash during execution.

☐ Do not refer to the value of a component of an array when that component has not previously been given a value. This can cause unexpected results to occur, since the value is indeterminate.

☐ Do not use a variable to specify the lowest or highest index for an array. Some languages allow this (particularly, interpreted BASIC), but not Modula-2.

☐ Use brackets for array components, not parentheses.

Check Your Understanding

1. Declare a type-identifier for an array of two REAL variables, one variable for each BOOLEAN value.

2. What would be the effect of replacing each of the three lines beginning FOR in Example 1.7B by FOR K := Size−1 TO 0 BY −1 DO?

3. For the formal parameter F: ARRAY OF INTEGER and the actual parameter A: ARRAY [−15..7] OF INTEGER, what is HIGH(F)? What is F[4]? What is F[10]?

4. (NA) Declare an array of 50 BOOLEAN variables with lowest index 150.

5. (NA) Write a function that finds the index of the smallest number in a given array of REALs.

6. (NA) Write a statement procedure that reverses the order of the values in an array of CARDINALs.

7. (NA) Write a function that tells the number of nonzero entries in a Matrix (as declared in this section).

8. (NA) Write a function that tells whether a given Matrix parameter is **upper-triangular**, that is, whether the values of all components indexed [I,J] with I > J are 0.

9. (NA) Write a statement procedure that **transposes** a given Matrix parameter. The transposition is accomplished by swapping the values at the components indexed [I,J] and [J,I] for each possible I,J pair.

1.8 CHARACTERS AND STRINGS

CHAR denotes the set of character values. There are normally either 128 or 256 character values, depending on the implementation. Each character has a number from 0 up to either 127 or 255, called its **ordinal number**. Those numbered from 32 to 126 can be typed directly on most keyboards; the others are often difficult to generate. On some keyboards, you can hold down the ALT key while typing a number; when you release the ALT key, the character with that ordinal number appears in the file you are typing. For instance, the character that rings a bell when it is printed is generated by holding down the ALT key while typing a 7. In Modula-2, the ASCII code is used for ordinal numbers; the ASCII values for the printable characters are given in Figure 8.

CHAR Type

A character literal can be denoted by a single character enclosed in quotes or in apostrophes, if the character is printable using your keyboard. Procedures named **Read** and **Write**, imported from InOut, allow you to read and write one character value.

Example 1.8A presents a program that reads one line of input and tells how many words are in it. This example imports the identifier **EOL** from InOut; EOL is a character constant that corresponds to the end-of-line marker in a file or to the RETURN key for input from the keyboard. The program makes use of the fact that every character value has an associated ordinal number, that the ordinal

	0	1	2	3	4	5	6	7	8	9	10	11	12	13	14	15
32		!	"	#	$	%	&	'	(	)	*	+	,	-	.	/
48	0	1	2	3	4	5	6	7	8	9	:	;	<	=	>	?
64	@	A	B	C	D	E	F	G	H	I	J	K	L	M	N	O
80	P	Q	R	S	T	U	V	W	X	Y	Z	[	\	]	^	_
96	`	a	b	c	d	e	f	g	h	i	j	k	l	m	n	o
112	p	q	r	s	t	u	v	w	x	y	z	{	|	}	~	

FIGURE 8. *Table of ASCII characters numbered 32 to 126 (32 is a blank).*

EXAMPLE 1.8A _____

```
MODULE WordCounter;
FROM InOut IMPORT WriteString, WriteLn, WriteCard, Done,
                  Read, Write, EOL;
    (* Count the number of words in one line of input from
       the keyboard.  We use a mechanical definition of
       a word, namely,  its characters are numbered higher
       than a blank and it's separated from other words
       by characters numbered no higher than a blank *)
    (* Written by William C. Jones, May 19-- *)
(* ********************************************************** )

PROCEDURE WordCount () : CARDINAL;
CONST
    Blank = ' ';
VAR
    Ch, SavedCharacter : CHAR;
    Count : CARDINAL;
BEGIN
    Count := 0;                    (* count the words seen *)
    SavedCharacter := Blank; (* pretend an initial blank *)
    Read (Ch);
    WHILE Done AND (Ch # EOL) DO
        IF (Ch > Blank) AND (SavedCharacter <= Blank) THEN
            Count := Count + 1;
        END;
        SavedCharacter := Ch;
        Read (Ch);
    END;
    RETURN Count;
END WordCount;
(* ********************************************************** )

BEGIN           (* WordCounter program *)

    WriteString ("Enter a line whose words I'll count: ");
    WriteLn;
    WriteCard (WordCount (), 1);
    WriteString (' words were on the line.');
    WriteLn;

END WordCounter.
```

numbers of characters impose an ordering on them, and that the ordinal number of a blank is less than that of any ordinary printable character.

This example does not actually count words, it counts the number of characters that begin a word. These are easier to find, since a criterion is that they are larger than a blank and follow something that is not larger than a blank. The only trouble is that the first word does not necessarily follow a word separator. I cannot simply add one to the count to allow for it, since the user might type a blank or two before typing the first word. So I initialize SavedCharacter to a blank; that is, I pretend that the user enters one more leading blank than is actually the case. In this situation, the lie does no harm and simplifies the logic. Such "white lies" are common in programming.

Another useful identifier imported from InOut is **termCH**, a CHAR variable that contains the most recently read character. ReadInt, ReadCard, and ReadReal take one character beyond the string of digits (or whatever) that form the number, so termCH will contain that following character; it must be a blank, tab, or end-of-line for the READ statement to be done successfully. You can use termCH to discard the latter part of a line of input, as follows (this roughly corresponds to the ReadLn statement in Pascal):

```
Ch := termCH;
WHILE Ch # EOL DO
    Read (Ch);
END;
```

Built-in Functions and Statements Useful with Characters

CAP(X) returns a CHAR value when X is any CHAR expression. The value returned is the capitalized form of X if X is a lowercase letter; otherwise the value returned is the given CHAR value.

ORD(X) returns the CARDINAL that tells the ordinal number of the value of X, when X is any CHAR expression.

CHR(X) returns the CHAR value that has the ordinal number of the value of X, when X is a CARDINAL expression in the range for ordinal numbers of characters.

INC(X, N) is a statement whose two parameters are a variable and a CARDINAL expression. The variable can be of any ordinal type including CHAR. The effect is to replace the value of X by the value that comes N steps later (using the ordinal number to count steps). The second parameter can be omitted when a step of 1 is wanted (that is, 1 is the default). INC stands for "increment." In Example 1.8A, the statement inside the IF statement could have been INC(Count).

DEC(X, N) is analogous to INC (X, N) except that DEC decrements (subtracts from) the value of X by N steps instead of incrementing it. When the second parameter is omitted, as in DEC(X), X is decremented by one step.

INC(X) is shorter than X := X+1 and has the same meaning when X is an INTEGER or CARDINAL variable. INC(X) is to be preferred, since it executes faster, especially when the variable is designated by something more complex than an identifier, as in INC(X[N]).

Strings

The **null character** is the character whose ordinal number is zero. It is often used as a sentinel value in Modula-2, especially when working with strings. The null character can be referred to as **0C** in a Modula-2 program (I will explain why in Section 1.11).

A **string variable** is an array of two or more characters whose lowest index is zero. Strings differ from, and are superior to, general arrays in only one respect: Constants of string type can be represented in a Modula-2 program using string literals. For example, assume you have the following declarations:

```
VAR  Word, Name  :  ARRAY [0..10] OF CHAR;
VAR  Address     :  ARRAY [0..20] OF CHAR;
VAR  Phrase      :  ARRAY [0..10] OF CHAR;
```

You can assign Word := 'hello' or Word := "hello Joe." The only restriction is that the string literal assigned to Word cannot have more than 10 characters. If, for instance, you assign Word := 'hello', those five characters will be assigned to Word[0] through Word[4] and 0C will be assigned to Word[5]; the rest of the characters of Word are indeterminate.

You can assign Word := Name, but you cannot assign Word := Phrase, since they are not the same type; two multiword type-denoters are never considered the same even if they are written the same. You should declare a type-identifier when you want to avoid this problem.

A string variable is called **null-terminated** if it is known to contain the null character as a sentinel value (Fig. 9). This implies that the values of components after the one containing 0C are irrelevant. For instance, if Word (declared above) is null-terminated, it can have at most 10 "actual" characters, since room must be left for the null character. When a string literal is the actual parameter for

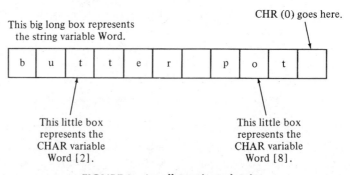

FIGURE 9. A null-terminated string.

ARRAY OF CHAR, the null character is added at the end of the string (but caution: Some implementations do not do this).

The InOut library module has the two procedures **ReadString** and **WriteString**, each of which accepts a string variable as a parameter. The parameter of Write-String is a VALUE parameter described as ARRAY OF CHAR, so any string variable or string literal can be the actual parameter; you have seen numerous uses of WriteString in the programs in this book. If the parameter contains 0C, only the characters before the first 0C are printed.

The ReadString procedure reads characters into an ARRAY OF CHAR until a character that is less than or equal to a blank is seen or until all but one of the components of the array are filled. Then 0C is put into the the next component of the array; the remaining components (if any) are left indeterminate. *Warning:* Several implementations of Modula-2 define ReadString somewhat differently. Some read to the end-of-line or the end of the array, whichever comes first; some read to the end-of-line even after the parameter is full, throwing away the excess; some do not put 0C in the array if the input has enough characters to fill it. So check your ReadString procedure before you rely on details of implementation.

Example 1.8B contains a procedure to illustrate the use of null-terminated strings. Some examples of how this ReadLine procedure could be used are as follows, assuming that Word is declared as ARRAY [0..6] OF CHAR and that | indicates an end-of-line marker:

ReadLine(Word) assigns "x y" to Word if the input is x y|

ReadLine(Word) assigns "abcdef" to Word if the input is abcdefgh|

EXAMPLE 1.8B _____

```
PROCEDURE ReadLine (VAR Data : ARRAY OF CHAR);
    (* Read the entire rest of the current line of input;
       store as many characters in Data (in order) as will
       fit, leaving room for 0C.  If the line is too short,
       leave the later values indeterminate *)
VAR
    K  : CARDINAL;
    Ch : CHAR;
BEGIN
    K := 0;
    Read (Ch);
    WHILE Done AND (Ch # EOL) DO
        IF K < HIGH (Data) THEN
            Data [K] := Ch;
            INC (K);
        END;
        Read (Ch);
    END;
    Data [K] := 0C;
END ReadLine;
```

Warnings

The following are some points that give people new to Modula-2 some difficulty:

☐ You cannot assign a string variable to another string variable unless they are exactly the same type; it is not enough that they are declared similarly.

☐ You cannot assign a string literal to a string variable that has a shorter length, although you can to a longer one.

☐ The effect of ReadString differs in various implementations.

Check Your Understanding

1. Write a program segment that writes every other capital letter from 'A' to 'Y', in that order.

2. Write a statement procedure that capitalizes all lowercase letters in a given array of characters. Use the CAP function.

3. (NA) Write a function that tells how many "actual" characters there are in a given null-terminated array of characters.

4. (NA) Write a function that tells whether two given null-terminated arrays of characters have the same "actual" characters.

5. (NA) Write a statement procedure that strips trailing blanks from any given null-terminated string variable by the simple expedient of putting the null character directly after the last nonblank.

6. (NA) Write a statement procedure that does a "shift left": It alters its null-terminated string parameter by copying each "actual" character into the component to its left, except that the value in component 0 becomes the last "actual" character.

1.9 RECORDS

In this section you will see how to declare a variable to consist of a number of different variables of *different* types. You can refer to each of these **fields** of the structured variable individually, or you can refer to the structure as a whole.

Declaring a Record Type

A **record** is a set of values that do not have to be all the same type (as opposed to an array, which is a set of values that do). Example 1.9A displays a plausible declaration of a student record, assuming we want to store information as to the

EXAMPLE 1.9A _____

```
CONST
    StrMax = 20;
TYPE
    ShortString = ARRAY [0..StrMax] OF CHAR;
    Information =
        RECORD
            ID, CreditHours : CARDINAL;
            AmtOwed         : REAL;
            Name            : ShortString;
            IsFullTime      : BOOLEAN;
        END;
TYPE
    LotsOfInfo = ARRAY [1..500] OF Information;
VAR
    ThisStudent : Information;
    School      : LotsOfInfo;
```

number of hours for which the student is registered, the amount of tuition owed, the name of the student, and a note as to whether the student is full-time or not. Each student has an ID number by which he or she is referenced. I have also provided declarations of variables using the Information type; I will be referring to those variables in this section.

This form of declaration makes it easy to see that the information in School consists of a number of students indexed from 1 to 500. Each record contains the information about one particular student. ThisStudent is just one such record.

The order in which the names of the components of the record are listed in the declaration of the record type is immaterial. The following is a declaration of a record type that is exactly the same in effect, although it has five **field sections** instead of four (the field sections are the phrases between RECORD and END that are separated by semicolons).

```
TYPE    Information = RECORD
                        Name        : ShortString;
                        CreditHours : CARDINAL;
                        IsFullTime  : BOOLEAN;
                        AmtOwed     : REAL;
                        ID          : CARDINAL;
                      END;
```

Accessing the Fields of a Record Variable

You cannot refer to a particular component of ThisStudent as ThisStudent[Name] or ThisStudent[ID], the way you do with arrays. Modula-2 syntax requires that you refer to these two components (normally called fields) using periods, namely as ThisStudent.Name and ThisStudent.ID. For example, the following procedure asks the user of a program for a student's ID:

```
PROCEDURE InputID (VAR ThisStudent : Information);
BEGIN
    WriteString ('Enter the ID: ');
    ReadCard (ThisStudent.ID);
END InputID;
```

This procedure could be called using the statement InputID(School[4]). Such a procedure call passes the fourth component of School as the actual parameter to the formal parameter ThisStudent; so the ID field of School[4], namely School[4].ID, is what is actually changed by this call.

You could use WriteString(School[57].Name) to write the name of the student at component 57 of the School array. You could count the letters in the null-terminated student's name with the following program segment:

```
K := 0;
WHILE ThisStudent.Name [K] # Null DO
    INC (K);
END;
```

A procedure to find the student with the largest amount owed in a LotsOfInfo array is shown in Example 1.9B. This procedure applies the common algorithm of searching through all components of the array, at each point recording the biggest debtor seen so far. When all components have been inspected, the biggest debtor

EXAMPLE 1.9B _____

```
PROCEDURE FindDebtor (VAR School  : LotsOfInfo;
                      VAR Culprit : Information);
    (* Find the record of the biggest debtor *)
VAR
    K : CARDINAL;
BEGIN
    Culprit := School [1];
    FOR K := 2 TO 500 DO
        IF School [K].AmtOwed > Culprit.AmtOwed THEN
            Culprit := School [K];
        END;
    END;
END FindDebtor;
```

EXAMPLE 1.9C _____

```
CONST
    StrMax = 20;
TYPE
    ShortString = ARRAY [0..StrMax] OF CHAR;
    StudentInfo =
        RECORD
            ID, CreditHours : CARDINAL;
            AmtOwed         : REAL;
            Parents : RECORD
                        MomsName, DadsName : ShortString;
                        MomsAge, DadsAge : CARDINAL;
                      END;
            Name            : ShortString;
            IsFullTime      : BOOLEAN;
        END;
```

seen so far must be the biggest debtor of all. The procedure assumes that there are exactly 500 students in the school. However, in most applications, the number of information values in an array varies during execution of a program; Chapter 2 presents techniques for managing such a situation.

Fields That Are Records

A field of a record can be of any type known to the processor at that point. In particular, it can also be a record. For example, you could use a more complex record as shown in Example 1.9C. Then ThisStudent.Parents is a record with two string fields and two cardinal fields; the mother's name is ThisStudent.Parents.MomsName and the father's age is ThisStudent.Parents.DadsAge.

Syntax and Semantics

Figure 10 depicts syntax diagrams for a record type and for the basic kind of field section. For a record type, an identifier that precedes the colon of one of its field sections is a **field-identifier** of that record type.

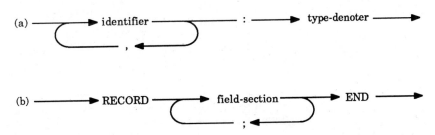

FIGURE 10. (a) Syntax diagram for the basic kind of field-section. (b) Syntax diagram for a record-type.

A **record variable** is any variable-designator of a record type. You access a value stored in a field of a record variable by writing the field-identifier directly after the record variable, with a period separating them. If X denotes a record variable and Y is an identifier of a field of its record type, X.Y can be treated in all ways as a variable of the type specified in its record section except as the control variable of a FOR statement. In particular, you can assign one record variable to another, as in the assignments to Culprit in Example 1.9C; this is more efficient and clearer than assigning individual fields.

PROGRAMMING STYLE

You should usually avoid choosing a field-identifier that is declared differently elsewhere in the program. The main principle of good programming style is to make your program as easy as possible for another reader to understand. Using an identifier in two different ways is usually confusing.

Bytes

The following discussion is correct for many computers; it is representative of most 16-bit microcomputers. The primary unit of storage for certain computers is 1 **byte**. You can store the equivalent of one eight-binary-digit number in 1 byte, which means that you can put any of 256 different values there (since the eighth power of 2 is 256). The ASCII numbering system for characters is based on 256: Codes from 0 to 127 are assigned characters by that numbering system, and the other 128 codes are left free for machine-dependent use. For instance, some machines have Greek, German, French, and Spanish characters coded with numbers above 127, as well as mathematical symbols and graphics characters. Boolean values are stored using 1 byte; that may sound wasteful, but packing the values in closer adds to execution time.

Two bytes of storage are used for values of INTEGER and CARDINAL types. That gives 65,536 different values that can be stored for integer and cardinal

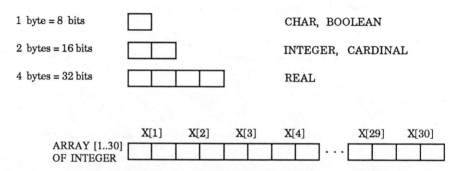

FIGURE 11. Typical space requirements for various types of values.

variables. The permissible range for CARDINAL values is 0 to 65,535, and the permissible range for INTEGER values is −32,768 to +32,767.

Four bytes of storage are used for REAL values (Figure 11). Three bytes are used to store the digits of the real number; the other byte is used to store information about the sign of the number and the location of the decimal point within the digits. Actually, it is not a decimal point at all, since base 2 or base 16 is used instead of base 8; you could call it a hexadecimal point.

Some applications require larger integers or more precise reals, so some implementations of Modula-2 provide a LONGINT or LONGCARD type (4 bytes providing more than 4,000,000,000 different values) or a LONGREAL type (8 bytes providing the equivalent of 13-decimal-digit accuracy).

Address Computations

The following declarations are chosen to make the next discussion clearer; you would rarely use such identifiers in a program:

```
TYPE    ArrayOf20Chars    = ARRAY [0..19] OF CHAR;
        ArrayOf30Integers = ARRAY [1..30] OF INTEGER;
        ArrayOf10Reals    = ARRAY [15..24] OF REAL;
        Array36of20Chars  = ARRAY [5..40] OF ArrayOf20Chars;
        Array14of10Reals  = ARRAY [-4..9] OF ArrayOf10Reals;
```

If a program declares VAR X1: ArrayOf20Chars, sufficient space for storing 20 characters is **allocated** (set aside or reserved) for X1 and its address in memory is recorded in the compiled form of the program. For instance, the compiler might place X1 at bytes number 4012 through 4031. If a reference is made to X1[2] in the program, the location of that variable would be computed as 4014; a reference to X1 would be interpreted as a reference to location 4024. For any index K used with X1, the corresponding location would be computed as K+4012.

If a program declares VAR X2: ArrayOf30Integers, sufficient space for storing 30 integers (at 2 bytes each) is allocated for X2, namely 60 bytes; for instance, locations 2750 through 2809 might be reserved for X2. If a reference is made to X2[2], the location would be computed as 2752 (since X2[1] is at locations 2750-2751); a reference to X2[17] would be 32 bytes higher than X2[1], namely at locations 2782-2783. The general rule is that X2[K] is at location $2*(K-1)+2750$, since K−1 tells how many integer components come before X2[K] in the array.

Similarly, if a program declares VAR X3: ArrayOf10Reals and the compiler stores X3 beginning at location 3000, locations 3000-3003 are reserved for the first component X3[15], locations 3004-3007 for X3[16], and so forth. If you want a formula for the general case, an array with indices Lo to Hi and components requiring B bytes each has (Hi−Lo+1) components and therefore needs B∗(Hi−Lo+1) bytes of storage. If FL is the first location allocated for the array, then component K is stored at location FL+B∗(K−Lo).

You can apply this rule to arrays of structured types. For instance, if a program declares VAR X4: Array36of20Chars and the compiler stores X4 beginning at location 2000, locations 2000-2019 are reserved for the first component X4[5], since that first component requires 20 bytes of storage. Locations 2020-2039 are allocated for the second component X4[6]; the last component X4[40] is stored beginning 35∗20 bytes above the initial byte, namely at locations 2700-2719. The second component of X4[40] is referenced as X4[40][1] or as X4[40,1], whichever you prefer; it is stored at location 2701.

If a program declares VAR X5: Array14of10Reals and the compiler stores X5 beginning at location 3720, each component of X5 takes 40 bytes of storage, so the first component X5[−4] is in locations 3720-3759. The third component of X5[−4] is X5[−4][17] (also written as X5[−4,17]); it is stored at locations 3728-3731.

Address computations for records are analogous to those for arrays. Assume, for example, that a program declares VAR R: Information (as given in Example 1.9A). Then R has two cardinal fields (2 bytes each), one real field (4 bytes), one 21-character field (21 bytes), and a Boolean field (1 byte). Thus each Information variable requires 30 bytes of storage. If the compiler allocates locations 1315-1344 for R, then R.ID will be in locations 1315-1316, R.AmtOwed will be in locations 1319-1322, R.Name will be in locations 1323-1343, and R.Name[3] will be in location 1326. The order of listing the field identifiers affects the order in which the compiler stores the values, although it has no effect on the semantics of the program.

Many computers measure storage in **words**, which is usually a larger unit than a byte. For instance, a 32-bit microcomputer would probably define a word to be 4 bytes, since that is 32 binary digits. The compiler is constrained to declare variables at word boundaries. Thus if we declare VAR X: ARRAY [0..10] OF CHAR, only 11 bytes of storage are used, but 12 bytes are allocated to make a whole number of words. If X is in locations 2000-2010, the next variable to be allocated will begin in location 2012; that is, all independently declared variables begin at a multiple of 4 bytes. Similarly, a record variable of Information type would be allocated 8 words (32 bytes) even if the last Boolean field were omitted from the declaration, since 29 bytes will not fit into 7 words.

Check Your Understanding

1. Declare a record type named StockRecord for storing information about one kind of item in stock in a store. The fields should be an ID number, a descrip-

tion of the item, the price of the item, the original cost of the item, and the number currently in stock.

2. Declare an array of 1000 kinds of items of StockRecord type, as described in Exercise 1.

3. Write a function that tells the total amount of profit to be earned if all items for a given StockRecord (from Exercise 1) are sold at the specified price.

4. Write a function that assigns to Total the total amount owed by all students, using the declarations for Example 1.9B.

5. Assume that a program declares X: ARRAY [10..20] OF RECORD A,B: REAL END. For the storage requirements described in this section, where is X[13].B if X begins at address 2000? Where is X[20].A?

6. (NA) Write a function that tells how many students are full-time. Use the declarations for Example 1.9B.

7. (NA) Write a function that gives the average number of hours for students registered. Use the declarations for Example 1.9B.

1.10 THE WITH STATEMENT

Often a statement or sequence of statements will refer to the fields of one record several times. The statements become cluttered with the name of the record variable and hard to read easily; the WITH statement lets you remove that clutter. Assume you write a program with the declarations given in Example 1.9A—School is an array of records with fields called Name, ID, CreditHours, and AmtOwed. Consider the following program segment:

```
FOR K := 1 TO 500 DO
    WriteString (School [K].Name);
    WriteCard   (School [K].ID, 8);
    WriteCard   (School [K].CreditHours, 8);
    WriteReal   (School [K].AmtOwed, 8);
END;
```

The following rephrases this coding using a WITH statement. The rephrased segment has exactly the same effect. WITH School[K] DO means that every instance of the identifiers Name, ID, CreditHours, and AmtOwed that occurs in the statement sequence of the WITH statement is to have "School[K]." prefixed to it. This is because they are fields of School[K] (I am ignoring the IsFullTime field in these examples for simplicity).

```
FOR K := 1 TO Size DO
    WITH School [K] DO  (* fields are ID, CreditHours,
                                AmtOwed, Name, IsFullTime *)
        WriteString (Name);
        WriteCard   (ID, 8);
        WriteCard   (CreditHours, 8);
        WriteReal   (AmtOwed, 8);
    END;
END;
```

Establishing the Reference for a WITH Statement

There is a danger in using WITH statements. Some students think that it would be easiest to phrase the given program segment as follows. This does *not* have the same effect.

```
(* ERRONEOUS REPHRASING *)
WITH School [K] DO  (* fields are ID, CreditHours,
                            AmtOwed, Name, IsFullTime *)
    FOR K := 1 TO Size DO
        WriteString (Name);
        WriteCard   (ID, 8);
        WriteCard   (CreditHours, 8);
        WriteReal   (AmtOwed, 8);
    END;
END;
```

If, say, K has the value 9 just before this segment is executed, then every reference to Name and the other fields will have "School[9]." prefixed to it. That is, the index K is evaluated at the time the WITH statement is executed. Thus the record being referenced does not change each time that K changes inside the FOR statement. When you want to have the storage location associated with School[K] recalculated each time that K changes, you must put WITH School[K] DO *inside* the FOR statement.

Syntax and Semantics of WITH

The WITH statement has the form WITH...DO...END, with a single record variable before DO and a statement sequence after DO. For a WITH X statement, each variable-access within the statement sequence that could have X prefixed to it using a period is to be interpreted as if it did. *Exception:* If either of two WITH statements could be applied, the innermost WITH statement is applied first.

The reference to a record variable is established on entering a WITH statement, for the entire duration of the WITH statement. For example, if the record variable is School[K], any assignment to K within the WITH statement does not change the record variable that is being accessed; the WITH statement has to be executed again to change the record variable.

▐▶ **PROGRAMMING STYLE**

It is a good idea to list the field-identifiers of a record variable in a comment to the right of DO in a WITH statement. That tells the reader which identifiers are qualified by the record variable and saves the trouble of looking in the type declaration for that information.

Warning

The most common error that students make when they write their first program using records is to refer to a field without giving the name of the record variable that contains that field. For example, they may refer to Size when they should refer to Data.Size. Of course, a properly used WITH statement permits the use of Size instead of Data.Size, but it is far too easy to use a WITH statement improperly. I suggest therefore: For your first program using records, do not use any WITH statements whatsoever. When you have the program working correctly, revise it using WITH statements properly. It will be much easier to debug, because you will know that new errors are caused by the added WITH statements. Thereafter, you should not have much trouble using WITH statements.

Check Your Understanding

1. Rewrite the procedure in Example 1.9B using WITH School[K] appropriately.

2. A program defines a record type Date = RECORD Day, Month, Year: CARDINAL; END. The date December 25, 1988, would be stored in X as X.Month := 12, X.Day := 25, and X.Year := 1988. Write a Boolean function that tells whether one Date is earlier than another. Use WITH for the first parameter.

3. (NA) Rewrite your answer to Exercises 3 and 4 of Section 1.9 using WITH appropriately.

1.11 INFREQUENTLY USED LANGUAGE FEATURES

The language features described in this section (LOOP, CASE, HALT, subrange types, enumeration types, octal notation for characters, and variant records) are used relatively little in this book. If you are getting overloaded on Modula-2 at this point, you can postpone this section for a week or two and come back to it when you need it.

Control Statements

You have seen the IF, WHILE, REPEAT, and FOR statements. There are several more statements that control the flow of execution. One is the **LOOP** statement; it is simply the reserved words LOOP and END with a statement sequence between them. The loop iterates until explicitly terminated, usually by a RETURN or **EXIT** statement. The effect of EXIT is to terminate the LOOP statement that most closely contains it and to continue execution from the point just after the END of the LOOP statement. The program segment in Example 1.11A is a revision of the statements in Example 1.6B using a LOOP statement.

The **CASE** statement chooses one of several alternative actions depending on the value of an ordinal expression given directly after the word CASE. The alternatives are separated by the vertical bar character. The CASE statement can have an ELSE clause at the END to handle all values of the given expression that do not fit any of the cases; you can expect the program to crash if no alternative applies and no ELSE clause is given. The following program segment illustrates the use of the CASE statement.

```
CASE Ch OF
     'A'..'Z' : WriteString ('It is uppercase');
  |  'a'..'z' : WriteString ('It is lowercase');
  |  '0'..'9' : WriteString ('It is a digit');
  |  ',', ':', ';', '.' : WriteString ('It is a punctuation');
                          WriteString (' character');
ELSE    WriteString ("I'm sorry, I do not recognize that");
        HasUnknownCharacter := TRUE;
END;
```

EXAMPLE 1.11A _____

```
(* sample of coding using LOOP and EXIT *)
     LOOP
          ReadInt (Value);
          IF NOT Done THEN
              EXIT;
          END;
          WriteInt (Value, 6);
          ReadCard (Junk);
          IF NOT Done THEN
              EXIT;
          END;
     END;
```

Coding in this book aligns the vertical bar with the word CASE, since it is logically equivalent to ELSIF. However, many people prefer to put the bar at the end of the preceding line.

HALT is a built-in procedure-identifier without parameters; execution of HALT causes the program to terminate. There are some situations where this is advantageous.

Subrange and Enumeration Types

Type declarations like the following are allowed in Modula-2:

```
TYPE    IndexValue = [ 20 .. 50 ];
        DayOfWeek = (Sun, Mon, Tue, Wed, Thr, Fri, Sat);
```

A **subrange type** consists of two constant expressions separated by a double dot and enclosed in brackets; the constant expressions must be values in the same ordinal base type. Two types have the same **base type** if they are the same type up to "subrangeness." In more technical terms, the base type of a type T is T itself unless T is a subrange type, in which case the base type of T is the largest type of which T is a subrange.

When either CARDINAL or INTEGER could be the base type, the compiler assumes CARDINAL. For instance, assume that you declare K: IndexValue; then K is much the same as a CARDINAL variable that at run time can only have values in the range from 20 to 50, inclusive. K can be combined in expressions with, or assigned to, any variables whose base type is CARDINAL. However, K can be the actual parameter for a VAR parameter only if the VAR parameter is also of type IndexValue. In particular, WriteCard(K,8) is legal but ReadCard(K) is not.

The DayOfWeek type is an **enumeration type**. It is a type that contains just the seven values specified. That declaration of DayOfWeek also declares each of the three-letter identifiers as a constant-identifier of that type. The ordinal number of each of these seven values is given by its position in the list, from ORD(Sun)=0 up to ORD(Sat)=6. The only operators that can be used on DayOfWeek values are the relational operators, which use the ordinal numbers of the values to determine greater, less than, and so forth.

Essentially the same effect could be obtained by declaring Sun=0, Mon=1,..., Sat=6, then defining DayOfWeek=[Sun..Sat]. However, the compiler would then fail to check that values of type DayOfWeek are not combined in CARDINAL expressions; this type-checking can be helpful in detecting logic errors at compile time.

Octal Notation for Characters

7C means the character whose ordinal number is 7, which happens to be the character that rings a bell; thus 7C is a character literal. So is 0C, the character whose ordinal number is 0. This notation is a useful way of referring to a character when it is not available on the keyboard.

You might think that 41C denotes the character whose ordinal number is 41, but that would be wrong. **Octal notation** (base 8) is used when characters are represented this way. That is, the position of a digit in the numeral indicates a power of 8, not a power of 10 as in everyday numerals. So 41C means "the character whose ordinal number is 4 eights plus 1"; that is character number 33, the exclamation mark. Similarly, 124C means "the character whose ordinal number is 1 sixty-four plus 2 eights plus 4"; since that comes to 84, it is the capital letter T (according to the ASCII table in Section 1.8).

Warnings

The following are some points that give people new to Modula-2 some difficulty.

☐ If you use a subrange type, the brackets are part of it.

☐ If in revising a program you insert a LOOP statement within an existing LOOP statement, be careful not to enclose an EXIT statement that is supposed to EXIT the outer LOOP instead.

Variant Records

There are situations in which it is valuable to be able to have an array containing two or more different kinds of records. **Variant records**, discussed next, allow you to do this. This facility can save space or simplify coding or both.

A small college maintains records on three kinds of employees. The kind of information stored for one kind of employee differs from the kind stored for another. Example 1.11B shows some plausible declarations of such records. In real life, there would be many more fields in each record, and several more kinds of records.

It is common to write several programs that deal with all three of these kinds of records at one time, as when making out paychecks; so you might want an array of employee records. But all elements of an array must be the same type.

Variant records provide a space-saving solution to this problem. They allow you to declare one record type that can hold any one of the three kinds of information, as shown in Example 1.11C. I have added one extra field for Person, of the enumeration type Category, so I can note which kind of employee a given record describes. The part of this definition from the word CASE down to its END is called the **variant-part** of the record. The variable Person is called the **tag field** of the variant record.

In general, the current value of Emp[K].Person determines which fields of Emp[K] are in existence. When a statement changes the value of Emp[K].Person,

EXAMPLE 1.11B _____

```
(* Sample of three different record declarations *)
TYPE
    String = ARRAY [0..StrMax] OF CHAR;
    StaffEmployee  =  RECORD
                        ID : CARDINAL;
                        BiweeklyPay : REAL;
                        YearsOfService : REAL;
                        Union, Supervisor : String;
                      END;
    TeacherEmployee = RECORD
                        ID : CARDINAL;
                        AnnualPay : REAL;
                        Tenured : BOOLEAN;
                        Department, Degree : String;
                      END;
    StudentEmployee = RECORD
                        ID : CARDINAL;
                        HourlyRate : REAL;
                        SourceOfFunding, Major : String;
                      END;
```

EXAMPLE 1.11C _____

```
(* Sample of a variant record type *)
TYPE
    String    = ARRAY [0..StrMax] OF CHAR;
    Category  = (Staff, Teacher, Student);
    Employee  =
        RECORD
            ID : CARDINAL;
            CASE Person : Category OF
                Staff   : BiweeklyPay : REAL;
                          YearsOfService : REAL;
                          Union, Supervisor : String;
              | Teacher : AnnualPay : REAL;
                          Tenured : BOOLEAN;
                          Department, Degree : String;
              | Student : HourlyRate : REAL;
                          SourceOfFunding, Major : String;
            END;
        END;
VAR
    Emp : ARRAY [1..NumberOfEmployees] OF Employee;
```

the fields for that new value can be referenced; the fields for other Categories should not be referenced.

To illustrate how you could work with an array of such records, the following program segment prints the annual pay of each employee in the array Emp. I assume that students work 20 hours a week for 30 weeks a year. The technique is to inspect the value of Person for a given component and compute annual pay from that value's pay field.

```
FOR K := 1 TO NumberOfEmployees DO
    WITH Emp [K] DO
        CASE Person OF
            Staff   : WriteReal (26.1 * BiweeklyPay, 12);
          | Teacher : WriteReal (AnnualPay, 12);
          | Student : WriteReal (600.0 * HourlyRate, 12);
        END;
    END;
END;
```

Space Requirements

Assume that storage space for values is as specified in Section 1.9 (1 byte for CHAR or BOOLEAN, 2 for CARDINAL, 4 for REAL). For the three separate record declarations in Example 1.11B, a String requires 31 bytes of space, so a StaffEmployee requires 72 bytes, a TeacherEmployee requires 69 bytes, and a StudentEmployee requires 68 bytes.

Similar computations of space requirements for the variant record declaration in Example 1.11C show that the first part of this kind of record requires 3 bytes, the staff part requires 70 bytes, the teacher part requires 67 bytes, and the student part requires 66 bytes. A compiler normally implements such a variant record by allocating 73 bytes (3 plus the largest of the other three numbers) and using the space after the first 3 bytes for all three parts. For instance, an assignment to a staff person's YearsOfService would put a REAL value in the fifth through the eighth bytes after the common part. For a teacher, the fifth byte would be used for the Boolean Tenured and the sixth, seventh, and eighth bytes would be the first three characters of the Department String. For a student, the fifth through the eighth bytes after the common part would be the first four characters of the SourceOfFunding String.

Other Possibilities

An alternative form of Example 1.11C is the **free union**. It is defined by omitting the word "Person" in the variant declaration in that example. This has the same effect as omitting the field created by the phrase "Person: Category;" in the amalgamated declaration. *Note:* Some compilers require you to omit the colon as well.

When a free union is used, you save the space taken up by that field. However, then you cannot inspect a variant record to determine which variant it is. This can often be disadvantageous.

The variant part of a record is much like a CASE statement, except that field sections are used in place of statements. You may list several constant expressions before a colon, or a subrange of constant expressions. For example, you could replace the phrase "Teacher" by "PartTimeTeacher, FullTimeTeacher." Then both kinds of teacher would have the same structure in their records.

You are allowed to omit the fields for a variant. For example, you could insert the following variant between the Staff and Teacher variants:

```
|    Retired : ;
```

Then records of retired persons would have an ID field but no other fields.

Check Your Understanding

1. What characters do the following represent, according to the ASCII table in Section 1.8? 53C 101C 141C

2. For the enumeration type WhatKind = (Negative, Zero, Positive), write a function procedure that tells WhatKind of INTEGER its parameter is.

3. Write a program segment that assigns to a variable Count the number of staff employees in Emp. Assume the variant record declaration given in Example 1.11C.

4. Consider the declaration TYPE X=RECORD ID: CARDINAL; Y: ARRAY [1..7] OF REAL; U,V,W: CHAR; END. Under the space requirement assumptions made in this section, tell the number of bytes in X and in an Information record as declared in Example 1.9A; then compute how many bytes it would be for a variant record with X and Information. Use a BOOLEAN tag field.

5. (NA) Write a statement procedure containing a CASE statement that prints the English word corresponding to its CARDINAL parameter ("one" for 1, "two" for 2, etc.), except that it prints "Out of range" for any cardinal larger than 4.

6. (NA) Convert each to octal notation: 7, 14, 28, 100, 231.

1.12 SOFTWARE ENGINEERING

Software engineering is the study of how to develop large programs or systems of programs to perform a given task. The development can be broken down into six stages (Fig. 12) that form what is called the **software development life cycle**: analyze, specify, design, code, test, and maintain.

Analyze: The objective in the analysis stage is to develop a clear statement of the requirements for a satisfactory solution of the problem. You have to find out what kind of data will be managed and what kind of results the program should produce. You have to see what resources are available in terms of hardware, people to operate the system, and money to develop and maintain the system. A significant aspect of this stage is to determine whether in fact a computer solution is desirable.

Specify: The objective of the specification stage is to describe in full detail *what* the software system will do, as it appears to the end user. In other words, you must develop a clear and detailed description of the task to be performed. For large, complicated projects, this tends to resemble a legal contract between the software engineers and the end user. The task to be

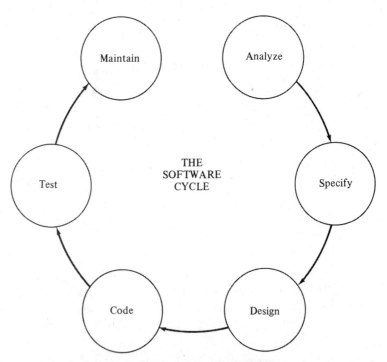

FIGURE 12. The software development cycle.

performed should be expressed in terms of the application for which it is to be used rather than in computer terminology. The overall criterion is that it should be understandable to the end user who knows nothing about computers and programming and has no wish to learn.

Design: The objective of the design stage is to describe *how* the software is to accomplish the task. The primary technique for developing the design is **top-down analysis**, also known as **stepwise refinement**. We use pseudocode to describe the algorithms. Each algorithm should be short and call on a number of other relatively independent algorithmic units that communicate with each other primarily through parameter lists. Then we develop those subalgorithms further. All ambiguities and contradictions found in the specifications are to be resolved at this stage. The detailed design should be expressed in terms of the capabilities of a computer. Still, it is best to keep it more general than a specific computer language; keep to ordinary English to the extent possible. The design should be explainable to an end user who knows little or nothing about programming but does not mind learning something about how computers work in general.

Code: The objective of the coding stage is to develop the program in a specific computer language. The primary goal is to produce correct results in an acceptable amount of execution time. A secondary goal, almost as important, is to develop a program that is easily understood by other people. Studies have shown that typically, for significant and worthwhile programs, at least twice as much time is spent working on a program after it is "finished" as before that point. The people who have to maintain and modify the program after this "up and running" stage may not be the ones who wrote it; if they cannot understand it, they may be forced to throw it out and start over. That would be a great waste of time and effort. Moreover, the programmer will find the debugging and testing of the program much easier if great care has been taken in writing the program clearly. This is why style principles relating to formatting, commenting, choice of identifiers, and so forth are so important.

Test: The objective of the testing stage is to eliminate logic errors and other conflicts with the specifications as much as possible. Quite often, **bottom-up testing** is used: First, individual units are tested; second, several modules are tested as a unit to see how well they work together; third, the completed system is tested by the end user. However, a **top-down approach** to testing often works better: The top levels of the system are coded and tested as early as possible, using "dummy procedures" in place of the real ones. These **procedure stubs** might have nothing but a number of WRITE statements, or they might assign their parameters some reasonable made-up values.

Maintain: The objective of the maintenance stage is to keep the system in a state such that it meets needs that arise after it is in use. Previously undetected logic errors may surface and need correcting. The computer or operating system may be replaced by a more modern one, requiring adaptations of the software. Or the user may want new features added or existing features improved.

Testing

Experience with large programming projects has shown that about two thirds of the errors arise in the design stage and only about one third in the coding stage. The time and effort required for the testing stage can be minimized if you are extremely careful in the design and implementation stages. Specifications must be detailed enough that test data can be developed for the software system. Most of the test data should be written up during the specification and design stages, before the coding begins. This should include the expected results of running the system with that test data. Every statement in the program must be tested by one or more test runs. For each IF condition, there should be a test run that makes it true and a test run that makes it false.

Consider a program that is to sort a list of from 1 to 10 items, putting them in increasing order. Then it should be tested with 1 item and with 10 items as well as for several numbers in between. Also, you should see what happens with 11 items or with none at all. The program should be tested with a list that is already in order, with a list that is in reverse order, with a list that is in order except that the first item is moved to the end, with a list that is in order except that the last item is moved to the front, and with several other special cases, as well as a few lists that are simply well mixed up.

It is often highly useful to put debugging statements in the program at the time the program is coded, to aid in later testing. These statements are removed or disabled when the program has been thoroughly tested. A simple technique is to use statements that print the values of certain key variables at certain key points. If you use such **tracing** statements, be sure to identify the key point; for instance, you could number those key points and write the number as well as the values of the variables. An example is:

```
WriteString ('At the point numbered 3, x = ');
WriteCard (x, 1);
WriteLn;
```

A more sophisticated method is to guard such a statement sequence with a test of a Boolean expression, as in: IF Debugging THEN... END. Debugging can be a Boolean constant with the value TRUE during test runs; on the last compilation, declare Debugging = FALSE to deactivate the traces. You may want several such debugging constants for testing different aspects of the program.

One way to avoid an excessive amount of output from tracing statements is to use an "assertion." This can be an expression that should be true at a certain key point if all is well. At key point 4 you could test the truth of the assertion X>=0 by using the procedure call Assert(X>=0, 4). This invokes a procedure along the following lines:

```
PROCEDURE Assert (Condition : BOOLEAN; Point : INTEGER);
BEGIN
    IF NOT Condition THEN
        WriteInt (Point, 1); ...
    END;
END Assert;
```

The statement sequence guarded by the IF can be as complex as you like. You might want to halt the program at some points when the assertion is false; you could pass a negative integer to the second parameter in such cases and use IF Point<0 THEN HALT; END after the WRITE statements.

CHAPTER REVIEW

It is inappropriate to summarize this whole chapter, since it is itself a summary of the essentials of a first course in programming. However, it is profitable to review those aspects of Modula-2 that might cause some trouble to people whose first course was in Pascal. This summary should be adequate to allow them to read this book if they are going to do all their programming assignments and tests in Pascal. *Note:* The hints on programming style in Sections 1.3, 1.6, and 1.7 are just as applicable in Pascal as in Modula-2.

CARDINAL is a set of nonnegative integers, usually ranging twice as high as the set of INTEGERs. X # 0 means X not-equal-to 0. INC(X) means to increment X by 1 unit; DEC(X) means to decrement X by 1 unit.

An operator cannot combine variables of different types, and an expression cannot be assigned to a variable of a different type, with two exceptions: (1) Types that are the same up to "subrangeness" are compatible for operators and assignments; (2) CARDINAL expressions can be assigned to INTEGER variables and vice versa. In particular, type conversions are required when REALs are mixed with either INTEGERs or CARDINALs in an expression. FLOAT converts an integer to a real.

There is no generalized READ or WRITE statement that accepts a varying number of parameters of varying types. The input and output procedures are subject to the same restrictions to which all other procedures are subject. Thus any particular READ procedure from InOut requires exactly one parameter, and there must be a different READ procedure for each type of variable into which you want to read a value. For instance, ReadCard has one CARDINAL parameter, ReadReal has one REAL parameter, and Read has one CHAR parameter. Every input and output procedure must be explicitly imported from a library module.

BEGIN is used only to begin the body of a program or procedure; it is never used after THEN or ELSE or DO. Every IF, WHILE, or FOR requires a matching END. Capitalization is significant; all reserved words and built-in identifiers are fully capitalized. The name of a procedure follows the END of that procedure.

If an expression of the form B AND C occurs and B is false, C is not evaluated. This partial-evaluation feature avoids certain kinds of crashes that must be guarded against in Pascal. Similarly, if B is true, then evaluation of B OR C does not cause evaluation of C.

Miscellaneous: Open array parameters are available. String variables can be assigned string constants of shorter length. The CASE statement has an ELSE clause. The word FUNCTION is replaced by PROCEDURE. RETURN terminates a function or statement procedure; it is required for functions.

PRACTICE TEST

The test that your instructor gives you on this chapter may include exercises for which you are to write a short program, procedure, or segment of a program. The following are some practice exercises. The answer to each of these is in this book (as indicated in the exercise) so you can check your answers easily. To prepare for a test, study the indicated examples thoroughly until you can be sure that you would earn a high grade on a test composed solely of these exercises. If you understand them well, you should have little trouble with the actual test questions.

1. Write a program that finds the largest of a list of cardinals read from an input file and then prints the result to an output file. [Example 1.4A simplified]

2. Write a function to find the least-common multiple of two given positive integers. [Example 1.6A]

3. Write a function that tells whether a given array of reals contains any negative number. [Example 1.7A]

4. Write a function that tells how many components of two given arrays of cardinals have equal values. [Example 1.7B]

5. Write a statement procedure that reads one full line of input and creates a null-terminated string containing everything up to the end-of-line (or as far as possible, if the line is too long). [Example 1.8B]

6. Write a statement procedure that capitalizes all lowercase letters in a given array of characters. [Exercise 2 in Section 1.8]

PROGRAMMING PROBLEMS

1. Revise Example 1.7B (Telepathy) so that two numbers are read before the data for each run: the ID number and also the number of cards in the run. The number of cards will never be more than 100. That is, the first run might be preceded by 4173 and 60, meaning that the run with the ID 4173 has only 60 cards. After the 120 cardinals that represent the data for that run, the next two numbers might be 2222 and 25, meaning that the run with the ID 2222 is next and has 25 cards. That pair of numbers would then be followed by the 50 cardinals for that run, and so forth.

2. Revise Example 1.7B so that, after the input file has been processed, the program reports the number of runs entered and the average number of matches per run.

3. Write a program to read a 10-by-10 matrix (as declared in Section 1.7) and tell whether it is a **magic square**. A magic square is a square matrix of integers in which the sum of entries for each row, for each column, and for each of the two diagonals are the same (that is, 22 sums are all equal to each other). The input will be 100 integers, one row at a time. For extra credit, tell whether the entries are the integers from 1 to 100, each used exactly once.

4. A matrix is said to have a **saddle point** at a component that is the largest value in its column and the smallest value in its row. Write a program to read a 10-by-10 matrix (as declared in Section 1.7) and find the coordinates of all saddle points.

5. Revise Example 1.8A (WordCounter) to read a text file and report the total number of words in the file, the total number of lines, and the average number of words per line.

6. Write a statistical program that reads a file and reports how many 1-character "words" there were, how many 2-character "words," how many 3-character "words," and so forth. Define a "word" to consist of characters with ordinal number higher than 32 and bounded by characters with ordinal number not higher than 32. You may assume that no word has more than 50 characters.

7. Write a LIAR program as follows: Tell the user of the program you have picked an integer from 1 to 10 and she is to guess it in as few guesses as she can. Give her nine guesses and say they are all wrong. Then tell her the correct answer (any number she did not pick) and insult her intelligence for taking so long to get it. *Implementation restriction:* Use an array of 10 Boolean values to record the guesses.

8. Write a program to read two lists of numbers from an input file. The first list has 30 integers, all different from each other; they are the ID numbers of workers at a certain company. The second list has an unknown number of integers, possibly including some duplicates; they are the ID numbers of workers who passed through the security entrance on a given day, in the order they came (some came and went several times). The program is to print all integers that occur in both lists (if any), except that no integer is to be printed more than once (this is the list of workers present that day). Store the first list in an array of 30 integers; use an array of 30 Boolean values to keep track of which integers have been printed.

9. An author sends a manuscript to his publisher. The copyeditor makes changes in the manuscript by prefixing each line with one of three 3-character codes: with "i   " if the copyeditor inserted it, with "d   " if the copyeditor wants it deleted, with "   " if there is no change. Write a program that accepts a manuscript edited this way and prints either the original manuscript or the manuscript with the revisions incorporated, as specified by the user of the program (but strip the first three characters off in either case).

Shorter Problems (can be done well with fewer than 15 statements)

10. Write a procedure that inserts a given null-terminated string G into another null-terminated string A starting with component number S of A. Thus A becomes longer by the number of "actual" characters in G. Make reasonable adjustments for out-of-range values without crashing.

11. Write a program that reads an input file and creates a new file that contains only those lines of the input file that begin with a capital letter. Leading blanks are to be ignored in deciding which lines to print. Use the ReadLine procedure in Example 1.8B appropriately.

12. Write a procedure that converts a positive integer to "octal notation." The two parameters should be the CARDINAL value to be converted to "octal notation," and VAR Result: ARRAY OF [0..6]. For instance, 157 should be converted to '000235'.

13. Write a procedure that converts "octal notation" for a number to the number itself. Assume the same parameters as in the previous problem, except that Result is a value parameter and the CARDINAL parameter is a VAR parameter.

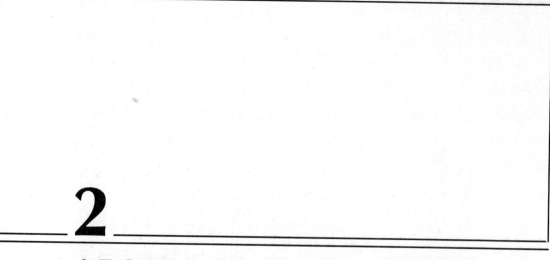

2

ABSTRACT DATA TYPES

In this chapter you will learn about the concept that is the heart of this text—abstract data types. This powerful concept is used to make large, complex programs much more manageable, much easier to develop, and less subject to error.

You will see two language features that facilitate working with abstract data types—library modules and opaque declarations. The latter are used only in library modules. These language features are the primary points of difference between Modula-2 and its predecessor Pascal.

A library module can be thought of as a part of a program that is compiled separately. One advantage of **separate compilation** is that it saves time. If you make a change in part of the program that does not affect any of several previously compiled library modules, recompilation does not take as long, since only part of the program is recompiled. Another advantage is that the compiled library module can be used in several different programs.

A good understanding of recursion is essential to further study of computer science. A full chapter could be written on the uses of recursion alone, if placed later in the book, but it seems the better course to introduce it in the latter part of this chapter and then use it wherever appropriate throughout the text. Each of the later chapters has several uses of recursion, especially Chapters 5 and 7.

2.1 CREATING LIBRARY MODULES

A library module is two separate compilation units, the **implementation module** and the **definition module**. The definition module contains only the headings of procedures; the full procedures are in the implementation module. A **client module** is a compilation unit that imports the identifiers declared in the library module; it may be either a program module or one of the two parts of another library module.

The programmer of a client module uses only the definition module, to find out what the procedures do and how they are invoked; the way they do what they do is hidden in the implementation module. Therefore, descriptive comments are even more important in a definition module than in normal program modules; *every* procedure must have a highly descriptive comment heading.

The Terminal Module

The Terminal module, available with almost all implementations of Modula-2, provides some elementary input/output procedures for communicating with the user via the screen and keyboard. The advantage of having the Terminal module available in addition to the InOut module is twofold: One is that importing from a library module increases the size of the compiled program accordingly; Terminal is much smaller than InOut, which can sometimes be crucial. In addition, the InOut module provides for only one input channel and only one output channel, so you cannot send messages to the user's screen as long as you have an external file open for output. You can use Terminal for such communications.

Terminal exports four procedures that are the same as those in InOut except they always apply to the screen and keyboard. Those four are WriteString, WriteLn, Write, and Read (the latter two for writing and reading a single character).

Qualidents

No doubt you are wondering how you can import WriteLn from Terminal and also from InOut without creating confusion for the compiler (confusion is anathema to a compiler). The answer is, you cannot. But you can import the identifiers Terminal and InOut using the following import sections; then you can refer to the two procedures as Terminal.WriteLn and InOut.WriteLn.

```
IMPORT Terminal;
IMPORT InOut;
```

Terminal.WriteLn is called a **qualident**, short for **qualified identifier**; the identifier WriteLn is qualified by the name of the module where it is declared. The foregoing import sections make it so that Terminal and InOut can be referenced unqualifiedly in your program, but not any of their identifiers. You could even declare WriteLn independently to mean something different and use it along with Terminal.WriteLn and InOut.WriteLn.

Modula-2 provides another way to be able to use both WriteLn procedures in your program. You can use the following import sections:

```
IMPORT Terminal;
FROM InOut IMPORT WriteString, WriteLn, WriteInt; (* for example *)
```

Now you can use WriteLn standing alone; it refers to the identifier declared in InOut. When you want to use Terminal's WriteLn procedure, you must qualify it: Terminal.WriteLn. For instance, to write the message "Start" to both an output file and the screen, you could use the following lines if you have the import sections just described:

```
WriteString ('Start');
WriteLn;
Terminal.WriteString ('Start');
Terminal.WriteLn;
```

Creating a Definition Module

The one thing I have found irritating about Terminal is that it provides no way to write an integer; I can often get along without the rest of the procedures from InOut. I do not want to bloat my programs by importing from InOut just to get WriteInt, so I wrote a helpful little library module to use in conjunction with Terminal. I call this module "Helpful."

I included a few useful constants: Blank is the blank character; it is obviously useful in making a program clear to the reader. Null is the null character (ordinal number 0), used as a sentinel value in a string of characters. EOL is the end-of-line marker, which is also in InOut. Since Null and EOL cannot be typed at a keyboard, I use Modula-2's octal (base 8) notation for characters—36C means "the character whose ordinal number is 3 eights plus 6." Example 2.1A contains the definition module. This module consists of everything but the statements to be executed.

EXAMPLE 2.1A _____

```
DEFINITION MODULE Helpful;
EXPORT QUALIFIED (* constants  *) Blank, Null, EOL,
                 (* procedures *) WriteInteger, CompareStr;
    (* Helpful identifiers to augment the Terminal module *)
    (* Written by William C. Jones, May 19-- *)
CONST
    Blank = ' ';
    Null = 0C;
    EOL = 36C;
(* *********************************************************** )

PROCEDURE WriteInteger (GivenInteger : INTEGER);
    (* Write an integer with no leading blanks, using
       the Write procedure from Terminal *)

PROCEDURE CompareStr (First  : ARRAY OF CHAR;
                      Second : ARRAY OF CHAR) : INTEGER;
    (* First and Second should be null-terminated strings.
       Return a positive integer if First > Second,
       a negative if First < Second, and zero if equal *)

END Helpful.
```

I added a procedure that allows me to compare two strings for equality or to see which is larger; I have often found such a procedure helpful, since Modula-2 does not allow relational operators with strings. Note that I used two different formal-parameter sections in the heading of CompareStr, instead of using First, Second: ARRAY OF CHAR. This allows the two parameters to be of different types. Two examples of the use of this CompareStr procedure are:

```
IF CompareStr (Word, X) > 0 THEN ...   (* see if Word > X *)
WHILE CompareStr (X, "hi") <= 0 DO ... (* test X <= "hi") *)
```

A definition module differs from a program module in five respects:

☐ It begins with the word DEFINITION.

☐ It has EXPORT QUALIFIED followed by the names of the identifiers to be exported from this module. This is the **export section**.

☐ Each procedure is stripped down to just its heading and semicolon.

☐ It has no action part (BEGIN statement-sequence).

☐ Opaque types are allowed but not priorities (you do not know about these yet; I just mention them to make this list of differences complete).

You would rarely have a need to declare an identifier in the definition module that you did not want to export to client modules. In fact, many implementations of Modula-2 automatically export all identifiers defined, in accordance with the most recent specifications for Modula-2. Such implementations do not require an EXPORT QUALIFIED section; if one is present, they should treat it as a comment.

The Helpful Implementation Module

After you complete a definition module, you compile it (e.g., on the VAX 780 you use *$MOD HELPFUL.DEF*, assuming you named the file HELPFUL.DEF). This allows you to compile any module that imports from this library module, although you cannot run a client module until you have prepared the implementation module. *Note:* In order to give you the flavor of the compilation process, I describe what you have to do on the VAX 780; your system will probably use a somewhat different procedure. The $ symbol is the prompt given by the VAX 780.

The next step is to write the corresponding implementation module. First you make a copy of the definition module in a different file (I would use *$COPY HELPFUL.DEF HELPFUL.IMP*). This new copy will be the implementation module. In the new copy, you replace the word DEFINITION by IMPLEMENTATION, omit the export and import sections, and add any other import sections you might need. Then you fill in the blocks for all procedures, adding additional global declarations as needed. Finally, you write the statement part of the module, if needed. Figure 1 shows the order of compilation.

Example 2.1B displays the Helpful implementation module. It makes use of the ASCII code, in which the digits are the characters numbered 48 (for '0') through 57 (for '9'). The logic for the WritePositive procedure is rather primitive, and it assumes that the maximum positive integer has only five digits. A much better implementation of WritePositive will be presented in Example 2.6B.

The statement part of the implementation module will be executed before any client module executes. For instance, if Helpful exported a Boolean variable

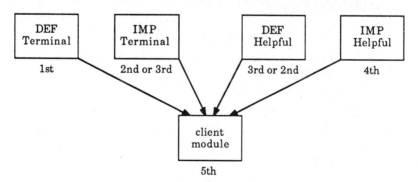

FIGURE 1. The order of compilation of interdependent modules.

EXAMPLE 2.1B _____

```
IMPLEMENTATION MODULE Helpful;
FROM Terminal IMPORT Write;
    (* Helpful identifiers to augment the Terminal module*)
    (* Written by William C. Jones, May 19-- *)
(*****************************************************************)

PROCEDURE WriteInteger (GivenInteger : INTEGER);
  (* Write an integer with no leading blanks, using Write*)
  (*---------------------------------------------------------*)

    PROCEDURE WritePositive (GivenCardinal : CARDINAL);
    BEGIN
        Write (CHR (48 + (GivenCardinal DIV 10000)));
        Write (CHR (48 + (GivenCardinal DIV 1000) MOD 10));
        Write (CHR (48 + (GivenCardinal DIV 100) MOD 10));
        Write (CHR (48 + (GivenCardinal DIV 10) MOD 10));
        Write (CHR (48 + GivenCardinal MOD 10));
    END WritePositive;
  (*---------------------------------------------------------*)

BEGIN         (* WriteInteger *)
    IF GivenInteger = 0 THEN
        Write ('0');
    ELSIF GivenInteger < 0 THEN
        Write ('-');
        WritePositive (-GivenInteger);
    ELSE
        WritePositive (GivenInteger);
    END;
END WriteInteger;
(*****************************************************************)

PROCEDURE CompareStr (First  : ARRAY OF CHAR;
                      Second : ARRAY OF CHAR) : INTEGER;
    (* First and Second should be null-terminated strings.
       Return a positive integer if First > Second,
       a negative if First < Second, and zero if equal *)
VAR
    K : CARDINAL;
BEGIN
    First [HIGH (First)] := Null;    (* to play it safe *)
    Second [HIGH (Second)] := Null;  (* ditto           *)
    K := 0;
    WHILE (First[K] = Second[K]) AND (First[K] # Null) DO
        INC (K);
    END;
    RETURN INTEGER (ORD (First [K])) -
           INTEGER (ORD (Second [K]));
END CompareStr;
(*****************************************************************)

END Helpful.
```

named Okay, you could put BEGIN Okay := TRUE just before END Helpful in the implementation module, which would initialize Okay. The declaration VAR Okay: BOOLEAN goes in the definition module.

Next you compile the implementation module. On the VAX, you use *$MOD HELPFUL.IMP*. If it compiles successfully, you need to **link** it with the modules from which it imports. On the VAX you use *$LINK HELPFUL*. If Helpful imported from another library module you had written, say EDLEE, you would use *$LINK HELPFUL,EDLEE*. Since the VAX keeps standard library modules such as Terminal and InOut in a special library that it has no trouble finding easily, you do not mention Terminal when linking Helpful. Of course, you do not run Helpful; it is not, after all, a program module.

Now you can compile, link, and run a program that imports identifiers from Helpful. On the VAX, this is done (assuming you have a program module in a file named CATHY.MOD) using *$MOD CATHY* then *$LINK CATHY,HELPFUL* then *$RUN CATHY*. If you make any changes in the implementation module, you do not recompile CATHY, but you have to relink it before running it. If you make any changes in the definition module, you must start over with all the compiling and linking.

You can test the procedures in the Helpful module by writing a **driver program**, that is, a program intended solely to "exercise" those procedures. For instance, the body of a driver program could prompt the user for two strings and write the result of calling CompareStr; then it could prompt the user for an integer and use WriteInteger to print it.

The Value of Library Modules

There are several good reasons for using library modules. One is that a library module can contain several related utility procedures that make it much easier to work with a given programming situation. The procedures are used in many different programs; this means that those client programs are significantly smaller in size and complexity than they would otherwise be, so they are easier to develop.

Another reason is that a library module can completely conceal a data structure from client modules, which provides a level of abstraction that simplifies programming; an example is the Terminal module. The programmer of a client module need not be at all concerned with how Terminal handles input and output, merely that it handles them properly. This is called **data abstraction** or **information hiding**; you will see many examples of it in this book. It is a key technique in the development of larger programs.

A third reason for using a library module is to isolate a global variable that is used too widely to pass as a parameter each time. You know, of course, that it is bad style for a procedure to cause a change in a variable that is declared outside the procedure, unless the variable is passed as a parameter to that procedure. But sometimes that means that a variable has to be passed to too many procedures, which is clumsy. In Modula-2, you can put the variable and the relevant procedures in a separate library module. Then anyone reading the program can easily see when the variable is changed. An example of this is the Boolean variable Done in the InOut library module.

A fourth reason for using a library module is that it can be compiled separately from the programs that use it and the compiled form used in several different programs. This greatly reduces debugging time when you make one small change in a program that is several hundred pages long (counting all the modules involved).

Library Modules for Pascal Programmers

If you are programming in Pascal, you can accomplish much of what Modula-2's library modules do if your compiler has two nonstandard features: One is an INCLUDE option, so you can put a group of related declarations in a separate file and have them included during compilation. The other feature is the ability to have declarations in a fairly arbitrary order, since you will be having several TYPE sections mixed in with several PROCEDURE sections.

Assume, for instance, that your program has declarations such as those indicated on the left of the following box, and that the three identifiers beginning with L have a common subject matter suitable for a library module. You should be able to reorder the declarations as shown on the right, with all L-declarations isolated in one group (the three indented lines). Then you cut the L-declarations out of your program, creating another file containing them (called perhaps LSTUFF.LIB). In their place in the program you put {$I LSTUFF.LIB} or {%INCLUDE 'LSTUFF.LIB'} or whatever your compiler specifies. This "compiler directive" means that the LSTUFF.LIB file, though physically separate from the file containing the program, is to be treated during compilation as if it were actually at that point in your program. That is, LSTUFF.LIB is physically but not logically separate.

```
PROGRAM X ...                    PROGRAM X ...
CONST A = ...                    CONST A = ...
TYPE  L1 = ...                       TYPE L1 = ...
      B = ...                        PROCEDURE L2 ...
PROCEDURE L2 ...                     PROCEDURE L3 ...
PROCEDURE C ...                  TYPE B = ...
FUNCTION  D ...                  PROCEDURE C ...
PROCEDURE L3 ...                 PROCEDURE D ...
PROCEDURE E ...                  PROCEDURE E ...
BEGIN (* program *) ...          BEGIN (* program *) ...
```

You may sometimes find it necessary to put some initialization code in an extra procedure that is called once by the client module as part of its own initialization. This is not as satisfactory as Modula-2's features, but it works.

The remarks just made on the value of library modules apply to such constructs in Pascal as well as in Modula-2. If this "library module" is included in several different client modules, as is usually the case, it is worthwhile to consider the included file the "implementation module" and develop a stripped-down form of it as the "definition module." The stripped-down form has the block of all procedures and functions removed and usually the part after the equals sign in type declarations. You only refer to the definition module when you write client programs in Pascal.

Check Your Understanding

1. Describe what would have to be added to Examples 2.1A and 2.1B to be able to export the ReadLine procedure of Example 1.8B from Helpful, after modifying ReadLine to import from Terminal instead of InOut.

2. How would the effect of CompareStr be changed if (First[K]#Null) were changed to (Second[K]#Null)?

3. (NA) Describe in detail how Helpful would be changed so that the function call Count( ) would return the number of times that WriteInteger has been called since program execution began. *Hint:* Declare a variable CountCalls global to the implementation module.

4. (NA) Rewrite the WHILE condition of the CompareStr procedure in Example 2.1B so the first and second statements can be omitted without taking a chance on a crash. Then write an essay discussing the pros and cons of doing this.

Reminder: Answers to all Check Your Understanding exercises are at the end of the book, except for those marked **NA** (for "no answer"). The NA ones may be assigned by your instructor for homework.

2.2 ABSTRACT DATA TYPES

A set of programs is being designed for working with student records for a school. During the development of the design, it is found that the programs need to be able to do the following things with student records: (1) Read one record from a file; (2) Write one record to a file; (3) Compare two records on the basis of ID numbers to see which comes first. None of these programs is directly concerned with the individual fields of a record, except as required for the three operations just listed.

The definition module in Example 2.2A provides three procedures that can be used by these client modules. This module is called InfoMan, because it provides

EXAMPLE 2.2A _____

```
DEFINITION MODULE InfoMan;
    (* These are some declarations that permit manipulation
        of one Information record *)
    (* Written by William C. Jones, May 19-- *)
EXPORT QUALIFIED Information, InputInfo, OutputInfo,
                Compare, Okay;

CONST
    StrMax = 20;
TYPE
    ShortString = ARRAY [0..StrMax] OF CHAR;
    Information =
        RECORD
            ID, CreditHours : CARDINAL;
            AmtOwed         : REAL;
            Name            : ShortString;
            IsFullTime      : BOOLEAN;
        END;
VAR
    Okay : BOOLEAN; (* tells whether Input was successful*)
    (************************************************************)

PROCEDURE InputInfo (VAR TheInfo : Information);
    (* Read all values into TheInfo;
        Okay := Done successfully *)

PROCEDURE OutputInfo (TheInfo : Information);
    (* Write all values from TheInfo in a form that
        can be properly read by InputInfo *)

PROCEDURE Compare (First, Second : Information) : INTEGER;
    (* Return a positive integer if First > Second;  return
        a negative if First < Second; return 0 if equal *)

END InfoMan.
```

for the manipulation of information records. The rest of this section gives some illustrations of how these procedures can be used, followed by the implementation for InfoMan.

The Compare procedure may require some explanation. It is often desirable to be able to tell whether one piece of information is the same as another; you would test Compare(X,Y)=0 to determine this. If you are keeping the information in order, Compare(X,Y)>0 tells whether X comes later in the ordering than Y. You would expect that the Compare function makes the comparison between the ID numbers of the two students.

If you write a program that manipulates information values as declared in this InfoMan definition module, and if you never refer to the internal structure of an information record (such as the specific field names), using only the procedures declared in InfoMan, then your program treats Information as an **abstract data type**. In general, an abstract data type consists of (1) a type-identifier for a class of objects and (2) sufficient procedures for working with objects of that type that a client module need not access the internal structure of the objects. InfoMan contains only one type-identifier, namely Information; and InfoMan has just three procedures. Actually, there are not too many programs that can manage with just these three procedures; abstract data types introduced later in this book will have a greater number and variety of procedures.

Counted Arrays

The majority of applications of arrays do not fill the arrays entirely. When working with arrays of characters, it is normal in Modula-2 to use the Null character as a sentinel value to mark the end of the portion you are using (examples are in Section 1.8). If you had an array of social security numbers, you could use 0 as a sentinel value, since 0 is not a "naturally occurring" social security number. For arbitrary arrays, however, this is often not reasonable; it can be difficult or impossible to find a value that cannot naturally appear, which is the criterion for a useful sentinel value. In such cases, it usually works well to keep a counter of how many of the first few components have valid values. The following record, called a **counted array**, could be used in such cases:

```
TYPE CountedArray =
        RECORD
           Item : ARRAY [1..1000] OF Information;
           Size : CARDINAL;   (* number of components in use *)
        END;
```

Consider, for instance, a program that works with an array of student records; it might be part of the administrative software for a small school. Assume that the enrollment at this school normally ranges between 600 and 800; then an array of 1000 records should be enough to allow for some growth. At any given time, the actual number of students might be 743 or 618 or 792; this number would be stored in the Size field. A small example of a Counted Array is shown in Figure 2.

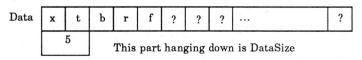

FIGURE 2. How a counted array with five values appears in memory.

If all the records in such an array are to be written out, the following program segment can be used (assuming the array is named Data):

```
FOR K := 1 TO Data.Size DO
    OutputInfo (Data.Item [K]);
END;
```

Note that the actual parameter of a procedure can be a component of an array that is part of a record variable, even though the formal parameter is a simple identifier. Some students have trouble remembering this.

If a new record is to be read in and added at the high end of such an array of records, the following program segment can be used:

```
InputInfo (Student);
IF Okay THEN
    INC (Data.Size);
    Data.Item [Data.Size] := Student;
END;
```

Note that it is legal to assign the whole record at once; you do not have to assign one field at a time. Alternatively, since it makes no difference what is in the components numbered higher than Size, you could use the following segment:

```
InputInfo (Data.Item [Data.Size + 1]);
IF Okay THEN
    INC (Data.Size);
END;
```

If this hypothetical school adminstration program keeps the list of students *in increasing order*, and if a new record named Student is to be added to the array, then the coding must be correspondingly more complex. The normal method is to move each record up one in the array, beginning from the record at component number Data.Size, until a record is seen that is not greater than Student. At that point, Student can be inserted in the array at the place vacated by the most recently moved record. Example 2.2B shows how this might be done.

EXAMPLE 2.2B _____

```
PROCEDURE InsertInOrder (Student  : Information;
                         VAR Data : CountedArray);
    (* Add the Student to the Data array, keeping records
       in increasing order.  Context: client of InfoADT *)
VAR
    K : CARDINAL;
BEGIN
    WITH Data DO  (* fields are Item and Size *)
        K := Size + 1;
        WHILE (K > 1) AND
              (Compare (Item [K - 1], Student) > 0) DO
            Item [K] := Item [K - 1];
            DEC (K);
        END;
        Item [K] := Student;
        INC (Size);
    END;
END InsertInOrder;
```

Sequential Search

The simplest algorithm for a **sequential search** for an information value named TheInfo is: Look through the array starting from the first value and progressing to the last in sequence. For each value inspected, if you find TheInfo, you are finished. If you come to the end of the array, TheInfo is not there, so you are finished. The coding is in Example 2.2C.

There are some delicate aspects to this coding. If the loop terminates when Index is less than or equal to Data.Size, it must be because the information values matched, so Index is correct. But if Index becomes greater than Data.Size, the first part of the WHILE condition is false and the loop terminates, so the second part is not evaluated (because of short-circuit evaluation of Boolean expressions). This is important, because there may not even be a component number Index in the array. Example 2.2B contains a similar use of short-circuit evaluation.

Searching through a Sorted Array

If you know that the values in the array are in order from lowest to highest, you can cut the search time significantly by writing the WHILE condition in Example

EXAMPLE 2.2C _____

```
PROCEDURE Search (TheInfo  : Information;
                      VAR Data : CountedArray) : CARDINAL;
      (* Use sequential search to find the Index of the first
         instance of TheInfo in the Data; return Size + 1
         if missing.  Context:  client of InfoADT *)
VAR
    Index : CARDINAL;
BEGIN
    Index := 1;
    WHILE (Index <= Data.Size) AND
          (Compare (TheInfo, Data.Item [Index]) # 0) DO
          INC (Index);
    END;
    RETURN Index;
END Search;
```

2.2C as follows:

```
WHILE (Index <= Data.Size) AND
      (Compare (TheInfo, Data.Item [Index]) > 0) DO
```

Now the loop also terminates if a value is seen that is greater than TheInfo. This requires an additional check after the WHILE statement, in place of the simple RETURN Index statement:

```
IF (Index <= Data.Size) AND
        (Compare (TheInfo, Data.Item [Index]) = 0) THEN
    RETURN Index;
ELSE
    RETURN Data.Size + 1;
END;
```

Notice that you must check that Index is in range first, since the loop could have terminated because you reached the end of the array.

It is worthwhile to estimate the time saved when the array is sorted. Consider a typical case in which you are searching through an array of about 800 values and the value TheInfo is near the middle (if it is there at all). Then the original WHILE loop (in Example 2.2C) would execute either 400 or 800 times, depending on whether the value TheInfo is present. The reformulation would average about 400 iterations whether TheInfo is present or not, plus an additional test in the IF statement. This is an insignificant increase in time when TheInfo is present, and a nearly 50% savings when it is not.

Each time through the WHILE loop you have to test a two-part condition. This can be avoided for a sorted array, causing the loop to execute up to one-third faster, by first checking whether TheInfo is beyond the end of the array. Begin by revising the coding as follows:

```
IF Compare (TheInfo, Data.Item [Data.Size]) > 0 THEN
    RETURN Data.Size + 1;
ELSE
    (* use the coding described earlier *)
END;
```

Now the coding described earlier can be simplified by removing the test (Index <= Data.Size) from the WHILE condition and from the IF condition.

An Implementation of InfoMan

Example 2.2D is a full implementation module for InfoMan. The InputInfo procedure simply reads the values for one field at a time, except for the Boolean field. For the procedure to work correctly, the amount owed must be followed by a single blank, then a capital T for TRUE or F for FALSE, then another blank, then the student's name. The blank after the amount owed is read by the ReadReal procedure. The OutputInfo procedure writes the values in each field in such a way that InputInfo can retrieve them.

The Compare function compares the IDs of the two given information records to see which is smaller; it returns 1 if First's ID is greater than Second's, -1 if First's ID is smaller, and 0 if they are the same. You might think that it would be simpler to replace the body of Compare by the single statement RETURN First.ID-Second.ID, and you would be right. However, that statement could crash the program when very large IDs are used. For instance, a typical 16-bit microprocessor would allow cardinals up to 65,535 and integers only up to 32,767; so comparing ID numbers of 50,000 and 1000 would cause problems.

IIII➡ PROGRAMMING STYLE

Some students ask about the declaration of CountedArray: "Why not use two separate variables—Item (the array of 500 components) and Size (the number of

EXAMPLE 2.2D _____

```
IMPLEMENTATION MODULE InfoMan;
FROM InOut      IMPORT ReadCard, WriteCard, Read, Done,
                       ReadString, WriteString, WriteLn;
FROM RealInOut IMPORT ReadReal, WriteReal;
(*****************************************************)

PROCEDURE InputInfo (VAR TheInfo : Information);
    (* Read all values into TheInfo; Okay := Done *)
VAR
    Ch : CHAR;
BEGIN
    ReadCard (TheInfo.ID);
    ReadCard (TheInfo.CreditHours);
    ReadReal (TheInfo.AmtOwed);
    Read (Ch);  (* T for true or F for false *)
    TheInfo.IsFullTime :=  Ch = 'T';
    Read (Ch);  (* a separating blank *)
    ReadString (TheInfo.Name);
    Okay := Done;
END InputInfo;
(*****************************************************)

PROCEDURE OutputInfo (TheInfo : Information);
    (* Write all values from TheInfo in a form that
       can be properly read by InputInfo *)
BEGIN
    WriteCard (TheInfo.ID, 10);
    WriteCard (TheInfo.CreditHours, 10);
    WriteReal (TheInfo.AmtOwed, 10);
    IF TheInfo.IsFullTime THEN
        WriteString (' T ');
    ELSE
        WriteString (' F ');
    END;
    WriteString (TheInfo.Name);
    WriteLn;
END OutputInfo;
(*****************************************************)

PROCEDURE Compare (First, Second : Information) : INTEGER;
    (* Return a positive integer if First > Second;  return
       a negative if First < Second; return 0 if equal *)
BEGIN
    IF First.ID = Second.ID THEN
        RETURN 0;
    ELSIF First.ID < Second.ID THEN
        RETURN -1;
    ELSE
        RETURN 1;
    END;
END Compare;
(*****************************************************)

END InfoMan.
```

components in use) instead of a record?" But Size is meaningless unless accompanied by Item, and Item is useless unless accompanied by Size; the two variables are "meant for each other." Think of RECORD... END as the bonds of matrimony; a record declaration binding them together is the only proper thing to do, considering their intimate relationship to each other.

Summary

The content of this section exemplifies a paradigm that you will see applied many times in this book:

1. Identify a data type as being useful in a programming situation, and describe a number of operations that need to be done with objects of the specified type. The operations must be powerful enough that no client module need access the internal structure of the data objects except by using the specified operations; this is what makes it an *abstract* data type.

2. Describe completely the operations using procedure headings and comment descriptions; this makes up the definition module.

3. Give some examples of coding that use the procedures, as illustrations of the use of the procedures.

4. Develop one or more implementation modules for the data type, to show how the procedures can be realized in coding.

FOR PASCAL PROGRAMMERS: Using your compiler's INCLUDE directive, you would have a separate file, perhaps called INFOMAN.LIB, in which you would put the CONST, TYPE, and VAR declarations from Example 2.2A and the full procedure declarations from Example 2.2D. If used in say 10 client programs, a change in the declarations need only be made in INFOMAN.LIB, and all client programs recompiled, to effect the change in all 10 of them consistently. Moreover, editing and printing a program or INFOMAN.LIB is made easier by this separation. This use is the primary reason why most decent Pascal compilers provide an INCLUDE directive. InputInfo and OutputInfo could have an additional file parameter in Pascal, as in InputInfo(Infile, Information) and OutputInfo(Outfile, Information). When you pass INPUT or OUTPUT as the actual parameters, communication is with the keyboard or screen.

Check Your Understanding

1. Write a program segment that prints every other information value in a counted array named Data, beginning with component 1. Assume the declarations used for Example 2.2B.

2. What changes should be made in Example 2.2B if the array of information values is to be kept in decreasing order?

3. What changes must be made in Examples 2.2A and 2.2D to add a function that returns the amount owed by a given student? Use the following function heading:

```
PROCEDURE DebtOf (Student : Information) : REAL;
```

4. What change should be made in Example 1.9B to use the DebtOf function (from Exercise 3) instead of referring to the AmtOwed field directly?

5. (NA) Write a function that tells how many students in a given counted array owe more than $100. Assume the change described in Exercise 3 has been made in InfoMan.

6. (NA) Revise the coding in Example 2.2B to execute faster by first comparing Student to Item[1] (analogous to the improvement described in the text for Example 2.2C).

2.3 ELEMENTARY USE OF POINTERS; OPAQUE TYPE DECLARATIONS

For each variable in a program, there is an identification number by which it can be referenced. This number is called the **address** of the variable. For example, a 64K machine has 65,536 storage locations (since 1K means 1024 locations, and 64 times 1024 is 65,536); these storage locations are normally numbered from 0 to 65,535. So far, you have not seen any way to refer directly to the address of a variable in a program. That is what is discussed in this section.

A Program Using Addresses Explicitly

The following discussion refers to Example 1.7B (the Telepathy program) for concreteness; but you need not look back to it. That program declared two arrays named Sender and Receiver of type LotsOfNumbers = ARRAY [0..Size−1] OF CARDINAL, where Size is 100. We will recode that program using addresses of arrays rather than the arrays themselves. That is, a LotsOfNumbers variable is to contain the address of an array of 100 cardinals. This requires that we insert the two words POINTER TO in the type declaration of LotsOfNumbers, as follows:

```
TYPE  LotsOfNumbers = POINTER TO ARRAY [0..Size - 1] OF CARDINAL;
```

Now the local declarations of Sender and Receiver as LotsOfNumbers variables in the PerformTask procedure do *not* create arrays; they create instead two variables that can contain the addresses of arrays. So we need a way to create the arrays themselves. That is done by putting the following two **NEW** statements just after the BEGIN of PerformTask:

```
NEW (Sender);
NEW (Receiver);
```

The statement NEW(Sender) does two things: It **allocates** (sets aside or reserves) suitable storage space for an array, and it stores the address of that storage space in Sender.

Obviously, we cannot refer to the array as Sender anymore; Sender is the name of the variable containing the address of the array. We need a notation for referring to the array itself. You have already seen two "compound" ways of referring to variables, namely X[Y] and X.Y. In Modula-2, we use the **caret** or arrow character ↑ when working with address variables. The two arrays of our revised Example 1.7B are referred to as Sender ↑ and Receiver ↑ ; so "Sender ↑ " can be read as "the array whose address is stored in Sender" (Fig. 3).

Note on terminology: Most people recognize that X[Y] is not an identifier; it is a combination of two identifiers and two brackets. But some people do not realize that X.Y and X ↑ are also not identifiers; X.Y is two identifiers separated by a

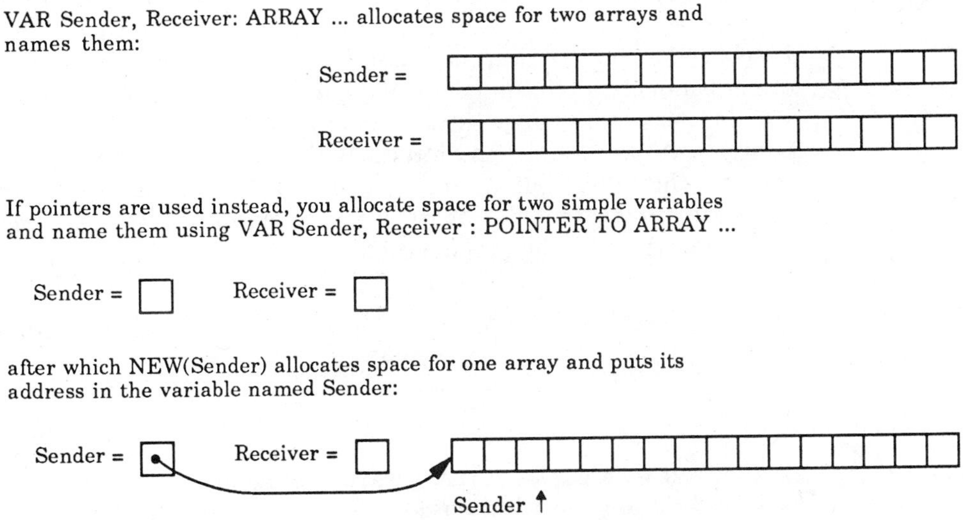

FIGURE 3. *Using pointers to arrays instead of the arrays.*

period, and X ↑ is an identifier followed by an arrow. An identifier consists only of letters and digits.

The formal parameter part of the ReadTwoArrays procedure is (VAR Sender, Receiver: LotsOfNumbers). You can see that these parameters contain addresses of arrays rather than the arrays themselves. Since Sender ↑ is an array, we refer to one of its components using Sender ↑ [K]. This means that a caret must be added in two lines of the ReadTwoArrays procedure as follows:

```
ReadCard (Sender↑ [K]);
ReadCard (Receiver↑ [K]);
```

Some changes are also needed in the NumberOfMatches function. Its formal parameter part is (VAR Sender, Receiver: ARRAY OF CARDINAL). That should be changed to (Sender, Receiver: LotsOfNumbers); the VAR is not necessary, since we are passing addresses rather than large arrays. Then two lines of the function should be modified, as follows:

```
FOR K := 0 TO Size - 1 DO
    IF Sender↑ [K] = Receiver↑ [K[ THEN
```

Alternatively, we could have left the NumberOfMatches procedure as it was and changed the procedure call in PerformTask to WriteCard(NumberOfMatches(Sender ↑ , Receive ↑), 1). That would be an inconsistent use of the identifiers Sender and Receiver, however, so we would also change the names of the formal parameters of NumberOfMatches.

Only one other change is required to make the program correct: Modula-2 requires that we include the following import for any module that uses NEW (actually, there are other alternatives, but they are too advanced to discuss here). **Storage** is a library module that contains procedures to permit management of storage locations by the programmer.

```
FROM Storage IMPORT ALLOCATE;
```

Now that we are done revising the program, you are probably asking yourself, "Why would anyone want to do this? It was simpler before." That is true. I present pointers in this simplest possible context to explain and illustrate them, not to justify them. Another context that provides justification for pointers comes later in this section, and many others in later chapters. Pointers are rarely used precisely in the way just described. If you just cannot wait to have a justification, consider this: If you are sorting information and you frequently execute a swap such as Save := First; First := Second; Second := Save, the algorithm will execute much faster if you are swapping pointers taking 2 bytes each instead of strings of characters taking perhaps hundreds of bytes each.

Two More Examples of Programs Using Pointers

The program in Example 1.1A can be revised so that POINTER TO CARDINAL is used instead of CARDINAL (Fig. 4). Doing this is overkill but instructive. It requires four simple modifications:

☐ Declare TYPE Pointer = POINTER TO CARDINAL;
   VAR NumberPurchased: Pointer;

☐ Replace NumberPurchased by NumberPurchased↑ in the three places where that variable is mentioned.

☐ Insert NEW(NumberPurchased) as the first statement; this creates the CARDINAL variable denoted by NumberPurchased↑.

☐ Put FROM Storage IMPORT ALLOCATE at the top to enable you to use the built-in NEW procedure.

As one additional example, Example 2.3A is a complete program that uses pointers.

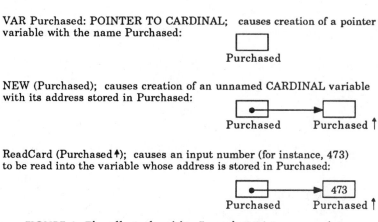

VAR Purchased: POINTER TO CARDINAL; causes creation of a pointer variable with the name Purchased:

Purchased

NEW (Purchased); causes creation of an unnamed CARDINAL variable with its address stored in Purchased:

Purchased   Purchased ↑

ReadCard (Purchased↑); causes an input number (for instance, 473) to be read into the variable whose address is stored in Purchased:

Purchased   473   Purchased ↑

FIGURE 4. The effect of revising Example 1.1A to use a pointer.

EXAMPLE 2.3A _____

```
MODULE IllustratePointers;
FROM InOut  IMPORT WriteString, ReadInt, WriteInt, WriteLn;
FROM Storage IMPORT ALLOCATE;
VAR
    Number : POINTER TO INTEGER;
BEGIN

    NEW (Number);
    WriteString ('Enter an integer: ');
    ReadInt (Number^);
    WriteString ('Its square is ');
    WriteInt (Number^ * Number^, 1);
    WriteLn;

END IllustratePointers.
```

Opaque Type Declarations

An opaque type declaration in a definition module consists of simply listing the type-identifier and postponing the full declaration to the implementation module. It is only allowed for addresses, cardinals, integers, and perhaps a few other simple types. Some processors only allow them for addresses, since that is all that standard Modula-2 requires. As an example, the TYPE section of a definition module could be as follows:

```
TYPE Location;
```

Then the TYPE section of the implementation module might be:

```
TYPE Location = CARDINAL;
```

This double definition means that Location and CARDINAL are names for the same thing, as far as the implementation module is concerned, but no client module can assume that. For instance, if X is a variable of type Location, then ReadCard(X) is a legal statement in the implementation module but not in any client module. The advantage is that the implementation module can later be replaced by a different implementation with a different definition for Location without requiring any changes in any client module.

An Example of an Opaque Type Declaration

Example 2.2A is a definition module for InfoMan; the implementation module is in Example 2.2D. The TYPE section of that definition module declares Information = RECORD ID: CARDINAL... END. I want to make it so that no client module can refer to the internal structure of an Information variable. But since the declaration is there for all to see, I cannot prevent it; any module that imports the type-identifier Information can use the field-identifiers of that record type.

Therefore, I will change this to an opaque type declaration. I must change the TYPE section in the definition module to "TYPE Information;", that is, I omit everything after the identifier being defined. This guarantees that no client module can refer to the internal structure of an Information variable.

I will call the revised library module **InfoADT**, since Information is an abstract data type (**ADT**). The Information data type is called *abstract* because, if I conceal the implementation module and only allow client modules to access the compiled form of it, no one will know what Information is really like. I must make the following four changes in the implementation module:

1. Declare Information as a pointer type. For InfoADT, I use:

```
TYPE  Information = POINTER TO InfoRecord;
      InfoRecord = RECORD
                        ID, CreditHours : CARDINAL;
                        AmtOwed         : REAL;
                        Name            : ShortString;
                        IsFullTime      : BOOLEAN;
                   END;
```

2. Append a caret to each mention of an Information variable in a statement, except as an actual parameter of a formal Information parameter. In InputInfo and OutputInfo, that requires changing "TheInfo." to "TheInfo ↑ ." in five different places, one for each field. In Compare it requires four carets, twice on First and twice on Second.

3. Use NEW(X) for each Information variable X before any reference to X ↑ is allowed. However, this creates a problem; a client module cannot use NEW(X) because the fact that X is a pointer type is hidden from client modules. The best solution I can think of is to add a new procedure (call it **CreateInfo**) to the InfoADT library module. I will give it the single statement NEW(TheInfo) (where TheInfo is the VAR parameter of CreateInfo). Since a client module would almost always want a new Information record created when reading an information value from a file, I also make NEW(TheInfo) the first statement in InputInfo.

4. Add the following import section: FROM Storage IMPORT ALLOCATE;

ShortString and StrMax are not used anywhere in the definition module, and I do not want to export them, so I will move their declarations to the implementation module also. With the changes described here, Example 2.2B and the program segments near it that use InfoMan can import from InfoADT instead with no difference in effect. However, Example 2.2B will execute significantly faster, since it moves address values around in the array instead of entire records; records take up more space and therefore require more time to move. This is an important advantage of using pointers.

The DISPOSE Procedure

Assume that you have a client module for InfoADT, one that contains a frequently called procedure with a local variable VAR Temp: Information. Then, as already mentioned, you must make CreateInfo(Temp) the first statement of the procedure. When execution of the procedure terminates, Temp (containing the address of the Information) will be disposed of, since it is local to that procedure. However, the Information record itself will remain in existence (i.e., the space for the address Temp is deallocated, but the space for the record Temp ↑ is not). The next time the procedure is called, the CreateInfo(Temp) statement will create an entirely different record variable and put its address in Temp. If this goes on for very long, you will have a large number of records for which space is reserved, although you cannot use them. You could even run out of space to finish the program, which would make the program crash. This is not good.

The procedure **DISPOSE** lets you recover the space for Temp ↑ simply by putting DISPOSE(Temp) as the last statement of every procedure that begins with CreateInfo(Temp); DISPOSE deallocates the storage space so it is free to be reused. The trouble is, DISPOSE requires an address variable, and no client module "knows" that Information is an address variable. The solution is to add to InfoADT another procedure, with the single statement DISPOSE(TheInfo) (where TheInfo is the VAR parameter). I will call this procedure **DestroyInfo**.

As a general rule, you should properly dispose of such variables if you may need the space later. This was not necessary for the modified Telepathy program described earlier, since termination of the PerformTask procedure terminates the program.

When you use both NEW and DISPOSE in a program, you must have the following import:

```
FROM Storage IMPORT ALLOCATE, DEALLOCATE;
```

Newer implementations of Modula-2 do not have NEW and DISPOSE as built-in procedures. Instead, you would use something like ALLOCATE(P, SIZE(P ↑)) for NEW(P) and DEALLOCATE(P, SIZE(P ↑)) for DISPOSE(P).

For Pascal Programmers: Steps 1, 2, and 3 for converting a program to using pointer types are the same, except that ↑ InfoRecord is used in place of POINTER TO InfoRecord. This is the only situation in Pascal when a caret is placed *before* an identifier (and it must be an identifier; ↑ ARRAY or ↑ RECORD is not allowed in Pascal). It is legal to use ↑ TypeIdentifier in a type declaration if the TypeIdentifier is declared later in the same TYPE section. There are no imports from Storage. NEW and DISPOSE are predefined and should work as described.

The InfoADT Library Module

You may have noticed one lack in the proposed module: It often happens that you want to copy one record variable into another so you can have two different record variables with identical contents. If X and Y are Information variables, X := Y will not do the job. That would just copy an address from Y to X, so X and Y would point to the same record variable; you would not have two *different* record variables. A reasonable solution is to add yet another procedure named **CopyInfo**; it copies information from one record variable into another, replacing the previous information. X := Y should be used only when you are willing to treat Y as indeterminate thereafter. This leads to the definition module shown in Example 2.3B. Figure 5 shows the effect of executing procedures from that example.

I have already described the implementation in sufficient detail, so I will not give the whole implementation module here. The bodies of the four key procedures are:

```
(* body of Compare *)              (* body of CreateInfo *)
IF First↑.ID = Second↑.ID THEN     NEW (TheInfo);
    RETURN 0;
ELSIF First↑.ID < Second↑.ID THEN  (* body of CopyInfo *)
    RETURN -1;                     TheInfo↑ := Source↑;
ELSE
    RETURN 1;                      (* body of DestroyInfo *)
END;                               DISPOSE (TheInfo);
```

Details of Compiler Construction

Assume that a procedure call of the form Pr(AP) is executed with AP as the actual parameter, and the formal parameter section is (VAR FP: REAL). Then the usual way that compilers implement such a VAR parameter is to use a VALUE parameter of pointer type. For example, the compiler may create a VALUE parameter named Edgar of type POINTER TO REAL, local to the procedure Pr. Then execution of Pr(AP) actually assigns the address of AP to Edgar, and any reference to FP within the procedure is replaced by a reference to Edgar ↑ .

EXAMPLE 2.3B _____

```
DEFINITION MODULE InfoADT;
EXPORT QUALIFIED Information, CreateInfo, CopyInfo, Okay,
       DestroyInfo, InputInfo, OutputInfo, Compare;
    (* These are some declarations that permit manipulation
       of one Information record.  Warning: CreateInfo must
       be used to allocate space for any Information before
       it   is   used   with   any   other   procedure   but
       InputInfo.  Do not assume  :=  gives  two  different
       copies of Information *)
    (* Written by William C. Jones, May 19-- *)
TYPE
    Information;
VAR
    Okay : BOOLEAN;
(************************************************************)

PROCEDURE CreateInfo (VAR TheInfo : Information);
    (* Allocate space for one Information variable *)

PROCEDURE CopyInfo (VAR TheInfo: Information;
                        Source    : Information);
    (* Replace the information in TheInfo by a copy of
       the information in Source *)

PROCEDURE DestroyInfo (VAR TheInfo : Information);
    (* Deallocate the space used by the record variable *)


PROCEDURE Compare (First, Second : Information) : INTEGER;
    (* Return a positive integer if First > Second;  return
       a negative if First < Second; return 0 if equal *)

PROCEDURE InputInfo (VAR TheInfo : Information);
    (* Create TheInfo, then read all values into it if
       possible;  Okay := done successfully *)

PROCEDURE OutputInfo (TheInfo : Information);
    (* Write all values from TheInfo in a form that
       can be properly read by InputInfo *)

END InfoADT.
```

You may be wondering why only POINTER types (and sometimes a very few other types) can be hidden (opaque) in Modula-2. The reason is that the compiler must know how much storage space to allocate for each variable when the definition module is compiled. The storage space required for a record depends on the number and types of fields, so you cannot hide a record type in the implementation module. But the storage space required for an address is independent of the type of variable to which the pointer points, so there is no problem with hiding such a type. If the compiler allocates the same amount of space for a CARDINAL

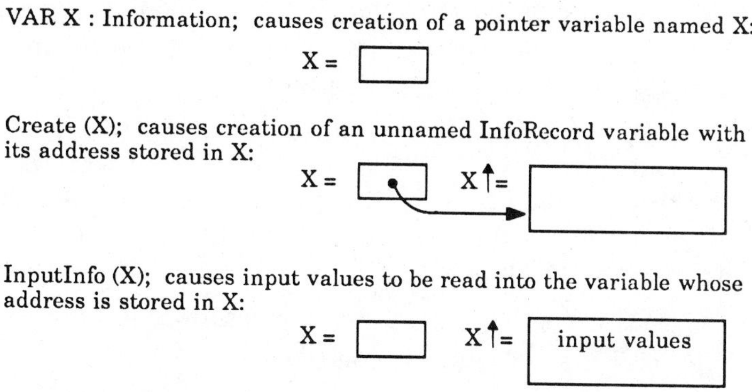

VAR X : Information; causes creation of a pointer variable named X:

X =

Create (X); causes creation of an unnamed InfoRecord variable with its address stored in X:

X =   X ↑=

InputInfo (X); causes input values to be read into the variable whose address is stored in X:

X =   X ↑=   input values

FIGURE 5. The effect of executing procedures from Example 2.3B.

or INTEGER or CHAR as it allocates for an address, then such types can also be opaque.

An interesting fact is that any client module of InfoADT can import from InfoMan instead and still work correctly, assuming that you add the three procedures CreateInfo, CopyInfo, and DestroyInfo to InfoMan. Their implementations do not need any statements (other than a simple assignment statement for CopyInfo), since allocation and deallocation are done automatically for the records:

	In InfoMan (no pointers)	In InfoADT (pointers)
CreateInfo:	(* no statements *)	NEW (TheInfo);
DestroyInfo:	(* no statements *)	DISPOSE (TheInfo);
CopyInfo:	TheInfo := Source;	TheInfo ↑ := Source ↑ ;

There are many applications in which you would want to have Information = POINTER TO RECORD... but still be able to access the internal structure of Information. In that case, you need only put the full declaration in the definition module in place of "TYPE Information;" and omit the declaration entirely from the implementation module.

Check Your Understanding

1. What recoding is required for Example 1.3A to use POINTER TO REAL instead of REAL, similar to what was described in the first part of this section? For each NEW include a matching DISPOSE, even when it really is not necessary.

2. A certain procedure declares a local variable P: POINTER TO INTEGER in its VAR section. The one statement in the procedure is NEW(P). What is the effect of executing this procedure?

3. (NA) What recoding is required for Example 1.6A to use POINTER TO INTEGER instead of INTEGER, similar to what was described in the first part of this section? For each NEW include a matching DISPOSE, even when it really is not necessary. First change the formal parameter part of LCM to be (First, Second: INTEGER).

4. (NA) Write the DebtOf function described in Exercise 3 of Section 2.2, assuming it is to be added to InfoADT.

2.4 TWO EXAMPLES OF ABSTRACT DATA TYPES

In several programming situations it is necessary to use extremely large cardinals with hundreds or thousands of digits. For instance, some methods of encrypting data (so that people who steal a computer file cannot decipher the information) require finding prime numbers with hundreds of digits. Since such a "big number" type is not built-in in most languages, it is necessary to design your own type. This section discusses a library module for such big numbers. The latter part of this section develops a library module that is adequate for many programs that use strings of characters.

Both these modules have the six procedures described for InfoADT (CreateInfo, CopyInfo, DestroyInfo; InputInfo, OutputInfo, and Compare), with the same specifications, but they have other procedures as well. If a program imports from more than one of these information-handling modules, qualidents (as described in Section 2.1) have to be used.

The BigCardADT Library Module

A library module for big cardinals should have the six InfoADT procedures described in Example 2.3B. In addition, this **BigCardADT** module should have procedures for adding two big numbers, for adding a big number to a small one (of type CARDINAL), for multiplying two big numbers, for multiplying a big number by a small one, and so forth. The following implementation is appropriate for compilers that have 65,535 as the largest CARDINAL value, which is typical for 16-bit microprocessors. Some of the choices made depend on the fact that the square of 256 is one more than the largest CARDINAL value.

If the programming situation requires you to work with only a few big numbers, a reasonable method is to use a counted array of perhaps 10,000 characters. Each character represents a two-digit number from 00 to 99, inclusive (in other words, you work in base 100). The reason for choosing this range is that you can multiply the numerical equivalent of two characters together and stay in the range for CARDINAL. That is, CARDINAL includes values up to 99∗99. This simplifies multiplication algorithms. CHAR is used instead of CARDINAL to store the two-digit numbers because that usually cuts storage requirements at least in half.

The array is accompanied by a Size field to indicate the point beyond which all base 100 digits of the number are 0. Each Item[K] is in the range CHR(0)..CHR(99), and represents the base 100 digit with the same ordinal number. Example 2.4A shows the coding of a library procedure to multiply a big number TheInfo by a CARDINAL Given. You should be able to see that the coding is correct, based on your understanding of how ordinary multiplication works.

EXAMPLE 2.4A _____

```
(* Context:   part of BigCardADT implementation module *)
CONST
    Base      = 100;
    SmallBase = 10;
    MaxSize   = 10000;
TYPE
    Information  = POINTER TO CountedArray;
    CountedArray = RECORD
                       Item : ARRAY [1..MaxSize] OF CHAR;
                       Size : CARDINAL;
                   END;
(*******************************************************)

PROCEDURE MultiplyCard (VAR TheInfo : Information;
                            Given   : CARDINAL);
    (* Multiply TheInfo by Given and store the result in
       TheInfo.  Write an appropriate error message if
       the result is too large to be Information *)
VAR
    Carry, K, Product : CARDINAL;
BEGIN
    WITH TheInfo^ DO           (* fields are Item and Size *)
        Carry := 0;
        FOR K := 1 TO Size DO
            Product := Given * ORD (Item [K]) + Carry;
            Item [K] := CHR (Product MOD Base);
            Carry := Product DIV Base;
        END;
        WHILE (Carry > 0) AND (Size < MaxSize) DO
            INC (Size);
            Item [Size] := CHR (Carry MOD Base);
            Carry := Carry DIV Base;
        END;
        IF Carry > 0 THEN
            WriteString ('Error; product is too large');
            WriteLn;
        END;
    END;
END MultiplyCard;
```

Some situations require you to frequently divide big numbers by 2 and 3. You can then use a multiple of 6 below 256 for the base (such as 216), instead of 100. This can significantly increase speed of execution and simplify the algorithms you have to code. To allow for this, the implementation module can declare a constant named Base that is 100 or 216 or whatever value is appropriate.

The Six Fundamental Procedures

CopyInfo and DestroyInfo are both one-statement procedures exactly like the ones for InfoADT: CopyInfo executes TheInfo ↑ := Source ↑ and DestroyInfo executes DISPOSE(TheInfo). To develop Compare, you should first check the Sizes of the two given information values; the one with the larger Size is the larger information value. If the Sizes are the same, you have to compare the array components beginning from Item[Size] and going toward Item[1]. If you see two components that differ, you can tell which information value is smaller; if none differ, the information values are equal. The details of the coding of Compare are left as an exercise.

The OutputInfo procedure appears to be straightforward—just write the Size and then write the values of Item[Size]..Item[1]. The reason for writing the components in reverse order is that it is the way people are used to thinking of them. The reason for writing the Size first is to allow InputInfo to use a FOR loop to read the number.

A serious problem with this approach is that characters numbered below 32 often have a special meaning to input/output procedures, so these characters should be avoided. A simple solution is to write the character numbered 32 higher than the character stored in the array. But some systems have trouble with characters numbered higher than 127. If you have such a system, and if no character above CHR(27) causes difficulties, you might want to use CHR(28)..CHR(127).

EXAMPLE 2.4B _____

```
PROCEDURE OutputInfo (TheInfo : Information);
    (* Write all values from TheInfo in a form that
       can be properly read by InputInfo *)
    (* Context:  array implementation of BigCardADT *)
VAR
    K : CARDINAL;
BEGIN
    WITH TheInfo^ DO          (* fields are Item and Size *)
        WriteInt (Size, 10);
        FOR K := Size TO 1 BY -1 DO
            WriteInt (ORD (Item [K]) DIV SmallBase, 2);
            WriteInt (ORD (Item [K]) MOD SmallBase, 1);
        END;
        WriteLn;
    END;
END OutputInfo;
```

However, it is likely that you would find it most useful to have the numbers written in the standard form using digits. That requires a little more effort and programmer time, but it is the approach I use here. The coding is in Example 2.4B. The coding of InputInfo is left as an exercise.

Documentation

An important principle for reducing errors is that the documentation for a proce-dure should be written carefully *before* the procedure is coded. That is, you should write a comment heading for the procedure before you start to code it. If you do not, you will often find that the coding has a bug in it. At least half of such bugs can be avoided by developing a careful description of what the procedure is to accomplish before you start the coding. Remember the old programming prin-ciple: **Code in haste, debug in leisure.**

When you write the description of what the procedure is supposed to accom-plish, you should think in terms of **preconditions** and **postconditions**. The pre-conditions for a procedure are the conditions that must be true when the proce-dure is called in order for the procedure to do its job correctly. The postconditions for a procedure are the conditions that should be true when the procedure termi-nates, assuming that the preconditions held and the procedure did its job cor-rectly. The postconditions are often stated in terms of the changes that the procedure causes.

The preconditions for Example 2.4A are that TheInfo denotes an information value and Given denotes a cardinal value. In particular, TheInfo↑.Size must be in the range 0..MaxSize and each of Item[1]..Item[Size] must be an ordinal value less than 100. The postconditions are that TheInfo denotes the information value that is the product of Given with the number denoted by the original TheInfo, unless that number has more than 20,000 decimal digits, in which case TheInfo is indeterminate and an appropriate message appears. No other change is to be effected by the MultiplyCard procedure. The comment heading in Example 2.4A is not this wordy, but it does correspond closely to this description.

Similarly, the precondition for OutputInfo in Example 2.4B is that the value in TheInfo denotes an information value. The postcondition is that a textual repre-sentation of that information value appears in the output channel; no other change is to be effected by the OutputInfo procedure.

The LineADT Library Module

In a large number of programming situations, you need to be able to manipulate lines of text. Many such situations do not require you to modify the structure of a line once it is read in. The **LineADT** library module developed next should satisfy the need. For times when this module is not adequate, a more extensive library module is developed in Chapter 8.

The same six fundamental procedures as in Example 2.3A are in this LineADT module, and two more besides. The **CharAt** function tells the Kth character in a

EXAMPLE 2.4C _____

```
DEFINITION MODULE LineADT;
EXPORT QUALIFIED Information, CreateInfo, CopyInfo,
                 DestroyInfo, InputInfo, OutputInfo,
                 Compare, CharAt, LengthOf, Okay;
    (* Comment heading of this module and of the first six
       procedures can be found in Example 2.3A *)
TYPE
    Information;
VAR
    Okay : BOOLEAN;
(***************************************************************)

PROCEDURE CreateInfo  (VAR TheInfo : Information);
PROCEDURE CopyInfo     (VAR TheInfo : Information;
                            Source : Information);
PROCEDURE DestroyInfo (VAR TheInfo : Information);
PROCEDURE Compare   (First, Second : Information): INTEGER;
PROCEDURE InputInfo    (VAR TheInfo : Information);
PROCEDURE OutputInfo      (TheInfo : Information);
(***************************************************************)

PROCEDURE CharAt (Pos    : CARDINAL;
                  TheInfo : Information) : CHAR;
    (* Return the character at position number Pos of
       TheInfo, if Pos is in the range 1..length-of-TheInfo
       Result is indeterminate if Pos is out of range *)

PROCEDURE LengthOf (TheInfo : Information) : CARDINAL;
    (* Return the number of characters in TheInfo *)

END LineADT.
```

particular line of characters, for values of K from 1 up to however many characters the line contains. But to use this function, you need to know how many characters the line contains, so the **LengthOf** function tells the number of characters in one line. The full definition module is in Example 2.4C.

As an example of how the procedures in this module can be used, the following coding prints all characters in a given line of nonblank characters:

```
FOR Pos := 1 TO LengthOf (OneLine) DO
    Ch := CharAt (Pos, OneLine);
    IF Ch # ' ' THEN
        Write (Ch);
    END;
END;
```

Example 2.2B and the two segments of program code just before it can be used with this LineADT module without change, even though they were written with student records in mind. One segment was written to print out an array of information values, and the other segment was written to read a single information value and add it to an array. Section 2.5 contains a complete program that imports from LineADT. Moreover, the program in Section 3.12 could be used with LineADT.

Implementations of LineADT

There are several possibilities for implementing LineADT. One is to use a pointer to a counted array again; this is left as a programming problem. Another possibility is to use a pointer to just an array of characters, not to a record. We can place the null character (0C) after the last character component that is in use as a sentinel value. Then the Compare function is coded much the same as CompareStr in the Helpful module (Example 2.1B), and the InputInfo procedure is coded much the same as the ReadLine procedure in Example 1.8B; the exact nature of the modifications can be found in the exercises. OutputInfo and CreateInfo require only two statements each:

```
(* body of OutputInfo *)          (* body of CreateInfo *)
WriteString (TheInfo↑);            NEW (TheInfo);
WriteLn;                           TheInfo↑ [0] := 0C;
```

CopyInfo and DestroyInfo are the same as they were for InfoADT in Section 2.3. The CharAt and LengthOf functions are in Example 2.4D.

The NoInfo Value

In some applications it is useful to have a special information value to use as a sentinel or for similar purposes. This **NoInfo** value should be recognizably different from all others; Compare should be able to differentiate. A suitable NoInfo value depends on the kind of information you have. For InfoADT, a student record with an ID of 0 would suffice. For BigCardADT, you could use a record with Size=0; the big cardinal 0 would have Size=1 and its first character CHR(0).

LineADT is more difficult, since you have to allow for empty lines; you could put CHR(1) in the first component, assuming that CHR(1) cannot occur naturally

EXAMPLE 2.4D _____

```
(* Context:  null-terminated implementation of LineADT *)
(* implementations of the CharAt and LengthOf functions  *)
CONST
    MaxSize = 100;
    Null    = 0C;
TYPE
    Information = POINTER TO ARRAY [0..MaxSize] OF CHAR;
(***********************************************************)

PROCEDURE CharAt (Pos     : CARDINAL;
                  TheInfo : Information) : CHAR;
    (* Return the character at position number Pos of
       TheInfo, if Pos is in the range 1..Length-of-TheInfo
       Result is indeterminate if Pos is out of range*)
VAR
    K : CARDINAL;
BEGIN
    K := 0;
    WHILE (K + 1 < Pos) AND (TheInfo^ [K] # Null) DO
        INC (K);
    END;
    RETURN TheInfo^ [K];
END CharAt;
(***********************************************************)

PROCEDURE LengthOf (TheInfo : Information) : CARDINAL;
    (* Return the number of characters in TheInfo *)
VAR
    K : CARDINAL;
BEGIN
    K := 0;
    WHILE TheInfo^ [K] # Null DO
        INC (K);
    END;
    RETURN K;
END LengthOf;
```

in the application. So you would declare VAR NoInfo: Information in the definition module and change the last line of the implementation module to:

```
BEGIN     (* body of LineADT impl. *)
    NEW (NoInfo);
    NoInfo↑ [0] := CHR(1);
    NoInfo↑ [1] := CHR(0);
END LineADT.
```

Check Your Understanding

1. What changes should be made in Example 2.4B on the assumption that CHR(28)..CHR(127) are written?

2. What addition could be made to Example 2.4B to have a number printed with less than 80 characters per line, so the output fits on a screen?

3. What changes should be made in the body of CompareStr (Example 2.1B) to obtain the coding for Compare for the null-terminated implementation of LineADT?

4. What changes should be made in the body of ReadLine (Example 1.8B) to obtain the coding for InputInfo for the null-terminated implementation of LineADT?

5. (NA) Write the Compare function for the CountedArray implementation of BigCardADT.

6. (NA) Modify Example 2.4A to be a procedure that adds two big numbers TheInfo and Given and stores the result in TheInfo.

7. (NA) Write procedure headings and detailed comment descriptions for three more useful procedures that could be in BigCardADT.

8. (NA) Write a version of OutputInfo for LineADT in which Size is not written. Instead, Item[Size]..Item[1] are written, then CHR(0) as a sentinel. Then write the corresponding version of InputInfo.

9. (NA) Write the body of InputInfo that corresponds to Example 2.4B.

10. (NA) Write the body of InputInfo that corresponds to Exercise 1.

2.5 APPLICATION: A SPELLING CHECKER

A person is sitting at a computer keyboard typing a paper for an English class when she realizes she does not know whether the correct spelling of "wierd" is "weird" or vice versa. So she activates a program that accesses a dictionary. She enters "wierd," and the program tells her it is not in the dictionary. She enters "weird," and the program tells her it *is* in the dictionary. So she goes back to working on her English paper, using the "weird" spelling. This section develops this spelling checker program, using imports from LineADT (discussed at the end of Section 2.4). The binary search algorithm is part of this program.

Definition Module and Driver Program

The spelling checker could be a procedure in a library module imported by the editing program. When the editing program is executed, the initialization part of the library module reads in a dictionary of words. When the user wants to check the spelling of a word, the editing program calls the main spelling checker procedure to see if the word is in the dictionary. The dictionary is assumed to have the words in normal alphabetic order.

The first thing I do is develop a driver program to test the spelling-checker procedure. This forces me to think about the kinds of declarations I will need in the spelling checker. All the driver has to do is repeatedly get one word from the user and tell the user whether it is in the dictionary. The user needs a way of terminating the driver; entering a word with no characters should work fine. The driver program is in Example 2.5A.

The structure of the driver program indicates that the concrete form of the spelling checker should be a Boolean function with one parameter, the word to be looked up. From this driver program, you can see that the definition module for the spelling checker need only export one identifier, the one for the Boolean function. The coding is straightforward and is in Example 2.5B.

EXAMPLE 2.5A _____

```
MODULE Driver;
FROM LineADT  IMPORT Information, LengthOf, InputInfo;
FROM Spelling IMPORT InDictionary;
FROM InOut    IMPORT WriteString, WriteLn;
    (* Exercise the Spelling module *)

VAR
    OneWord : Information;
BEGIN

    WriteString ('Enter a word to look up.');
    WriteString ('  Simply press RETURN to quit: ');
    InputInfo (OneWord);
    WHILE LengthOf (OneWord) > 0 DO
        IF InDictionary (OneWord) THEN
            WriteString ('In the dictionary.');
        ELSE
            WriteString ('Not in the dictionary.');
        END;
        WriteLn;
        WriteString ('Enter another word (or RETURN): ');
        InputInfo (OneWord);
    END;

END Driver.
```

EXAMPLE 2.5B _____

```
DEFINITION MODULE Spelling;
FROM LineADT IMPORT Information;
EXPORT QUALIFIED InDictionary;

    (* Initialization code reads an alphabetized list into
       a data structure.  InDictionary accesses the list *)
    (* Written by William C. Jones, March 19-- *)

PROCEDURE InDictionary (TheInfo : Information) : BOOLEAN;
    (* Tell whether TheInfo is in the dictionary *)

END Spelling.
```

The Spelling Checker Implementation Module

The first thing to decide is the data structure in which the dictionary is to be stored. For simplicity, I use a counted array:

```
VAR   Data : RECORD
                Item : ARRAY [1..MaxSize] OF Information;
                Size : CARDINAL;
             END;
```

The body of the spelling checker module is to read the dictionary into this array. This is a standard logic—you read one information value at a time, storing them in Item[1], Item[2],... until there are no more values to read. Size is assigned the number of values read. That leaves only the logic of the InDictionary function to develop. We use a fast way of searching an ordered array for a value, called the **binary search** algorithm.

Binary Search

The basic logic of binary search is that you pick an index about halfway between 1 and Size and look at the value of the component there. If TheInfo is greater than the value seen (using Compare), you know that TheInfo does not occur below that middle value, so you can remove the *first* half of the array from further consideration. If, on the other hand, TheInfo is *not* greater than the value seen, you know that TheInfo does not occur above that middle value, so you can remove the *second* half of the array from further consideration. Either way, you cut your work in half.

Algorithm for Binary Search (values in increasing order)

1. Initialize an integer variable Bottom to 1;
2. Initialize another integer variable Top to Size;
3. Do repeatedly until time to stop:
   - 3.a. STOP if Top equals Bottom;
     Note: If TheInfo is in the array, then Item [Bottom[<= TheInfo <= Item [Top];
   - 3.b. Choose a number Middle that is about halfway between Bottom and Top;
   - 3.c. Replace Bottom by Middle + 1 if TheInfo > Item[Middle], otherwise replace Top by Middle (then TheInfo <= Item[Top]);
     Note: If TheInfo is in the array, then TheInfo = Item [Top];
4. Return TheInfo = Item [Top] as the function result.

The purpose of the two notes in this algorithm is to help readers prove to themselves that this algorithm accomplishes the search correctly. A person who reads the algorithm without the notes will understand what it is doing but will not be sure that it will produce the correct result in all circumstances. The notes point the way to that reasoning.

The loop in this algorithm translates easily to a WHILE statement. The obvious question is, "Why not use WHILE in writing the pseudocode algorithm instead of the format shown?" The answer is that an algorithm should be expressed in **computer-adaptable English**, that is, instructions in English that can be easily translated to any reasonable high-level language. The WHILE construct does not occur in ordinary English. A more important reason is that it is best to postpone the question of which looping construct to choose (normally WHILE, REPEAT, or FOR) until the coding stage; that choice is irrelevant when designing the algorithm to accomplish a given task. You can do this by always expressing a loop as shown (often with the STOP condition in a different place). The coding for this algorithm is in Example 2.5C.

SAMPLE RUN. Assume that the ordered array is ('art', 'but', 'by', 'do', 'go', 'me', 'pie', 'tea'), Size = 8, and TheInfo = 'me'(Figure 6). Then the following happens:

```
Bottom := 1;          Top := 8;                        (* look in 1 thru 8 *)
WHILE: 8 > 1, so:     Middle := 4 ((8 + 1) DIV 2);
                      Item[4] < 'me', so Bottom := 5;  (* look in 5 thru 8 *)
WHILE: 8 > 5, so:     Middle := 6 ((8 + 5) DIV 2);
                      Item[6] >= 'me', so Top := 6;    (* look in 5 thru 6 *)
WHILE: 6 > 5, so:     Middle := 5 ((6 + 5) DIV 2);
                      Item[5] < 'me', so Bottom := 6;  (* look in 6 thru 6 *)
WHILE:  Both Top and Bottom are 6, so the loop terminates;
Item[6] is 'me', so RETURN TRUE.
```

EXAMPLE 2.5C _____

```
IMPLEMENTATION MODULE Spelling;
FROM LineADT IMPORT Information, InputInfo, DestroyInfo,
                    Compare, Okay;
FROM InOut   IMPORT OpenInput, CloseInput;
    (* Read an alphabetized list of less than MaxSize words
       into a data structure.  Accept words from the user
       and tell whether they are in the alphabetized list*)
    (* Written by William C. Jones, March 19-- *)
CONST
    MaxSize = 10000;
VAR
    Data : RECORD
                Item : ARRAY [1..MaxSize] OF Information;
                Size : CARDINAL;
           END;
(*****************************************************)

PROCEDURE InDictionary (TheInfo : Information) : BOOLEAN;
    (* Use Binary Search to tell whether TheInfo is in
       the nonempty Data structure *)
VAR
    Bottom, Middle, Top : CARDINAL;
BEGIN
    WITH Data DO    (* fields are Item and Size *)
        Bottom := 1;
        Top := Size;
        WHILE Top > Bottom DO
                (* If TheInfo is in the array, then
                   Item [Bottom] <= TheInfo <= Item [Top]*)
            Middle := (Bottom + Top) DIV 2;
                (* so Bottom <= Middle < Top *)
            IF Compare (TheInfo, Item [Middle]) <= 0 THEN
                Top := Middle;
            ELSE
                Bottom := Middle + 1;
            END;
        END;
        RETURN Compare (TheInfo, Item [Top]) = 0;
    END;
END InDictionary;
(*****************************************************)

BEGIN          (* Spelling Checker *)
    OpenInput ('');
    WITH Data DO      (* fields are Item and Size *)
        Size := 0;
        InputInfo (Item [Size + 1]);
        WHILE Okay AND (Size < MaxSize - 1) DO
            INC (Size);
            InputInfo (Item [Size + 1]);
        END;
        DestroyInfo (Item [Size + 1]);
    END;
    CloseInput;
END Spelling.
```

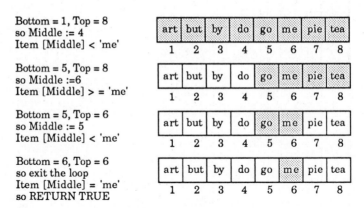

Bottom = 1, Top = 8
so Middle := 4
Item [Middle] < 'me'

Bottom = 5, Top = 8
so Middle :=6
Item [Middle] > = 'me'

Bottom = 5, Top = 6
so Middle := 5
Item [Middle] < 'me'

Bottom = 6, Top = 6
so exit the loop
Item [Middle] = 'me'
so RETURN TRUE

FIGURE 6. Sample run for binary search algorithm, searching for me.

If TheInfo had been 'ham', the same thing would have happened in the loop, but the function would have returned FALSE.

The binary search algorithm is an example of a **divide and conquer** algorithm: You divide the data to be processed into two roughly equal parts and then process each half. In this case, one half can be immediately removed from consideration, since it can be seen not to contain the value you are looking for. If you have 1000 items to be searched, you can do it with only about 10 iterations. For a million items, you can do it with only about 20 iterations.

⬛➡ PROGRAMMING STYLE

Some people modify the binary search to terminate the loop as soon as Item[Middle] equals TheInfo. This requires a third alternative in the IF structure in the loop. This actually slows the algorithm, because if TheInfo is not in the array, time is wasted, and even if it is, half the time we do not see it as Item[Middle] until the last iteration of the loop. Thus it is not worth making the extra comparison.

Another good reason for not terminating the loop when Item[Middle] is equal to TheInfo is that TheInfo may occur more than once in the array, and Item[Middle] may not be the first component that contains TheInfo. The function of Example 2.5C always finds the *first* component that contains TheInfo. This is important in some applications.

Advantages of Using an Abstract Data Type for the Spelling Checker

A typical situation is that the average word in the dictionary has 7 characters and the longest word has 20 characters. If you use the array implementation of

LineADT described in the previous section, the dictionary would require storage for more than 10,000 times 20 characters, which can easily strain your computing resources. If you could store only the characters in the words, the dictionary would require storage for only 10,000 times 7 characters. Later in this book you will see ways to come close to this goal. If you make such a change, you only need to change the coding in LineADT; the spelling checker and the editing program do not change one iota. This is the primary advantage of using an abstract data type.

Note that the spelling checker library module is ignorant of the true nature of the information it is storing and retrieving. You could replace LineADT by BigCardADT to obtain a library module for storing and retrieving a list of prime numbers, for instance. Or you could replace it by the InfoADT described in Section 2.3 to obtain a library module for storing and retrieving registration information about student records. This is another advantage of using an abstract data type.

The client module is ignorant of how the spelling checker stores its information. It does not even know there is a variable named Data in the spelling checker; Data is private. This means that, if you find a more efficient way to store and retrieve information, you can replace the spelling checker implementation module by another one without revising any other module. *Note:* Actually, it would be reasonable to consider the spelling checker as dealing with an abstract data structure (the dictionary) rather than an abstract data type, since the unit does not export a type.

Check Your Understanding

1. Trace the InDictionary function for the array ('at', 'can', 'fib', 'fib', 'hi', 'no', 'see', 'yes') when TheInfo is 'fib'.

2. Rewrite Example 2.5C so that the loop terminates when Item[Middle] is TheInfo.

3. How many iterations will the WHILE loop in Example 2.5C perform if Size is 20? What if Size is 400? *Hint:* There are two answers for each question.

4. (NA) Trace Example 2.5C for the array (1, 4, 5, 12, 12, 12, 12, 17, 18) when TheInfo is 12 (assuming imports from BigCardADT instead of LineADT).

5. (NA) In Example 2.5C, the program crashes if the dictionary is empty. In some situations, you would have to guard against this possibility and return FALSE. Modify the coding accordingly.

6. (NA) In Example 2.5C, the coding accepts at most MaxSize−1 values. Modify it to accept MaxSize values.

2.6 RECURSION

It is permissible in Modula-2 for any statement to call any procedure. In particular, a statement within a procedure can call that same procedure. This is called **recursion**. The recursive procedure in Example 2.6A, though only four statements long, requires careful study. The key fact about recursion is that, when a procedure is activated, a *new copy* of the called procedure is created, with its local variables stored in different locations from any other variables in the program (even if those local variables have the same name as other ones being used). *Note:* Calling a procedure is also known as activating it or **invoking** it.

If this procedure is invoked when the input is "strange stuff," the output will be "egnarts". For a detailed analysis, assume that the ReadAndWrite procedure is invoked when the input is "Hi Ed." Then:

- ☐ A copy of the procedure is created; I will call it ReadAndWrite #1. This #1 copy reads the 'H' into its local variable Ch and sees it is not a blank. So it invokes ReadAndWrite and then writes the 'H'.

- ☐ That invocation of ReadAndWrite creates a *new* copy, which I will call ReadAndWrite #2, with its own local variable Ch, which I will call Ch #2. This #2 copy reads the 'i' into its local variable (Ch #2) and sees it is not a blank. So it invokes ReadAndWrite and then writes the 'i'.

- ☐ That invocation creates a third copy, which I will call ReadAndWrite #3, with its own local variable Ch, which I will call Ch #3. This #3 copy reads the blank into its local variable (Ch #3) and sees it is a blank. So that third copy terminates (it has nothing else to do).

The sequence of reads, calls, and writes in the order in which they happen for the input "Hi Ed." can be described as follows:

- ☐ Some procedure (call it P) calls copy #1;
- ☐ Copy #1 reads 'H' into Ch #1 and calls copy #2;

EXAMPLE 2.6A _____

```
PROCEDURE ReadAndWrite;
    (* Read all characters down to the next blank;
       then print them in reverse order *)
VAR
    Ch : CHAR;
BEGIN
    Read (Ch);
    IF Ch # ' ' THEN
        ReadAndWrite;
        Write (Ch);
    END;
END ReadAndWrite;
```

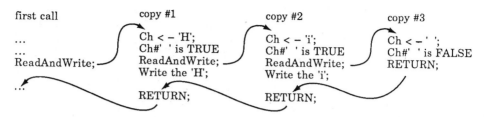

first call   copy #1   copy #2   copy #3

FIGURE 7. *Chart of recursive calls for Example 2.6A with input "Hi Ed."*

☐ Copy #2 reads 'i' into Ch #2 and calls copy #3;

☐ Copy #3 reads ' ' and terminates, which returns control to #2;

☐ Copy #2 writes 'i' and terminates, which returns control to #1;

☐ Copy #1 writes 'H' and terminates, returning control to P;

☐ Procedure P continues execution.

At the point where copy #3 reads the blank, the situation could be drawn as shown in Figure 7. The tiny arrows are supposed to indicate that Ch is assigned the value shown. Follow down a column until an exiting arrow is seen, then follow that arrow to the top of the next column and continue as before. When you get to the end of a column, follow the exiting arrow back to the point where the procedure was called.

Actually, the only difference between one call of the procedure and the next is the variables. Therefore, a compiler would in practice produce only a copy of the storage locations used by the procedures and a note of the place in the calling procedure where execution was temporarily suspended, rather than a copy of the whole procedure. I will continue to use the word "copy" with this understanding.

Example: Print an Integer One Character at a Time

Example 2.1B presented a procedure named WritePositive that prints a given positive integer. The procedure can only use the Write statement (for one character), not the WriteCard procedure. The procedure is rather clumsy, and only works for integers less than 99,999. If you have an implementation of Modula-2 that allows larger numbers, that WritePositive# procedure does not work. The next example presents a replacement for the WritePositive procedure that works for positive integers of any size.

If the given cardinal is 256, I want to write the digit '2' followed by the digit '5' followed by the digit '6'. If the given cardinal is 8, I just want to write the digit '8'. This procedure is difficult to write without recursion and still be independent of the implementation. By contrast, it is easy to print the digits backward without recursion; the following program segment will do it for any positive integer:

```
REPEAT
    Write (CHR (48 + GivenCardinal MOD 10));
    GivenCardinal := GivenCardinal DIV 10;
UNTIL GivenCardinal = 0;
```

This program segment requires a little explaining. For any positive number X, X MOD 10 is the remainder after dividing X by 10. The ASCII code for the digit 0 is 48, for the digit 1 is 49,..., for the digit 9 is 57. Thus the ASCII code for the last digit of X is 48 + X MOD 10. When we divide X by 10 and discard the remainder (which is what DIV does), we "lose" the last digit. We keep going until we get to 0.

To print the digits in the correct order, we must somehow reverse the order of operations. For instance, to print the digits of 256, we want to print the digits of 25 and then print the '6'; to print the digits of 25, we want to print '2' and then print the '5'. The procedure is given in Example 2.6B. Figure 8 shows the order in which "copies" of the procedure are created and statements are executed. Follow exiting arrows where they occur, otherwise go down in a column.

It is best to try a few sample runs to see how this procedure works:

☐ For WritePositive(2), the IF condition is FALSE, so CHR(48+2) is printed, which is the digit '2'. The procedure works similarly for any other number less than 10.

☐ For WritePositive(25), the IF condition is TRUE, so WritePositive(2) is executed (which prints '2' as just shown) and then CHR(48+5) is printed, which is the digit '5'.

☐ For WritePositive(256), the IF condition is TRUE, so WritePositive(25) is executed (which prints '25' as just shown) and then CHR(48+6) is printed, which is the digit '6'.

☐ For WritePositive(2569), the IF condition is TRUE, so WritePositive(256) is executed (which prints '256' as just shown) and then CHR (48+9) is printed, which is the digit '9'.

EXAMPLE 2.6B _____

```
PROCEDURE WritePositive (GivenCardinal : CARDINAL);
    (* Write the positive GivenCardinal using only Write *)
BEGIN
    IF GivenCardinal >= 10 THEN
        WritePositive (GivenCardinal DIV 10);
    END;
    Write (CHR (48 + GivenCardinal MOD 10));
END WritePositive;
```

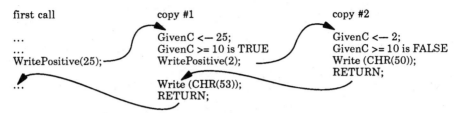

FIGURE 8. Chart of recursive calls for WritePositive (25).

Example: A Complete Binary Tree

This next example is the foundation of a number of algorithms that are used later in this book. First, you need to know what a "complete binary tree" is. Figure 9 shows three complete binary trees: the 1-level tree (on the left), the 2-level tree (in the middle), and the 3-level tree (on the right). There is only one complete binary tree for any given number of levels.

For numbers higher than 3, the definition of the N-level **complete binary tree** is that it consists of two (N − 1)-level complete binary trees with the number N centered above them (other applications may have different values written in). I want to write a procedure to print all the numbers that occur in the complete binary tree of a given number of levels, in order from left to right. For instance, for the 3-level tree, I want the following sequence of numbers: 1 2 1 3 1 2 1. The algorithm for doing this follows directly from the definition (Example 2.6C).

As a sample run for this procedure, assume it is invoked with the parameter 2. This first copy of PrintTree executes the ELSE clause, which invokes a second copy of PrintTree with the parameter 1. This second copy executes the THEN clause (writing the number 1) and then returns control to copy #1. Copy #1 writes the number 2 and then invokes another copy of PrintTree. This other copy executes the THEN clause (writing the number 1) and then returns control to copy #1. That completes execution of copy #1, so it returns control to the procedure that called it, having caused the writing of 1 2 1. Figure 10 charts this sequence of actions.

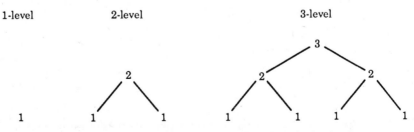

FIGURE 9. The complete binary trees for 1, 2, and 3 levels.

EXAMPLE 2.6C

```
PROCEDURE PrintTree (Levels : CARDINAL);
    (* Print the numbers in the complete binary tree with
       the given number of Levels in order left to right *)
BEGIN
    IF Levels <= 1 THEN (* it's the 1-level tree *)
        WriteCard (Levels, 1);
        WriteLn;
    ELSE
        PrintTree (Levels - 1);
        WriteCard (Levels, 1);
        WriteLn;
        PrintTree (Levels - 1);
    END;
END PrintTree;
```

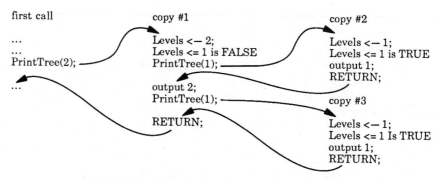

FIGURE 10. *Chart of recursive calls for PrintTree(2).*

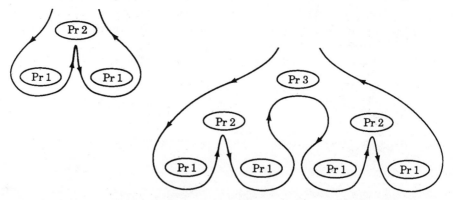

FIGURE 11. *Recursion trees for PrintTree(2) and PrintTree(3). Pr is an abbreviation for "Print." Each circle is an activation of PrintTree; the arrows show the order of activation.*

Figure 11 diagrams the recursive calls in another way. The figure on the left is for PrintTree(2); the one on the right is for PrintTree(3). This kind of diagram is called a **recursion tree**.

Application: The Towers of Hanoi Game

The output from the complete binary tree procedure is the solution to a solitaire game called the **Towers of Hanoi**. As shown in Figure 12, this game consists of three pegs on a board, with five rings on one of the pegs. The rings are numbered 1 through 5, reading from the top down. That is, ring 1 is on top of ring 2, which is on top of ring 3, and so forth. The objective is to make legal moves so you end up with the five rings on a different peg. A legal move consists of moving one ring from one peg to another peg without putting it on a lower-numbered ring.

The previous paragraph is a full description of the rules, but if you have not seen the game before, you will probably need to try it out to see what I mean. You can use three piles of pieces of paper, with a number on each piece. *Note:* In some forms of the game, the rings are different sizes instead of being numbered, with the smaller sizes corresponding to the smaller numbers. Also, some forms have 6 or 8 rings.

The best solution to the game is: (1) Think of the pegs as being labeled A, B, C, with the rings initially on A; (2) Move the rings in the order given by the Print-Tree procedure; (3) Ring 1 always goes from A to B or from B to C or from C to A. If you try it, you will see that this description gives you exactly one choice of a legal move each time and that you win the game in 31 moves with 5 rings; it would take 255 moves for 8 rings. Thus a program that tells the user how to win the Towers of Hanoi game can easily be written using the PrintTree procedure:

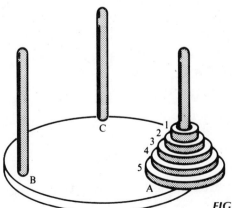

FIGURE 12. Drawing of the Towers of Hanoi setup.

```
(* body of program to solve the Towers Of Hanoi game *)
VAR
    NumberOfRings : CARDINAL;
BEGIN
    WriteString ('Enter the number of rings to be moved ');
    ReadCard (NumberOfRings);
    WriteString ('You move the rings in this order: ');
    PrintTree (NumberOfRings);
END TowersOfHanoi.
```

IIII➡ PROGRAMMING STYLE

Perhaps Example 2.6C puzzled you by using the condition Levels<=1 instead of Levels=1. There is a good reason for the former. The only difference occurs when Levels is 0. The programmer should assure that the procedure is not called in such a case. However, if the programmer makes such a mistake, it is better to print a reasonable answer (the number 0) instead of crashing the program (which is what would happen if the condition were Levels=1). In general, it is better to write procedures so that they do not crash, as long as it takes no more effort.

Check Your Understanding

1. Revise Example 2.6A so it makes a ripple pattern as indicated by the following sample runs:
   An input of "Modula " produces output of "Modula aludoM"
   An input of "pot " produces output of "pot top"

2. What changes would be required to have Example 2.6B print values in base 8?

3. How would the effect of Example 2.6B change if you made the error of writing the > symbol instead of the >= symbol?

4. Describe as succinctly as possible the result of computing F(N) for any positive integer N, when F is defined as follows. *Hint:* Compute F(1), then compute F(2), then compute F(3), and so forth.

```
PROCEDURE F (Given : CARDINAL) : CARDINAL;
BEGIN
    IF Given <= 1 THEN
        RETURN 1;
    ELSE
        RETURN 2 * F (Given DIV 2);
    END;
END F;
```

5. What change could be made in Example 2.6C to have it print a different sequence of numbers, as follows: If Levels is 1, you print 1. If Levels is 2, you print 2 1 1. If Levels is 3, you print 3 2 1 1 2 1 1. In general, the sequence for Levels is the number Levels followed by two copies of the sequence for Levels−1.

6. (NA) Use the following function procedure to compute F(N) for each N up to 20. For extra credit, describe as succinctly as possible the result of computing F(N) for any positive integer N.

```
PROCEDURE F (Given : CARDINAL) : CARDINAL;
BEGIN
    IF Given <= 4 THEN
        RETURN Given;
    ELSIF ODD (Given) THEN
        RETURN F (2 * Given);
    ELSE
        RETURN F (Given DIV 3);
    END;
END F;
```

7. (NA) Write out a logical argument to show that the solution for the Towers of Hanoi game does in fact give you exactly one choice for each move.

8. (NA) For the following procedure, what is the result of executing PrintNumbers(1,7)? Of executing PrintNumbers(1,15)?

```
PROCEDURE PrintNumbers (Top, Limit : CARDINAL);
BEGIN
    IF Top <= Limit THEN
        WriteCard (Top, 1);
        WriteLn;
        PrintNumbers (2 * Top, Limit);
        PrintNumbers (2 * Top + 1, Limit);
    END;
END PrintNumbers;
```

9. (NA) Answer the previous exercise after moving the first call of PrintNumbers up to just after the THEN.

2.7 MORE ON RECURSION

A palindrome is a word or phrase that reads the same left to right as it does right to left. Some examples are "ADA" and "PEEP" and "ABLE WAS I ERE I SAW

ELBA" (Napoleon's epitaph). Assume you are given an array of characters named Data and are asked to find out whether the 13 components numbered 5 through 17 (for instance) form a palindrome. You could write a Boolean function to be activated as follows:

```
IF IsOkay (Data, 5, 17) THEN...
```

The recursive development of this function is straightforward once you decide how the property of being a palindrome depends on a smaller phrase being a palindrome. If the string of characters has fewer than two characters, obviously it is a palindrome. Otherwise, you only need check that (1) the first and last characters are equal, and (2) the rest of the string (between the first and last characters) is also a palindrome. Thus the IsOkay function could be written as shown in Example 2.7A. Figure 13 shows a chart of the recursive calls of IsOkay when the phrase is "LEVEL".

Verifying a Recursive Algorithm

When one copy of the ReadAndWrite procedure in Example 2.6A activates a second copy of ReadAndWrite, the number of characters before the next blank is less than it was when the first copy was activated. That is, each additional level of recursion has a smaller number of consecutive nonblanks to process (assuming there is a blank in the input).

When one copy of the WritePositive procedure in Example 2.6B activates a second copy of WritePositive, the value of the parameter is less than the value of the parameter when the first copy was activated. That is, each additional level of recursion receives a smaller value of GivenCardinal.

For every recursive procedure you write, you should verify that it is **self-terminating** by finding some "entity" such that: (1) For each additional active call of the procedure, the size of the entity is less; and (2) There is no additional call of

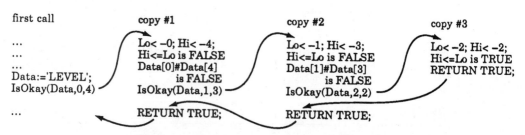

FIGURE 13. Chart of recursive calls for IsOkay('LEVEL',0,4).

EXAMPLE 2.7A _____

```
MODULE Palindrome;
FROM InOut IMPORT ReadString, WriteString, WriteLn;
    (* Tell whether a given phrase is a palindrome *)
    (* Written by Emord Nilap, December 19-- *)

CONST
    StrMax = 60;
TYPE
    Phrase = ARRAY [0..StrMax] OF CHAR;
(***********************************************************)

PROCEDURE IsOkay (Data   : Phrase;
                  Lo, Hi : CARDINAL) : BOOLEAN;
    (* Tell whether Data[Lo]...Data[Hi] is a palindrome *)
BEGIN

    IF Hi <= Lo THEN
        RETURN TRUE;
    ELSIF Data [Lo] # Data [Hi] THEN
        RETURN FALSE;
    ELSE
        RETURN IsOkay (Data, Lo + 1, Hi - 1);
    END;

END IsOkay;
(***********************************************************)

VAR
    Data : Phrase;              (* a putative palindrome    *)
    K    : CARDINAL;            (* counts characters in Data *)

BEGIN       (* Palindrome *)

    WriteString ('Propose a putative palindrome: ');
    ReadString (Data);

    K := 0;
    WHILE (K <= StrMax) AND (Data [K] # 0C) DO
        INC (K);
    END;

    IF IsOkay (Data, 0, K - 1) THEN
        WriteString ('Passes as a palindrome.');
    ELSE
        WriteString ('Pardon, that is not a palindrome.');
    END;
    WriteLn;

END Palindrome.
```

the procedure when the size of the entity becomes small enough (you should also be able to find out what "small enough" is).

In Example 2.6A, the entity is the number of characters before the next blank at the beginning of the activation, since there is no additional call of the procedure when a blank occurs in the input. This procedure is self-terminating only if there is a blank in the input (the "small enough" number is 0).

In Example 2.6B, the entity is the value of the parameter at the beginning of the activation, since there is no additional call of the procedure when GivenCardinal is less than 10 (the "small enough" number is 9). This procedure is unconditionally self-terminating. In the IsOkay function of Example 2.7A, the entity is Hi−Lo; when Hi−Lo is small enough (0 or −1), there are no further calls of the function. An interesting point is that, owing to the short-circuit evaluation feature of Modula-2, the body of IsOkay could be written as one statement:

```
RETURN (Hi <= Lo) OR (Data [Lo] = Data [Hi]) AND
                IsOkay (Data, Lo + 1, Hi - 1)
```

Delocalization

When a procedure is called recursively, each activation of the procedure has its own separate copies of the local variables and parameters. For instance, Example 2.6A works because each activation has its own copy of Ch for storing a character while waiting for other activations to terminate. And Example 2.6B works because each activation has its own copy of GivenCardinal for storing the number until after other activations terminate.

It often happens that one or more of the local variables and parameters need not be replicated; that is, it is sufficient for all activations to access the same copy of the variable. In that case, you can save storage space and execution time by using just one copy. This requires that the copy be declared globally to the recursive procedure.

The **delocalization technique** for a recursive procedure is to declare a subprocedure that (1) does all the recursion but (2) refers to one or more variables declared in the procedure and not passed as parameters, in order to (3) save time and space. This often causes the subprocedure to have side effects, which normally makes a program much harder to understand. However, clarity must sometimes be sacrificed to save space in primary memory; besides, when the side effects are restricted to a subprocedure of a not-very-large procedure (preferably not more than one page long), clarity usually suffers little if at all. This is the only kind of situation in the first six chapters of this book where side effects are permitted.

Example 2.7B shows how the palindrome function from Example 2.7A can have Data delocalized in this manner. The lines marked (∗+∗) have been added, and the line marked (∗change∗) has been changed by omitting Data as a parame-

EXAMPLE 2.7B _____

```
PROCEDURE IsOkay (Data   : Phrase;
                  Lo, Hi : CARDINAL) : BOOLEAN;
   (* Tell whether Data[Lo]..Data[Hi] is a palindrome *)
  (*--------------------------------------------------------*)

    PROCEDURE CheckOut (Lo, Hi : CARDINAL) : BOOLEAN; (*+*)
    BEGIN
        IF Hi <= Lo THEN
            RETURN TRUE;
        ELSIF Data [Lo] # Data [Hi] THEN
            RETURN FALSE;
        ELSE
            RETURN CheckOut (Lo + 1, Hi - 1);      (*change*)
        END;
    END CheckOut;                                     (*+*)
  (*--------------------------------------------------------*)

BEGIN          (* IsOkay *)                           (*+*)
    RETURN CheckOut (Lo, Hi);                         (*+*)
END IsOkay;
```

ter; otherwise the function is the same as in Example 2.7A. The entire purpose of the subprocedure is to omit Data as a parameter. This saves execution time and space in primary memory, at a price of little or no sacrifice of clarity.

The following are common situations in which delocalization of a variable X in a recursive procedure is possible.

☐ X is a formal VAR parameter, and the corresponding actual parameter in each call of the recursive procedure is also X.

☐ X is a formal VALUE parameter, and the corresponding actual parameter in each call of the recursive procedure is also X, and X is not changed by the recursive procedure.

☐ X is a local variable of the recursive procedure, and X is not referred to by the procedure after any recursive call of itself.

Check Your Understanding

1. If you change the <= symbol to the < symbol in the IsOkay function of Example 2.7B, how does that change the effect of the function?

2. If you change the <= symbol to the = symbol in the IsOkay function of Example 2.7B, how does that change the effect of the function?

3. Find the "entity" and "small enough number" for Example 2.6C, as described in the subsection on verification.

4. (NA) Write a function to test whether a part of a phrase is a multipalindrome, which is defined as follows: If it has less than four characters, it must be a palindrome; otherwise, both the first half and the second half must be multipalindromes. *Note:* In considering the first and second halves, ignore the character in the middle if any.

5. (NA) Declare TYPE Numbers = ARRAY [1..100] OF [1..100]. Write a recursive Boolean function that accepts a Numbers array X and an integer N below 100 and tells whether X[1]..X[N] are all odd. Use just one statement.

6. (NA) Same as the previous exercise, except tell, for given X and N and integer Total, whether there is any combination of X[1]..X[N] that gives a total of Total, using each entry in X at most once. Again, use just one statement. *Application:* If each entry in X represents a denomination of bills or coins, this function tells whether you can pay Total cents exactly without making change. For example, if X contains 10, 10, 25, 100, you have two dimes, a quarter, and a dollar (assuming U.S. denominations). The function should return TRUE for 0, 10, 20, 25, and certain other values.

7. (NA) Same as the previous exercise, except allow the use of any entry in X as many times as you want. *Question:* With what application related to units of money does this function help?

2.8 THE FIBONACCI AND ACKERMANN-PÉTER FUNCTIONS

This section introduces two functions that are valuable in the study of computer science. They are introduced at this point to provide more experience with recursion.

The Fibonacci Function

The Fibonacci function has one value parameter, a positive integer. The full definition in mathematical notation is given in the following three lines:

☐ Fib (1) = 1;
☐ Fib (2) = 2;
☐ Fib (x) = Fib (x − 1) + Fib (x − 2) when x is greater than 2.

At first it may seem that the definition is defective; how can a function be defined in terms of itself? The idea is that, when you want to calculate Fib(6), you first calculate Fib(3), then Fib(4), then Fib(5), then Fib(6), in that order. That way, each function value is defined in terms of values that have already been computed. Thus:

   ☐ Fib(3) = Fib(2) + Fib(1), which is 2 + 1, which is 3;

   ☐ Fib(4) = Fib(3) + Fib(2), which is 3 + 2, which is 5;

   ☐ Fib(5) = Fib(4) + Fib(3), which is 5 + 3, which is 8;

   ☐ Fib(6) = Fib(5) + Fib(4), which is 8 + 5, which is 13.

The definition given is essentially an abbreviated presentation of an algorithm to compute the function value. Compare it with the coding at the top of Example 2.8A. This coding is extremely wasteful of execution time. For instance, Fib(6) calls Fib(4) after it calls Fib(5), which also called Fib(4). The better way to code this is to follow the algorithm implicit in the method just used to find Fib(6), as shown in the lower part of Example 2.8A. Note that the FOR statement gives the correct answer when x = 3, since it performs no iterations in that case.

The Ackermann-Péter Function

The Ackermann-Péter function was defined in 1935 by the Hungarian mathematician Rosza Péter, as a simplification of a function developed by Wilhelm Acker-

EXAMPLE 2.8A _____

```
PROCEDURE Fib (x : CARDINAL) : CARDINAL;
    (* Compute Fibonacci numbers recursively -- bad *)
BEGIN
    IF x <= 2 THEN
        RETURN x;
    ELSE
        RETURN Fib (x - 1) + Fib (x - 2);
    END;
END Fib;
(***************************************************************)

PROCEDURE Fib (x : CARDINAL) : CARDINAL;
    (* Compute Fibonacci numbers NONrecursively *)
VAR
    ThisFib, TheFibBefore, K, Saved : CARDINAL;
BEGIN
    IF x <= 2 THEN
        RETURN x;
    ELSE
        ThisFib := 3;              (* for x = 3 *)
        TheFibBefore := 2;         (* for x = 2 *)
        FOR K := 4 TO x DO
            Saved := ThisFib;
            ThisFib := ThisFib + TheFibBefore;
            TheFibBefore := Saved;
        END;
        RETURN ThisFib;
    END;
END Fib;
```

mann. The Ackermann-Péter function, hereafter abbreviated AP, is an interesting example of double recursion. It is important in the theory of computability. The function discussed in this section is a slight simplification of the original AP function.

AP has two value parameters x and y, both of which must be positive integers. The full definition is given in the following three lines:

☐ AP (1, y) = y + 2 for any positive y;

☐ AP (x+1, 1) := AP (x, AP (x, 1)) for any positive x;

☐ AP (x+1, y+1) := AP (x, AP (x+1, y)) for any positive x and y.

This definition is probably not too clear to you, since the format is unfamiliar. It is actually nothing more than a somewhat abbreviated description of a recursive algorithm computing the value of the function. Compare the definition with the following coding:

```
PROCEDURE AP (x, y : Positive) : Positive;
BEGIN
    IF x = 1 THEN
        RETURN y + 2;
    ELSIF y = 1 THEN
        RETURN AP (x - 1, AP (x - 1, 1));
    ELSE
        RETURN AP (x - 1, AP (x, y - 1));
    END;
END AP;
```

The coding of this function is extremely wasteful of execution time for the same reason that the Fibonacci function was wasteful; the same value of the function is computed many times in the process of working out a given value. The following analysis of the nature of the AP function leads to a faster-executing algorithm, although it is less clear.

When x is greater than 1, the value of the function is defined in terms of its values for x − 1. Therefore, it is easiest to compute the first few values of the AP function for one particular value of x before computing a value for the next higher value of x. The following table lists several values of the function. For any given value in this table, the number at the far left of the table is the value of x used and the number at the top of the table is the value of y used. For instance, AP(1,3) = 5, AP(2,1) = 5, AP(2,5) = 13, and AP(3,2) = 29.

y=	1	2	3	4	5	6	7	8	9	10	11	12	13	14
x = 1	3	4	5	6	7	8	9	10	11	12	13	14	15	16
2	5	7	9	11	13	15	17	19	21	23	25	27	29	31
3	13	29	61	125	253	509								

If you study the connection between the defining equations and this table, you should see a pattern. You can compute the AP(2,y) values (row 2 of the table) as follows, using the fact that AP(1,y) is y + 2:

AP(2,1) is AP(1, AP(1,1)), which is AP(1,3), which is 5.
AP(2,2) is AP(1, AP(2,1)), which is AP(1,5), which is 7.
AP(2,3) is AP(1, AP(2,2)), which is AP(1,7), which is 9.
AP(2,4) is AP(1, AP(2,3)), which is AP(1,9), which is 11.
AP(2,5) is AP(1, AP(2,4)), which is AP(1,11), which is 13.

In general, AP(2,y) is 2*y+3. Row 3 of the table, which contains the AP(3,y) values, is now somewhat more laboriously calculated as follows:

AP(3,1) is AP(2, AP(2,1)), which is AP(2,5), which is 2*5 +3 = 13.
AP(3,2) is AP(2, AP(3,1)), which is AP(2,13), which is 2*13+3 = 29.
AP(3,3) is AP(2, AP(3,2)), which is AP(2,29), which is 2*29+3 = 61.
AP(3,4) is AP(2, AP(3,3)), which is AP(2,61), which is 2*61+3 = 125.

The rules for constructing any row (for x > 1) can be expressed as follows: AP(x,1) is obtained by looking at the value just above it in the table, finding the column with that number at the top, and using the value in that column and in the x − 1 row. For y > 1, AP(x,y) is obtained by looking at the value to its left in the table, finding the column with that number at the top, and using the value in that column and in the x − 1 row. You can rephrase this algorithm as follows (for x > 1):

To compute AP(x,1):
    Let v denote the value above where it goes in the table;
    Extend row x − 1 of the table to column v, finding AP(x − 1, v);
    Return that value;
To compute AP(x,y) for y greater than 1:
    Let v denote the value to the left of where it goes in the table;
    Extend row x − 1 of the table to column v, finding AP(x − 1, v);
    Return that value;

To implement this algorithm for AP, you can establish an array Val[1], Val[2],..., Val[x] to contain the most recently computed value in row 1, 2,..., x, respectively. For instance, assume you want to compute AP(4,7):

☐ You first compute AP(1,1)=3. This is Valopen[1].

☐ Now you compute AP(2,1) by moving to column 3 of row 1, obtaining Val[1]=5, so Val[2]=5. Actually, you should keep track of the column for which the value applies. Thus Col[1]=3 and Col[2]=1, since the 5 is in column 3 of row 1 and in column 1 of row 2.

EXAMPLE 2.8B _____

```
PROCEDURE AP (x, y : Positive) : Positive;
    (* The Ackermann-Peter function *)

TYPE
    Vector = ARRAY [1..MaxSize] OF Positive;
  (*--------------------------------------------------------*)

    PROCEDURE MoveRightInRow (x, y : Positive;
                             VAR Col, Val : Vector);
        (* Given that Val[1]...Val[x] are all equal,
           change Col[x] to y and compute the corresponding
           Val[x].  Change Val[1]...Val[x-1] so they all
           equal Val[x] *)

    VAR
        K : Positive;

    BEGIN

        IF x = 1 THEN
            Val [1] := y + 2;
            Col [1] := y;
        ELSE
            FOR K := Col [x] + 1 TO y DO
                MoveRightInRow (x - 1, Val [x], Col, Val);
                Val [x] := Val [x - 1];
            END;
            Col [x] := y;
        END;

    END MoveRightInRow;
  (*--------------------------------------------------------*)

VAR
    K : Positive;
    Col, Val : Vector;

BEGIN           (* AP *)

    Val [1] := 3;
    Col [1] := 1;
    FOR K := 2 TO x DO  (* go down column 1 to row x *)
        MoveRightInRow (K - 1, Val [K - 1], Col, Val);
        Val [K] := Val [K - 1];
        Col [K] := 1;
    END;
    MoveRightInRow (x, y, Col, Val);
    RETURN Val [x];

END AP;
```

☐ Next you compute AP(3,1) as follows: Move right in row 2 to column Val[2] (which is 5), so now Col[2]=5 and Val[2]=13. Then assign Col[3]=1 and Val[3]=13.

☐ Next you compute AP(4,1): Move right in row 3 to column Val[3] (which is 13), where you find 65,533, so that causes Col[3]=13 and Val[3]=65,533.

☐ Now that you have filled in the first column, AP(4,7) is found by moving right in row 4 to column 7.

It should be obvious that the numbers involved are going to become very large very fast. That is what makes the Ackermann-Peter function interesting. The more efficient recursive coding is in Example 2.8B, but to actually run this procedure for large values of x and y, you would have to declare Positive to be a type that allows extremely large values.

Check Your Understanding

1. Find Fib(8), Fib(9), and Fib(10).

2. Compute AP(3,7). *Hint:* Study the table given.

3. Change the definition of the Fibonacci sequence to start with 3,4 instead of 1,2. What are the next five numbers?

4. (NA) Change the definition of the Fibonacci sequence to start with 2,4 instead of 1,2. What is its relation to the original sequence?

5. (NA) Trace the action of the recursive function in Example 2.8A when called with x = 8. Tell what value is assigned to what variable for each execution of an assignment statement.

6. (NA) The MoveRightInRow procedure of Example 2.8B would execute faster if you handled the special case of x = 2 separately, instead of recursively. Rewrite it to do so.

7. (NA) Apply the delocalization technique described at the end of the previous section to the Col and Val parameters of MoveRightInRow. There is no need in this case to have a separate subprocedure, since the whole AP function is fairly short.

2.9 RECURSION VERSUS EFFICIENCY

You have seen a number of algorithms that have been coded recursively, and you will see many more in this text. There are many situations in which recursion is by far the best approach. However, some students get carried away with recursion, using it with wild abandon. This section considers the question of when recursion should be used and when it should not.

The first principle is that recursion should not be used when a nonrecursive solution is just as clear, about as fast, and nearly as compact. For instance, Example 2.9A gives recursive and nonrecursive solutions to the problem of finding the sum of the values in an array of integers. The nonrecursive solution is the time-worn method that everyone is familiar with, but it takes a little time to understand the recursive solution. Since clarity of coding is one of the most important considerations in programming, the nonrecursive solution is preferred.

The recursive procedure in this example carries out the same sequence of additions as the nonrecursive procedure. For instance, a call of the recursive procedure with Size=3 causes a second activation with Size=2, which causes a third activation with Size=1, which causes a fourth activation with Size=0.

☐ The fourth activation returns 0, which corresponds to Ans := 0.

☐ The third activation adds that 0 to Ary[1] (which is what happens in the nonrecursive form when K = 1) and returns it to the second activation.

☐ The second activation adds the returned value to Ary[2] (which is what happens in the nonrecursive form when K = 2) and returns it to the first activation.

EXAMPLE 2.9A _____

```
TYPE
    BigArray = ARRAY [1..MaxSize] OF INTEGER;
(*************************************************************)

PROCEDURE Sum (Ary : BigArray; Size : CARDINAL) : INTEGER;
    (* Add Ary[1]...Ary[Size] recursively *)
BEGIN
    IF Size = 0 THEN
        RETURN 0;
    ELSE
        RETURN Ary [Size] + Sum (Ary, Size - 1);
    END;
END Sum;
(*************************************************************)

PROCEDURE Sum (Ary : BigArray; Size : CARDINAL) : INTEGER;
    (* Add Ary[1]...Ary[Size] NONrecursively *)
VAR
    Answer, K : INTEGER;
BEGIN
    Answer := 0;
    FOR K := 1 TO Size DO
        Answer := Ary [K] + Answer;
    END;
    RETURN Answer;
END Sum;
```

☐ The first activation adds the returned value to Ary[3] (which is what happens in the nonrecursive form when K = 3). Then it returns that answer to the calling procedure, just as the nonrecursive form does.

Iteration versus Recursion

The iterative language constructs in Modula-2 are WHILE, REPEAT, FOR, and LOOP statements. You probably know already that any coding can be readily transformed to use WHILE and IF; WHILE and IF are the basic control statements. In a sense, recursion is a more basic kind of operation than iteration. That is, any coding using WHILE and IF can be readily transformed to use recursion and IF; but some coding using recursion and IF is quite difficult to transform to use WHILE and IF.

To transform a WHILE construct to a recursive construct, you begin by putting the WHILE statement in a procedure by itself. If Pr is the name of the procedure and you let Condition and Statements stand for the essential parts of the WHILE statement, the iterative and recursive forms are:

```
PROCEDURE Pr;                    PROCEDURE Pr;
BEGIN                            BEGIN
    WHILE Condition DO               IF Condition THEN
        Statements;                      Statements;
                                         Pr;
    END;                             END;
END Pr;                          END Pr;
```

In general, a recursive procedure for which only the last action taken in any activation is a recursive call can be written nonrecursively without too much trouble. Such a situation is called **tail recursion**. For instance, the next example shows a recursive and a nonrecursive solution to the problem of finding the greatest common divisor of two numbers. Both algorithms depend on the fact that, for any number K, Large-K∗Small is divisible by any number that divides both Large and Small. Since (Large MOD Small) is by definition of the form Large-K∗Small, the greatest common divisor of Small and Large is the greatest common divisor of Small and (Large MOD Small).

The algorithm in Example 2.9B calculates the greatest common divisor of 24 and 87 as follows: Replace 24 and 87 by 15 and 24, since 87 MOD 24 is 15; then replace those by 9 and 15, since 24 MOD 15 is 9; then replace 9 and 15 by 6 and 9, which are replaced by 3 and 6, which are replaced by 0 and 3. Since one of the numbers is now 0, the other is the greatest common divisor of the original numbers 24 and 87.

EXAMPLE 2.9B _____

```
PROCEDURE GCD (Small, Large : CARDINAL) : CARDINAL;
    (* Find the greatest common divisor of Large and
       Small recursively, where Small <= Large *)
BEGIN
    IF Small = 0 THEN
        RETURN Large;
    ELSE
        RETURN GCD (Large MOD Small, Small);
    END;
END GCD;
(**********************************************************)

PROCEDURE GCD (Small, Large : CARDINAL) : CARDINAL;
    (* Find the greatest common divisor of Large and
       Small NONrecursively, where Small <= Large *)
VAR
    Remainder : CARDINAL;
BEGIN
    WHILE Small # 0 DO
        Remainder := Large MOD Small;
        Large := Small;
        Small := Remainder;
    END;
    RETURN Large;
END GCD;
```

Excessive Number of Activations

As stated previously, you do not use recursion when an iterative solution is just as easy and just as clear. So the question is, if a situation is easier to code recursively, should you do so? The answer depends primarily on the number of recursive calls that are generated and the amount of storage space required.

If a recursive algorithm requires many more recursive calls than an iterative algorithm requires iterations, the iterative algorithm should be used. You can generally tell when this is the case. For instance, the top procedure in Example 2.8A is one of the worst uses of recursion known. *Reminder:* The Fibonacci numbers are 1, 2, 3, 5, 8, 13, 21, 34, and so on, where each number is the sum of the two before it (except for the starting values 1 and 2).

The nonrecursive procedure in Example 2.8A has a FOR statement with $N - 3$ iterations. The recursive procedure in that example causes a number of iterations greater than the (half-of-N)th power of 2, when N is at least 4. For instance, Fib(8) requires 5 iterations nonrecursively, but 44 activations recursively. Fib(10) requires more than twice as many activations as Fib(8); in general, Fib(N) requires more than twice as many activations as Fib(N−2), for N larger than 3. This can be seen to be true as follows: Calculation of Fib(N) requires calculation of Fib(N−1) and Fib(N−2). Since Fib(N−1) also requires calculation of Fib(N−2), the total number of activations for Fib(N) is more than twice that required for Fib(N−2).

Space Requirements of Recursion

Another reason for using a nonrecursive solution instead of a recursive one is to save storage space. Each procedure activation requires a certain small amount of space; but the main culprits are usually the procedure parameters, since each of those requires a certain amount of space. For instance, in Example 2.9A, the recursive GCD procedure has two local variables named Large and Small. GCD(24,87) causes six activations of the procedure, each with its own two local variables. The recursive MoveRightInRow procedure in Example 2.8B has four parameters, each of which requires space in each activation.

These space demands can often be avoided by using the delocalization technique described at the end of Section 2.7. A value parameter or local variable can be "delocalized" if its value is not accessed by the recursive procedure after it makes a recursive call. This was the case for the Data parameter of IsOkay in Example 2.7A. A VAR parameter can be "delocalized" if the actual parameter of a recursive call is the same as the formal parameter. This was the case for the Col and Val parameters of MoveRightInRow in Example 2.8B.

The final consideration in deciding whether to use recursion or iteration is execution time. However, modern compilers are usually built so that "good" uses of recursion do not take significantly longer than iteration. In fact, a recursive solution can execute faster than an iterative solution on machines that have a "stack architecture." This assumes that you delocalize where feasible, since passing parameters adds to execution time.

Techniques for Removal of Recursion

Any program that uses recursion can be rewritten without using recursion. There are some standard techniques for doing so, but if none of the considerations mentioned earlier in this section apply, it is best not to do so. However, you may be programming in a language that does not permit recursion; then you have no choice. For instance, most dialects of FORTRAN and COBOL do not allow recursion.

Languages that do not support recursion offer GOTOs as a rather poor substitute. If you have an algorithm that naturally uses recursion, and you need to adapt it to a recursionless language, you can use a "stack" (to be described in the first section of the next chapter). You establish a stack of records, where each record holds the values of local variables and parameters for a given call of the recursive procedure, as well as a **return address**, a cardinal explained later in this paragraph. At each point in the procedure where a recursive call occurs, replace it by statements that push a new record on the stack and GOTO the beginning of the procedure. Put a statement label directly after the replacement statements. At the end of the procedure, pop a record off the stack, restore values from the record, and GOTO to the statement label indicated by the return address in the record. However, if the stack is empty, simply exit the procedure. You often have to use a CASE statement that has an appropriate GOTO for each return address.

The result of all this is usually a procedure that is several times as big and extremely difficult to comprehend. There is an even easier method of removing recursion that usually suffices: First you determine the maximum number of copies of the procedure that can be active under recursion. For instance, assume you are executing the PrintTree procedure of Example 2.6C with a parameter of 13; then there will be 13 levels of recursion. So you simply make 12 more copies of the procedure with names such as Proc1, Proc2,..., Proc12. Then have the procedure call Proc1 instead of itself; Proc1 calls Proc2 instead of itself; and so forth. This requires more storage space for the program, but that can be reduced by replacing large blocks of nonrecursive code in the procedure by a call to an auxiliary procedure. The additional storage space is the only disadvantage; clarity of coding is retained, and very little programming effort is required.

Check Your Understanding

1. Trace the action of Example 2.9B when the recursive GCD function is called using GCD(21,27).

2. Calculate the number of activations of the recursive Fib function in Example 2.8A when it is called using Fib(12).

3. What changes should be made in Example 2.8A to obtain recursive and nonrecursive functions that compute the number of activations of the recursive Fib function (note the answer to Exercise 2)?

4. (NA) Trace the action of Example 2.9B when the recursive GCD function is called using GCD(150,220).

5. (NA) Show how a WHILE statement can be replaced by recursion by rewriting Example 1.8B.

2.10 THE HALTING PROBLEM (A READ-ALOUD STORY)

This book discusses various kinds of algorithms to a great extent. Algorithms are compared for efficiency using several criteria. To put this discussion in the proper perspective, you should be aware that there are certain programming situations for which no algorithm can be developed to solve the problem. This story presents such a situation.

Once upon a time there were two hotshot programmers named Ginny and Cathy. Their job at the company where they worked was as follows: From time to time, other company programmers would submit to them a floppy disk with a program file and a data file. Ginny and Cathy would run tests and eventually report one of two results: "This program will fall into an infinite loop with this data," or "This program will eventually halt execution with this data." Since the programs produced by this company tended to run excessively long times on very expensive computer equipment, the company boss considered this job crucial, so Ginny and Cathy were paid much better than the other programmers and given many company perks, including their own private parking spaces.

Another programmer named Ed Lee was jealous of Ginny and Cathy. One day he came to them and said, "I've secretly developed a program that does what the two of you have been doing, and the boss is running tests on it now. It has already checked out over a dozen programs that you two had previously checked, and it came up with the same answers you did. When the testing is done and my program is proven correct, I'll be the one to have all the company perks and you ladies will be out on your cans."

Ginny and Cathy went to Paula, the boss, and said, "Ed's program is a crock. There was no need for you to test out all those programs; let us look at Ed's program and we'll have a test case for you this afternoon that will show that his program has a logic error. The problem is that you have been doing **black-box testing**; you haven't been looking at the internal structure of the program and choosing test cases on that basis." So Paula gave them a copy of Ed's program with which to work.

Ginny studied the program and found that there were only two kinds of output statements in it. There were hundreds of places where it printed "infinite loop" and hundreds of other places where it printed "program halts." They modified Ed's program by replacing each statement that printed "program halts" by a new statement REPEAT(* wait *)UNTIL 2+2=5; this is obviously an infinite loop. They also replaced each "infinite loop" output statement by one that printed "Ed is a dork." They put two copies of this modification on a floppy disk, then went back to Paula and said, "Okay, here is a program file and a data file for which Ed's program gives the wrong answer."

Paula ran the modification on one computer and ran Ed's program analyzing the modification on another computer. She waited and waited. They both kept on running, but that did not prove anything; after all, it could be days or weeks before they halted, if they would ever halt. She said, "How am I ever going to know whether Ed's program has a bug? If it says Ginny's program halts, I will never be able to tell; it might just be taking an inordinate amount of time before it stops. If it says Ginny's program will run forever and the program is still running years from now, I won't really know; it may be about to halt."

Then Cathy explained what Ginny had done and the implications of it. If Ed's program says Ginny's program halts, Ginny's program will go through exactly the same steps that Ed's program does until Ed's program gets to the output statement that says the program halts. At that point Ginny's program will execute the statement REPEAT(* wait *)UNTIL 2+2=5, which is an infinite loop. That is wrong, so Ed's program has a bug in it (assuming it says that Ginny's program halts).

If, on the other hand, Ed's program says Ginny's program has an infinite loop, Ginny's program will go through exactly the same steps that Ed's program does. The REPEAT statement will never be reached in Ginny's program, because the "program halts" output statement is never reached in Ed's program. Ginny's program will print the phrase "Ed is a dork" and then halt execution. Thus Ed's program gives the wrong answer if it says that Ginny's program has an infinite loop.

After a good deal of thought, Paula could see that what Cathy said was true. She exclaimed, "How did you ever figure that out?" Ginny and Cathy explained that they and Ed had gone to the same school, but Ed had taken only easy courses. In particular, he had bypassed the course on Church's thesis in favor of a COBOL course. **Church's thesis** states that there is no reasonable programming language in which you can write a program that correctly tells, for any program in that language, whether it halts for a given input. So Paula raised both their salaries several thousand dollars, gave them a key to the executive washroom, and fired Ed.

MORAL OF THIS STORY. Take courses where you learn a lot, even if they are a lot of work. Do not just get your degree, like Ed did. And when your instructor assigns lots of hard problems to solve, thank him or her for giving you a good education.

Notes: The foregoing discussion proves that, in the programming language Ginny and Cathy were using, there cannot be a program that tells, for any program in that language, whether the program halts for a given input. Church's thesis says there is no algorithm in *any* programming language that correctly tests every program in a given reasonable programming language to see if it halts. In essence, the thesis says that there are many kinds of programs that cannot be debugged in Pascal or in Modula-2. Church's thesis cannot be proven; you cannot list all possible programming languages and test each one. However, most people who go deeply into the subject feel that Church's thesis is true. The thesis is based on Goedel's theorem, which says that there are certain facts about numbers that no one can prove are true, although they *are* true.

CHAPTER REVIEW

A library module is a pair of separately compiled units that can be considered extensions of the program you are writing. This allows you to use an extensive library of procedures in several different programs without having to write them over again each time. It also cuts compilation time enormously for large programs. But the major advantage is that it allows you to hide the implementation of a data type used in the program, which makes it easier to design your program.

A pointer type is of the form POINTER TO T where T is some type-denoter. A variable of this pointer type can contain the address of a variable of type T. If P is of type POINTER TO T, NEW(P) allocates space for a variable of type T and puts its address in P; you can refer to that variable by using P ↑ . You can deallocate the space by using DISPOSE(P). Most Modula-2 compilers allow you to use NEW and

DISPOSE if you have FROM Storage IMPORT ALLOCATE, DEALLOCATE in your program.

You can give just the name of an exported type in a definition module if you declare that type in the implementation module as a pointer type. This opaque declaration allows you to hide from a client module the structure of variables accessed by pointers.

InfoMan contains a declaration of Information and some procedures to manipulate variables of Information type; InfoADT is similar except that Information is a pointer to a record instead of the record itself (although in some applications Information may not be a record). The six procedures common to the information-handling modules discussed in this chapter are CreateInfo, CopyInfo, DestroyInfo, InputInfo, OutputInfo, and Compare.

Recursion is what happens when, at some point during execution of a procedure, that procedure is activated again. Any use of recursion should be closely checked to see that it must eventually terminate.

PRACTICE TEST

To prepare for a test, study the indicated examples thoroughly until you can be sure that you would earn a high grade on a test composed solely of these exercises.

1. Write a procedure to insert a given information value in a counted array whose values are in increasing order, maintaining the order. [Example 2.2B]

2. Write the function procedure Compare, which has two Information parameters and returns 0 if the IDs are equal, 1 if the ID of the first is larger, -1 if the ID of the first is smaller. Assume that Information is a record with a CARDINAL ID field. [Example 2.2D]

3. Revise Example 1.3A using POINTER TO REAL instead of REAL. Use DISPOSE for each NEW. [Exercise 1 in Section 2.3]

4. Write the OutputInfo procedure for the CountedArray implementation of big cardinals in which the decimal digits of the number are written with a blank before each pair of digits. [Example 2.4B]

5. Write the CharAt function for the null-terminated array implementation of LineADT. The function returns the character at a given position in a given string of characters. [Example 2.4D]

6. Write a recursive procedure that prints the numbers in the complete binary tree with a given numbers of levels, in order from left to right. [Example 2.6C]

7. Write a recursive Boolean function that accepts an array of characters and two indices in the array, then tells whether the string of characters indicated by those indices is a palindrome. [Example 2.7A or 2.7B]

8. Write a nonrecursive function to compute the Nth Fibonacci number. [Example 2.8A]

9. Write a recursive procedure to compute the greatest common divisor of two given cardinals, where the first is no larger than the second. [Example 2.9B]

PROGRAMMING PROBLEMS

1. Write a program that reads an input file with three numbers per line, two integers and a real, until the end of the file is reached. Each line represents one entry on a sales receipt, sent from a cash register to a central computer: The first number is the ID number of a stock item, the second is the quantity of that item that has been sold, and the third (real) is the price of that item. There will usually be many duplicates for a given ID number (all with the same price), but there will not be more than 500 lines in the file. Print a list of all distinct ID numbers mentioned, in order from lowest to highest, with the total quantity sold and the price for each ID. *Implementation restrictions*: Use the InsertInOrder procedure (Example 2.2B) without change; compute totals for each ID during the printing stage. Also follow the implementation restrictions given for Problem 3.

2. Modify the previous problem by assuming an unknown number of lines in the file, but at most 500 different ID numbers. *Implementation restrictions*: As each line is read, use binary search to find out whether the ID number is already listed. If not, insert it in the list before reading the next line; otherwise, just add the quantity.

3. Write a program that reads a file of one day's sales, the output from Problem 2. Then it reads another file with three cardinals per line: an item's ID, the minimum number of that item that should be kept in inventory, and the number on hand not counting the sales recorded in the first file. Have the program create a reorder file telling how many units of which items should be ordered to fill out the inventory and the cost of reordering those units (but only for IDs in the first file for which a reorder is necessary). Then print the total cost of all those reorders. The IDs in the first file will be a subset of those in the second file; there will not be more than 500 different ID values in the first file; IDs in each file will be in increasing order; there will be no duplicate IDs within either file. *Implementation restrictions:* Call on InfoADT (Information = POINTER TO RECORD ID, QuantitySold: CARDI-

NAL; PricePerItem: REAL; END), but add three functions to Example 2.3B: IdOf, QuanOf, and PriceOf, each returning the value of a field of a given Information parameter. Put the information for the first file in a CountedArray as described in Section 2.2. The values in the second file are to be read into three simple variables, not stored in an array.

4. Write a program that repeatedly accepts two integers, the numerator and denominator of a fraction, and prints the fraction reduced to lowest terms. It calls the GCD function to find the number to divide out of both the numerator and denominator. Note that the program is little more than a driver program for the function.

5. Write a program that accepts two positive integers less than 10000, the first less than the second. Then it prints one line for each number K between those two given numbers (inclusive of the two). Each line contains 12 numbers. The first number in a line is the K for that line. Each number after the first is the "Ziel" of the one before. The "Ziel" of a number from 0001 to 9999 is obtained by reversing the four digits of the given number (after filling in leading zeros for numbers below 1000) and subtracting the smaller from the larger. *Example:* Two lines could be:

   1452 1089 8712 6534 2178 6534 2178 6534 2178 6534 2178 6534
   4723 1449 7992 4995 999 8991 6993 2997 4995 999 8991 6993

6. Modify Problem 5 as follows: First make reasonable guesses as to the behavior of this Ziel function. Then modify your program to test your guesses on long series of numbers generated in this fashion. For example, is it always true that every case of repeats will repeat by twos or by fives (the divisors of 10)? *Note:* This is very hard.

7. Modify Problem 5 by changing the definition of Ziel as follows: The Ziel of a number 0001 to 9999 is obtained by rearranging the digits in increasing order and also in decreasing order, then subtracting the former from the latter.

8. Write a program to accept as input any positive integer and print the thirtieth power of the given number (which is of course larger than the largest cardinal). *Implementation restrictions:* Use the BigCardADT implementation module described at the end of Section 2.3. Include a pair of procedures for each of addition, multiplication, subtraction, and division.

9. It is easy to find a power of 3 that is 1 less than a power of 2, namely 3 < 4. Find all other such cases with less than 10000 digits. *Implementation restrictions:* Same as for the previous problem.

10. Write an elementary line editor for a file with 0 or more lines, each with at most 80 characters. At all times during this program, no line exceeds 80 characters in length and the total number of lines never exceeds 600. The

program should continually assure that these conditions are satisfied. First read all lines from the file into an array of lines and display on the screen line number 1. Then accept one-letter commands that do the following (N is the number of the line that is currently displayed, so initially N is 1):

M: Modify line number N by replacing it with a new line (entered at the keyboard), and display this new line number N.

D: Delete line number N from the array, display the new line number N (formerly line number N+1).

I: Insert a new line (entered at the keyboard) before line number N in the array; display the new line number N+1 (the old line N).

A: Advance one line, that is, display line number N+1.

E: Exit from the editor, that is, write the revised array of lines to the file.

Make reasonable allowance for what to display when there are no more lines, so that "I" will insert new lines at the end of the file. The program should never crash. Use imports from LineADT.

11. Modify the preceding problem by allowing these additional commands:

B: (Begin) resets the current line to line number 1.

J+: Jump 20 lines forward in the array.

J−: Jump 20 lines backward in the array.

F: Find the next occurrence of a given three-character string in the file, advancing to the line that contains it.

12. Rewrite the AP function in Example 2.8B without using recursion.

13. You are given a deck of 6 cards numbered 1 through 6, inclusive. You are to first put them in increasing order: 1 2 3 4 5 6. Then you are to perform a perfect riffle shuffle, which consists of dividing the cards exactly in half and interleaving the halves so you end up with the ordering 1 4 2 5 3 6. You are to repeat the perfect riffle shuffle until the cards are again in the original order: The second shuffle yields 1 5 4 3 2 6, the third shuffle yields 1 3 5 2 4 6, and the fourth shuffle yields 1 2 3 4 5 6.

Write a program that does this not only for 6 but for each even number of cards from 2 up to 100 and reports, for each such even number, the number of perfect riffle shuffles required to obtain the original order. For instance, 2 cards require 1 shuffle, 4 cards require 2 shuffles, 6 cards require 4 shuffles, and 8 cards require 3 shuffles. This problem is designed to give you practice with arrays and nested loops.

14. The screen of a particular kind of computer monitor can be considered to be a square array of dots, 320 dots wide and 200 dots tall. Figures are formed on the screen by lighting certain of the dots. Write a program to read in a 200-by-320 array of cardinals that are either 0 (for an unlighted dot) or 1 (for a lighted dot) and compute the area of one particular object on the screen (i.e., the number of lighted dots in the figure). The object under study is specified by giving the indices of one of its lighted dots. For instance, if the given lighted dot is at [40,100], you would compute the area by counting that lighted dot and the lighted dots connected to it and the lighted dots connected to those, and so forth. At most four dots are connected to any given dot, namely, the ones north, south, east, and west of it. *Implementation restriction:* As each dot is counted, change the value of the component from 1 to 2. Use recursion.

15. Expand on the program just described by reading in a 200-by-320 array of cardinals and printing out the number of objects on the screen as well as, for each object, the area of the object and the indices of one of its lighted dots (the latter is for identification purposes).

16. Modify the program in Problem 14 to tell whether the given object (or rather, the object that includes the given lighted dot) touches the border of the screen. If it does, print a sequence of indices of connected lighted dots that lead from the given dot to the border. If the screen is considered to be a maze in which you can only go where a 1 is, this problem amounts to finding a path from a given point in the maze to the outside of the maze.

17. Do any of the previous three problems with the understanding that each dot is connected to at most eight dots; allow dots that are to the northeast, northwest, southeast, and southwest of the given dot.

3

FUNDAMENTAL DATA STRUCTURES WITH ARRAY IMPLEMENTATIONS

The subject matter of this chapter is several fundamental data structures, presented as abstract data types. A **data structure** is a collection of information values with a certain relationship to one another, where the collection can be treated as a unit.

"Stacks," "queues," and "tables" occur in a large number of situations, particularly situations that arise in constructing compilers and operating systems. A more general data structure is the "linear list," which I also analyze here. I discuss several implementations of each of these data structures in this chapter and the next.

The emphasis for the rest of this book is on collections of information values, not on the internal structure of the information values themselves. The coding assumes that imports are made from an information-handling library module named InfoADT that exports CreateInfo, CopyInfo, DestroyInfo, InputInfo, OutputInfo, and Compare. In practice, you would import from LineADT, BigCard-ADT, or whatever information-handler you wanted to use.

Some applications of the data structures are discussed in this chapter. If you would like to see some more complex applications, Section 7.1 can be covered after Section 3.3, Section 7.2 after Section 3.5, and Section 7.3 after Section 3.7.

141

3.1 STACKS

The first data structure you learn about in this chapter is a "stack," perhaps the most fundamental data structure in computing. You can put information on a stack, and you can remove information from a stack, with the condition that the only information value you can remove is the one you *most recently* put on. I begin by describing some programs in which a stack would be useful.

The AlgebraicExpression Program

Consider a program to read one or more lines of input each containing what is supposed to be a legal expression in algebra. The program is to tell whether the characters on each line actually form a legal algebraic expression. Part of the program might be a Boolean function IsLegal that tells whether the characters in a given string form a legal algebraic expression. Such an expression might indicate grouping of symbols using brackets ([   ]) and braces ({   }) as well as parentheses ((   )). You can have a large number of these grouping symbols in an expression, and you have to check to see if they are properly nested.

A good way of doing this is with a **stack**. Visualize a cart that holds a stack of serving trays in a restaurant (Figure 1). Each time a tray is added, a spring mechanism allows the whole stack to move down. Each time a tray is removed, the spring moves the rest of the stack up. Thus the top tray on the stack is always at a fixed height independent of the number of trays on the stack, unless the stack is empty or full.

For this algebraic expression program, you could use a stack that contains parentheses, brackets, and braces instead of trays. You look at each character in the expression, proceeding from left to right. Each time you see a left parenthesis, bracket, or brace, you put it on top of the stack for safekeeping until you find its mate. Each time you see a right parenthesis, bracket, or brace, you compare it with the character on the top of the stack. If they do not match, the algebraic expression is illegal. If, however, the one you take off the stack matches the one you compared with it, you discard both of them and continue the algorithm. The stack of grouping symbols must be empty when you reach the end of the expression.

FIGURE 1. A restaurant cart with trays.

The StockHolder Program

Consider the situation of a wealthy person who buys and sells large amounts of stock in various companies. For federal tax purposes, she is required to compute her profit and loss by assuming that any share she sells was the one she most recently purchased, when shares in that company were purchased at several different prices. This is called **LIFO** accounting, which stands for *Last-In-First-Out*.

For example, assume the following sequence of transactions for the stock in one particular company: She buys 40 shares for $150 each in February; then she buys 25 shares for $120 each in May; then she sells 20 shares for $140 each in August. The tax rule says she sold the May shares, not the February shares. So she is required to declare a profit of $20 each for tax purposes, instead of a loss of $10 each; that makes a net profit of $400. If she had sold 60 shares instead of 20, she would have had a profit of $20 on each of 25 shares and a loss of $10 on each of 35 shares. That would be a net profit of $150.

Stacks are appropriate for such a program. You can use one stack for each company in which the person holds stock. Each time she buys shares, you put the information about it on top of the stack for that company (this is called **pushing** information on the stack). Thus at any given time the most recently purchased shares are on top of the stack. When she sells stock, you take the shares from the top of the appropriate stack. This is called **popping** information from the stack.

Use of Stacks in Compilers

Yet another situation in which stacks are useful is that of procedure calls in programs. Initially, the processor pushes information about the program on an "activation stack." The program's **activation record** contains the global variables and a note as to which statement to execute next. Each time a statement is executed, the activation record is updated. Each time a procedure is called, the processor pushes an activation record for that procedure on the top of the activation stack. When a procedure terminates execution, the activation record on top of the stack is removed and execution continues in the procedure whose activation record is below it. This is what makes recursion possible.

There is even a popular and powerful computer language called Forth that is based on stacks. For example, addition is implemented by using a one-word statement that pops two numbers off the main stack, adds them together, and pushes the result back on the main stack. Any mention of a variable pushes its address on the stack; then a separate "load" command pops the address off the stack and replaces it by the value stored at that address.

The Stack Operations

We need procedures with which we can manipulate a stack. The standard terminology for putting an item on a stack is **Push**; **Pop** is used for taking an item off a

			4		
		8		7	7	7
	3	3	3	3	3	3	3
5	5	5	5	5	5	5	5
Empty	Push 5	Push 3	Push 8	Pop 8	Push 7	Push 4	Pop 4	Pop 7

FIGURE 2. *How a stack changes for a sequence of pushes and pops.*

stack. These two names have an obvious connection with the restaurant cart of trays image.

We need a function to tell us whether the stack is empty, so we can avoid the mistake of trying to Pop an item from an empty stack; I call this Boolean function **IsEmpty**. We occasionally need a procedure that lets us look at the item on top of the stack without actually changing the stack; I call this procedure **Peep**. Figure 2 illustrates the use of Push and Pop for one particular stack.

We want to be able to use the stack-handling module without change in several different situations, so we import from another module (InfoADT or Info-Man, described in Chapter 2) the kind of item to be pushed or popped, called Information for full generality. For example, the AlgebraicExpression program could declare TYPE Information=POINTER TO CHAR or perhaps Information=CHAR; the ShareHolder program could declare Information as a pointer to a record type with fields for the number of shares, the price per share, the date of purchase, and so forth.

The Abstract Data Type

To see how the parameters of the procedures should be declared, we look at an application of the procedures. In the AlgebraicExpression program, part of the algorithm might be as follows:

Algorithm for matching parentheses and the like:
1. IF ThisCharacter is one of '(', '[', or '{', then:
      1.a. Push ThisCharacter on the Stack;
    OTHERWISE IF ThisCharacter is one of ')', ']', or '}', then:
      1.b. IF the Stack is empty, return FALSE (illegal);
      1.c. Pop TopCharacter from the Stack;
      1.d. IF ThisCharacter and TopCharacter do not match, return FALSE.

This gives a good idea of what the parameters should be for our stack manipulations, sufficient to write the definition module (Example 3.1A). In essence, this

EXAMPLE 3.1A _____

```
DEFINITION MODULE StackADT;
FROM InfoADT IMPORT Information;
EXPORT QUALIFIED Stack,   Push,   Pop,   Peep,
                  IsEmpty, Create, Destroy;
    (* Module to implement stack manipulations indepen-
        dently of the kind of Information being put on the
        stack.  Warning:  Every Stack must be initialized
        before anything else can be done with it. *)
    (* Written by Dr. William C. Jones, October, 19-- *)
TYPE
    Stack;
(* ********************************************************** )

PROCEDURE Push (TheInfo : Information;   VAR Data : Stack);
    (* Put TheInfo on top of Data *)

PROCEDURE Pop (VAR TheInfo : Information;
               VAR Data    : Stack);
    (* Remove TheInfo from the top of Data if Data is
        not empty; no effect if Data is empty *)

PROCEDURE Peep (VAR TheInfo : Information;   Data : Stack);
    (* Access the Information on top of Data if Data is
        not empty; no effect if Data is empty *)


PROCEDURE IsEmpty (Data : Stack) : BOOLEAN;
    (* Tell whether Data is empty *)

PROCEDURE Create (VAR Data : Stack);
    (* Initialize Data as an empty structure *)

PROCEDURE Destroy (VAR Data : Stack);
    (* Deallocate the space for the empty structure *)

END StackADT.
```

definition module describes the abstract data structure called a stack. This is data abstraction; no client module is to reference a stack except through this library module.

The definition module for StackADT exports two additional procedures analogous to CreateInfo and DestroyInfo in InfoADT. We need to be able to initialize a stack to the empty state; for that we need a procedure that we call **Create**. We also provide a procedure named **Destroy** to complement Create; when the implementation is as a pointer to a variable, we need to be able to deallocate space for stacks that are only used for a short time.

Assume that you have a nonempty Stack and you want to dispose of all the information on it. The following coding does this:

```
REPEAT
    Pop (TheInfo, Data);
    DestroyInfo (TheInfo);
UNTIL IsEmpty (Data);
```

Example 3.1B gives another illustration of how a program could use these stack manipulation procedures. It displays a procedure that could be in a client module (i.e., a module that imports declarations from StackADT). The task performed by this procedure is turning a given stack upside down, that is, reversing the order of the information values on the stack. The algorithm is: Create a local stack; move information from the given stack to the local stack one value at a time, which reverses the order of the information; then destroy the given stack and assign the local stack to it.

When you use these StackADT procedures, you should keep in mind that none of them create or destroy information values. It helps to think of Push(TheInfo, Data) as giving TheInfo to Data, so you cannot then change TheInfo without risking a change in what is on the stack. Similarly, Pop(TheInfo, Data) moves information from the stack to TheInfo, and Peep(TheInfo, Data) lets you look at what is on the stack. Create and Destroy change the number of stacks in existence.

Preconditions and Postconditions

A **valid Stack value** is defined by:

- [ ] Execution of Create returns a valid Stack value.
- [ ] Execution of Destroy for a valid Stack value returns an invalid Stack value.
- [ ] Execution of any other procedure in StackADT for a valid Stack value returns a valid Stack value.
- [ ] There are no other valid Stack values.

The precondition for a procedure, as described in Section 2.4, is the condition that must be true when the procedure is called, otherwise programming errors can occur. The postcondition for a procedure is what else is guaranteed to be true when the procedure terminates, if the precondition was met. The comments in StackADT describe the preconditions and postconditions informally; the rest of this subsection formalizes them.

The precondition for each of the StackADT procedures except Create is that the Stack parameter have a valid Stack value; Create does not have a precondition (or you could say that it has an empty precondition). The postcondition for Destroy is that the Stack parameter has an invalid Stack value. The postcondition

EXAMPLE 3.1B _____

```
PROCEDURE Reverse (VAR Data : Stack);
    (* Replace Data by a stack with the same items in
       the opposite order *)
    (* Context:  client of StackADT *)
VAR
    LocalStack : Stack;
    TheInfo    : Information;
BEGIN
    Create (LocalStack);
    WHILE NOT IsEmpty (Data) DO
        Pop (TheInfo, Data);
        Push (TheInfo, LocalStack);
    END;
    Destroy (Data);
    Data := LocalStack;
END Reverse;
```

for each of the other StackADT procedures is that the Stack parameter has a valid Stack value and moreover:

☐ For IsEmpty, the Boolean value returned tells whether the Stack has had as many information values taken away as have been added.

☐ For Create, IsEmpty returns true.

☐ For Push, the Stack has one more information value than it had before, namely the information parameter.

☐ For Peep, if IsEmpty were to return false, then the value of the information parameter is the information value most recently added to the Stack parameter.

☐ For Pop, if IsEmpty were to return false, the value of the information parameter is the information value most recently added to the Stack parameter, and the Stack has one less information value than it had before, namely the value of the information parameter.

Utility Procedures

A **utility procedure** in a library module is a procedure whose effect could be accomplished by calling on other procedures in the module. That is, the procedure is made part of the library module, although it could be written outside the library module. The reason for having a utility procedure is speed of execution, since putting it inside the library module allows its algorithm to access the internal makeup of the data structure. In many applications of Stacks, the seven procedures described in Example 3.1C are utility procedures (i.e., they are made part of StackADT).

EXAMPLE 3.1C _____

```
(* Some reasonable utility procedures for Stacks *)

PROCEDURE Join (VAR First, Second : Stack);
     (* First becomes the new structure composed of the
        information from First in front of the information
        from Second, with the order of the items of each
        structure unchanged.  Dispose of Second properly *)

PROCEDURE Shift (VAR Data, Source : Stack);
     (* Take one information value from Source and put it
        in Data; no effect if Source is empty *)

PROCEDURE Copy (VAR Data, Source : Stack);
     (* Make Data a duplicate copy of Source.  Data must
        initially be empty.  No effect if Source is empty.
        Import CreateInfo and CopyInfo from InfoADT *)

PROCEDURE ReadAll (VAR Data : Stack);
     (* Initialize Data; read information from a file and
        put it in Data in the order read, first thing read
        on top, until end-of-file is reached.  Import from
        InfoADT:  InputInfo, DestroyInfo, Okay *)

PROCEDURE WriteAll (Data : Stack);
     (* Write all information records from Data to a file,
        in the order they occur in Data.  Do not change
        Data.  Import OutputInfo from InfoADT *)

PROCEDURE DestroyAllInfo (VAR Data : Stack);
     (* Destroy all information in Data, leaving it empty.
        Import DestroyInfo from InfoADT *)

PROCEDURE SizeOf (Data : Stack) : CARDINAL;
     (* Tell how many items are in the Data structure *)
```

In this section and in the exercises, algorithms for these procedures are presented using the six **primitives** given in Example 3.1A. Later, when we see various implementations of StackADT, the algorithms will be discussed in terms of the implementations.

The coding for DestroyAllInfo using imports from StackADT and InfoADT was given earlier in this section. The Shift procedure could be coded as follows, using a local Information variable named TheInfo:

```
Pop (TheInfo, Source);
Push (TheInfo, Data);
```

The Copy procedure can be easily implemented recursively using imports from StackADT. Procedure calls are implemented by the compiler as a stack; we can take advantage of that by declaring local variables OldInfo and NewInfo and using the following coding for Copy:

```
IF IsEmpty (Source) THEN
    Create (Data);
ELSE
    Pop (OldInfo, Source);
    Copy (Data, Source);   (* recursive call *)
    CreateInfo (NewInfo);
    CopyInfo (NewInfo, OldInfo);
    Push (NewInfo, Data);
    Push (OldInfo, Source);
END;
```

Each time Copy calls itself, a new set of local variables is created for storing the information taken from the Source. When the Source is empty, the recursion "unwinds," pushing values onto both Data and Source in the proper order.

If a utility procedure is added to StackADT, its description should include a list of all imports it needs (as shown for ReadAll, DestroyAllInfo, and WriteAll). Remember that the InfoADT module given in Example 2.3B is merely a sample; different applications have different exports from InfoADT. The six primitive procedures given for StackADT do not import anything from InfoADT except the Information type.

Example 3.1D displays a simple program that shows the power that derives from having the procedures from InfoADT and StackADT available for use. The task performed by this program is reading information values from a file and writing them to another file in the opposite order of how they occurred in the first file. Notice that the logic of such a program is easy to develop when you have the right imports. First you read one information value at a time and push each on a stack. After you come to the end of the input file, you pop one information value at a time from the stack and write each to the file. You do not have to concern yourself with any of the messy little details of reading and writing a complex record; the InfoADT procedures take care of that for you.

Check Your Understanding

1. Complete the following procedure, using imports from StackADT:

```
PROCEDURE SwapTopTwo (VAR Data : Stack);
(* Change Data by swapping its top and next-to-top items; but
   do nothing if there are fewer than two items in Data *)
```

EXAMPLE 3.1D _____

```
MODULE Invert;
FROM InOut    IMPORT OpenInput,  CloseInput,
                     OpenOutput, CloseOutput;
FROM InfoADT  IMPORT Information, Okay, DestroyInfo,
                     InputInfo,   OutputInfo;
FROM StackADT IMPORT Stack, Create, IsEmpty, Push, Pop;
    (* From a given file of information, create a new file
       with the same values in the opposite order *)
    (* Written by William C. Jones, October 19-- *)
(*********************************************************)

VAR
    Data : Stack;
    TheInfo : Information;

BEGIN          (* program *)

(* read all information from the input file, put on stack*)
    Create (Data);
    OpenInput ('');
    InputInfo (TheInfo);
    WHILE Okay DO
        Push (TheInfo, Data);
        InputInfo (TheInfo);
    END;
    DestroyInfo (TheInfo); (* created but not filled *)
    CloseInput;

(* move all information from the stack to the output file*)
    OpenOutput ('');
    WHILE NOT IsEmpty (Data) DO
        Pop (TheInfo, Data);
        OutputInfo (TheInfo);
    END;
    CloseOutput;

END Invert.
```

2. Write a Boolean function that tells whether a given stack has at least two information values in it. Import from StackADT.

3. Complete the following procedure using StackADT:

```
PROCEDURE SplitOddsAndEvens (VAR Odds, Evens : Stack);
(* The stack named Odds is to be divided in two parts.
   The first, third, fifth, etc. items originally on Odds
   are to end up on Odds, and the second, fourth, sixth,
   etc. items originally on Odds are to end up on Evens *)
```

4. (NA) Complete the ReadAll procedure described in Example 3.1C, importing from StackADT and InfoADT as needed. *Hint:* Use a local Stack.

5. (NA) Complete the WriteAll procedure described in Example 3.1C, importing from StackADT and InfoADT as needed.

6. (NA) Complete the Join procedure described in Example 3.1C, importing from StackADT as needed. *Hint:* Shift the information in First to a local Stack variable.

7. (NA) Complete the Copy procedure described in Example 3.1C, importing from StackADT and InfoADT as needed, without using recursion. *Hint:* First shift the information to a local stack variable.

8. (NA) Complete the SizeOf procedure described in Example 3.1C, importing from StackADT as needed.

9. (NA) Write a procedure that removes the last (bottom) Information record from its Stack parameter (no effect if the Stack is empty).

10. (NA) Revise the body of Example 3.1B so that you copy the given stack to the local stack and then transfer information values one at a time back to the given stack.

11. (NA) Show that Peep is really a utility procedure of StackADT rather than a true primitive. Discuss why the other five procedures are all primitives.

3.2 APPLICATION: EVALUATING EXPRESSIONS IN POLISH NOTATION

Some calculators use what is called **postfix notation** for entering expressions. The basic idea is that an operator is entered *after* the two operands it is to combine. The following examples should clarify this:

4 3 +	yields 7, which is 4 plus 3.
5 2 −	yields 3, which is 5 take away 2.
7 8 *	yields 56, which is 7 times 8.
4 3 + 8 *	yields 56, since 4 3 + is 7 and 7 8 * is 56.
4 3 8 + *	yields 44, since 3 8 + is 11 and 4 11 * is 44.
10 7 − 2 −	yields 1, since 10 7 − is 3 and 3 2 − is 1.
10 7 2 − −	yields 5, since 7 2 − is 5 and 10 5 − is 5.
3 4 * 14 2 / −	yields 5, since 3 4 * is 12, 14 2 / is 7, and 12 7 − is 5.

An algorithm for evaluating a postfix expression is to repeat the following sequence of actions until only one number remains:

1. Find the first (leftmost) triplet consisting of two numbers followed *directly* by an operator.

2. Replace those three things by the result of the operation normally denoted by putting the operator between the two numbers.

An expression is said to be in legal postfix notation if this algorithm eventually produces a single number from the expression. The second step refers to "things" because English does not have any word for a thing that can be either a number or an operator; standard computer science terminology for such a semantic unit is *token*, so I use that word in place of "thing" from now on.

Evaluating a Postfix Expression

Consider a program to evaluate a postfix expression. A reasonable approach is apparently to read tokens (numbers and operators) from left to right, making some computations from time to time. The problem is to decide what computations to make when. You need some way to store an arbitrary number of values for later retrieval; this need is clear when you consider the postfix expression 1 2 3 4 5 6 7 + + + + + +, which is 28. You do not make any computation for this expression until you see the first plus sign, at which point you evaluate 6 7 + to obtain 13. The next plus sign tells you to evaluate 5 13 +, which is 18. The next plus sign tells you to evaluate 4 18 +, etc.

From this example and earlier ones, you should be able to see that, when reading a postfix expression from left to right, you stop and make a calculation each time you see an operator. The operator applies to the two most recent numbers, so a stack seems a likely data structure to use. Each time you see a number, you push it on the stack. Each time you see an operator, you take the top two numbers off the stack and perform the operation. The result replaces the two numbers and the operator, so you can put it on the stack and continue. Once you realize that this process produces the correct value for every legal postfix expression, you have the following algorithm:

Algorithm to evaluate a legal postfix expression
1. Create an empty stack and do any other initializing necessary;
2. DO the following repeatedly until time to stop;
    2.a. Get one token (number or operator);
    2.b. STOP if there was nothing to get;
    2.c. IF the token is a number, then:
        Push the number on the stack;
      OTHERWISE, it is an operator, so:
        Pop two numbers off the stack;
        Combine them using the operator;
        Push the result on the stack;

3. Pop the number off the stack and print it, since that is the overall value of the postfix expression.

Further Considerations for this Program

At this point in the development of the program you should be realizing that the specifications for the program are highly inadequate. You have to know what form the input will have, in order to be able to get the next number or operator. You also have to know what action is to be taken if the expression is found to be illegal as a postfix expression. I do not plan to develop the design of this program much further; it is left as a programming problem. If your instructor assigns it, he or she will give you the additional specifications. If these specifications require one or more blanks between tokens (numbers and operators), or else that each token consist of just one character, the problem will be significantly easier to solve.

Step 2.a of the algorithm is the InputInfo procedure. This subalgorithm has to return a value that is either an operator or a number. The easiest way to do this is to return a string of characters. The first character of the string tells you what kind of token it is: A digit implies a number, one of $+ - * /$ implies an operator, and anything else implies an illegal symbol (and therefore an illegal expression). *Exception:* Some special character can be used to indicate that the end of the expression was reached. This can serve as a signal to exit the loop and print the result.

It is probably better, however, to shove more of the work down to a lower level. The information returned by Step 2.a can have three values: One is a Boolean that tells whether a number or an operator was read. The other two are a numeric value and a character value, only one of which is assigned a value (depending on the Boolean). Two special characters can be returned, one for "illegal input" and the other for "end of input." Even better would be one of seven values in an enumeration type such as (Plus, Minus, Times, Divide, Numeric, Unknown, EndOfExpression). Then you only need have one additional value, an integer that is given a value when the first parameter is Numeric.

```
Information = RECORD
              Symbol : (Plus, Minus, Times, Divide,
                        Numeric, Unknown, EndOfExpression);
              Number : INTEGER;
          END;
```

The program has to be able to access values in both fields and to change values in both fields. Thus it is simplest if Information is not declared as an opaque type, so the fields can be accessed directly. This means that Information is not an abstract data type for this program. The Number value is indeterminate if the Symbol value is not Numeric.

Prefix Notation

There is also a **prefix notation**, in which the operator is *prefixed* to the pair of numbers on which it is to operate. The normal notation that you are familiar with is called **infix notation**, because the operator is *in* between the two numbers on which it is to operate. The prefix and postfix notations are also called **Polish notation** and **reverse Polish notation**. The Polish forms are used by many language compilers as an intermediate step in converting infix expressions to machine language. Pascal and Modula-2 compilers usually do not, however; they use "recursive descent," described in Chapter 7.

In prefix notation, the expression $*$ + 2 3 4 yields 20, since + 2 3 is 5 and $*$ 5 4 is 20; the expression + $*$ 2 3 $*$ 7 4 yields 34, since $*$ 2 3 is 6, $*$ 7 4 is 28, and + 6 28 is 34. To evaluate any legal prefix expression, you can scan the expression from left to right, putting each token (number or operator) on a stack, until you have two numbers in a row on top of the stack. At that point you pop them and the operator just below them on the stack, evaluate the operator on those two numbers, and push the result back on the stack. If that makes two numbers on top of the stack, do it again.

An interesting point about prefix and postfix expressions is that parentheses are not needed to make the meaning clear. With infix notation, 2 + 3 $*$ 4 requires either parentheses or a common agreement (such as what you learned in your algebra classes) as to whether the addition or the multiplication is to be done first. Postfix notation would write this as either 2 3 + 4 $*$ or as 2 3 4 $*$ +, each of which can be evaluated in only one way.

Another interesting point is that an infix expression can be converted to postfix by the following algorithm: (1) Put the appropriate pair of parentheses in the expression for each operator; (2) Move each operator next to its right parenthesis; (3) Omit all parentheses. The same algorithm, with "right" replacing "left," converts an infix expression to prefix notation. Two examples for postfix notation are:

Expression to convert →	(2 + 3) − 4 $*$ 1	2 + 3 $*$ 4
1. Fully parenthesize:	((2 + 3) − (4 $*$ 1))	(2 + (3 $*$ 4))
2. Move op to right paren:	((2 3 +) (4 1 $*$)−)	(2 (3 4 $*$)+)
3. Omit all parentheses:	2 3 + 4 1 $*$ −	2 3 4 $*$ +

Check Your Understanding

1. Convert the following postfix expressions to infix notation, then evaluate them: (a) 20 3 2 − 5 $*$ / (b) 4 2 4 2 4 2 $*$ + $*$ + $*$

2. Convert the following prefix expressions to infix notation, then evaluate them: (a) $* - 7 / 8\ 4\ 2$ (b) $- 1 - 2 - 3 - 4 - 5\ 6$

3. Convert the following infix expressions to prefix notation; do not evaluate: (a) $(7 - 4) * (6 + 3)$ (b) $2 + 3 * (4 + 5 * (6 + 7))$

4. (NA) Write a Boolean function that accepts a Stack as a parameter and tells whether it represents a valid prefix expression. Assume that Information is the record declared in this section, that Unknown and EndOfExpression do not occur in the information in the stack, and that the stack was obtained by reading values and pushing them as read, with no popping. *Hint:* In a valid prefix expression, the number of numbers in any right-hand part of the expression is more than the number of operators, and the total number of numbers in the expression is 1 more than the number of numbers in it.

3.3 AN IMPLEMENTATION OF StackADT

There are several possible ways that the abstract data type Stack can be implemented. I describe the simplest here, the **simple array implementation**, and save the others for later.

First I choose an upper limit on the size of the stacks I use; I call it MaxSize. I use an array of MaxSize Information variables to store the items on the stack. The bottom item on the stack is kept in component 1 of the array, the second-to-bottom item is kept in component 2, and so forth. I must keep track of the top of each stack, so I use the following declarations (Size is to be the index of the top item on the stack):

```
CONST   MaxSize = 50;
TYPE    Stack = POINTER TO CountedArray;
        CountedArray = RECORD
                          Item : ARRAY [1..MaxSize] OF Information;
                          Size : CARDINAL;
                       END;
```

It is worth noting that the use of abstract data types means that the procedure in Example 3.1B does not mention NEW, DISPOSE, or ↑, although with this implementation it may involve a pointer to a record containing an array of pointers to records that contain arrays of characters.

In each Stack, Size is the index of the item most recently pushed on the stack; Size is 0 when the Stack is empty. This implies that the statement sequence of IsEmpty is simply RETURN Data ↑ .Size=0. Create requires that we create the array variable (using NEW(Data)) and then set Data ↑ .Size to 0. Destroy is simply DISPOSE(Data).

The definition module for stacks assumes that stacks are unlimited in size; any number of information values can be pushed onto a given stack. In practice, the programmer must estimate the storage requirements of the program and choose the implementation accordingly. If the implementation sets a limit that is exceeded during execution of a client module, that is a defect of the implementation. Some people would say that the implementation should halt the program at that point. However, I think it is enough to print a warning message and continue operations. Although the results will probably not be correct, there may be valuable information that can be recovered from the execution of the program so far. Thus the algorithm for Push writes messages using the Terminal module (in case the output channel has been changed through InOut).

Algorithms for Push, Pop, and Peep

The algorithm for Push is easily developed for this implementation. You check first that the array is not full. If it is, you write a message to the terminal; otherwise you increment Size and assign the given Information to Item[Size]. The algorithm for Pop is just the reverse: You check first that the Stack is not empty. If it is empty, you do nothing; otherwise, you assign Item[Size] to the VAR Information parameter and then decrement Size. Peep is even simpler: Assign Item[Size] to the parameter if Size is acceptable. You may assume that Size is not greater than MaxSize, since the preconditions for the procedures specify that the Stack must be initialized before it can be used. The full implementation module is in Example 3.3A.

Note that Pop and Peep do not write messages if the given Stack is empty; that would be a violation of the specifications given in Example 3.1A. *No effect* is required in such a situation, and writing a message would be an effect.

ⅢⅢ➡ PROGRAMMING STYLE

In general, a library module should be established on the **separation of powers principle**: There should be one particular kind of activity that only the module does. In this case, the activity is working with the internal structure of a Stack. Nothing outside this module should depend in any way on the actual internal structure of a Stack.

Check Your Understanding

1. Write the SizeOf function (described in Example 3.1C) as a utility in the simple array implementation of StackADT.

2. Write the WriteAll procedure (described in Example 3.1C) as a utility procedure in the simple array implementation of StackADT.

EXAMPLE 3.3A _____

```
IMPLEMENTATION MODULE StackADT;
FROM InfoADT  IMPORT Information;
FROM Storage  IMPORT ALLOCATE, DEALLOCATE;
FROM Terminal IMPORT WriteString, WriteLn;
    (* Module to implement Stack manipulations independently
       of the kind of Information being put on the Stack  *)
    (* The simple array implementation of StackADT *)
    (* Written by William C. Jones, October 19-- *)
CONST
    MaxSize = 50;
TYPE
    Stack = POINTER TO CountedArray;
    CountedArray =
        RECORD
            Item : ARRAY [1..MaxSize] OF Information;
            Size : CARDINAL;
        END;
(******************************************************)

PROCEDURE Push (TheInfo : Information;  VAR Data : Stack);
    (* Put TheInfo on top of Data *)
BEGIN
    WITH Data^ DO  (* fields are Item, Size *)
        IF Size = MaxSize THEN
            WriteString (' Stack is too full');
            WriteLn;
        ELSE
            INC (Size);
            Item [Size] := TheInfo;
        END;
    END;
END Push;
(******************************************************)

PROCEDURE Pop (VAR TheInfo: Information;  VAR Data: Stack);
    (* Remove TheInfo from the top of Data if Data is
       not empty; no effect if Data is empty *)
BEGIN
    WITH Data^ DO  (* fields are Item, Size *)
        IF Size >= 1 THEN
            TheInfo := Item [Size];
            DEC (Size);
        END;
    END;
END Pop;
(******************************************************)

PROCEDURE IsEmpty (Data : Stack) : BOOLEAN;
    (* Tell whether Data is empty *)
BEGIN
    RETURN Data^.Size = 0;
END IsEmpty;
(******************************************************)

(* continued on next page *)
```

157

```
(* EXAMPLE 3.3A continued *)


PROCEDURE Peep (VAR TheInfo : Information;  Data : Stack);
        (* Access the Information on top of Data if Data is
           not empty; no effect if Data is empty *)
BEGIN
    WITH Data^ DO  (* fields are Item, Size *)
        IF Size >= 1 THEN
            TheInfo := Item [Size];
        END;
    END;
END Peep;
(*************************************************************)

PROCEDURE Create (VAR Data : Stack);
        (* Initialize Data as an empty structure *)
BEGIN
    NEW (Data);
    Data^.Size := 0;
END Create;
(*************************************************************)

PROCEDURE Destroy (VAR Data : Stack);
        (* Deallocate the space for the empty structure *)
BEGIN
    DISPOSE (Data);
END Destroy;
(*************************************************************)

END StackADT.
```

3. Write the DestroyAllInfo procedure (described in Example 3.1C) as a utility procedure in the simple array implementation of StackADT.

4. In Example 3.3A, omit the two words POINTER TO. What other changes must then be made in that example? You may ignore the fact that Modula-2 requires moving the declaration of CountedArray to the definition module.

5. (NA) Write the ReadAll procedure (described in Example 3.1C) as a utility procedure in the simple array implementation of StackADT.

6. (NA) Write the Push procedure for an implementation of stacks in which there should never be more than three items on a stack at any time, so a Stack is declared as follows (Size records the number of items on the stack):

```
TYPE Stack = POINTER TO
          RECORD
              First, Second, Third : Information;
              Size : CARDINAL;
          END;
```

7. (NA) Write the Pop procedure under the same assumptions as in the preceding exercise.

3.4 QUEUES

The next data structure we consider is a **queue** (pronounced just like the letter "Q"). This data structure contains a number of items, as does a stack. From time to time an item can be added to the queue or taken from the queue, as with a stack. The only difference is that the only item you can take from a queue is the one that has been on the queue the *longest*. By contrast, the only item you can remove from a stack is the item that has been on the stack the *shortest* period of time.

Applications of Queues

When you see the "Take a number" sign at a bakery, you are being asked to join a queue; the number indicates your position in the queue. People standing in line to buy movie tickets or to register for classes (Fig. 3) normally form a queue. A person who "cuts in line" is violating the fundamental property of a queue, that those who have waited longest are served first.

Queues are important in situations involving computer hardware. A computer system designed for use by several people at the same time involves a number of resources that can only be used by a limited number of programs at a time. If too many programs require the use of memory space or a printer, the processor usually puts them on a queue to wait their turn.

In the Stockholder program described in Section 3.1, the LIFO method of accounting was discussed. The tax laws allow a person to choose either the LIFO

FIGURE 3. A registration queue.

method (which uses stacks) or the **FIFO** method (*First-In-First-Out*), which uses queues.

The Queue Operations

We need procedures with which we can manipulate a queue. For instance, we need a procedure to **Enqueue** (append) a given item on the *rear* of a queue. We also need a procedure to **Dequeue** (remove) an item from the *front* of a queue. We need a Boolean function **IsEmpty** to tell us whether the queue is empty, so we can avoid the mistake of trying to Dequeue an item from an empty queue. We occasionally need a procedure **Peep** to allow us to see the item at the front of the queue without changing the queue. Figure 4 shows how a queue (initially empty) grows and shrinks as a number of Enqueue and Dequeue operations are performed on it.

It is desirable to keep *all* queue operations in a separate module, so we will develop a library module **QueueADT** containing Enqueue, Dequeue, Peep, and IsEmpty. We also need **Create** and **Destroy**, to allow for the possibility that a Queue is a pointer. We want to use this module without change in several different situations, so we import Information, the kind of item to be enqueued or dequeued, from InfoADT or from InfoMan. Some or all of the procedures in Example 3.1C are often added to QueueADT as utility procedures, with "Stack" changed to "Queue" throughout.

The first step in writing the library module is to write the definition module; this is in Example 3.4A. In essence, this describes the abstract data structure called a queue. Notice that it differs from the StackADT module only in that Enqueue and Dequeue have replaced Push and Pop (and, of course, the word Stack is replaced by the word Queue). In fact, if you make those replacements of names in the subsection on pre- and postconditions in Section 3.1, and if you replace "most recently" by "least recently" in that subsection, then you will have the pre- and postconditions for Queues.

Empty	Enq 5	Enq 3	Enq 8	Deq 5	Enq 7	Enq 4	Deq 3	Deq 8
	5	5	5	3	3	3	8	7
		3	3	8	8	8	7	4
			8		7	7	4	
						4		

FIGURE 4. How a queue changes for a sequence of enqueues and dequeues. Each column depicts the queue as it looks after each change (specified at the top) is made to it. The front of the queue is at the top of the picture. Think of the bar as a box office at a theater.

EXAMPLE 3.4A _____

```
DEFINITION MODULE QueueADT;
FROM InfoADT IMPORT Information;
EXPORT QUALIFIED Queue,   Enqueue, Dequeue, Peep,
                 IsEmpty, Create,  Destroy;
    (* Written by William C. Jones, October 19-- *)
    (* Module to implement queue manipulations independently
       of the kind of Information being put on the queue.
       Warning:  Every Queue must be initialized before
       anything else can be done with it *)
TYPE
    Queue;
(* * * * * * * * * * * * * * * * * * * * * * * * * * * * * * * * * * * * * * * * * * * * * * * * * * * * * * * * * *)

PROCEDURE Enqueue (TheInfo  : Information;
                   VAR Data : Queue);
    (* Put TheInfo on the rear of Data *)

PROCEDURE Dequeue (VAR TheInfo : Information;
                   VAR Data    : Queue);
    (* Remove TheInfo from the front of Data if Data is
       not empty; no effect if Data is empty *)

PROCEDURE Peep (VAR TheInfo : Information;  Data : Queue);
    (* Access the Information at the front of Data if
       Data is not empty; no effect if Data is empty *)

PROCEDURE IsEmpty (Data : Queue) : BOOLEAN;
    (* Tell whether Data is empty *)

PROCEDURE Create (VAR Data : Queue);
    (* Initialize Data as an empty structure *)

PROCEDURE Destroy (VAR Data : Queue);
    (* Deallocate the space for the empty structure *)

END QueueADT.
```

Using the Queue Primitives

For an example of how the procedures in QueueADT work together, consider the following task: You have a queue named Source and an information value named TheInfo. Your job is to create a new queue named Data that contains the first few values from Source, removing those values from Source. Specifically, you are to transfer from Source to Data values down to but not including the first value on Source that matches TheInfo (using Compare). *Boundary situations:* If the first value on Source matches TheInfo, Data is to be an empty queue and Source is to be unchanged. If no value on Source matches TheInfo, all values are to be moved to Data, leaving Source empty. The following coding accomplishes this task:

```
Create (Data);
Peep (TopOne, Source);
WHILE NOT IsEmpty (Source) AND (Compare (TopOne, TheInfo) # 0) DO
    Dequeue (TopOne, Source);
    Enqueue (TopOne, Data);
    Peep (TopOne, Source);
END;
```

Note in this coding how advantageous it is to be allowed to peep at the front value on an empty queue without crashing or receiving a written message. The WHILE condition is carefully written to avoid errors when peeping an empty queue.

A Simple Implementation of Queues

There are several possible ways in which this data structure can be implemented. I begin with the simplest and most obvious here; it models what happens in a queue at the movies. This implementation executes more slowly than others; its primary advantage in practical programming is in **rapid prototyping**, that is, producing functional software quickly so the end user can test it to see if the specifications should be changed.

First I choose an upper limit on the size of the queues; I call it MaxSize. I use an array of MaxSize Information variables to store the items on the queue. The first item on the queue (also known as the front of the queue) is put in component 1 of the array, the second item is put in component 2, and so forth. Whenever I remove an item from the queue, I take it from component 1 and then move all the other items down one in the array. Thus component 1 corresponds to the spot at the movie ticket office right at the window, component 2 corresponds to the spot just behind that, and so forth. I need to keep track of the size of each queue, so I use the following declarations:

```
CONST   MaxSize = 50;
TYPE    Queue = POINTER TO CountedArray;
        CountedArray = RECORD
                            Item : ARRAY [1..MaxSize] OF Information;
                            Size : CARDINAL;
                        END;
```

In each Queue, Size is the index of the item most recently appended to the queue, so Size is 0 when the Queue is empty. Thus the bodies of Peep, Create, Destroy, and IsEmpty are the same as those for stacks. The algorithm for Enqueue is the same as the one for Push with stacks.

The algorithm for Dequeue is more complicated. We check first that the Queue is not empty. If it is not, we assign Item[1] to the VAR Information parameter and then decrement Size. But we must also shift each item remaining on the queue to the component with the next lower index. The rest of the implementation module is exactly the same as Example 3.3A, except the word Stack is changed to the word Queue. Example 3.4B shows just the Enqueue and Dequeue procedures.

Reminder: Create and Destroy change the number of queues in existence, but no procedure affects an information value. Think of Enqueue as giving up the information to the Queue and Dequeue as retrieving the information from the Queue. Be careful not to change the information obtained by Peep, since it is (presumably) still on the queue.

EXAMPLE 3.4B _____

```
(* Context:  simple array implementation of QueueADT *)
PROCEDURE Enqueue (TheInfo  : Information;
                      VAR Data : Queue);
     (* Put TheInfo on the rear of Data *)
BEGIN
    WITH Data^ DO  (* fields are Item, Size *)
        IF Size = MaxSize THEN
            WriteString (' Queue is too full');
            WriteLn;
        ELSE
            INC (Size);
            Item [Size] := TheInfo;
        END;
    END;
END Enqueue;
(* *******************************************************)

PROCEDURE Dequeue (VAR TheInfo : Information;
                      VAR Data    : Queue);
     (* Remove TheInfo from the front of Data if Data is
        not empty; no effect if Data is empty *)
VAR
    K : CARDINAL;
BEGIN
    WITH Data^ DO  (* fields are Item, Size *)
        IF Size >= 1 THEN
            TheInfo := Item [1];
            FOR K := 2 TO Size DO
                Item [K - 1] := Item [K];
            END;
            DEC (Size);
        END;
    END;
END Dequeue;
```

A More Efficient Implementation of Queues

Each time you Dequeue Item[1] you have to shift all the other items down. This adds greatly to the execution time, though not as badly as if you had to move whole Information records instead of just pointers to them. You could instead leave everything where it is and make a note that the front of the Queue is now Item[2]. The next time you Dequeue an item, you take it from Item[2] and make a note that Item[3] is now the front of the Queue. This suggests the following declaration, with Front telling the index of the front of the Queue and Rear telling the index of its rear:

```
TYPE    Queue = POINTER TO PartOfArray;
        PartOfArray = RECORD
                          Item : ARRAY [1..MaxSize] OF Information;
                          Front, Rear : CARDINAL;
                      END;
```

Now the basic idea is, Enqueue adds 1 to Rear and Dequeue adds 1 to Front. The Create procedure can be coded as follows, to make Front be correct the first time something is put on an empty Queue:

```
NEW (Data);
Data↑.Front := 1;
Data↑.Rear := 0;
```

This approach saves execution time during Dequeue, but it introduces other complications. A serious problem is that you tend to run out of room for the Queue. Say you initially append three items to an empty Queue, then you repeatedly Dequeue and Enqueue one item at a time. After a while, Front=48 and Rear=50 (assuming MaxSize is 50). You Dequeue Item[48], so now Front=49. Then you try to Enqueue an item, but there is no room, even though the Queue is short.

The solution is straightforward: There is room in the lower part of the Item array. So you set Rear to 1 and Enqueue at Item[1]. The next time Enqueue is called, you Enqueue at Item[2]. Eventually Front will also creep past 50 to 1. Figure 5 illustrates how the values in the array change for a particular sequence of Enqueue and Dequeue operations in this **circular array implementation** of QueueADT.

Unfortunately, this solution causes problems elsewhere in the implementation. Let us assume that you have an empty Queue for which you perform the

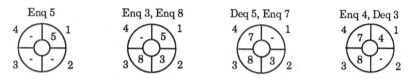

Empty	Enq 5	Enq 3	Enq 8	Deq 5	Enq 7	Enq 4	Deq 3	Deq 8
f ?	f r 5	f 5	f 5	?	?	r 4	r 4	r 4
?	?	r 3	3	f 3	f 3	f 3	?	?
?	?	?	r 8	r 8	8	8	f 8	?
?	?	?	?	?	r 7	7	7	f 7

It may help to visualize the array as if it were circular:

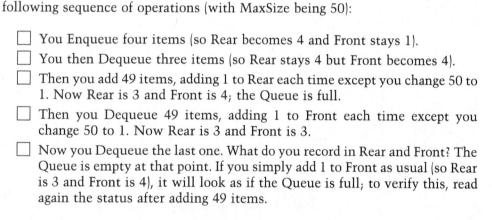

FIGURE 5. *How a queue changes for a sequence of enqueues and dequeues. This is the array implementation in which Front and Rear are recorded and MaxSize is 4. "?" denotes an indeterminate or irrelevant value. "f" and "r" mark the front and rear components, respectively.*

following sequence of operations (with MaxSize being 50):

- ☐ You Enqueue four items (so Rear becomes 4 and Front stays 1).
- ☐ You then Dequeue three items (so Rear stays 4 but Front becomes 4).
- ☐ Then you add 49 items, adding 1 to Rear each time except you change 50 to 1. Now Rear is 3 and Front is 4; the Queue is full.
- ☐ Then you Dequeue 49 items, adding 1 to Front each time except you change 50 to 1. Now Rear is 3 and Front is 3.
- ☐ Now you Dequeue the last one. What do you record in Rear and Front? The Queue is empty at that point. If you simply add 1 to Front as usual (so Rear is 3 and Front is 4), it will look as if the Queue is full; to verify this, read again the status after adding 49 items.

There are several possible solutions to this problem. One is to add a Boolean variable to the Queue record to keep track of whether the Queue is empty. Another is to limit the Queue to at most MaxSize−1 items. However, it is easiest simply to reset Rear to 0 and Front to 1 when you Dequeue the last item from a Queue. That is, an empty Queue is signified by having Rear be 0. I use that method here. The corresponding Dequeue procedure is shown in Example 3.4C; the other modifications of QueueADT are left as a programming problem.

Check Your Understanding

1. Write the Join procedure described in Example 3.1C, except join two Queues instead of two Stacks. Import from QueueADT as needed.

EXAMPLE 3.4C _____

```
PROCEDURE Dequeue (VAR TheInfo : Information;
                   VAR Data     : Queue);
     (* Remove TheInfo from the front of Data if Data is
         not empty; no effect if Data is empty *)
     (* Context: circular array implementation of QueueADT,
                 in which Rear=0 denotes an empty queue *)
BEGIN
    WITH Data^ DO  (* fields are Item, Front, Rear *)
        IF Rear # 0 THEN
            TheInfo := Item [Front];
            IF Front = Rear THEN
                Rear  := 0;
                Front := 1;
            ELSIF Front = MaxSize THEN
                Front := 1;
            ELSE
                INC (Front);
            END;
        END;
    END;
END Dequeue;
```

2. Write the WriteAll procedure described in Example 3.1C, except use a Queue instead of a Stack. Assume that the procedure is to be part of the circular array implementation of QueueADT (as in Example 3.4C).

3. Write the procedure SizeOf described in Example 3.1C, for a Queue instead of a Stack. Import from QueueADT as needed. *Hint:* Shift the information to a local queue.

4. Write the ReadAll procedure described in Example 3.1C, except read a Queue instead of a Stack. Import from QueueADT and InfoADT as needed.

5. (NA) Write a procedure that removes the rear item from its Queue parameter (no effect if the Queue is empty). Import from QueueADT as needed. *Hint:* Use a local Queue variable to which you move every item but the last one.

6. (NA) Write the Peep procedure for an implementation of queues in which there should never be more than three items on a queue at any time, so a Queue is declared as follows (Size records the number of items on the Queue):

```
TYPE   Queue = POINTER TO RECORD
                   First, Second, Third : Information;
                   Size : CARDINAL;
               END;
```

7. (NA) Write the Copy procedure described in Example 3.1C, for queues instead of stacks. Assume the procedure is to be a utility procedure in the circular array implementation of QueueADT.

8. (NA) Write the Join procedure described in Example 3.1C, except join two Queues instead of two Stacks. Assume the procedure is to be a utility procedure in the circular array implementation of QueueADT.

9. (NA) Just before the discussion of implementations of queues in this section, there is a segment of code that removes values from a queue down to but not including a given information value. Rewrite it so that you never call Peep when the queue is empty. Which way do you think is better?

3.5 LINEAR LISTS

A **linear list** is a number of items arranged in a certain order, just as is a stack or a queue. However, you can do more with a linear list than you can with a stack or queue. In particular, you can look at an item at any location on the list and you can insert or remove an item at any location on the list. *Note:* Some people use the term **sequential list** for a linear list.

The Linear List Operations

In order to manipulate linear lists, we need procedures that are the analogs of the six procedures for stacks and the six for queues. ListADT uses **Insert** in place of Push or Enqueue, **LookAt** in place of Peep, and **Delete** in place of Pop or Dequeue. It has **Create** and **Destroy** with much the same meaning as before. As with stacks and queues, we keep these five linear list operations in a separate module and import Information from InfoADT or InfoMan.

The new aspect of a linear list is that you have to specify the location on the list where you want to insert, delete, or look at a value. That is, each of these three procedures has an extra parameter that tells the location on the list. This location can be at the beginning of the list, at the end of the list, or anywhere in between. For many implementations, the location is indicated by a CARDINAL. This need not always be the case, so we must declare the Location type in the library module.

To use this feature properly, we need some way to initialize a Location variable to the first location on the list, and we need some way to change the value of a Location variable. We cannot just add 1 to the value, because the Location is not a CARDINAL in some implementations (as you will see in Chapter 4). We use three function procedures **FirstLocation**, **NextLocation**, and **InList**. InList is a Boolean function that tells us whether there is information at the given Location. When InList returns FALSE, we can Insert at that location but we cannot Delete or LookAt there (since there is no information there). It may help to keep in mind

```
Start with this Data list:      3    9    7    2
L := FirstLocation (Data);     ③    9    7    2
L :=NextLocation (L, Data);     3   ⑨    7    2
Delete (X, L, Data);            3   ⑦    7    2        (* now X contains 9 *)
L := NextLocation (L, Data);    3    7   ②
L := NextLocation (L, Data);    3    7    2    ◯     (* InList is false *)
Insert (X, L, Data);            3    7    2    9
```

FIGURE 6. *How a list changes as various operations are performed. Read lists from left to right, that is, the leftmost item is the first. The circle shows which item L is currently indicating.*

that a list with N items on it has N + 1 possible locations: at any one of the N items or after the last one. Figure 6 illustrates the use of these procedures; Example 3.5A contains the complete definition module.

Assume that you execute Where := FirstLocation(Data) and then execute Where := NextLocation(Where, Data) K − 1 times (where K is some cardinal constant). This puts you at the Kth item on the list. That is, LookAt and Delete act on item K of the list, unless there are fewer than K items on the list, in which case InList(Where, Data) is false, so LookAt and Delete have no effect. Also, Insert creates a new item K on the list, inserted before the former item K on the list, unless there were fewer than K items on the list, in which case Insert creates a new last item on the list.

Preconditions and postconditions can be stated for ListADT procedures as was done for stacks and queues. Most of the specifications are tediously similar to the ones given earlier. The new part is that preconditions for procedures involving locations specify that all location values used be valid for the List parameter. That means that the location value must be assigned using FirstLocation and NextLocation with the List parameter, and that no insertion or deletion has since taken place earlier in the list. Exact descriptions of pre- and postconditions are left as an exercise.

Examples of Uses of ListADT Procedures

In some applications, such as sorting, it may be necessary to swap some given information (named, say, TheInfo) with the information at a particular location Where on a given list Data. This can be accomplished as follows:

```
IF InList (Where, Data) THEN
    Delete (OtherInfo, Where, Data);
    Insert (TheInfo, Where, Data);
    TheInfo := OtherInfo;
END;
```

When you want to test whether a list named Data is empty, you can test the condition InList(FirstLocation(Data),Data). The following coding could be used to

EXAMPLE 3.5A _____

```
DEFINITION MODULE ListADT;
FROM InfoADT IMPORT Information;
EXPORT QUALIFIED (* types *) List, Location,
   (* st procs  *) Insert, Delete, LookAt, Create, Destroy,
   (* functions *) InList, FirstLocation, NextLocation;
(* Written by Dr. William C. Jones, October, 19-- *)
(* Linear List manipulations. Warning: Every List must be
   initialized before anything else can be done with it *)
TYPE
    List;
    Location;
(* **************************************************** *)
(* If Where indicates the Kth item, execution of Insert, *)
(* Delete, or LookAt at or after that location leaves    *)
(* Where indicating the (possibly new) Kth item, if any. *)

PROCEDURE Insert (TheInfo : Information;
                  Where   : Location;  VAR Data : List);
     (* Put TheInfo at location Where of Data *)

PROCEDURE Delete (VAR TheInfo : Information;
                  Where : Location;  VAR Data : List);
     (* Take TheInfo from location Where of Data if
        any information is there; no effect otherwise *)

PROCEDURE LookAt (VAR TheInfo : Information;
                  Where : Location;  Data : List);
     (* Access TheInfo at location Where of Data if
        any information is there; no effect otherwise *)
(* **************************************************** *)
(*  Procedures controlling the Location.  A List with   *)
(*  N items has N + 1 Locations, one at each item plus  *)
(*  a Location after the last item on the List          *)

PROCEDURE InList (Where : Location; Data : List) : BOOLEAN;
     (* Tell whether information is at Location Where
        in Data; if not, only Insert works *)

PROCEDURE FirstLocation (Data : List) : Location;
     (* Return the location of the first item in Data *)

PROCEDURE NextLocation (Where : Location;
                        Data  : List) : Location;
     (* Return the location of the item in Data after the
        one Where currently indicates, unless already
        past the last one in Data *)
(* **************************************************** *)

PROCEDURE Create (VAR Data : List);
     (* Initialize Data as an empty structure *)

PROCEDURE Destroy (VAR Data : List);
     (* Deallocate the space for the empty structure *)

END ListADT.
```

assign to Where the location at the very end of a given Data list, after all the information in the list:

```
Where := FirstLocation (Data);
WHILE InList (Where, Data) DO
    Where := NextLocation (Where, Data);
END;
```

The operations just described can often be executed much faster if they are utility procedures exported from ListADT. Example 3.5B contains a description of six often-used utility procedures for ListADT. Coding for Modify and LastLoca-

EXAMPLE 3.5B _____

```
(*    six reasonable utility procedures for ListADT    *)

PROCEDURE Modify (VAR TheInfo : Information;
                  Where       : Location;
                  VAR Data    : List);
    (* Swap the information at location Where of Data for
       TheInfo if any information is in that location *)

PROCEDURE LastLocation (Data : List) : Location;
    (* Return the location after the last item in Data *)

PROCEDURE Seek (Pos : CARDINAL;  Data : List) : Location;
    (* Return the Location of the information in position
       number Pos on the List.  If Pos is too large, return
       a Location that makes InList false *)

PROCEDURE MoveInfo (FromLoc, ToLoc : Location;
                    VAR Data        : List);
    (* Move the Information at FromLoc to be at Location
       ToLoc, with all in-between information values moved
       one place to compensate.  No effect if
       InList (FromLoc, Data) is false *)

PROCEDURE Search (TheInfo : Information;
                  Data     : List) : Location;
    (* Return the Location of TheInfo if it is in Data.  In
       case of a tie, return the Location of the first one.
       If not there, Return a Location that makes InList
       false.  Import Compare from InfoADT *)

PROCEDURE Sort (VAR Data : List);
    (* Rearrange the information values in Data so they are
       in increasing order, using Compare from InfoADT *)
```

tion has just been given. Coding for Sort using imports from ListADT is in Example 6.4A (which you could study now if you wish).

The procedures in Example 3.1C are also useful utility procedures, when "Stack" is changed to "List" throughout. For instance, the WriteAll procedure for a list writes each information value on a given list in order, without changing the list. The logic is similar to the familiar algorithm for writing out the first few values in an array until a sentinel value is seen. The coding of WriteAll for a list named Data, using imports from ListADT and InfoADT, is:

```
Where := FirstLocation (Data);
WHILE InList (Where, Data) DO
    LookAt (TheInfo, Where, Data);
    OutputInfo (TheInfo);
    Where := NextLocation (Where, Data);
END;
```

Note that calling FirstLocation is analogous to initializing an integer variable to 1, and that calling NextLocation is analogous to adding 1 to the integer variable. In fact, for some implementations of ListADT, Location values are integer values from 1 on up. For some other implementations of ListADT, described in Chapter 4, Locations are pointer values. The FirstLocation and NextLocation functions provide an abstraction of initializing and incrementing. InList provides an abstraction of going too far.

Assume that a client module wants to print the values on a list in reverse order—the last one, then the next-to-last, and so forth. This can be done by executing the statement PrintReverse(FirstLocation(Data), Data) if the client module declares the recursive procedure in Example 3.5C. The logic of this procedure is as follows: To print in reverse order all the values from a certain point on,

EXAMPLE 3.5C _____

```
PROCEDURE PrintReverse (Where : Location;  Data : List);
    (* Print all values at Where and later,
        in reverse order *)
    (* Context:  client of ListADT *)
VAR
    TheInfo : Information;
BEGIN
    IF InList (Where, Data) THEN
        PrintReverse (NextLocation (Where, Data), Data);
        LookAt (TheInfo, Where, Data);
        OutputInfo (TheInfo);
    END;
END PrintReverse;
```

you first check to make sure that the list has an information value at that point. If it does not, you do not need to do anything. Otherwise, you can print all the values that come after that point, then you can print the value at that point.

This recursive procedure has a parameter that does not change from one activation to the next, namely Data. Moreover, we do not need to have a separate copy of TheInfo for each activation of procedure; we can use the same local TheInfo variable for all activations. In such cases, it is more efficient to *delocalize* the procedure, which means to use a subprocedure that (1) does all the recursion and (2) has side effects on variables that are local to the overall procedure but that (3) saves execution time and primary memory storage. This requires three changes in the PrintReverse procedure of Example 3.5C:

1. Insert the following line before BEGIN:

```
PROCEDURE PrintAtLocation (Where : Location);
```

2. Insert the following two lines before END PrintReverse:

```
END PrintAtLocation;
BEGIN
        PrintAtLocation (Where);
```

3. Change the call of PrintReverse(NextLocation(Where, Data), Data) to:

```
PrintAtLocation (NextLocation (Where, Data));
```

Check Your Understanding

1. Describe in English what the following is testing for:
   WHILE InList (NextLocation (FirstLocation (Data), Data),Data) DO...

2. Write a segment of code that deletes all but the last two information values in a list named Data. *Hint:* See Exercise 1.

3. Write the Seek procedure described in Example 3.5B, importing from ListADT as needed.

4. Write the SizeOf procedure described in Example 3.1C (but replace "Stack" by "List"), importing from ListADT as needed.

5. (NA) Write the Search procedure described in Example 3.5B, importing from ListADT and InfoADT as needed.

6. (NA) Write the ReadAll procedure described in Example 3.1C (but replace "Stack" by "List"), importing from ListADT and InfoADT as needed.

7. (NA) Write the Join procedure described in Example 3.1C (but replace "Stack" by "List"), importing from ListADT as needed.

8. (NA) Show that LookAt is actually a utility procedure for ListADT rather than a true primitive, by calling other procedures in ListADT to accomplish its task.

9. (NA) Write a procedure that creates a new list that contains copies of all information values that are on both of two given lists. Neither of the two given lists is to be changed. Import from InfoADT and ListADT as needed.

10. (NA) Write a procedure that removes from a given list all information values that match earlier information values in that same list, importing from InfoADT and ListADT as needed.

11. (NA) Give complete pre- and postconditions for each of the eight procedures in ListADT.

12. (NA) Write a recursive procedure that counts the number of information values X in a given list for which X is not smaller than any information value that comes later in the list.

3.6 THE SIMPLE ARRAY IMPLEMENTATION OF ListADT

The List data type can be implemented in several ways; let us begin with the one closest to what we did with stacks and queues. We choose an upper limit Max-Size for the size of the lists we use. We use an array of up to MaxSize information records to store the items on the list. The first item on the list is put in component 1 of the array, the second item is put in component 2, and so forth. Size is the number of items on the list, and the Location of an item on the list is its index in the array.

For this **simple array implementation**, whenever we delete an item from the linear list, we take it from the position indicated and then move all the higher items down by one component (see Fig. 7). Whenever we insert an item on the list, we first shift a number of items up by one component. We put the following

16 information values (marked "a" through "p") in a 30-component array.
The front is at component 1 and the rear is at component 16.

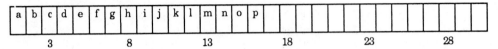

Insert a new value (marked "u") at the fourth location Seek (4, Data):

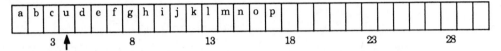

Delete the value marked "f" from the seventh location Seek (7, Data)

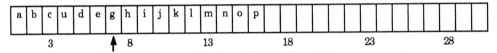

FIGURE 7. *A list in the simple array implementation.*

declarations in the implementation module:

```
CONST   MaxSize = 50;
TYPE    List = POINTER TO CountedArray;
        CountedArray = RECORD
                        Item : ARRAY [1..MaxSize] OF Information;
                        Size : CARDINAL;
                       END;
```

In each List, the items are in components Item[1] to Item[Size]. Size is the index of the item at the rear of the list; Size is 0 when the List is empty. This implies that the statement sequences of Create and Destroy are the same as they were for the analogous implementation of stacks and queues (in Example 3.3A).

The algorithms for FirstLocation, NextLocation, and InList are simply a matter of returning 1, returning 1 more than the location given (if it is not already more than Size), and testing whether Where is less than or equal to Size. For instance, the body of NextLocation could be:

```
IF Where < Data↑.Size + 1 THEN
    RETURN Where + 1;
ELSE
    RETURN Data↑.Size + 1;
END;
```

EXAMPLE 3.6A _____

```
PROCEDURE Insert (TheInfo  : Information;
                  Where    : Location;
                  VAR Data : List);
    (* Put TheInfo at location Where of Data *)
    (* Context: simple array implementation of ListADT *)
VAR
    K : CARDINAL;
BEGIN
    WITH Data^ DO          (* fields are Item, Size *)
        IF Size = MaxSize THEN
            WriteString (' List is too full');
            WriteLn;
        ELSE
            INC (Size);
            FOR K := Size TO Where + 1 BY -1 DO
                Item [K] := Item [K - 1];
            END;
            Item [Where] := TheInfo;
        END;
    END;
END Insert;
```

That leaves only the Delete, LookAt, and Insert procedures to develop. Delete and LookAt are left as exercises. The algorithm for Insert consists of four steps: First make sure that Size is such as to permit the insertion at location Where; this requires that the list not be full. Then increment Size by 1 (since we are adding information), move the values in Item [Where]... Item[Size−1] up one component to Item[Where+1]... Item[Size], and put the given Information at location Where. The coding is in Example 3.6A.

Many Modula-2 compilers do not allow you to have CARDINAL as an opaque type. They require you to use Location: ADDRESS instead, which is a type that allows the same operations as CARDINAL. For this you must also have the import section FROM SYSTEM IMPORT ADDRESS.

You should not think that there is anything sacrosanct about the particular eight procedures I have chosen for ListADT. Their headings and descriptions of behavior are the result of **design decisions** I have made. Other authors may present a different set of procedures with different specifications that allow a client module much the same capability.

Summary

An **abstract list** consists of N Information values (N >= 0) and N + 1 Location values, each of which can be considered as being numbered from 1 on up. For K = 1..N, Location K is used for actions involving Information K. Location N + 1 is where an Information value can be inserted but not deleted or looked at.

In the simple array implementation of lists, a **concrete list** consists of a record with two fields: a cardinal and an array of Information components. The cardinal field has the value N (the number of Information values on the list). For K = 1..N, the Kth information value is stored in the Kth component of the array field. This implementation fails if N exceeds the number of components in the array. Subject to that stipulation, a *List* is a pointer to a concrete list and, for K = 1..N, *Location K* is the index in the array of Information K; Location N+1 is the index N+1.

Reminder: A procedure in an implementation of an abstract data type should write a message to the user only if (1) the comment describing the task to be accomplished by the procedure says that a message is to be written, or (2) the implementation fails. Note that the implementation of Insert in Example 3.6A writes a message when the List is too full; this is because the implementation should ideally not limit the size of a List, so the implementation is defective if MaxSize is exceeded. However, the Delete procedure is not to write any message in any circumstances, even if asked to delete from an empty list. The comment in Example 3.5A that describes Delete does not say that anything will be done if there is no information to delete, so *nothing* is to be done, not even writing a message to the effect that the List is empty.

▐▌▌➡ **PROGRAMMING STYLE**

You may think that it is necessary to check that Where is between 1 and Size+1 in the Insert procedure, to be sure that the indices are in range. But that can only be a problem if the list or the location has not been properly initialized, which means that the programmer of the client module has made a programming error. In that case, it is best to let the programmer know of the error as soon as possible, by letting the program crash. The basic principle of **defensive programming** is to guard against errors by the *user* of a program as much as is feasible. But that is a completely different matter from guarding against programming errors.

A primary reason that it is important not to guard against programming errors is that it penalizes the good programmer. For instance, a good programmer will check that a list is properly initialized before passing it to Insert. So another check within Insert duplicates the programmer's coding, which adds to the execution time and the size of the compiled program. Besides, you cannot guard against all programming errors anyway; a List that is not properly initialized will have indeterminate values in it, which may in some cases be within the range of 1 to Size.

In an IF statement that involves ELSE or ELSIF, it is usually best to put first the alternative that has the shorter statement sequence. This brings the ELSE or ELSIF clause closer to the line containing IF, which makes it a little easier for the reader to see. Compare Example 3.6A with the Push procedure in Example 3.3A.

Warning

In Modula-2, you must be careful with CARDINALs to write Where<Size+1 instead of Where−1<Size. The difference is that the latter condition crashes the program if

Where is 0. The reason is that it is a CARDINAL expression, since Where is a CARDINAL. So Where−1 is required to have a CARDINAL value, and −1 is not a CARDINAL value.

Classification of Parameters

You will often find it helpful, when studying the effect of a particular procedure, to classify each of its parameters in one of three categories:

☐ The procedure **uses the value** of the parameter: The procedure refers to the value the parameter had when the procedure was called and does not give the parameter a value. This is called an **in parameter**, since it brings a value into the procedure.

☐ The procedure **returns the value** of the parameter: The procedure gives the parameter a value and does not refer to any value the parameter might have had when the procedure was called. This is called an **out parameter**, since it takes a value out of the procedure.

☐ The procedure **modifies the value** of the parameter: The procedure refers to the value the parameter had when the procedure was called, but it also contains a statement that gives the parameter a value. Such a parameter is called an **in-out parameter**.

In the eight procedures of ListADT, the List parameter is an in-out parameter for Create, Destroy, Insert, and Delete; it is an in parameter for LookAt, InList, FirstLocation, and NextLocation. The Information parameter is an in parameter for Insert and an out parameter for LookAt and Delete. The Location parameter is an in parameter for all procedures; a Location value can be obtained only when it is returned by the FirstLocation or NextLocation function. A VALUE parameter can only be an in parameter. A VAR parameter can be any one of the three kinds.

Check Your Understanding

1. Write the SizeOf utility for the simple array implementation of ListADT.

2. Write the LookAt procedure for the simple array implementation of ListADT.

3. Classify all eight parameters in Example 2.3B as in, out, or in-out.

4. Write the Delete procedure for the simple array implementation of ListADT.

5. (NA) Write the Join utility described in Example 3.1C (but replace "Stack" by "List") for the simple array implementation of ListADT.

6. (NA) Write the MoveInfo procedure described in Example 3.5B, importing from ListADT as needed. Then write it for the simple array implementation of ListADT. Discuss why it is worthwhile having it as a utility procedure.

7. (NA) Assume that you perversely decide to code FirstLocation as RETURN 0 and NextLocation as follows:

```
IF Where < Data↑.Size THEN
    RETURN Where + 1;
ELSE
    RETURN Data↑.Size;
END;
```

List all other changes that have to be made in the coding for the other six procedures in the simple array implementation of ListADT.

3.7 TABLES

The two data structures Stack and Queue differ from each other only in that the former has Push/Pop and the latter has Enqueue/Dequeue; that is, only the procedures that insert and delete an Information value differ. The difference is that Pop takes the most recently inserted item, and Dequeue takes the least recently inserted item. Thus the way you identify the item to be deleted is by when it was inserted. By contrast, the Delete procedure for a List identifies the item to be deleted by its position in the list.

A **table** has yet another definition of deletion: The deletion procedure for tables removes an information value that has previously been specified by another procedure we call **Find**. Find requires that its Information parameter contain a means of identifying the Information that is to be deleted, typically an ID field. The deletion procedure for Tables is called **TakeOut,** and the insertion procedure is called **PutIn**. *Note:* Some books call this data structure a **dictionary** or a **set** instead of a table.

Applications of Tables

A business might have several hundred customers, with one information record for each. From time to time a customer is put in or taken out of the data structure. The primary use of the structure is to maintain information on the customers for retrieval. When you want to obtain information about a certain customer, you provide the name or other identification of the customer to Find the record and then **Inspect** retrieves the rest of the information about that customer.

Another application of tables is found in computer language compilers. As a program is compiled, each identifier that is declared in the program is stored in a table, along with information as to the type of object declared (constant, variable, procedure, etc.), the block for which that declaration is valid, the value if it is a constant, and so forth. When you see an already declared identifier during compilation of the program, you supply it to the Find procedure, so you can then Inspect the information about that identifier.

A compiler will often erase all entries for a given procedure once the end of the procedure is reached. One way that this can be accomplished is to create a new table for each procedure, then destroy it when the end of the procedure is compiled; a Stack of Tables might even be used. In practice, however, it is better to add two procedures to the TableADT module: **Mark**(Data) can be called at any time; it marks the beginning of a new subtable (one subtable per procedure). When **Release**(Data) is executed, all information in the most recent subtable is deleted, that is, all information added since the most recent call of Mark(Data). When these two procedures are available, the compiler does not use TakeOut at all.

The Find Procedure

The InfoADT module contains a procedure named Compare that can tell whether two given information records are equal and, if not, can tell which is earlier (in some sense). Typically, the information is a record with a field (which we call ID) that determines the ordering. For instance, the ID might contain a social security number, a cardinal number that can be directly compared. Or the ID might contain the last name of a person or company. The record might even contain a first name and a last name; ordering is determined by the last name except when two records have the same last name, in which case the first name determines the ordering. Or the information might consist of nothing more than an array of characters, rather than a number of different fields. We will not be concerned with the details of the ordering, only that the Compare procedure give us access to that ordering relation.

The heading of the Find procedure for a Table is:

```
PROCEDURE Find (TheInfo : Information; VAR Data : Table);
```

You may treat the Find procedure as if it makes a note of the ID (or whatever) of TheInfo. The TakeOut procedure deletes the information from Data that the Compare procedure says has that ID and returns the full record. There are two problems that can arise. One is that there might be no such record. To test for this, we have a Boolean function InTable(Data) that tells whether the most recent Find operation was successful. If it was not successful, the TakeOut procedure has no effect. The second problem that can arise is that there are two or more Information records that match the information value provided to Find (for instance, they might have the same ID). In that case, I adopt the convention that the most recently added Information is to be deleted (since this is what the compiler application requires). Many other applications of TableADT do not have duplicate IDs in the table, in which case that problem does not arise. The Inspect procedure is the same as TakeOut except that the information is not deleted from the table.

Similarities between TableADT and StackADT

In essence, a table can be treated as a collection of stacks, one for each ID—PutIn finds the appropriate stack and does a push operation; Find simply finds the appropriate stack. Inspect and TakeOut are the same as Peep and Pop for the most recently found stack. InTable tests whether the most recently found stack is nonempty, opposite to the IsEmpty function.

The only other procedures in TableADT are Create and Destroy, which are the same as those for stacks, *mutatis mutandis* (to save you looking that one up, it means "making the required changes"; in this case, just change "Stack" to "Table").

The definition module for TableADT is in Example 3.7A. Note that the only difference from StackADT (other than replacing "Stack" by "Table") is the use of PutIn, TakeOut, and Inspect in place of Push, Pop, and Peep, and the availability of Find and InTable but not IsEmpty. Keep in mind that the "marker" described in the comments is only to aid your understanding; an implementation is not required to actually have one. The next section discusses an implementation that records the marked information value and another implementation that does not.

Design Considerations

The specifics of TableADT result from design decisions I have made. For example, I could instead have decided to have TableADT export an Information variable used to communicate between client modules and the TakeOut and Inspect procedures, thus eliminating the need for Find. I could have exported a Boolean variable that is set by Find instead of having the InTable function; but that would expose the data structure to the possibility that the client module changes the value of the variable. I could have given Find a Boolean VAR parameter to return the result of the search, which would also eliminate the need for InTable; but that would be a little more trouble for the client module. I could have said that TheInfo for Inspect and TakeOut is an in-out parameter and required the client module to supply at least an ID; but then the implementation would need to import DestroyInfo from InfoADT, and it is best to make the connections between abstract data types as few as possible.

This TableADT module would be more useful if it provided a way to progress through the values in the table one at a time in order. However, that is more restrictive than what many applications need and eliminates some otherwise excellent implementations. An abstract data type with such additions will be

EXAMPLE 3.7A _____

```
DEFINITION MODULE TableADT;
FROM InfoADT  IMPORT Information;
EXPORT QUALIFIED Table,   PutIn,    Find,    InTable,
                 Inspect, TakeOut, Create, Destroy;
   (* Written by William C. Jones, October 19-- *)
   (* Module to implement table manipulations independently
      of the kind of Information being put in the table.
      Warning:  Every Table must be initialized before any-
      thing else can be done with it.  InfoADT must export
      Compare to determine matching information values.  *)
   (* Hypothetically speaking, each table is considered
      to have a "marker" that sometimes "marks" an
      information value in the table *)

TYPE
    Table;
(* ****************************************************** *)

PROCEDURE PutIn (TheInfo  : Information;
                 VAR Data : Table);
       (* Put TheInfo in Data and "mark" it *)

PROCEDURE Find (TheInfo  : Information;
                VAR Data : Table);
       (* "Mark" the most-recently-added information value
           that matches TheInfo using Compare, if any;
           else no information value is marked.
        TheInfo only needs to have the hypothetical ID
           "filled in," to allow the use of Compare *)

PROCEDURE InTable (Data : Table) : BOOLEAN;
       (* Tell whether any there is any information value
           in the table that is "marked" *)

PROCEDURE Inspect (VAR TheInfo : Information;
                   Data        : Table);
       (* Retrieve the "marked" information value, if any;
           but no effect if InTable would return FALSE. *)

PROCEDURE TakeOut (VAR TheInfo : Information;
                   VAR Data    : Table);
       (* Same as Inspect, except that TheInfo is also
           removed from Data if it is there.
        The "marker" is moved to the matching information
           value added next after the deleted one, if any;
           else no information is "marked." *)

PROCEDURE Create (VAR Data : Table);
       (* Initialize Data as an empty structure *)

PROCEDURE Destroy (VAR Data : Table);
       (* Deallocate the space for the empty structure *)

END TableADT.
```

described in the next section, after you have had a chance to become familiar with TableADT.

The File Clerk Analogy

It may help to think of a Table as a file clerk with a large number of filing cabinets. Information can be visualized as a file folder with an ID number written on the outside and several sheets of filled-out forms inside (telling a person's name, employment history, wages, etc.). The file clerk theoretically has some kind of marker that can be clipped onto a file folder.

☐ PutIn(TheInfo, FileCabinets) means: You give a file folder to the file clerk, who puts it somewhere in the file cabinets, presumably in such a way that it will be easy to find later. The marker goes on that file folder.

☐ Find(TheInfo, FileCabinets) means: The file clerk puts the marker on the most recently added information value that matches TheInfo; if there is none, the marker is laid to one side.

☐ InTable(FileCabinets) returns TRUE if the marker is on a file folder, FALSE if it is laid to one side.

☐ Inspect(TheInfo, FileCabinets) means: The file clerk gives you a copy of the currently marked file folder. But if the marker is laid to one side, the file clerk does nothing.

☐ TakeOut(TheInfo, FileCabinets) means: The file clerk removes the currently marked file folder from the file cabinets and gives it to you, and the marker is moved to the one after it (or laid to one side if no other file folder matches that one). However, nothing happens if the marker was already laid to one side.

☐ Create(FileCabinets) acquires the cabinets and hires the file clerk.

☐ Destroy(FileCabinets) dumps the cabinets and fires the file clerk.

Note the "separation of powers" in action here: On the one hand, you do not know what filing system is used. PutIn could amount to putting your file at the front of the next empty drawer, so the other procedures just hunt through the drawers until a match is found; or a sophisticated filing system could be used that allows very fast retrieval. On the other hand, the file clerk is not concerned with what is inside the folders; she does not even have to be able to read, except for recognizing ID numbers.

Preconditions and Postconditions

Create does not have a precondition; its postcondition is that the Table parameter contains a valid Table value. The precondition for each of the TableADT procedures except Create is that the Table parameter have a valid Table value. The postcondition for Destroy is that the Table parameter contains an invalid Table value. The postcondition for each of the other TableADT procedures is that the Table parameter has a valid Table value and moreover:

- [ ] For PutIn, the Table has one more information value than it had before, namely the information parameter, and the marker is on it.
- [ ] For Find, the marker is on the most recently added matching value in the Table, if any; otherwise the marker is not on a value.
- [ ] For Inspect, either (1) the marker was not on a value, or (2) the information parameter contains the most recently added matching information value in the Table.
- [ ] For TakeOut, the same as for Inspect plus, if the marker was on a value, the returned information value is no longer in the Table and the marker is on the next most recently added matching value still in the Table, if any.

Using Tables

The Modify procedure is an excellent utility procedure for TableADT. It replaces information currently in the table by updated information with the same (hypothetical) ID (replacing the most recently inserted one in case of ties). The old information (if any) is returned in its Information parameter, and the marker is set to the new information. Thus the procedure call Modify(TheInfo, Data) has the same effect as the following sequence of statements:

```
Find (TheInfo, Data);
IF InTable (Data) THEN
    TakeOut (OtherInfo, Data);
    PutIn (TheInfo, Data);
    TheInfo := OtherInfo;
END;
```

A simple way in which a Table could be used is to retrieve information at the request of the user, once the ID for the information is supplied. The coding could be:

```
InputID (TheInfo);
Find (TheInfo, Data);
IF InTable (Data) THEN
    Inspect (TableInfo, Data);
    OutputToUser (TableInfo);
ELSE
    WriteString (' That information is not available.');
END;
```

The library module in Example 2.5C is used to check the spelling of a word when the user is in a word-processing program. The implementation module is simple when imports from TableADT are used: The initialization is little more than repeatedly reading values and calling PutIn until the end of the file is reached, although normally TableADT would have a utility ReadAll procedure that can be used instead. The InDictionary procedure is just two statements:

```
Find (TheInfo, Data);
RETURN InTable (Data);
```

Example 3.7B gives a more complex illustration of how a client module might use the procedures in TableADT. This DeleteOldest procedure deletes from a table the *least* recently added information value that matches a given information value. Its LookFurther subprocedure is called recursively as many times as there are matching values in the table. Each activation of LookFurther has a local Information variable in which a value from the table is stored. The recursion creates a stack of activations of LookFurther with their saved values until a call of

EXAMPLE 3.7B _____

```
PROCEDURE DeleteOldest (VAR TheInfo : Information;
                        VAR Data    : Table);
     (* Like TakeOut, except if two or more match,
        delete and return the least-recently-added one *)
     (* Context:  client of TableADT *)
   (*-----------------------------------------------------*)

   PROCEDURE LookFurther;
       (* The one we want is still in the table *)
   VAR
       Saved : Information;
   BEGIN
       Saved := TheInfo;
       TakeOut (TheInfo, Data);
       IF InTable (Data) THEN
           LookFurther;
       END;
       PutIn (Saved, Data);
   END LookFurther;
   (*-----------------------------------------------------*)

BEGIN           (* DeleteOldest *)
    TakeOut (TheInfo, Data);
    IF InTable (Data) THEN
        LookFurther;
    END;
END DeleteOldest;
```

InTable returns FALSE. Then, as the recursion "unwinds," each activation of LookFurther inserts its information value back into the table, so the original order of insertion is kept.

Perhaps the best way to make sure you understand this procedure is to trace its action four different times: when there is no matching information in the table, then when there is only one, then when there are two, then when there are three matching information values in the table. That should be enough to convince you of its correctness.

Note that two variables have been delocalized in Example 3.7B: Data and TheInfo are not passed as VAR parameters, since they are the same variable on each activation of the LookFurther procedure.

In designing this procedure, recursion was deliberately chosen as a way to establish a temporary stack structure to store an unknown number of Saved values. A nonrecursive method would be to establish a local Table variable and store values there until the last is found, then transfer all but the last back. This would work because a table acts like a number of stacks, one for each different ID (or whatever criterion Compare uses).

Check Your Understanding

1. Write a segment of code that imports from TableADT and deletes from a table named Data all information values that match TheInfo. All the matching values are to be destroyed.

2. Write a segment of code that imports from TableADT and inserts TheInfo in a table named Data only if no matching value is already in the table.

3. Rewrite the DeleteOldest procedure nonrecursively using a local Table variable.

4. (NA) Trace the action of DeleteOldest, assuming that there are three information values in the table with the given ID. Call those values A, B, and C in the order they were originally inserted in the table.

5. (NA) Write a recursive function that counts how many information values in a given table match TheInfo. The function should leave the table unchanged except for the marker. Use imports from TableADT.

3.8 IMPLEMENTATIONS OF TableADT; ORDERED TABLES

Why should we go to a lot of work developing an implementation for tables when we can do everything with a list that we can do with a table (and then some)? What we will do is import almost everything we need from ListADT. Then any implementation of ListADT provides a corresponding implementation of TableADT, including the ListADT implementations you will see in Chapter 4. The advantage of importing from ListADT is that the programming effort needed is much less; the disadvantage is that execution time is somewhat greater. A library module that does most of its work by importing from other library modules is called **layered software**.

We declare a Table to be a List plus a Location in that List. The Location indicates the "marked" value. To create or destroy a table, we just call the procedures of the same name in ListADT. To put something in a table, we just put it at the front of the list. To Find something in a table, we search through the list (starting from the front) until we find the location of a matching information value. If we do not find it, the location will be such as to make InList false, so InTable tests InList.

This naive concept needs some fine tuning. How do we keep track of the current location in the list that Find finds so that Inspect can inspect there and TakeOut can take information out there? It is reasonable to declare a Table to be a pointer to a record consisting of a List plus a Location. Create initializes everything:

```
TYPE    Table = POINTER TO RECORD
                    Lst : List;
                    Loc : Location;
                END;
(* body of Create *)
    NEW (Data);
    ListADT.Create (Data↑.Lst);
    Data↑.Loc := FirstLocation (Data↑.Lst);
```

Now PutIn puts information at the first location on the list and sets Data ↑ .Loc to that first location. Find goes through the list until it finds the information it is given and sets Data ↑ .Loc to that location; if the search fails, Data ↑ .Loc ends up not being in the list, which makes InList false, so InTable returns InList(Data ↑ .Loc, Data ↑ .Lst). If you had Search as a utility in ListADT, you could just use Data ↑ .Loc := Search(TheInfo, Data ↑ .Lst). Inspect just calls LookAt, and TakeOut just calls Delete.

One problem arises with this implementation—if you delete an information value that is not the last item on the list, Data ↑ .Loc will still be in the list. Thus another call of TakeOut will succeed, removing whatever value happens to follow the one you just took out, although it does not match. The obvious solution is to move the location further down in the list, looking for the next matching value. Example 3.8A presents the implementation module for this **naive layered implementation**.

EXAMPLE 3.8A _____

```
IMPLEMENTATION MODULE TableADT;
FROM InfoADT IMPORT Information, Compare;
FROM ListADT IMPORT List, Location, InList, FirstLocation,
                    NextLocation, Insert, Delete, LookAt;
FROM Storage IMPORT ALLOCATE, DEALLOCATE;
IMPORT ListADT;
    (* implement Table using ListADT procedures for
       a naive layered implementation *)
    (* Written by William C. Jones, October 19-- *)
TYPE
    Table = POINTER TO RECORD
                  Lst : List;
                  Loc : Location;
             END;
(***********************************************************)

PROCEDURE Create (VAR Data : Table);
BEGIN
    NEW (Data);
    ListADT.Create (Data^.Lst);
    Data^.Loc := FirstLocation (Data^.Lst);
END Create;
(***********************************************************)

PROCEDURE Destroy (VAR Data : Table);
BEGIN
    ListADT.Destroy (Data^.Lst);
    DISPOSE (Data);
END Destroy;
(***********************************************************)

PROCEDURE PutIn (TheInfo : Information;  VAR Data : Table);
BEGIN
    Data^.Loc := FirstLocation (Data^.Lst);
    Insert (TheInfo, Data^.Loc, Data^.Lst);
END PutIn;
(***********************************************************)

PROCEDURE Find (TheInfo : Information;  VAR Data : Table);
    (* Set Data^.Loc to the location of the first matching
       information.  NOT InList if none matches.  *)
VAR
    Where : Location;
    ListInfo : Information;
BEGIN
    Where := FirstLocation (Data^.Lst);
    LookAt (ListInfo, Where, Data^.Lst);
    WHILE InList (Where, Data^.Lst) AND
              (Compare (TheInfo, ListInfo) # 0) DO
        Where := NextLocation (Where, Data^.Lst);
        LookAt (ListInfo, Where, Data^.Lst);
    END;
    Data^.Loc := Where;
END Find;
(***********************************************************)
```

(* continued on next page *)

187

```
(* EXAMPLE 3.8A continued *)


PROCEDURE InTable (Data : Table) : BOOLEAN;
BEGIN
    RETURN InList (Data^.Loc, Data^.Lst);
END InTable;
(***********************************************************)

PROCEDURE Inspect (VAR TheInfo : Information;
                       Data     : Table);
BEGIN
    LookAt (TheInfo, Data^.Loc, Data^.Lst);
END Inspect;
(***********************************************************)

PROCEDURE TakeOut (VAR TheInfo : Information;
                   VAR Data     : Table);
BEGIN
    Delete (TheInfo, Data^.Loc, Data^.Lst);
    Find (TheInfo, Data);
END TakeOut;
(***********************************************************)

END TableADT.
```

Additional Implementations of TableADT

Execution time for TakeOut could be improved by beginning the search at the point of deletion; this is left as an exercise. Another time-waster with this implementation is that the work of searching further after a TakeOut is wasted if Find or PutIn is called next. The smart thing is to wait and see. You can add a Boolean field to the Table record: If this field is TRUE, it means that a re-search is needed before Inspect or TakeOut or InTable can be used, owing to a previous use of TakeOut. However, you will not have the proper information value for the re-search, so you need to save the value in another field of the Table record after each deletion. This **wait-and-see layered implementation** is left as a programming problem.

If you implemented TableADT directly using the simple array implementation, you would only save a small amount of execution time for the procedure calls and the indirect references. This could be done with the naive implementation or the wait-and-see implementation. For the **wait-and-see array implementation**, a Table could be declared as:

```
TYPE    Table = POINTER TO RECORD
                    Item : ARRAY [1..MaxSize] OF Information;
                    Size, Loc : CARDINAL;
                    ResearchNeeded : BOOLEAN;
                    CopyOfDeletedInfo : Information;
                END;
```

Another idea is to keep the array of information values in increasing order at all times. Then binary search (illustated in Example 2.5C) can be used to find a value, and re-search would not be necessary. For this **ordered array implementation**, you could use the following simpler declaration:

```
TYPE    Table = POINTER TO RECORD
                    Item : ARRAY [1..MaxSize] OF Information;
                    Size, Loc : CARDINAL;
                    IsThere : BOOLEAN;
                END;
```

The IsThere field is assigned FALSE when you delete a value and there is no later matching value, and when you call Find and the value sought is not found. In other words, you have a nonexistent information value at Loc, but Loc is the index of the component where the information would be if it were put in the table. This lets you use Find to do much of the work for PutIn. InTable(Data) simply returns Data ↑ .IsThere and Inspect is as follows:

```
IF Data↑.IsThere THEN
    TheInfo := Data↑.Item [Data↑.Loc];
END;
```

DictiADT

The ordered array implementation is suitable for a form of TableADT in which you can find the first or "smallest" information value in the table (as determined by Compare) or the "next smallest" after a given information value. This permits you to go through the list alphabetically (or however Compare determines the ordering). This capability has such wide application that it deserves its own name—I call it DictiADT. This is reasonable because you can look up information in it easily, as in a dictionary. A large part of Chapter 5 is devoted to implementations of DictiADT. The definition module for DictiADT is the same as TableADT with the addition of four procedures, described in Example 3.8B. The FindX procedures simply reset the "marker."

Example 3.8B includes two utility procedures WriteTable and ReadTable. These procedures are used when the information in the table is stored in external files between runs of a program. ReadTable can be assumed to work correctly only with files written by WriteTable. For instance, WriteTable may write the values in increasing order, after writing the number of values. By contrast, ReadAll has to allow for unordered information values. ReadAll can be used for reading from the keyboard, and WriteAll can write to the screen; ReadTable and

EXAMPLE 3.8B _____

```
DEFINITION MODULE DictiADT;
    (* "Alphabetically" means "according to Compare."
    Declarations are those in TableADT plus the
    following four procedures  *)
    (* Written by William C. Jones, February 19-- *)
PROCEDURE FindFirstIn (VAR Data : Table);
    (* "Mark" the alphabetically (or whatever) first
    information value in Data, if Data is not empty *)

PROCEDURE FindNextIn (VAR Data : Table);
    (* "Mark" the information value in Data that is
        alphabetically directly after the one currently
        "marked," treating the values as if the more
        recently added of matching values comes earlier.
        Exception 1:  If no value is marked because of a
        deletion, mark the one following the one deleted.
        Exception 2:  If no value is marked because Find
        failed, mark the one following the one sought.
        Exception 3:  If there is no next value, leave
        all information unmarked.  *)
(* *****************************************************)

(* The following are utility procedures for DictiADT *)

PROCEDURE WriteTable (VAR Data : Table);
    (* Write the information in Data to a file for future
    access by ReadTable; destroy Data *)

PROCEDURE ReadTable (VAR Data : Table);
    (* Read a file written by WriteTable and create
    Data containing those values *)

END DictiADT.
```

WriteTable should be thought of as strictly for permitting long-term storage. In implementations where the amount of data is too great for internal memory, ReadTable will not even read all the information; it may simply establish connections to the file so it can store and retrieve individual information values in it.

Warning

Some compilers have difficulty with library module names that are more than eight characters in length. For instance, the VAX compiler could not handle SpellingChecker as the name of the library module in Section 2.5; the error was eliminated by simply changing the name to Spelling. That is the reason why I use the name DictiADT instead of DictionaryADT.

Ordered Array Implementation of DictiADT

For the ordered array implementation of DictiADT, the FindFirstIn procedure initializes Data ↑.Loc to 1. However, the IsThere field must always be maintained so that InTable only has to test it. So FindFirstIn should assign TRUE to IsThere if the table is nonempty and FALSE otherwise.

The FindNextIn is a little more complicated. Basically, you just need to increment Data ↑.Loc. However, you must first check that you are not at the end of the list; if so, nothing is there. There is one other thing you have to watch out for—if Find was tried and failed, you want the information value that comes after the one sought, which is what Data ↑.Loc indicates already. See Example 3.8C for the coding. You must make a similar adjustment for most uses of TakeOut. The adjustment consists in first checking that IsThere is true and, if not, just make it true and do not change Data ↑.Loc.

The two FindX procedures make it easy to process the information values in a table in increasing order. For instance, the following segment will write all values in order:

```
FindFirstIn (Data);
WHILE InTable (Data) DO
    Inspect (TheInfo, Data);
    OutputInfo (TheInfo);
    FindNextIn (Data);
END;
```

Using Lists for Stacks, Queues, and Tables

Some programs are sufficiently complex that they use stacks, queues, and linear lists. This can be managed by using IMPORT StackADT, QueueADT, ListADT in the import section of the program module. But then you would have to refer to the various Create procedures using qualidents, that is, StackADT.Create, QueueADT.Create, and ListADT.Create (and similarly for other procedures).

A simpler way is to consider stacks and queues as restricted forms of linear lists, similar to what was done with TableADT. Then you can just import ListADT into StackADT and declare your own Pop procedure that executes the statement Delete(TheInfo, FirstLocation(Data), Data). Push would also be simple: Insert(TheInfo, FirstLocation(Data), Data). You have two ways to go for queues: Dequeue could be the same as Pop and Enqueue could put values in the last location on the list; or Enqueue could be the same as Push and Dequeue could take the last information value on the list.

This *augmented ListADT module* could have not only the basic eight procedures from ListADT (Create, Destroy; Insert, Delete, LookAt; InList, FirstLocation, NextLocation), but also Push, Pop, Enqueue, Dequeue, Peep, IsEmpty; Join,

EXAMPLE 3.8C _____

```
IMPLEMENTATION MODULE DictiADT;
    (* Key parts of the ordered array implementation *)
TYPE
    Table = POINTER TO RECORD
                Item : ARRAY [1..MaxSize] OF Information;
                Size, Loc : CARDINAL;
                IsThere : BOOLEAN;
            END;
(************************************************************)

PROCEDURE FindFirstIn (VAR Data : Table);
BEGIN
    Data^.Loc := 1;
    Data^.IsThere := Data^.Size > 0;
END FindFirstIn;
(************************************************************)

PROCEDURE FindNextIn (VAR Data : Table);
BEGIN
    IF Data^.IsThere AND (Data^.Loc <= Data^.Size) THEN
        INC (Data^.Loc);
    ELSE
        Data^.IsThere := (Data^.Loc <= Data^.Size);
    END;
END FindNextIn;
(************************************************************)

PROCEDURE WriteTable (VAR Data : Table);
VAR
    K : CARDINAL;
BEGIN
    WriteCard (Data^.Size, 1);
    WriteLn;
    FOR K := 1 TO Data^.Size DO
        OutputInfo (Data^.Item [K]);
    END;
END WriteTable;
(************************************************************)

PROCEDURE ReadTable (VAR Data : Table);
VAR
    K : CARDINAL;
BEGIN
    NEW (Data);
    ReadCard (Data^.Size);
    Data^.Loc := 1;
    Data^.IsThere := FALSE;
    FOR K := 1 TO Data^.Size DO
        InputInfo (Data^.Item [K]);
    END;
END ReadTable;
(************************************************************)

END DictiADT.
```

Seek, Search, ReadAll, and WriteAll. That would give you maximum flexibility in using any combination of stacks, queues, tables, and linked lists. The Search procedure would be used primarily for operations involving table structures.

Check Your Understanding

1. Modify TakeOut in Example 3.8A to speed up the algorithm by starting the search from where the deletion took place.

2. Write a utility function for the naive layered implementation of TableADT: The function tells how many information values in a given Table match a given information value, without changing the "marker."

3. Modify the InDictionary function in Example 2.5C to obtain a Find procedure for the ordered array implementation of DictiADT using binary search (Example 3.8C).

4. Explain why the Create procedure in Example 3.8A has to initialize Data ↑ .Loc, although Data ↑ .Lst is empty.

5. Write the Create procedure for the ordered array implementation of DictiADT (Example 3.8C).

6. (NA) Write the Mark and Release procedures (described near the beginning of Section 3.7) as procedures exported from the implementation of TableADT given in Example 3.8A. Assume that InfoADT exports an information value called NoInfo that is distinguishable from all other information values. Put NoInfo in the list whenever Mark is called.

7. (NA) Write the PutIn procedure for the ordered array implementation of DictiADT; call on Find as needed.

8. (NA) Write the TakeOut procedure for the ordered array implementation of DictiADT with binary search.

9. (NA) Write a utility procedure for DictiADT that deletes all information values for which there is a more recently added information value that matches it.

3.9 MORE IMPLEMENTATIONS OF ListADT

This section presents two additional implementations of ListADT using arrays. In certain circumstances, these implementations allow a program to execute significantly faster than with the simple array implementation.

Reverse Array Implementation of ListADT

In many applications of lists, insertions and deletions are almost always made at or near the beginning of the list. In fact, some applications really use the list as a stack except that they occasionally look at or modify values below the top of the stack. The simple array implementation for lists causes a lot of movement of data for such applications. If we store the information values in the array in the reverse order of the simple array implementation, we obtain a faster-acting implementation. That is, when a list named Data contains N items, they are stored in Data $\uparrow$ .Item[1] through Data $\uparrow$ .Item[N], but the first one is in Data $\uparrow$ .Item[N] and the end one is in Data $\uparrow$ .Item[1]. Data $\uparrow$ .Size is still N.

This implementation is not fully specified until we decide what a Location is. We define the Location of an item to be its position number in the list for this **reverse array implementation of ListADT**. Thus the body of FirstLocation is simply RETURN 1. The NextLocation and InList functions are also coded exactly the same as for the simple array implementation (Section 3.6). An illustration of the effect on the other procedures is LookAt(TheInfo, Where, Data), which can be implemented as:

```
IF Where <= Data↑.Size THEN
    TheInfo := Data↑.Item [Data↑.Size + 1 - Where];
END;
```

If the list has the five values 'A', 'B', 'C', 'D', and 'E' in that order, with 'A' the first information value on the list and 'E' the last one on the list, then Size is 5, 'A' is stored at index 5 in the array, 'C' is stored at index 3, and 'E' is stored at index 1 in the array. The procedure call Insert('X', 3, Data) puts 'X' in the component of index 4 after moving 'A' to component 6 and 'B' to component 5. See Figure 8 for more examples.

The rest of this implementation is left as a programming problem. Note that this reverse array implementation is faster than the simple array implementation only when the average position for insertions and deletions is in the first half of the list. In particular, if all insertions are at one end of the list and all deletions at the other end, as with queues, the two implementations are about the same in execution time. But for the simpler implementations of TableADT described in the previous section, the reverse array implementation is faster.

The primary disadvantage of this reverse array implementation is that reading a large number of values and inserting them one at a time in the list takes much more time than it does for the simple array implementation. However, if you use a utility ReadAll procedure, you can recover almost all the extra time. The trick is to first read all the information values into the wrong end of the array and then move them down to the components with small indices.

16 information values (marked "a" through "p") in a 30-component array.
The front is at component 16 and the rear is at component 1.

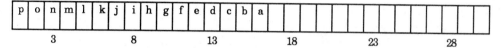

Insert a new value (marked "u") at the fourth location Seek (4, Data):

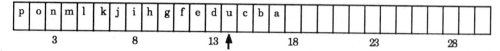

Delete the value marked "f" from the seventh location Seek (7, Data)

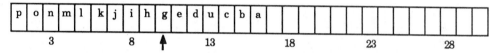

FIGURE 8. A list in the reverse array implementation.

You might think that a better choice for the definition of a Location would be the index in the array. Thus FirstLocation would return Data ↑ .Size and NextLocation would subtract 1. However, this definition cannot be used because it violates the specifications in ListADT. For instance, if you have 10 items on a list and execute the following three statements, you should delete the second and third items on the list; but the statements would instead delete the second and first items on the list.

```
Where := NextLocation (FirstLocation (Data), Data);
Delete (TheInfo, Where, Data);   (* would delete item 2  *)
Delete (TheInfo, Where, Data);   (* would delete item 1  *)
```

Deques, Rings, and Priority Queues

A **deque** is a data structure for which Insert, Delete, and LookAt are only allowed at the beginning or end. Thus it is intermediate between stacks and queues on the one hand and lists on the other. Some applications use only deques. The procedures could be named InsertFront, DeleteFront, LookAtFront, InsertRear, DeleteRear, and LookAtRear; you would also need Create, Destroy, and IsEmpty. Deque is short for "double-ended queue" and is pronounced either as one syllable ("deck") or as two ("DQ"). The development of the library module for dequeues by importing from ListADT is left as a programming problem.

A **ring** can be visualized as a data structure with information arranged in a ring, so each information value is followed by an information value and no information value is "first." You should also visualize a marker placed on one particular information value in the ring. The primitive operations on a ring, in addition to Create, Destroy, and IsEmpty, are (1) Peep, which accesses the marked value; (2) Dering, which removes the marked value; (3) Enring, which inserts a new information value after the marked value (if the ring is empty, the new information value is marked); and (4) Advance, which moves from one marked value to the next. These can be implemented using queue procedures, in which the marked value is the one at the front of a queue. Then Dering is Dequeue, Enring is Enqueue, Peep is Peep, and Advance corresponds to a Dequeue followed by an Enqueue of the same value. A ring has applications in computer networks and time-sharing.

A **priority queue** is a data structure in which each information value in the structure has a **priority number**. The deletion procedure always takes the information value with the lowest priority number; so if the priority numbers are positive integers, priority 1 is deleted soonest. In case of ties, deletion takes the least recently added item.

A priority queue module should have six procedures corresponding to those for Queues. Since insertion and deletion act differently, they should have different names; let us call them EnPriQ and DePriQ. The names and specifications for the other four procedures can be left unchanged.

A priority queue can be implemented in any of several ways. One way is to code EnPriQ the same as Enqueue and replace the logic of Dequeue so it takes the item with the smallest priority number. Another way is to code DePriQ the same as Dequeue and replace the logic of Enqueue so it inserts items in increasing order of priority numbers.

If the priority number of an information value is determined by the Compare function from InfoADT, the priority queue is a **sorted list** in which values are kept in increasing (or perhaps decreasing) order. If the priority number is determined solely by the order of insertion, the priority queue is a normal stack or queue, depending on whether the more recent insertions are given lower or higher priority numbers than are earlier insertions.

Circular Array Implementation of ListADT

The main problem with array implementations of ListADT is the amount of time required to move items when an insertion or deletion occurs at an inconvenient place. The problem is essentially unavoidable as long as we keep items physically next to each other in storage. The next chapter describes a way around this; it does not use arrays. There is, however, one way that the time can be cut almost in half with arrays. It is a generalization of the circular array implementation for queues.

The **circular array implementation for ListADT** can be described as follows: Think of the array as a circle, with component MaxSize curved around so that it is directly followed by component 1. Keep the list in a sequence of components in

16 information values (marked "a" through "p") in a 30-component array.
The front is at component 18 and the rear is at component 3.

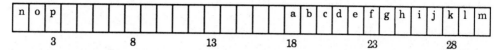

Insert a new information value (marked "u") as the fourth one in the list.

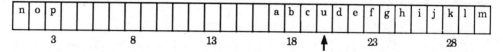

Insert another new value (marked "v") as the third-to-last in the list.

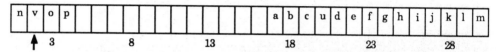

FIGURE 9. A list in the circular array implementation.

this circular array. When you insert or delete on either end, do not move the other items. When you insert or delete close to the rear, move only the later items to make room. When you insert or delete close to the front, move the earlier items to make room. In general, insertion or deletion should move only the items on the shorter end of the list (Fig. 9).

You should have a Front field, telling the index of the front item, and a Rear field telling the index of the rear item. If MaxSize is 50, Front is 8, and Rear is 20, it follows that there are 13 items on the list: Item[8] is the first, Item[9] is the second, . . . , Item[20] is the last. If MaxSize is 50, Front is 20, and Rear is 8, then the list has "wrapped around" the end of the array. Item[20] is the first item on the list, Item[21] is the second, . . . , Item[50] is the thirty-first, Item[1] is the thirty-second, so Item[8] is the thirty-ninth. Thus there are 39 information values on the list.

It is highly convenient in the coding to have a third field that tells the number of items on the list. This Size field is redundant, since it can be computed from the Front and Rear fields as Size=Rear+1−Front (if there is no wrap around) or Size=Rear+1+MaxSize−Front (with wrap around). Actually, with these three fields, Front, Rear, and Size, any one of them is redundant; for instance, you could do without the Rear field and compute it when you need it. Thus we declare a List as:

```
TYPE   List = POINTER TO RECORD
                 Item : ARRAY [1..MaxSize] OF Information;
                 Size, Front, Rear : CARDINAL;
              END;
```

An empty list can be denoted by setting Size to 0; Front and Rear are irrelevant, although Front should be initialized as 1 more than Rear, since that shortens execution time overall. A Location can be the position number of the item on the list. Thus FirstLocation merely returns 1 and LastLocation returns Size, regardless of the values of Front and Rear. InList simply tells whether the given location is less than or equal to Size. The really interesting procedures are Insert, Delete, and LookAt, since they have to worry about whether the information is wrapped around the end. For instance, the body of LookAt could be coded as follows:

```
WITH Data↑ DO  (* fields are Item, Size, Front, Rear *)
    IF Where <= Size THEN
        Spot := Where + Front - 1;
        IF Spot <= MaxSize THEN
            TheInfo := Item [Spot];
        ELSE
            TheInfo := Item [Spot - MaxSize];
        END;
    END;
END;
```

The Insert procedure is left as a programming problem. Delete is understandably complicated—if you want to double the speed with which a procedure is executed, you usually have to put in more programming effort and you often need to use more storage space. After you make sure that the given Location is from 1 to Size, it is best to first compute the index in the array of the information to be deleted. You count up from Front to the given Location, wrapping around if necessary, to find the appropriate spot. Then you remove the information from that component. Next you look to see whether it is faster to shift the lower values in the list up or to shift the higher values down, and then you make the appropriate shifts. Finally, you subtract 1 from the Size. The coding for this algorithm is in Example 3.9A.

To shift a group of values by one component, you have to first check whether wraparound occurs within the group. If not, shifting can be accomplished by a simple FOR loop. If wraparound interferes, you should do the shifting in three stages: Shift the group at one end of the array, then move one value from the other end to this end, then shift the group at the other end of the array.

Check Your Understanding

1. Write the DePriQ procedure to delete the smallest item from a nonempty priority queue, importing from ListADT and InfoADT. Assume that information is always inserted in the first location on a list.

EXAMPLE 3.9A _____

```
PROCEDURE Delete (VAR TheInfo : Information;
                  Where : Location;  VAR Data : List);
     (* Context:  circular array impl. of ListADT *)
 (*----------------------------------------------------------*)

    PROCEDURE TakeFromRear (Spot       : CARDINAL;
                            VAR Data : List);
    VAR
        K : CARDINAL;
    BEGIN
        WITH Data^ DO (* fields: Item, Size, Front, Rear *)
            IF Spot > Rear THEN      (* wrapped around *)
                FOR K := Spot TO MaxSize - 1 DO
                    Item [K] := Item [K + 1];
                END;
                Item [MaxSize] := Item [1];
                Spot := 1;
            END;
            FOR K := Spot TO Rear - 1 DO
                Item [K] := Item [K + 1];
            END;
            IF Rear = 1 THEN
                Rear := MaxSize;
            ELSE
                DEC (Rear);
            END;
        END;
    END TakeFromRear;
 (*----------------------------------------------------------*)

    PROCEDURE TakeFromFront (Spot      : CARDINAL;
                             VAR Data : List);
    END TakeFromFront;    (* left as an exercise *)
 (*----------------------------------------------------------*)

VAR
    Spot : CARDINAL;
BEGIN          (* Delete *)
    WITH Data^ DO  (* fields are Item, Size, Front, Rear *)
        IF Where <= Size THEN
            IF Where + Front - 1 <= MaxSize THEN
                Spot := Where + Front - 1;
            ELSE
                Spot := Where + Front - 1 - MaxSize;
            END;
            TheInfo := Item [Spot];
            IF Where > Size DIV 2 THEN (* take from rear *)
                TakeFromRear (Spot, Data);
            ELSE
                TakeFromFront (Spot, Data);
            END;
            DEC (Size);
        END;
    END;
END Delete;
```

199

2. Write the body of the TakeFromFront subprocedure of Delete for the circular array implementation of ListADT. *Hint:* It has exactly the same "shape" as the TakeFromRear subprocedure.

3. (NA) Write the Create procedure for the circular array implementation of ListADT.

4. (NA) Write the Modify utility procedure (described in Example 3.5B) for the circular array implementation of ListADT.

5. (NA) Discuss why execution time is shortened overall if the Create procedure of the circular array implementation of ListADT initializes Front and Rear so that Front = Rear+1 as well as setting Size to 0.

3.10 IMPLEMENTATIONS OF TableADT: TABLE LOOKUP, HASHING

The simple array implementation for TableADT is fine when there are only 10 or 20 items in the table, but it is horribly slow when there are hundreds. Many applications require greater speed. This section discusses a method of implementing TableADT that gives very fast access to the information in the table, as long as you know something about the IDs (or their equivalents) of the information values with which you are working. We start with the simple array declaration of Table:

```
TYPE  Table = POINTER TO RECORD
                Item : ARRAY [1..MaxSize] OF Information;
                Size, Loc : CARDINAL;
              END;
```

Pure Table Lookup

In the most desirable sort of situation, the ID is a cardinal up to some number that is not too much larger than the number of information records that are in the table. An example is the following situation: Each employee of a certain company is given an ID number when hired. The number given is always chosen to be the smallest positive integer not currently possessed by an employee. When the system was first instituted, each of the 274 employees was given an ID number in the range 1 through 274. When three more were hired, they were given numbers 275, 276, and 277. When five people quit, that freed the numbers 4, 82, 147, 195, and 201. So when two more people were hired, they were given the numbers 4 and 82. At this point, the IDs range from 1 through 277 for the 274 employees.

In a situation like this, the best possible implementation for TableADT is an array of perhaps 400 Information values (to allow for future expansion) with the Information for the employee with ID K stored in component K. Then Find(TheInfo, Data) could set the current location in the array to TheInfo ↑ .ID. PutIn(TheInfo, Data) can just put the information at Data ↑ .Item[TheInfo ↑ .ID]. However, we keep all references to the internal structure of Information isolated in InfoADT, so we cannot refer to TheInfo ↑ .ID within TableADT. Therefore, we have InfoADT export an additional procedure that tells the ID of a given information record. The heading of this procedure could be:

```
PROCEDURE Hash (TheInfo : Information;
                Maximum : CARDINAL) : CARDINAL;
(* Return a positive integer up to Maximum, depending solely on
   Maximum and the ID (or its equivalent), computed in such a way
   that the cardinals returned for all the information records
   are spread fairly evenly over the range from 1 to Maximum *)
```

This procedure heading is probably not what you expected at this point, since it is written to be applicable both to this situation and others discussed later. The reason for the Maximum parameter is to assure you that the number returned by the function is in the range of indices you have for your array. The comment about being spread evenly and the name Hash will be explained shortly.

This **hashing function** provides what you need for the **pure table lookup** situation just described (i.e., where Hash does not return the same number for two different information values). For instance, PutIn consists of just the one statement Data ↑ .Item[Hash(TheInfo, MaxSize)] := TheInfo. However, you cannot simply use TheInfo := Data ↑ .Item[Data ↑ .Loc]) to Inspect TheInfo in the Data table. What if the information is not in the table? Then Inspect would return an indeterminate value. You need some way of telling whether the information with a given ID is in the table. One way is to attach a Boolean variable to each Information component, as follows:

```
TYPE    Table = POINTER TO RECORD
                  Item : ARRAY [1..MaxSize] OF Information;
                  InfoThere : ARRAY [1..MaxSize] OF BOOLEAN;
                  Loc : CARDINAL;
                END;
```

Loc records the index of the value for which a search was last made. Now Create initializes every component of InfoThere to FALSE and Loc to 1. PutIn executes

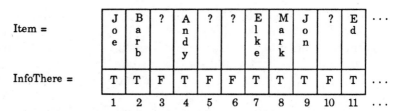

J o e	B a r b	?	A n d y	?	?	E l k e	M a r k	J o n	?	E d	...

Item =

InfoThere =

T	T	F	T	F	F	T	T	T	F	T	...
1	2	3	4	5	6	7	8	9	10	11	...

FIGURE 10. Hash table with Boolean field to tell whether information is there.

the statement Data ↑ .InfoThere[Hash(TheInfo, MaxSize)] := TRUE as well as putting the information at that component (Fig. 10). The other procedures are coded accordingly. For instance, Inspect can be:

```
IF Data↑.InfoThere [Data↑.Loc] THEN
    . TheInfo := Data↑.Item [Data↑.Loc];
END;
```

Another solution is to have InfoADT export an Information variable named NoInfo. This variable is initialized in the statement part of the implementation module and never changed; it indicates the absence of information. For instance, NoInfo might have an ID of 0 if positive integers are used. Then Create initializes every component of Item to NoInfo and Inspect is different from the foregoing coding only in testing Compare(Data ↑ .Item [Data ↑ .Loc], NoInfo)#0.

Hashing Functions

Many applications do not provide such convenient IDs. Common situations are that the ID is a name or a social security number. In such situations, there are zillions of possible IDs, although only a few hundred may be in use for the particular application.

As a concrete example, the company with 274 employees might use social security numbers as IDs instead of making up their own numbers. A social security number has 9 digits (currently), so there are slightly under a billion possible IDs. An application might instead use 10 letters as IDs—the first 9 characters of the last name, padded on the right with the @ symbol if necessary, except that employees with the same last name are given an arbitrary additional letter to distinguish them. Even if only capitals are used, the number of possibilities is nearly 27 to the tenth power.

Note: I use the @ symbol because it comes just before capital A using the ASCII code, which can simplify some computations.

In such a case, the Hash function is to compute from the ID an integer in the range 1..400 (or whatever we are using for MaxSize). For instance, if the ID is the social security number, the Hash function could return that number MOD 400, plus 1. This is called the **division method** using a divisor of 400. If the ID is a string of 10 characters that can be either capital letters or the @ sign, the ordinal number of each character ranges from 64 to 90; so you could compute a number from 1 to 400 using the ordinal numbers of all the characters, or you could use just three arbitrary characters, as in (for example):

```
(ORD (ID [0]) + 5 * ORD (ID [3]) + 11 * ORD (ID [8])) MOD MaxSize + 1
```

If you are lucky enough that the IDs used for the 274 employees (or whatever) give you 274 different values for the MaxSize you choose (such as 400), you can use the table lookup method just described with no change whatsoever. However, such luck is almost impossible, even if you were to use an array of 1000 items for 274 employees. Almost certainly there will be at least two employees whose IDs "hash" to the same number. Did you know that among 24 randomly chosen people, the probability is more than 50% that at least two of them will have the same birthday (month and day)? That is the same sort of situation as having 24 employees with their 366 different birthdays as their IDs.

The method of computing the Hash value from the ID should spread the returned values as evenly as possible over the whole range, just as a good cook making hash mixes the ingredients uniformly throughout the mixture (that is the origin of the name Hash). The even spread cuts down on the number of **collisions** (two IDs hashing to the same number).

An interesting way of hashing values is called **folding**. For instance, if a social security number is stored using three cardinal values, you can "fold" them together to make up a new cardinal by using a 1 in the binary notation for the result wherever an odd number of the three cardinals has a 1 in that place for its binary notation, using a 0 elsewhere, and then using the MOD operator to find the remainder after division by MaxSize. For instance, if the binary notation for three cardinals is 0011010110, 0010111010, and 0001001011, they are folded together to obtain 0000100111, for which the decimal notation is 39. In Modula-2, that folding is accomplished by:

```
CARDINAL ( BITSET(First) / BITSET(Second) / BITSET(Third) )
         MOD MaxSize + 1
```

In practice, however, the division method has been found to give excellent results as long as the divisor is a prime number, so the more intricate methods such as folding are often not worth developing.

Collisions

You have to be able to handle the situation where two IDs hash to the same number. The basic logic for PutIn using NoInfo is:

```
H := Hash (TheInfo, MaxSize);
IF Compare (Data↑.Item [H], NoInfo) = 0 THEN
    Data↑.Item [H] := TheInfo;
    Data↑.Loc := H;
ELSE
    PutItSomewhereElseInTheArray (TheInfo, Data, H);
END;
```

The problem is to decide where the somewhere else is. An easy way is to put it at component H+1 or, if that already has information, at component H+2 or, if that already has information, at component H+3, and so forth. (We count indices modulo MaxSize+1; that is, after MaxSize comes 1, then 2, etc.) This is called **linear probing**. It works, but unless the number of information values is under half of MaxSize, you end up with long **clusters** of values in the array, which means you could "probe" several dozen locations before you find an empty one. Example 3.10A shows a Find procedure for linear probing using the InfoThere field.

A much better way of probing is a **double hashing**: When a collision occurs at index H, you compute a new hash value NH from the key. Then you look at H+NH, then H+2*NH, then H+3*NH, and so forth until you find an empty spot. This works quite well as long as MaxSize is a prime number. As a simple example, if H is the remainder after division, NH could be the quotient.

Another way to "probe" is **quadratic probing**: Try component H+1 or, if full, try H+4 or, if that is full, try H+9 or, if that is full, try H+16, and so on, using consecutive square numbers. This avoids the clusters that linear probing gives, but it only works well if MaxSize is a prime number, and even then an adjustment has to be made if more than half the positions are probed without finding anything. The mathematical analysis is beyond the scope of this book, as are the multitudinous other probing methods.

The name for the situation in which information is stored in an array as determined by a hashing function that may return the same value for different information records is **open addressing**. I have not even mentioned all the difficulties caused by a mixture of deletions and insertions in open addressing. For instance, if TakeOut simply puts NoInfo in the appropriate component, Inspect would have to search the entire array if the given information value is not in the table. A reasonable solution is for every procedure except TakeOut to assume that no deletions have occurred, and for TakeOut to act in such a way that this assumption does no harm. That makes the algorithm for the TakeOut procedure extremely complicated, but it keeps the others simple.

EXAMPLE 3.10A _____

```
TYPE
    Table = POINTER TO RECORD
                    Item : ARRAY [1..MaxSize] OF Information;
                    InfoThere : ARRAY [1..MaxSize] OF BOOLEAN;
                    Loc : CARDINAL;
                END;
(***********************************************************)

PROCEDURE Find (TheInfo : Information; VAR Data : Table);
    (* Context:  hash table with open addressing and an
       InfoThere field.  Use linear probing *)
VAR
    K, StartingPoint : CARDINAL;
BEGIN
    Data^.Loc := 0;  (* in case it is not found *)
    StartingPoint := Hash (TheInfo, MaxSize);
    K := StartingPoint;
    IF Data^.InfoThere [K] THEN
        REPEAT
            IF Compare (Data^.Item [K], TheInfo) = 0 THEN
                Data^.Loc := K;  (* save the most recent *)
            END;
            IF K = MaxSize THEN
                K := 1;   (* circle around to the front *)
            ELSE
                INC (K);
            END;
        UNTIL (K = StartingPoint) OR
              NOT Data^.InfoThere [K];
    END;
END Find;
```

Open addressing with linear probing has a particular advantage when the information is stored externally, since the disk head often does not have to move so much. A variation called **bucket hashing** works as follows: Assume that the operating system reads and writes records four at a time and you feel that a hash table of size 800 is adequate for the number of records you have. Instead of having MaxSize=800, use MaxSize=200 (one fourth of 800). For a given hash number H, start linear probing at location 4*H−3. For instance, if the information hashes to 13, you use linear probing beginning with 49; if the information hashes to 111, you use linear probing beginning with 441. Each group of four locations is called a **bucket**. The advantage is that you can search four locations before the system must read in another block of records.

A completely different way of solving the collision problem is called **chaining**: You use an array of lists, with approximately as many lists as there are information records to store. Now collisions are no problem, because you simply put a value on the list given by its hash number. Some lists may have several items on them, but the average length of a list is 1, so searching is fast. However, array implementations of lists are inappropriate owing to the amount of space they require; you would use an implementation described in the next chapter.

Check Your Understanding

1. Write the Find procedure for pure table lookup using NoInfo.

2. Write the TableADT InTable function for open addressing with linear probing, assuming that no deletions have been made and the InfoThere field is used.

3. Write the TableADT Inspect procedure for open addressing with linear probing, assuming that no deletions have been made.

4. (NA) What is the result of "folding" the integers 17, 24, and 10 using the method described for binary notation?

5. (NA) Write the TableADT PutIn procedure for open addressing with a form of double hashing, assuming that no deletions have been made.

6. (NA) Write an essay discussing the problems involved in constructing the algorithm for the TableADT TakeOut procedure for open addressing with quadratic probing in such a way that it does no harm for the other procedures to assume that no deletions have taken place.

3.11 IMPLEMENTATION OF InfoADT WITH CURSORS

A number of popular computer languages do not have pointers available. This section discusses an alternative method of implementing InfoADT, the **cursor method,** which accomplishes much the same thing. This method resembles the way a compiler normally handles the NEW and DISPOSE operations.

The Cursor Method

If a computer language does not have pointers as a language feature, it is not difficult to do what has been described for InfoADT, but it is clumsy. Instead of List=POINTER TO RECORD Item... Size... END, you could declare List=RECORD Item... Size... END. And instead of Information=POINTER TO RECORD ID... END, you could use Information=RECORD ID... END. The problem is that a great deal of space is wasted, since a list now has MaxSize "large" Information variables instead of MaxSize "small" address variables plus Size "large" record variables. Also, it takes much more execution time to move the information in "large" variables rather than the information in "small" variables.

As a typical concrete example, make the following assumptions: One information record requires about three lines of type on the average page, equivalent to about 240 characters (i.e., 240 bytes of space), and an integer value or a pointer value just requires 2 bytes. You are programming a situation in which you keep track of stock certificates. The stockholder normally has around 100 certificates, never more than 200 at any one time. The certificates may be spread thinly among many companies, but never more than 100 companies. Or the certificates may be concentrated in just a few companies, but never more than 50 certificates for any one company.

If you use one list for each company, you need 100 lists with up to 50 certificates per list. The simple array implementation of ListADT using pointers in InfoADT (Section 3.6) requires at most 58,200 bytes: 200*240 for the up to 200 information records, plus 50*2+2 for each of 100 lists. By contrast, a straightforward implementation of a List without pointers to Information requires about 1,200,200 bytes: 50*240+2 for each of 100 lists.

Using a cursor, the space requirements can be reduced to 58,200 bytes. A **cursor** is merely an index in an array used as a substitute for a pointer. You create a large array of 200 records of 240 bytes each, which can be called StoreRoom. Each list consists of Size plus an array of 50 cardinals Item[1]... Item[Size] as before, but now the information values are the indices of the components of StoreRoom that contain the information for that list. Figure 11 shows how things might be for two lists, one with 4 items on it and the other with 2 items on it.

Algorithms for Cursors Using Boolean Markers

The primary problem to consider is how to tell which components of the StoreRoom array are available for use when a new Information record is called for. Perhaps the most straightforward way is to mark each component TRUE or FALSE. That is, you can use a Boolean array and, for instance, mark the thirteenth component TRUE or FALSE depending on whether component 13 is in use. When you want to "create" a new information record, you search until you find an unoccupied component, then mark it TRUE and return the index of that

Assume that at a certain point in the program List A has 4 items, which happen to be stored in components 3, 6, 1, 4 of the StoreRoom array, in that order. Assume that List B has 2 items, in components 5 and 8. We use an arrow to indicate the component of which a particular list element is the index:

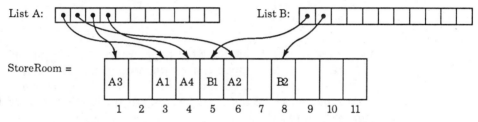

FIGURE 11. *A list as an array of cursors into a large StoreRoom array.*

component. When you want to "destroy" an information record, you mark it
FALSE. The key declarations for this implementation could be:

```
TYPE  Information = CARDINAL;
VAR   StoreRoom : ARRAY [1..MaxInfos] OF
         RECORD
               Info : RECORD ... (whatever is appropriate) END;
               Occupied : BOOLEAN;
         END;
```

Just before the END InfoADT in the implementation module, you initialize the
StoreRoom to have all components unoccupied. This initialization code will be
executed before any client module begins execution:

```
BEGIN  (* body of InfoADT implementation module *)
    FOR K := 1 TO MaxInfos DO
        StoreRoom [K].Occupied := FALSE;
    END;
END InfoADT.
```

The procedure call CreateInfo(TheInfo) is supposed to return an indicator of a
record in which information can be stored. The following coding should work
(albeit slowly) for the body of CreateInfo:

```
FOR K := 1 TO MaxInfos DO  (* UNTIL RETURN *)
    IF NOT StoreRoom [K].Occupied THEN
        TheInfo := K;
        StoreRoom [TheInfo].Occupied := TRUE;
        RETURN;
    END;
END;
```

This coding does not provide for what happens when all components are occupied. This should never happen if the programmer has correctly calculated the
maximum space requirements. But just in case, you should append statements to
this coding that write an appropriate message to the terminal, as in the Push
procedure of Example 3.3A.

The procedure calls DestroyInfo(TheInfo) and CopyInfo(TheInfo, Source) need only execute one statement each. The bodies of the procedures would be:

```
DestroyInfo:   StoreRoom [TheInfo].Occupied := FALSE;
CopyInfo:      StoreRoom [TheInfo].Info := StoreRoom [Source].Info;
```

The other procedures in InfoADT are highly dependent on the structure of an information record. In general, references to TheInfo↑ in the pointer form of InfoADT would simply be replaced by references to StoreRoom[TheInfo].Info in the cursor form. For instance, ReadCard(StoreRoom[TheInfo].Info.ID) is used in place of ReadCard(TheInfo↑.ID). In other words, you refer to "the information whose index is in TheInfo" instead of "the information whose address is in TheInfo." *Note:* For compilers that disallow CARDINAL as an opaque type, you would have to declare TYPE Information=ADDRESS; but you can still do CARDINAL arithmetic with ADDRESS values.

Cursor Implementation Using a Stack

For the implementation just described, the CreateInfo procedure is very slow. If CreateInfo is called when 150 of the 200 components are in use, almost all the 150 will be at the beginning of the array, so the FOR loop may have to make 150 iterations before it finds an unoccupied spot. One solution is to have CreateInfo start its search from where it left off last. This requires a private global variable to keep track of that spot, initialized to 1 in the body of InfoADT. Another solution is to keep all unoccupied spots in a stack. CreateInfo then pops an available information record off the stack and DestroyInfo pushes one onto the stack. This speeds up CreateInfo enormously, slows DestroyInfo only slightly, and has no effect on the other procedures. I discuss this method next.

In the declaration of StoreRoom, replace the Boolean Occupied field by a CARDINAL field named Link. This Link field is to contain the index of the StoreRoom component that is below it in the stack of available nodes (assign it 0 if it is on the bottom of the stack). Assume that Available is a private global variable that keeps track of the index of the StoreRoom component on the top of the stack. Then CreateInfo can be coded as:

```
TheInfo := Available;
Available := StoreRoom [Available].Link;
```

As mentioned before, we could allow for running out of space in the array by guarding this two-statement sequence by IF Available#0 THEN and writing appropriate messages to the terminal in the ELSE part. The DestroyInfo procedure would return a component to the stack of available components:

```
StoreRoom [TheInfo].Link := Available;
Available := TheInfo;
```

This implementation of InfoADT (Fig. 12) obviously executes much faster. Available has to be properly initialized to the index of the top of a stack containing all the records, but that only takes about as long as the initialization for the Occupied implementation did (see Check Your Understanding). This implementation also uses a certain amount of space for the Link fields, at least as much as the Occupied values took. But if you declare StoreRoom as an array of variant records, that space would not be lost, since the Link field is used only when the Info field is not being used. In fact, the only change would be in the declaration of StoreRoom; the statements of the implementation do not change at all.

These techniques can be applied to any pointer type, not just Information. For instance, Chapter 4 discusses TYPE PointerToNode = POINTER TO Node, where Node is a record type. You can use cursors instead if you declare PointerToNode = CARDINAL, declare an array of Nodes, and manage your own storage. If you are using a language that does not allow an array of records, you use several arrays, one for each field.

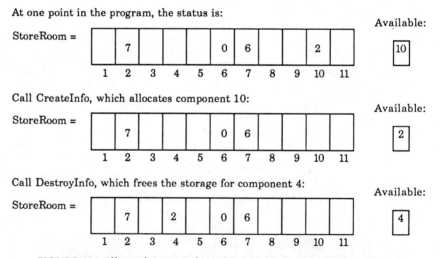

FIGURE 12. Effect of CreateInfo and DestroyInfo using the StoreRoom.

Check Your Understanding

1. Assume that each information record requires 300 bytes of storage, an integer or pointer requires 2 bytes, and the application requires at most 40 lists with never more than 60 items on any one list and never more than 300 items altogether. Compute the amount of space required for the direct implementation (no cursors or pointers) versus the amount required for a cursor implementation.

2. Write the body of InfoADT using the Link/Available implementation, to initialize the stack appropriately.

3. Write the CopyInfo procedure using the Link/Available implementation.

4. (NA) Write the CreateInfo procedure and the body of InfoADT for the variation of the Occupied implementation in which CreateInfo begins the sequential search for an unoccupied spot at the point where it last left off.

3.12 APPLICATION: APPOINTMENT BOOK

The program in this section maintains an appointment book as a linear list of names, dates, and locations. However, the program is written with sufficient generality that Information could be any type. Also, the program can be used for other kinds of lists besides appointments.

Some of the programming problems at the end of this chapter and the next ask you to write a particular implementation for ListADT; the program developed in this section is useful for testing your implementation, since it calls on all the primitive procedures in ListADT. It also calls on the Seek and ReadAll utility procedures, so you need to have those in your ListADT modules as well.

The Overall Logic of the Program

The first time that the user runs this program, she enters various appointments in a list and saves them on a floppy disk. From time to time, the user runs the program again, inserting and deleting various appointments on the list, then saves the updated list in an external file. So the overall logic is:

Algorithm for the Appointment Book Program
1. Create an empty list in which to store various appointments;
2. Read the current list of appointments from a file, if desired;
3. Make whatever changes in the list the user requests;
4. Write the updated list to a file.

In Modula-2, the OpenInput procedure lets the user provide the name of the file that contains the data, so the file can be read. If the user does not provide a name, or if the name provided is invalid, the reading should be omitted.

The Create procedure and the ReadAll and WriteAll utility procedures take care of all but Step 3 of the overall algorithm. I have included the WriteAll procedure in the program using imports from ListADT as a way of testing some of the ListADT procedures.

Making Changes in the List as Requested

Now we can consider accepting requests from the user for changes in the list. The user should be allowed to insert or delete one appointment at any one position in the list. Obviously, the user is going to want to see what appointments are in the list from time to time, so we should also provide that option. Therefore, we ask the user to indicate which of four choices she wishes:

- ☐ Insert at a particular position on the current list.
- ☐ Delete at a particular position on the current list.
- ☐ Show what the entire list looks like at this point.
- ☐ Exit from the program.

The easiest way to handle a choice like this is with a **menu**: Tell the user the permissible choices and ask for a single character that indicates the choice. I will use 'i', 'd', and 's' for "insert," "delete," and "show," respectively. To simplify things, any other choice indicates a wish to exit the program. If the user chooses 'i' or 'd', she must also choose the position in the list where the change is to be made. The easiest way to do that is to ask for a position number and convert that to a Location. Seek is the utility function that makes the conversion.

Algorithm for making changes at the user's request
DO until time to STOP:
    1. Ask user for a single character: 'i', 'd', 's', or other;
    2. IF it is 's', then:
        Show the entire list as it currently stands;
      OTHERWISE, IF it is 'i' or 'd', then:
        Ask for the position number where the change is to be made;
        Make the change: insert if 'i', delete if 'd';
      OTHERWISE:
      STOP.

If the user requests 's' for show, you write the entire list using the WriteAll procedure. If the user requests an insertion, you have to get the information from the keyboard and insert it in the list at the specified position. If the user requests a deletion, you have to first check that the specified position is in the current list. If it is, you delete the information and display it on the screen; if not, you give an appropriate message. Example 3.12A contains the complete program.

Check Your Understanding

1. What changes would be necessary in Example 3.12A to allow the user to enter 'e' and have information she enters be enqueued on the list (i.e., put at the rear of the list)?

2. Why is the call of DestroyInfo in the MakeThisOneChange subprocedure? Why is there no call of CreateInfo before calling InputInfo in that subprocedure?

3. When the list is fairly long, the WriteAll procedure should print a line number at the beginning of each line of output. What changes would be required to accomplish this? Note that, if an Information value is a string of characters, this makes Example 3.12A into a primitive line editor.

4. (NA) What changes would be necessary in Example 3.12A to allow the user to enter 'q' and have information she enters be dequeued from the list (i.e., taken from the front of the list)?

5. (NA) The REPEAT statement in Example 3.12A tests Ch against each of 'i', 'd', and 's' twice for each input. A WHILE statement cannot avoid this redundancy, but a LOOP statement can easily. Revise the REPEAT statement as a LOOP statement appropriately.

3.13 AXIOMATICS

The various definition modules given in this chapter export certain types and certain procedures. A client module is not to do anything with an object of one of the exported types except through the procedures provided. Since the implementation is not available, it is crucial that the effect and interaction of the various procedures be clearly described. I have done that by referring to concepts with which everyone should be familiar, such as restaurant trays and standing in line at a movie. However, there is a chance that some people might think something slightly different is intended; it would be best if the meaning could be given so there is no question what is meant. Axiomatics provides this possibility.

EXAMPLE 3.12A _____

```
MODULE AppointmentBook;
(* Read a list from a file, make changes as directed by the
    user, and then write the revised list to a new file. *)
(* Written by William C. Jones, October 19-- *)
FROM InOut   IMPORT OpenInput, CloseInput, WriteString,
                    WriteLn, OpenOutput, CloseOutput,
                    ReadCard, Read, Done;
FROM InfoADT IMPORT Information, DestroyInfo,
                    InputInfo, OutputInfo;
FROM ListADT IMPORT List, Location, Create, Destroy,
                    FirstLocation, NextLocation, InList,
                    LookAt, Insert, Delete, Seek, ReadAll;
(***********************************************************)

PROCEDURE WriteAll (Data : List);
    (* Copy the List to the output file, in order *)
VAR
    TheInfo : Information;
    Where   : Location;
BEGIN
    Where := FirstLocation (Data);
    WHILE InList (Where, Data) DO
        LookAt (TheInfo, Where, Data);
        OutputInfo (TheInfo);
        Where := NextLocation (Where, Data);
    END;
END WriteAll;
(***********************************************************)

PROCEDURE ModifyListAsToldByUser (VAR Data : List);
  (*  Insert and Delete information as specified by user *)
  (*---------------------------------------------------*)

    PROCEDURE MakeThisOneChange (TheChange : CHAR;
                                 Where     : Location);
        (* Insert or delete at the specified location *)
    VAR
        TheInfo : Information;
    BEGIN
        IF TheChange = 'i' THEN
            WriteString ('Enter the information now: ');
            InputInfo (TheInfo);
            Insert (TheInfo, Where, Data);
        ELSIF InList (Where, Data) THEN
            Delete (TheInfo, Where, Data);
            WriteString ('The information there was: ');
            OutputInfo (TheInfo);
            DestroyInfo (TheInfo);
        ELSE
            WriteString ('No information at that place.');
            WriteLn;
        END;
    END MakeThisOneChange;
  (*---------------------------------------------------*)


(* continued on next page *)
```

```
(* EXAMPLE 3.12A continued *)


VAR
      Ch, Junk : CHAR;
      Position : CARDINAL;

BEGIN         (* ModifyListAsToldByUser *)

    REPEAT
        WriteString ('Enter:  i = insert, d = delete, ');
        WriteString ('s = show list, other to quit: ');
        Read (Ch);
        Read (Junk);   (* the end-of-line *)

        IF Ch = 's' THEN
            WriteAll (Data);
        ELSIF (Ch = 'i') OR (Ch = 'd') THEN
            WriteString ('At what position number? ');
            ReadCard (Position);
            MakeThisOneChange (Ch, Seek (Position, Data));
        END;
    UNTIL (Ch # 'i') AND (Ch # 'd') AND (Ch # 's');

END ModifyListAsToldByUser;
(*********************************************************)

VAR
    Data : List;

BEGIN         (* program *)

    OpenInput ('');
    IF Done THEN
        ReadAll (Data);
        CloseInput;
    ELSE
        Create (Data);          (* start with an empty list *)
    END;

    ModifyListAsToldByUser (Data);

    OpenOutput ('');
    WriteAll (Data);
    CloseOutput;

END AppointmentBook.
```

Rephrasing of Definition Modules

This material is much easier to discuss when all procedures exported from the definition module are function procedures. That is obviously not the case for the modules in this chapter. It is worthwhile rewriting these definition modules to accomplish this. However, the redefinitions in this section are not used anywhere else in this book.

Consider **StackAX**, a definition module much the same as StackADT except that all exported procedures are function procedures with no VAR parameters. It is also convenient to have StackAX export the Information type. The exports from StackAX are:

```
DEFINITION MODULE StackAX;
TYPE Information;
TYPE Stack;
PROCEDURE Create () : Stack;
PROCEDURE IsEmpty (D : Stack) : BOOLEAN;
PROCEDURE Push (x : Information;  D : Stack) : Stack;
PROCEDURE Peep (D : Stack) : Information;
PROCEDURE Pop (D : Stack) : Stack;
END StackAX.
```

This StackAX module is missing Destroy, since I want to ignore it for this section (it is only used for space-saving purposes, anyway). Otherwise, all the capabilities of StackADT are included here. To initialize an empty Stack, you use D := Create() instead of Create(D). IsEmpty is the same as in StackADT. To Push the Information x onto the Stack D, you use D := Push(x,D) instead of the statement Push(x,D). To Peep at the Information on the top of the stack, you use x := Peep(D) instead of Peep(x,D). Pop does not return an information value, it only returns the slightly smaller stack. However, you can get the information by using Peep. Thus, instead of using Pop(x,D) you use two statements: x := Peep(D); D := Pop(D). *Note:* Functions cannot be used in place of statement procedures if either Stack or Information is declared as a record type; both are expected to be declared as pointer types.

Axioms for StackAX

A set of axioms is a group of statements about the results of calling certain functions for certain values, which as a group give a complete specification of the meaning of those functions. Now, did that make much sense on first reading? You really have to see some examples of axioms to understand what is going on. For instance, the following is a complete set of four axioms for StackAX:

1. When you Create a Stack, that Stack is empty.
2. When you Push something on a Stack, that Stack is not empty.
3. When you Push something on a Stack and then Pop that resulting Stack, the Stack you get is the Stack with which you started.
4. When you Push something on a Stack and then Peep that resulting Stack, the Information you get is the Information you pushed.

This phrasing of the axioms still leaves a little to be desired, since it refers to "on" a Stack, which makes reference to the intuitive concept of a Stack. Axioms should be more abstract than that. The following list is a restatement of the four axioms. Note that the first-in-first-out property of stacks is embodied in axioms 3 and 4.

AXIOMS FOR StackAX. For any Information value x and any valid Stack value D:

```
IsEmpty ( Create() ) = TRUE.
IsEmpty ( Push(x,D) ) = FALSE.
Pop ( Push(x,D) ) = D.
Peep ( Push(x,D) ) = x.
```

The definition of a valid Stack value is:

1. Create() is a valid Stack value.
2. Pop(x,D) and Push(x,D) are valid Stack values if D is.
3. No other value is a valid Stack value.

Testing and Using Axioms

The question arises, "How can you prove that this group of statements completely describes the properties of stacks?" The answer is, you cannot. You can study them to make sure you agree they should be true about any implementation of stacks. You can test a set of axioms to see if they are adequate to prove other statements that should be true about any implementation of stacks. But a set of axioms is the starting point for proofs and not subject to proof itself.

For a small example of testing the axioms, consider this statement: If you create a stack, execute Push twice for that stack, then execute Pop twice for that stack, you should end up with an empty stack. That is, you should be able to prove the following statement from the axioms (the marks below the statement are just there to facilitate the discussion):

```
IsEmpty ( Pop ( Pop ( Push (x, Push (y, Create() ) ) ) ) ) = TRUE
        .        |              ,                    ,      |  .
```

The part between the | marks is of the form required by axiom 3, with the part between the commas in the role of D. Thus Axiom 3 says that the part between | marks can be replaced by the part between commas, which gives you:

```
IsEmpty ( Pop ( Push (y, Create() ) ) ) = TRUE
         .        ,                    , .
```

Now the part between periods is of the form required by axiom 3, with Create() in the role of D. Thus Axiom 3 says that the part between periods can be replaced by Create(), which gives you:

```
IsEmpty ( Create() ) = TRUE
```

Axiom 1 tells you this statement is true, so the set of axioms is adequate to prove the original statement is true.

What else are axioms good for? They can help you verify that a particular implementation is correct. For instance, the simple array implementation for StackADT, with slight modifications for StackAX, can be shown to be logically correct. Create assigns 0 to Data ↑ .Size and IsEmpty tests Data ↑ .Size=0. Therefore IsEmpty(Create()) is TRUE. Push adds 1 to Data ↑ .Size when it is less than MaxSize. Since Data ↑ .Size is a CARDINAL and you cannot get 0 by adding 1 to any cardinal, it follows that IsEmpty(Push(x,S)) will be false unless MaxSize is 0. That shows that MaxSize must be a positive number for the implementation to be correct.

To verify that axiom 3 holds for this implementation, note that a Push followed by a Pop executes four statements: Add 1 to Size, assign x to Item[Size], assign Item[Size] to x, and subtract 1 from Size. That verifies axiom 3 except in the case when Size=MaxSize. Therefore, the implementation violates the axioms if a Push is attempted when Size=MaxSize. The check for axiom 4 is similar.

The conclusion is: The simple array implementation of StackAX is a valid implementation as long as MaxSize is a positive integer and Push is not executed for any stack with MaxSize information values.

QueueAX

The **QueueAX** definition module is exactly the same as StackAX except that "Stack" changes to "Queue" and Push/Pop change to Enqueue/Dequeue.

```
DEFINITION MODULE QueueAX;
TYPE Information;
TYPE Queue;
PROCEDURE Create () : Queue;
```

```
PROCEDURE IsEmpty (D : Queue) : BOOLEAN;
PROCEDURE Enqueue (x : Information;  D : Queue) : Queue;
PROCEDURE Peep (D : Queue) : Information;
PROCEDURE Dequeue (D : Queue) : Queue;
END QueueAX.
```

A reasonable set of axioms for QueueAX is more complex than one for StackAX. The following set is analogous to the ones given earlier. The translation to ordinary English is left as an exercise.

AXIOMS FOR QUEUEAX. For any Information value x and any valid Queue value D:

```
IsEmpty ( Create() ) = TRUE.
IsEmpty ( Enqueue(x,D) ) = FALSE.
IF IsEmpty (D) THEN
    Dequeue ( Enqueue (x,D) ) = D
ELSE
    Dequeue ( Enqueue (x,D) ) = Enqueue (x, Dequeue(D) )
END.
IF IsEmpty (D) THEN
    Peep ( Enqueue (x,D) ) = x
ELSE
    Peep ( Enqueue (x,D) ) = Peep (D)
END.
```

A valid Queue value is defined as for Stacks, except that Enqueue and Dequeue replace Push and Pop in the definition.

Axioms 3 and 4 embody the first-in-first-out property of queues. Further discussion of QueueAX and a set of axioms for ListAX is going too far afield from the scope of this book.

Check Your Understanding

1. (NA) Write a translation of the axioms for QueueAX in ordinary English, similar to the list that occurs just before the axioms for StackAX.

2. (NA) Show that all capabilities of QueueADT except Destroy are available through QueueAX.

CHAPTER REVIEW

A Stack is a data type for which the distinguishing operations are Push and Pop. A Queue has the corresponding operations Enqueue and Dequeue. For a List they are called Insert and Delete; for a Table they are called PutIn and TakeOut. In addition, each of the four library modules contains Peep (or LookAt or Inspect), Create, and Destroy. IsEmpty is in StackADT and QueueADT; TableADT has Find and InTable instead.

Create, Destroy, IsEmpty, and InTable have just one parameter, the data structure. Each of the other procedures in StackADT, QueueADT, and TableADT has an Information parameter and a data structure parameter. For ListADT, each of Insert, LookAt, and Delete has an additional Location parameter that tells where the action is to take place.

The item deleted (popped) from a Stack is the one most recently put on the Stack. The item deleted (dequeued) from a Queue is the one least recently put on the Queue. The item deleted from a Table is the one with the ID (or whatever) you specify; in case of ties, the most recently inserted one is deleted.

The item deleted from a List is the one at the location you specify. For this reason, ListADT has three additional procedures for manipulating locations, namely FirstLocation, NextLocation, and InList. Lists are the most general form of structure presented in this chapter, in the sense that an implementation of any of the other structures can easily be obtained by importing from ListADT.

Overall, StackADT and QueueADT each have six primitive procedures; TableADT has seven, and ListADT has eight. Several utility procedures are commonly added to these library modules, among which are:

- [ ] ReadAll(Data) creates Data and then reads all information (using InputInfo) and inserts it in Data in the order read, with the first information value at the beginning (top or front) of the list.

- [ ] WriteAll(Data) writes all information in Data (using OutputInfo) without changing Data; the order is determined by Pop for stacks, by Dequeue for queues, and from the first location on down for lists.

- [ ] Search(TheInfo,Data) for ListADT returns the location of TheInfo in Data.

You studied the simple array implementation of each of these four abstract data types. This is probably the easiest implementation to understand. You also saw the Front/Rear implementation of QueueADT, the ordered array and hashing implementations of TableADT, the reverse and circular array implementations of ListADT, and the cursor implementation of InfoADT. Later chapters contain more implementations of these library modules.

DictiADT adds two procedures to TableADT: FindFirstIn(Data) finds the "smallest" value, and FindNextIn(Data) advances to the next smallest one. The ordered array implementation can be used for DictiADT. Two additional utility procedures, ReadTable and WriteTable, facilitate long-term storage.

A hash function accepts an information value and a positive number and returns a cardinal from 1 up to the given positive number. This is used for implementations of TableADT in which each information value is put in an array at the component whose index is the number the hash function returns. This is the fastest implementation of TableADT as long as there are no collisions (two information values with the same hash result). Collisions make life much more difficult.

Additional sections in this chapter presented Polish notation, discussed an application of ListADT to make an appointment book, and gave a brief introduction to the concept of axiomatics.

PRACTICE TEST

To prepare for a test, study the indicated examples thoroughly until you can be sure that you would earn a high grade on a test composed solely of these exercises.

1. Write the Reverse procedure importing from StackADT—reverse the order of the values in a given stack. [Example 3.1B]

2. Write the Pop procedure within StackADT using the simple array implementation. [Example 3.3A]

3. Write the Dequeue procedure within QueueADT using the simple array implementation. [Example 3.4B]

4. Write the Dequeue procedure within QueueADT using the circular array implementation. [Example 3.4C]

5. Write the Join procedure importing from QueueADT. [Exercise 1 of Section 3.4]

6. Write the recursive PrintReverse procedure, which prints all values at Where and later in reverse order, importing from ListADT. [Example 3.5C]

7. Write the Insert procedure within ListADT using the simple array implementation. [Example 3.6A]

8. Write the Find procedure for the naive layered implementation of TableADT. [Example 3.8A]

9. Write the FindFirstIn procedure for the ordered array implementation of DictiADT. [Example 3.8C]

PROGRAMMING PROBLEMS

1. Write the stockholder program described at the beginning of Section 3.1. Import from StackADT and InfoADT as needed.

2. Write the postfix evaluation program described in Section 3.2.

3. Write the prefix evaluation program described in Section 3.2.

4. Write a full implementation module for QueueADT based on the circular array implementation used for Example 3.4C; or use one of the alternative implementations with a Boolean variable or a restriction of MaxSize-1 on the number of items, as your instructor specifies.

5. Write a full implementation module for QueueADT based on the circular array implementation used for Example 3.4C, except that when it is time to add an item and Rear=MaxSize, you shift all records down so that Front becomes 1.

6. Write a full implementation module for either StackADT, QueueADT, DequeADT (for deques), or PrioQADT (for priority queues), using imports from ListADT, as your instructor specifies.

7. Write a full definition and implementation module for RingADT, to implement rings as described in Section 3.7. Take special care with the comments in the definition module; they are very important. Use an array implementation that is efficient under the assumption that Advances will occur hundreds of times more frequently than Enrings and Derings, and write a short paper defending your choice of implementation.

8. Rewrite the DeleteOldest procedure in Example 3.7B nonrecursively, using a local Table variable in which to store all information values matching the given one. When you have removed them all, put all but the last one back in the original table.

9. Write a full library module to replace TableADT with different semantics, as follows: Include Modify as a utility but omit Find; add a Boolean out parameter to TakeOut, Inspect, and Modify. Export an Information variable Ident that is initialized to a fixed information record. Each call to TakeOut, Inspect, or Modify must be preceded by filling that record in sufficiently to allow the use of Compare to find the matching record. None of TakeOut, Inspect, or Modify directly affects the contents of the fixed information record. Instead, TakeOut moves a record from the list to TheInfo; Inspect stores the address of a record in TheInfo; and Modify swaps the record in the Table with TheInfo (TheInfo can be Ident for the Modify procedure). This way, TakeOut does not destroy any information record.

10. Write a full wait-and-see array implementation for TableADT, as described in Section 3.8.

11. Write a full implementation module for ListADT using the reverse array implementation discussed in Section 3.9. Include the Push, Pop, Enqueue, Dequeue, Peep, Join, ReadAll, and Seek utilities. Use the program in Example 3.12A to test your module.

12. At a military base, people put their ID cards in a slot by the gate each time they go in or out. A computer program records the information on the card. That information includes an ID number unique to that person, as well as the name, rank, and department (strings of 1 to 20 characters). Not more than 400 different ID cards exist, but there may be thousands of card usages in a given day (people going out for lunch, etc.) The program maintains at all times a list of all people currently inside the base. Insertion of a special card with an ID number of 0 causes the up-to-date list to be printed. The program runs continuously on a dedicated microcomputer. Write the program, using TableADT and InfoADT. Simulate insertions of ID cards by reading from a text file.

13. Write a driver program to test out a specific implementation of TableADT. This program can be similar to the program in Example 3.12A. It should accept 'i', 'd', 'p', or 'm' as commands and call PutIn, TakeOut, Inspect, or the utility Modify accordingly. The program should also accept 'w' as a command and write out the entire contents of the table (using a utility). An information value can be an integer. You can test the driver with an implementation of TableADT described in this chapter, then save it to test the search tree implementation of TableADT described in Chapter 5.

14. Write the Insert procedure for the circular array implementation of ListADT described in Section 3.9.

15. Write the full implementation module for TableADT assuming pure table lookup with either the InfoThere array or the NoInfo variable, as your instructor specifies. See Section 3.10 for definitions.

16. Write the full implementation module for TableADT using open addressing with quadratic probing. *Implementation restriction:* Write TakeOut so that the other procedures can assume that no deletions have been made.

17. Write an implementation module for ListADT that imports from QueueADT (assuming you already have an implementation for QueueADT) and declares: List = POINTER TO RECORD Q: Queue; Size, Loc: CARDINAL; END; Location=CARDINAL. Size tells the number of items in the list, which is also the number of items in the queue. The queue consists of the values at locations number Loc through Size of the list followed by the values at locations number 1 through Loc−1. Thus Insert(X, 5, Data) enqueues X if Loc

is 5 (and adds 1 to Size and Loc); but if Loc=2, Insert(X, 5, Data) will dequeue three values and re-enqueue them before enqueueing X.

18. Write a program to write out all partitions of a given positive integer. A **partition** of N is a listing of one or more positive integers in nondecreasing order with the sum N. For instance, the seven partitions of 5 are: 5, 1+4, 2+3, 1+1+3, 1+2+2, 1+1+1+2, 1+1+1+1+1. Use a stack, and generate partitions in the order indicated by this example.

4

LINKED LIST IMPLEMENTATIONS OF FUNDAMENTAL DATA STRUCTURES

The use of an array to store a list in consecutive storage locations has two big disadvantages: One is that the insertion or deletion of an item usually requires moving many other items to make room; sometimes you have to move all of them. The other disadvantage is in space requirements; if you have L lists each of which could have as many as N items on it, you need space for L*N information values, even though the total number of information values in existence at any given time might be much less.

Pointers can be used to create a data structure whose size changes during execution of the program and whose elements are not stored in consecutive storage locations; this avoids both disadvantages. Section 4.1 develops the logic behind such a use of pointers, with an implementation of StackADT. Section 4.2 discusses applications of pointers, including some stack utilities and an implementation of TableADT. The next two sections are devoted to developing an implementation of ListADT using linked lists, which is given in its complete form in Example 4.4A. This is called the **standard linked list implementation**. Later sections discuss alternative implementations of several abstract data types.

This is the first chapter with emphasis on the development of complex algorithms, so the chapter also reviews tactics for developing algorithms easily. Presumably, you have learned such tactics to a significant extent in an earlier course. *Note:* To reinforce concepts involving pointers, Section 4.1 begins with a review of most things said earlier about them.

4.1 DEFINITION OF A LINKED LIST

You can use a built-in procedure NEW to create variables as needed. These variables stay in existence until the built-in procedure DISPOSE is called to free the space used. Thus you can change the amount of computer memory you are using during execution of the program. A variable created using NEW is called a **dynamic variable**. By way of contrast, a variable that is declared in a VAR section is called a **static variable**. In the following discussion, I take as an example variables of InfoRecord type, declared as follows:

```
TYPE    InfoRecord =
            RECORD
                ID, CreditHours : CARDINAL;
                AmtOwed         : REAL;
                Name            : ARRAY [0..StrMax] OF CHAR;
                IsFullTime      : BOOLEAN;
            END;
```

Using Pointer Variables

We use a type of variable in which we can store the *address* of the variable that we create, that is, a reference to the location in the computer's memory where the value of that variable is stored. A variable that contains an address is called a **pointer variable**, because it "points to" another variable.

For example, assume that P is the identifier of a variable that can contain the address of an InfoRecord variable. This requires the declaration VAR P: POINTER TO InfoRecord. Then the statement NEW(P) does two things: It causes the creation of a brand-new dynamic variable of InfoRecord type and it assigns to P the address of that InfoRecord variable. We can then refer to the address of this InfoRecord variable using P.

The way we refer to the InfoRecord whose address is stored in P is P ↑ . For instance, if X is an identifer for an InfoRecord, a reasonable sequence of statements would be NEW(P); P ↑ := X. These two statements create a new InfoRecord and then assign the contents of X to that new variable. It would be a logic error to execute X := P ↑ immediately after creating P ↑, because P ↑ contains no known value at that point; it is indeterminate. But the following sequence of statements would be reasonable:

```
NEW (P);
P↑.ID := GivenID;
P↑.IsFullTime := TRUE;
P↑.Name := 'Ed Lee';
P↑.AmtOwed := 13747.32;
P↑.CreditHours := 3;
X := P↑;
```

The Cardboard Box Analogy

It would perhaps be helpful to imagine a variable of InfoRecord type as a large cardboard box suitable for storing one InfoRecord (Name, ID, etc.). Imagine also a pointer variable to be a tiny cardboard box suitable for storing a sheet of paper with an address written on it. When you declare X as an InfoRecord variable in a VAR section, you are creating an empty large cardboard box and writing the name "X" on the outside of that box. Similarly, declaring P as POINTER TO InfoRecord creates an empty tiny cardboard box and writes the name P on the outside of that box.

The statement NEW(P) creates an empty large cardboard box but does not write any name on the outside of that box—the box remains *anonymous*. Instead, the address of that newly created box is written on a sheet of paper and placed in the tiny cardboard box named P. If there was already a sheet of paper in that tiny box, it is crumpled up and thrown away. The statement P ↑ := X copies all the information from the large box named X into the anonymous large box whose address is stored in the tiny box named P.

If P and Q are both pointers to InfoRecord variables, the statement P := Q makes a copy of the sheet of paper in Q and puts that copy in P (if there was already a sheet in P, it is crumpled up and thrown away). But the statement P ↑ := Q ↑ copies all the information from the large box whose address is stored in Q into the large box whose address is stored in P. P ↑ := Q ↑ does not change the addresses stored in P and Q, and P := Q does not change the contents of any InfoRecord variable. The statement DISPOSE(P) takes the large box whose address is written on the sheet of paper in P and throws that box back into a storeroom of boxes (the place where NEW goes to look for an empty box).

Creating New Pointer Variables Dynamically

Each InfoRecord variable that is created dynamically must have its address stored in a pointer variable. So if the number of pointer variables is limited at the time of compilation, the number of usable InfoRecord variables is also limited. The solution to this problem is to declare a new kind of record, called a **node** in common parlance. It has two fields: One field is for storing an InfoRecord, and the other is a pointer variable. That pointer variable will contain the address of a node.

```
TYPE    PointerToNode = POINTER TO Node;
        Node = RECORD
                    Info : InfoRecord;
                    Link : PointerToNode;
               END;
```

It is permissible to use a type-identifier directly following POINTER TO before that identifier is declared. This is an exception to the general rule that an identifier must be declared before it is used in another declaration; but you are required to declare that type-identifier within the same TYPE section.

With these declarations, you can create as many InfoRecord variables as you wish, simultaneously creating pointers for them. First you create one PointerToNode in a VAR section. Then you use NEW to create a Node and store its address in that one PointerToNode variable. Then you use NEW again to create a *second* Node and store its address in the Link field of the *first* Node. Then you use NEW again to create a *third* Node and store its address in the Link field of the *second* Node. Then you use NEW again to create a *fourth* Node and store its address in the Link field of the *third* Node, and so on.

This creates a chain of InfoRecords with each one linked to the next. Such a chain is called a **linked list**. You can then access the whole list of (possibly hundreds of) InfoRecords by starting from the one PointerToNode and progressing through the list, using the Link fields.

The NIL Value

There is no point in creating a linked list of records unless you are going to access the information in some way. The obvious method is to start at the beginning of the linked list and process each InfoRecord until you get to the end of the list. But how do you tell when you are at the end of the list?

The last Node on the list is not to have the address of a Node in its Link field. You indicate this "address of no Node" by assigning the built-in constant value **NIL** to that pointer variable. In the cardboard box analogy, NIL corresponds to a blank sheet of paper stored in a tiny cardboard box. In many applications, it serves as a sentinel value.

Assume, for instance, that the linked list is to have only four nodes in it, as shown in Figure 1. The Link field of the fourth node is then assigned the value NIL. When anything is done with the list, going from one node to the next, the

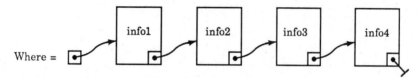

Where =

FIGURE 1. *This is how things look after NEW has been used four times. Each little box holds the address of the next big box. The address of a big box is denoted by an arrow pointing to that big box. The last little box contains NIL.*

value NIL in the Link field of the fourth node will be used by the algorithm to determine that it is time to stop. This is a linked list in "standard form"—the Link field in each node contains the address of the next node, except that the last node has NIL in its Link field.

Implementing StackADT Using Linked Lists

A stack is easily implemented using a linked list. We use one node for each information value in the stack. The first node contains the Information on top of the stack, that is, the one that is obtained when Pop or Peep is called. The second node contains the Information that would be obtained on the second of two consecutive calls of Pop, and so forth. *Note:* Henceforth I make no assumptions about whether Information is a record (such as InfoRecord, defined earlier) or is a pointer to such a record or has some other structure.

A Stack is defined to be the address of the first node in the linked list. If you have an empty stack, it should of course have no nodes. This is indicated by assigning NIL to the Stack variable. Thus the following type declarations (or their equivalent) are used:

```
TYPE    PointerToNode = POINTER TO Node;
        Stack = PointerToNode;
        Node = RECORD
                    Info : Information;
                    Link : PointerToNode;
               END;
```

StackADT exports six procedures as well as the declaration of Stack: Create, IsEmpty, Destroy, Peep, Push, and Pop. The implementations of four of these procedures are fairly trivial:

☐ Create is supposed to cause a given Stack variable Data to indicate an empty stack. So it has the single statement Data := NIL.

☐ IsEmpty is to tell whether a given Stack variable Data is currently empty. So it need only execute RETURN Data=NIL.

☐ Destroy is to deallocate dynamic space taken up by an empty Stack named Data. Since an empty stack has no nodes, Destroy does not need any statements at all in this implementation.

☐ Peep is to return the Information on top of the Data Stack, if Data is not empty. Since the Information in the first node is referred to as Data ↑ .Info, Peep should execute TheInfo := Data ↑ .Info after checking that Data is not NIL. So the coding can be as follows:

```
IF Data # NIL THEN
    TheInfo := Data↑.Info;
END;
```

Coding for Push and Pop

Push has two parameters—TheInfo and Data. The task to be performed is the addition of TheInfo to the top of the Data Stack. In this implementation, you have to create a node in which to store TheInfo. A local PointerToNode variable P is often useful in such situations:

```
NEW (P);
P↑.Info := TheInfo;
```

Now that you have the node, you have to link it in at the front of the list. There are apparently two cases: If Data is empty, P ↑ will also be the last node on the list, so we execute two statements:

```
P↑.Link := NIL;
Data := P;
```

If, on the other hand, Data already has nodes, you want to assign the address of the first node to the Link field of P ↑ and then store the address of P ↑ in Data:

```
P↑.Link := Data;
Data := P;
```

Note that the preceding pair of statements differs only in that it assigns Data instead of NIL to P ↑ .Link. Since NIL is assigned only when Data is NIL, you can use the preceding pair of statements whether the stack is empty or not. So the full coding for the Push procedure is as follows:

```
(* body of Push for standard linked lists *)
NEW (P);
P↑.Info := TheInfo;
P↑.Link := Data;
Data := P;
```

Figure 2 shows what happens if Push is called when the linked list has three nodes. The arrows from a small box to a node indicate that the address of the node is stored in the small box. Some people find it easier to see a drawing with actual "addresses" shown, as in Figure 3.

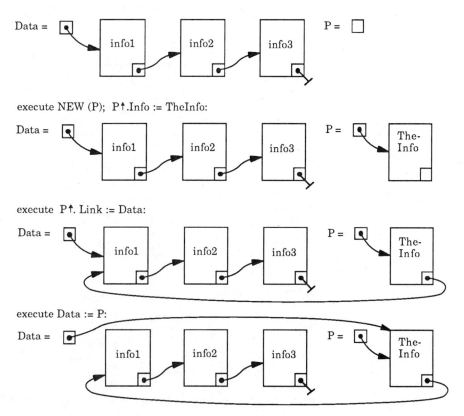

FIGURE 2. Insert at the front of a linked list: Push in StackADT.

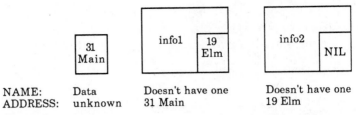

NAME:	Data	Doesn't have one	Doesn't have one
ADDRESS:	unknown	31 Main	19 Elm

FIGURE 3. A linked list with two nodes and two information values.

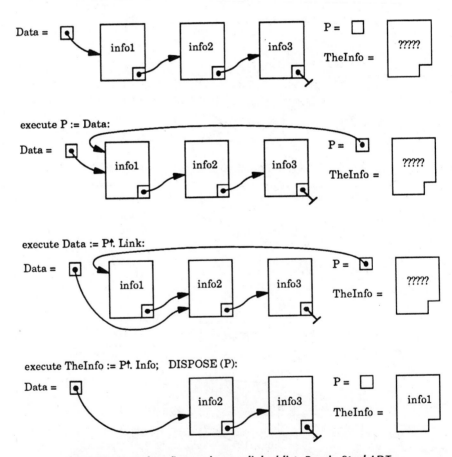

FIGURE 4. Delete first node on a linked list: Pop in StackADT.

Pop is only a little more complicated. It also has the two parameters TheInfo and Data. If the Stack is empty, you return without doing anything. Otherwise you could go ahead and detach the first node from the linked list and make the second node (if any) on the linked list the first one (Fig. 4). This can be accomplished by the following coding, using a local PointerToNode variable P to hold the address of the node to be deleted:

```
IF Data # NIL THEN
    P := Data;
    Data := Data↑.Link;
    (* see later for this coding *)
END;
```

The missing part of this coding is to assign its Information value to TheInfo and dispose of the unwanted node. These two statements do that:

```
TheInfo := P↑.Info;
DISPOSE (P);
```

You might be wondering whether some adjustment has to be made if there is no second node. But in that case, Data ↑ .Link is NIL; so Data is assigned NIL by one of the foregoing statements, which indicates an empty stack.

Check Your Understanding

1. Consider a program with these declarations:

```
TYPE  PointerToNode = POINTER TO Node;
VAR   P, Head : PointerToNode;
      X, Y : Node;
```

Which of these are legal Modula-2 statements?

NEW(P);   NEW(X);   NEW(P ↑);

2. Using the declarations from Exercise 1, which of these are legal Modula-2 statements?

P := Head;   P   := X;   P ↑ := X;

P := ↑ X;   P ↑ := Head ↑ ;   X   := Y;

3. Write a program segment that assigns to TheInfo the second Information value in a linked list named Data (instead of the first, as Peep does). But the coding should do nothing if there are not two nodes in the list.

4. Write a program segment that exchanges the information in the first and second nodes of a linked list Data that is known to have more than two nodes in it.

5. (NA) Illustrate the result of adding two more nodes to the situation shown in Figure 3. Make up two more addresses.

6. (NA) Write a function that removes the second Information value in a linked list (instead of the first, as Pop does). But the function should do nothing if there are not two nodes in the list.

4.2   ELEMENTARY ALGORITHMS FOR LINKED LISTS

Programs that work with stacks and also read data from a file often want the information to be on the stack in the reverse order of that obtained by Push. That is, the first information value in the file is to be on the top of the stack, and the last information value in the file is to be on the bottom of the stack. This can be done by pushing each value onto the stack as it is read and then reversing the stack (as shown in Example 3.1B). But it is more efficient to use a utility ReadAll procedure, developed in this section.

Reminder: The InputInfo procedure (imported from InfoADT) reads one information value from a file. If the file contains no information at that point, InputInfo simply assigns FALSE to the Boolean variable Okay (also imported from InfoADT); otherwise it assigns TRUE.

Pretracing

Pretracing is an important technique in developing algorithms. It consists of making up some sample data and deciding what the algorithm will do at each point for that data. For the following discussion, the sample data comprise three sets of information. It suffices to call them first, second, and third, since InputInfo handles the details of each set of information. Three nodes will be created; for purposes of this discussion, it helps to gives them the names Anne, Beth,

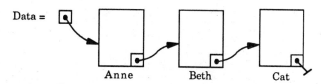

FIGURE 5. A complete linked list with three Nodes on it. Of the four names shown, only "Data" can be used in the program.

and Cat, although you cannot use these names to refer to them in a program (Fig. 5).

At each point in the pretracing, you try to state what the algorithm will do as one of five possibilities: a READ statement, a WRITE statement, an assignment, a call to some procedure, or the testing of a condition to decide what to do next.

READ into TheInfo;	reads first Information value.
SEE THAT Okay is TRUE, so:	
NEW (Data);	creates one Node (call it Anne).
Data ↑ .Info := TheInfo;	puts the first Information value in Anne.
P := Data;	for convenience in later coding.
READ into TheInfo;	reads second Information value.
SEE THAT Okay is TRUE, so:	
NEW (P ↑ .Link);	creates Beth; Anne's Link <− Beth's address.
P := P ↑ .Link;	P <− Beth's address.
P ↑ .Info := TheInfo;	puts the second Information value in Beth.
READ into TheInfo;	reads third Information value.
SEE THAT Okay is TRUE, so:	
NEW (P ↑ .Link);	creates Cat; Beth's Link <− Cat's address.
P := P ↑ .Link;	P <− Cat's address.
P ↑ .Info := TheInfo;	puts the third Information value in Cat.
READ into TheInfo;	reads fourth Information value, but fails.
SEE THAT Okay is FALSE, so:	
P ↑ .Link := NIL;	Cat's Link <− NIL (sentinel value).

Note: Technically, a READ or WRITE is a call to a procedure, so there are actually only three kinds of actions to consider: CALL, ASSIGN, or TEST. However, most people find it easier to think of READ and WRITE as separate categories when writing a pretrace.

This pretrace makes it easy to develop the coding for the ReadAll procedure. The basic feature is clearly a WHILE loop of the form WHILE Okay DO, with a call to InputFromInfo just before the WHILE statement and also as the last statement between DO and END. The coding that begins with NEW(Data) is different from that following the other tests of Okay, so that has to be handled separately (Example 4.2A).

EXAMPLE 4.2A _____

```
PROCEDURE ReadAll (VAR Data : Stack);
    (* Read all information remaining in the file using
        InputInfo and Okay.  Create a Stack of those
        information values with the first-read on top *)
    (* Context:  standard linked list StackADT utility *)
  (*-----------------------------------------------------*)

    PROCEDURE MakeTheList (P : PointerToNode);
        (* Create a linked list of Nodes and store the
            address of the first in the Link field of P^ *)
    VAR
        TheInfo : Information;
    BEGIN
        InputInfo (TheInfo);
        WHILE Okay DO
            NEW (P^.Link);
            P := P^.Link;
            P^.Info := TheInfo;
            InputInfo (TheInfo);
        END;
        P^.Link := NIL;
    END MakeTheList;
  (*-----------------------------------------------------*)

VAR
    TheInfo : Information;

BEGIN            (* ReadAll *)

    InputInfo (TheInfo);
    IF Okay THEN
        NEW (Data);
        Data^.Info := TheInfo;
        MakeTheList (Data);
    ELSE
        Data := NIL;
    END;

END ReadAll;
```

Testing a Loop for Termination

Any time you write a WHILE loop, you should check that the loop is guaranteed to terminate. In Example 4.2A, the check is as follows: Each iteration must read something from the file, since InputInfo is one of the statements subordinate to the WHILE. Thus the end of the file must eventually be reached. That sets Okay to FALSE, and the WHILE condition prevents reiteration when Okay is FALSE. Such a loop can be called a **read-controlled loop**.

By contrast, the Search procedure in Example 2.2C has what is called an **add-controlled loop**. The condition of its WHILE statement prevents reiteration when

Index is more than Size. Since each iteration adds 1 to Index and has no other effect on Index, Index must eventually exceed Size, so this loop is self-terminating.

An add-controlled loop depends on the existence of two expressions, called the **control expression** (*CE*) and the **limiting expression** (*LE*). In Example 2.2C, the control expression is Index and the limiting expression is Size. In the InsertInOrder procedure of Example 2.2B, the control expression is K and the limiting expression is 2; −1 is added on each iteration. The general definition of an add-controlled loop is that it satisfies one of the following four groups of properties:

1. (a) Each iteration of the statement sequence subordinate to the loop statement adds at least 1 to the CE;
   (b) No iteration changes the LE;
   (c) The WHILE or UNTIL condition (or its equivalent) prevents reiteration when the CE is larger than the LE;
2. (a) At least 1 is subtracted from the CE on each iteration;
   (b) No iteration changes the LE.
   (c) Reiteration is prevented when the CE is smaller than the LE;
3. (a) At least 1 is added to the CE on each iteration;
   (b) No iteration changes the LE;
   (c) Reiteration is prevented when the CE equals the LE, and the value of the CE is initially not larger than the LE;
4. Same relation to 2 as 3 has to 1.

For the Search procedure, case 1 applies; for the InsertInOrder procedure, case 2 applies.

Each FOR statement forms an add-controlled loop, so it is impossible for a FOR statement to be an "infinite loop." Standard Modula-2 compilers guarantee that FOR statements are self-terminating by enforcing the restriction that the control variable cannot be modified inside the FOR statement. You should verify that all other loops in your programs are self-terminating before you run the program.

Recursive Formulation of ReadAll

A procedure like Example 4.2A is usually written using recursion, because it is shorter and easier to understand. The key point to notice is that the MakeTheList subprocedure does just what ReadAll does, except the pointer to the list is put in Data ↑ .Link instead of in Data. Thus the procedure call MakeTheList(Data) can be replaced by ReadAll(Data ↑ .Link), as shown in Example 4.2B.

Any time you write a recursive procedure, you should verify that it is self-terminating. For Example 4.2B, the check is as follows: Each additional recursive call is made with less distance to the end of the file than the procedure that called it had, since the calling procedure first executes InputInfo. When the distance to the end of the file becomes zero, Okay will be assigned FALSE, which prevents any additional recursive calls.

EXAMPLE 4.2B _____

```
PROCEDURE ReadAll (VAR Data : Stack);
    (* Read all information remaining in the file using
       InputInfo and Okay.  Create a Stack of those
       information values with the first-read on top *)
    (* Context:  standard linked list StackADT utility *)
VAR
    TheInfo : Information;
BEGIN
    InputInfo (TheInfo);
    IF NOT Okay THEN
        Data := NIL;
    ELSE
        NEW (Data);
        Data^.Info := TheInfo;
        ReadAll (Data^.Link);
    END;
END ReadAll;
```

This use of recursion is valuable in producing shorter and clearer coding. The key concept is that two segments of coding are the same except for the name of the variable on which they act. Passing the name of the variable to a VAR parameter in a recursive call allows you to use the same code segment for both situations.

Progressing through a Linked List

The WriteAll procedure is a utility procedure that writes to a file all the information values on a given linked list in the order they occur on the list. The basic logic is to first see whether the given pointer is NIL. If it is, the list is empty, so nothing need be done. Otherwise, there is information there, so you write it out and then look at its Link pointer. If that is NIL, you can stop; otherwise you write out the information in the second node and then look at the Link field for that node. This continues until you see NIL.

Apparently a WHILE loop is needed for the coding of this algorithm, with the condition being P#NIL. P can be a local variable that moves along the list. Figure

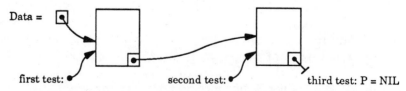

FIGURE 6. *Value of P at each of the three times when P#NIL is tested in the WriteAll procedure, assuming a two-node list.*

EXAMPLE 4.2C _____

```
PROCEDURE WriteAll (Data : Stack);
    (* Write the information in each Node on the Stack *)
    (* Context:  standard linked list StackADT utility *)
VAR
    P : PointerToNode;
BEGIN
    P := Data;
    WHILE P # NIL DO
        OutputInfo (P^.Info);
        P := P^.Link;
    END;
END WriteAll;
```

6 shows how a two-node linked list looks at each point in the execution of Example 4.2C when P#NIL is tested.

The WriteAll procedure contains a statement that compares P and NIL to see whether they are equal. It is legal to compare two addresses for equality but not to see which one is smaller. It is also legal for a function to return an address value, but you cannot put a caret on that returned function value.

Implementing TableADT

Linked lists can be used for a simple implementation of TableADT, using a record with a pointer to the first node on a linked list and a pointer to a node on the list indicating the current position.

```
TYPE    PointerToNode = PointerToNode;
        Table = RECORD
                        Head, Loc : PointerToNode;
                END;
```

All that PutIn has to do is add each new information at the front of the linked list. Find then goes through the list from front to rear to find the first information value that matches the given value; if there are two, the most recently inserted value will be seen first. Since an empty table is denoted by having a NIL value, the Destroy procedure has no statements and the Create procedure is just Data.Head := NIL; Data.Loc := NIL. The PutIn procedure is much the same as Push from Section 4.1. Find, Inspect, and TakeOut are left as exercises. Note that there is a big problem with TakeOut: When you delete a node in the middle of the linked list, how do you hook the two parts back together? This question is the subject of the next section.

Warning

One of the worst errors that people make with linked lists is failure to assign a value to every field of a Node shortly after the Node is created. Later, when a reference is made to an indeterminate field, weird things happen. If it is an address field, some references can crash the whole operating system of the computer, not just the program. This means that you have to shut down the computer and restart it. You should check each algorithm involving NEW to be sure that a value is assigned to all fields of the newly created variable. This can save you a lot of grief.

Previously I mentioned add-controlled loops and read-controlled loops. Example 4.2C illustrates a third common variety of loop: The control variable P contains an address; each iteration changes P to the value in the Link field of the node P currently indicates; the termination condition is that P become NIL. This works only if you have made sure to assign each Link field properly, especially the last one. You could call this kind of loop a **link-controlled loop**.

Check Your Understanding

1. What would be the effect of calling the WriteAll procedure in Example 4.2C if the two statements subordinate to the WHILE were switched?

2. Write the Shift utility procedure (described in Example 3.1C) for the standard linked list implementation of StackADT.

3. Write the SizeOf utility function (described in Example 3.1C) for the standard linked list implementation of StackADT.

4. Write the Inspect procedure for the implementation of TableADT described at the end of this section.

5. Write the Find procedure for the implementation of TableADT described at the end of this section.

6. (NA) Write a utility procedure for the standard linked list implementation that finds the next-to-last information value on a given Stack. The formal parameters are VAR TheInfo: Information; Data: Stack. The value of TheInfo is to be indeterminate if the list has fewer than two Nodes on it.

7. (NA) Write out a reasoned argument proving that every Node created by NEW in Example 4.2B has both fields assigned a value within that procedure.

8. (NA) Write the TakeOut procedure for the implementation of TableADT described at the end of this section.

4.3 LOCATIONS ON A LINKED LIST

We now get into the details of developing an implementation module for List-ADT (Example 3.5A) using linked lists. The standard design is analogous to what was done for StackADT: Define a List variable to be a pointer to the first Node on the linked list (NIL if the list is empty). For instance, if Data is a List, then Data ↑ .Info is the first Information on the list, and Data ↑ .Link ↑ .Info is the second Information on the list. This makes two procedures very easy to code:

☐ To Create a List named Data, simply assign NIL to Data.

☐ Destroy does not need any statements at all, since an empty list takes up no dynamic storage space.

Appropriate type declarations are:

```
TYPE    PointerToNode = POINTER TO Node;
        Location = PointerToNode;
        List = PointerToNode;
        Node = RECORD
                   Info : Information;
                   Link : PointerToNode;
               END;
```

I will discuss the algorithms for all but Insert and Delete in ListADT in this section. The full implementation module is in the next section, so I do not write out any procedures formally in this section.

The Location of Information on a Linked List

The obvious way to give the location of information on a list is to give a pointer to the Node containing it. Then FirstLocation(Data) would merely return Data. If Where has been assigned a location on Data, then NextLocation(Where, Data) would return a pointer to the Node after the one that Where points to, that is, it would return Where ↑ .Link. Of course, if Where=NIL, then Where is past the rear of the list, so NextLocation would just return NIL. Also, LookAt(TheInfo, Where, Data) would return Where ↑ .Info if Where is not NIL.

This design decision is workable, but it is quite wasteful of execution time when something must be inserted or deleted. For instance, assume that Where is the location of the tenth Node on the list. Then Delete(TheInfo, Where, Data) should delete that tenth Node and link the ninth Node to the eleventh one. This requires a change in the Link field of the ninth Node. The only way to get to the ninth Node is to start at the beginning of the list and come down. That takes a lot of time. Sometimes the time can be saved by a trick: To insert a node N0 between nodes N1 and N2, you can put the information from N2 into the newly created N0, put the new information in N2, and then link N0 into the list *after* N2. A similar trick helps for some deletions. However, we need something that works fast all the time.

The problem is that you need to access the Link field of the Node before the one where the change is to be made. The standard solution to this problem is to maintain a pointer to the Node containing the Link field to be changed. Thus the "Location" of the tenth Information value is a pointer to the ninth Node, and the "Location" of the fourth Information value is a pointer to the third Node. This greatly speeds up insertion and deletion.

With this solution, the first Node requires special handling, since there is no preceding Node. In this case we set Where to NIL. Thus the procedure call FirstLocation(Data) simply returns NIL, regardless of the value that Data has. LookAt(TheInfo, Where, Data) normally returns Where $\uparrow$ .Link $\uparrow$ .Info, since Where $\uparrow$ .Link is normally the Node that contains the desired Information value. NextLocation(Where, Data) still sets Where to Where $\uparrow$ .Link, unless that value is NIL. Figure 7 should help clarify this description.

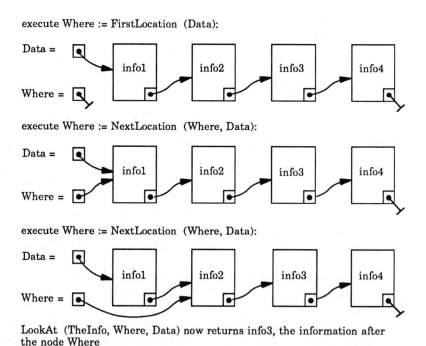

LookAt (TheInfo, Where, Data) now returns info3, the information after the node Where

FIGURE 7. *Result of executing FirstLocation and NextLocation for a standard linked list.*

The standard linked list implementation of an abstract list of N information values (N >= 0) and N + 1 Location values can be summarized as follows: A *concrete list* consists of N nodes, each with an Information field and a link. For K = 1..N−1, node K contains the Kth Information value and its link is the address of node K+1. Node N contains the Nth Information value and its link is NIL. A *List* is the address of node 1; if the abstract list is empty, the List value is NIL. Location 1 is NIL; for K = 2..N+1, *Location K* is the address of node K − 1.

For a given list, a **valid Location value** is (1) a value returned by FirstLocation or (2) a value returned by NextLocation when given a valid location value. Each valid location value has a corresponding position number, computed as follows:

☐ If you apply FirstLocation to a list, you get a valid location value with the position number of 1.

☐ If InList is true for that location value and list, and if you apply NextLocation again, you get a valid location value with the position number of 2.

☐ If InList is true for that location value and list, and if you apply NextLocation again, you get a valid location value with the position number of 3; and so on.

An Algorithm for the NextLocation Function

The procedure call NextLocation(Where, Data) is to return the Location of the Node after the one for which Where is the Location. Normally, that is just Where ↑ .Link. However, you cannot return Where ↑ .Link when Where is NIL (i.e., when you are actually thinking of the first information on the list). In that case, NextLocation should return a pointer to the first Node on the list (since you want the second information on the list). There is also a special case to consider when you are at the rear of the list; then you should not change Where. This situation is recognized by seeing that Where ↑ .Link is NIL.

> Algorithm for NextLocation
> IF Where is NIL, you are at the front of the list, so:
> Return a pointer to the first Node;
> OTHERWISE, IF Where's Link is NIL, you are past the rear, so:
> Return the Where you were given;
> IN ALL OTHER CASES:
> Return Where's Link.

Some people find it useful to think of Location this way: The third Location is the address of the "pre-third node" (the node before the one with the third information value). The seventh Location is the address of the "pre-seventh node"; and so on. Thus the first Location is NIL because there is no "pre-first node."

An Algorithm for the LookAt Procedure

Normally, LookAt(TheInfo, Where, Data) should return Where $\uparrow$ .Link $\uparrow$ .Info in TheInfo. *Challenge:* See if you can describe all cases where this is not to be done before reading further.

It is illegal to evaluate Where $\uparrow$ when Where is NIL. In that case, you want to look at the first information on the list, so you should execute TheInfo := Data $\uparrow$ .Info. But first you should check that Data is not NIL; if it is, the list is empty, so you do nothing.

The overall algorithm for LookAt is an IF statement: If Where is NIL, take the action just described, otherwise you can look at Where $\uparrow$ .Link. In that case, you had better check that it is not NIL before you try to return the information there. If it is NIL, you do nothing, since Where's Link field is NIL when you are at the end of the list. A direct translation of this algorithm for LookAt gives you the following coding:

```
(* body of the LookAt procedure for standard linked lists *)
IF Where = NIL THEN
    IF Data # NIL THEN
        TheInfo := Data↑.Info;
    END;
ELSIF Where↑.Link # NIL THEN
    TheInfo := Where↑.Link↑.Info;
END;
```

▐▐▐▶ PROGRAMMING STYLE

It is poor programming style to have IF statements within IF statements if it can be easily avoided. Often it is possible to revise the coding so that you have a three- or four-alternative IF statement (using ELSIF) where the alternatives are simpler. This is usually easier for a reader of the program to comprehend, and the objective of good programming style is to make the program comprehensible to a reader. Consideration of the IF statement just given for LookAt indicates that it can be recoded as the following simpler statement. This recoding may execute a bit more slowly, since one extra condition is tested in some cases. But speed of execution is usually not as important as clarity.

```
IF (Where = NIL) AND (Data # NIL) THEN
    TheInfo := Data↑.Info;
ELSIF (Where # NIL) AND (Where↑.Link # NIL) THEN
    TheInfo := Where↑.Link↑.Info;
END;
```

Some programmers prefer to avoid compound conditions, so they would write the body of LookAt as follows. Other programmers would rather go to some lengths to avoid an empty statement sequence after THEN. The question of whether the following coding is an improvement should be an interesting topic for class discussion:

```
IF Data = NIL THEN
    (* do nothing *)
ELSIF Where = NIL THEN
    TheInfo := Data↑.Info;
ELSIF Where↑.Link # NIL THEN
    TheInfo := Where↑.Link↑.Info;
END;
```

An Algorithm for InList

InList(Where, Data) tells whether you can delete at location Where. Apparently that is the same as saying that Where ↑ .Link is not NIL. However, you have to check that Where is not NIL before you refer to Where ↑ .Link. If Where is NIL, you are to delete the first information on the list; so you are at the end only if the Data list is empty. Thus the coding for InList could be either of the two following segments, depending on how comfortable you feel with the concept that calculations can be made with Booleans just as they are with numbers:

```
RETURN (Data # NIL) AND        IF Where = NIL THEN
       ((Where = NIL) OR           RETURN Data # NIL;
       (Where↑.Link # NIL));    ELSE
                                    RETURN Where↑.Link # NIL;
                                END;
```

Check Your Understanding

1. After execution of the following statements, what Nodes are on the AList, the BList, and the CList? Identify them by calling them Anne, Beth, Cathy, and Dawn in the order in which they were created.

```
NEW (AList);
InputInfo (AList↑.Info);
NEW (BList);
InputInfo (BList↑.Info);
BList↑.Link := NIL;
NEW (AList↑.Link);
InputInfo (AList↑.Link↑.Info);
NEW (CList);
CList↑.Info := AList↑.Info;
CList↑.Link := NIL;
DISPOSE (AList);
```

2. After execution of the statements in Exercise 1, what sets of information are on the AList, the BList, and the CList? Identify them by calling them One, Two, and Three in the order in which they were read from the file.

3. Write the LastLocation utility (described in Example 3.5B) for the standard linked list implementation of ListADT.

4. Write the Seek utility (described in Example 3.5B) for the standard linked list implementation of ListADT.

5. (NA) Rewrite the coding of LookAt beginning with IF Data #NIL THEN.

6. (NA) Under what conditions could the two code segments given for LookAt in the subsection on programming style produce different results?

7. (NA) Write Search (described in Example 3.5B) as a utility function for the standard linked list implementation of ListADT.

8. (NA) Complete the following utility procedure to be added to ListADT. Use the standard linked list implementation.

```
PROCEDURE Strip (TheInfo : Information;  VAR Data : List);
(* Remove all information from Data that matches TheInfo, leaving
   the remaining information in its original order in Data *)
```

4.4 IMPLEMENTATION MODULE FOR ListADT USING LINKED LISTS

The only algorithms we have left to develop are those of Insert and Delete, which are opposites of each other to some extent. The full implementation module for ListADT is at the end of this section. *Remember:* In the standard linked list implementation of ListADT, if Spot is a Location on a list with more than one information value, then:

☐ The *third* location value is the address of the second node, because it contains a link to the node with the *third* information value. This makes it easy to change the link when deleting the third information value.

☐ The *second* location value is the address of the first node, because it contains a link to the node with the *second* information value. This makes it easy to change the link when deleting the second information value.

☐ The *first* location value is NIL, to distinguish it from the other location values. You do not change links when deleting the first information value; you simply assign a new address to Data.

Keep the following in mind when Where is a Location not at the beginning or end of the list: LookAt asks you to look at the node *after* Where ↑ ; Insert asks you to insert a new node *after* Where ↑ ; and Delete asks you to delete the node *after* Where ↑ .

The Insert Procedure

The Insert procedure allows you to create a Node to hold some given Information and insert that Node on a given linked list at a given Location. The overall algorithm is apparently to create a new Node, put the given Information in it, and link that Node into the list. The first two steps are straightforward, but we need a subalgorithm for fixing the links. As usual, we have to treat Where=NIL as a special case, so we need an IF statement. If Where is NIL, we link that Node at the beginning of the list, otherwise we link it after Where ↑ (Fig. 8).

```
NEW (P);
P↑.Info := TheInfo;
IF Where = NIL THEN
    P↑.Link := Data;
    Data := P;
ELSE
    P↑.Link := Where↑.Link;
    Where↑.Link := P;
END;
```

Algorithm Development

Notice how the algorithm is easier to develop when we take it one stage at a time. First we see it as a sequence of three steps: Create a new Node, then fix the Info

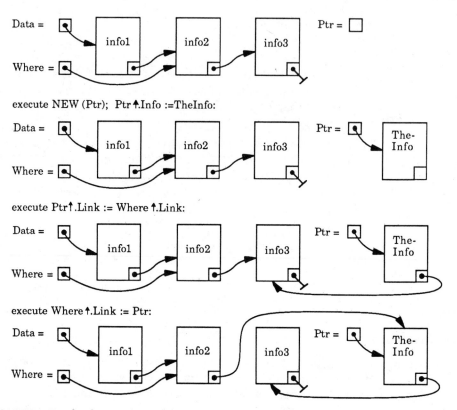

FIGURE 8. Result of executing Insert when the list has three information values and Where points to the second node on the list.

field, then fix the Link field. The third step is the only one that requires more than one or two statements, so we develop it further: We see it as a selection of two courses of action, depending on whether Where is NIL. Each of these two courses of action can be expressed in one or two statements, so we can code them directly.

There will also be situations in which the algorithm is properly seen as a repetition of a statement sequence. In general, any algorithm can be expressed as either a *sequence,* a *selection,* or a *repetition* of actions. This was proven by Bohm and Jacopini in 1966 (the **Structure Theorem**).

Top-down analysis consists of developing the algorithm to perform a given task by expressing it concisely in terms of subtasks, then developing subalgorithms for those subtasks in the same way. This continues until each subalgorithm is so close to the target programming language that it can be translated directly to one or two program statements. This top-down approach is the most valuable technique in the efficient development of algorithms for large, complex programs and procedures.

Perhaps the most difficult part of top-down analysis is to decide what algorithm will accomplish the given task to be performed. The Structure Theorem is useful for this. It is often best to ask yourself: Can I accomplish this task by repeating a sequence of actions over and over again until it is time to stop? Or does the action to be taken depend on whether such-and-such is true? Or can I just go about straightforwardly performing action A, then action B, then perhaps action C as well (for appropriate actions A, B, and C)?

Another very useful technique for developing the algorithm from the given task to be performed is to choose a particular case of the task and simply do it. For instance, if the task to be performed is to read any list of any number of reals and find the smallest, you can choose the list 3.2, 7.52, −3.875, 9.634, 1.0 and carry out the task one step at a time for that list. As you perform the task, you will be applying an implicit algorithm. Now all you have to do is make that algorithm explicit, generalizing it so it applies to any list of any number of reals.

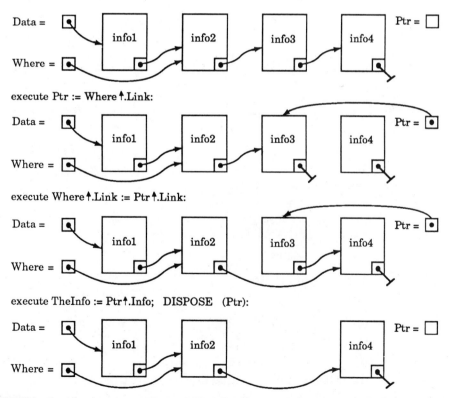

FIGURE 9. *Result of executing Delete when the list has four information values and Where points to the second node on the list.*

The Delete Procedure

The Delete procedure allows you to delete a Node from a given linked list at a given spot (Fig. 9). The algorithm is roughly as follows: First be sure that the given linked list is not empty and that the given Location is not past the rear of the list. If those conditions are met, the links have to be fixed to remove the Node in question from the linked list. Then the information can be removed from the Node and the Node disposed of. The links for the list should be fixed before you delete the Node. The reason is that you have to refer to the address in the Link field of the Node, and you cannot do that after the Node has been disposed of.

In the subalgorithm for fixing the links, there are two cases, since the beginning of the list requires special treatment: If Where is NIL, delete the Node at the front of the list, otherwise delete the Node after Where ↑ . Notice that the coding of Delete in Example 4.4A, after the check for the existence of the Node, is the mirror image of the coding of Insert.

An interesting quirk of Modula-2 is that you have to declare the type-identifier Node in this module even though you never use it. The reason is that you cannot declare PointerToNode=POINTER TO RECORD... because one of its fields is of type PointerToNode and you cannot use the identifier you are declaring in the declaration itself.

Warning

After you execute the following sequence of statements, what value is in A ↑ .Link?

```
NEW (A);
A↑.Link := A;
B := A;
B↑.Link := NIL;
```

If you said A, the address of the created node, you need to draw a few pictures to see why the answer should be NIL. This is a common error.

Check Your Understanding

1. Write the Modify procedure (described in Example 3.5B) as a utility in the standard linked list implementation of ListADT.

2. Write a Boolean function that tells whether a given location is the location of the last information value on a given list.

3. Write a recursive utility procedure in the standard linked list implementation of ListADT, to put a given information value at the end of a list.

EXAMPLE 4.4A _____

```
IMPLEMENTATION MODULE ListADT;
FROM InfoADT IMPORT Information;
FROM Storage IMPORT ALLOCATE, DEALLOCATE;
    (* Written by William C. Jones, October 19-- *)
    (* Procedures to permit fundamental manipulations of
        linear lists.  Every List must be initialized
        before anything else can be done with it *)
TYPE
    PointerToNode = POINTER TO Node;
    Location = PointerToNode;
    List = PointerToNode;
    Node = RECORD
                Info : Information;
                Link : PointerToNode;
            END;
(***********************************************************)

PROCEDURE Insert (TheInfo : Information;
                  Where   : Location;  VAR Data : List);
    (* Put TheInfo at location Where of Data *)
VAR
    P : PointerToNode;
BEGIN
    NEW (P);
    P^.Info := TheInfo;
    IF Where = NIL THEN
        P^.Link := Data;
        Data := P;
    ELSE
        P^.Link := Where^.Link;
        Where^.Link := P;
    END;
END Insert;
(***********************************************************)

PROCEDURE Delete (VAR TheInfo : Information;
                  Where       : Location; VAR Data : List);
    (* Take TheInfo from location Where of Data if
        any information is there; no effect otherwise *)
VAR
    P : PointerToNode;
BEGIN
    IF (Data # NIL) AND
            ((Where = NIL) OR (Where^.Link # NIL)) THEN
        IF Where = NIL THEN
            P := Data;
            Data := P^.Link;
        ELSE   (* Where^.Link is not NIL *)
            P := Where^.Link;
            Where^.Link := P^.Link;
        END;
        TheInfo := P^.Info;
        DISPOSE (P);
    END;
END Delete;
(***********************************************************)
```

```
(* EXAMPLE 4.4A continued *)


PROCEDURE LookAt (VAR TheInfo : Information;
                     Where         : Location;  Data : List);
       (* Access TheInfo at location Where of Data if
          any information is there; no effect otherwise *)
BEGIN
    IF (Where = NIL) AND (Data # NIL) THEN    (* first one *)
        TheInfo := Data^.Info;
    ELSIF (Where # NIL) AND (Where^.Link # NIL) THEN
        TheInfo := Where^.Link^.Info;
    END;
END LookAt;
(*****************************************************)

PROCEDURE InList (Where : Location; Data : List) : BOOLEAN;
      (* Tell whether information is at Location Where *)
BEGIN
    RETURN (Data # NIL) AND
           ((Where = NIL) OR (Where^.Link # NIL));
END InList;
(*****************************************************)

PROCEDURE FirstLocation (Data : List) : Location;
       (* Return the location of the first item on Data *)
BEGIN
    RETURN NIL;
END FirstLocation;
(*****************************************************)

PROCEDURE NextLocation (Where : Location;
                          Data  : List) : Location;
       (* Return the location of the item on Data after the
          one Where indicates, but not past the end one *)
BEGIN
    IF Where = NIL THEN
        RETURN Data;
    ELSIF Where^.Link = NIL THEN
        RETURN Where;
    ELSE
        RETURN Where^.Link;
    END;
END NextLocation;
(*****************************************************)

PROCEDURE Create (VAR Data : List);
       (* Initialize Data as an empty structure *)
BEGIN
    Data := NIL;
END Create;
(*****************************************************)

PROCEDURE Destroy (VAR Data : List);
       (* Deallocate the space for the empty structure *)
END Destroy;  (* no action required *)
(*****************************************************)

END ListADT.
```

4. Write the Join procedure (described in Example 3.1C) as a utility in the standard linked list implementation of ListADT.

5. (NA) Write this procedure to be added to ListADT as a utility in the standard linked list implementation:

```
PROCEDURE Reverse (VAR Data : List);
(* Change Data to be the list consisting of the same
   Information records in the opposite order *)
```

6. (NA) Write a procedure that accepts a pointer to a linked list as a value parameter, disposes of Nodes 2, 4, 6, 8, 10, and so forth, and leaves the remaining Nodes linked in the order 1, 3, 5, 7, 9, and so forth. That is, every other Node, starting from the second one, is disposed of. Use recursion and DestroyInfo appropriately.

7. (NA) Write the Copy procedure (described in Example 3.5B) as a utility in the standard linked list implementation of ListADT.

8. (NA) Write the MoveInfo procedure (described in Example 3.5B) as a utility in the standard linked list implementation of ListADT.

9. (NA) Recode the Delete procedure in Example 4.4A using just one IF statement. Discuss which coding is better.

4.5 IMPLEMENTATIONS: LINKED LISTS WITH HEADER AND TRAILER NODES

For several procedures in the standard linked list implementation for ListADT (Example 4.4A), the overall algorithm has been coded as an IF statement. The reason is that there are two or three special cases to consider, since the beginning of the list has to be treated differently and so does the end of the list. The primary cause of this is that Where normally gives the predecessor of the information value we are actually thinking of, and the first information value on the list has no predecessor. If it did, algorithms would be so much simpler.

The solution is straightforward: Give the first information value on the list a predecessor. This predecessor is called the **header node** for the list. We leave the Info field of the header node indeterminate; only the Link field is significant. Thus, in this **basic header node implementation**, every List is to have one more node on it (at the beginning of the list) than in the standard linked list implementation described earlier. The first location on the list is the address of the header node.

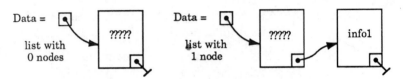

FIGURE 10. Two short linked lists with header nodes.

The Create procedure must create a list named Data with one node (the header) on it, as in Figure 10, so the coding for Create is:

```
NEW (Data);     (* makes the header node *)
Data↑.Link := NIL;
```

The WriteAll utility procedure for header nodes is exactly the same as the WriteAll in Example 4.2B except that we begin by executing P:=Data ↑ .Link instead of P:=Data. You may want to trace the logic through for the list shown in Figure 11.

The Delete procedure in Example 4.4A is particularly messy in the standard linked list implementation. With header nodes, the two cases are merged into one. All we have to guard against is that there is actually something to delete, that is, Where ↑ .Link cannot be NIL. Where itself should never be NIL, since part of the precondition for Delete is that Where is a valid location on Data. The coding for Delete is revised as:

```
(* Delete for the basic header node implementation *)
IF Where↑.Link # NIL THEN
    P := Where↑.Link;          (* P↑ is to be deleted *)
    Where↑.Link := P↑.Link;
    TheInfo := P↑.Info;
    DISPOSE (P);
END;
```

SUMMARY. In the basic header node implementation of ListADT, a *concrete list* of N information values is a linked list of N + 1 nodes. For K = 1..N, node K + 1 contains the Kth information value. A *List* is the address of node 1. *Location K* is the address of node K.

The code segment just given for Delete illustrates a very useful tactic in the development of programs: **Don't reinvent the wheel.** If you already have a program segment that does what you want to do or something very close to it, study

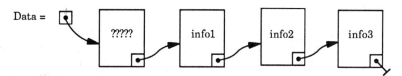

FIGURE 11. A linked list with a header node and three information values.

it to see how it should be changed to accomplish your task. This principle is the motivation for developing library modules that are as complete and flexible as possible. Then they can be used in many different client modules, thereby simplifying the programming.

Time, Space, and Effort

When you compare the header node implementation with the standard implementation, you can see that each list requires somewhat more *space for storage*. The amount of space can be significant in applications that work with many lists, such as the StockHolder program described in Section 3.1. This is especially true if static information variables are used instead of pointers to information records, since each header node has a wasted Info field.

Execution time for the Create procedure is slightly more using a header node, but execution time for the Delete procedure is slightly less (since fewer comparisons have to be made). On the whole, you would find that execution time for a client module using either of the two implementations is roughly the same. Execution time for both Create and Delete is not affected by the number of values on the linked list. By comparison, execution time for Delete is much greater for the simple array implementation when the list has more that just a few values on it, since its average execution time is proportional to the number of values on the list.

Programmer effort in developing the header node implementation is significantly less than for the standard implementation. Any time you can cut down on the number of control statements in a program, you make it easier to develop, easier to debug, and easier to maintain. The amount of effort required of the programmer is often the determining factor in program design decisions.

Efficiency of coding depends on these three factors: space requirements in the computer's storage media, speed of execution, and programming effort. These are the prime considerations in choosing from among several different ways of performing a given task. An important part of making the decision is to determine how often each of the procedures will be called. Speed of execution of an application program often depends heavily on the speed with which two or three procedures are executed. An application in which insertions and deletions are frequent and searches for given information are rare suggests a linked list. If the application spends most of its time searching the list for information and very little time inserting and deleting, a sorted array with binary search may be best.

Storing Values in the Header Node

Many applications require frequent access to the rear of a list (such as for queues) or need to know how long the list is. In the simple linked list implementation, you would have to start from the front of the list and go through it one node at a time until you reach the end. The speed of execution can be greatly increased by storing additional information with each list. A reasonable place for keeping this list information is in the header node, since that makes the information easy to find.

For example, assume that the header node has an extra field named Rear, which always contains the address of the last node on the list. Then you can easily add TheInfo to the rear of Data by using the following coding:

```
NEW (Data↑.Rear↑.Link);
Data↑.Rear := Data↑.Rear↑.Link;
Data↑.Rear↑.Info := TheInfo;
Data↑.Rear↑.Link := NIL;
```

Unfortunately, there are disadvantages to this implementation. Each change in the list requires that we update the Rear value to reflect the change. For instance, in the Delete coding given earlier in this section, the following statements should be added just before the DISPOSE statement:

```
IF P = Data↑.Rear THEN   (* deleted the rear node *)
    Data↑.Rear := Where;
END;
```

Warning

Assume that you have a procedure with a List parameter Data. This procedure removes the first information value from Data and later puts it back at the front of Data. Thus Data is the same when the procedure terminates as it was when the procedure began. Does that mean that Data can be a value parameter of the procedure?

Assume that the actual parameter is named Actual. Although the formal parameter Data has the same information values in the same order that Actual has, Data may be a different value. For the standard linked list implementation, Actual initially contains the address of the first node on the list. This node Actual ↑ has been disposed of and replaced by a new node Data ↑ containing the same information value. So you cannot thereafter reference Actual ↑ . This problem does not arise for the header node or the counted array implementation of lists, unless the procedure calls Destroy for the parameter.

The general principle is that if a procedure makes any change in an abstract structure, even if the values are later restored, the structure must be passed as a VAR parameter instead of as a value parameter. For an example of this, you could study Section 7.2 now.

Implementation of DictiADT

For the ordered array implementation of DictiADT (Section 3.8), we added two values to each list: A Boolean value IsThere to tell whether the most recent Find succeeded, and a location Loc to tell the location of the current information. For the **ordered linked list with header implementation** of DictiADT, we could add the same values to the header node. Then Create begins by allocating one node and assigning NIL to its link, as before. It must also initialize Loc to the header (the only location on an empty list with header) and IsThere to FALSE. PutIn executes Find to assign to the Loc field the address of the node that is to be linked to the new node (Fig. 12). The node is inserted and IsThere is set to TRUE. This coding is in Example 4.5A.

Using a Variant Node (Optional)

This subsection is included for those who know something about variant records. You can skip it completely without loss of continuity.

The trouble with the DictiADT implementation just described is that each node has four fields instead of two. In most implementations of Modula-2, that means that each node will require twice as much space as is needed for standard linked lists, if Information is a pointer value. The header node does not use the Info field, and the other nodes do not use the Loc and IsThere fields. You could avoid this loss of space by declaring a Table to be a pointer to a special header record with Loc, Link, and IsThere fields, and leave Node with just the two fields

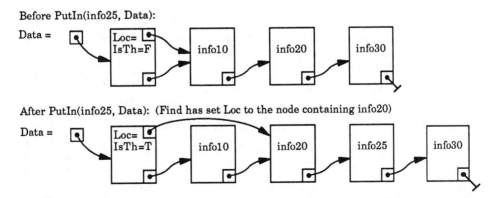

FIGURE 12. A list using a header node with Loc and IsThere fields, before and after calling PutIn(info25, Data).

EXAMPLE 4.5A _____

```
(* Context: ordered linked list/header impl. of DictiADT *)
TYPE
    PointerToNode = POINTER TO Node;
    Table = PointerToNode;
    Node = RECORD
              Info      : Information;
              Link, Loc : PointerToNode;
              IsThere   : BOOLEAN;
           END;
(**********************************************************)

PROCEDURE Create (VAR Data : Table);
BEGIN
    NEW (Data);
    Data^.Link := NIL;
    Data^.Loc := Data;
    Data^.IsThere := FALSE;
END Create;
(**********************************************************)

PROCEDURE PutIn (TheInfo : Information; VAR Data : Table);
VAR
    P : PointerToNode;
BEGIN
    Find (TheInfo, Data);
    NEW (P);
    P^.Info := TheInfo;
    P^.Link := Data^.Loc^.Link;
    Data^.Loc^.Link := P;
    Data^.Loc := P;
    Data^.IsThere := TRUE;
END PutIn;
```

Info and Link. But then you would lose the simplicity of coding that characterizes having a header node.

You can have both simplicity and compactness if you declare Node as a variant record. When it is the header node, it contains Loc and IsThere fields; otherwise it contains an Info field. In any case, it contains the Link field. The declaration is made as follows:

```
TYPE Node = RECORD
               Link : PointerToNode;
               CASE BOOLEAN OF
                    TRUE  : Info : Information;
                  | FALSE : Loc      : PointerToNode;
                            IsThere : BOOLEAN;
               END;
            END;
```

The coding of the procedures does not change except for the NEW and DIS-POSE statements. For Create in Example 4.5A, the NEW statement must be NEW(Data, FALSE), since you are creating a header node. For PutIn, the NEW statement must be NEW(P, TRUE). In TakeOut, you use DISPOSE(P, TRUE); in Destroy, you use DISPOSE(Data, FALSE). In other words, you use FALSE for a header node and TRUE for any other node.

You have to obey a restriction when you use this variant record: You should not refer to the Info field if the node was created using FALSE, and you should not refer to the Loc or IsThere field if the node was created using TRUE. Some Modula-2 compilers require you to have a colon after CASE in the declaration of Node, since there is no tag field. Some Modula-2 compilers do not have NEW and DISPOSE, so you must use ALLOCATE and DEALLOCATE with the appropriate sizes.

Trailer Nodes

The trailer node implementation of linked lists simply adds an extra node at the *end* of each list. The information in this node is irrelevant; it is there just to simplify the algorithms (Fig. 13). The Create procedure has the following two statements:

```
NEW (Data);
Data↑.Link := NIL;
```

One advantage of this implementation is the same as for the header node implementation: A list with N information values has N + 1 nodes. Therefore, it is easy to write a WHILE statement to process all the nodes on a list, since executing the statement sequence of a WHILE statement N times requires that the WHILE condition be evaluated N + 1 times, and there are N + 1 nodes for which the condition can be evaluated.

A Location in this implementation is more naturally defined—it is a pointer to the node containing the information rather than to the preceding node; the Location is at the end when it points to the trailer node. Thus FirstLocation re-

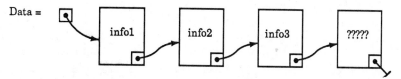

FIGURE 13. A linked list with a trailer node and three information values.

turns Data, InList returns Where ↑ .Link#NIL, and LookAt is simply TheInfo :=
Where ↑ .Info.

When a deletion is to be made at a certain location, there will always be a
following node. The technique is to copy the information from that following
node into the node whose information is to be deleted, then delete the following
node. This solves the problem with changing links that occurs for the standard
linked list implementation. Similarly, when an insertion is to be made before
node X, you instead insert a node after X, move the information from X to that
following node, then put the given information in node X.

This implementation executes very quickly as long as Information is a pointer
to a record rather than the record itself. For instance, the coding for Insert is:

```
NEW (P);                        (* make a copy of Where↑    *)
P↑.Info := Where↑.Info;         (*            ''             *)
P↑.Link :=Where↑.Link;          (*            ''             *)
Where↑.Link := P;               (* link P↑ after Where↑     *)
Where↑.Info := TheInfo;         (* put TheInfo in Where↑    *)
```

Check Your Understanding

1. Write the Join procedure (described in Example 3.1C) for the basic header node implementation of ListADT.

2. Write the Seek function for the basic header node implementation of ListADT (the heading is in Example 3.5B).

3. Write the TakeOut procedure for the ordered linked list with header node implementation of DictiADT, either with or without using a variant record, as you prefer.

4. Write the Seek function for the trailer node implementation of ListADT.

5. Write the NextLocation function for the trailer node implementation of ListADT.

6. (NA) Write the ReadAll procedure for the basic header node implementation of ListADT (the heading is in Example 3.1C).

7. (NA) Write the Find procedure for the ordered linked list with header node implementation of DictiADT.

8. (NA) Define "concrete list" for the trailer node implementation of ListADT, following the pattern in the beginning of this section.

4.6 IMPLEMENTATIONS: CIRCULAR AND DOUBLY LINKED LISTS

This section describes two more implementations of ListADT, variations on the standard linked list implementation. In one implementation, the last node is linked to the first node; this lets queue operations execute quickly. In the other implementation, each node is linked to the node before it as well as to the node after it.

Circular List Implementation of ListADT

A popular variation on the standard linked list implementation is reminiscent of a snake swallowing its tail: The Link field of the last Node on the List contains the address of the first Node on the List instead of containing NIL. Only one other change is made: Data contains the address of the last Node on the List instead of the first Node (Fig. 14). This implementation is called the **circular list implementation**.

The first thing to note is that it is still possible to tell where the list begins and ends. When going through the Nodes from beginning to end, the first Node to process is Data ↑ .Link ↑ ; the last one to process is Data ↑ . The second thing to note is that, given Data, it is very easy to find the last Node on the List and almost as easy to find the first Node on the List. This lets queue operations execute quickly, since you can easily add a node to the end of the list; that is the main advantage of the circular implementation. You obtain greater speed (in accessing the last node) at the cost of more programming effort (algorithms are more complex) but at no cost in space. By contrast, header and trailer nodes reduce programming effort at a cost in space, but execution time is not greatly affected.

There are applications in which a list should be treated as if it were circular; for instance, you might want to write a program about people who sit around a campfire and toast marshmallows. The circular list implementation is useful for such applications. A famous problem of this type is presented later in this section.

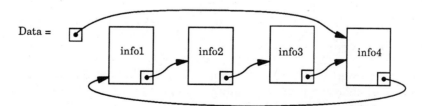

FIGURE 14. A circular list with four information values.

Some Coding for the Circular List Implementation

The Create procedure is just Data := NIL. A Location value is still a pointer to the preceding Node; it is NIL when Data is NIL or when we mean to indicate the first node on the list. Thus FirstLocation is just RETURN NIL and InList is just RETURN (Data#NIL) AND (Where#Data). Destroy still has no statements. That takes care of the four easy procedures.

The NextLocation function is not too complicated. Normally you return Where ↑ .Link. The only cases in which this does not apply are when Where is NIL (since that is the Location for the first item, so to move on to the next item you return Data ↑ .Link) or when Where is Data (since that is the Location after the last item on the list, you leave Where unchanged). The coding is:

```
IF (Data # NIL) AND (Where = NIL) THEN
    RETURN Data↑.Link;
ELSIF Where = Data THEN
    RETURN Where;
ELSE
    RETURN Where↑.Link;
END;
```

In general, actions at a Location Where on a circular linked list should check four conditions, since the action depends on whether Data#NIL, Where=NIL, Where=Data, or otherwise. The Insert procedure can be developed by studying the one for the standard linked list implementation (Example 4.4A) and seeing what modifications have to be made. You can still begin by creating the Node and storing the given Information in it. The only other thing that has to be done is change a few pointers to link the new Node into the list and be sure that Data still contains the address of the last Node on the list. The rest of the coding for circular lists is left as a programming problem.

SUMMARY. In the circular list implementation of ListADT, a *concrete list* of N information values is a linked list of N nodes, except that node N links to node 1. For K=1..N, node K contains the Kth information value. A *List* is the address of node N; it is NIL if N is 0. For K=2..N+1, *Location K* is the address of node K − 1. Location 1 is NIL.

The ONE POTATO Problem

A group of children playing baseball have broken a neighbor's window. They have to choose one of their number to face up to the neighbor and arrange to make restitution. So they stand around in a circle and chant "1 potato, 2 potato, 3 potato, 4; 5 potato, 6 potato, 7 potato, more." One of the children points to each child in turn during the chant; the one last pointed to (the eighth one counted off) leaves the circle and the chant begins again. This continues until there is only one child left, who then gets stuck with the undesirable task.

This problem can be easily solved using a circular list. The information could be the children's names. The primary input is the number of children, the number of positions the pointing finger moves around the circle each time (8 in the illustration), and the child with whom to start. After you construct a list containing the names, you count around the circle a fixed number of times, delete the Node at that point, and repeat. When the list has just one Node left, that is the chosen one.

The program can be written as a client module of ListADT, which does not take advantage of the circular implementation. You can write a procedure that goes on to the next item on the list in a circular fashion by executing the following statements:

```
Where := NextLocation (Where, Data);
IF NOT InList (Where, Data) THEN
      Where := FirstLocation (Data);
END;
```

It is much better, however, to have a utility procedure for ListADT that is invoked by something like Advance(N, Where, Data), which goes around the circle N positions. This way you can take advantage of the increase in speed due to the circular implementation.

Circular Lists with Header/Trailer

A variation on the simple circular linked list uses a trailer node that links to the first node: The List variable points to the trailer node. A Location is a pointer to the node containing the desired information rather than to the node before. Insertions and deletions are made as described in Section 4.5 for trailer nodes. This design simplifies several algorithms, thus reducing programmer effort, but it takes more storage space than the simple circular linked list implementation. An alternative is to have a Location be a pointer to the node before; in that case, the dummy node inserted between the first and last nodes is technically a header node (see Fig. 15).

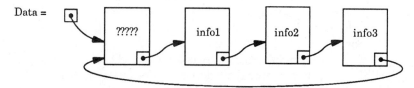

FIGURE 15. A circular list with a header node and 3 information values.

One primary advantage of having the list be circular is that it allows enqueueing easily. You can enqueue TheInfo on Data as follows:

```
NEW (P);                       (* create a new node            *)
P↑.Link := Data↑.Link;         (* link it after the dummy node  *)
Data↑.Link := P;               (* "                             *)
Data↑.Info := TheInfo;         (* put TheInfo in the former dummy *)
Data := P;                     (* the new node is now the dummy  *)
```

Another advantage of having a circular list with a dummy node is that the time required for a sequential search through the entire list for information matching TheInfo can be cut by up to one third by first putting TheInfo in the dummy node. This means you can simplify the WHILE condition by avoiding the test to see if you are at the end of the list. The following coding finds the address of the node containing the matching information, except it finds the address of the dummy node if no information in the list matches TheInfo. It differs from the naive searching algorithm in that the first statement has been added and the WHILE condition does not include the phrase AND (P # Data).

```
Data↑.Info := TheInfo;
P := Data↑.Link;
WHILE Compare (TheInfo, P↑.Info) # 0 DO
    P := P↑.Link;
END;
```

Doubly Linked Lists

There are several applications where it is highly advantageous to be able to access the information that precedes a given information value, or to be able to go through the values on a list in reverse order easily. For such applications, ListADT should export a utility function PriorLocation that returns the location just before a given location on a given list. Then an implementation for ListADT can be chosen that executes PriorLocation quickly.

The **doubly linked list** implementation provides quick execution of PriorLocation, but at a cost in space. Each node has two pointers, a Link pointer to the next node and a Prior pointer to the node before it in the list. In the simplest implementation, the Link value for the last node on the list is NIL and the Prior value for the first node on the list is also NIL; Data is a pointer to the first node. An alternate implementation is doubly circular with a header node that is also a trailer node: The last node's Link is to the header node, which has a Link to the first node, and the first node's Prior value is the address of the header node, whose

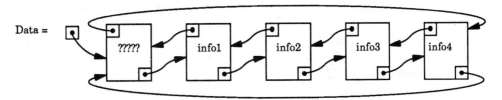

FIGURE 16. *A doubly linked list with four information values and header.*

Prior value is the address of the last node (Fig. 16). A Location is a pointer to the Node where the change is to be made, since the double pointers make it easy to fix the links (the Location value is the address of the header node when an insertion is to be made at the end of the list). The declaration of a Node is:

```
TYPE   PointerToNode = POINTER TO Node;
       List = PointerToNode;
       Location = PointerToNode;
       Node = RECORD
                Info : Information;
                Link, Prior : PointerToNode;
              END;
```

The coding for the Create procedure in the **doubly linked list with header node** implementation is more complex than usual, since the header node should be doubly linked to itself: NEW(Data); Data ↑ .Link := Data; Data ↑ .Prior := Data. FirstLocation returns Data ↑ .Link, and InList tells whether the given Location is not the header node. PriorLocation returns Where ↑ .Prior, and NextLocation returns Where ↑ .Link.

The Insert and Delete procedures are straightforward but a little tedious. To insert some information at a given Location, you create a new node and link it just after the node indicated. Note that the following coding for Insert is simplified by having a header node, since you do not have to treat the end nodes as special cases.

```
(* Insert procedure for a doubly linked list with header *)
NEW (P);
P↑.Link   := Where;           (* link new node to others    *)
P↑.Prior := Where↑.Prior;     (*    "                       *)
Where↑.Prior   := P;          (* link other nodes to new one *)
P↑.Prior↑.Link := P;          (*    "                       *)
P↑.Info    := Where↑.Info;    (* adjust the info values      *)
Where↑.Info := TheInfo;       (*    "                       *)
```

You might think it better to put TheInfo in the new node and link it before the one at Where, but that would be a violation of the specifications for ListADT, which say that the value of location K is not to change when the Kth information value is inserted or deleted. The rest of the coding for doubly linked lists is left as a programming problem.

Check Your Understanding

1. Write the LookAt procedure for the circular list implementation of ListADT.

2. Write a function that imports from ListADT and tells whether a given List has just one item on it. This is useful for the ONE POTATO program.

3. Write the utility WriteAll procedure for the circular list implementation of ListADT (the heading is in Example 3.1C).

4. Write the Push procedure, putting a given Information value at the beginning of a given List, as a utility for the doubly linked list implementation of ListADT with header node.

5. (NA) Write the utility Modify procedure for the circular list implementation of ListADT (the heading is in Example 3.5B).

6. (NA) Write the Delete procedure for the doubly linked list implementation of ListADT with header node.

7. (NA) Write the utility Copy procedure for the circular list implementation of ListADT (the heading is in Example 3.1C).

8. (NA) Write the utility Seek function for the circular list implementation of ListADT (the heading is in Example 3.5B).

4.7 PROGRAM VERIFICATION

This section introduces some concepts in program verification, particularly loop invariants. Illustrations of loop invariants are given for both array and linked list implementations. Some FOR statements have been rephrased as WHILE statements, since this discussion is easier with WHILE statements than with FOR statements.

Analysis of a WHILE Statement

Consider an array named Item with integer indices. Assume that some numbers have been stored in a part of the array, namely the part from Item[StartingIndex] up through Item[Size], where StartingIndex is not more than Size. Then the following program segment embodies the usual method for finding the position of the smallest number:

```
(A) Position := StartingIndex;
    K := StartingIndex + 1;
    WHILE K <= Size DO
        IF Item [K] < Item [Position] THEN
            Position := K;
        END;
        INC (K);
    END;
```

How do you know that this coding really does find the position of the smallest number? Consider the following statement:

(B) Each time the WHILE condition in (A) is evaluated, Position is the index of the smallest number in Item[StartingIndex]... Item[K−1].

The WHILE statement in (A) terminates only when the WHILE condition is evaluated and K is more than Size. So if you can show that statement (B) is true, and also show that the loop in (A) terminates eventually, you have shown that the coding in (A) finds the position of the smallest number in Item[Starting-Index]... Item[Size].

This WHILE loop is an add-controlled loop; K increases on each iteration of the loop, and the loop cannot reiterate when K increases past Size. That shows that the loop terminates, so you only have to show that statement (B) is true. Consider the following statement, a part of (B):

(C) Position is the index of the smallest number in
    Item[StartingIndex]... Item[K−1].

There is a straightforward two-step method for showing that this statement (C) is true each time the WHILE condition in (A) is evaluated. The method is called *proof by induction*:

1. Show that (C) is true the first time the WHILE condition is evaluated.
2. Show that if (C) is true at a given time when the WHILE condition is evaluated and found true, it follows that (C) is also true the next time the WHILE condition is evaluated.

For Step 1: The first time the WHILE condition is evaluated, K is StartingIndex + 1, so (C) says that Position is the index of the smallest number in Item[Start-ingIndex]... Item[StartingIndex], which is obviously true, since Position is initialized to StartingIndex.

For Step 2: Assume that (C) is true at a given time when the WHILE condition is evaluated and found true. Then if Item[K] is smaller than Item[Position], Item[K] is the smallest of Item[StartingIndex]... Item[K] and Position is assigned K. If Item[K] is not smaller than Item[Position], Item[Position] is the smallest of Item[StartingIndex]... Item[K] and Position does not change. Either way, Position becomes the index of the smallest number in Item[StartingIndex]... Item[K]. Execution of INC(K) then makes it again true that Position is the index of the smallest number in Item[StartingIndex]... Item[K−1].

Loop Invariants

A **loop invariant** for a WHILE statement is a statement LI with the following three properties:

1. LI is true the first time the WHILE condition is evaluated.
2. If LI is true at a given time when the WHILE condition is evaluated and found true, it follows that LI is also true the next time the WHILE condition is evaluated.
3. It is easy to see that, if LI is true at a time when the WHILE condition is evaluated and found false, the objective to be accomplished by the loop is in fact accomplished.

Since (C) is true when the WHILE condition becomes false, that means that K is greater than Size. Therefore, Position is the index of the smallest number in Item[StartingIndex]... Item[Size]. The statement (C) is therefore a loop invariant of the WHILE statement in (A). Remember that the first and second properties listed imply that LI is true every time the WHILE condition is evaluated.

Loop Invariant for a Standard Linked List

Before we can discuss loop invariants for a standard linked list, we have to have an explicit definition of a standard linked list. A standard linked list is defined by:

- ☐ Each standard linked list contains a specific number of nodes.
- ☐ NIL is a standard linked list with 0 nodes.
- ☐ If P ↑ is a node for which P ↑ .Link is a standard linked list with K nodes, then P is a standard linked list with K + 1 nodes (for any cardinal K).
- ☐ Nothing else is a standard linked list.

This definition bars circular lists. For instance, if Data ↑ is a node for which Data ↑ .Link equals Data, then Data and Data ↑ .Link are the same list; thus Data does not fit the definition of a standard linked list, since if it did, Data would have both K nodes and K + 1 nodes, a contradiction.

The following program segment is some coding for a variant of the WriteAll utility for a standard linked list. The objective to be accomplished by this segment (D) is to write all information values in a standard linked list named Data and to tell how many there are:

```
(D)  P := Data;
     Count := 0;
     WHILE P # NIL DO
          OutputInfo (P ↑ .Info);
          P := P ↑ .Next;
          INC (Count);
     END;
     WriteInt (Count, 1);
```

A reasonable loop invariant for segment (D) is the following statement:

(E) There are Count information values on the Data list that are not on the P list, and all of them have been written out.

To show that (E) is in fact a loop invariant, we have to show that the three properties of loop invariants hold. The statement (E) is true the first time the WHILE condition is evaluated: There are 0 nodes on Data that are not on P, since P equals Data; Count is 0, and 0 information values have been written out. Now if (E) is true at a given time when the WHILE condition is evaluated and found TRUE, three actions are carried out:

☐ The OutputInfo statement writes P ↑ .Info, so the first Count+1 information values on Data have been written out, namely, all those that are not on the P ↑ .Link list.

☐ Then P is assigned P ↑ .Link, so now there are Count+1 information values on Data that are not on P, all of which have been written out.

☐ Finally, Count is incremented, so now there are Count information values on the Data list that are not on the P list, all of which have been written out. Thus (E) is true again, just in time for the next evaluation of the WHILE condition.

It is easy to see that, if (E) is true at a time when the WHILE condition is evaluated and found FALSE, P is NIL and thus has 0 nodes, so all the information values on the Data list have been written out. This verifies that all three properties of loop invariants hold.

Note that in proving statements about segment (D) I assumed that the OutputInfo procedure works correctly. In general, you verify a given procedure on the assumption that other procedures work correctly. If they do not, you will discover that when you try to verify those other procedures.

The Value of Loop Invariants

When you have to develop an algorithm to accomplish a given task, it can be very helpful to first develop a good loop invariant if the task is not too trivial. For instance, if the task is to sort the numbers in an array Item[1]... Item[Size], you might decide on the following loop invariant:

(F) All the values in Item[1]... Item[K] are in increasing order.

Then you write a WHILE statement for which (1) this statement is true every time the WHILE condition is evaluated, and (2) K increases until it eventually becomes Size. At that point, the array will be sorted.

Obviously, statement (F) will be true when K is 1. So the overall form of the WHILE statement could be:

(G) K := 1;
       WHILE K < Size DO
             INC (K);
             SortItems1ToKGivenThatItems1ToKminus1AreAlreadySorted;
       END;

The key to developing the algorithm for sorting Item[1]... Item[K] given that Item[1]... Item[K−1] are already in order is to recognize that the values in Item[1]... Item[K−1] must keep their position relative to each other and that the value in Item[K] must be inserted in the appropriate place in that sequence. This means that we can use the InsertInOrder procedure in Example 2.2B.

Another use of a loop invariant is: Suppose that you have developed a fairly complex algorithm whose overall logic is a looping statement. The logic feels right to you, but you are not absolutely sure it gives the correct result in every case. Write down an appropriate loop invariant and then verify that it really is appropriate. This is not as hard as it sounds, since you could not have developed the algorithm without an implicit concept of the loop invariant; you just have to make it explicit. In the process of verifying the loop invariant, you may see a logic error and be able to correct it. When the loop invariant is verified, you can have much more confidence in the correctness of the algorithm. Then write the loop invariant in the comments for the coding, to make the reasoning of the algorithm clear to the reader.

For instance, consider the algorithm presented in Section 2.5 for searching an array Item[1]... Item[Size] to find TheInfo. A reasonable loop invariant for the Binary Search coding is:

(H) If TheInfo is in the array, it is in Item[Bottom]... Item[Top].

Initially, Bottom is 1 and Top is Size, so the first property of a loop invariant is satisfied. When the loop terminates, Bottom equals Top, so it is easy to test whether TheInfo is in the array; that satisfies the third property of a loop invariant. The second property takes some careful logical reasoning, which is typical for loop invariants.

A Taste of Program Verification

Program verification is easiest when the only control statements involved are WHILE (no FOR or REPEAT) and IF...ELSE...END (no ELSIF). That is why I rewrote FOR statements as WHILE statements in the previous discussion. Consider again the initial example, the coding (A) for finding the Position of the smallest value in an array. Example 4.7A illustrates a fuller verification of that coding. I rewrite the IF statement with an ELSE clause, although I simply put an empty statement in that ELSE clause.

Each numbered assertion (1 to 10) in this example can easily be shown to be true at the point where it occurs in the coding. For instance, the IF condition will

EXAMPLE 4.7A _____

```
(* Example of verification of coding *)
(* Define statement C(X) to be:  Position is the index of
   the smallest of Item[StartingIndex]... Item[X]        *)

   Position := StartingIndex;
                    (* 1.    C(StartingIndex) is true  *)
   K := StartingIndex + 1;
                    (* 2.    C(K-1) is true             *)
   WHILE K <= Size DO
                    (* 3.    C(K-1) is true, K <= Size *)
      IF Item [K] < Item [Position] THEN
                    (* 4.    C(K-1) is true and         *)
                    (*       Item[K] < Item[Position]   *)
         Position := K;
                    (* 5.    C(K) is true               *)
      ELSE
                    (* 6.    C(K-1) is true and         *)
                    (*       Item[K] >= Item[Position] *)
         (* empty statement *);
                    (* 7.    C(K) is true               *)
      END;
                    (* 8.    C(K) is true               *)
      INC (K);
                    (* 9.    C(K-1) is true             *)
   END;
                    (*10.    C(K-1) is true, K > Size  *)
(* THEREFORE:  C(Size) is true. *)
```

be either true or false, so one of the two subordinate statement sequences will be executed. One makes statement 5 true and the other makes statement 7 true. Since statements 5, 7, and 8 are identical, it follows that statement 8 is true after execution of that IF statement.

The following segment of Example 4.7A is typical in the verification of assignment statements; the *postcondition* 2 follows from the *precondition* 1 by replacing K by StartingIndex+1 in the postcondition:

```
                      (*  1.    C(StartingIndex) is true      *)
       K := StartingIndex + 1;
                      (*  2.    C(K-1) is true                 *)
```

I suggest you spend a few minutes studying this example to get a feel for what is going on. I do not use this material anywhere else in this book, but you can expect to see more on the subject as you progress further in computer science.

Check Your Understanding

1. Find a reasonable loop invariant for the WHILE statement of the CompareStr procedure in Example 2.1B.

2. Find a reasonable loop invariant for the WHILE statement in Example 1.3A.

3. (NA) Find a reasonable loop invariant for the FOR statement in Example 1.7A, after rewriting it as:
   K := 0; WHILE K <= HIGH(GivenArray) DO ... INC (K); END

4.8 IMPLEMENTING TableADT: HASH TABLE WITH CHAINING

You have to have studied Section 3.10 on Hashing to understand this section, which describes several efficient implementations of TableADT and DictiADT when you have one large table rather than many small tables. The methods described here are practical only if lists are implemented as linked lists rather than as arrays. They are designed for several hundred or several thousand records.

Hash Table with Chaining to Implement TableADT

Assume that InfoADT exports an Information variable named NoInfo to be used to indicate the absence of information and also exports a function with the following heading:

```
PROCEDURE Hash (TheInfo : Information;
                Maximum : CARDINAL) : CARDINAL;
```

This Hash function returns a number from 1 to Maximum that is computed from the ID or whatever Compare uses. The values returned should be spread fairly evenly over the range from 1 to Maximum. Maximum should be chosen to be at least as large as the number of different information values in the list, possibly two or three times as large.

The implementation of TableADT presented in Section 3.10 was: Declare an array of MaxSize Information variables and initialize each component to NoInfo. To insert TheInfo in the table, put it in the component with index Hash(TheInfo, MaxSize). To find TheInfo in the table, look in the component with index Hash(TheInfo, MaxSize); if you see NoInfo, then TheInfo is not there. Serious problems with this method arise when two or more information variables have the same hash number.

An excellent solution is to have an array of MaxSize linked lists rather than an array of information variables. You let the list at component H contain all the information variables for which Hash returns H. Some lists will be empty and some will contain several values. But if the number of lists is approximately equal to the number of information values, the average size of each list will be 1, so a sequential search of a list should not take long. Also, you do not need to have the NoInfo value when you use this **hash table with chaining** solution (Figure 17).

Normally, you should choose MaxSize to be close to the maximum number of information values you expect to have in the table. However, the nice thing about this implementation of TableADT is that any positive integer for MaxSize will work, though with less efficiency. If you make a mistake about the number of information values or someone uses the program for a number greatly different from what you intended, that will not cause the program to crash or give wrong answers. For instance, if this table is used in a compiler to store all the identifiers

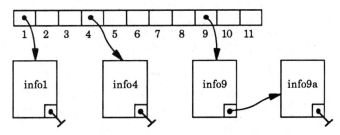

FIGURE 17. A hash table with chaining.

in a program, a reasonable choice for MaxSize might be 500. That should handle programs on the order of 50 pages reasonably efficiently. If the compiler processes a program with only 20 identifiers, it is wasting space with very little increase in speed; if a program declares several thousand identifiers, it might compile two or three times as slowly per page, but at least it will compile.

Coding for Hash Table with Chaining

The list at component H in the array can be used with the naive layered implementation of tables for the information values with the hash value H. The following declaration could be used in TableADT, with Lists implemented however you like, although the standard linked list implementation is usually best.

```
TYPE Table = POINTER TO RECORD
                Lst   : ARRAY [1..MaxSize] OF List;
                Index : CARDINAL;
                Loc   : Location;
             END;
```

The "marker" on the current information value is indicated by giving the index of the list it is in and the location in that list. If the marker is not on any information value, you set Index to 0. The Create procedure in TableADT will contain initialization code to create MaxSize empty lists and lay the "marker" to one side:

```
(* TableADT.Create for hash table with chaining *)
NEW (Data);
Data↑.Index := 0;
FOR K := 1 TO MaxSize DO
    ListADT.Create (Data↑.Lst [K]);
END;
```

The PutIn procedure puts the given information value on the front of the appropriate list, so it can be coded as:

```
(* TableADT.PutIn for hash table with chaining *)
Data↑.Index := Hash (TheInfo, MaxSize);
Data↑.Loc := FirstLocation (Data↑.Lst [Data↑.Index]);
Insert (TheInfo, Data↑.Loc, Data↑.Lst [Data↑.Index]);
```

The Find procedure searches for the given information on the list at component Hash(TheInfo, MaxSize); if it does not find the information, Data ↑ .Index is assigned 0. Thus InTable is just RETURN Data ↑ .Index#0, and Inspect is coded as:

```
IF Data↑.Index # 0 THEN
    LookAt (TheInfo, Data↑.Loc, Data↑.Lst [Data↑.Index]);
END;
```

Execution time for PutIn, Find, TakeOut, and Inspect depends only on the relation between MaxSize and the number of information values. In other words, if program X differs from program Y only in that X has MaxSize 10 times as large, X can handle 10 times the number of information values that Y can with no decrease in speed.

The only significant disadvantage to this method, in comparison with a hash table with open addressing, is the cost in space when you use pointers to information values rather than the information values themselves. For a total of N information values you should have an array of approximately N pointers to short linked lists. Each node on a list contains not only a pointer to an information value but a pointer to the next node on the list, so there are 2*N pointers in nodes, for a total of 3*N pointer values in addition to the space required for the N information values. A hash table with open addressing, as described in Section 3.10, is quite efficient when there are twice as many array components as there are information values. That requires 2*N pointers to information values instead of 3*N pointer values. The difference may be important in certain applications.

Hash Table with Chaining to Implement DictiADT

Many applications of tables require that the information be stored in order. For instance, a decent compiler should offer the option of having a **cross-reference listing** printed out. This listing gives all identifiers in alphabetic order with the numbers of all lines on which they are referenced. One way to do this is to sort them at the end of the compilation phase and then print them out. This takes quite a while, however. Time is saved if the identifiers are kept in sorted order in the table, especially if the sortedness can be used to save time in searching.

The Hash function could be designed to reflect the ordering of the information values. If all values in Lst[1] come first, then all values in Lst[2], and so on, you can implement DictiADT by keeping each linked list in increasing order. For instance, if the ID is a person's name or other alphabetic information, using only capital letters with "@" as a filler for words that are too short, the Hash function could return a number from 1 to 702 as follows:

```
RETURN 27 * (ORD (ID [0]) - 65) + (ORD (ID [1]) - 64) + 1
```

This formula depends on the fact that "@" comes just before "A" in the ASCII code; if a blank were used as the filler, an adjustment would have to be made. The first term gives a multiple of 27: 0, 27, 54, 81, and so on (assuming that "@" cannot be the first character of the ID). The second term gives a number from 0 to 26; with the 1 added, you get a number from 1 to 27. Thus words beginning with "A" have hash numbers from 1 to 27; "A" goes to 1, "AA..." goes to 2, "AB..." goes to 3,... "AZ..." goes to 27. Words beginning with "B" have hash numbers from 28 to 54; and so on. The last group would be "ZZ...", which has a hash number of 27*25+26+1 = 702.

If you feel that 702 is far too many, you could use only the first letter (to have 26 lists) or divide the second term by 3 (which gives you 234 lists) or make some other such modification. The objective is to have lists with an average size of about 1. Then you can print the whole table in order by going through the lists in order of hash numbers.

The real problem with this means of hashing is that it does not spread the values out evenly, so some of the lists will be much longer than others. For instance, how many people's names or identifiers in a program begin with QR or KB? As an example of the imbalance possible, a certain commercially available 130-page word-processing program names all its editor-feature procedures beginning with the word Edit, as in EditBlockMove or EditExit. That means that about 5% of all identifiers in this humongous program would go in the ED list of the alphabetized hash table.

Check Your Understanding

1. Write the TakeOut procedure for the implementation of TableADT using hashing with chaining.

2. Write the Destroy procedure for the implementation of TableADT using hashing with chaining.

3. (NA) Make a reasonable adjustment in the hashing formula given for keeping alphabetic IDs in order, assuming that a blank (CHR(32)) is used to fill out short words instead of "@".

4. (NA) Write the Find procedure for the implementation of TableADT using hashing with chaining.

4.9 IMPLEMENTATION OF DictiADT: INDEXED SEQUENTIAL ACCESS

The following paragraphs describe an implementation of DictiADT that maintains the table as an array of lists (although it may not look that way at first). This implementation is a variation in which the individual lists are roughly the same size, with much better uniformity than for a hash table with chaining. However, it uses binary search to find the correct component, so execution time may be slightly more than for the hash table. This method is called an **indexed sequential access method**.

The basic idea is that you use the ordered linked list with header node implementation described in Section 4.5. In addition, you keep an index, which is an array that initially records the address of perhaps every seventh node in the linked list. As insertions and deletions occur, the distances between nodes addressed by the array varies somewhat. For this implementation, you do not need a Hash function or a NoInfo value; you only use the Compare procedure to find something. The method works quickly if, during any one run of the program, there are not too many insertions and deletions as a percentage of the total number of information values in the original data structure (otherwise the index becomes unbalanced).

A Concrete Example

In a typical application, a company has a large amount of data in written records that it wants converted for computerized access; perhaps the company has grown past the point where it can efficiently work with written records. A secretary enters all the data in alphabetic order in a disk file, using a word processor or using a data-entry program designed for that purpose. In fact, the program described next can be used as long as the user exits the program and reenters it whenever it becomes irritatingly slow, perhaps every 20 or 30 entries.

This company's data forms a data base of perhaps 1000 records. Each day, your program is to read all the data into memory and permit the user to make numerous modifications in the data, including perhaps 20 to 50 insertions and deletions. After each day's activities, all the updated information is written to the disk file in order, in preparation for the next day's activities. The number of records in the data base gradually increases over time, by perhaps 50 records a month.

For this indexed sequential method, the table is essentially an array of lists with at least one seventh as many lists as there are records. The reason for the one seventh is that a sequential search of seven records is at least as fast as a binary search on the average, since in either case an average of four records have to be inspected. For instance, we might use an index array of size 500 for the initial data base of 1000 records, with the intention of increasing the size of the index and recompiling the program in a few years when the data base grows to more than 3500 records (which would make one seventh as many lists as records).

Assume that we implement DictiADT using the usual declarations of Node as a record with Information and PointerToNode fields. The implementation module declares a Table as:

```
TYPE    Table = POINTER TO RECORD
                    Head, Loc : PointerToNode;
                    Index : ARRAY [1..MaxSize] OF PointerToNode;
                    Size : CARDINAL;        (* size of the index *)
                    IsThere : BOOLEAN;      (* tested by InTable *)
                END;
```

The following describes the behavior of the program on a typical day when there are 1350 records in the data base, assuming MaxSize is 500: The program initially determines the file containing the data and the number of records in the file (1350). Then it calls ReadTable, which creates a linked list with header node Data ↑ .Head and reads the ordered information from the file into the list. Data ↑ .Loc is initialized to the header node, and Data ↑ .IsThere is initialized to FALSE. Since there are 1350 values, the program computes 1350 DIV 500 and rounds up, obtaining 3. Thus ReadTable assigns the address of every third node to the Index array, those containing information values 3, 6, 9, and so on (Fig. 18). Index[450] contains the address of the 1351st node, which contains the 1350th information value. The index-making procedure called by ReadTable is in Example 4.9A.

When these preliminaries are finished, the program announces it is ready for the day's activities. Each time the user requests a record by giving the ID, the Find procedure performs a binary search on the 450 records in its index (there is no information in the header node) until it finds the record that comes *just before* the given record. The binary search should be preceded by a test to see if the information at Index[1] is less than the given information value. If not, the sequential search will begin with the header node.

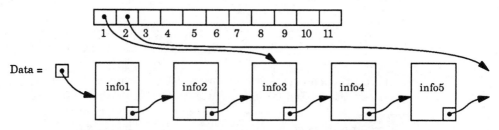

FIGURE 18. Part of a linked list with an index every three nodes.

EXAMPLE 4.9A _____

```
PROCEDURE MakeIndex (NumValues : CARDINAL;
                     VAR Data  : Table);
VAR
    Where          : PointerToNode;
    GroupSize, K : CARDINAL;
BEGIN
    GroupSize := (NumValues + MaxSize - 1) DIV MaxSize;
    WITH Data^ DO  (* fields include Head, Index, Size *)
        Size := 0;
        Where := Head;
        FOR K := 1 TO NumValues DO
            Where := Where^.Link;
            IF K MOD GroupSize = 0 THEN
                INC (Size);
                Index [Size] := Where;
            END;
        END;
    END;
END MakeIndex;
```

After Find determines the proper address, it does a sequential search in the list of 1350 ordered records from that point on. Data ↑ .Loc is assigned the address of the node just before the one sought or, if not there, of the record that would come directly before it if it were there. Then PutIn, TakeOut, or Inspect can easily be performed. When the WriteTable procedure is called at the end of the day's activities, the revised information is written back to the file and the information in memory is disposed of. The coding for PutIn does not affect the index array at all:

```
(* body of PutIn *)
Find (TheInfo, Data);
NEW (P);
P↑.Info := TheInfo;
P↑.Link := Data↑.Loc↑.Link;
Data↑.Loc↑.Link := P;
Data↑.IsThere := TRUE;
```

The FindNextIn procedure has the job of moving Data ↑ .Loc on to the next location, if it is not at the end of the linked list. However, an adjustment must be made if the previous Find operation failed (indicated by Data ↑ .IsThere being FALSE). In that case, the current location does not change.

```
(* body of FindNextIn *)
IF Data↑.IsThere AND (Data↑.Loc↑.Link # NIL) THEN
    Data↑.Loc := Data↑.Loc↑.Link;
END;
Data↑.IsThere := Data↑.Loc↑.Link # NIL;
```

You can think of the Index array as dividing the main list into 450 sublists, each originally having three records. As the day goes on, insertions and deletions in the list cause some sublists to have more or less than three records, but that should almost never cause any noticeable degradation in performance. On the average, a search requires 10 comparisons (using binary search) to find the right index record and 2 comparisons (using sequential search) to find the right information on a list of three records, which takes only a fraction of a second. In fact, if you forget to increase the size of the array from 500 and the list grows to 10,000 records over a period of years, the average number of comparisons grows to only 10+11, which takes less than twice as long.

A number of improvements can be made in this design to improve execution time. For instance, the index can be created as the file is read. Another way to speed things up is to declare the index array with components 0..MaxSize and assign the given information value to the header node; you can save an extra comparison during the binary search that way. Even better, if InfoADT exports a NoInfo value that is smaller than all legitimate information values, you can put NoInfo in the header node and consider it one of the index components.

Deletions in the Indexed Sequential Method

If one of the index nodes is deleted, the corresponding component in the index array must be adjusted. You can assign it the node before it or the node after it in the linked list, whichever you prefer. You also have to allow for the possibility that the list becomes empty during execution of the program.

With any kind of reasonably distributed sequence of insertions and deletions, the addresses in the index array will stay approximately three places apart at all times (or whatever the GroupSize is). In any case, as long as you maintain the property that the information at Index[K+1] never comes before the information at Index[K], you avoid incorrect results; there is no harm in having two or more consecutive index addresses be the same.

Keeping the Information in External Storage

In practice, the method just described often fails because of lack of memory. A typical record for a customer of a company might require 100 to 1000 bytes of storage, so a thousand such records might be pushing it. The following discussion shows a way around this problem. *Note:* Skip this subsection unless you read Section 3.11 on cursors.

Most programming languages have the facility for accessing disk files as if they were arrays. That is, they have procedures for using **random-access files** that allow you to read one record from a given position in the file or to write one record to a given position in the file. Each record has a position number from 1 up to however many records there are in the file. Such a file can be many times larger than what you could store in the computer's memory.

The whole file can be considered to be one giant linked list. Each record in this file corresponds to a node on a linked list in memory; it contains the information and also a Link field, which gives the position number of the next node (in the file) in the linked list. In place of NIL, you use a position number of 0. When a program creates a table, it does not have to read the records to create the linked list Data ↑ .Head, because the linked list already exists in the file.

For the illustration with 1350 records, the program initially reads every third record into memory and stores its ID (or whatever Compare uses) in the index array of 450 values. The reason for storing only the ID is to save storage space in memory.

The program cannot use NEW and DISPOSE to manage storage in a file, so it has to keep track of extra "nodes" in the file. The easiest way is a linked list of unused nodes, such as was discussed in Section 3.11: A variable named Available contains the position number of the first node on a linked list (actually a stack) of nodes that have been discarded. When a deletion is made, the node is unhooked from the main linked list in the usual manner and pushed onto the stack of available nodes. When an insertion is made, the program first checks to see if Available is nonzero. If so, it pops the top node from the available list and hooks it into the main list. If Available is 0, the program extends the file to make room for a new node.

Reading information from a file takes much more time than retrieving it from memory, so it would be a good idea to store the up to 500 records of the index in memory, or at least their IDs. It is highly convenient for the whole file to have a special header node with some kind of dummy ID (such as 0 or all blanks) that precedes (using Compare) all real ID values. This header node is valuable because no information about the linked list has to be stored in a separate file: The header node can always be in position 1 (so the program knows where to find it) and can contain a note of the number of records in the file (so the program can determine NumValues) and a note of what value Available currently has.

This indexed sequential method works well for several hundred to several thousand records. When you have hundreds of thousands of records, the method is too slow. In that case, you can use an index that gives you access to any of a large number of indexes that give you access to records. The various indexes should be stored in external memory so they do not have to be rebuilt each time. The section on B+ trees in Chapter 5 presents techniques along these lines.

Check Your Understanding

1. For the indexed sequential implementation (Example 4.9A), assume that Max-Size is 255 and there are currently 1800 records. Which records are put in the index? How many records are in the index? What is the average number of comparisons needed to find a particular record?

2. In Example 4.9A, explain why you cannot assign (NumValues−1) DIV Max-Size + 1 to GroupSize. Also explain why evaluation of K MOD GroupSize cannot crash the program because of division by zero.

3. Write the FindFirstIn procedure for the implementation of DictiADT using the indexed sequential method.

4. (NA) Redo Exercise 1 on the assumption that MaxSize is 127 and there are currently 600 records.

4.10 APPLICATION: POLYNOMIAL ARITHMETIC

Consider a program in which a large amount of work is done with polynomials. For instance, you might have to add two polynomials or multiply them together. The following computations illustrate polynomial addition and multiplication as a reminder for those of you who are a bit rusty.

$$
\begin{array}{r}
3x^2 - 5x + 9 \\
+\ \underline{\qquad 7x - 11} \\
3x^2 + 2x - 2
\end{array}
\qquad\qquad
\begin{array}{r}
3x^2 - 5x + 9 \\
\ast\ \underline{\qquad 7x - 11} \\
-33x^2 + 55x - 99 \\
\underline{21x^3 - 35x^2 + 63x \qquad} \\
21x^3 - 68x^2 + 118x - 99
\end{array}
$$

A polynomial is the sum of a number of *terms* ($7x - 11$ is considered to be the sum of the two terms $7x$ and -11). Each term has an *exponent* (the power on x) and a *coefficient* (the constant multiplier). The exponent in the term $7x$ is 1 (since the first power of x is x) and the exponent in the term -11 is 0 (since the zeroth power of x is 1). A reasonable way to implement polynomials in a computer program is to have Information indicate one term and have a List of terms represent a polynomial. Since we may have several forms of InfoADT for various programs, I will call this one TermADT to distinguish it from the others.

The ListADT library module remains unchanged, as it should, except for the addition of some utility procedures such as Copy, Modify, Join, and LastLocation (since I anticipate using them with some frequency) and the replacement of each reference to InfoADT by a reference to TermADT. A decision has to be made about how to arrange the terms in a given list. The two obvious possibilities are increasing and decreasing order of exponents; I opt for the former.

The TermADT Module

TermADT will of course export the Information type as well as the fundamental CreateInfo, CopyInfo, and DestroyInfo procedures. The nature of the coefficient will usually be REAL or INTEGER; we can maintain flexibility by declaring TYPE Domain=REAL and using Domain everywhere. Then if we later want the coefficients to be of INTEGER type, we only need change the declaration of Domain and recompile the module. TermADT should also provide a way to inspect both the coefficient and the exponent of a given term and a way to assign values to either of them. The following four procedures provide this capability:

```
TermADT exports Information, Domain, CreateInfo, CopyInfo,
        DestroyInfo, and:
PROCEDURE SetCoefficient (VAR TheInfo : Information; Given : Domain);
PROCEDURE SetExponent (VAR TheInfo : Information; Given : CARDINAL);
PROCEDURE CoefficientOf (TheInfo : Information) : Domain;
PROCEDURE ExponentOf (TheInfo : Information) : CARDINAL;
```

The only significant parts of a term are the coefficient and exponent, so these seven procedures yield a completely adequate library module. In fact, the CopyInfo procedure is a utility; its function can be accomplished using the other procedures, as follows:

```
SetCoefficient (TheInfo, CoefficientOf (Source));
SetExponent (TheInfo, ExponentOf (Source));
```

You might want to have a Compare function to compare two terms to see whether the exponents match, but you can test the condition ExponentOf(First) = ExponentOf(Second) just as easily and somewhat more naturally. The only reason I can think of for keeping Compare is so you can have Sort as a ListADT utility without change.

Some additional utilities might be a good idea. In general, you should strike a reasonable balance between including procedures that are used in many different situations and keeping the library module down to a reasonable size. The best idea is to use the basic module in designing two or three programs before you decide on the best choice of utilities. ReadTerm and WriteTerm might be useful, but I suggest just one additional utility for now: **NewTerm**. This function accepts a coefficient and an exponent and creates a term for them. Granted, this can be done easily with other procedures, but I expect it to occur frequently enough to justify having it as a utility.

Using the TermADT and ListADT Modules

There are many different sorts of things that a client module might want to do with polynomials. Some fundamental ones would be to read a polynomial, write a polynomial, add two polynomials, multiply a polynomial by a constant, and differentiate a polynomial. I will discuss the algorithm for adding two polynomials and leave the rest as exercises.

A reasonable way to obtain the sum of two polynomials without changing either of the given polynomials is to make a copy of the second one in a Sum parameter and then add the first polynomial to Sum. The overall logic could be:

Algorithm for adding two polynomials:
1. Create in Sum a duplicate copy of the second polynomial;
2. Consider the first term (if any) of the first polynomial;
3. DO repeatedly until there is no term under consideration:
    3.a. Let s denote the location in Sum where that term should go;
    3.b. IF the term at s (if any) has the same exponent, then:
        Add the coefficients;
    OTHERWISE:
        Insert a copy of the term under consideration in the Sum;
    3.c. Consider the next term (if any) of the first polynomial.

Further refinements of this logic can lead to the coding in Example 4.10A.

An alternative approach to this problem is to join the two polynomials, sort them in increasing order of exponents, and then go through the result and merge adjacent terms with the same exponent. That may be even more trouble, however.

Check Your Understanding

1. Revise Example 4.10A to omit the use of NewTerm, so you can see how handy it is to have NewTerm.

2. What changes should be made in Example 4.10A to obtain a procedure that subtracts the Second polynomial from the First?

3. (NA) Write a function to evaluate a given polynomial at a given real number and return the result.

EXAMPLE 4.10A _____

```
PROCEDURE AddPolys (VAR Sum        : List;
                        First, Second : List);
    (* Add the two polynomials First and Second together to
       obtain a new polynomial, to be stored in Sum *)
VAR
    FirstTerm, SumTerm : Information;
    f, s : Location;
BEGIN
    Create (Sum);
    Copy (Sum, Second);
    s := FirstLocation (Sum);
    LookAt (SumTerm, s, Sum);

    f := FirstLocation (First);
    WHILE InList (f, First) DO

        LookAt (FirstTerm, f, First);

        (* set s to point to where FirstTerm goes *)
        WHILE InList (s, Sum) AND (ExponentOf (SumTerm)
                      < ExponentOf (FirstTerm)) DO
            s := NextLocation (s, Sum);
            LookAt (SumTerm, s, Sum);
        END;

        (* add FirstTerm to Sum *)
        IF NOT InList (s, Sum) OR (ExponentOf (SumTerm)
                          > ExponentOf (FirstTerm)) THEN
            Insert (NewTerm (CoefficientOf (FirstTerm),
                        ExponentOf (FirstTerm)),
                        s, Sum);
        ELSE   (* they are equal *)
            SetCoefficient (SumTerm, CoefficientOf(SumTerm)
                          + CoefficientOf (FirstTerm));
            Modify (SumTerm, s, Sum);
        END;

        f := NextLocation (f, First);

    END;
END AddPolys;
```

4. (NA) Write the full implementation module for TermADT using Information= POINTER TO RECORD Coef: Domain; Exp: CARDINAL; END.

5. (NA) Write a procedure to modify a given polynomial by multiplying it by a given term.

6. (NA) Write a procedure to find the derivative of a given polynomial.

4.11   ADDRESS AND PROCEDURE TYPES

The eight procedures in ListADT require only the import of Information from InfoADT, not any of the other procedures such as Compare and CreateInfo. Almost every time you have a new application using ListADT, you will need to revise InfoADT. Since ListADT imports from InfoADT, that means you have to recompile ListADT, which means it can no longer be used for a previous application. A solution is to have several identical copies of ListADT (with different names, of course), but that is wasteful of space and time.

Modula-2 has a number of features that many other languages do not have. Among these features are ones that make it possible to have the ListADT library module independent of the InfoADT module. They require, however, that Information be a pointer type. Thus you sacrifice some flexibility, but you cannot expect something for nothing in computer science.

The ADDRESS Type

The only change required in ListADT is to omit FROM InfoADT IMPORT Information and replace it by the following two lines:

```
FROM SYSTEM IMPORT ADDRESS;
TYPE Information = ADDRESS;
```

SYSTEM is the name of a library module that every Modula-2 compiler should have. Actually, it is not a free-standing library module at all; it is part of the compiler. In a way, ADDRESS is the same as a built-in identifier except that you must explicitly "build it in" by importing it from SYSTEM. The use of ADDRESS often causes a program to be dependent on a particular implementation, that is, not be **portable** to another machine and compiler; so Modula-2 requires you to acknowledge explicitly the implementation-dependency in the program by an import from SYSTEM.

ADDRESS is a type that is compatible with all pointer types. Thus Information can be declared in InfoADT as POINTER TO anything and imported by a client module; that Information will be accepted as an actual parameter for a formal ADDRESS parameter in ListADT. You can assign any pointer value to an ADDRESS variable and compare two ADDRESS values for equality.

To summarize: If you replace the import section as just described in the ListADT definition module, you only need to compile it and its implementation module once and for all. You can have several different client modules that use different pointer definitions of Information, all importing from the same

ListADT module. List is then said to be a **generic type**. The same thing applies to QueueADT, StackADT, and TableADT.

Values of ADDRESS type can use the operators and numerals that CARDI-NALs use. Thus the following statements are legal when A is declared to be a variable of ADDRESS type: A := 1; A := A+1. However, some compilers may require you to use A := ADDRESS(1) for the first statement, since they consider a 1 by itself on the right of := to be a CARDINAL expression, and a CARDINAL cannot be assigned to an ADDRESS.

You can also import a function ADR from SYSTEM. This function accepts a variable of any type and returns the ADDRESS of its storage location. For instance, If you declare VAR A: ADDRESS; R: REAL, execution of A := ADR(R) assigns to A the address of the location where R is stored (using the machine's internal numbering system).

Note: Modula-2 provides a way to have Information be a static variable instead of a pointer variable and still make ListADT independent of InfoADT. The method requires that you replace references to Information parameters by references to ARRAY OF WORD, where WORD is imported from SYSTEM. However, development of this approach is beyond the scope of this book.

Procedure Types

What if you want to add a few utility procedures to ListADT, procedures that use Compare or CreateInfo from InfoADT, for instance? This can also be done without having to recompile ListADT for each different InfoADT. The trick is to avoid importing anything from InfoADT. The language feature that makes this trick possible is that each global procedure declaration is treated as declaring a **constant of a procedure type**. You can also declare procedure variables and procedure type-identifiers. For instance, you can add the following declarations to the ListADT definition module:

```
TYPE  InfoProcessor = PROCEDURE (VAR Information);
VAR   CompareInfo : PROCEDURE (Information, Information) : INTEGER;
      MakeInfo, UnmakeInfo, ReadInfo, WriteInfo : InfoProcessor;
```

You have now declared five procedure variables. A client module can import Compare (a procedure constant) from an information-handling library module or declare Compare itself as a procedure constant; then it imports the CompareInfo variable from ListADT, executes the assignment statement CompareInfo := Compare, and calls a utility Sort or Search procedure. The implementation of the

Sort or Search procedure refers to the CompareInfo variable, which has the value given it by the client module, namely the Compare procedure.

Similarly, the utility module ReadAll shown in Example 4.2A can be rewritten in terms of ReadInfo and UnmakeInfo. The client module can import these two procedure variables from ListADT and assign the equivalent of InfoADT.InputInfo and InfoADT.DestroyInfo to them, which allows ReadAll to work properly. These two procedures are both of the same **procedure type**; they have one parameter, which is a VAR Information parameter, and that is the definition of the InfoProcessor type. Note that, for simplicity, I have said that WriteInfo is also of type InfoProcessor; that means that InfoADT.OutputInfo cannot be used without changing its formal value parameter to a VAR parameter.

Modula-2 provides another way that procedures can be accessed in ListADT without importing them. It requires the declaration of InfoProcessor, but not of the global procedure variables such as CompareInfo. For an example, you can rewrite the heading of ReadAll as follows:

```
PROCEDURE ReadAll (VAR Data : List;
                   ReadInfo, UnmakeInfo : InfoProcessor);
```

Now you can call the ReadAll procedure from a client module with a statement like the following:

```
ReadAll (Data, InfoADT.InputInfo, InfoADT.DestroyInfo);
```

This statement assigns the two procedure constants declared in InfoADT to the two procedure parameters declared in the heading of ReadAll. Personally, I like the first way of doing things better; it keeps the old familiar headings for the utility procedures. But it should only be used if the values of the procedure variables never change for any one client module.

One restriction that applies to the use of procedure types is that any procedure constant (i.e., the actual procedure value) assigned to a procedure variable or passed to a procedure parameter must be declared globally to some normal module; it cannot be local to another procedure, or a built-in procedure, or imported from SYSTEM.

For Pascal Programmers. The equivalent of ADDRESS and ADR are not available in Pascal. However, a primitive equivalent of procedure types is available. The difference is that you have to describe the procedure type explicitly in the heading of the procedure. For instance, you could have the following procedure heading for ReadAll:

```
PROCEDURE ReadAll (VAR Data : List;
                   PROCEDURE InputInfo (VAR X : Information);
                   PROCEDURE DestroyInfo (VAR X : Information));
```

Now you can call the ReadAll procedure from a client module with a statement like the following:

```
ReadAll (Data, InputInfo, DestroyInfo);
```

Check Your Understanding

1. Write a ProcessAllInfo utility procedure for the standard linked list implementation of ListADT. It executes a given InfoProcessor for each information value on a given list, so there are two parameters. Note that this is a generalization of the WriteAll utility.

2. What changes would have to be made in the TableADT definition module (Example 3.7A) so you could compile it once and for all and have various client modules use it with different Information pointer types?

4.12 STORAGE MANAGEMENT: StoreADT

This section discusses some methods of allocating and deallocating storage for dynamic variables. The methods are presented by considering possible implementations of the ALLOCATE and DEALLOCATE procedures. These implementations provide further practice with linked lists. It is assumed throughout this section that the processor measures storage in units called words, which may be 2 or 4 bytes or some other amount.

Managing Your Own Storage

When you use NEW or DISPOSE in a Modula-2 program, the compiler replaces those procedure calls by calls to ALLOCATE and DEALLOCATE, respectively, adding as a second parameter the number of words of storage to be allocated. In this section, a new library module named StoreADT is developed. To use it, you would replace imports from STORAGE by imports from StoreADT, as follows:

```
FROM StoreADT IMPORT ALLOCATE, DEALLOCATE;
```

When you have this import section, the imports come from the library module shown in Example 4.12A. The headings for the two procedures are the same as for the ones in the Storage module, which is normally used. However, the implementation is the one developed here, not the one developed by the team that wrote the compiler.

The built-in SYSTEM library module exports four identifiers that we use in this section: ADDRESS, WORD, ADR, and TSIZE. A formal parameter of type ADDRESS can have any pointer value as the actual parameter, which is the reason we use it in the ALLOCATE and DEALLOCATE procedures.

A WORD is the standard unit of storage for your particular computer. We begin by reserving a large amount of space that this library module will control, handing it out and taking it back as requested. The easiest way to do that is to make the following declaration:

```
VAR Store : ARRAY [1..50000] OF WORD;
```

EXAMPLE 4.12A _____

```
DEFINITION MODULE StoreADT;
    (* storage management *)
    (* Written by William C. Jones, March 19-- *)

FROM SYSTEM IMPORT ADDRESS;

PROCEDURE ALLOCATE (VAR Addr : ADDRESS;
                    NumWords : CARDINAL);
    (* Allocate a block with NumWords words, beginning at
       the address returned in Addr.  Crash if no space is
       available  *)

PROCEDURE DEALLOCATE (VAR Addr : ADDRESS;
                      NumWords : CARDINAL);
    (* Return to available storage the block with NumWords
       words, beginning at the address in Addr  *)

END StoreADT.
```

The 50000 is arbitrary and depends on the particular computer that is being used, so of course we use a constant-identifier for that number, to make conversions for other computers easy.

ADR(Store) is the address of the first word of the variable Store. We need this address in order to compute addresses of various words within the Store array. For instance, if we want to allocate the words in the range Store[10].. Store[14], we pass ADR(Store)+10 back in the Addr parameter of ALLOCATE and 5 in its NumWords parameter.

The only other import from SYSTEM that is used here is the **TSIZE** function. This function tells the number of words required for a variable of a given type. To implement a linked list, we declare a Node type, as usual. Then TSIZE(Node) is the number of words required for one Node variable.

The Linked List of Available Storage

When we have a block of storage that is available for use, we want to keep track of it on a linked list. There are other ways of managing storage, but the library module presented here uses one linked list. The nodes for the linked list also take up storage, so we have to allocate space for them. This can be complicated unless we adopt a standard technique—we make the first part of the block be the list node. We store in each node the size of the block of storage and a link to the next node in the linked list. We do not need to make a note of the starting address of the block of storage, since that is the address of the node itself. However, we do need to be sure that each block is large enough to store the information for one node. So we always allocate at least TSIZE(Node) words of storage in each block. The client module does not have to be aware of this; the implementations of ALLOCATE and DEALLOCATE handle this aspect of storage management.

It is easiest to have a header node on a linked list, although that takes up extra space. Since we will have only one list of available nodes, the one extra node is insignificant. So we begin by choosing a name for the pointer to the head of the list; I call it Avail. Avail is the address of the node of size TSIZE(Node) at the beginning of the Store array; so we assign PointerToNode(ADR(Store)) to Avail. The purpose of the PointerToNode identifier is to cause a type transfer, since ADR(Store) is of type ADDRESS and Avail is of type PointerToNode. If we leave out the type identifier, some compilers may fail to compile the program because of a type mismatch.

The link field of Avail ↑ points to the one block of storage initially available, of size 50000−TSIZE(Node). The address of that one block is ADR(Store)+ TSIZE(Node), since it is TSIZE(Node) words down from the beginning of the Store array. Note that Avail ↑ .Link is a Node with just a few words of space, but it is also the address of the beginning of a very large block of space. The link field of the Avail ↑ .Link node is assigned NIL, since it is the last node on the linked list (Fig. 19).

Example 4.12B contains a full implementation module for StoreADT. You should study the declarations of that module and the body of the module now.

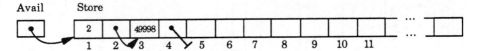

FIGURE 19. Initial configuration of storage.

EXAMPLE 4.12B _____

```
IMPLEMENTATION MODULE StoreADT;
    (* First-Fit method of storage management *)
    (* Written by William C. Jones, March 19-- *)

FROM SYSTEM IMPORT ADDRESS, WORD, ADR, TSIZE;
    (* Method:  Avail is a linked list with header node.
      Each node on the list records the amount of storage
      beginning at its address, and is available for
      allocation.  Initially, Store is allocated and all
      of it except for the first part (for the header
      node) is one block.  Requested space is taken from
      the smallest node of sufficient size, and returned
      space is pushed onto the front of the available
      list.  There is no coalescing -- very primitive. *)

CONST
    MaxWords = 50000;
TYPE
    PointerToNode = POINTER TO Node;
    Node = RECORD
                Size : CARDINAL;
                Link : PointerToNode;
            END;
VAR
    Store : ARRAY [1..MaxWords] OF WORD;
    Avail : PointerToNode;
(******************************************************)

PROCEDURE DEALLOCATE (VAR Addr : ADDRESS;
                          NumWords : CARDINAL);
VAR
    P : PointerToNode;
BEGIN
    IF NumWords < TSIZE (Node) THEN
        NumWords := TSIZE (Node);
    END;
    P            := PointerToNode (Addr);
    P^.Size      := NumWords;
    P^.Link      := Avail^.Link;
    Avail^.Link  := P;
    Addr         := NIL;
END DEALLOCATE;
(******************************************************)
```

(* continued on next page *)

292

```
(* EXAMPLE 4.12B continued *)


PROCEDURE ALLOCATE (VAR Addr     : ADDRESS;
                    WordsNeeded : CARDINAL);
  (*--------------------------------------------------------*)

    PROCEDURE FindBigEnoughBlock (WordsNeeded : CARDINAL;
                                  VAR Parent : PointerToNode);
       (* Find the address of the node that links to
          a node that has at least WordsNeeded words *)
    BEGIN
        Parent := Avail;
        WHILE (Parent^.Link # NIL) AND
              (Parent^.Link^.Size < WordsNeeded) DO
            Parent := Parent^.Link;
        END;
        IF Parent^.Link = NIL THEN
            HALT;
        END;
    END FindBigEnoughBlock;
  (*--------------------------------------------------------*)

VAR
    Parent, Child : PointerToNode;

BEGIN  (* ALLOCATE *)

    IF WordsNeeded < TSIZE (Node) THEN
        WordsNeeded := TSIZE (Node);
    END;

    FindBigEnoughBlock (WordsNeeded, Parent);
    Child := Parent^.Link;

    IF Child^.Size >= WordsNeeded + TSIZE (Node) THEN
        Child^.Size := Child^.Size - WordsNeeded;
        Addr        := ADDRESS (Child) + Child^.Size;
    ELSE
        Parent^.Link := Child^.Link;
        Addr         := Child;
    END;

END ALLOCATE;
(*********************************************************************)

BEGIN          (* initialization *)

    Avail := PointerToNode (ADR (Store));
    Avail^.Size := TSIZE (Node);
    Avail^.Link := PointerToNode (ADR (Store) +
                         TSIZE (Node));
    Avail^.Link^.Size := MaxWords - TSIZE (Node);
    Avail^.Link^.Link := NIL;

END StoreADT.
```

Remember that the body of an implementation module is executed before any module that imports from it is executed. Also, since Avail and Store are variables global to the implementation module, they maintain their value even when no procedure in the module is activated.

The First-Fit Method

Now we consider what method to use to obtain a suitable amount of storage when it is requested by a call to ALLOCATE. The simplest method is called the **First-Fit method**. The general idea is to find the first available block that is at least as big as the requested amount and allocate that; however, if it is too big, we keep the excess available for future requests.

There are several details to consider before this can be considered an algorithm. What if the number of words requested is smaller than TSIZE(Node)? Then we should change it to TSIZE(Node), otherwise, when it is returned we cannot use it in the linked list. Similarly, if the block is only a little larger than the amount requested, so that what is left is not big enough for a Node, we should allocate the whole block, deleting the Node from the linked list of available blocks.

What if there is no block that is big enough? We follow the normal procedure, which is to halt the program at that point. The coding of ALLOCATE corresponding to this development is in Example 4.12B. Do not read the coding for DEALLO-CATE yet.

DEALLOCATE has the task of returning the given block to the available storage list. The easiest way to do this is to put it on the linked list directly after the header node. But first we check to be sure it is at least as large as a Node. If not, we must have allocated some extra space at the time ALLOCATE was executed, so we can safely assume the block has TSIZE(Node) words. Again we have to use a type transfer to convert the given ADDRESS value to a Pointer-ToNode value, to avoid a type mismatch.

Study Example 4.12B carefully now. Can you see how the algorithm occasionally loses track of a small piece of storage? Specifically, if a block of size 20 is requested and a block of size 21 is found, and if TSIZE(Node) is greater than 1, the whole block of 21 words is allocated. When the block is deallocated, it is assumed to have only 20 words; the extra word is lost. This is a defect of the implementation, but the objective has been to develop a workable implementation, not a superefficient one. One solution is to make all blocks a multiple of MinSize, but that wastes space in many applications. The rest of this section discusses some other storage management methods.

Fragmentation

Storage requests can best be met if the available storage consists of a few large blocks rather than many small blocks. There are two reasons: One is that searching for a block takes less time, since there are fewer blocks to inspect and they are more likely to be big enough; another reason is that a request for a 100-word block when only a large number of blocks of less than 100 words are available would halt the program. The presence of a large number of not-very-large blocks is called **external fragmentation**.

By this reasoning, if a request is received for a block of 100 words, and we have blocks of 140 and 100, it is best to allocate the 100-word block instead of the 140-word block. It is better to leave one 140-word block available than two blocks of sizes 100 and 40. So apparently it is worthwhile to search the list for the *smallest* block that is at least the size requested. This is called the **Best-Fit** method, and of course requires more time for searching the list of available blocks. It can also fail when the First-Fit method does not. For instance, if you have blocks of 50, 40, and 30 words on the available list, and if you have requests for blocks of 40, 10, 35, and 30 words in that order, the Best-Fit method fails and the First-Fit method works.

External fragmentation can be minimized by arranging to **coalesce** (merge) two adjacent available blocks into one large block whenever possible. The problem is to find two adjacent available blocks quickly. A reasonable way is to keep the blocks stored on the available list in increasing order of memory address. Then, when you see an available block such that its starting address plus its size is the value in its Link field, you have found two adjacent available blocks you can coalesce. Of course, maintaining the ordering on the linked list takes extra execution time and programmer effort.

External fragmentation and search time are both greatly reduced if you use the **buddy system**. In one standard form of the buddy system, the size of each available and each allocated block is always a power of 2: 1, 2, 4, 8, 16, 32, and so on. An array of linked lists of blocks is kept, one list for each power of 2. For instance, component 5 of the array would contain a pointer to a linked list of blocks of size 32. The lists are not kept in any particular order.

When a request for a block is made, it is satisfied from the appropriate list if possible. If not, a block is taken from the next higher nonempty list and split into two available blocks, called *buddies*. This is repeated until a block of the appropriate size is made, namely, the power of 2 at or just above the size requested.

When a block is deallocated, you first check its buddy to see if it is also available. If so, you coalesce the two buddies and repeat the check. The advantage of this method is that you can easily compute the buddy of any given block of storage without searching through a list.

The problem with this method is that **internal fragmentation** is severe. This means that the amount of unused but unavailable storage in allocated nodes is excessive. For instance, a request for a 36-word block allocates a 64-word block, which wastes 28 words of storage.

Many other methods for managing storage have been developed, most of them more complicated that the ones described in this section. The usual trade-offs between time, space, and effort are central to the analysis of the various methods.

Check Your Understanding

1. Rewrite Example 4.12B to make FindBigEnoughBlock into a function.

2. Rewrite Example 4.12B to find the smallest available block of storage that is big enough for the requirements (the Best-Fit method).

3. (NA) Rewrite the body of ALLOCATE in Example 4.12B to allocate the first part of the available block instead of the last part, when the block is larger than is needed. Discuss which way is better.

4. (NA) Rewrite Example 4.12B to use a ring—a circular linked list without a header node in which you do not bother to keep track of the front of the list, since you can start looking for a block at any point in the circle. Halt the program if the list becomes empty.

5. (NA) Describe the formula that computes the buddy of a given block from the starting address and size of the block.

CHAPTER REVIEW

NIL is a constant that can be compared with any pointer value; thus its type is context-dependent, just as for small nonnegative integers and one-character strings. It is legal to declare a type POINTER TO T when T is a type-identifier declared later in the same type section. This is of importance when you declare a type of variable that involves pointers to variables of that same type.

A linked list is essentially a number of pairs of values, one being an information value on the list and the other being an indicator of another such pair of values. The list is organized in such a way that you can begin from the first information value and reach any other information value by following the indicators. The complete implementation module for ListADT using the standard linked list design is in Example 4.4A.

Top-down analysis can be defined as "the iterative decomposition of a problem into a small number of subproblems until all the problems are small." It is the most useful approach to the solution of large problems. I discussed techniques helpful in carrying out top-down analysis and aspects of efficiency considerations: time, space, and programmer effort.

The header node linked list implementation maintains one extra node at the beginning of the list with no information in it. The circular linked list implementation has the last node linked to the first node; a List is a pointer to the last node. In the doubly linked list implementation, each node has an extra link to the node before; this allows a Location to be a pointer to the node containing the desired information rather than to the node before it, and it allows traversal of a list in reverse order.

Two fast-executing implementations of TableADT use an array of very short lists. In hashing with chaining, a hash function returns a cardinal for each information value, which is the index in the array of the list where you should find the information. In the indexed sequential implementation, you build an index into one large ordered list, consisting of evenly spaced Location values. This index can be searched using Binary Search to find a good starting point for a short sequential search of the large list.

PRACTICE TEST

1. Write the recursive form of the ReadAll utility procedure using the standard linked list implementation. [Example 4.2B]

2. Write the WriteAll utility procedure using the standard linked list implementation. [Example 4.2C]

3. Write the NextLocation function procedure using the standard linked list implementation. [Example 4.4A]

4. Write the LookAt procedure using the standard linked list implementation. [Example 4.4A]

5. Write the Insert procedure using the standard linked list implementation. [Example 4.4A]

6. Write the Join procedure for the basic header node implementation. [Exercise 1 of Section 4.5]

7. Write the LookAt procedure for the circular list implementation. [Exercise 1 of Section 4.6]

PROGRAMMING PROBLEMS

For the problems requiring you to write an implementation module for ListADT, consider adding several utility procedures such as ReadAll, WriteAll, Push, Pop, Peep, Enqueue, Dequeue, Join, Search, and Seek.

1. Rewrite the entire implementation module for ListADT with Where indicating the Node where the information is instead of the Node before it. Where feasible, use the following trick to insert information between nodes N1 and N2: Put N2's information in a new node N0, put the new information in N2, and insert N0 after N2. A similar trick can be used for deletion. Where that does not work, start from the top of the list and work down.

2. Complete the entire implementation module for ListADT using basic header nodes as described at the beginning of Section 4.5.

3. Complete the entire implementation module for ListADT using header nodes in the variant record form as described in Section 4.5.

4. Modify the ListADT implementation module (standard linked list form) in such a way that each procedure except Create that changes a Node (namely Insert, Delete, and Destroy) first checks that it is a valid Node and, if not, refuses to change it. A valid Node is one that has been Created but not yet Destroyed. One rather slow method is to maintain a linked list of security nodes each of whose Info field is simply a pointer to a valid Node. Then you can go down the list to check a given Node. This device prevents a common error, namely, assigning a value to P ↑ when P's value is indeterminate. Such an error can crash the entire operating system of a microcomputer.

5. Complete the entire implementation module for ListADT using a circular linked list as described in Section 4.6.

6. Complete the entire implementation module for ListADT using a circular linked list as described in Section 4.6, except that you maintain a pointer to the first node on the list instead of to the last node on the list.

7. Complete the entire implementation module for ListADT using doubly linked nodes with a header node, as described in Section 4.6.

8. Complete the entire implementation module for ListADT using doubly linked nodes without a header node, as described in Section 4.6.

9. Write a limited program formatter. The input is a Modula-2 program. Assume that MODULE, TYPE, CONST, PROCEDURE, VAR, BEGIN, WHILE, FOR, IF, ELSE, ELSIF, REPEAT, UNTIL, WITH, CASE, LOOP, and END occur only at the beginning of a line, often with leading blanks. Your program should produce as output a program indented according to the indentation rules used in this book and also check that ENDs, UNTILs, ELSIFs, and ELSEs match. Your instructor may specify a different set of indentation rules. *Suggested algorithm:* Use a stack where BEGIN, WHILE, FOR, IF, REPEAT, WITH, CASE, and LOOP are pushed when seen. When UNTIL or END is seen, pop a word from the stack and verify that it is or is not REPEAT, respectively. For ELSIF, verify that the popped word is IF and then repush it. For ELSE, verify that the popped word is IF and then push the ELSE.

10. Write the ONE POTATO program as a client module of ListADT (see Section 4.6 for a description).

11. Write the ONE POTATO program using circular linked lists directly (see Section 4.6 for a description).

12. Complete the entire implementation module for TableADT using a hash table of lists (chaining), as described in Section 4.8.

13. Complete the entire implementation module for DictiADT using the indexed sequential method, as described in Section 4.9.

14. The user of a program has a number of coins, all of which weigh the same except one is either lighter or heavier. The user also has a balance scale that will tell whether one group of coins is heavier or lighter or the same weight as another group of coins. Write an interactive program that gives directions to the user on what coins to weigh when in order to determine which coin is different and whether it is lighter or heavier. The fewer weighings, the better the program. Use recursion, and assume there are more than 12 coins. The beginnings of a sample run might be as follows:

> PROG: How many coins do you have?
> USER: 15
> PROG: Consider the coins to be numbered from 1 to 15, inclusive. Weigh 1...5 (on the left) against 6...10 and tell me the result, using one of three letters: B = balance, L = left side low, R = right side low.
> USER: L
> PROG: Now you know that 11..15 are okay.

15. Rewrite Example 4.12B to keep available blocks in increasing order of memory address and to coalesce adjacent blocks whenever possible. Use the ring implementation described in Exercise 4 of Section 4.12, but also keep another pointer to the available block with the lowest address, to speed up coalescing. When these improvements are used, you have a fairly nice method of managing storage.

16. Write a full StoreADT implementation module using the buddy system, as described in Section 4.12.

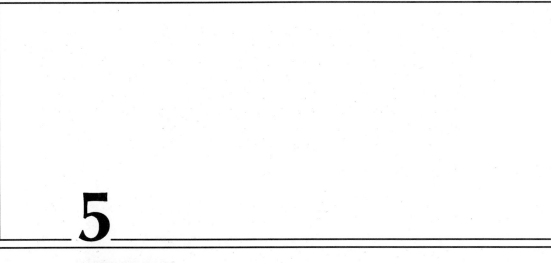

5

TREES

A list is an arrangement of information values so that they have a certain relationship to one another. Specifically, a nonempty list always contains a first information value, and you can get to any other information value on the list by starting from the first one and repeatedly going on to the next one until you get to the one for which you are looking. Moreover, there is only one way to get to a specific information value in the list starting from the first one.

A **binary tree** is also an arrangement of information values so that they have a certain relationship to one another, but the relationship is more complicated. An information value in a binary tree can be "followed by" *two* information values (the word "binary" refers to "two"). An information value can have a "left follower" and a "right follower." A nonempty binary tree always contains a first information value, and you can get to any other information value in the binary tree by starting from the first one and repeatedly going on to a follower until you get to the one for which you are looking. Moreover, there is only one way to get to a specific information value in the binary tree starting from the first one.

When data is stored in a tree structure instead of a list structure, it can greatly speed up searching algorithms. Figure 1 is an example of a binary tree. The followers of an information value are indicated by arrows pointing downward.

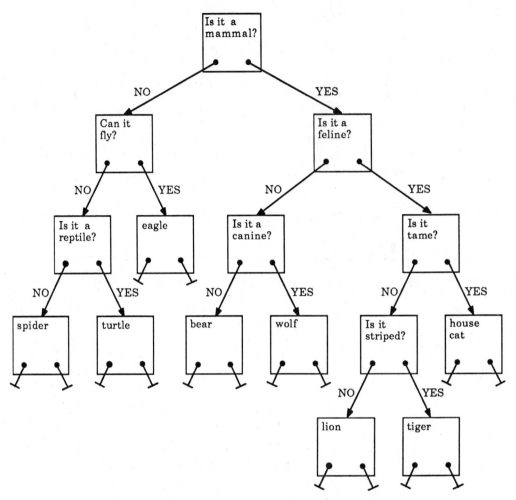

FIGURE 1. A game tree for Twenty Questions.

5.1 APPLICATION AND DEFINITIONS FOR BINARY TREES

The context in which I introduce binary trees is a game program that learns. The user thinks of a specific kind of animal, and the computer attempts to guess what it is in 20 yes/no questions or fewer.

The easiest way to specify the task to be performed is to give part of a sample run (i.e., a partial pretrace). In this sample run, "PROG:" denotes what the program writes and "USER:" denotes the user's response ("Y" for "Yes" and "N" for "No"). The user has been running the program for a while. At the point in the program where the data structure is that shown in Figure 1, the conversation goes as follows:

PROG: You must think of a kind of animal.
PROG: I will try to guess what it is. Let's start.
PROG: Is it a mammal?
USER: N
PROG: Can it fly?
USER: N
PROG: Is it a reptile?
USER: Y
PROG: I guess a turtle
PROG: Was I right?
USER: Y
PROG: Great! I got it!
PROG: Will you play again?
USER: Y
PROG: You must think of a kind of animal.
PROG: I will try to guess what it is. Let's start.
PROG: Is it a mammal?
USER: Y
PROG: Is it a feline?
USER: N
PROG: Is it a canine?
USER: Y
PROG: I guess a wolf
PROG: Was I right?
USER: N
PROG: Oh, rats! What was it?
USER: chihuahua
PROG: What question should I have asked to distinguish
    between your choice and my guess?
USER: Is it tiny?
PROG: What is the correct answer for your choice?
USER: Y
PROG: Thanks, I'll remember that.
PROG: Will you play again?
USER: N
PROG: Oh, rats! Please?
USER: N
PROG: Double rats!! Goodbye.

Establishing a Suitable Data Structure

The program must store the new information it obtains during the game so that it will know better next time. An appropriate data structure for this program might look like Figure 1 at the point when we started our excerpt from the sample run. Each box in this figure represents a node. It is a different kind of node from the kind used for linked lists, because each node contains *two* pointers as well as the Information. The Information in each node is a string of characters, either a question or a kind of animal. If it is a kind of animal, both pointers in that node are NIL. If it is a question, neither pointer in that node is NIL.

The whole structure is called a **binary tree**. It is called a *tree* because it looks sort of like a tree, at least if you turn it upside down. We could implement these nodes by the following type declarations:

```
TYPE    PointerToNode = POINTER TO Node;
        Node = RECORD
                    Info         : Information;
                    Left, Right  : PointerToNode;
               END;
```

The Left value would indicate the Node to the left of the current Node, which corresponds to a "No" answer. Similarly, the Right value would indicate the Node that corresponds to a "Yes" answer. To keep track of the tree, we have to record the **root** of the tree (the Node at the very top).

Algorithms for the Twenty Questions Game

To start the program, we "plant" a *tiny* tree. As the game progresses, the tree grows larger (and thus the computer becomes "smarter"). We can initialize the tree as shown in Figure 2.

It will often be necessary to create new Nodes as the game goes on. A new Node will have a kind of animal in it, and its pointer values will be NIL. Such a Node is called a **leaf** of the tree. We will be able to tell the Nodes containing animals from the Nodes containing questions by whether or not they are leaves.

The body of the game program can consist of initializing the binary tree and then determining whether the game will be played. If it is, a PlayGame procedure is called to do the actual playing. That is all we should expect the main algorithm to accomplish, because of all the chatter in the sample run.

The question is, what is the algorithm for playing the game? We begin by looking at the root Node. If that Node contains a question, we ask it; if the answer is Yes, we move to the right in the tree, otherwise we move to the left in the tree. And what do we do at that point? The same thing again. Thus the

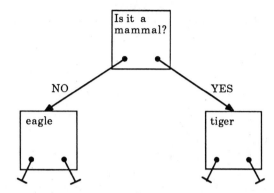

FIGURE 2. An initial game tree for the Twenty Questions program.

PlayGame procedure is a prime candidate for recursion. The overall structure of PlayGame could be as follows:

```
IF ThisNode↑.Left = NIL THEN (* it is a leaf *)
    SeeIfCorrect (ThisNode);
ELSE
    AskChar (ThisNode↑.Phrase, Response);
    IF Response = 'N' THEN
        PlayGame (ThisNode↑.Left);
    ELSE
        PlayGame (ThisNode↑.Right);
    END;
END;
```

Of course, eventually we reach a leaf (i.e., an animal instead of a question). In that case, we do not call the PlayGame procedure again. Instead, we make our guess. If we are right, we are done. If not, we want to find out the correct answer and augment the tree accordingly.

How do we make the tree larger? In our sample run, we want to get sufficient information from the user so that we can replace the Node on the left of Figure 3 by the "subtree" on the right.

Among the permissible operations for binary trees should be a procedure that inserts a given information value in a tree to the left or right of a given Node, when there is nothing there already. When we ask the user for the user's choice and for the question that would distinguish the user's choice from the computer's guess, we add two Nodes to the tree. These two Nodes will be leaves containing the user's choice and the computer's guess. The Node that formerly contained the computer's guess will contain the question and also pointers to the two

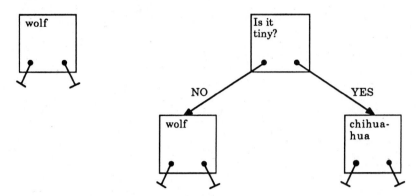

FIGURE 3. *The node on the left is replaced by the subtree at the right.*

answer Nodes. A handy binary tree procedure would be one that lets you swap the question for the answer that is at a Node.

Definitions

A binary tree consists of a finite number of nodes. The **empty binary tree** has no nodes. A nonempty binary tree consists of a node (called its root) that has a **left subtree** and a **right subtree**. Each subtree is also a binary tree; either subtree can be empty. If both subtrees of a node are empty, the node is called a leaf. The root of the left subtree of node X is said to be the **left child** of X. The root of the right subtree of node X is said to be the **right child** of X. X is called the **parent** of its left and right children. The **descendants** of X are all the nodes in the left and right subtrees of X.

The root of a binary tree is said to be at **level 0** in that tree. The left child and the right child of the root are said to be at **level 1** in the tree. A child of either of those two nodes is said to be at level 2 in the tree. In general, the child of a node at level K is said to be at level K + 1. The **height of a tree** is the largest level number of the nodes in the tree.

Figure 4 shows a small binary tree of height 3. The seven nodes in this tree are labeled from A to G for easy reference, and the level of each node is given beside it. Node A is the root of this tree. Its left child is node B, which has two children, nodes C and D, both of which are leaves at level 2. The right child of node A is node E. Node E has no right child; its left child is node F. Node F has no left child; its right child is node G, which is a leaf. Node G is at level 3.

A **complete binary tree** is a binary tree for which (1) all leaves are on the same level, and (2) no node has just one child. Figure 9 in Chapter 2 shows complete binary trees of heights 0, 1, and 2. The tree in Figure 1 of this chapter is not complete, because the leaves are on different levels. It is, however, a special kind of binary tree called a **2-tree**, since no node has just one child.

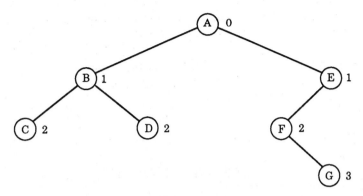

FIGURE 4. A tree with the levels marked for each node.

A **path** in a tree is a sequence of nodes for which each (other than the last) is the parent of the one after it. The **length of a path** is 1 less than the number of nodes in it.

To study binary trees, you need to learn about logarithmic notation using base 2. First, some examples: The third power of 2 is 8 and the fourth power of 2 is 16; so we say the logarithm of each number from 9 to 16, inclusive, is 4. The fifth power of 2 is 32, so we say the logarithm of each number above 16 but not above 32 is 5. That is, the logarithm is 5 for any number that is above 2^4 but not above 2^5. In general, the **logarithm of N** is the exponent on the smallest power of 2 that is at least as large as N.

The notation for the logarithm of N is **lg(N)**. For instance, lg(8) = 3 and lg(9) = 4. The number of levels in a complete binary tree is lg(N + 1), where N is the number of nodes in the tree. *Note:* Many people prefer to define lg as the logarithm base 2 allowing fractional values [e.g., lg(3) is approximately 1.585]; what this book calls lg(N) is obtained by rounding upward for such fractional values.

Check Your Understanding

1. How many leaves are in the complete binary tree of height 4? How many nodes are there altogether in that tree?

2. How many leaves are in the tree in Figure 1?

3. How many different paths of length 3 are there in Figure 1?

4. According to Figure 1, if you are thinking of a tiger, what is the sequence of questions the program asks you?

5. How many 2-trees are there with 3 nodes? How many with 4 nodes? How many with 5 nodes?

6. Find lg(N + 1) when N is any of 2, 3, 4, 5, 6, 7, 8.

7. (NA) Draw the complete binary tree of height 3.

8. (NA) Draw all possible binary trees that have at most three nodes. There are nine of them, including the empty tree.

9. (NA) Write the level number beside each node in Figure 1.

5.2 DEFINITION MODULE FOR BINARY TREES

You should now have some concept of the procedures you need in a definition module for binary trees. I call this module **BinADT** and the identifier for a binary tree type **BinTree**. The procedures come in four colors, analogous to the ones for linear lists:

1. You need the usual Create and Destroy procedures, with no change in meaning, just in the parameter type.

2. You need a way to indicate a location in the tree, and you should be able to change that location (analogous to the list procedures FirstLocation, NextLocation, and InList). These tree functions are called Root, Left, and Right. You test whether a location is in the tree by comparing it with a NoNode value.

3. You need a procedure corresponding to the list procedure LookAt. The one in BinADT is called See. There is also a Swap procedure that replaces the information at a location by new information.

4. You need procedures for inserting and deleting values. These are more complex than for lists, because you have to specify whether you want it done at the root, to the left of a given location, or to the right of a given location. Thus we have three of each kind of tree procedure: Insertion is performed by PutRoot, PutLeft, and PutRight; deletion is performed by TakeRoot, TakeLeft, and TakeRight.

Using Locations in a Binary Tree

You can think of a **Location** in a binary tree as a place where you have a node whose contents you can look at or a place where you can insert a new node (as a child of an existing node). Instead of the FirstLocation function, the **Root** function returns the location for the root of the tree. If the tree is empty, the location returned will be **NoNode**, exported from the BinADT module. You do not need an IsEmpty procedure, since you can test the condition Root(Data)=NoNode.

In place of the NextLocation function, the functions **Left** and **Right** move you down in the tree to the left or right of your previous location. If X is the location of a node in the tree named Data, then Left(X, Data) is the location of the left child of that node. But when there is no left child, Left returns NoNode and you cannot do anything at that location. You do not need an InList function, since you can test the location to see if it is NoNode.

The same sort of thing is true for the Right function. For instance, if Data is the tree in Figure 4 of the previous section, X := Root(Data) sets X to the location of A; X := Left(X, Data) sets X to the location of B; then X := Right(X, Data) sets X to the location of D; then X := Left(X, Data) assigns NoNode to X.

See and **Swap** are precisely analogous to the LookAt and Modify procedures for lists. They have the same three parameters with the same purposes: an Information parameter in which to return the information value, a Location that tells where the action is to take place, and a Data parameter for the data structure.

PutLeft and **PutRight** have the same three parameters as Insert for lists: an Information value to insert, the location below which it is to be inserted, and the Data structure being modified. **PutRoot** puts a given information value at the root of a given binary tree. For all three of these insertion procedures, the subtree that was previously at the point of insertion becomes the right subtree of the newly inserted value, and its left subtree is empty. Most applications tend to insert a leaf, in which case both subtrees of the newly inserted value are empty. *Note:* I could have designed BinADT to put the subtree on the left, or simply throw it away, or have the PutX procedures refuse to allow insertion where there is a nonempty subtree. But I think that moving the subtree to the right works best. These considerations did not arise for lists, since each node has just one "sublist" (the part of the list that comes after it).

TakeLeft, **TakeRight**, and **TakeRoot** have the same parameter structure as the corresponding PutX procedures: Information and BinTree, plus a Location for TakeLeft and TakeRight. Then we have the problem of what to do with the subtrees of the newly deleted node. The solution used here is as follows: If the node has one nonempty subtree, let it replace the node in the tree; with two nonempty subtrees, refuse to make any change in the tree; with both subtrees empty, replace the node by an empty subtree.

When making an insertion or deletion, you have to specify the parent of a node so adjustments can be made there. This is not as clean as specifying the node itself, but it saves the implementation a lot of work. An alternative for this design decision would be to have the implementation keep a record of the parent of each node in the node itself; but this is not commonly done, and I want to stay with the classic implementation of binary trees. Besides, it would still cause problems when inserting at the bottom of the tree. Figure 5 shows some examples of the use of these Put and Take procedures.

Note that a Put followed by the corresponding Take leaves the tree as it was. A call of Take followed by the corresponding Put would leave the tree the same only if the original node had an empty left subtree; if it were an empty right subtree, the left subtree would shift sides.

You could consider a list to be a special case of a binary tree in which all left subtrees are empty. Then the use of PutRight for any node in that tree is analo-

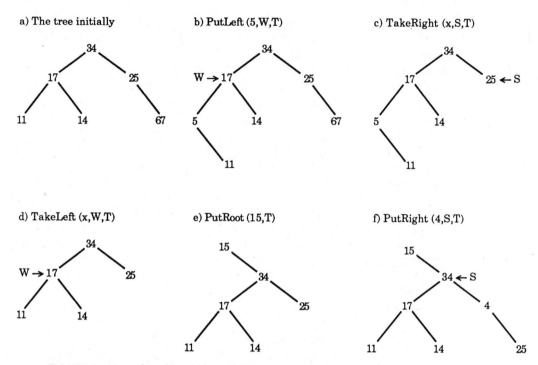

FIGURE 5. *Examples of insertion and deletion in a binary tree T. Arrows indicate the node for which W or S is the location.*

gous to ListADT.Insert; it shifts the "sublist" formerly at that point down one to make room. Similarly, the use of TakeRight is analogous to ListADT.Delete; it shifts the "sublist" below the deleted node back up to close up the list. This provides some justification for the design decisions I have made (Example 5.2).

The constant NoNode is of type Location, which I want to keep hidden from client modules. Therefore, I declare a variable named NoNode and initialize it in the implementation module. This is a tiny defect in Modula-2; it would be nicer if we could declare hidden constants the way we can declare hidden types.

Sample Uses of BinADT

Assume that you have a tree named Data and you want to swap the information at the root with the information in its left child. This can be done with the following statement sequence. Note that there is no need to check Eve#NoNode; the Left function does that for you. Figure 6 shows the tree at two stages in the execution of this code.

EXAMPLE 5.2A _____

```
DEFINITION MODULE BinADT;
FROM InfoADT IMPORT Information;
EXPORT QUALIFIED BinTree, Location, NoNode, See, Swap,
          PutRoot,  PutLeft,  PutRight, Root, Left, Right,
          TakeRoot, TakeLeft, TakeRight, Create, Destroy;
   (* Written by Dr. William C. Jones, October 19-- *)
   (* Binary tree manipulations.  Every BinTree must be
      initialized before anything else can be done with it*)
TYPE
    BinTree;
    Location;   (* a node in a given binary tree, or a value
                   that indicates no node in the tree *)
VAR                         (* actually a constant; it is *)
    NoNode : Location;      (* the value indicating that  *)
                            (* no node is at a location   *)
(* Note:  No procedures except the three PutX procedures
   have any effect if NoNode is at the given Location *)
(*******************************************************)

PROCEDURE See (VAR TheInfo : Information;
                   Where : Location;  Data : BinTree);
      (* Access TheInfo at the Location Where in Data *)

PROCEDURE Swap (VAR TheInfo : Information;
                   Where : Location;  VAR Data : BinTree);
      (* Exchange the information at Where for TheInfo *)

PROCEDURE PutRoot (TheInfo  : Information;
                   VAR Data : BinTree);
      (* Put TheInfo at the root of Data.  The subtree that
         was there becomes the right subtree of TheInfo;
         the left subtree of TheInfo is empty.  *)

PROCEDURE PutLeft (TheInfo : Information;
                   Parent  : Location; VAR Data : BinTree);
      (* Put TheInfo to the left of Parent in Data.  The
         subtrees of TheInfo determined as for PutRoot *)

PROCEDURE PutRight (TheInfo : Information;
                   Parent : Location; VAR Data : BinTree);
      (* Put TheInfo to the right of Parent in Data.  The
         subtrees of TheInfo determined as for PutRoot *)

PROCEDURE TakeRoot (VAR TheInfo : Information;
                   VAR Data    : BinTree);
      (* If one subtree is empty, remove TheInfo from the
         root of Data and replace it by the other subtree.
         No effect if both subtrees are nonempty.  *)

PROCEDURE TakeLeft (VAR TheInfo: Information;
                   Parent : Location; VAR Data : BinTree);
      (* Remove TheInfo to the left of Parent in Data,
         subject to subtree conditions as for TakeRoot *)

(* continued on next page *)
```

```
(* EXAMPLE 5.2A continued *)


PROCEDURE TakeRight (VAR TheInfo: Information;
                     Parent : Location; VAR Data : BinTree);
     (* Remove TheInfo to the right of Parent in Data,
        subject to subtree conditions as for TakeRoot *)

PROCEDURE Root (Data : BinTree) : Location;
     (* Return the location of the root of Data *)

PROCEDURE Left (Where : Location;
               Data  : BinTree) : Location;
     (* Return the location of the left child of the node
        in Data that Where currently indicates; return
        NoNode if no node at Where or no left child *)

PROCEDURE Right (Where : Location;
                Data  : BinTree) : Location;
     (* Return the location of the right child of the node
        in Data that Where currently indicates; return
        NoNode if no node at Where or no right child *)

PROCEDURE Create (VAR Data : BinTree);
     (* Initialize Data as an empty structure *)

PROCEDURE Destroy (VAR Data : BinTree);
     (* Deallocate the space for the empty structure *)

END BinADT.
```

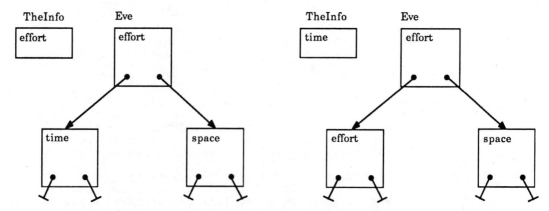

FIGURE 6. *How a tree looks before and after execution of Swap (TheInfo, Left(Eve,Data), Data).*

```
Eve := Root (Data);   (* auxilary variable for efficiency *)
IF Left (Eve, Data) # NoNode THEN
    See (TheInfo, Eve, Data);
    Swap (TheInfo, Left (Eve, Data), Data);
    Swap (TheInfo, Eve, Data);
END;
```

Assume that you want to have a function that tells whether there is a leaf at a given location Where in a given tree Data. Then the following statement would serve as the body of the function:

```
RETURN (Where # NoNode) AND (Left  (Where, Data) = NoNode)
                        AND (Right (Where, Data) = NoNode)
```

Assume that you have a node Ersa with one child, the right one, which is a leaf. Assume also you want to make it the left child instead. Then the following statements would accomplish this task:

```
TakeRight (TheInfo, Ersa, Data);
PutLeft (TheInfo, Ersa, Data);
```

Assume that you want to write a function that tells how many nodes are in a given tree or subtree. You might want to use NumNodes(Root(Data), Data) to obtain the number of nodes in a tree named Data, for instance. One way is to count the nodes in the left subtree of the root, then count the nodes in the right subtree of the root, then add these two numbers together and add 1 for the root itself. How do you count the nodes in a subtree? You use the function just described. Recursion is often used in algorithms involving binary trees.

Each algorithm involving recursion should be checked to be sure that it is self-terminating, that is, it cannot continue indefinitely. Under what circumstances would you not apply the algorithm just described? When the subtree is empty, since then you know the count is 0 without having to call the function again. Each time the function calls itself, the called function counts the nodes in a smaller subtree of Data than the calling function did. When the subtree has no nodes, the function does not call itself again. This checks that the recursion eventually terminates. The function could be:

```
PROCEDURE NumNodes (Where : Location; Data : BinTree) : CARDINAL;
BEGIN
    IF Where = NoNode THEN
        RETURN 0;
    ELSE
        RETURN 1 + NumNodes (Left  (Where, Data), Data)
                 + NumNodes (Right (Where, Data), Data);
    END;
END NumNodes;
```

The IF statement indicates that, as far as this NumNodes function is concerned, there are only two kinds of binary trees—empty ones and nonempty ones. An empty tree is usually easy to manage; in this case, we just return 0, since it has no nodes. A nonempty binary tree has three parts—the root, the left subtree, and the right subtree. The ELSE part of this function calculates the number of nodes for each of the three parts. It is easy to calculate for the root—just add 1. And it is easy to calculate for each subtree—just call NumNodes again.

The following coding illustrates how the BinADT definition module could be used for the game program described in Section 5.1. Let us assume that InfoADT declares TYPE Information = ARRAY [0..StrMax] OF CHAR, instead of as an opaque type. Then the following statements serve to initialize the tree for the game:

```
Create (Data);
PutRoot ('Is it a mammal?', Data);
PutLeft ('eagle', Root (Data), Data);
PutRight ('tiger', Root (Data), Data);
```

Warning

Some compilers have a defect that forces a change in some of the foregoing coding. Specifically, the VAX and Logitech compilers do not allow a client module to compare two variables for equality when they are of an opaque type. This is illogical, of course. Only simple types can be opaque types, and all simple types allow comparison for equality. Moreover, Niklaus Wirth specifies for Modula-2, "Assignment and test for equality are applicable to all opaque types."

If your compiler has this defect, you cannot use IF Where=NoNode or IF Left(Eve, Data)#NoNode as shown herein, since Location is an opaque type. A reasonable solution is to add the following Boolean function to BinADT:

```
PROCEDURE Equal (First, Second : Location) : BOOLEAN;
    (* Return TRUE if they are equal, FALSE if they are not *)
```

If you make this change, you might also want to make NoNode a Location-valued function instead of a variable. That prevents any client module from accidentally changing the value of NoNode. *Note:* A few applications of ListADT may also need the Equal function for some compilers.

Traversals of a Binary Tree

Assume that you have a binary tree named Data and you want to print all the information in a subtree of Data headed by Spot. Again, recursion is useful, and the overall approach is similar to that used for the NumNodes function. We have two alternatives: Either the subtree is empty or it is not. If it is empty, there is nothing to do; so the body of the procedure can simply be IF Spot # NoNode THEN... END. If the subtree is nonempty, we have three things to write—its root, its left subtree, and its right subtree. Since the order was not specified, let us write the information in the left subtree first and the information in the right subtree last. Writing the information in the root is just a matter of calling See and then OutputInfo. Writing the information in the subtrees can be done by calling this procedure again, as shown in Example 5.2B.

The WriteAll utility procedure can then simply consist of one statement: WriteSubtree (Root (Data), Data). This is called **inorder traversal** of the tree because the root is processed in between the processing of the left and right subtrees. Inorder traversal is the most common way of traversing an entire tree, processing one node at a time. The recursion is self-terminating because (1) each time the WriteSubtree procedure calls itself, the subtree parameter has fewer nodes, and (2) when the subtree parameter has no nodes, the procedure cannot call itself. Note that the first value printed is in the **leftmost node** of the tree, found by going left from the root until you find a node with an empty left subtree.

Two other ways of traversing a binary tree are called **preorder traversal** and **postorder traversal**. Preorder traversal processes each node just *before* all the node's descendants are processed. Postorder traversal processes each node just *after* all of the node's descendants are processed. For example, Figure 7 contains a drawing of a binary tree in which leaf nodes contain numbers and nonleaf nodes

EXAMPLE 5.2B _____

```
PROCEDURE WriteSubtree (Spot : Location;
                        Data : BinTree);
VAR
    TheInfo : Information;
BEGIN
    IF Spot # NoNode THEN
        WriteSubtree (Left (Spot, Data), Data);
        See (TheInfo, Spot, Data);
        OutputInfo (TheInfo);
        WriteSubtree (Right (Spot, Data), Data);
    END;
END WriteSubtree;
```

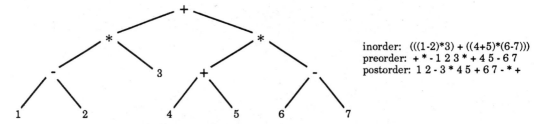

inorder: (((1-2)*3) + ((4+5)*(6-7)))
preorder: + * - 1 2 3 * + 4 5 - 6 7
postorder: 1 2 - 3 * 4 5 + 6 7 - * +

FIGURE 7. A binary expression tree with various traversals.

contain operators that have two operands. Such a tree is called a **binary expression tree**. Preorder, inorder, and postorder traversals of this tree are given at the right of the figure. Preorder traversal yields the prefix form of an expression, postorder traversal yields the postfix form of the same expression, and inorder traversal yields the normal infix form of the same expression. I put parentheses in the inorder traversal to make the order of precedence clear.

Preconditions and Postconditions

The precondition for each of the 13 procedures in Example 5.2A except Create is that all Location and BinTree values be valid. Create has an empty precondition. A BinTree value is valid if it has been returned by any procedure in BinADT other than Destroy and that procedure's preconditions were met. A Location value is valid if it has been returned by any function in BinADT for the corresponding BinTree and no deletion or insertion has since taken place at or above that location and that procedure's preconditions were met.

The postcondition for Destroy is that the BinTree value it returns is invalid. The postcondition for PutRight is as follows: No change if the given Location is NoNode; otherwise, TheInfo is on the right of the Parent, the right subtree of TheInfo is the former right subtree of the Parent, and the left subtree of TheInfo is empty. Postconditions for other situations are left as an exercise.

Check Your Understanding

1. Write the contents of the nodes of Figure 4 in preorder traversal; then do it using inorder traversal and postorder traversal.

2. Write a function that tells whether a given binary tree has more than two nodes. Use imports from BinADT for this and the following exercises.

3. Write a function Leftmost that returns the location of the leftmost node in a given binary tree. It is not to be NoNode unless the tree is empty.

4. Write a recursive Boolean function to tell whether a given binary tree contains a given information value.

5. (NA) Write a function NumberLevels that returns the number of levels in a given binary tree.

6. (NA) Draw four different binary trees with seven nodes for which postorder traversal yields A B C D E F G in that order.

7. (NA) Write a procedure that prints the information in the top three nodes of a binary tree (no effect if the tree is empty).

8. (NA) Write a recursive function that returns the Location of a given information value in a given tree; return NoNode if it is not there.

9. (NA) Write a procedure that deletes the leftmost node in a binary tree (no effect if the tree is empty).

10. (NA) For the code segment that swaps the information at Eve with the information at its left child, discuss the effect of replacing the call to See by a call to Swap. Remember to take into account that Information might be a record or it might be a pointer to a record.

11. (NA) Write a recursive procedure that finds the parent of a given node, using imports from BinADT and the following heading:

```
PROCEDURE Parent (Where : Location; Data : BinTree) : Location;
```

12. (NA) Assume that BinADT exports the utility Parent described in Exercise 11. Write a function that returns the next location in inorder traversal after a given location in a given BinTree. Alternatively, write a function that returns the preceding location in inorder traversal.

13. (NA) Write out complete postconditions for each of the procedures in BinADT that your instructor specifies.

5.3 TWO APPLICATIONS OF BinADT

This section presents two situations in which imports from BinADT can profitably be used. Both examples develop part of the coding for their programs; the rest is left as programming problems. Section 7.5 on Huffman codes discusses a much larger program that uses BinADT, but that section assumes the addition of four utility procedures that allow you to easily insert and delete entire subtrees of a binary tree.

The Geneology Program

You are to develop a program that reads a file of information telling who is whose mother or father for the direct antecedents of a particular person named, say, Ed. Then the program is to answer questions about this data base of information. The questions include (where X could be any person): (1) Who is X's child? (2) Who is X's mother? (3) List the descendants from X down to Ed.

Your first job is to find out how the file is constructed. Assume that you determine that:

- ☐ The name of the person at the root is on the first line in the file.
- ☐ Each other line begins with 'M', 'F', or 'X'.
- ☐ A line beginning 'M' is followed by two names A and B, where A is the mother of B and B was the first name on some preceding line.
- ☐ A line beginning 'F' is followed by two names A and B, where A is the father of B and B was the first name on some preceding line.
- ☐ A line beginning 'X' denotes the end of the file.

Your program can read this file and construct a binary tree in which the mother of a person goes on the left of that person in the tree and the father goes on the right. This leads directly to the coding shown in Example 5.3A.

The AddToTree procedure requires that you look at a given spot in the tree, initially the root. If the Child is there, you put the Parent on one side or the other. If the Child is not there, you look through the left subtree to find the Child and add the connection. If you do not find the Child in the left subtree, you look through the right subtree to find the Child and add the connection. The way you look through a subtree is the way that was just described, so recursion is appropriate.

A problem arises in deciding whether to look through the right subtree. You need some way of noting whether the Child was found in the left subtree. The logical method is to use a Boolean value to keep track of that—you can initialize StillLooking to TRUE, then set it to FALSE when you find the Child. The coding is in Example 5.3B. Note the delocalization of six variables to save time and space in the recursion.

The AnswerQuestions procedure is left as a programming problem. Note that the program contains no guards against bad input. This is poor. If you complete the development of the problem, be sure to add appropriate guards so the program cannot crash or produce nonsensical answers for any input.

The ExpressionTree Program

You are to develop a program that reads an arithmetic expression in correct prefix notation and writes it out in either infix or postfix notation. You may assume that InfoADT exports not only the usual subprograms including InputInfo for

EXAMPLE 5.3A _____

```
MODULE Geneology;
FROM BinADT  IMPORT BinTree, Location, Create, See,
                    PutRoot, PutLeft, PutRight,
                    Root, Left, Right;
FROM InfoADT IMPORT Information, InputInfo, OutputInfo,
                    Compare;
FROM InOut   IMPORT OpenInput, CloseInput, Read, Write;
    (* Build a data base consisting of geneological
       information and answer questions on it *)
    (* Written by William C. Jones, March 19-- *)

CONST
    Mother = 'M';
    Father = 'F';
    Exit   = 'X';
(*-- procedures AddToTree and AnswerQuestions go here --*)

VAR
    Data            : BinTree;
    Parent, Child : Information;
    Ch              : CHAR;

BEGIN           (* program *)

    Create (Data);
    OpenInput ('');
    InputInfo (Parent);
    PutRoot (Parent, Data);

    Read (Ch);
    WHILE Ch # Exit DO
        InputInfo (Parent);
        InputInfo (Child);
        AddToTree (Parent, Child, Ch, Data);
        Read (Ch);
    END;

    CloseInput;
    AnswerQuestions (Data);

END Geneology.
```

reading an operator or operand, but also a Boolean function IsOp that tells whether a given information value is an operator (as opposed to a simple operand). You may also assume that each operator has two operands, as is normal.

A reasonable algorithm is: (1) Read the information into a binary expression tree, a 2-tree in which each simple operand is at a leaf node and each operator has two children, its first operand and its second operand; (2) Ask the user whether infix or postfix notation is wanted; (3) Print the infix or postfix notation, which-

EXAMPLE 5.3B _____

```
PROCEDURE AddToTree (Parent, Child : Information;
                     Ch             : CHAR;
                     VAR Data       : BinTree);
    (* Add Parent on left of Child if Ch = Mother,
       on right if Ch = Father *)
VAR
    TheInfo       : Information;
    StillLooking  : BOOLEAN;
  (*--------------------------------------------------------*)

    PROCEDURE TryThere (Spot : Location);
    BEGIN
        See (TheInfo, Spot, Data);
        IF Compare (TheInfo, Child) = 0 THEN
            IF Ch = Mother THEN
                PutLeft (Parent, Spot, Data);
            ELSE
                PutRight (Parent, Spot, Data);
            END;
            StillLooking := FALSE;
        ELSE
            TryThere (Left (Spot, Data));
            IF StillLooking THEN
                TryThere (Right (Spot, Data));
            END;
        END;
    END TryThere;
  (*--------------------------------------------------------*)

BEGIN            (* AddToTree *)
    StillLooking := TRUE;
    TryThere (Root (Data));
END AddToTree;
```

ever was specified. Figure 7 at the end of the previous section shows an example of an expression tree. Printing the expression requires a tree traversal (Fig. 8).

Reading the expression into a tree consists of creating the tree and reading the first information value into its root. If the value is an operator, you then read its first operand into the left subtree of the root and its second operand into the right subtree of the root. This algorithm is simple to code; see Example 5.3C. The coding for ReadLeftSubtree is in the answers to the exercises, and ReadRightSubtree is analogous.

Now that you have read and constructed the expression tree, you ask the user whether infix or postfix notation is wanted. You then call one of two procedures. If the user chooses infix notation, you have to use parentheses to avoid ambiguity. A reasonable algorithm is to print a pair of parentheses around any subexpression formed with an operator and two operands; you do not print parentheses around a simple operand.

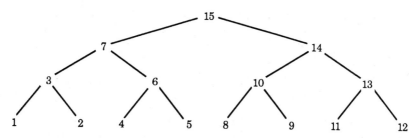

FIGURE 8. A complete binary tree with four levels. What kind of traversal produces the numbers in order?

A procedure to print the expression in infix notation thus has two alternatives, depending on whether the information value at the node under consideration is an operator or a simple operand. If it is a simple operand, you simply print it. If it is an operator, you print a left parenthesis, the first operand (which may be a complex expression), the operator, the second operand, and then the right parenthesis. The method of printing either operand is the same as just described, so recursion is appropriate here. The coding is in Example 5.3D. The rest of the program is left as a programming problem.

Check Your Understanding

1. Rewrite Example 5.3B to omit the StillLooking variable. Instead, set Ch to Exit when the Child is found.

2. Example 5.3B is easy to modify for one of the tasks in AnswerQuestions, namely, finding the mother or father of a given person. Do so.

3. Write the ReadLeftSubtree subprocedure for Example 5.3C.

EXAMPLE 5.3C

```
PROCEDURE ReadTree (VAR Data : BinTree);
VAR
     TheInfo : Information;
BEGIN
     Create (Data);
     InputInfo (TheInfo);
     PutRoot (TheInfo, Data);
     IF IsOp (TheInfo) THEN
          ReadLeftSubtree (Root (Data), Data);
          ReadRightSubtree (Root (Data), Data);
     END;
END ReadTree;
```

EXAMPLE 5.3D _____

```
PROCEDURE PrintInfix (Spot : Location;  Data : BinTree);
VAR
    TheInfo : Information;
BEGIN
    See (TheInfo, Spot, Data);
    IF IsOp (TheInfo) THEN
        Write ('(');
        PrintInfix (Left (Spot, Data), Data);
        OutputInfo (TheInfo);
        PrintInfix (Right (Spot, Data), Data);
        Write (')');
    ELSE
        OutputInfo (TheInfo);
    END;
END PrintInfix;
```

4. (NA) Example 5.3B is easy to modify for one of the tasks in AnswerQuestions, namely, printing the chain of people between the person at the root and a specified person. Do so.

5. (NA) Write the PrintPostfix procedure similar to Example 5.3D.

5.4 IMPLEMENTATION MODULE FOR BinADT

The **standard two-pointer implementation for binary trees** is similar to that used for linked lists, with Nodes and pointers to Nodes. The primary difference is that a Node contains two pointers named Left and Right, as well as an Information field. The implementation module must initialize the NoNode "constant" properly, for which we use NIL. Example 5.4A displays all of the implementation except for the 13 procedures.

Create, Destroy, and See are all very short procedures:

```
Create:   Data := NIL;
Destroy:  (* no statements needed, since the tree is empty *)
See:      IF Where # NoNode THEN
              TheInfo := Where↑.Info;
          END;
```

The body of the Swap procedure is the usual exchange algorithm:

```
IF Where # NoNode THEN
    Saved := Where↑.Info;
    Where↑.Info := TheInfo;
    TheInfo := Saved;
END;
```

Three Procedures Controlling the Location in a Tree

The Root function can just RETURN Data, since the distinction between Bin-Tree and Location is only made on the abstract level (i.e, the Modula-2 compiler will not allow a client module to assign a Location to a BinTree, since the definition module implies they are of different types). The Left function returns a pointer to the Node on the left of the given node, except that if Left is given NoNode, it should return NoNode. The Right function is analogous except with "Left" replaced by "Right". Note in the following coding that I use NoNode instead of NIL, since I think it is a little more natural and therefore clearer.

```
(* body of Left function *)        (* body of Right function *)
IF Where # NoNode THEN             IF Where # NoNode THEN
    RETURN Where↑.Left;                RETURN Where↑.Right;
ELSE                               ELSE
    RETURN NoNode;                     RETURN NoNode;
END;                               END;
```

EXAMPLE 5.4A _____

```
IMPLEMENTATION MODULE BinADT;
FROM InfoADT IMPORT Information;
FROM Storage IMPORT ALLOCATE, DEALLOCATE;
   (* Binary tree manipulations.  Every BinTree must be
      initialized before anything else can be done with it*)
   (* Written by William C. Jones, October 19-- *)
TYPE
    PointerToNode = POINTER TO Node;
    BinTree = PointerToNode;
    Location = PointerToNode;
    Node = RECORD
                Info : Information;
                Left, Right : PointerToNode;
           END;
(* The 13 procedures go here; see later discussion *)

BEGIN          (* body of implementation module *)
    NoNode := NIL;
END BinADT.
```

The TakeX Procedures

The TakeX procedures are to delete a node that does not have two nonempty subtrees. To remove the node to the left of a given node, you just remove the root of the left subtree of that node; similarly for nodes on the right. Thus the body of TakeLeft could be coded as follows; for TakeRight, just change "Left" to "Right."

```
(* body of TakeLeft *)
IF Parent # NoNode THEN
    TakeRoot (TheInfo, Parent↑.Left);
END;
```

For the TakeRoot algorithm, coded in Example 5.4B, you check to see which subtree of the node to be deleted is empty. If neither is, or if there is no node to be deleted, you do nothing; otherwise you move the other subtree up in place of the specified node and put the information in TheInfo. Since you have now removed all the information you needed from that node, you can dispose of it properly.

Similarly, the PutLeft and PutRight procedures can simply call PutRoot after guarding against a NIL Parent pointer. The PutRoot procedure is left as an exercise. *Note:* The cursor implementation described in Section 3.11 can be modified to implement tree nodes instead of using this pointer implementation.

EXAMPLE 5.4B _____

```
PROCEDURE TakeRoot (VAR TheInfo : Information;
                    VAR Data    : BinTree);
    (* Context:  standard 2-pointer impl. of BinADT *)
VAR
    Del : Location;
BEGIN
    Del := Data;  (* save address of node to delete *)
    IF Del = NoNode THEN
        RETURN;     (* there is no node to be deleted *)
    ELSIF Del^.Left = NoNode THEN
        Data := Del^.Right; (* move right subtree up *)
    ELSIF Del^.Right = NoNode THEN
        Data := Del^.Left;  (* move left subtree up *)
    ELSE
        RETURN;       (* no effect, since two subtrees *)
    END;
    TheInfo := Del^.Info;
    DISPOSE (Del);
END TakeRoot;
```

Implementing ListADT with Binary Trees

The standard two-pointer implementation of binary trees can be revised to provide a very efficient implementation of ListADT. You arrange the Nodes in the binary tree so that inorder traversal gives you the list items in the proper order. Then you add another field Count to each Node that tells 1 more than the number of Nodes in its left subtree. A List is a PointerToNode, and a Location is a cardinal that tells the ordinal number of the item in the list; so FirstLocation returns 1 and NextLocation returns Where+1.

To find item 12, for instance, look at the root's Count field. If Count is 12, item 12 is at the root, else if Count is more than 12, item 12 is in the left subtree, else item 12 in the whole tree is item number 12−Count in the right subtree. Figure 9 shows two different binary trees used to represent the same list of 12 information values. The information values are assumed to be letters; the figure shows both the information value and the Count for each node.

This implementation of ListADT has the advantage that any subtree of the overall tree represents a sublist of the overall list; thus recursion can be used to great advantage. This is because *the Count field in a node tells the position number of the node's information in an inorder traversal of the subtree of which the node is the root.* This would not be true if we instead recorded the position number of the information on the whole list. Then an insertion or deletion could require changing the Count value for most of the nodes, instead of for just a few.

In this implementation of ListADT, it is often easier to write procedures using recursion, even in situations where a looping statement executes just as quickly. For instance, a function SizeOf to tell the number of information values in the list can be developed quite naturally as follows: The size of the list is the number of nodes in the left subtree of the root plus the number in the right subtree of the root, plus 1 for the root itself (unless, of course, there is no root, in which case the size is 0). The Count field of the root contains the number of nodes in the left

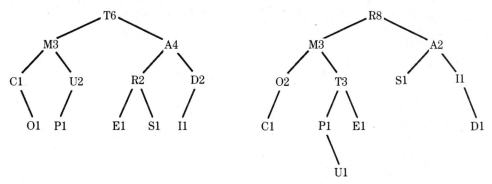

FIGURE 9. *Two different binary trees that represent the same list using the Count field. Information (letters) and Counts are shown. Inorder traversal produces the list items in the order COMPUTERSAID; T is 6th, R is 8th, A is 10th, D is 12th.*

subtree plus 1 for the root. So you can compute the size of the list by adding the Count value of the root to the size of the list represented by the right subtree of the root (except just compute 0 for an empty list). Thus the coding of the body of the utility function SizeOf(Data: List): CARDINAL would be:

```
IF Data = NoNode THEN
    RETURN 0;
ELSE
    RETURN Data↑.Count + SizeOf (Data↑.Right);
END;
```

If you think about what happens when this SizeOf function is called for either of the trees shown in Figure 9, you will realize that it just adds up the Counts in all nodes seen when you start at the root and keep going to the right. Thus it computes $6+4+2$ for the first tree and $8+2+1+1$ for the second tree in Figure 9. Therefore, the following coding for SizeOf should give the correct answer about

EXAMPLE 5.4C _____

```
(* Context:  Tree-with-Count implementation of ListADT *)
TYPE
    List = POINTER TO Node;
    Location = CARDINAL;
    Node = RECORD
                Info : Information;
                Left, Right : List;
                Count : CARDINAL;
            END;
(* ************************************************************ *)

PROCEDURE LookAt (VAR TheInfo : Information;
                      Where      : Location;
                      Data       : List);
    (* LookAt procedure for ListADT.  Location is
       a CARDINAL for this ListADT *)
BEGIN
    IF Data = NIL THEN
        (* do nothing *)
    ELSIF Where = Data^.Count THEN
        TheInfo := Data^.Info;
    ELSIF Where < Data^.Count THEN
        LookAt (TheInfo, Where, Data^.Left);
    ELSE
        LookAt (TheInfo, Where - Data^.Count,
                Data^.Right);
    END;
END LookAt;
```

as quickly:

```
Total := 0;
WHILE Data # NoNode DO
    Total := Total + Data↑.Count;
    Data := Data↑.Right;
END;
RETURN Total;
```

In many cases, a recursive solution is much simpler than using a loop. For instance, the LookAt procedure can be coded recursively as shown in Example 5.4C. It is easy to see that this coding gives the correct answer; a nonrecursive algorithm would be more complex.

With these definitions, search algorithms such as the one used in LookAt work reasonably quickly. For instance, if you are searching through the complete binary tree that contains 1023 information values on 10 levels, you would only have to look at 10 Nodes to find the information for which you are looking.

As another implementation of ListADT, you could store at a node the number of nodes in its whole subtree, instead of the Count just described. However, most algorithms would take somewhat longer to execute.

Advanced Uses of Binary Trees

Right-threading consists of putting in the Right field a pointer to the next Node in inorder traversal sequence when it would otherwise be NIL; but then you have to add a Boolean field to the Node to note what kind of address is stored in the Right field (right subtree versus next inorder Node). If you name that Boolean field HasNodesOnRight, the coding to find the **inorder successor** of a node is:

```
P := Where↑.Right;
IF Where↑.HasNodesOnRight THEN
    WHILE P↑.Left # NIL DO
        P := P↑.Left;
    END;
END;
RETURN P;
```

Full threading of a binary tree consists in also putting in the Left field a pointer to the previous node in inorder traversal sequence when it would otherwise be

NIL, and adding a second Boolean field (named perhaps HasNodesOnLeft) to the node to note what kind of address is stored in the Left field. Full threading is often used in conjunction with a header node for each binary tree.

Partial or full threading permits faster execution of some algorithms and requires very little additional space, although it requires significantly more programming effort. However, for many computer systems, adding even one Boolean field to a record that otherwise contains only addresses takes just as much storage per node as if you added another address. If such is the case, or if space is not at a premium, it is generally better to add one extra Parent field, telling the parent of the node. You can use this Parent field to find the inorder successor of the node in less than half again the time required with right threading, and you can also use it to find the inorder predecessor just as quickly. Moreover, there are many applications in which you need to find the parent of a given node quickly, and even full threading does this clumsily. A fairly efficient implementation of ListADT can be obtained by using a right-threaded tree or by adding a Parent field to binary tree nodes.

Check Your Understanding

1. Write a utility procedure in the standard two-pointer implementation of BinADT: Transpose accepts two Locations in a given binary tree and swaps the information values that are in those two Nodes. Take no action if either Location is NoNode.

2. Write the PutRight procedure for the standard two-pointer implementation of BinADT, calling on PutRoot.

3. Write a recursive utility procedure in the standard two-pointer implementation of BinADT: Reflect changes a given binary tree into its mirror image.

4. Rewrite the body of Example 5.4C using a WHILE statement instead of recursion. Use WHILE (Data # NIL) AND (Where # Data ↑ .Count) DO.

5. Write the PutRoot procedure for the standard two-pointer implementation of BinADT. *Hint:* It is similar to TakeRoot.

6. (NA) Write a utility procedure in the standard two-pointer implementation of BinADT that swaps the left and right subtrees of a given tree.

7. (NA) Write a recursive utility procedure in the standard two-pointer implementation of BinADT: DestroyAllInfo deallocates all space taken up by a binary tree, including that taken up by its information values. Import DestroyInfo from InfoADT.

8. (NA) Write a recursive utility procedure in the standard two-pointer implementation of BinADT: Copy makes a duplicate copy of a given binary tree.

9. (NA) An alternative to the design used for Example 5.4C is to have Count be the ordinal number of the item on the list (thus store 23 in Count for item number 23 in inorder traversal). Discuss why this design would in general not execute as fast as the given design.

10. (NA) Show that having a Parent field permits an algorithm that finds the inorder successor of a given node by looking at less than two other nodes on the average, if the binary tree is complete.

11. (NA) Compute how much faster the procedure in Example 5.4C executes, if any, when the two ELSIF clauses are switched (so the comparison for equality is not made first) for a complete binary tree of 15 nodes. Repeat the computation for 31 nodes. Can you see the pattern?

5.5 IMPLEMENTATION: TableADT USING BINARY SEARCH TREES

When a large amount of information is stored in order in an array, a particular information value can be found quickly (using binary search), but additional information can be inserted or deleted only by a large amount of shifting of information to the left or right. If a linked list is used to store the information, insertion and deletion only require changing a few pointers; but searching must be done sequentially, which wastes time. A "binary search tree" combines the benefits of both. It is a data structure in which you can quickly find information that is there, or find the location where it should be if you want to insert it in the structure. It is a special kind of binary tree, so insertion and deletion only require changing a few pointers.

This section develops an implementation of TableADT (described in Example 3.7A) using a binary search tree. *To review:* TableADT contains the Create and Destroy procedures as does ListADT, with the same meaning. There are no procedures that control the location in a table; when you use PutIn, the implementation decides where to put information. You set an internal "marker" by using Find and test it by using InTable. Inspect and TakeOut retrieve the value at the marker, if any.

Definition of a Binary Search Tree

A **binary search tree** is a binary tree in which the information at the root of each subtree is, in a sense, close to the middle value of all the information in the whole subtree. Consider a node X in the binary search tree. Then all information in the left subtree of X must be "smaller" than the information in X (as dictated by the Compare procedure). And none of the information in the right subtree of X can be "smaller" than the information in X. We allow for the possibility that some of the information in the right subtree of X matches X (using Compare). Figure 10 shows

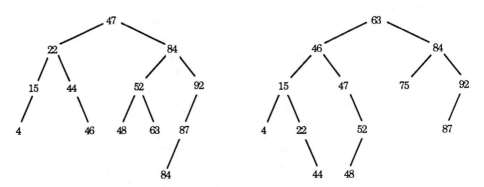

FIGURE 10. *Two binary search trees with integers as information.*

two examples of binary search trees in which the information is assumed to be a single cardinal. Note that, if you read a binary search tree from left to right, the numbers are in increasing order.

Assume that you have a binary search tree with 199 information values in it, and assume that the tree is reasonably **balanced** (i.e., the left and right subtrees of each node have approximately the same number of nodes). Assume further that you want to insert in the tree some new information that does not match any information already there (according to Compare). So you compare the given information with the information at the root of the tree. If the given information is "smaller," you know that it goes somewhere in the left subtree, which should have about 99 information values. Thus you avoid any comparisons with the approximately 99 information values in the right subtree. On the other hand, if the given information is "larger" than the information at the root, you avoid any comparisons with the information in the left subtree, which should have about 99 information values. Either way, you cut your work in half with this one comparison.

If the tree is very nicely balanced, you can expect to need only about 8 comparisons in order to find out where that information goes. (Can you see how I calculated the number 8?) Then you can change a few links to put it in the tree. Of course, this compares very favorably with the 100 comparisons (on average) you have to make with linked lists; it more than makes up for the extra programming effort required. This is an instance of the *divide-and-conquer* tactic.

The following development of TableADT does not make any effort to keep the tree balanced. It has been found that, if the records read in are in a random order, the method described here is reasonably efficient even without trying to maintain balance. You can normally expect to make about 10 to 13 comparisons in order to search a tree of 199 records, instead of the 8 mentioned. This is still a big improvement over the 100 comparisons (on average) for linked lists.

Binary Search Tree Implementation of TableADT

For a table, you have to keep track of the whole data structure and of the current location within that structure. A record with three fields works well:

- ☐ The root node of the binary search tree (the whole data structure).
- ☐ The current location; use NIL when the "marker" is "laid aside".
- ☐ The parent of the node where the information is; the parent is defined only when the current location is not NIL and not the root.

A Table must be declared as a pointer to such a record, so it can be an opaque type in the library module.

Create executes NEW(Data) and initializes two fields to NIL (the parent field need not be initialized, since there is no current information). Destroy executes a DISPOSE statement. InTable tests whether the current location is NIL. Inspect returns the information value at the current location, if a node is there. That leaves the implementations of PutIn, Find, and TakeOut. PutIn and Find are developed in this section; TakeOut is sufficiently interesting that the entire next section is devoted to it. Example 5.5A shows the implementation module using a binary search tree, except that the three nontrivial procedures are postponed until later.

The choice of the fields to establish for a table is not trivial. You could omit the Parent field and just keep track of the Child. This somewhat simplifies the Create, Find, and PutIn procedures, but it forces the TakeOut procedure to search through the tree again to find the parent of the node it is deleting. You could add a fourth field, a Boolean value that tells whether the Child node is to the left or to the right of the Parent node. But this does not help, since you can test Parent ↑ .Left = Child almost as easily as you can test whether the Boolean value is TRUE or FALSE.

The Find Procedure

The Find procedure is to search through the binary tree for the given information and set the Child and Parent fields accordingly. You start by setting a pointer to the root node and seeing whether the information there matches TheInfo. If so, you have found the Child. If not, you set the pointer to the left or right child of that node, depending on whether the result of the comparison was smaller or larger than 0. Since you want to set the Parent field, you first assign the node to Parent in case it is the one containing the information. That way, when you find the right node, the Parent field will contain the correct value.

The value in the pointer that moves down the tree is to be assigned to the Child field of the table when you find the given information, so you might as well use the Child field as the moving pointer. The only problem that can arise with this approach is that the information might not be in the tree. But in that case,

EXAMPLE 5.5A _____

```
IMPLEMENTATION MODULE TableADT;
FROM InfoADT IMPORT Information, Compare;
FROM Storage IMPORT ALLOCATE, DEALLOCATE;
    (* RootNode is a binary search tree;
        Child is the node containing the current information
            (NIL if not in the tree)
        Parent is the parent of Child (if not the root) *)
    (* Written by William C. Jones, April 19-- *)

TYPE
    PointerToNode = POINTER TO Node;
    Table = POINTER TO RECORD
                    RootNode, Parent, Child : PointerToNode;
                END;
    Node  = RECORD
                    Info : Information;
                    Left, Right : PointerToNode;
                END;
(***********************************************************)

PROCEDURE Create (VAR Data : Table);
BEGIN
    NEW (Data);
    WITH Data^ DO
        RootNode := NIL;
        Child := NIL;
    END;
END Create;
(***********************************************************)

PROCEDURE Destroy (VAR Data : Table);
BEGIN
    DISPOSE (Data);
END Destroy;
(***********************************************************)

PROCEDURE InTable (Data : Table) : BOOLEAN;
BEGIN
    RETURN Data^.Child # NIL;
END InTable;
(***********************************************************)

PROCEDURE Inspect (VAR TheInfo: Information; Data: Table);
BEGIN
    IF Data^.Child # NIL THEN
        TheInfo := Data^.Child^.Info;
    END;
END Inspect;
(***********************************************************)

(* The 3 procedures PutIn, Find, and TakeOut go here;
   see later examples *)

END TableADT.
```

you will eventually find NIL to the left or right of a node. At that point, you can stop—Child is NIL, as it should be, and the value of Parent is irrelevant. The overall logic of Find (Example 5.5B) is therefore:

1. Initialize Child to the RootNode;
2. DO until time to stop:
   2.a. STOP if Child is NIL;
   2.b. STOP if Child contains the given information value;
   2.c. Set Parent to Child;
   2.d. Set Child to the Left or Right value for Parent, depending on whether the given information value is smaller than or larger than the one at the Parent.

The PutIn Procedure

The PutIn procedure creates a new node to hold some given Information and puts that node in a given binary search tree at the correct spot. The hard part is to find the correct spot. To change the links properly, you must access the Left or Right field of the node that is directly above where the new node goes, except when the tree is empty.

A nice way of handling this situation is to have a recursive subprocedure with a VAR PointerToNode parameter. The subprocedure is to create a new node in the tree whose root is pointed to by the parameter. The parameter is initially the root of the whole binary search tree. If that tree is empty, the node is created and its address is assigned to the parameter. If the given information value is smaller than the value at the root node, you have to create a new node in its left subtree, so you call the subprocedure with the Left pointer of the root node as the parame-

EXAMPLE 5.5B _____

```
PROCEDURE Find (TheInfo : Information; VAR Data : Table);
    (* Context:  binary search tree impl. of TableADT *)
BEGIN
    WITH Data^ DO
        Child := RootNode;
        WHILE (Child # NIL) AND
                (Compare (TheInfo, Child^.Info) # 0) DO
            Parent := Child;
            IF Compare (TheInfo, Child^.Info) < 0 THEN
                Child := Parent^.Left;
            ELSE
                Child := Parent^.Right;
            END;
        END;
    END;
END Find;
```

ter. If the given information value is larger, you call the subprocedure with the Right pointer of the root node as the parameter.

Since the parameter is a VAR parameter, any assignment to it is actually an assignment to the Left or Right field of the node above it, or to Data ↑ .RootNode if it happens on the first activation. This way, you do not have to have three large segments of code that differ only in that they refer to the Left, Right, or RootNode pointers.

A problem arises when you allow matching information values in the tree. The Find procedure stops at the first information value that matches the one it is looking for. That means that, if X and Y are matching information values for which X was inserted before Y, Y has to be higher up in the tree than X is. So X must be in the right subtree of Y (since all information values to the left of Y must be smaller). The logic of the PutIn procedure can be adjusted to allow for this as follows: If, while searching down the tree, you find a matching information value, swap it with the one you are trying to insert and go to the right in the tree. That way, the older one will be below and to the right of the newer one. Example 5.5C contains the coding.

It is instructive to see an example of how the PutIn procedure works using the algorithm just described. Assume that you start with an empty tree and that the information is just a CARDINAL. Say a client module calls PutIn six times, with the cardinals 8, 12, 6, 11, 8, and 15 in that order. Then Figure 11 shows how the tree grows.

One way to reduce the complexity of PutIn is to change the rules; we could specify that a Table cannot have two different matching sets of information. There are many situations in which this condition holds. But one of the most useful situations for a Table occurs during compilation of a program; the identifiers mentioned in the program can be stored in a Table. If two procedures declare the same identifier and one procedure contains the other, any reference to the identifier within the inner procedure is to be taken as a reference to its own

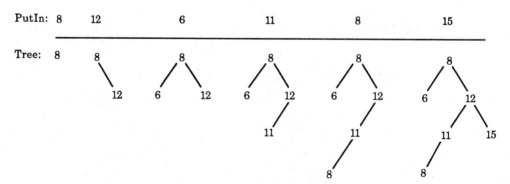

FIGURE 11. Examples of TableADT.PutIn for an initially empty binary search tree, using the values 8, 12, 6, 11, 8, 15 in that order.

EXAMPLE 5.5C _____

```
PROCEDURE PutIn (TheInfo : Information; VAR Data : Table);
    (* Context:  binary search tree impl. of TableADT *)
VAR
    Saved : Information;
  (*------------------------------------------------------------*)
    PROCEDURE MakeNewNode (VAR Spot : PointerToNode);
    BEGIN
        NEW (Spot);
        Spot^.Info  := TheInfo;
        Spot^.Left  := NIL;
        Spot^.Right := NIL;
        Data^.Child := Spot;
    END MakeNewNode;
  (*------------------------------------------------------------*)
    PROCEDURE PutInSearchTree (VAR Spot : PointerToNode);
    BEGIN
        IF Spot = NIL THEN
            MakeNewNode (Spot);
        ELSE
            Data^.Parent := Spot;
            IF Compare (TheInfo, Spot^.Info) < 0 THEN
                PutInSearchTree (Spot^.Left);
            ELSE
                IF Compare (TheInfo, Spot^.Info) = 0 THEN
                    Saved := Spot^.Info;
                    Spot^.Info := TheInfo;
                    TheInfo := Saved;
                END;
                PutInSearchTree (Spot^.Right);
            END;
        END;
    END PutInSearchTree;
  (*------------------------------------------------------------*)
BEGIN           (* PutIn *)
    PutInSearchTree (Data^.RootNode);
END PutIn;
```

declaration. That declaration will have been inserted more recently, assuming the compiler processes the program in the order it is written.

Changing the rules would only decrease the complexity of PutIn; it would not significantly change the speed of execution. The only change required is to omit the IF statement in Example 5.5C. The other procedures are not affected by having matching information values.

This implementation of TableADT could be rewritten as one that imports from BinADT and does nothing with the Left, Right, and Info fields directly. In that case, the Create procedure would be:

```
NEW (Data);
BinADT.Create (Data↑.RootNode);
Data↑.Child := NoNode;
```

InTable would just return Data ↑ .Child#NoNode, and Inspect would execute BinADT.See(TheInfo, Data ↑ .Child).

Check Your Understanding

1. If the number 49 is inserted in the binary search tree on the right in Figure 10, what is the sequence of information values seen on the way to where the 49 goes?

2. Write a utility procedure for this implementation of TableADT: Print the information in all the nodes in a binary search tree, in order from highest to lowest.

3. Rewrite the PutIn procedure (Example 5.5C) so that Compare is never called for the same two sets of information (in order to save execution time).

4. In the Create procedure of Example 5.5A, why not move the NEW statement inside of the WITH statement?

5. Revise the coding in this section by omitting the Parent field of a Table.

6. (NA) Draw a picture of the binary search tree that results when the PutIn procedure is called seven times for the information 6, 3, 8, 4, 5, 4, and 7, in that order. Start with an empty tree.

7. (NA) Write the Find procedure using imports from BinADT as described at the end of this section.

8. (NA) Write the PutIn procedure using imports from BinADT as described at the end of this section.

9. (NA) Rewrite the PutIn procedure of Example 5.5C without using recursion.

5.6 THE TakeOut PROCEDURE FOR A BINARY SEARCH TREE

The TakeOut procedure begins by checking that there is information to be removed and, if not, does nothing. Otherwise it puts the information in its information parameter. This is just what Inspect does. The problem is, what do we do with the empty node? We cannot just leave it there, and we cannot simply dispose of it without losing both its subtrees. If one of its subtrees is empty, the problem is simplified, since we can just move its other subtree up into its place and then dispose of it.

Challenge. I will discuss why this does not affect the ordering property of the binary search tree later in this section; take a few minutes now to see if you can reason it out on your own before you read it.

Algorithm for TakeOut

The logic for deleting one node is simplified if you do not have to treat the three cases of the Left field of the Parent, its Right field, and the root of the whole tree separately. So you can begin by seeing which case applies and calling a subprocedure with the Left or Right field as a VAR parameter (or Data↑.RootNode if you are deleting the root). This subprocedure is to make the appropriate change in its VAR parameter, which you can call Spot.

The overall algorithm I decided on for deleting one node is a selection of two alternatives, depending on whether the node has an empty right subtree.

- ☐ If Spot has an empty right subtree, replace Spot by its left subtree and dispose of the node that was there.

- ☐ If Spot has a nonempty right subtree, look through that right subtree to find the smallest information value in it. Call that node X. Then copy the information from X into the Spot node and delete X. X will be easy to delete because X must be the leftmost node in Spot's right subtree (I will explain why shortly), so its own left subtree must be empty. So replace X by its right subtree and dispose of X.

Figure 12 displays a binary search tree. Assume that TakeOut is called twice, with the cardinals 11 and 12 in that order. Then the middle and righthand parts of Figure 12 show the two stages in which the tree shrinks using this algorithm. Note that the 13 replaces the 12 for the second deletion.

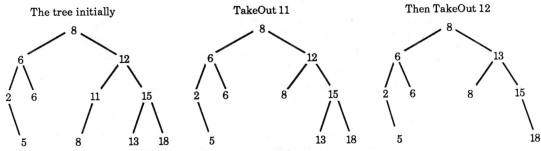

FIGURE 12. Examples of TableADT.TakeOut using a binary search tree.

When you delete the information from the tree, the Child field of the table should be reset to NIL. The only exception occurs when there is a matching information value in the tree. In that case, it will be the information in the leftmost node of the right subtree of Data ↑ .Child. So, if the right subtree of the Child is nonempty, you should test the information you move up to the Child node to see if it matches the information value you are taking out. If so, do not set Child to NIL. The coding for the TakeOut procedure is in Example 5.6A.

There are now four logical arguments that I have to supply in this section, to justify this algorithm: I have to show that the smallest information in a binary search (sub)tree is in its leftmost Node, and I have to show that replacing the information in a Node by the smallest information in its nonempty right subtree keeps it a binary search tree. I have to tell you why I chose the right subtree rather than the left subtree, and I have to show that replacing any node by its only nonempty subtree keeps the whole tree a binary search tree.

Why the Leftmost Node Contains the Smallest Information

The TakeOut procedure produces a new (slightly smaller) binary tree from a given binary search tree. This new tree purports to also be a binary search tree. I have to give some logical reasoning to show that it is. The *key fact* is that, in any given nonempty subtree T of a binary search tree, all information values that are smaller than the information at the root of T are in the left subtree of T (and only those smaller values). That is the definition of a binary search tree. In particular, every subtree of a binary search tree is also a binary search tree.

It is necessary to show that the leftmost Node in every nonempty binary search tree contains the smallest information in that tree, in the sense that no other information in that tree is smaller. There is a standard technique for proving such statements, called the **Induction Principle**. It goes like this: Pretend there is at least one tree for which that statement is not true. Let T denote the "smallest" of all such trees, that is, the one with the least number of nodes. Show that the statement really is true for T. Then this shows that you have pretended something that is logically impossible; the statement really is true for *all* trees. Think about that for a minute to be sure you accept the validity of such an argument.

Therefore, I start by letting T denote the smallest nonempty binary search tree for which the leftmost node does *not* contain the smallest information value. Since T is nonempty, it has a root node. None of the nodes in the right subtree of T contain smaller information than that at the root of T (according to the "key fact"), so the smallest information in T must be either at its root or in its left subtree. There are two cases to consider:

☐ If the left subtree of T is empty, that means that the smallest information in T must be at its root, and it also means that its root is the leftmost Node in T.

EXAMPLE 5.6A _____

```
PROCEDURE TakeOut (VAR TheInfo : Information;
                   VAR Data     : Table);
    (* Context:  binary search tree impl. of TableADT *)
VAR
    Subtree : PointerToNode;
  (*--------------------------------------------------------*)

    PROCEDURE DeleteLeftmost (VAR Spot : PointerToNode);
        (* Move the information in the leftmost node up to
           Child^.Info and delete that leftmost node *)
    BEGIN
        IF Spot^.Left # NIL THEN
            DeleteLeftmost (Spot^.Left);
        ELSE          (* empty left subtree *)
            Data^.Child^.Info := Spot^.Info;
            IF Compare (TheInfo, Spot^.Info) # 0 THEN
                Data^.Child := NIL;
            END;
            Subtree := Spot^.Right;
            DISPOSE (Spot);
            Spot := Subtree;
        END;
    END DeleteLeftmost;
  (*--------------------------------------------------------*)

    PROCEDURE DeleteOneNode (VAR Spot : PointerToNode);
        (* Delete one node and replace Spot^.Info *)
    BEGIN
        IF Spot^.Right # NIL THEN
            DeleteLeftmost (Spot^.Right);
        ELSE           (* empty right subtree *)
            Data^.Child := NIL;
            Subtree := Spot^.Left;
            DISPOSE (Spot);
            Spot := Subtree;
        END;
    END DeleteOneNode;
  (*--------------------------------------------------------*)

BEGIN          (* TakeOut *)
    WITH Data^ DO
        IF Child # NIL THEN
            TheInfo := Child^.Info;
            IF Child = RootNode THEN
                DeleteOneNode (RootNode);
            ELSIF Child = Parent^.Left THEN
                DeleteOneNode (Parent^.Left);
            ELSE
                DeleteOneNode (Parent^.Right);
            END;
        END;
    END;
END TakeOut;
```

☐ If the left subtree of T is not empty, let us call it L. Then the smallest information in T must be the smallest information in L. L is a binary search tree with fewer Nodes than T has, so the statement is true of L. Thus the leftmost Node in L contains the smallest information in L, which is therefore the smallest information in T. Since I go left from the root of T to get to L, and then keep going left to get to the leftmost Node in L, that Node must also be the leftmost Node in T.

This proves the statement for the "let's pretend" T. The Induction Principle implies that the statement is therefore true for any binary search tree: The smallest information is in the leftmost node.

Why Shifting the Information Up is Okay

The second assertion to prove is that replacing the information of a Node N in a binary search tree by the smallest information in N's right subtree keeps it a binary search tree. The following arguments should suffice:

☐ None of the information to the right of N is smaller than the new information at N, since we chose the smallest information to the right of N.

☐ All the information to the left of N is smaller than the new information at N, since all that information is smaller than what was formerly at N and the new information is not smaller than what was formerly at N.

☐ For any other Node in the tree, all information in its left subtree was in its left subtree before the deletion and thus is smaller than the information at its root. Also, all information in its right subtree was in its right subtree before the change, and thus is not smaller than the information at its root.

Why Replacing a Node by its Only Subtree is Okay

Assume that N is a Node with only one subtree. Assume also that you change things so that the Parent of N points to the root of that subtree (on the same side) instead of to N and you dispose of N. Then the whole tree remains a binary search tree. You can see this by considering any Node X in the whole tree and showing that (1) all Nodes to its left are smaller, and (2) no Node to its right is smaller. There are two possibilities:

☐ If N was in a subtree of X, N's subtree was in that same subtree of X, and it still is. Thus properties (1) and (2) still hold.

☐ If N was not in a subtree of X, the subtrees of X have not changed, so properties (1) and (2) must still hold.

Why Using the Left Subtree Is Not Okay

The fourth reasoning to give is to show why I took the smallest (leftmost) information value in the right subtree instead of the largest (rightmost) information value in the left subtree. The trouble is that the left subtree may contain two sets of matching information that are both the largest information value in that left subtree. If I were to move one of them up to the root, then the other one would be in its left subtree, though it would not be smaller. This is contrary to the definition of a binary search tree.

By contrast, assume that the leftmost information value in some right subtree R matches some other information value in R that was put in earlier. Then that other earlier information must be in the leftmost's right subtree, and it will still be in its right subtree after it is moved up. So future searches down through the tree will find the more recently inserted information value first, as they should.

Implementation of DictiADT

This implementation of TableADT cannot be extended to an implementation of DictiADT by just adding the FindFirstIn and FindNextIn procedures. The trouble is that you have to keep track of the current location in the tree even when there is no information there. You can do this by keeping track of the place where a leaf node would be inserted, either on the left or right of a Parent node. So you add an additional field to a Table, such as a Boolean OnRight field that tells whether you would insert to the right of the Parent node. This greatly complicates several of the seven procedures already developed, although InTable and Inspect would not change.

The coding is simplified by having the equivalent of a header node: Create allocates space for a RootNode and makes its left subtree empty; all the information goes in the left subtree of the RootNode. Create then initializes Parent to the RootNode and OnRight to FALSE. The rest of this implementation is left as a programming problem.

Check Your Understanding

1. Assume that the procedure in Example 5.6A is used to delete the number 46 from the binary search tree on the right of Figure 10 in Section 5.5. How does that change the tree?

2. Assume that no two information values in the table are supposed to match, and your algorithms can ignore this possibility. How much can you speed up the execution of TakeOut in that case?

3. Describe all changes that would have to be made in all procedures in the binary search tree implementation of TableADT if, for any Node N, all infor-

mation values in N's right subtree are larger than the information at N but no information values in N's left subtree are larger.

4. The tree at the left of Figure 12 was obtained from the one on the right of Figure 11 by performing five insertions. What can you deduce about the order in which those insertions were made?

5. (NA) Can you speed up execution of the TakeOut procedure by checking whether a node's left subtree is NIL and, if so, avoiding the search for the leftmost node in its right subtree? Does that keep the whole tree a binary search tree in which the higher of matching information values is the most recently added? If it does, what changes in the coding must be made?

6. (NA) Rewrite the TakeOut procedure using imports from BinADT, as described at the end of the previous section.

7. (NA) Give a logical argument using the Induction Principle to show that no Node in a binary search tree is larger than the rightmost Node of that binary search tree.

8. (NA) Give a logical argument using the Induction Principle to show that less than half of all Nodes in a nonempty binary tree have two children.

9. (NA) Give a logical argument using the Induction Principle to show that the leaf nodes of a tree are processed in the same order when using inorder traversal as when using preorder traversal.

10. (NA) Give a logical argument using the Induction Principle to show that, if inorder traversal of two trees gives the same information values in the same order, and if postorder traversal of the two trees gives the same information values in the same order, the two trees must be identical copies of each other.

11. (NA) Give a logical argument using the Induction Principle to show that, if every node in a binary tree has an equal number of nodes in its left and right subtrees, the total number of nodes in the tree is 1 less than a power of 2.

5.7 IMPLEMENTATION: BinADT USING ARRAYS

An array implementation of binary trees is not so straightforward as it was for lists. For lists, we do not store information about where to find the follower of a given information value; instead, we have a formula to compute the index of the follower of X from the index of X, namely adding 1. This does not work for binary trees, since each value has two followers. We need a simple formula to do this for trees.

The Standard Array Implementation of BinADT

Consider the complete binary tree of height 3 shown on the left in Figure 13. Each node has a number from 1 to 15. If you study it for a while, you will see that the left child of node number K has the number $2*K$ and the right child has the number $2*K+1$. From this is derived the standard numbering method for the nodes in the top four levels of *any* tree: Use the number shown in Figure 13 unless there is no node there, in which case consider it to be NoNode. Thus, for the complete tree of height 2, the nodes are numbered 1 to 7 as shown on the right in Figure 13.

If a tree has height 4, the bottom level can have up to 16 nodes, so we number the nodes on the bottom level from 16 to 31, working from left to right and omitting numbers where there are no nodes. For height 5, some or all of the numbers from 32 to 63 are used for the bottom level, with 16 to 31 for the next-to-bottom level. In general, the bottom level of a tree of height N has up to 2-to-the-Nth nodes. Two examples are shown in Figure 14.

For the array implementations of lists, we set an upper limit on the number of information values that can be in the list at any one time. For binary trees, we do the same; but we also stipulate that no node can be used whose number is higher than MaxSize in the following numbering method:

1. Number the root 1;
2. Do until time to STOP:
   2.a. STOP if all nodes are numbered;
   2.b. If a numbered node has an unnumbered left child, then:
        Number that left child using twice as much;
   2.c. If a numbered node has an unnumbered right child, then:
        Number that right child using 1 more than twice as much.

Note: Technically, this is not an algorithm, because it does not tell you how to choose from several numbered nodes with unnumbered children. However, the choice is immaterial.

In the **standard array implementation of binary trees**, we declare an array with components numbered 1 to MaxSize. We put each information value of the tree

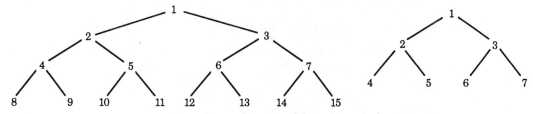

FIGURE 13. Standard numbering of two complete binary trees.

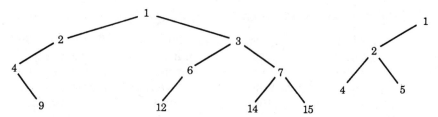

FIGURE 14. *Standard numbering of two trees of heights 3 and 2.*

in the component whose index is the number computed by the foregoing method. The problem is that this gives us MaxSize nodes, and most trees do not have that many nodes in use. We need some way of marking a node as "nonexistent."

One solution to this problem is available when InfoADT exports a constant that indicates the absence of information. For instance, InfoADT could export NoInfo, which must be distinguishable from all true information values. Then we could assign NoInfo to an array component to indicate that there is no information there (and thus no true Node there). For a pointer implementation, NoInfo could be NIL; if Information is an entire record with a string as the ID, NoInfo could be a record with an ID that is all blanks. This design is left as a programming problem.

Another solution to this problem does not require anything of InfoADT except that it export the Information type. However, it requires more space for a binary tree: Each array component can be a record with two values; one is a Boolean that

EXAMPLE 5.7A _____

```
IMPLEMENTATION MODULE BinADT;
FROM InfoADT IMPORT Information;
    (* standard array implementation of binary trees *)
    (* The left child of component K is at index 2*K;
       the right child of component K is at index 2*K+1 *)
CONST
    MaxSize = 1000;        (* so up to 10 levels *)
TYPE
    BinTree = POINTER TO ARRAY [1..MaxSize] OF
        RECORD
            IsANode : BOOLEAN;
            Info : Information;
        END;
    Location = CARDINAL;

(* ALL 13 procedures go here; see later discussions *)

BEGIN         (* initialization *)
    NoNode := 0;
END BinADT.
```

tells whether there is a true Node at that component, and the other is an Information value (which is indeterminate if the Boolean value indicates that there is no true Node there).

An obvious design decision is to let a Location in a tree be the index in the array of the Node in question. The NoNode value could be any number that cannot be an index; the obvious choice is 0. An implementation module for this design is in Example 5.7A, without the procedures; it allows up to 10 levels in a tree.

The Thirteen Binary Tree Procedures

The procedure call Create(Data) executes NEW(Data) and then initializes Data ↑ [1].IsANode to FALSE. This allows us to test Data ↑ [1].IsANode to find out whether a tree is empty. The procedure call Destroy(Data) executes the one statement DISPOSE(Data). The coding for Root(Data) could be:

```
IF NOT Data↑ [1].IsANode THEN
        RETURN NoNode;
ELSE
        RETURN 1;
END;
```

The Left function is only slightly more complicated; we have to make sure that we are not out of the permissible range for indices of the array. So the body of the function Left(Where, Data) could be as follows. Note how the partial evaluation feature of Modula-2 is heavily used here.

```
(* body of Left for standard array implementation of BinADT *)
Child := 2 * Where;
IF (Where >= 1) AND (Child <= MaxSize) AND
            Data↑ [Where].IsANode AND Data↑ [Child].IsANode THEN
    RETURN Child;
ELSE
    RETURN NoNode;
END;
```

The body of the Right function is the same as that of the Left function except that the first statement is replaced by Child := 2*Where+1.

The See procedure can be coded as:

```
IF (Where >= 1) AND Data↑ [Where].IsANode THEN
    TheInfo := Data↑ [Where].Info;
END;
```

The Swap, PutX, and TakeX procedures are left as exercises. Some of them are fairly challenging. It might be best if all three PutX procedures did little but call a procedure that puts a given information value at a given index in the array; this procedure would not be exported, since it is private to the implementation.

A Different Array Implementation of BinADT

Figure 15 shows the complete binary trees of heights 2 and 3. Their nodes are numbered as implied by inorder traversal. For instance, a tree of up to 4 levels would have its nodes numbered as shown on the left of Figure 15, except that nonexistent nodes would be considered to be NoNode. When MaxSize is 15, the root node is numbered 8, and the children of node 8 are numbered 4 and 12. In general, when MaxSize is 1 less than a power of 2, the root node is numbered (MaxSize+1) DIV 2, the left child of the node numbered N is numbered N DIV 2, and the right child of the node numbered N is numbered 3∗N DIV 2.

With this **powers-of-two numbering**, the BinADT implementation module is the same as shown in Example 5.7A; only the bodies of some of the procedures are different. For instance, Create, Destroy, Root, See, and Swap are exactly the same. The coding for the Left function differs only in that Child is computed as Where DIV 2. Similarly, the only change for the Right function is to compute Child as 3∗Where DIV 2. The PutX and TakeX procedures are also little different from the original array implementation described.

This numbering is a natural one, in a sense. If you perform a binary search of an array of 15 items, the first one you look at is item 8. Next you look at item 4 or 12, depending on the comparison with item 8. If you review Exercise 2 of Section 2.5, you will see that the coding for the binary search algorithm corresponds to this numbering. That exercise refers to the algorithm in which you stop as soon as you see the item for which you are searching.

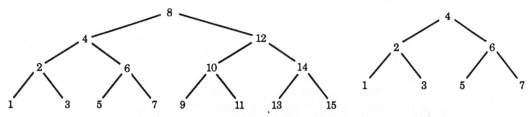

FIGURE 15. Powers-of-two numbering of two complete binary trees.

Several other array implementations of binary trees are feasible. For instance, you can store the information in preorder sequence, where each array component also has a notation of the index in the array of the root of its right subtree (0 if the right subtree is empty, −1 if no value is at that index). This implementation is left as a programming problem. You might try to develop a reasonable array implementation using the postorder sequence.

Check Your Understanding

1. Write the utility Transpose procedure (described in Exercise 1 of Section 5.4) for the standard array implementation of BinADT.

2. Write the Swap procedure for the standard array implementation of BinADT.

3. Rewrite the IF condition for the Left function (standard array implementation) so that it can be followed by THEN RETURN NoNode ELSE RETURN Child END. Then explain why you do not have to guard against Where>MaxSize.

4. Write the Copy utility procedure (described in Example 3.1C) for the standard array implementation of BinADT.

5. (NA) Write a function that finds the location of the parent of the node at a given location, using the powers-of-two array implementation of BinADT. Make appropriate adjustments for locations without parents.

6. (NA) Write the PutRoot procedure for the standard array implementation of BinADT.

7. (NA) Write the TakeRoot procedure for the standard array implementation of BinADT.

8. (NA) Rewrite the coding for the Left function in the standard array implementation of BinADT without taking advantage of partial evaluation. You need this skill in some other programming languages.

9. (NA) Give a logical argument based on the Induction Principle to show that the loop for the text's "algorithm" for the standard numbering of tree nodes will always terminate, however one chooses a numbered node with an unnumbered child.

5.8 PERFECTLY BALANCED BINARY TREES

The task to be considered in this section is putting a sequential list of information values into a binary tree structure. The values should be placed so that inorder traversal of the binary tree goes through the values in the same order that they occurred on the list. Moreover, the values should be placed so that the resulting binary tree is as balanced as possible.

For instance, you might have a file of values stored in increasing order; when the task just described has been accomplished, you will have a binary search tree that can be searched very quickly for a given value. This is essentially the task that the ReadTable procedure is to accomplish for DictiADT. As another instance, you might have a List of values (as declared in ListADT) from which you obtain values one at a time (normally using NextLocation and LookAt) and put them in the tree. Then inorder traversal of the resulting tree gives the values in the proper order.

To make this task more concrete, we will assume that you use InputInfo from InfoADT to obtain the next information value in sequence, and that Size is the number of information values to be obtained and put in the binary tree. The task is to be performed using the standard two-pointer implementation of binary trees.

Definition of Balance

"Balance" in a binary tree means that, for any node in the tree, its left and right subtrees are close to being the same size. This "definition" has to be made more precise before it can be of any use. A **perfectly balanced tree** is one in which the left and right subtrees of any node are within 1 of each other in number of nodes. The reason for not requiring that the subtrees have exactly the same number of nodes is that it would exclude, for instance, trees with an even number of nodes.

A 3-level binary tree can have up to 7 nodes in it. A 4-level binary tree can have up to 15 nodes in it. A 5-level binary tree can have up to 31 nodes in it. In general, N nodes require a tree with at least $\lg(N+1)$ levels [$\lg(N+1)$ was defined in Section 5.1 as the exponent on the power of 2 just above N]. There are applications in which it is advantageous to have the number of levels in a tree be as small as possible. For example, there should be 4 levels if there are 8 to 15 nodes in the tree, and there should be 5 levels if there are 16 to 31 nodes in the tree. This consideration arises when using an array implementation of binary trees, as discussed in Section 5.7. It so happens that every perfectly balanced tree has the minimum number of levels possible. This can be shown using the Induction Principle, discussed in Section 5.6.

Algorithm for Creating a Perfectly Balanced Binary Tree

Assume that you have 19 information values to read into a perfectly balanced binary tree. Then you have to put the first 9 in the left subtree of the root, the last 9 in the right subtree of the root, and the tenth one as the root. The requirement of perfect balance dictates the 9-and-9 split. Inorder traversal of the tree will go through the left subtree before it gets to the root, which is why the 9 in the left subtree have to be the *first* 9.

In the left subtree L of that tree, the 9 values have to be split up so that the first 4 are in the left subtree of L, the last 4 are in the right subtree of L, and the fifth one is at the root of L. The reasoning is the same as just given for the 19 in the whole tree. The same 4-and-4 split applies to the right subtree of the whole tree.

In the left subtree of L, there are 4 nodes. These have to be split 2-and-1, but you are free to choose whether the two are on the left or on the right. It is standard operating procedure to put the larger number on the left when you have a choice. Thus the first two go on the left, the third one goes at the root, and the fourth one goes on the right. By applying this standard decision procedure at each step, you arrive at the tree shown in Figure 16. That figure also displays the tree you would get if you had six information values to put in the tree. The numbers at the nodes are the numbers of the information values in the order they were read.

This discussion leads to the following algorithm for creating a perfectly balanced binary tree from the next N information values read from a file (assuming N is not 0):

1. Create a new node for the root of the tree;
2. Create a perfectly balanced binary tree containing the next N DIV 2 values from the file and make it the left subtree of the root;
3. Put the next information value at the root;
4. Create a perfectly balanced binary tree containing the rest of the values from the file and make it the right subtree of the root.

This algorithm is obviously recursive; the coding is in Example 5.8A. Note that this algorithm produces the only possible binary tree for a given number of information values subject to the two conditions (1) inorder traversal of the tree gives the original order of the values, and (2) the left subtree of each node has the same number of nodes as the right subtree or else one more node than the right subtree.

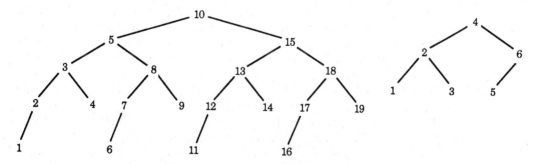

FIGURE 16. Two perfectly balanced trees, of sizes 19 and 6.

EXAMPLE 5.8A _____

```
PROCEDURE MakeBalancedTree (Size     : CARDINAL;
                            VAR Data : BinTree);
    (* Make a perfectly balanced binary tree from an empty
            tree by using InputInfo Size times; store the
            information so that inorder traversal gives the
            original order *)
    (* Context:  utility in the standard two-pointer
                    implementation of BinADT *)
VAR
    SizeOnLeft : CARDINAL;
BEGIN
    IF Size = 0 THEN
        Data := NIL;
    ELSE
        NEW (Data);
        SizeOnLeft := Size DIV 2;
        MakeBalancedTree (SizeOnLeft, Data^.Left);
        InputInfo (Data^.Info);
        MakeBalancedTree (Size - 1 - SizeOnLeft,
                            Data^.Right);
    END;
END MakeBalancedTree;
```

Variations on the Basic Algorithm

For the implementation of ListADT using a binary tree plus a Count field (Example 5.4C), assume that the ReadAll utility procedure can obtain the Size of the list to be read, either by asking the user or reading it from a file that was written at the same time the information values were written. Then ReadAll can call a slight variant of Example 5.8A in which the part after the NEW statement is replaced by:

```
Data↑.Count := Size DIV 2 + 1;
MakeBalancedTree (Data↑.Count - 1, Data↑.Left);
InputInfo (Data↑.Info);
MakeBalancedTree (Size - Data↑.Count, Data↑.Right);
```

This MakeBalancedTree procedure can also be written using imports from BinTree instead of as a utility procedure. The logic is much the same, although clumsier when you cannot access the internal structure of a tree. For one thing, you cannot create a new node without providing some information to go in it; but you do not have the information until after you have read information for the left subtree. So you have to insert garbage as information at the root, then fill up the left subtree, then swap the garbage for the correct information.

Another problem is that you cannot pass the Left or Right field of a node as a VAR parameter in the recursion. This means you have to delay the recursive call until after you have put information at the root of the subtree you want to read. A third problem is that you cannot read directly into the Info field of a node—you have to read into a local Information variable and call Swap (to swap the information for the garbage). The coding is in Example 5.8B.

EXAMPLE 5.8B _____

```
PROCEDURE MakeBalancedTree (Size     : CARDINAL;
                            VAR Data : BinTree);
    (* Make a perfectly balanced binary tree from an empty
        tree by using InputInfo Size times; store the
        information so that inorder traversal gives the
        original order *)
    (* Context:  client of BinADT *)
VAR
    TheInfo : Information;
  (*----------------------------------------------------*)

    PROCEDURE ReadTree (Size : CARDINAL; Spot : Location);
        (* Size >= 1 and there is a node at the Spot *)
    VAR
        SizeOnLeft : CARDINAL;
    BEGIN
        IF Size >= 2 THEN
            SizeOnLeft := Size DIV 2;
            PutLeft (TheInfo, Spot, Data);
            ReadTree (SizeOnLeft, Left (Spot, Data));
        END;
        InputInfo (TheInfo);
        Swap (TheInfo, Spot, Data);
        IF Size >= 3 THEN
            PutRight (TheInfo, Spot, Data);
            ReadTree (Size - 1 - SizeOnLeft,
                      Right (Spot, Data));
        END;
    END ReadTree;
  (*----------------------------------------------------*)

BEGIN           (* MakeBalancedTree *)
    Create (Data);
    IF Size >= 1 THEN
        PutRoot (TheInfo, Data);        (* garbage for now *)
        ReadTree (Size, Root (Data));
    END;
END MakeBalancedTree;
```

Check Your Understanding

1. If Example 5.8A is called with Size=4, how many times does it call itself and with what values of Size on each call?

2. What variables, if any, have been delocalized in Example 5.8B?

3. Assume that Example 5.8A is never called from outside itself with Size=0. Rewrite it to execute faster by having it never call itself with Size=0.

4. (NA) Give a logical argument to show that only complete binary trees have the property that the left and right subtrees of every node have the same number of nodes.

5. (NA) Use the Induction Principle to prove that any perfectly balanced tree has the minimum possible number of levels for the number of nodes that it has. *Hint:* Consider first the case where the number of nodes is odd, then the case where it is even.

6. (NA) Write a Boolean function telling whether a given binary tree is perfectly balanced, using imports from BinADT.

5.9 OTHER BALANCING ACTS

For some applications, it is desirable to create a binary tree in which:

1. The tree has the minimum number of levels possible for the number of nodes it has.
2. The tree has the minimum number of nodes possible on the bottom level.
3. All nodes on the bottom level are to the left in the tree.

This defines an **almost-complete binary tree**. The first requirement means that such a tree is reasonably balanced. The third requirement means that it does not fit the definition of "perfectly balanced," although the time required to access a node in the tree averages the same as for a perfectly balanced tree. The standard array implementation of a binary tree, described in Section 5.7, will have all nodes in the components indexed from 1 to N (where N is the number of nodes) precisely when the tree satisfies the three requirements just listed. Figure 17 shows the almost-complete binary trees for 19 and for 5 nodes. The numbers at the nodes indicate the order in which nodes are produced using inorder traversal. Consider the task of reading a given number of information values and creating the almost-complete binary tree containing them, where inorder traversal produces the values in order. For instance, assume that you have 19 values. You need a tree with 5 levels, since lg(19+1) = 5 (32 is the power of 2 just above 19). 15 values go on the first 4 levels, and the remaining 4 values go on the fifth level as

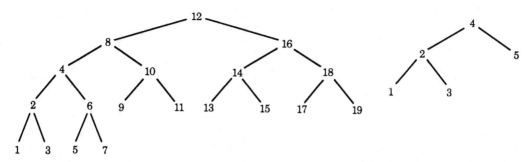

FIGURE 17. Two almost-complete trees, of sizes 19 and 5.

far to the left as possible. If you look at Figure 17 again, you can see that the left subtree of the root has 11 nodes and the right subtree has 7 nodes. So you create the whole tree by reading 11 values and making the left subtree out of them, then reading the twelfth value and putting it at the root, then reading the remaining 7 values and making the right subtree out of them.

The 7 nodes in the right subtree form a complete binary tree. The 11 nodes in the left subtree L will have the "extra" 4 on the bottom level as far to the left as possible. That means that the left subtree of L will have 7 nodes and the right subtree of L will have 3 nodes.

Each subtree of an almost complete binary tree is also an almost complete binary tree. For 24 to 31 nodes, the first 15 will be in the left subtree, the sixteenth will be the root, and the remaining 8 to 15 will be in the right subtree. For 16 to 23 nodes, the last 7 will be in the right subtree and the first 8 to 15 will be in the left subtree.

Consideration of examples such as the foregoing leads to the following general rule: For a given number N of nodes, where Power is the power of 2 just above N, there are two cases to consider: If N >= Power∗3 DIV 4, the left subtree is complete with Power DIV 2 − 1 nodes and the right subtree is almost complete. If N < Power∗3 DIV 4, the right subtree is complete with Power DIV 4 − 1 nodes and the left subtree is almost complete. You should try out various number of nodes until you see that this is true.

This indicates that an algorithm for creating an almost-complete binary tree from input values can be obtained from Example 5.8A or 5.8B by simply changing the value computed for SizeOnLeft. The statement SizeOnLeft := Size DIV 2 can be replaced by the following coding:

```
Power := ThePowerOfTwoJustAbove (Size);
IF Size >= Power * 3 DIV 4 THEN
    SizeOnLeft := Power DIV 2 - 1;
ELSE
    SizeOnLeft := Size - Power DIV 4;
END;
```

This implies that you have to write a function to compute the power of 2 just above a given number, but in practice you compute it once before you call the MakeBalancedTree procedure for the first time and pass it as a parameter on each call of the procedure. Execution time is cut a little if you pass one fourth of that Power instead of the power itself. You may have been puzzled by the computation of SizeOnLeft in the ELSE clause; remember that the size of the left subtree is the given Size minus 1 for the root and minus the size of the right subtree.

Other Algorithms for Creating a Nearly Balanced Tree

The two algorithms described so far require you to know how many values are to be read. For instance, in creating a perfectly balanced tree, you do not know whether to put the tenth information value at the root unless you know that there will be 8 or 9 more information values to read. The utility ReadAll procedure performs the task we have been discussing except that the number of values is not known in advance. This keeps us from using one of the forms of MakeBalancedTree just described.

There are two possible ways to create a balanced binary tree with the original ordering when we do not know how many values there are. One is to design an algorithm that does not require knowing the number of values. The other is to first read all the values in and count them as they are read and then call MakeBalancedTree.

For the first method, study the sequence of binary trees given in Figure 18 and look for the pattern. There is one tree shown for each number of nodes from 1 to 7; the pattern can be extended as far as you like. Each tree has the minimum number of levels possible. The number at each node is the number of the information value read in and put at that node.

You could design an algorithm to create that one of these trees that corresponds to the number of information values to be read. The advantage is that each tree is obtained from the one before by adding a node and assigning values to its pointers, but only changing one other pointer value at most. In other words, the amount of work to be done in creating such a tree from an unknown number of information values is very little more than the amount necessary for a perfectly balanced or an almost-complete tree when the number of nodes is known in advance. A general description of these trees is as follows: For N nodes, consider

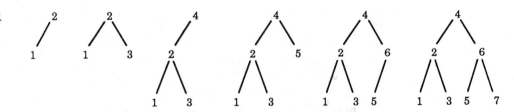

FIGURE 18. A sequence of 7 nearly balanced binary trees.

the smallest complete binary tree with at least N nodes. Number the nodes of that complete tree in accordance with inorder traversal. Delete nodes numbered higher than N. If that deletes a node without completely deleting its left subtree, move that left subtree up where the node was. The algorithm and coding for generating such a tree is left as a programming problem.

Another way of performing ReadAll is to read the information values and put them on a queue of nodes, counting them as they are read. It is most efficient to use tree nodes and use the right pointers as links for the queue (leaving the left pointers indeterminate). When the whole file has been read, you can call a modification of MakeBalancedTree with an additional parameter, a pointer to the first node on the queue that has not yet been put in the tree. The algorithm is similar to Example 5.8A; the coding is left as a programming problem.

AVL Trees

In many applications, it is important to keep a binary tree nearly balanced while insertions and deletions occur in random order, interspersed with frequent searches of the tree for a particular value. The definitions given previously in this section are not suitable. If you tried to maintain perfect balance or almost-completeness, it would require too much reordering of the nodes. An easier goal is to try to keep the tree an "AVL tree" at all times. An **AVL tree** is a binary tree in which, for any node, the number of levels in its two subtrees differ by at most 1. Every perfectly balanced tree and every almost-complete tree is an AVL tree. Figure 19 shows three **Fibonacci trees**; it can be shown that these are the most unbalanced AVL trees possible. The definition of a Fibonacci tree for a larger number of nodes is that it is obtained by making the previous one its left subtree and the one before that its right subtree. *Note:* AVL stands for Adelson-Velskii and Landis, the people who came up with this definition.

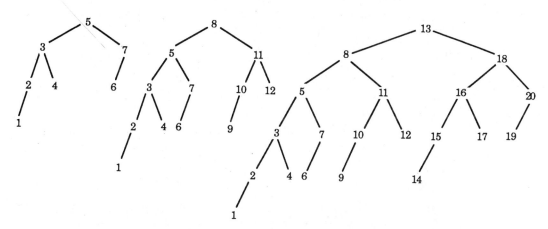

FIGURE 19. The Fibonacci AVL trees for levels 4, 5, and 6.

A common use of AVL trees (also known as **height-balanced trees**) is in maintaining a binary search tree for an implementation of TableADT or in implementing ListADT. In the latter case, we often add a Count field to keep track of 1 more than the number of nodes in the left subtree of each node, to make it easy to find the Kth item on the list. Each time a node is inserted or deleted, it must be done so that inorder traversal of the tree produces the correct result (increasing order for a binary search tree, linear list order for an implementation of ListADT).

To make it easier to check an AVL tree for balance and rebalance it when needed, it is common to add a Balance field to each node. The Balance value for a node is the number of levels in its right subtree minus the number of levels in its left subtree. The insertion and deletion procedures are complicated, so they are left as programming problems. The insertion algorithm is described in the next paragraph. Evidence from many test runs indicates that, if insertions and deletions are made randomly, rebalancing is necessary about once every two insertions and about once every five deletions.

Assume that an AVL tree is being used as a binary search tree and an insertion is made, creating a new leaf node for the inserted information value. The Balance value for the new node is 0, since it has empty left and right subtrees. The Balance value of the parent of the new leaf is corrected by adding 1 to it if the insertion was made on its right, subtracting 1 from it if the insertion was made on its left. No rebalancing is necessary at the parent node, since the tree was an AVL tree before the insertion. At each node on the path back from the new node to the root, the Balance is recalculated until the root is reached or a node is given a Balance value of 2 or -2. In the latter case, rebalancing at that node, done as described next, will leave the balance unchanged at all other nodes in the AVL tree.

The left side of Figure 20 shows the rebalancing that should be done when node A becomes unbalanced by an insertion in the right subtree of its right child. T1, T2, T3, and T4 denote subtrees. Either all four are empty subtrees, or else one of the two original subtrees of C has one less level than the other three subtrees. The indicated change causes the subtree shown to have the same number of levels as it had before the insertion and its root to have a Balance value of 0.

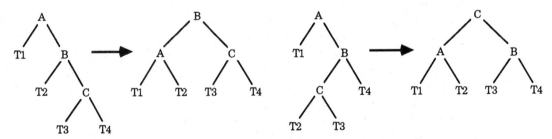

FIGURE 20. Rebalancing an AVL tree when an insertion is made in the subtree at C. All subtrees T1, T2, T3, T4 are empty, or else one of the two original subtrees of C has one less level than the other three after the insertion and before rebalancing.

The right side of Figure 20 shows the rebalancing that should be done when node A becomes unbalanced by an insertion in the left subtree of its right child (node B). The same assertions can be made as in the preceding paragraph. Any insertion in the left subtree of a node that unbalances the node is analogous to one of the two situations described for right subtrees.

Internal Path Length and Search Time

One reason for keeping a tree reasonably balanced is that it cuts down on the amount of time it takes to find a particular node. The following discussion applies to trying to find a particular node in a binary search tree or to trying to find node K in a binary tree implementation of ListADT using a Count field.

To find a particular node X, the number of nodes at which you have to look is 1 more than the level number for X. The sum of the level numbers for all nodes in a tree is called the **internal path length** of the tree. So the average number of nodes at which you have to look to find a particular node is 1 more than the internal path length divided by the number of nodes in the tree. This computation gives a measure of the **search time** for a given tree.

Let us look at a few examples of search time. For the complete binary tree of height 1, there are 3 nodes; the search time is $(1+2+2)/3$, which is 5/3. For the complete binary tree of height 2, there are 7 nodes; the search time is $(1+2+2+4*3)/7$, which is 17/7. For the complete binary tree of height 3, the search time is $(17+8*4)/15 = 49/15$. For the complete binary tree of height 4, the search time is $(49+16*5)/31 = 129/31$. For the perfectly balanced or almost-complete binary tree with 19 nodes, the search time is $(1+2+2+4*3+8*4+4*5)/19 = 69/19$. In general, it can be shown that the search time for a perfectly balanced tree or almost-complete tree (which includes complete trees) with N nodes is approximately 1 less than the exponent on the power of 2 that equals $N + 1$, allowing fractional powers of 2.

The search time for the Fibonacci tree with 20 nodes (Figure 19) is $(1+2+2+4*3+7*4+5*5+1*6)/20 = 76/20$. A large number of tests with AVL trees indicates that the average search time for AVL trees is less than 1 more than it is for perfectly balanced trees with the same number of nodes. It can be shown that the worst possible search time for an AVL tree cannot be over 28% more than that of the best possible search time for any tree with the same number of nodes. This indicates that an AVL tree provides acceptable efficiency in search algorithms.

The search time for a binary tree with 19 nodes and no left subtrees in it is $(1+2+3+4+...+18+19)/19 = 190/19 = 10$. This extreme case shows how bad things can get. However, it can be proven mathematically that, if a binary search tree is created by the insertion and deletion algorithms given in Sections 5.5 and 5.6, the average search time for all binary search trees is only 1.39 times the search time for a perfectly balanced binary search tree with the same number of nodes. In case you are curious, the 1.39 is twice the natural logarithm of 2.

Check Your Understanding

1. How many nodes are in the Fibonacci tree with eight levels?

2. The tree on the far right of Figure 12 is an AVL tree. What adjustment should be made if the value 4 is inserted in it?

3. (NA) Find the two Fibonacci trees that precede the ones in the sequence given in Figure 19.

4. (NA) Give a logical argument to show that the Fibonacci trees are the most unbalanced AVL trees possible, in the sense that they have the fewest nodes for a given number of levels.

5. (NA) Write a Boolean function telling whether a given binary tree is almost-complete, using imports from BinADT.

6. (NA) Rewrite Example 5.8A to make an almost-complete binary tree, passing the power of 2 just above Size as an additional parameter to a recursive subprocedure.

5.10 GENERAL TREES

A general tree is a tree in which each node can have any number of children, instead of being limited to just two. A formal definition of a general tree is as follows: A nonempty **tree** consists of a node (the root of the whole tree) together with 0 or more smaller trees in a specific order. None of these subtrees is to contain the root of the whole tree or a node that is in some other subtree of the root of the whole tree.

The root of one of the subtrees is called a **child** of the root of the whole tree. The definitions of leaf, parent, level, subtree, and height apply to general trees as well as to binary trees. The **degree of a node** in a tree is the number of children it has. Thus a leaf is a node of degree 0. The **degree of a tree** is the largest of the degrees of its nodes.

Probably you are thinking that a binary tree can therefore be defined as a tree of degree at most 2. That is almost true, but not quite. There are two different binary trees with two nodes: one where the root has a nonempty left subtree, and the other where the root has a nonempty right subtree. By contrast, there is only one *tree* with two nodes; it consists of the root and the only child of that root. We do not call that only child a left child or a right child.

The subtrees of a given node in a tree are assumed to be ordered in some way. For instance, if a given node has three children, one of them is the **oldest child**, one is the youngest child, and one is the middle child. I will use the term **younger sibling** to refer to the next child (in order of "age") after a given child.

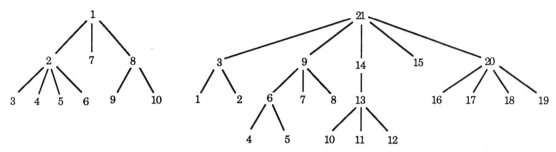

FIGURE 21. Two examples of general trees.

Figure 21 shows two trees. The one on the left has 10 nodes on 3 levels; its height is 2. The one on the right has 21 nodes on 4 levels; its height is 3. Each node has a number in it to make it possible to refer to it easily. In the tree on the left, the node numbered 7 is the younger sibling of the oldest child (node 2) of the root (node 1); it is at level 1 and has degree 0; it is a leaf. In the tree on the right, the node numbered 13 is the oldest (and only) child of the third child (node 14) of the root (node 21). Node 13 has degree 3, node 14 has degree 1, and node 21 has degree 5.

Two trees are said to have **the same tree structure** if (1) the degrees of their roots are equal, and (2) the subtrees rooted at the Kth child of each root have the same tree structure, for each K from 1 up to the degree of the root, inclusive. *Note:* Some books discuss unordered trees, in which there is no order assigned to the children of a node. This book does not.

A tree can obviously be used to store information about the direct descendants of a given person. Less obviously, a tree can be used to store the outline for a book. For instance, the root node of a tree could represent this book; the 8 children of the root represent Chapter 1, Chapter 2,..., Chapter 8; Chapter 1 has 13 children: Section 1.1,..., Section 1.12, and the end material (chapter review, practice test, and problems). The node representing Section 1.5 has 6 children: one for the introductory paragraph, one for each subsection heading, and one for the exercises.

Canonical Representation of a General Tree

Each general tree can be represented by a binary tree in which (1) the number of nodes is the same, (2) the root of the binary tree is the root of the general tree, (3) the left child of a node in the binary tree is the oldest child of that node, and (4) the right child of a node in the binary tree is the younger sibling of that node. This is called the **canonical binary tree representation** of the given general tree. Figure 22 shows the canonical binary tree representation of the trees in Figure 21.

This canonical representation gives us an easy way to implement a TreeADT library module—we simply import the necessary procedures from BinADT to manipulate the corresponding canonical binary tree. The procedures

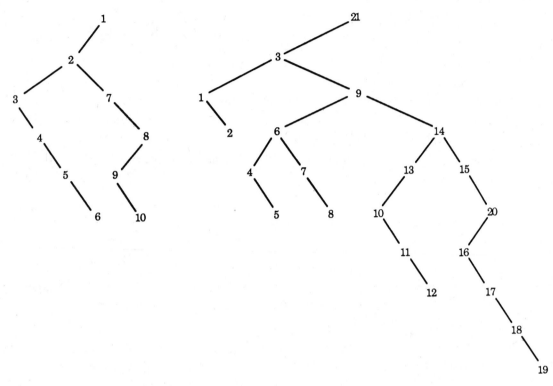

FIGURE 22. Canonical binary trees for the two trees in Figure 21.

TreeADT.Create, TreeADT.Destroy, and TreeADT.Root are the same as the BinADT procedures of the same name. Locations in a general tree can denote a node or NoNode, as in BinADT. Then TreeADT.OldestChild can be the same function as BinADT.Left, and TreeADT.YoungerSibling can be the same function as BinADT.Right. TreeADT.See and TreeADT.Swap are the same as the BinADT procedures of the same name.

The BinADT procedures for insertion and deletion are adequate, so a simple change of name gives adequate facilities for manipulating trees. Thus PutRight is renamed PutYoungerSibling, TakeLeft is renamed TakeOldestChild, PutRoot is left as PutRoot, and so forth.

To summarize: A reasonable definition module for general trees can be obtained from the BinADT definition module by making the following name changes in Example 5.2A: Change "BinADT" to "TreeADT", "Left" to "Oldest-Child", "Right" to "YoungerSibling", "BinTree" to "GenTree", and "Parent" to "ElderPerson". An implementation module is obtained with exactly the same changes.

Traversals of General Trees

There are three commonly used means of traversing a general tree: **preorder, inorder,** and **postorder tree traversal**. Each is defined to be the preorder, inorder, and postorder traversal of the corresponding canonical binary tree. Thus preorder traversal of a general tree consists of (1) processing the root of the tree, then (2) preorder-traversing the subtrees rooted at the children of the root in order from oldest to youngest child. You may need to think about this for a while to see that it is true. It may help to compare the first tree in Figure 21 with its canonical binary tree representation in Figure 22; the numbering of the nodes is the order obtained by preorder traversal.

It may take some deep thought to realize that inorder traversal of a general tree consists of inorder-traversing the subtrees rooted at the children of the root in order from oldest to youngest child, then processing the root of the tree. As an example, the numbering of the nodes of the second tree in Figure 21 is the order obtained by inorder traversal; the second tree in Figure 22 shows that this is true.

Ternary Tree Representation

Consider a situation in which information about the hierarchical structure of a certain large corporation is to be stored. The corporation consists of dozens of divisions, each of which consists of scores of departments, each of which consists of hundreds of employees. This organization can be considered a general tree, with employees being children of departments, which are children of divisions, which are children of the corporation node. If the canonical binary tree representation is used, all the employees of a given department are in essence on a linked list. This is fine for sequential processing, but slows up searching algorithms. A binary search tree containing the employees of a given department would make searching much faster than a linked list. Of course, the divisions would also be organized as a binary search tree, as well as the departments of each division.

The implementation would naturally have three fields for each node in addition to the Information field: For a given division, two pointers would be the usual left and right pointers to other divisions of the corporation, and one would be a pointer to the binary tree of departments in that division. Similarly, a given department would have left and right pointers to other departments in its division, as well as a pointer to the binary tree of its employees. This representation of the general tree is called the **ternary tree representation**.

Tries

Another kind of tree is called a **trie** (pronounced "try") or sometimes a **digital search tree**. Assume, for instance, you want to store a dictionary of about 30,000 words averaging seven characters each in a structure for fast access. You could use declarations as follows:

```
TYPE    PointerToNode = POINTER TO Node;
        Node          = ARRAY ['@'..'Z'] OF PointerToNode;
VAR     Root    : PointerToNode;   (* root of the trie *)
        Present : PointerToNode;   (* special sentinel value *)
```

This kind of structure does not have an information value stored in each node. The presence of the word 'ACE' in the dictionary would be indicated as follows: First, we pretend that the word is 'ACE@'; that is, every word is assumed to end in '@'. The 'A' component of the root node is Root ↑ ['A']; it contains a pointer to a node whose 'C' component contains a pointer to a node whose 'E' component contains a pointer to a node whose '@' component has the value Present. That is, Root ↑ ['A'] ↑ ['C'] ↑ ['E'] ↑ ['@'] = Present.

To store the word 'AD', the 'A' component of the root node points to a node whose 'D' component points to a node whose '@' component points to Present. That is, Root ↑ ['A'] ↑ ['D'] ↑ ['@'] = Present. By contrast, Root ↑ ['A'] ↑ ['C'] ↑ ['@'] is NIL, which means that the word 'AC@' is not in the dictionary. Also, Root ↑ ['A'] ↑ ['C'] ↑ ['B'] is NIL, which means that no word beginning 'ACB' is in the dictionary. Figure 23 shows the nodes in a very small trie.

In a trie, eight comparisons are needed for an average 7-letter word, which is distinctly better than the 15 comparisons (lg(30,000)) for a well-balanced binary search tree or around 21 comparisons for a random binary search tree. But actually, execution time is much better than that suggests. A comparison with a word in a binary search tree often requires comparing several letters of the word before

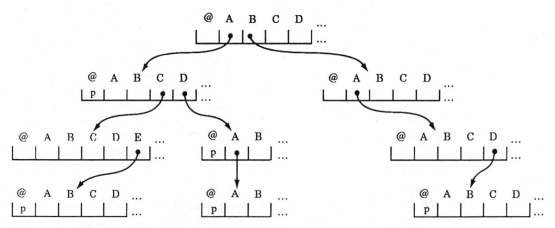

FIGURE 23. *A small trie with the words 'ACE', 'A', 'AD', 'ADA', 'BAD'. p denotes a special sentinel named Present. Empty boxes indicate NIL.*

you find that there is no match; in a trie, only one letter has to be compared before you know what to do.

The primary disadvantage of using a trie is the amount of space it requires. There are more nodes than there are words, sometimes several times as many nodes. Each node contains 27 pointer values; so if a pointer value takes 2 bytes of space, you need well over 54 bytes of space per word stored. By contrast, a binary search tree requires about 14 bytes per word, since each node contains three pointer values and the words can be stored in an array with an average of 8 characters per word (7 for its characters plus 1 for an end marker).

Check Your Understanding

1. Give the degree and level number of each node in the tree on the left of Figure 21.

2. List the nodes in the first tree in Figure 21 in inorder sequence.

3. Draw the general tree whose canonical representation is the tree on the far right of Figure 19, except first add a root node with the number 21 and with the node numbered 13 as its left child.

4. (NA) Give the degree and level number of each node in the tree on the right of Figure 21.

5. (NA) Draw all trees that have 4 nodes. *Hint:* There are 5 of them.

6. (NA) List the nodes in the second tree in Figure 21 in postorder sequence.

7. (NA) Describe as succinctly as possible postorder traversal of a general tree, without explicitly referring to the corresponding binary tree.

8. (NA) Draw the general tree whose canonical representation is the tree on the far left of Figure 17, except first add a root node with the number 20 and with the node numbered 12 as its left child.

9. (NA) Let Bin(N) denote the number of binary trees with N nodes, and let Gen(N) denote the number of general trees with N nodes. Find the relation between these two functions and discuss why it is so.

10. (NA) Draw a ternary tree representation of each of the two general trees in Figure 21. Use the almost-complete binary tree for each group of children of a node.

11. (NA) Write a recursive procedure to find the location of the parent of the node with a given location in a given general tree. Use imports from TreeADT. *Warning:* This is difficult.

5.11   B-TREES

A **2-3 tree** is a tree for which (1) all leaves are on the same level, and (2) all nonleaves have either 2 or 3 nonempty subtrees. A 2-3 tree can have either one or two information values stored in each node; a nonleaf has two information values if and only if it has three subtrees. These information values are used in ternary (3-way) search algorithms to decide which of the subtrees to look at next. It is standard to arrange things as follows, a generalization of a binary search tree with no equal information values:

- ☐ The information values in the tree are all different from one another.
- ☐ The information values in each node are in increasing order.
- ☐ The number of nonempty subtrees of a nonleaf node is 1 more than the number of information values in that node.
- ☐ The information values in the first subtree of a node are all less than the first information value in the node.
- ☐ The information values in the last subtree of a node are all greater than the last information value in the node.
- ☐ If a node has three nonempty subtrees (and hence two information values), the information values in the middle subtree are all between the first and second information values in that node.

A 2-3 tree is also known as a **B-tree of order 3**, since each node has a maximum of three subtrees. Figure 24 displays a 2-3 tree with 8 nodes. The height of the tree is 2. Information is assumed to be ordered on a 1-letter field, which is given in the nodes. The nodes with the information values q and n each have 2 subtrees. The node with the information values t,w has 3 subtrees. All other nodes have 0 subtrees.

The advantage of using a 2-3 tree to store information is that the number of nodes accessed in a search of the tree is less than the number accessed in using a

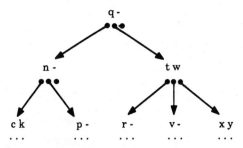

FIGURE 24.   *An example of a 2-3 tree. Letters represent information. A dot represents an empty subtree, and a hyphen represents no-info.*

binary search tree. Of course, processing one node takes a little longer than in a binary search tree.

Implementation of DictiADT Using 2-3 Trees

An implementation of DictiADT using 2-3 trees proceeds along the same lines as it did using binary search trees. It is useful for insertion and deletion algorithms to have each Node record the address of its parent, so you can declare a Node as follows, assuming MaxSubtrees=3 and PointerToNode = POINTER TO Node:

```
TYPE    Node = RECORD
               Parent   : PointerToNode;
               NumInfos : CARDINAL;
               Info : ARRAY [1..MaxSubtrees - 1] OF Information;
               Addr : ARRAY [1..MaxSubtrees] OF PointerToNode;
           END;
```

A Table should record the location of the current information, or the location where it would be if it were to be inserted. The latter is necessary for the added capabilities of DictiADT. For nonexistent information, it suffices to keep track of the leaf node where it would be inserted and the index in that leaf node; you also need a Boolean that tells whether that information is in the table. So a Table can be declared as:

```
TYPE    Table = POINTER TO RECORD
               RootNode, Loc : PointerToNode;
               Index : CARDINAL;
               IsThere : BOOLEAN;
           END;
```

The Find procedure searches through a 2-3 tree for a given information value; its job is to set Loc, Index, and IsThere appropriately. Thus for the 2-3 tree in Figure 24, Find('x', Data) should set Loc= <the x,y node> and Index=1. Finding 'y' should find the same Loc value with Index=2; in both cases, IsThere is assigned TRUE. Finding 'u' should set Loc= <the v node> and Index=1, but also set IsThere to FALSE. This Find procedure is in Example 5.11A.

Insertion into a 2-3 tree should, of course, retain the properties of the 2-3 tree. For instance, if o is to be placed in the 2-3 tree of Figure 24, it should go in the p node as the first information, moving p to the second information component. If instead g is placed in that tree, it should go in the c,k node, except there is not

EXAMPLE 5.11A _____

```
PROCEDURE Find (TheInfo : Information; VAR Data : Table);
    (* Set the Loc, Index, and IsThere fields *)
BEGIN
    WITH Data^ DO
        Loc := RootNode;
        LOOP
            Index := 1;
            WHILE (Index <= Loc^.NumInfos) AND
             (Compare (TheInfo, Loc^.Info [Index]) > 0) DO
                INC (Index);
            END;
            IF (Index <= Loc^.NumInfos) AND
             (Compare (TheInfo, Loc^.Info[Index]) = 0) THEN
                IsThere := TRUE;
                RETURN;
            ELSIF Loc^.Addr [Index] = NIL THEN
                IsThere := FALSE;
                RETURN;
            END;
            Loc := Loc^.Addr [Index];
        END;
    END;
END Find;
```

enough room. So we can split the c,k node into two nodes containing c and k, respectively, with g placed in the parent n node.

For a more complicated example, assume we place z in the 2-3 tree of Figure 24. The x,y node is full, so we can split it into two nodes containing x and z, respectively, and put y (the middle value of x,y,z) in the parent t,w node. However, that t,w node is already full, so we split it into two nodes containing t and z, respectively, and put w (the middle value of t,w,z) in their parent node. The new t node has the r and v nodes as its children; the new y node has the x and z node as its children. In some cases, we end up splitting the root, which makes the tree one level higher. Figure 25 illustrates a sequence of insertions of information values in an originally empty 2-3 tree.

The general algorithm for the insertion in a 2-3 tree of TheInfo is as follows, assuming TheInfo is not in the tree. *Terminology:* The subtree "before" Info[K] is Addr[K] and the subtree "after" it is Addr[K+1].

1. Find the appropriate leaf node;
2. IF that leaf node is not full, then:
    2.a. Put TheInfo in it in such a way as to maintain the ordering of the Info values, with a NIL subtree before and after it;
3. OTHERWISE:
    3.a. Split that node into two nodes, with the first information value in

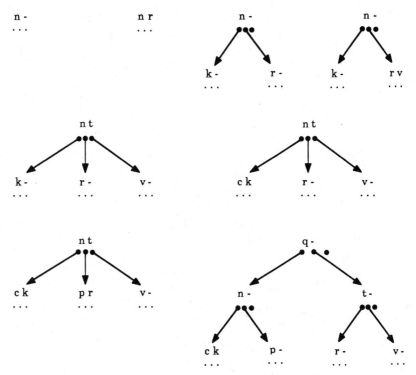

FIGURE 25. Insert n, r, k, v, t, c, p, q in that order in a 2-3 tree. A dot represents an empty subtree; a hyphen represents no-info. Then inserting w, x, y leads to the tree in Figure 22.

the left-hand node L and the last information value in the right-hand node R;

3.b. IF that node had a parent, then:
Insert the middle information value in the parent as described in this algorithm, maintaining order in the Info values, with L before it and R after it;

3.c. OTHERWISE:
Create a new root with that middle information value in it, L before it and R after it.

Deletion from a 2-3 tree is more complex than insertion. If the value you want to delete is not in a leaf, it must have an immediate predecessor in the tree (i.e., it cannot be the first value; prove it for yourself) and that immediate predecessor must be in a leaf (you can prove that also if you try), so you can move its immediate predecessor up into its place. Either way, you end up deleting a value in a leaf. If that leaf (call it X) had two information values, you do not have to do anything more. Otherwise X has no information in it, which is not allowed.

Choose an adjacent leaf Y, and find the information value IV in the parent node for which X and Y are before and after it. If Y has two information values, take one from there, move it up in place of IV, and move IV down to X. Otherwise move IV to Y and dispose of X. If that leaves the parent node with no information, repeat the process you used for X. Occasionally this implosive effect will work its way back to the root, causing the tree to shrink in height.

B-trees

A B-tree of order 14 is a tree in which all leaf nodes are on the same level, each nonleaf node has from 7 to 14 nonempty subtrees (except the root is permitted to have as few as 2 nonempty subtrees), and each nonleaf node has 1 less information value than it does nonempty subtrees (so 6 to 13); a leaf node must also have 6 to 13 information values (except the root can have as little as 1 information value). In general, a nonempty **B-tree of order N** is a tree in which all information values are different and:

1. All leaf nodes are on the same level.
2. Each node has at most $N - 1$ information values.
3. Each nonleaf node has 1 more nonempty subtree than it has information values.
4. Each node except the root has at least $(N-1)$ DIV 2 information values.
5. The tree has the **search property**: The information values in each node are in increasing order, and the Kth information value in a node is larger than all values in the Kth subtree but smaller than all values in the $(K+1)$th subtree.

The declarations of Node and PointerToNode required for a B-tree of order 14 are the same as for a 2-3 tree; we just define MaxSubtrees=14 instead of 3. In fact, the coding of the Find procedure is completely unchanged. The algorithm for insertion is also the same as it was for 2-3 trees, except that splitting an overly full node yields two nodes of 6 and 7 information values instead of 1 and 1. Similarly, deletion causes the merging of two nodes when one would otherwise have 5 information values. These algorithms apply to B-trees of any order at least 3.

Using B-trees for Accessing External Storage

The time and space requirements for a B-tree are in general greater than they are for a binary search tree, as long as only internal memory is being used. The real advantage of using B-trees comes when the amount of information is too much for internal memory. Consider, for instance, a group of about a million records, each with a 10-character ID. Assume that this amount of data is stored on one optical disk that is divided into **blocks** of 256 characters each, and that each record fits into one 256-byte block. The computer accesses information on the disk one block at a time. The address of each block on the optical disk is a 4-byte integer. Two bytes will not do, since that would only allow addresses up to 65,536; 4 bytes allow more than 4 billion addresses. Most Modula-2 implementations have a LONGCARD or LONGINT type that occupies 4 bytes.

You can use a B-tree of order 14 to access this information. Information can be defined as a record consisting of a 10-byte ID and a 4-byte address specifying where the full block of information can be found on the optical disk. Each node will occupy one block. It will contain 14 addresses of child nodes at 4 bytes each (56 bytes), 13 Information records at 14 bytes each (182 bytes), the address of the parent node (4 bytes), and a NumInfos value (2 bytes). That makes a total of 244 bytes, which will fit easily into one block. In fact, the leftover 12 bytes could be used to speed up execution of the coding or to store additional information. For instance, you could use 10 bytes to store an extra ID; that extra space can simplify insertions because it leaves room to insert an ID in a full node just before you split the node.

When you want to access one of these million records, you read the root block, which tells you which of up to 14 other blocks to read, which tells you which of up to 14 other blocks to read, and so on. The number of blocks on the sixth level of the tree can be as high as the fifth power of 14, which is 537,824. Since each of those blocks can contain 13 Information values, you have the capacity to select any one of more than six million records in only 7 accesses of blocks on the disk. Since accessing a block takes much more time than the computations involved in processing the arrays of information values and pointers, this is a great savings over a binary search tree, which would require about 20 accesses of blocks to find one in a million records.

If the data base never has any insertions or deletions made in it (**read-only data**), each node can be filled with 13 information values to obtain the maximum use of the available space. Even if insertions and deletions are permitted, the average node may contain perhaps 10 information values, which means there will be about 100,000 information values on the sixth level of the tree, and any one of a million can be found in 7 accesses.

Check Your Understanding

1. Assuming 1024-byte blocks, 4-byte addresses, social security numbers as 4-byte IDs, and read-only data on 3 million federal government employees, what order of B-tree gives the minimum number of block accesses?

2. Same as the previous exercise, but assume 512-byte blocks.

3. How many 2-3 trees are there with 3 nodes? With 4? With 5? With 6?

4. Describe in detail all binary trees that are also 2-3 trees.

5. (NA) Give a logical argument to show that an information value that is in a nonleaf of a 2-3 tree cannot be the smallest value in the tree and that its immediate predecessor in the tree must be in a leaf.

6. (NA) Draw the tree that results from inserting b in the 2-3 tree in Figure 24.

7. (NA) Draw the tree that results from deleting q in the 2-3 tree in Figure 24.

8. (NA) Rewrite Example 5.11A to execute faster. Do not use a LOOP statement.

5.12 B+ TREES IN EXTERNAL STORAGE

This section describes an advanced method of quickly accessing a very large mass of data stored externally. This method is the heart of VSAM (Virtual Sequential Access Method). It is an improvement over B trees because it simplifies processing the information values in order as well as accessing them at random. I develop the declarations and coding for a significant part of an implementation of DictiADT, sufficient for you to complete the implementation as a programming project.

B+ Trees

A B+ tree is an improvement on a B tree. We have the same restrictions on the structure of the tree, except that it is possible for the root to be empty. The primary difference is that the leaf nodes contain the IDs for *all* the records in the data file; any ID in a nonleaf node that corresponds to an information value is usually duplicated in a leaf node. Thus the subtree to the left of an ID in a nonleaf node can contain that ID; the only time it does not is when there is no record in the file for the ID in the nonleaf node. Another difference is that the last pointer in each leaf node points to the next leaf node.

The B+ tree only stores the key or ID value for an information value, plus a pointer to the block of external storage that contains the information, not the entire record. The pointer to the information's block is only in the leaf nodes; the nonleaf nodes contain pointers to other nodes in the B+ tree.

Figure 26 shows a B+ tree of order 4 with 3 levels and 11 information values. A completely full B+ tree of order 4 with 3 levels would have 48 information values—3 in each of 16 leaf nodes. Each leaf node would have 3 pointers to blocks containing information plus 1 pointer to the next leaf (NIL for the sixteenth leaf). The 48 IDs in the leaves would be in increasing order. Each group of 4 leaf nodes would have a common parent with 3 ID values, perhaps the last ID in each of its first 3 children. The root would have 4 children, which are the 4 parents of the leaves. The root might contain the last ID in the fourth child of each of the root's first three children.

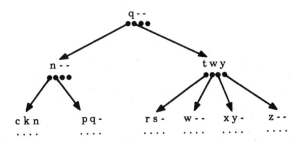

FIGURE 26. An example of a B+ tree of order 4. A dot represents an empty subtree; a hyphen represents no-info.

The easiest way to understand the B+ tree structure is to consider a concrete example. Assume that the data is stored in 1K blocks—1024 characters each. We use one block for each node and fill it as full as possible; this minimizes the number of block accesses. Assume that a block pointer requires 4 bytes of storage and that an ID requires 10 bytes of storage. The number of pointer values in a node must be one more than the number of ID values. Some trial and error shows that a node has room for just 72 IDs and 73 pointer values: 10∗72 = 720, 4∗73 = 292, for a total of 1012 bytes of space. Each node will therefore have between 36 and 72 IDs, and between 37 and 73 subtrees. This will be a B+ tree of order 73. Each node must keep track of the number of IDs actually stored in the node.

The following declarations could be used for a B+ tree of order 73:

```
CONST   MaxSubtrees = 73;
        MinSubtrees = 37;     (* for all but the root *)
TYPE    IDType = ARRAY [0..9] OF CHAR;
        Node   = RECORD
                     NumIDs : CARDINAL;
                     ID     : ARRAY [1..MaxSubtrees - 1] OF IDType;
                     Addr   : ARRAY [1..MaxSubtrees] OF BlockAddress;
                 END;
```

Each nonleaf node has NumIDs+1 children. Addr[K] is the address of the block containing the Kth child of the node. The IDs in that child node are all less than or equal to ID[K], except when K is NumIDs+1. All IDs in the block whose address is Addr[K] are less than those in the block whose address is Addr[K+1]; that is, the IDs on any one level are in increasing order when read left to right.

The leaf nodes (on the bottom level of the tree) contain all IDs of all records in the data structure. For these leaf nodes, Addr[K] is the address of the block where the information with ID[K] can be found, and Addr[MaxSubtrees] is the address of the block where the leaf node with the next higher IDs can be found (NoAddress for the last leaf node). This makes it easy to progress through the information values in order.

Basic Facilities for B+ Trees

Working with external storage requires more facilities than internal storage does. We assume the existence of two procedures for accessing blocks, one for reading them in and the other for writing them out. A block can be storage for either a node or an information value (or the first part of an information value, since one information value may require several blocks). That makes it difficult to declare the type of the block. We get around this by using a formal parameter of type ARRAY OF WORD, which means that any actual parameter is allowed.

We also need a way of asking the system to allocate a block for storing information. Correspondingly, we need a way of returning a no-longer-needed block to the system. These procedures are obvious parallels to NEW and DISPOSE. Finally, we need a way of telling the system to record the table for future reference and to access a previously recorded table. The OpenAccess procedure might ask the user for an eight-character name and find the corresponding root block and number of levels; if it does not find the name in its list of names, it allocates a new block and makes the number of levels 1. The CloseAccess procedure could then update its reference list with a given root block and number of levels.

We collect the declarations for Blocks in a library module (Example 5.12A; NoAddress corresponds to NIL). How this module is implemented is not the concern of this section. If you develop the programming project for B+ trees, your compiler should have library modules from which you can import to implement these declarations. Alternatively, you could simulate block operations using dynamic variables in internal memory.

For any given Table, we keep a record of the path through the B+ tree to the information for which we have most recently searched. This is kept in Block [1.. NumLevels], with the number of the child on the search path in Index [1.. NumLevels]. We declare sufficient array components to handle trees of any reasonable depth. Block, Index, and NumLevels are fields of the Table variable. In addition, we need a way to access the block that contains the root node, so we have a Root field to store its address. We also need to record the address of the block containing the current information value. The Loc field is used for that; it is NoAddress if there is no current information.

```
CONST   MaxLevels = 10;
VAR     Table = POINTER TO RECORD
                  Block      : ARRAY [1..MaxLevels] OF Node;
                  Index      : ARRAY [1..MaxLevels] OF CARDINAL;
                  NumLevels  : CARDINAL;
                  Root, Loc  : BlockAddress;
                END;
```

EXAMPLE 5.12A _____

```
DEFINITION MODULE BlockADT;
FROM SYSTEM IMPORT WORD;
EXPORT QUALIFIED BlockAddress, NoAddress,
                 ReadBlock,    WriteBlock, CreateBlock,
                 DestroyBlock, OpenAccess, CloseAccess;
    (* declarations for accessing external storage *)
    (* Written by William C. Jones, February 2, 19-- *)
TYPE
    BlockAddress;
VAR
    NoAddress : BlockAddress;

PROCEDURE ReadBlock (Addr       : BlockAddress;
                     VAR Block : ARRAY OF WORD);
    (* Copy block at the given BlockAddress into Block *)

PROCEDURE WriteBlock (Addr  : BlockAddress;
                      Block : ARRAY OF WORD);
    (* Replace block at the given BlockAddress by Block *)

PROCEDURE CreateBlock (VAR Addr : BlockAddress);
    (* Allocate space for a block in external storage;
       return its address in Addr *)

PROCEDURE DestroyBlock (Addr : BlockAddress);
    (* Deallocate space for a block in external storage *)

PROCEDURE CloseAccess (VAR Addr  : BlockAddress;
                       NumLevels : CARDINAL);
    (* Terminate access to the file or group of blocks for
       which this block is the reference block; record
       the number of levels associated with this block *)

PROCEDURE OpenAccess (VAR Addr       : BlockAddress;
                      VAR NumLevels : CARDINAL);
    (* Access a group of blocks as a unit, returning the
       address of the "first" or reference block and the
       associated number of levels; create the block and
       return 1 if it is a previously uncreated group *)

END BlockADT.
```

To simplify the logic, let us assume that an empty table always has a tree with just one node, the root, and NumIDs = 0 for that node; then we can have Levels=1 for the empty table. The root is the only leaf, and thus the last leaf, so we set Addr[1] to NoAddress, to indicate that there is no following node. We assume for every table that an up-to-date copy of the root block is stored in Block[1].

Finally, since the data structure is to be saved in external storage for use on another run of the program, or for use by another program, the ReadTable and WriteTable procedures are provided. When a program wants to use an existing

EXAMPLE 5.12B _____

```
(* Four DictiADT procedures for a B+ tree implementation*)

PROCEDURE Create (VAR Data : Table);
BEGIN
    NEW (Data);
    Data^.Block [1].NumIDs := 0;
    Data^.Block [1].Addr [1] := NoAddress;
    OpenAccess (Data^.Root, Data^.NumLevels);
    WriteBlock (Data^.Root, Data^.Block [1]);
    Data^.Loc := NoAddress;
END Create;
(*******************************************************)

PROCEDURE Destroy (VAR Data : Table);
BEGIN
    WriteTable (Data);
END Destroy;
(*******************************************************)

PROCEDURE ReadTable (VAR Data : Table);
    (* re-establish connection to existing external Table*)
BEGIN
    NEW (Data);
    OpenAccess (Data^.Root, Data^.NumLevels);
    ReadBlock (Data^.Root, Data^.Block [1]);
END ReadTable;
(*******************************************************)

PROCEDURE WriteTable (VAR Data : Table);
    (* sever connection to existing external Table *)
BEGIN
    WriteBlock (Data^.Root, Data^.Block [1]);
    CloseAccess (Data^.Root, Data^.NumLevels);
    DISPOSE (Data);
END WriteTable;
```

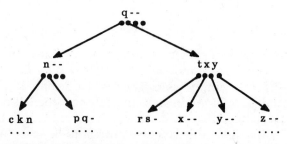

FIGURE 27. Deletion of w from the B+ tree of order 4 in Figure 26. Bring x over from following leaf and adjust IDs in parent.

Table, it executes ReadTable(Data) instead of Create(Data). The coding of the ReadTable, WriteTable, Create, and Destroy procedures for DictiADT is in Example 5.12B. Figure 27 illustrates deletion in a B+ tree.

Searching through the B+ Tree

The first thing you need to do is to develop the Find procedure, which searches through the file to find the address of the block containing some given information. This Find procedure can be used by several of the exported TableADT procedures. It requires two additional procedures exported from the InfoADT module, since we have to work directly with the ID of an information value: GetID returns the ID of a given information value, and CompareID compares two IDs.

A reasonable algorithm for Find is as follows: Given an ID and a Table, you first look through Block[1] to find the first ID that is not smaller than the given ID. The search should continue with the subtree to the left of the ID you find. If the given ID is larger than any ID in the node, the search continues with the rightmost subtree. In other words, use Addr[K] when ID[K] is greater than or equal to the given ID; use Addr[NumIDs+1] if all ID[K] are smaller. When you find the correct block address, you read the block. Repeat for Block[2], Block[3], and so on until you get to a leaf. When you search that block, you should find the ID you are looking for and the address of the block where its information is stored. If it turns out not to be there, you can return NoAddress as the answer, to indicate you could not find it. see Example 5.12C for this coding.

The reason that Find is not written as a function is that finding the block address is actually a minor part of its job. The most important thing that Find does is to record the path to the ID in the Block and Index arrays. FindAddress should of course use Binary Search for greater speed; this is left as an exercise.

Now it is straightforward to write the DictiADT procedures that do not modify the tree. Example 5.12D contains the coding for Inspect and the top-level coding for PutIn.

Reminder: Some compilers have the defect that you cannot compare values of an opaque type, as in Data ↑ .Loc # NoAddress. You can allow for this by providing a Boolean function named Equal and using NOT Equal(Data ↑ .Loc, NoAddress).

Sequential Processing of Records

To allow for processing the records in order, DictiADT has two additional procedures: FindFirstIn finds the first information value, and FindNextIn finds the next information value after the previous one. The objective of this section has been to introduce you to B+ trees and to get you started on a programming project. You now have to finish FindFirstIn, FindNextIn, PutIn, and TakeOut. Putting an information value in a leaf where there is room is not too much trouble; the

EXAMPLE 5.12C _____

```
PROCEDURE Find (TheInfo  : Information;
                VAR Data : Table);
    (* Context:  B+ tree implementation of DictiADT *)
  (*----------------------------------------------------------*)

    PROCEDURE FindLoc (TheID    : IDType;
                       Level    : CARDINAL;
                       VAR Data : Table);
        (* Search the ID entries in Block [Level]
           to find the first one greater-equal TheID *)
    VAR
        K : CARDINAL;
    BEGIN
        WITH Data^ DO (* fields include Block, Index, Loc*)
            WITH Block [Level] DO (* fields are NumIDs,
                                                ID, Addr *)
                K := 1;
                WHILE (K <= NumIDs) AND
                        (CompareID (TheID, ID [K]) > 0) DO
                    INC (K);
                END;
                Index [Level] := K;
                Loc := Addr [K];
            END;
        END;
    END FindLoc;
  (*----------------------------------------------------------*)

VAR
    K : CARDINAL;
    TheID : IDType;

BEGIN           (* Find *)

    WITH Data^ DO (* fields include Block, NumLevels, Loc*)

        GetID (TheInfo, TheID);
        FOR K := 1 TO NumLevels - 1 DO
            FindLoc (TheID, K, Data);
            ReadBlock (Loc, Block [K + 1]);
        END;
        FindLoc (TheID, NumLevels, Data);

        K := Index [NumLevels];
        IF (K > Block [NumLevels].NumIDs)
                OR (CompareID (TheID,
                        Block [NumLevels].ID [K]) # 0) THEN
            Loc := NoAddress;
        END;

    END;

END Find;
```

EXAMPLE 5.12D _____

```
PROCEDURE Inspect (VAR TheInfo: Information;  Data: Table);
    (* Context:  B+ tree implementation of DictiADT *)
BEGIN
    IF Data^.Loc # NoAddress THEN
        ReadBlock (Data^.Loc, TheInfo);
    END;
END Inspect;
(*****************************************************)

PROCEDURE PutIn (TheInfo : Information;  VAR Data : Table);
    (* procedures PutInLeaf and SplitLeaf go here *)
BEGIN
    Find (TheInfo, Data);
    IF Data^.Block [Data^.NumLevels].NumIDs
                    < MaxSubtrees - 1 THEN
        PutInLeaf (TheInfo, Data);
    ELSE
        SplitLeaf (TheInfo, Data);
    END;
END PutIn;
```

difficulty comes if you have to split a leaf. This can be done recursively. When you delete an information value, you can leave the deleted value's ID in a nonleaf node without harm. Deletion of an information value that leaves fewer than MinSubtrees in a nonroot node requires taking an ID from an adjacent node or, if there are not enough there, collapsing the two nodes into one node.

Some thought about the structure of the B+ tree of order 73 should make it clear that very little space is wasted by not having direct access from a nonleaf node to an information value. The leaves must have at least 36 times as many information values as there are on the next level up, so all but 3% of the IDs have to be on the bottom level anyway. If you added pointers to information values from nonleaf nodes, you would only be able to store 56 IDs per node, so you would lose more than you would gain.

You should also be able to see that the B+ tree is always at least half full of IDs. On the average, a B+ tree tends to be about 69% full, the natural logarithm of 2. There is a variation on the B+ tree, called a **B* tree**, in which you do not split a full node if a neighboring node on the same level is not full; instead, you spread the IDs between the two nodes. When both are full, you split the two into three nodes, each two-thirds full.

Check Your Understanding

1. Rewrite Find (Example 5.12C) using Binary Search.

2. What would MaxSubtrees and MinSubtrees be if each block held 2048 bytes, all other storage assumptions in this section remaining the same?

3. (NA) Discuss the problems involved in maintaining a B∗ tree so that every node except the root is at least two-thirds full at all times.

4. (NA) An equivalent form of a B+ tree is to put the *smallest* ID from each node (except the leftmost node on each level) in the parent node, instead of the largest. Discuss the effect that this modification would have on the coding in this section.

5. (NA) Discuss the problems involved in allowing two different information values in a B+ tree to have the same ID. Consider the case in which two different leaves contain matching IDs.

5.13 APPLICATION: GAME TREES

In this section, you will learn something about the analysis of games such as Chess, Checkers, Othello, Go, Kalah, and Tic-Tac-Toe. These are all instances of "two-person zero-sum full-knowledge games." That phrase means that two people play against each other; that what one wins, the other loses; and that each player on her turn has a number of choices, any of which she is allowed to freely choose and all of which her opponent knows about. Consequently, there are no chance elements such as dice and no concealed knowledge such as hidden hands of cards.

You will see that any such game can be analyzed so that the person who decides who goes first can be guaranteed never to lose. Unfortunately, the analysis often takes more computer time and space than is available. For instance, it has been computed that the full analysis of chess would require more space than is available in our galaxy, even if one chess position (including the board) were written on each molecule. *Note:* This section requires that you have read Section 5.10; it uses the TreeADT library module, an exact analog of BinADT.

The GameRules Library Module

No game can be analyzed unless you know the rules of the game. For one thing, you have to know how to set up the board (or whatever) at the beginning of play. For another, you have to know the possible moves for a given placement of pieces on the board (or whatever is appropriate to the game), and the effect on a given board position of making a specified move. The use of a program to work with the game means that you have to have a procedure that prints out the current status of the board (or whatever). Finally, the algorithms described in this section require a procedure that evaluates a board position on the assumption that the game has just ended and returns a number that is a measure of how advantageous it is to have moved to that position.

All these assumptions are described more precisely in Example 5.13A, which collects together all procedures that depend on the particular game being played.

EXAMPLE 5.13A

```
DEFINITION MODULE GameRules;
EXPORT QUALIFIED BoardStatus, MoveChoice, InitializeBoard,
              GetNextMove, Destroy, Advantage, WriteBoard,
              GetUsersMove, GetFirstMove, IsSentinel;
    (* Written by William C. Jones, February 19-- *)

TYPE
    BoardStatus;    (* full description of the current state
                       of the game, including whose turn it
                       is to move next and the move that was
                       last made *)
    MoveChoice;     (* a set of values that comprise all the
                       possible moves that can be made.
                       The values are ordered *)

PROCEDURE InitializeBoard (VAR Board : BoardStatus);
    (* Create the Board with the normal starting position
       for this game or, optionally in sophisticated
       programs, with a position specified by the user *)

PROCEDURE GetNextMove (CurrentBoard : BoardStatus;
                       VAR Move     : MoveChoice;
                       VAR NewBoard : BoardStatus);
    (* Create a NewBoard that is the result of making the
       legal move next following Move when given the
       CurrentBoard.  Also set Move to that legal move *)

PROCEDURE GetFirstMove (CurrentBoard : BoardStatus;
                        VAR Move     : MoveChoice;
                        VAR NewBoard : BoardStatus);
    (* Same as GetNextMove except the first legal Move is
       returned.  Move does not need to be initialized *)

PROCEDURE IsSentinel (Move : MoveChoice) : BOOLEAN;
    (* Tell whether Move is the sentinel value *)

PROCEDURE Destroy (VAR Board : BoardStatus);
    (* Deallocate space used for this Board *)

PROCEDURE Advantage (Board : BoardStatus) : REAL;
    (* Return a number that indicates the advantage of the
       given board status to the player who moved to it *)

PROCEDURE WriteBoard (Board : BoardStatus);
    (* Print out the current status of the board, including
       a description of the move that reached that status*)

PROCEDURE GetUsersMove (Board    : BoardStatus;
                        VAR Move : MoveChoice);
    (* Ask the user at the terminal what move he or she
       wishes to choose for the given BoardStatus *)

END GameRules.
```

In essence, this GameRules library module completely describes the game you are playing. You only need change the implementation module of GameRules to obtain results for Checkers instead of Othello, for instance. The terminology indicates that a board (typically 8-by-8) is used, but this need not be the case.

This example probably has a few surprises for you; I did not say anything about a sentinel value for moves. My design makes GetFirstMove, GetNextMove, and IsSentinel analogous to the List procedures FirstLocation, NextLocation, and NOT InList, respectively. The basic idea is that, for any given board position, there is a list of possible legal moves that can be made. You initialize Move by calling GetFirstMove; you also obtain the NewBoard position resulting from that move. Then you call GetNextMove, which finds the next legal move after the given one and also produces the new board that results from making that next legal move. If you call GetNextMove again, with the same CurrentBoard and the revised Move, you will obtain the next legal move in order and the result of making that move. If there is no next legal move, Move is set to the sentinel value and NewBoard is left indeterminate. As an example, the following coding displays all possible board positions, one at a time, that can result from making a legal move from a given CurrentBoard.

```
GetFirstMove (CurrentBoard, Move, NewBoard);
WHILE NOT IsSentinel (Move) DO
    WriteBoard (NewBoard);
    GetNextMove (CurrentBoard, Move, NewBoard);
END;
```

Example: The Game of TakeAway

Consider the following game of TakeAway: Two people each put 15 nickels in a common pot. Then each person in turn must take either 5, 10, or 15 cents. Whatever you take, you get to keep, except that the person who takes the last nickel collects 50 cents from the opponent as a prize. If you think this is too simple a game to analyze, see if you can figure out the best strategy before you read further.

Figure 28 displays the top part of the game tree for this game. Each node has five groups of a letter and an integer. The root has P150 F0 S0 W2 M20, which is code for this initial setup: "The Pot has 150 cents, First player has 0 cents, Second player has 0 cents, Who-just-moved = player 2, and the Move that reached this point was 20" (an arbitrary value). First player has three possible moves, represented by the three children of the root. For instance, the third child is P135 F15 S0 W1 M15, which means: "The Pot now has 135, First has 15, Second has 0, Who-just-moved is player 1, and the Move was to take 15 cents." The three children of the second child of the root are also shown.

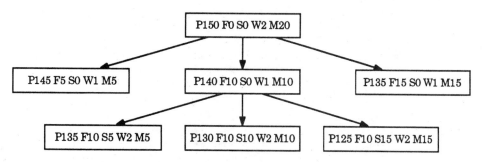

FIGURE 28. *The top part of the game tree for the TakeAway game.*

For this game of TakeAway, a BoardStatus could be an array of five cardinals and a MoveChoice could be any of 5, 10, 15, or 20 (the 20 being the sentinel value). InitializeBoard assigns the array (150,0,0,2,20) to Board. GetFirstMove normally creates a new array from the current one with 5 less in P, 5 more for F or S depending on W, change W to 3−W, and set M to 5. GetNextMove normally does the same except using M+5 instead of 5. IsSentinel tells whether the given Move is 20. Of course, some adjustment must be made for the end of the game. Advantage might just compute F−S (which tells how much more First has than Second) when W=1 (so First made the move) and compute S−F (which tells how much more Second has than First) when W=2 (so Second made the move).

Program for Arbitrary Game Trees

For the standard method of analyzing such a game, you set a **look-ahead level** that tells how much of the tree to construct for the analysis (since most games have too large a tree to construct completely). Then you create the game tree with that many levels. Finally, you analyze the game tree to find the best possible move for whoever is to move next and what the advantage of that move is to the person who makes the move. Since a full game-playing program is too much for this section, I only develop a program (Example 5.13B) to find the best move from a given initial position. InitializeBoard can be made sophisticated enough to accept any given board position and analyze it, which means that this program can be used to give good advice on the best move at any stage of a game.

The CreateAllDescendants procedure called by Example 5.13B has the job of creating the game tree. The FindAdvantage procedure has the job of computing the advantage of each possible move and finding the BestMove (the one with the highest advantage). Both these procedures are in later examples, to be discussed shortly.

Initially, the game tree has just a root node. The CreateAllDescendants procedure first checks to be sure that the number of levels to be added is positive; otherwise it does nothing (which, of course, accomplishes the objective of adding 0 levels to the tree). Then it obtains the first move possible from the board

EXAMPLE 5.13B _____

```
MODULE GameAnalysis;
FROM InOut     IMPORT WriteString, WriteLn, ReadCard;
FROM RealInOut IMPORT WriteReal;
FROM GameRules IMPORT BoardStatus, MoveChoice,
                      InitializeBoard, GetNextMove,
                      Destroy, Advantage, WriteBoard,
                      GetFirstMove, IsSentinel;
FROM TreeADT   IMPORT GenTree, Location, NoNode, Create,
                      See, PutRoot, PutOldestChild,
                      PutYoungerSibling, Root, OldestChild,
                      YoungerSibling;
    (* Written by William C. Jones, February 19-- *)
(********************************************************)

PROCEDURE FindBestMove (VAR BestMove    : BoardStatus;
                        VAR Profit      : REAL;
                        LookAheadLevel : CARDINAL);
    (* Find the BestMove from an initial position and the
       advantage involved in making that best move *)
(*--- CreateAllDescendants and FindAdvantage go here ---*)

VAR
    Board : BoardStatus;
    Tree : GenTree;
BEGIN
    Create (Tree);
    InitializeBoard (Board);
    PutRoot (Board, Tree);
    CreateAllDescendants (Tree, Root (Tree),
                          LookAheadLevel);
    FindAdvantage (Tree, Root (Tree), BestMove, Profit);
END FindBestMove;
(********************************************************)

VAR
    BestMove : BoardStatus;
    Profit : REAL;
    LookAheadLevel : CARDINAL;

BEGIN          (* GameAnalysis *)

    WriteString ('What look-ahead level should I use? ');
    ReadCard (LookAheadLevel);

    FindBestMove (BestMove, Profit, LookAheadLevel);
    WriteBoard (BestMove);

    WriteString ('That move evaluates as ');
    WriteReal (Profit, 1);
    WriteLn;

END GameAnalysis.
```

position at the given node in the tree. If that is the sentinel value, it indicates that there are no moves possible from that position; that is, the game is over and the procedure has accomplished its job.

If it is possible to move from the given position, the procedure puts the resulting board in the tree as the oldest child of the given node. Then it repeats the following sequence of actions (like preorder traversal) until a board position is obtained that results in the sentinel move: (1) Call the CreateAllDescendants procedure to create the nodes descendent from that child; (2) Get the board position that follows the one for that child; (3) Put it in a node as the younger sibling of that child.

IIII➡ PROGRAMMING STYLE

As is usual with any recursive procedure, you should verify that the recursion is self-terminating. When the CreateAllDescendants procedure calls itself (Example 5.13C), it supplies a LevelsToAdd value that is 1 less than the one it is given. The reason is that, if a node is to have at most L levels of descendants, its children are to have at most L−1 levels of descendants. Thus LevelsToAdd must decrease for each additional copy of the procedure that is active. The initial IF condition guards against additional recursive calls when LevelsToAdd becomes 0, so the number of copies of the CreateAllDescendants procedure that can be active at any one time cannot exceed LookAheadLevel+1.

Computing the Best Move

Now that the tree is constructed, we can perform the analysis. There are two key points about finding the best move. One is that we act on the assumption that a move that has no children is the end of the game, and the Advantage function tells the true outcome of that game. This is, of course, not true, since we have chopped off the tree after a certain number of levels. However, it is the best we can do; we can only hope that pruning the tree has not distorted the outcomes too much.

The other key point is as follows: If a move M has children, and if the highest advantage of all the children of M is X, then the advantage of making move M is −X. This takes a little thought to understand. The idea is, say I want to know what I gain if I make move M. I just look at all the possible responses my opponent can make to M. If there is one that is worth X, and if all the other responses are worth no more than X, then I will be pessimistic and assume my opponent will make the choice that is worth X. So my making move M allows my opponent to win X but no more than X. And that means that I lose X by making move M. *Note:* This does not mean that all moves are losing moves; it is often the case that X is a negative number. For instance, if my opponent has three possible responses to M, which have advantages of −4, −7, and −3, respectively, I assume that my opponent minimizes the loss by choosing the one that earns −3, so I earn 3 by making move M. This is called **minimax strategy**.

EXAMPLE 5.13C _____

```
PROCEDURE CreateAllDescendants (VAR Tree     : GenTree;
                                    Where      : Location;
                                    LevelsToAdd : CARDINAL);
    (* Create all descendants of the node at location Where
         in the game Tree, down to LevelsToAdd more levels *)
VAR
    NewBoard, CurrentBoard : BoardStatus;
    Move : MoveChoice;
BEGIN
    IF LevelsToAdd > 0 THEN

        (* verify that there is some move possible *)
            See (CurrentBoard, Where, Tree);
            GetFirstMove (CurrentBoard, Move, NewBoard);
            IF IsSentinel (Move) THEN
                RETURN;  (* no moves possible; game over *)
            END;

        (* the node has at least one child *)
            PutOldestChild (NewBoard, Where, Tree);
            Where := OldestChild (Where, Tree);
            CreateAllDescendants (Tree, Where,
                            LevelsToAdd - 1);
            GetNextMove (CurrentBoard, Move, NewBoard);
            WHILE NOT IsSentinel (Move) DO
                PutYoungerSibling (NewBoard, Where, Tree);
                Where := YoungerSibling (Where, Tree);
                CreateAllDescendants (Tree, Where,
                            LevelsToAdd - 1);
                GetNextMove (CurrentBoard, Move, NewBoard);
            END;

    END;
END CreateAllDescendants;
```

These two key points give us a way of evaluating two kinds of moves—those that have children in the tree and those that do not. Since those are the only kinds of move there are, we can evaluate every move to find its advantage. The algorithm for FindAdvantage is therefore: See if the board at the given location in the tree has children. If not, compute the advantage of the board in that location and return it as the answer. Otherwise, compute the advantage of each of its children using the two key points, find the largest of those advantages, and return the negative of that largest number as the answer. We should also return the Board-Status that is in the child node that produces the largest advantage. The coding is in Example 5.13D.

EXAMPLE 5.13D _____

```
PROCEDURE FindAdvantage (Tree          : GenTree;
                         Where         : Location;
                         VAR BestMove  : BoardStatus;
                         VAR Profit    : REAL);
   (* BestMove is that one of the given location's children
      that produces the greatest advantage for the person
      whose turn it is next to move, unless there are no
      children.  Profit is the advantage to the person who
      made the move to the given position *)
VAR
    XBoard  : BoardStatus;
    XProfit : REAL;
BEGIN

(* evaluate profit of this move directly if no children *)
        IF OldestChild (Where, Tree) = NoNode THEN
           See (XBoard, Where, Tree);
           Profit := Advantage (XBoard);
           RETURN;
        END;

(* find largest of the profits for opponent's moves *)
        Where := OldestChild (Where, Tree);
        FindAdvantage (Tree, Where, XBoard, Profit);
        See (BestMove, Where, Tree);
        Where := YoungerSibling (Where, Tree);
        WHILE Where # NoNode DO
           FindAdvantage (Tree, Where, XBoard, XProfit);
           IF XProfit > Profit THEN
              Profit := XProfit;
              See (BestMove, Where, Tree);
           END;
           Where := YoungerSibling (Where, Tree);
        END;

(* return negative of opponent's largest profits *)
        Profit :=  - Profit;

END FindAdvantage;
```

Additional Considerations

The techniques presented in this section, though adequate to solve the problem given subject to space and time limitations, are rather crude. As one improvement, you can avoid space limitations almost entirely, without any sacrifice in time, by computing the profit for a given node at the time you create it. In TakeAway, for instance, at the time you create the first child of the root and all its descendants, you also compute the profit for that child. As the recursion "unwinds," you deallocate the space taken up by its descendants, since you already have all the information you wanted from them. Then you process the next child, then the next, until done. Recursively applying the same calculation of profits and deallocation of space for each of the children of that child means that, in effect, you only have two or three boards in storage for each level at any given time. In chess, for instance, the game tree tends to become unstorable past the top 5 or 6 levels; but the technique just described allows you to go hundreds of levels deep without running out of storage space. Of course, time limitations intervene. Sad to say, evaluation of every chess position in the game tree at the rate of one creation/calculation/deallocation cycle per nanosecond would still take longer than the expected lifetime of the sun.

A technique that cuts down on the time drastically is called **alpha-beta pruning**. It is best explained with an illustration: Assume that move M has been calculated to have a profit of 5. You go on to evaluate a sibling S of M. In looking at the children of S, you find one for which the profit is −4. You can then ignore S and the rest of its children. The reason is that the maximum profit of the children of S is at least −4 (and could even be −2 or better), so the profit of S is at most 4. This means that M is a better move than S, regardless of the outcome for the other children of S.

The most profitable way to improve the results of analyzing a game tree is to develop a computation for Advantage that is highly accurate. This can strongly compensate for using only a few levels. For instance, in chess, you count a certain amount for each piece depending on its rank (such as 1 for pawn, 3 for bishop, 9 for queen), but you can also add or subtract some to allow for the solidity of the pawn defense, how close the knights are to the center of the board, and so forth.

Check Your Understanding

1. Show that the recursion in Example 5.13D is self-terminating.

2. Explain fully the tactics to maximize your profits in TakeAway.

3. A lot of time is wasted in FindAdvantage owing to the number of calls of See made at all levels of the tree when most of them are unnecessary. How would you rewrite the procedure to fix this?

4. (NA) Find the advantage for each of the three children of the root of the game tree for TakeAway. *Hint:* Check the answer for Exercise 2.

5. (NA) Display all grandchildren of the middle child of the root in Figure 28, with connections from the children of that middle child.

6. (NA) Display the full game tree for a game of TakeAway in which you must take either 10 cents or 20 cents at each turn and you start with 50 cents in the pot; the one who takes last pays 20 cents to the other. Find the advantage of every node in the tree.

7. (NA) What variables, if any, can be delocalized in Examples 5.13C and 5.13D? Make the appropriate changes.

CHAPTER REVIEW

A binary tree is a data structure in which each node has up to two children, called its left child and its right child; the node is called the parent of its children. A node with no children is called a leaf.

Each binary tree has a node called the root node. You can get from the root node to any other node in the tree by repeatedly going from parent to child; there is only one way to do that for any given node. The part of a tree consisting of a node and all its descendants is called a subtree of that tree. The level of a node is the number of moves you make as you go from the root to that node following parent-to-child connections; the level of the root is 0.

The definition module BinADT has Create and Destroy procedures analogous to those in ListADT. It has insertion, deletion, inspection, and modification procedures, but with a different parameter structure. It has Root, Left, and Right functions for working with locations within a BinTree. An analog for InList is not needed, because a special Location value named NoNode is used to indicate the absence of a node at a specified Location.

The standard two-pointer implementation of BinTree is as a pointer to a Node, which is defined as a record with three fields, namely Info, Left, and Right. The standard array implementation of BinTree (discussed in Section 5.7) is as (a pointer to) an array of information values, sufficient to hold the almost-complete binary tree of a specified number of nodes. The root is at component 1; the left child of component X is at component $2*X$ and the right child is at component $2*X+1$. A special value NoInfo can be used to indicate when the node is nonexistent.

An efficient implementation of the TableADT module can be obtained using binary search trees. The distinguishing property of binary search trees is that, for any information value X, all information in X's left subtree is smaller than X, but no information in X's right subtree is smaller than X. We have to assure that, with matching information values, only the most recently inserted one is accessed by the procedures. This can be done as follows: When searching down the tree to insert an information value, if you find a matching value, swap it with the one you are inserting and carry that older one along as you go further down the tree. This assures that the more recent ones are higher in the tree.

The TakeOut procedure is the messiest of those needed for binary search trees. The basic algorithm is: If the node being deleted has only one subtree, put that subtree in its place. Otherwise move the leftmost information in its right subtree up in its place and delete the node that originally contained that leftmost information. This algorithm requires a certain amount of logical reasoning to show that the resulting smaller tree is in fact a binary search tree with the more recent of matching information values still higher in the tree. A key principle in reasoning about binary trees and other structures is the Induction Principle.

A primary technique in obtaining a balanced tree is to use all of a complete binary tree except for some of the nodes on the bottom level. Another is to use an AVL tree, for which the left and right subtrees of any node in the tree differ by at most 1 in height.

In a general tree, a node can have any number of subtrees. A reasonable definition module uses three functions Root, OldestChild, and YoungerSibling analogously to the Root, Left, and Right functions for binary trees. Create, Destroy, See, and Swap are the same as for binary trees; so are the PutX and TakeX procedures, with only a small name change. Some particular general trees discussed were B-trees (of which 2-3 trees are a special case), B+ trees for fast access to external storage, and game trees.

PRACTICE TEST

To prepare for a test, study the indicated examples thoroughly until you can be sure that you would earn a high grade on a test composed solely of these exercises.

1. Write a function that returns the location of the leftmost node in a given binary tree. [Exercise 3, Section 5.2]

2. Write a recursive Boolean function that tells whether a given binary tree contains a given information value. [Exercise 4, Section 5.2]

3. Write the recursive TakeRoot procedure for the standard two-pointer implementation of BinADT. A sample procedure call is TakeRoot(TheInfo, Data). [Example 5.4B]

4. Write the recursive LookAt procedure for the two-pointer implementation of ListADT with a Count field. Count tells 1 more than the number of nodes in the left subtree. A sample procedure call is LookAt(TheInfo, Where, Data). [Example 5.4C]

5. Write Find for the binary search tree implementation of TableADT. A sample procedure call is Find(TheInfo, Data). [Example 5.5B]

6. Write PutIn for the binary search tree implementation of TableADT. A sample procedure call is PutIn(TheInfo, Data). [Example 5.5C]

7. Write a procedure to delete the leftmost information and its node from a binary search tree. [Subprocedure of Example 5.6A]

PROGRAMMING PROBLEMS

1. Complete the TwentyQuestions game program described in Section 5.1.

2. Complete the Geneology program described in Section 5.3.

3. Complete the Expression Tree program described in Section 5.3.

4. Redesign the BinADT definition module on the assumption that the PutX and TakeX procedures can be implemented efficiently having only the Location of the Node itself rather than the indication of Parent. This is true of the array implementation, for instance.

5. Revise the implementation module for BinADT using a header node implementation analogous to the first one described in Section 4.5.

6. Write an implementation module for BinADT in which each Node has an additional field, namely 1 more than the count of the number of Nodes in its left subtree (discussed at the end of Section 5.4). Add a utility procedure to return the count for a particular node and another to return the Location of the next Node in inorder traversal. Then write an implementation module for ListADT that imports from this augmented BinADT module; include the Seek utility function in ListADT.

7. Write an implementation module for ListADT using the standard two-pointer implementation of binary trees, except each Node should have the Count field described in the preceding problem. Alternately, use a field that tells the number of nodes in the whole subtree rooted at the node, or use a Parent field, or use right-threading, as your instructor specifies.

8. Write an implementation module for BinADT in which each Node has an additional field, namely a pointer to the next Node in inorder traversal. Add a utility procedure to return the Location of the next Node in inorder traversal.

9. Write an implementation module for BinADT in which each Node has an additional field, namely a pointer to the parent of the Node. Add a utility procedure to return the Location of the parent of a given Node, another to return the Location of the next Node in inorder traversal, and a third to return the location of the previous Node in inorder traversal.

10. Replace the coding for TakeOut in Example 5.6A by the following logic: If the node to be deleted has at least one empty subtree, move the other subtree up into its place. Otherwise, delete the node (call it N) after you move N's left subtree to become the left subtree of the leftmost node in N's right subtree and move N's right subtree to become N's parent's subtree in place of N. Then give a logical argument that this preserves all necessary properties of the binary search tree. *For extra credit:* Discuss the relative merits of the two deletion algorithms.

11. Write an implementation of TableADT using binary search trees, but import the tree-handling procedures from BinADT instead of dealing with tree pointers directly.

12. Write an implementation of TableADT using binary search trees, except add an extra Num field to each node that tells the number of nodes in the subtree for that node. Keep the tree reasonably balanced at all times by making sure that no node has two subtrees that differ by more than two nodes. Add extra procedures that find the Kth smallest or Kth largest information value for any K and a procedure that prints the values in the tree in order.

13. Write a full implementation module for BinADT on the assumption that InfoADT exports NoInfo; use the standard array implementation.

14. Write an implementation module for BinADT in which the information is stored at the front of an array in preorder sequence. Each array component is a record with two fields: Information and the index of the root of its right subtree (0 if the right subtree is empty, −1 if there is no information there).

15. Write the ReadAll utility procedure for BinADT to read an unknown number of values and put them in a binary tree so that (1) the tree has the minimum possible number of levels, and (2) inorder traversal of the tree yields the values in the order they were read. Use an algorithm that produces the trees in the sequence of Figure 18.

16. Write the insertion procedure for maintaining a binary search tree as an AVL tree, assuming that no two information values are equal (see Section 5.9).

17. Write the deletion procedure for the situation described in the preceding problem.

18. Write a program that tells how many binary trees there are for each number of nodes from 0 up to 30. *Hint:* Calculate them in the order 0, 1, 2, 3..., 29, 30, storing the results in an array of 31 cardinals for later reference.

19. Write a simplified spelling checker. Your program should read a file of a large number of words, store them in a trie or a balanced binary search tree (as your instructor specifies), and then read a second file of words, telling which ones are misspelled (i.e., not in the dictionary).

20. Write an implementation module for TreeADT (Section 5.10) in which the information is stored at the front of an array in postorder sequence. Each array component is a record with two fields: Information and the number of children that the node has.

21. Design a nice definition module for B-trees, with all the capabilities of BinADT and then some (definitions in Section 5.11).

22. Develop a full game-playing program for Kalah or Tic-Tac-Toe from the material in Section 5.13.

23. Rewrite the program in the examples of Section 5.13 so that each node is evaluated for advantage as it is generated, as described toward the end of that section. This permits you to avoid storing more than just a few of the board positions.

24. Write a procedure that prints all the information values in a binary tree using one of preorder, inorder, or postorder traversal, depending on whether the value of a CARDINAL parameter is 1, 2, or 3. Import the OutputInfo procedure from InfoADT and other procedures from BinADT.

25. Write a program that reads two files written by the program described in the preceding problem, one for preorder traversal and the other for inorder traversal with the same binary tree, then creates that same binary tree, and then prints it out in postorder traversal.

26. Write a procedure that finds the location in a given binary tree of the youngest common ancestor of two given locations in that tree.

27. Revise the PutIn procedure for binary search trees (Example 5.5C) so it simply rejects duplicate information values. Use the revised TableADT module to write a program that reads a file of information values and writes it out in sorted order with all duplicates removed.

28. Assume that InfoADT exports NoInfo, a value different from all "true" information values. Write the ReadTree and WriteTree utilities for BinADT as follows: WriteTree writes the values recursively in preorder traversal with NoInfo written after the first recursive call. ReadTree reads the output from WriteTree and recreates the tree. For instance, the tree on the right of Figure 16 would be written as follows if NoInfo is 0: 4 2 1 0 0 3 0 0 6 5 0 0. Show by the Induction Principle that your ReadTree creates the same tree.

29. Complete the DictiADT module described in Section 5.12 for B+ trees. To test your module, you may want to implement a BlockADT module that simulates a disk file by using pointers for block addresses.

6

SORTING ALGORITHMS

The subject matter of this chapter is algorithms that start with a number of values in possibly random order and rearrange them so that they are in increasing order of the ID field (or whatever other basis for comparison is appropriate to the situation; the Compare procedure abstracts this aspect of the problem).

The emphasis of this chapter is on efficiency in terms of space and time; the objective is to find sorting algorithms that execute quickly and/or do not use too much computer memory. The three sorting methods described in the first two sections are the simplest ones, but they are among the slowest algorithms. They eventually get the job at hand done, but many applications cannot afford to wait as long as it would require for them to work. If time and space were unimportant, you could skip everything in this chapter after the first section.

The usual trade-offs apply to sorting algorithms: Speed is obtained at the cost of either space or programmer effort, usually the latter. In fact, the complexity of the algorithms is such that the "faster" algorithms are only faster when there are many items to sort; for instance, the Insertion Sort, described in Section 6.1, is usually faster than all the algorithms considered here when you have less than 20 items to sort. You will learn how to compare different algorithms for speed. The algorithms you will see in this chapter include the Insertion Sort, the Selection Sort, the Bubble Sort, the Tree Sort, the Quicksort, the Merge Sort, the Shell Sort, the Radix Sort, and the Heap Sort.

6.1 THE INSERTION SORT

The **Insertion Sort** has the following logic: Repeatedly add a new value to an already sorted list at the place where it should go so that the resulting list is still in order. I assume throughout this chapter that Information is imported from InfoADT (Example 2.3B) or its equivalent; this provides full generality. Remember that Compare(X,Y) is an INTEGER function of two Information values; it returns a negative if X is less than Y and 0 if X equals Y.

For this section and the next, assume that a List is declared as a counted array and that you are designing a utility sorting procedure for ListADT:

```
TYPE   List = POINTER TO CountedArray;
       CountedArray = RECORD
                       Item : ARRAY [1..MaxSize] OF Information;
                       Size : CARDINAL;  (* components in use *)
                     END;
```

Illustration of the Insertion Sort

For an Insertion Sort using a counted array, after you have sorted Item[1]... Item[Index], you insert Item[Index+1] into that list in the appropriate place, so that you have Item[1]... Item[Index+1] sorted. You repeat this for each value of Index from 1 up to but not including the number of items to be sorted. The following **walk-through** for an array with six values should clarify this algorithm. To start with, assume you have the following array:

Current Status: Array = (18,13,11,19,12,16)

You are to put the first *two* in order. 13 goes below 18, so you swap the first and second values. The array is now sorted through item 2.

Current Status: Array = (_13,18_,11,19,12,16)

You are to put the first *three* in order. The third one (the 11) is less than the two numbers to its left, so you "pick up" the 11, shift the 18 and the 13 to the right (thereby vacating component 1), then put the 11 in component 1. The array is now sorted through item 3.

Current Status: Array = (_11,13,18_,19,12,16)

You are to put the first *four* in order. The fourth one (the 19) is greater than the one before it, so the array is already sorted through item 4.

Current Status: Array = (11,13,18,19,12,16)

You are to put the first *five* in order. The fifth one (the 12) is less than the three numbers to its left, so you "pick up" the 12, shift the 19, the 18, and the 13 to the right (thereby vacating component 2), then put the 12 in component 2. The array is now sorted through item 5.

Current Status: Array = (11,12,13,18,19,16)

You are to put the first *six* in order. The sixth one (the 16) is less than the two numbers to its left, so you "pick up" the 16, shift the 19 and the 18 to the right (thereby vacating component 4), then put the 16 in component 4. The array is now sorted through item 6.

Current Status: Array = (11,12,13,16,18,19)

Since there are no more components to sort, you are done. From this walk-through, the algorithm can be explicitly written out as:

Algorithm for the Insertion Sort
 DO the following for each component Item[2]... Item[Size] whose value is smaller than the one below it:
 Note: The part below that component is already sorted;
 1. Save the value of that component in a variable named Saved;
 2. Set K to the index of that component;
 3. DO repeatedly until time to stop:
   3.a. Copy into Item[K] the value of the component below it;
   3.b. Subtract 1 from K;
   3.c. STOP if Saved is at least as large as the value of the component below Item[K] or if there is none below it;
 4. Transfer the value from Saved to Item[K].

An advantage of this particular algorithm is that, if the numbers happen to be ordered already, the procedure executes very quickly. The algorithm is implemented in Example 6.1A.

The order of the two operands of OR is important. You cannot write the condition as in UNTIL (Compare(Saved, Item[K−1])>=0) OR (K=1); when K is 1, the processor would attempt to evaluate the first operand. That would crash the program, since there is no Item[0]. But with the order of operands shown, having

EXAMPLE 6.1A _____

```
PROCEDURE Sort (VAR Data : List);
    (* Algorithm: Insertion Sort *)
    (* Context:   simple array impl. of ListADT *)
VAR
    Index, K : CARDINAL;
    Saved    : Information;
BEGIN
    WITH Data^ DO        (* fields are Item and Size *)
        FOR Index := 2 TO Size DO
            IF Compare (Item [Index],
                        Item [Index - 1]) < 0 THEN
                Saved := Item [Index];
                K := Index;    (* so K > 1 *)
                REPEAT
                    Item [K] := Item [K - 1];
                    DEC (K);
                UNTIL (K = 1) OR
                      (Compare (Saved, Item [K - 1]) >= 0);
                Item [K] := Saved;
            END;
        END;
    END;
END Sort;
```

K = 1 prevents the evaluation of the comparison, owing to the *partial evaluation* feature of Modula-2.

Note that the CopyInfo procedure from InfoADT is not used. CopyInfo is necessary only when two distinct copies of the information are needed. You need only one copy of each Information record; you are just switching pointers to records. This can make the sorting procedure several times faster when one Information record requires a large amount of storage.

▐▶ PROGRAMMING STYLE

Consider the add-controlled loop in Example 6.1A: REPEAT... DEC(K); UNTIL (K=1) OR.... If you write (K<=1) instead of (K=1), the effect is the same. The advantage in writing (K<=1) is that a reader of the program can easily see that the loop is self-terminating, since only one statement subordinate to the REPEAT changes K. Otherwise the reader would have to look further to verify that K is set to a value larger than 1 immediately before the REPEAT. The disadvantage in writing (K<=1) is that the reader wonders if he or she misunderstood something; perhaps there are conditions under which K can be less than 1. This conflict occasionally arises when you try to be as clear as possible. That is why I put the comment (* so K>1 *) just before the REPEAT.

Check Your Understanding

1. What changes would be required to make the coding of the Insertion Sort arrange the values in decreasing order?

2. What changes would be required in the coding of the Insertion Sort to have the parameters be (VAR Item: ARRAY OF Information; Size: CARDINAL) as the formal parameter part?

3. Make changes in Example 6.1A so that it would work correctly even if partial evaluation were not available. Try to make the revisions in the coding execute as quickly as possible.

4. (NA) Trace Example 6.1A when the array is (50,54,52,40,45). Show the current status at the end of each iteration of the main loop, similar to what was done at the beginning of this section.

5. (NA) Revise Example 6.1A to sort from the top down; in particular, replace the line beginning FOR by FOR Index := Size−1 TO 1 BY −1 DO.

6. (NA) Assume that Data ↑ .Item is declared with a component 0 in which no information is stored. Show how you can use this extra space instead of the variable Saved to make the coding in Example 6.1A execute more quickly.

6.2 THE SELECTION SORT AND THE BUBBLE SORT

Another elementary method for sorting an array is called the **Selection Sort**. The algorithm is: Go through the array from Item[1] to Item[Size], looking for the smallest value. Switch it with the value in Item[1]. Now you need only sort Item[2]... Item[Size], so you repeat, except find the smallest of Item[2]... Item[Size] and switch it with Item[2]. Then repeat with 3, then with 4, and so on until done. Thus at each iteration you are selecting the smallest value in that part of the array that you have not yet sorted and putting it at the beginning of that part.

Example 6.2A displays the corresponding Sort procedure, assuming a program with declarations of Information, Compare, and List as used in Section 6.1. Note that, at the beginning of each iteration of the overall loop, the values in Item[1]... Item[Index] are sorted, and none of them are larger than any of those in the rest of the array.

A sample run with the array (13,16,17,15,11,19) causes the following sequence of actions, assuming Size is 6:

Index := 1; Position := 1;
The inner FOR loop sets Position to 5, the index of 11;
Switch Item[1] with Item[5], so the array becomes (11,16,17,15,13,19);

EXAMPLE 6.2A _____

```
PROCEDURE Sort (VAR Data : List);
    (* Algorithm: Selection Sort *)
    (* Context:   simple array impl. of ListADT *)
VAR
    Index, K, Position : CARDINAL;
    Saved              : Information;
BEGIN
    WITH Data^ DO     (* fields are Item and Size *)
        FOR Index := 1 TO Size - 1 DO
            Position := Index;
            FOR K := Index + 1 TO Size DO
                IF Compare (Item [K],
                            Item [Position]) < 0 THEN
                    Position := K;
                END;
            END;
            Saved := Item [Position];
            Item [Position] := Item [Index];
            Item [Index] := Saved;
        END;
    END;
END Sort;
```

Index := 2; Position := 2;

The inner FOR loop sets Position to 5;

Switch Item[2] with Item[5], so the array becomes (11,13,17,15,16,19);

etc. See Figure 1.

There is some similarity of the Insertion and Selection Sorts to two commonly used methods of sorting a bridge hand: A bridge player picks up 13 playing cards and sorts them into suits, ordered within each suit. If the player picks up one card at a time and inserts it in the proper place, that is similar to the Insertion Sort. If instead the person picks up all the cards at one time and picks out the highest card and puts it on the left, then the next highest, and so on, that is similar to the Selection Sort.

The Selection Sort evaluates Compare more often than the Insertion Sort does, but it moves the information around much less. Thus the Selection Sort works faster than the Insertion Sort when the information takes up a large amount of storage space. If the information consists of simple values or of pointers to records, Insertion Sort works faster than the Selection Sort.

The Bubble Sort

Yet another elementary method for sorting an array is called the **Bubble Sort**, or sometimes the **Exchange Sort**. The algorithm is: Go through the entire array from

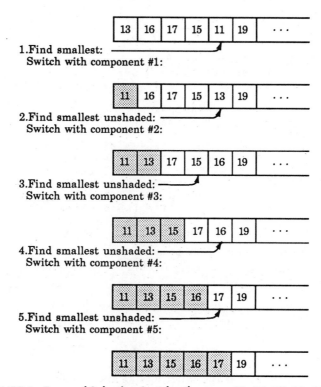

FIGURE 1. *Trace of Selection Sort for the array 13, 16, 17, 15, 11, 19.*

Item[Size] down to Item[2], comparing each component with the one below it. Whenever you find two adjacent components whose values are out of order, switch them around. When you are done, the smallest value will be in Item[1] (think about that for a while to see why). Then repeat, except only go down as far as Item[3]. Then repeat with 4, then with 5, and so on until done. The coding is in Example 6.2B.

⫸ PROGRAMMING STYLE

You may be wondering why I used the same name (Sort) for all three sorting procedures in Sections 6.1 and 6.2, instead of calling them InsertionSort, SelectionSort, and BubbleSort. The reason is that the name of a procedure should reflect the task that it accomplishes rather than the algorithm used to accomplish the task. To modules that call the procedure, all that counts is that the procedure sorts, not how it sorts. An advantage is that, if you have a number of programs that call a given Sort procedure and you decide to replace the algorithm in that procedure by a better one, you do not have to change any of the calling statements.

EXAMPLE 6.2B _____

```
PROCEDURE Sort (VAR Data : List);
    (* Algorithm: Bubble Sort *)
    (* Context:   simple array impl. of ListADT *)
VAR
    Index, K : CARDINAL;
    Saved    : Information;
BEGIN
    WITH Data^ DO    (* fields are Item and Size *)
        FOR Index := 1 TO Size - 1 DO
            FOR K := Size TO Index + 1 BY -1 DO
                IF Compare(Item [K], Item [K - 1]) < 0 THEN
                    Saved := Item [K];
                    Item [K] := Item [K - 1];
                    Item [K - 1] := Saved;
                END;
            END;
        END;
    END;
END Sort;
```

Speed of Execution

If it happens that the inner loop of the Bubble Sort is executed without making any switches, the array must be in order. Thus we need not increase Index and repeat. We can attempt to make this sorting algorithm execute somewhat faster in such cases by writing the outer loop as a REPEAT loop, controlled by a Boolean variable that tells whether a switch was made on the prior iteration. In general, however, this "improvement" actually slows execution down somewhat, since few iterations are saved and more must be done on each iteration.

Although the coding of the Bubble Sort is physically shorter than that of the Selection Sort or the Insertion Sort (due primarily to the power of the FOR statement), the Bubble Sort is in general the slowest of the three. In fact, the only reason for introducing it here is to provide a comparison with the other two sorting methods.

Check Your Understanding
_____

1. What changes must be made in Example 6.2A to have it sort the values in decreasing order?

2. What changes must be made in Example 6.2A to put the largest values on top instead of putting the smallest values on the bottom?

3. Trace Example 6.2A for the array (2,6,2,3,1).

4. (NA) Same as Exercise 1, except use Example 6.2B.

5. (NA) Trace Example 6.2B for the array (1,2,3,5,4).

6. (NA) Discuss the advantages and disadvantages of guarding the three statements involving Saved in Example 6.2A by IF Position # Index THEN.... Consider a typical case of sorting 20 values.

7. (NA) Modify the Selection Sort in Example 6.2A so that, on each pass through the array, you find both the smallest and the largest values and put them in their places. Show that this algorithm executes significantly faster.

6.3 TIME ANALYSIS OF ALGORITHMS

The problem in analyzing an algorithm for execution time is that the time required for even the simplest statement varies widely with the compiler and the machine used. We have to find a way to "factor out" the machine-dependent times to obtain a result that depends only on the number of items being processed and the structure of the algorithm. Such a method does not give exact execution times, but it does give a good measure by which to compare different algorithms.

The measure presented in this section can be used to show that a super computer using any sorting algorithm presented in Sections 6.1 and 6.2 cannot sort as fast as a microcomputer using any sorting algorithm presented later in this chapter, when you have a large number of items to sort. The reason, of course, is that the earlier sorting algorithms execute much more slowly than the later sorting algorithms for a large number of items.

Time Analysis of the DestroyAllInfo Procedure

Throughout this section, N denotes the number of items on the list being processed. I begin by analyzing coding for a utility procedure for the standard linked list implementation of ListADT. The DestroyAllInfo utility procedure accepts a List named Data as a VAR parameter and deallocates the space used by all information values in the List. It can be coded as:

```
WHILE Data # NIL DO
    P := Data;
    Data := Data↑.Link;
    DestroyInfo (P↑.Info);
    DISPOSE (P);
END;
```

I want to find out how long it takes this coding to execute. If the list has no items on it, the condition is evaluated and found false, so the algorithm terminates. If the list has one item on it, the condition evaluates as true, one iteration occurs that sets Data to NIL, then the condition evaluates as false, so the algorithm terminates. In general, the condition is evaluated N + 1 times and the subordinate statement sequence is executed N times, so the execution time for this algorithm can be expressed as:

(A) $(N+1)*$TimeToEvaluateCondition $+ (N*$TimeForStatementSequence$)$

It is time to introduce some new notation: Any single small letter in one of these time formulas represents a time period (usually very tiny) that depends only on the compiler and the machine. For instance, the time to evaluate the condition Data#NIL can be represented by the letter c. This lets me write the execution time for the DestroyAllInfo algorithm as:

(B) $(N+1)*c + (N*$TimeForStatementSequence$)$, or
(C) $N*(c+$TimeForStatementSequence$)+c$

The subordinate statement sequence consists of two assignment statements, a call to DestroyInfo that executes DISPOSE (for dynamic variables) or does nothing (for static variables), and an execution of DISPOSE. The time for each of these four statements depends only on the compiler and the machine, not on the number of items on the list. So I can use the small letters d, e, f, g to represent these four time periods:

(D) execution time for DestroyAllInfo $= N*(c+d+e+f+g)+c$

This looks like algebra, but it is actually much easier than algebra. Note that $(c+d+e+f+g)$ can be represented by another small letter k, since $(c+d+e+f+g)$ is independent of the number of items on the list. So I can simplify the expression to:

(E) execution time for DestroyAllInfo $= N*k+c$

Thus you see that the execution time is a first-degree polynomial in N, the number of items on the list. To summarize: *Execution time for DestroyAllInfo is a linear function of the number of items on the list.*

Execution in Constant Time

For the standard linked list implementation of ListADT, the body of the FirstLocation function is simply RETURN NIL, which is just one statement that depends on the machine (and the compiler too, of course, but that is rather a mouthful, so if you do not mind, in the future I will just say "depends on the machine" or even "machine-dependent" to save time, with the understanding that it depends on the compiler too), so:

(F) execution time for FirstLocation = c

Thus execution time for FirstLocation is a constant function, independent of the number of items on the list. The body of the InList function is:

```
RETURN (Data # NIL) AND ((Where = NIL) OR (Where↑.Link # NIL));
```

Let a, b, and c represent the time to evaluate the three simple conditions, and let d and e represent the time to evaluate AND and OR. Then the total execution time for InList is (a + d) if Data is NIL, but it can be as much as (a + b + c + d + e). So we can say:

(G) a+d <= execution time for InList <= a+b+c+d+e

We can always replace the sum or product of several small letters by a single small letter to simplify these expressions, so we have:

(H) g <= execution time for InList <= g+h

This is awkward to express; it would be much easier to say "execution time is so-and-so" than to say "execution time is somewhere between so-and-so and such-and-such." There is some more notation that permits this: The execution time for InList is said to be **big-oh of 1** because it is between two constant multiples of 1 (i.e., the multipliers depend only on the machine). Note that FirstLocation is also big-oh of 1, since its execution time is $c*1$, which is between $(c-1)*1$ and $(c+1)*1$. In symbols, "big-oh of 1" is expressed as $\mathbf{O(1)}$.

Big-oh Notation

Execution time is said to be big-oh of N if it is between two constant multiples of N (where N is the number of items on the list). Execution time for DestroyAllInfo was seen to be $N*k+c$, which is between $N*k$ and $N*(k+1)$ whenever N is larger than c. Since c is sure to be a fraction of a second, that means whenever N is at least 1. In general, execution time is **big-oh of N** (written $\mathbf{O(N)}$) if it is between two constant multiples of N for all sufficiently large values of N. So a summary of the results so far is:

execution time for DestroyAllInfo is big-oh of N
execution time for InList and FirstLocation is big-oh of 1

An alternative to saying an execution time is big-oh of some function is to say it is **proportionately asymptotically bounded by** that function. "Asymptotically" means "for sufficiently large N" and "proportionately" means "except for a constant multiplier." Another alternative phrasing is to say that the execution time is of the **same order of magnitude** as that function. For instance, the execution time for DestroyAllInfo is of the same order of magnitude as N.

Consider the following coding (from Example 4.4A) for Insert and NextLocation. They can both be seen to be big-oh of 1. For Insert, you execute NEW, then an assignment, then test a condition, then execute two assignments. This can be written as $(a+b+c+d+e)$, but why bother? Just say it is big-oh of 1, since it is a constant multiple of 1. Similarly, NextLocation tests one or two conditions and then returns a value, so its execution time is between $(a+b)$ and $(a+c+d)$, so it is also big-oh of 1.

```
(* body of Insert *)              (* body of NextLocation *)
NEW (P);                          IF Where = NIL THEN
P↑.Info := TheInfo;                   RETURN Data;
IF Where = NIL THEN               ELSIF Where↑.Link = NIL THEN
    P↑.Link := Data;                  RETURN Where;
    Data := P;                    ELSE
ELSE                                  RETURN Where↑.Link;
    P↑.Link := Where↑.Link;       END;
    Where↑.Link := P;
END;
```

The utility LastLocation function executes the following coding when the list has more than one item on it. The body of the WHILE loop executes $N-2$ times and the condition is evaluates $N-1$ times, so the total execution time is big-oh of N. To see this, calculate as follows: $b+(N-1){\star}c+(N-2){\star}d+e = N{\star}(c+d)+(b-c-2d+e)$, which is between $N{\star}(c+d-1)$ and $N{\star}(c+d+1)$ when N is very large (namely, larger than the absolute value of $b-c-2d+e$).

```
(* body of LastLocation function *)
Where := Data;
WHILE Where↑.Link↑.Link # NIL DO
    Where := Where↑.Link;
END;
RETURN Where;
```

Maybe you thought the execution time should be big-oh of $N-1$, but that is actually the same thing as big-oh of N. The calculation just given also comes out to be $(N-1) \cdot (c+d) + b - d + e$. It is best to choose the simplest expression for big-oh, so we always say big-oh of N rather than big-oh of $N-1$.

It is useful to keep in mind the following *general principles for computing big-oh:*

1. Big-oh for a statement that depends only on the machine is 1.
2. Big-oh for a sequence of statements is the sum of the big-ohs for each statement.
3. Big-oh for an IF statement with a machine-dependent condition is the larger of the big-ohs for each subordinate statement sequence, at most (and is sometimes less).
4. Big-oh for a loop is the number of times it executes multiplied by the big-oh for the subordinate sequence, as long as the condition for reiteration is just machine-dependent.

The first principle follows directly from the definition of big-oh. The second principle just means that the time required to execute a sequence of statements, one after the other, is found by adding up the execution times for each statement. The third principle is true because the execution of the IF condition is followed by execution of one subordinate statement sequence, so the total time is therefore at most 1 plus the larger execution time; adding 1 to a big-oh value does not change the big-oh value. The fourth principle is a generalization of the earlier discussion of the DestroyAllInfo procedure.

Big-oh for the Selection Sort

The coding for the Selection Sort (Example 6.2A) has the following structure (I use N instead of Size, to be consistent with the notation for this section):

```
FOR Index := 1 TO N - 1 DO
     Position := Index;
     FOR K := Index + 1 TO N DO
         (* only machine-dependent statements here *)
     END;
     (* only machine-dependent statements here *)
END;
```

The innermost machine-dependent statements execute in O(1) time. The average value for Index inside the loop is N/2 (averaging 1 and $(N-1)$), so the statements within the inner FOR loop execute N/2 times on the average. Multiply this by the O(1) to see that the inner FOR loop is O(N/2). Add O(1) for the other machine-dependent statements inside the outer loop to see that the body of the outer loop is O(N/2). Multiply by the number of times those statements are executed (N−1 times) to see that the overall coding is:

big-oh of (N−1)∗N/2, which is
big-oh of (N²)/2−N/2, which is
big-oh of N².

That last assertion might have thrown you—where did everything else go? The next-to-last line shows that execution time is between (N²)/3 and N² when N is at least 3. Thus the execution time for the Selection Sort is between two constant multiples of N² for N sufficiently large (namely, at least 3), so it is **O(N²)**. This is also known as **quadratic execution time**.

Big-oh for Recursive Algorithms

Consider the recursive PrintReverse procedure from Example 3.5C, whose body is:

```
IF InList (Where, Data) THEN
    PrintReverse (NextLocation (Where, Data), Data);
    LookAt (TheInfo, Where, Data);
    OutputInfo (TheInfo);
END;
```

Assume this procedure is called with a list of N items. If N is 0, all it does is evaluate a condition and then stop. If N is positive, it evaluates the condition, calls PrintReverse with a list of N−1 items, then executes two O(1) statements and stops. Thus there will be a total of N+1 activations of the procedure, each of which executes in O(1) time, not counting what the other activations do. That means that the execution time for this procedure is O(N+1), which is the same as O(N). As a general rule, if all activations of the recursive procedure have the same big-oh time exclusive of what other activations do, you multiply that time by the number of activations to find the overall big-oh time.

Note that the primary advantage of computing the execution time in terms of big-oh is that we obtain a measure of how fast execution time grows with the size of the list. If execution time is O(1), then tripling the size of the list makes no significant difference in the execution time. For a O(N) algorithm, tripling the size of the list approximately triples the execution time; the reason is that the execution time increases from about N∗k to about (3N)∗k for some constant k independent of N. For a O(N²) algorithm, tripling the size of the list multiplies the execution time by about 9; the reason is that the execution time increases from about N²∗k to about 3N²∗k for some constant k independent of N.

Logarithmic Execution Time

The coding for the binary search (Example 2.5C) is:

```
Bottom := 1;
Top := N;
WHILE Top > Bottom DO
    Middle := (Bottom + Top) DIV 2;
    IF Compare (TheInfo, Item [Middle]) <= 0 THEN
        Top := Middle;
    ELSE
        Bottom := Middle + 1;
    END;
END;
RETURN Compare (TheInfo, Item [Top]) = 0;
```

The statement sequence of the WHILE loop in this coding is big-oh of 1, so the overall execution time is the number of times the loop executes (the machine-dependent statements outside the loop are inconsequential). The value of (Top−Bottom+1) is cut approximately in half on each iteration. If you try out various possibilities for N, you will see that there will be either 2 or 3 iterations when N is from 5 to 8; there will be either 3 or 4 iterations when N is from 9 to 16; there will be either 4 or 5 iterations when N is from 17 to 32, and so on. In general, the number of iterations is either $\lg(N)$ or $\lg(N)-1$, depending on the location of the item for which you are searching. Thus the binary search algorithm is **big-oh of $\lg(N)$**. This is also known as **logarithmic execution time**.

Proper Definition of Big-oh

A sequential search through a list executes a loop with a $O(1)$ statement sequence somewhere between 1 and N times, depending on the location of the item for which you are searching. Does this mean that it is big-oh of 1, or big-oh of N, or big-oh of some function between those two?

The problem is that execution time for a sequential search varies depending on the information values involved. The definition of big-oh requires that we use the worst-case time unless average time is explicitly stated. Thus sequential-search executes in big-oh of N. Similarly, the Insertion Sort executes a FOR Index := 2 TO N loop where each iteration can require up to Index comparisons. Thus the worst-case execution time is proportional to $(2+3+\cdots+N)$, which makes Insertion Sort a big-oh of N-squared algorithm.

If we assume that the chance of any one item on the list being the subject of the search is the same as for any other item, the loop executes an average of $(N+1)/2$ times, so the average execution time for the sequential search algorithm is also big-oh of N. But it does not always happen that the average-case time has the same big-oh value as the worst-case time. In particular, the Quicksort sorting algorithm presented later in this chapter executes in N-squared time for its worst case and in N∗lg(N) time for its average time.

The technical definition of big-oh states that a function f(N) is big-oh of some other function g(N) if f(N) is asymptotically proportionally *less than or equal to* some constant multiple of g(N). For instance, since the sequential search is big-oh of N, it would technically be correct to say it is also big-oh of N-squared and big-oh of N∗lg(N). However, you should normally specify the smallest simple function of N.

Check Your Understanding

1. Find the execution time for the WriteAll procedure in Example 4.2C.

2. Find the execution time for the Find procedure in Example 5.5B, assuming the binary tree is very well balanced.

3. Write a function to compute lg(N) for any given positive N.

4. (NA) Find the execution time for the Insert procedure in Example 3.6A.

5. (NA) Find the execution time for the recursive ReadAll procedure in Example 4.2B.

6. (NA) Find the execution time for the Bubble Sort in Example 6.2B.

6.4 FRAMEWORK FOR CONSIDERING SORTING ALGORITHMS

The three sorting algorithms in Sections 6.1 and 6.2 were written as utility procedures for the simple array implementation of ListADT. Another context in which you could use an Insertion Sort is in a client module of ListADT. Example 6.4A demonstrates the appropriate coding after it is converted from Example 6.1A. Allowance has been made for the fact that it is much easier to go forward in a List than backward by moving from smaller to larger information values until the correct spot is found.

This algorithm is difficult to implement without using a second List variable. You could use recursion, but that would make heavy demands on the available space for a large list; the body of the Sort procedure could consist of the one statement SortAtSpot(FirstLocation(Data), Data)), and the recursive SortAtSpot subprocedure could look like the following:

```
IF InList (Spot, Data) THEN
    SortAtSpot (NextLocation (Spot, Data), Data);
    Delete (TheInfo, Spot, Data);
    (* then comes coding to put the information at Spot where
       it goes in the lower part of the list *)
END;
```

The Insertion Sort has the advantage of being an **incremental sorting** algorithm. That is, the resulting Data structure is sorted after each value is added to the structure (in Example 6.4A, Data is sorted at each point when the WHILE

EXAMPLE 6.4A _____

```
PROCEDURE Sort (VAR Data : List);
    (* Algorithm: Insertion Sort *)
    (* Context:   client of ListADT *)
   (*--------------------------------------------------------*)

    PROCEDURE InsertInOrder (TheInfo : Information;
                             VAR Data : List);
    VAR
        Spot        : Location;
        WhatsThere : Information;
    BEGIN
        Spot := FirstLocation (Data);
        LookAt (WhatsThere, Spot, Data);
        WHILE InList (Spot, Data) AND
                 (Compare (TheInfo, WhatsThere) >= 0) DO
            Spot := NextLocation (Spot, Data);
            LookAt (WhatsThere, Spot, Data);
        END;
        Insert (TheInfo, Spot, Data);
    END InsertInOrder;
   (*--------------------------------------------------------*)

VAR
    OriginalList : List;
    TheInfo      : Information;
    Where        : Location;

BEGIN         (* Sort *)
    OriginalList := Data;
    Create (Data);
    Where := FirstLocation (OriginalList);
    WHILE InList (Where, OriginalList) DO
        Delete (TheInfo, Where, OriginalList);
        InsertInOrder (TheInfo, Data);
    END;
    Destroy (OriginalList);
END Sort;
```

condition in the body of Sort is evaluated). This is valuable for implementations of TableADT.

The Insertion Sort is also a **stable sorting** algorithm; if there are two matching information values in the original list, the one that comes *earlier* in that original list will be placed *earlier* in the sorted list. This is necessary for some applications of TableADT. Some of the sorting algorithms we discuss in this chapter are not stable, so they would not be suitable for all applications of TableADT. The Selection Sort is not a stable sorting algorithm, nor is it an incremental sorting algorithm. *Note:* Some applications, such as a table of identifiers generated during compilation of a program, require stability in the sense that the earlier of matching values be *later* in the sorted list. This can be called **reverse stability** as opposed to **normal stability**. This book discusses primarily normal stability (the first kind of stability mentioned), but it is trivial to switch from one kind of stability to the other. Similarly, almost everything said about increasing order could be said about decreasing order, mutatis mutandis.

The Tree Sort

It is easy to tell whether a list is sorted: Look at each information value on the list, starting at the first location and going on to the next location each time, until you arrive at the end. If each one you look at (after the first one) is greater than or equal to the previous one you looked at, the List is sorted; otherwise it is not sorted.

Now consider the binary search tree implementation of TableADT, described in Section 5.5. Is this data structure sorted? In general, under what conditions can we say that a table is sorted, other than when it is implemented as a list?

A binary search tree is considered sorted; in fact, creating a binary search tree to hold information is commonly called the **Tree Sort**, which is a stable incremental sorting algorithm. The reason it is considered sorted is that we can produce all the information values in the tree in increasing order very quickly (i.e., in big-oh of N time); inorder traversal of the binary search tree does this. Example 6.4B shows how the logic of the Tree Sort can be used for a stable sort of a Stack.

Note that a reverse form of inorder traversal of the tree must be used to obtain a stack in increasing order. The coding of PutInSearchTree is a simplified form of Example 5.5C. Execution time for PutInSearchTree is big-oh of lg(N) on the average, so the WHILE statement in Example 6.4B is big-oh of N*lg(N). The TransferToStack procedure is big-oh of N, so the overall execution time for the Tree Sort is big-oh of N*lg(N) on the average. However, if the original stack is already sorted, the execution time will be big-oh of N-squared (this is its worst-case performance).

In discussing sorting algorithms in this chapter, I will assume that ListADT exports certain utility procedures that help make the overall logic of the sorting algorithms clearer. For instance, if I assume that ListADT exports Push, Pop, and IsEmpty as utilities and declares TYPE Stack=List, Example 6.4B can be used for lists. Also, Example 6.4A can be made a little clearer by using Pop instead of

EXAMPLE 6.4B _____

```
PROCEDURE Sort (VAR Data : Stack);
    (* Algorithm: Tree Sort *)
    (* Context:   client of StackADT *)
TYPE
    BinTree = POINTER TO Node;
    Node = RECORD
                Info : Information;
                Left, Right : BinTree;
           END;
VAR
    TheInfo : Information;
   (*-----------------------------------------------------*)

    PROCEDURE PutInSearchTree (VAR Spot : BinTree);
        (* Put TheInfo in the search tree in a leaf *)
    BEGIN
        IF Spot = NIL THEN
            NEW (Spot);
            Spot^.Info := TheInfo;
            Spot^.Right := NIL;
            Spot^.Left := NIL;
        ELSIF Compare (TheInfo, Spot^.Info) < 0 THEN
            PutInSearchTree (Spot^.Left);
        ELSE
            PutInSearchTree (Spot^.Right);
        END;
    END PutInSearchTree;
   (*-----------------------------------------------------*)

    PROCEDURE TransferToStack (Root : BinTree);
        (* Move all information from this subtree to the
           stack using the reverse of inorder traversal *)
    BEGIN
        IF Root # NIL THEN
            TransferToStack (Root^.Right);
            Push (Root^.Info, Data);
            TransferToStack (Root^.Left);
            DISPOSE (Root);
        END;
    END TransferToStack;
   (*-----------------------------------------------------*)

VAR
    HoldingTree : BinTree;

BEGIN           (* Sort *)
    HoldingTree := NIL;
    WHILE NOT IsEmpty (Data) DO
        Pop (TheInfo, Data);
        PutInSearchTree (HoldingTree);
    END;
    TransferToStack (HoldingTree);
END Sort;
```

Delete. A ListADT module with a fair number of such utilities could be called an augmented ListADT module.

Check Your Understanding

1. Give an example of a list of integers that proves that the Selection Sort is not a stable sort.

2. Revise Example 6.4A for efficiency by treating the first item on the given list separately from the rest.

3. Revise Example 6.4B to produce a procedure for a stable sort of a Queue, assuming imports from QueueADT.

4. (NA) Complete the recursive Insertion Sort procedure (using SortAtSpot) described early in this section.

5. Rewrite Example 6.4A on the assumption that it is a utility procedure in the standard linked list implementation of ListADT (Example 4.4A).

6. (NA) Rewrite Example 6.4A on the assumption that there is a MoveInfo utility procedure in ListADT as described in Example 3.5B. Do not use a second List.

7. (NA) Write the Selection Sort using imports from ListADT, assuming that there is a MoveInfo utility procedure in ListADT as described in Example 3.5B. Do not use a second List.

8. (NA) Write a short paper discussing two questions relative to Example 6.4B: the stability of the sorting algorithm and the proper placement of the DISPOSE(Root) statement.

6.5 THE MERGE SORT

The Merge Sort algorithm is an application of the divide-and-conquer method: You divide the problem to be solved into two parts, usually of about the same size. Then you solve the problem for each part. Finally, you use the results for each part to solve the problem for the whole. The way in which the Merge Sort does this is:

1. Split the structure to be sorted into two parts of equal size (or differing by 1, if you have an odd number of values).

2. Sort each half in increasing order.

3. Combine the two halves into a structure in increasing order.

An algorithm for splitting a structure into two equal parts is not hard to develop, assuming you know how many items are on the list; you just divide that number by 2 and shift that many items to the first list, then put the rest on the second list. If the number of items is odd, one of the halflists has to have 1 more item than the other; it might as well be the first halflist. For instance, 17 items would be split so that 9 are on the first halflist and 8 are on the second halflist.

Sorting one halflist can be done by a reapplication of the Merge Sort (i.e., recursively), although it is faster to use a simpler sort when the halflist is small. The recursion is self-terminating if we check that the list has at least two information values for each recursive call; that is another reason for keeping track of the number of values on each halflist.

Combining the two halves in increasing order can be done quickly when you take advantage of the fact that each halflist is already sorted: You repeatedly look at the top one on each halflist and move the smaller of the two to the whole list. Figure 2 shows the major stages in a Merge Sort for 10 numbers (although, in practice, 10 is too small for an efficient Merge Sort). Note that this is a stable sorting method.

The coding using imports from ListADT is given in Example 6.5A. It is interesting to note that the only ListADT procedures needed for the Merge Sort are the Queue procedures. This coding assumes (for compactness) that the SizeOf utility is also available. The use of the SizeOf utility or, if not available, simply counting the information values in a loop that goes to the end of the overall list, cuts execution time for the Merge Sort significantly. The splitting into two equal lists should execute much faster than it would without the initial count. Remember that Peep has no effect at all if the list is empty.

Figure 3 (on page 416) displays two trees of recursive calls; the numbers in each tree indicate the number of items to be sorted for a particular call of Sort. For instance, if asked to sort 10 values, the procedure calls Sort twice with 5 values. Each time Sort is called with 5 values, it calls Sort once with 3 values and once with 2 values. Sorting with 2 values does not cause any further recursive calls, but sorting with 3 values causes one more recursive call with a 2-item list.

Fastest Possible Algorithms for Sorting by Comparisons

If you have five items to sort, there are 120 = 5! different orders in which they can occur. Any algorithm to sort five items has to decide which of these 120 possibilities occurs. A comparison of items gives a yes/no answer, so it takes at least seven yes/no answers to classify a given list of five items as one of the 120 possibilities (since the seventh power of 2 is 128). The general rule is that the worst-case performance of any sorting method that depends only on comparisons requires at least lg(N!) comparisons to sort N items.

It can be shown mathematically that lg(N!) is approximately N*lg(N) − 1.5*N + 0.5*lg(N) + 1.25, which is big-oh of N*lg(N). Thus the fastest possible sorting methods that depend only on comparisons are big-oh of N*lg(N). The Merge Sort depends only on comparisons. The number of levels of recursion in

```
Given 10 unsorted numbers:    67  42  84  13  53  22  39  75  47  64
Split into two halflists*:    /  67  42  84  13  53  /  22  39  75  47  64
Sort each halflist:           / (13) 42  53  67  84  /  22  39  47  64  75
Look at the front two:
Move smaller to whole list:   13  /  42  53  67  84  / (22) 39  47  64  75
Look at the front two:
Move smaller to whole list:   13  22  /  42  53  67  84  / (39) 47  64  75
Look at the front two:
Move smaller to whole list:   13  22  39  / (42) 53  67  84  /  47  64  75
Look at the front two:
Move smaller to whole list:   13  22  39  42  /  53  67  84  / (47) 64  75
Look at the front two:
Move smaller to whole list:   13  22  39  42  47  / (53) 67  84  /  64  75
Look at the front two:
Move smaller to whole list:   13  22  39  42  47  53  /  67  84  / (64) 75
Look at the front two:
Move smaller to whole list:   13  22  39  42  47  53  64  / (67) 84  /  75
Look at the front two:
Move smaller to whole list:   13  22  39  42  47  53  64  67  /  84  / (75)
Look at the front two:
Move smaller to whole list:   13  22  39  42  47  53  64  67  75  /  84  /
One halflist is now empty, so
Move rest of other halflist:  13  22  39  42  47  53  64  67  75  84  /  /
```

*Each of the two halflists of 5 numbers is sorted by a (recursive) call of Merge Sort. The sequence of actions for the first halflist is:

```
Given 5 unsorted numbers:     67  42  84  13  53
Split into two halflists:     /  67  42  84  /  13  53
Sort each halflist:           /  42  67  84  / (13) 53
Look at the front two:
Move smaller to whole list:   13  / (42) 67  84  /  53
Look at the front two:
Move smaller to whole list:   13  42  /  67  84  / (53)
Look at the front two:
Move smaller to whole list:   13  42  53  /  67  84  /
One halflist is now empty, so
Move rest of other halflist:  13  42  53  67  84  /  /
```

FIGURE 2. Merge Sort for 10 numbers.

EXAMPLE 6.5A _____

```
PROCEDURE Sort (VAR Data : List);
    (* Algorithm: Merge Sort *)
    (* Context:   client of ListADT with Dequeue, Enqueue,
                  Peep, IsEmpty, and SizeOf *)
  (*-------------------------------------------------------*)

    PROCEDURE MergeSort (VAR Data: List;  Total: CARDINAL);
    VAR
        AList, BList : List;
        Half, K      : CARDINAL;
        AInfo, BInfo : Information;
    BEGIN

    (* split Data into two lists of equal size *)
        Half := Total - (Total DIV 2);
        Create (AList);
        FOR K := 1 TO Half DO
            Dequeue (AInfo, Data);
            Enqueue (AInfo, AList);
        END;
        BList := Data;
        Create (Data);

    (* sort each of the two lists *)
        IF Half >= 2 THEN
            MergeSort (AList, Half);
            IF Total >= 4 THEN
                MergeSort (BList, Total - Half);
            END;
        END;

    (* combine AList and BList to form the sorted Data *)
        Peep (AInfo, AList);
        Peep (BInfo, BList);
        FOR K := 1 TO Total DO
            IF IsEmpty (BList) OR (NOT IsEmpty (AList) AND
                          (Compare (AInfo, BInfo) < 0)) THEN
                Dequeue (AInfo, AList);
                Enqueue (AInfo, Data);
                Peep (AInfo, AList);
            ELSE
                Dequeue (BInfo, BList);
                Enqueue (BInfo, Data);
                Peep (BInfo, BList);
            END;
        END;
        Destroy (AList);
        Destroy (BList);

    END MergeSort;
  (*-------------------------------------------------------*)

BEGIN           (* Sort *)
    MergeSort (Data, SizeOf (Data));
END Sort;
```

415

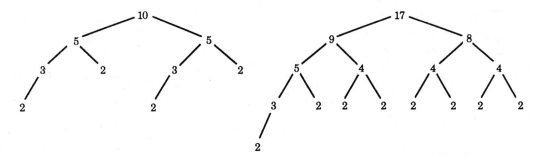

FIGURE 3. Tree of recursive calls in Merge Sort for 10 and 17 items.

the Merge Sort algorithm is lg(N), and the total number of comparisons made on each level is less than N. Thus the Merge Sort is big-oh of N∗lg(N), the best possible result.

A Linked List Implementation of the Merge Sort

Consider the Merge Sort as a utility procedure in the standard linked list implementation module for ListADT (Example 4.4A). It translates directly from Example 6.5A, except in the part where the two halflists are merged together. At that point, the loop can be made to execute faster when Data and the two halflists are all known to have at least one information value. This is true if you handle the first shift to Data before beginning the loop and you terminate that loop when one of the halflists becomes empty. This complicates the coding a little, but you have to expect that when you try to save execution time. The coding is in Example 6.5B. Note that the body of the Sort procedure checks that there are at least two items on the list before calling the MergeSort procedure. Note also that only link values are changed, never information values; linked implementations can save a large amount of time when information values require a large amount of space.

An Array Implementation of the Merge Sort

Consider the modifications that would have to be made in Example 6.5A to make it a utility procedure in the simple array implementation of ListADT (Example 3.6A). Remember that a List is declared as follows:

```
TYPE  List = POINTER TO CountedArray;
      CountedArray = RECORD
                          Item : ARRAY [1..MaxSize] OF Information;
                          Size : CARDINAL;
                      END;
```

If, for instance, the array has 17 items in it, the procedure makes its first recursive call to sort items 1..9 and its second recursive call to sort items 10..17, then merges the two halflists. That second call generates recursive calls for items 10..13 and items 14..17. So what changes on each call is just the indices of the range of values to be sorted. The easiest way to implement the procedure is to pass to the MergeSort subprocedure two cardinals Lo and Hi that tell the lowest and highest indices of the subrange of Information values to be sorted. The subprocedure is not to change any Information values outside the range Lo..Hi. So the formal parameter part of MergeSort is (Lo, Hi: CARDINAL) and the body of Sort is just a check that Data has at least two items followed by execution of MergeSort(1, Data ↑ .Size).

For the body of the MergeSort subprocedure, the logic is made clearer by using a local variable (call it Middle) to store the index of the halfway point. The body of MergeSort is roughly as follows:

```
Middle := (Lo + Hi) DIV 2;
MergeSort (Lo, Middle);
MergeSort (Middle + 1, Hi);
(* Coding to merge the two halves of the array *)
```

EXAMPLE 6.5B _____

```
PROCEDURE Sort (VAR Data : List);
    (* Algorithm: Merge Sort *)
    (* Context:   standard linked list ListADT utility *)
   (*--------------------------------------------------------------*)

    PROCEDURE MergeSort (VAR Data: List;  Total: CARDINAL);
    (*- - - - - - - - - - - - - - - - - - - - - - - -*)

        PROCEDURE ShiftSmaller (VAR LinkField, A, B: List);
            (* Shift node with smaller info to LinkField *)
        BEGIN
            IF Compare (A^.Info, B^.Info) < 0 THEN
                LinkField := A;
                A := A^.Link;
            ELSE
                LinkField := B;
                B := B^.Link;
            END;
        END ShiftSmaller;
    (*- - - - - - - - - - - - - - - - - - - - - - -*)

(* continued on next page *)
```

```
(* EXAMPLE 6.5B continued *)


    VAR
        Tail, AList, BList : Location;
        Half, K            : CARDINAL;

    BEGIN           (* MergeSort *)

    (* split Data into two lists of equal size *)
        Half := Total - (Total DIV 2);
        Tail := Data;
        FOR K := 2 TO Half DO
            Tail := Tail^.Link;
        END; (* Tail^ is now node number Half on Data *)
        BList := Tail^.Link;
        Tail^.Link := NIL;
        AList := Data;

    (* sort each of the two lists *)
        IF Half >= 2 THEN
            MergeSort (AList, Half);
            IF Total >= 4 THEN
                MergeSort (BList, Total - Half);
            END;
        END;

    (* combine two sorted lists to form the sorted Data *)
        ShiftSmaller (Data, AList, BList);
        Tail := Data;                   (* last node on Data *)
        WHILE (AList # NIL) AND (BList # NIL) DO
            ShiftSmaller (Tail^.Link, AList, BList);
            Tail := Tail^.Link;     (* last node on Data *)
        END;
        IF AList = NIL THEN
            Tail^.Link := BList;
        ELSE
            Tail^.Link := AList;
        END;

    END MergeSort;
  (*-------------------------------------------------------*)

VAR
    P     : Location;
    Count : CARDINAL;

BEGIN           (* Sort *)

    IF (Data # NIL) AND (Data^.Link # NIL) THEN
        P := Data^.Link^.Link;
        Count := 2;
        WHILE P # NIL DO
            P := P^.Link;
            INC (Count);
        END;
        MergeSort (Data, Count);
    END;
END Sort;
```

The logic for merging the two halves could be similar to the linked list implementation except for one problem: It seems impossible to move values around within the one array to get them in order. So you declare a local array variable into which the values can be copied. When you have them in order, you copy them back into the Data array. This coding is in Example 6.5C.

The use of the second array doubles the amount of space required for sorting, compared with the elementary sorts in Sections 6.1 and 6.2. That can still be too much for some applications. This is the primary disadvantage of the Merge Sort algorithm in array implementations. It also takes a good deal of time to copy information between arrays, but that can be avoided (at the cost of additional programming effort) by something along the following lines: Let recursive calls continue until the number of items to be sorted is less than 20 and the number of recursion levels is *even*. Sort the remaining values using the Insertion Sort (a very fast sort when there are so few items to sort). The merges at the deepest level of recursion take place from Item to HelperArray; at the next-deepest level, merge from HelperArray to Item; and so forth. When all recursion is terminated, the values will be in Item, where they should be.

Check Your Understanding

1. Assume that you do a Merge Sort for a list of 32 items. (a) How many times does Example 6.5B execute X := X ↑ .Link (for any X) outside the putting-together part of the procedure? (b) How many times, at most, inside that part? (c) Answer the first question for 2 to any positive power N.

2. In the middle part of Example 6.5A (the recursive part), the inner IF statement could be placed after the outer IF statement instead of within it. That would only slow down execution a little. Study Figure 3 and compute how many extra tests of Total>=4 are saved by keeping one IF statement within the other.

3. Rewrite Example 6.5C to call a procedure named InsertionSort whenever there are fewer than 20 values to sort.

4. (NA) The procedure in Example 6.5B checks that the given list has at least two information values before it calls the MergeSort subprocedure; the procedure in Example 6.5A does not. Explain the discrepancy.

5. (NA) Rewrite Example 6.5A so that it does not first count the number of information values on the entire list. Discuss how much more time your coding takes as opposed to that given in Example 6.5A.

6. (NA) Show that all three forms of the Merge Sort in the examples are stable sorting algorithms.

EXAMPLE 6.5C _____

```
PROCEDURE Sort (VAR Data : List);
    (* Algorithm: Merge Sort *)
    (* Context:   simple array impl. ListADT utility *)
VAR
    HelperArray      : ARRAY [1..MaxSize] OF Information;
    AList, BList, K : CARDINAL;
  (*---------------------------------------------------------*)

    PROCEDURE MergeSort (Lo, Hi: CARDINAL);
        (* Sort Item [Lo]..Item [Hi] in the Data array *)
    VAR
        Middle : CARDINAL;
    BEGIN
        WITH Data^ DO

        (* split into lists of equal size and sort them *)
            Middle := (Hi + Lo) DIV 2;
            IF Middle > Lo THEN
                MergeSort (Lo, Middle);
                IF Hi > Middle + 1 THEN
                    MergeSort (Middle + 1, Hi);
                END;
            END;

        (* combine two sorted lists in the HelperArray *)
            AList := Lo;
            BList := Middle + 1;
            FOR K := Lo TO Hi DO
                IF (BList > Hi) OR ((AList <= Middle) AND
                        (Compare (Item [AList],
                                    Item [BList]) < 0)) THEN
                    HelperArray [K] := Item [AList];
                    INC (AList);
                ELSE
                    HelperArray [K] := Item [BList];
                    INC (BList);
                END;
            END;

        (* copy the values back into the original array *)
            FOR K := Lo TO Hi DO
                Item [K] := HelperArray [K];
            END;

        END;
    END MergeSort;
  (*---------------------------------------------------------*)

BEGIN          (* Sort *)
    IF Data^.Size >= 2 THEN
        MergeSort (1, Data^.Size);
    END;
END Sort;
```

7. (NA) Revise Example 6.5A so that the MergeSort subprocedure does not use BList. Instead, let Data be the second part of the list, a parameter for the second recursive call of MergeSort.

8. (NA) Rewrite the merging-together logic in Example 6.5C to execute faster, as follows: Use a WHILE statement that executes until one list is empty, then put the rest of the other list where it goes in Data ↑ .Item.

9. (NA) Rewrite Example 6.5A along the lines indicated by the previous exercise.

10. (NA) The Merge Sort for an array can be written using FOR statements without recursion. Do so for the case when the number of items to be sorted is a power of 2.

11. (NA) The trees in Figure 3 lend credence to the hypothesis that the tree of recursive calls for any number of items N over 1 is perfectly balanced (left subtree of each node has either the same number or 1 more node than its right subtree) with $N-1$ nodes. Determine whether this is true and prove your conclusion.

6.6 THE QUICKSORT

The Quicksort algorithm for the standard linked list implementation is similar to the Tree Sort algorithm, but the Quicksort only requires one pointer variable in each node instead of two. However, you cannot sort incrementally, that is, in such a way that you sort each item into the structure before you go on to the next item. Incremental sorting was done with the Insertion Sort and the Tree Sort. The Quicksort procedures here require that you have the entire list available before you start sorting, as with the Selection Sort and Merge Sort.

Overall Logic of Quicksort

Quicksort, like Merge Sort, is a divide-and-conquer algorithm. After a check to be sure that there are at least two items on the list (since otherwise the list is already sorted), Quicksort has three main steps, illustrated in Figure 4:

1. Create two lists; call them AList and BList. All information values other than the first one (called Pivot) are to go on one of these two lists. All values that are less than the Pivot go on the AList; all values that are greater than or equal to the Pivot go on the BList.

2. Sort the AList and also the BList, using Quicksort.

3. Join the AList to the BList with the Pivot in the middle.

Given 10 unsorted numbers: 67 42 84 13 53 22 39 75 47 64
Split with 67 as the pivot: 67 / 42 13 53 22 39 47 64 / 84 75
Sort each halflist*:   67 / 13 22 39 42 47 53 64 / 75 84
Hook 67 in the middle: 13 22 39 42 47 53 64 ⓺⓻ 75 84

*Each of the two halflists (7 and 2 numbers, respectively) is sorted by a (recursive) call of Quicksort. The sequence of actions for the first halflist (with 7 numbers) is as follows:

Given 7 unsorted numbers: 42 13 53 22 39 47 64
Split with 42 as the pivot: 42 / 13 22 39 / 53 47 64
Sort each halflist: 42 / 13 22 39 / 47 53 64
Hook 42 in the middle: 13 22 39 ㊷ 47 53 64

FIGURE 4. Quicksort for 10 numbers.

The logic here can be compared with that of the Merge Sort. Both logics divide the list into two parts. The criterion for the Merge Sort is that the two sublists should be the same length (or off by 1 if necessary); the criterion for the Quicksort is a comparison with the Pivot information. Consequently, the division step is more complex for the Quicksort than for the Merge Sort. The fact that Quicksort sets the Pivot aside from both sublists should not obscure the overall similarity; there are even some variations of Quicksort that do not do this.

Sorting the two sublists is a simple matter of two recursive procedure calls for both the Merge Sort and the Quicksort. Putting the two sorted lists back together is much easier for the Quicksort, since the crucial work has already been done in the first step—the criterion for the division into two lists was chosen so that no comparisons need be made in putting the lists back together.

It is easy to hook the Pivot to the rear of the AList. If the Join utility is available in ListADT, it can be used to hook the BList to the rear of the new AList. The coding using imports from ListADT is given in Example 6.6A. To clarify the logic, I assume that ListADT has the utility procedures Enqueue, Dequeue (taking from the front of the list), and Join (Join attaches one list to the end of another list).

It is essential to verify each use of recursion to make sure that it is self-terminating. The recursive calls of Sort in the body of Sort are each made with only a part of the list with which the procedure was called. Neither list contains the Pivot, so even if one of AList and BList is empty, the other contains one less information value. Thus additional recursive calls reduce the number of information values in the list. The QuickSort procedure is guarded by IF statements that prevent further recursive calls when the given list has less than two information values, so recursion terminates when the given list becomes small enough.

EXAMPLE 6.6A _____

```
PROCEDURE Sort (VAR Data : List);
    (* Algorithm: QuickSort *)
    (* Context:   client of ListADT with Join, Dequeue,
                  Enqueue, and IsEmpty *)
  (*-------------------------------------------------------*)

    PROCEDURE QuickSort (VAR Data    : List;
                             PivotInfo : Information);
    VAR
        AList, BList : List;
        TheInfo      : Information;

    BEGIN

    (* split Data into two roughly equal sublists *)
        Create (AList);
        Create (BList);
        REPEAT
            Dequeue (TheInfo, Data);
            IF Compare (TheInfo, PivotInfo) < 0 THEN
                Enqueue (TheInfo, AList);
            ELSE
                Enqueue (TheInfo, BList);
            END;
        UNTIL IsEmpty (Data);

    (* sort each of the two lists *)
        Sort (AList);
        Sort (BList);

    (* combine AList/PivotInfo/BList to form sorted Data *)
        Destroy (Data);
        Data := AList;
        Enqueue (PivotInfo, Data);
        Join (Data, BList);

    END QuickSort;
  (*-------------------------------------------------------*)

VAR
    PivotInfo : Information;

BEGIN          (* Sort *)
    IF NOT IsEmpty (Data) THEN
        Dequeue (PivotInfo, Data);
        IF IsEmpty (Data) THEN
            Enqueue (PivotInfo, Data);
        ELSE
            QuickSort (Data, PivotInfo);
        END;
    END;
END Sort;
```

Linked List Implementation of Quicksort

The standard linked list implementation of Quicksort parallels Example 6.6A fairly directly. The primary difference is that direct access to the implementation makes it easy to check that Data has at least two information values before trying to sort it (since otherwise it is already sorted). Thus it is not necessary to dequeue a value and then, if the list is empty, immediately put it back. Example 6.6B displays the coding that results from modifying Example 6.6A. In the process of making the conversion, it turned out to be more advantageous to push values onto the sublists rather than enqueue them. It also turned out to be easy to have the Quicksort subprocedure call itself directly after checking that the sublists have at least two items.

The defect of the Quicksort is that the pivot value could be the largest or the smallest value on the list. In that case, one of the two sublists is empty and the next recursive call is made with only one less information value than the current one. If this happens each time, as it will if the list is already sorted in either order, what we have is a very slow form of Insertion Sort. The Tree Sort has the same defect, of course. Moreover, the number of recursive calls in such a worst-case situation is approximately equal to the number of information values on the list, which is quite wasteful of memory. By contrast, the worst-case behavior of the Merge Sort is $N*lg(N)$, just as is the average-case behavior of both Quicksort and Merge Sort.

In practice, the Quicksort algorithm is one of the fastest known methods of sorting values in an array when nothing helpful is known about their distribution, as far as how it works on the average. The Merge Sort is one of the fastest known methods for linked lists when nothing helpful is known about the distribution of information values. It can be proven mathematically that the average case for Quicksort takes only about 39% longer to execute than the best possible case (which is when the pivot is the middle value in every case). There are several variations that can be made in the details of the algorithm. Most variations are attempts to find a pivot value that is close to the middle.

Finding the Kth Smallest Item on a List

Some applications require you to find the median of a list of values. The **median** is the value for which half the other values are smaller and half the other values are larger. Of course, if you have an even number of values on the list, one of the halves has to be 1 smaller than the other. This problem is a particular instance of the more general problem of finding the seventh smallest or hundredth smallest or whatever item on the list.

The Quicksort can be easily modified to solve the problem of finding the Kth smallest item on the list for any K. The overall procedure is to choose a pivot value and split the list in two parts as usual. Count the number of items on the

EXAMPLE 6.6B _____

```
PROCEDURE Sort (VAR Data : List);
    (* Algorithm: QuickSort *)
    (* Context:   standard linked list ListADT utility *)
 (*----------------------------------------------------*)

    PROCEDURE QuickSort (VAR Data : List);
    VAR
        AList, BList, Spot, Saved : List;
    BEGIN

    (* split data into two roughly equal sublists *)
        AList := NIL;
        BList := NIL;
        Spot := Data^.Link;  (* Data^ is the pivot node *)
        REPEAT
            Saved := Spot^.Link;
            IF Compare (Spot^.Info, Data^.Info) < 0 THEN
                Spot^.Link := AList;
                AList := Spot;
            ELSE
                Spot^.Link := BList;
                BList := Spot;
            END;
            Spot := Saved;
        UNTIL Spot = NIL;

    (* sort each of the two lists *)
        IF (AList # NIL) AND (AList^.Link # NIL) THEN
            QuickSort (AList);
        END;
        IF (BList # NIL) AND (BList^.Link # NIL) THEN
            QuickSort (BList);
        END;

    (* link sorted AList and BList to form sorted Data *)
        Data^.Link := BList;
        IF AList # NIL THEN
            Spot := AList;
            WHILE Spot^.Link # NIL DO
                Spot := Spot^.Link;
            END;
            Spot^.Link := Data;
            Data := AList;
        END;

    END QuickSort;
 (*----------------------------------------------------*)
BEGIN         (* Sort *)
    IF (Data # NIL) AND (Data^.Link # NIL) THEN
        QuickSort (Data);
    END;
END Sort;
```

425

list of values smaller than the pivot. There are three possible outcomes:

- [ ] If that count turns out to be K − 1, the pivot is the Kth smallest item.
- [ ] If that count is more than K − 1, you should look for the Kth smallest item on the list of values smaller than the pivot. You ignore the list of larger values for the rest of the algorithm.
- [ ] If that count is less than K − 1, subtract it from K − 1 to obtain a number J; then find the Jth smallest item on the list of values larger than the pivot. You ignore the list of smaller values for the rest of the algorithm.

This algorithm is similar to the one used to search a binary tree for the Kth item in the tree in inorder traversal, assuming that each node contains a count of 1 more than the number of nodes in its left subtree. The coding is left as an exercise.

Check Your Understanding

1. When does the Quicksort procedure in Example 6.6B execute faster—when the original list was sorted in increasing order, or when it was sorted in decreasing order? Assume that no two information values are equal (as determined by Compare).

2. What changes would you make in Example 6.6A so that the list comes out in decreasing order?

3. Example 6.6B can be easily revised for linked lists with header nodes. What changes would you make?

4. In Example 6.6B, some of the List variables local to Quicksort can be delocalized. Which ones? Why?

5. (NA) Write a logical argument to show that the coding for Quicksort in Example 6.6A is stable.

6. (NA) Rewrite Example 6.6A to find the Kth item on a given list, where K is passed as a value parameter to the procedure.

7. (NA) Rewrite Example 6.6A (adding much to its length) so the Quicksort subprocedure calls itself directly instead of calling Sort.

8. (NA) Rewrite Example 6.6B to find the Kth item on a given list, where K is passed as a value parameter to the procedure.

9. (NA) Rewrite Example 6.6B to make it a stable sort.

6.7 AN ARRAY IMPLEMENTATION OF QUICKSORT

This section develops Quicksort as a utility procedure for the simple array implementation of ListADT. The first step is to note that the algorithm applies to a sublist of a list, not to a whole list. The body of the Sort procedure will call its Quicksort subprocedure with two parameters that tell the lowest and highest indices of the information values to be sorted; the statement is Quicksort(1, Data ↑ .Size). The Quicksort subprocedure will check that there are at least two items to be sorted before it does anything.

Details of the Algorithm

As before, we choose the first information value as the pivot and separate the rest of the information into two sublists, those smaller than the pivot and those not. But now we have the problem of storing the sublists in a contiguous range of components. A straightforward method is to shift all the smaller values to the low part of the array and all the larger values to the high part of the array, then put the pivot between those two parts. Values that match the pivot can go in either sublist. Keep in mind that we want to avoid using a duplicate of the array for temporary storage, since that is wasteful of space. The algorithm is correspondingly more complex.

You can visualize the algorithm used as follows: Pick up the pivot value and set it aside. That leaves an empty space in the low part of the array, to which you could move a smaller value. So look through the high part of the array (starting from the highest index and coming down) until you find a value smaller than the pivot. Move that value to the empty space. That creates an empty space in the high part of the array, and all values above it are greater than the pivot.

Now look through the low part of the array, working upward from where you last put a smaller value. When you see a value higher than the pivot, move it to the empty space. That leaves the empty space in the low part of the array again, and all values below it are smaller than the pivot. Then look through the high part of the array, working downward from where you last put a larger value. When you see a value lower than the pivot, move it to the empty space. That leaves the empty space in the high part of the array, and all values above it are larger than the pivot.

Repeat the preceding paragraph until you have the empty space placed so that all smaller values are below the empty space and all larger values are above it. That empty space is where the pivot goes. Put it there. Then you can sort the part below the pivot and the part above the pivot separately. Then you are done.

When you find a value that matches the pivot, you could put it on either list. In the linked list implementation, you always moved it to the right-hand list. In this second algorithm, it is a little faster to leave a matching information value in whichever sublist you find it in.

EXAMPLE 6.7A _____

```
PROCEDURE Sort (VAR Data : List);
    (* Algorithm: QuickSort *)
    (* Context:    simple array impl. of ListADT *)
VAR
    Pivot : Information;
  (*---------------------------------------------------------*)

    PROCEDURE FindSpotWherePivotGoes (Low, High : CARDINAL;
                                      VAR Spot : CARDINAL);
    VAR
        LowComponentIsEmpty : BOOLEAN;
    BEGIN
        WITH Data^ DO  (* only relevant field is Item *)
            LowComponentIsEmpty := TRUE;
            REPEAT
                IF LowComponentIsEmpty AND
                   (Compare (Item [High], Pivot) >= 0) THEN
                    DEC (High);
                ELSIF LowComponentIsEmpty THEN
                    Item [Low] := Item [High];
                    INC (Low);
                    LowComponentIsEmpty := FALSE;
                ELSIF Compare (Item [Low], Pivot) <= 0 THEN
                    INC (Low);
                ELSE
                    Item [High] := Item [Low];
                    DEC (High);
                    LowComponentIsEmpty := TRUE;
                END;
            UNTIL High = Low;
            Spot := Low;
        END;
    END FindSpotWherePivotGoes;
  (*---------------------------------------------------------*)

    PROCEDURE Quicksort (Lo, Hi : CARDINAL);
    VAR
        Spot : CARDINAL;
    BEGIN
        IF Lo < Hi THEN
            Pivot := Data^.Item [Lo];
            FindSpotWherePivotGoes (Lo, Hi, Spot);
            Data^.Item [Spot] := Pivot;
            Quicksort (Lo, Spot - 1);
            Quicksort (Spot + 1, Hi);
        END;
    END Quicksort;
  (*---------------------------------------------------------*)

BEGIN          (* Sort *)
    Quicksort (1, Data^.Size);
END Sort;
```

Given 10 unsorted numbers:		67	42	84	13	53	22	39	75	47	64
Set aside the pivot 67:	67	Lxx	42	84	13	53	22	39	75	47	H64
Move small number down:	67	64	L42	84	13	53	22	39	75	47	Hxx
No move, since small at L:	67	64	42	L84	13	53	22	39	75	47	Hxx
Move large number up:	67	64	42	Lxx	13	53	22	39	75	H47	84
Move small number down:	67	64	42	47	L13	53	22	39	75	Hxx	84
No move, since small at L:	67	64	42	47	13	L53	22	39	75	Hxx	84
No move, since small at L:	67	64	42	47	13	53	L22	39	75	Hxx	84
No move, since small at L:	67	64	42	47	13	53	22	L39	75	Hxx	84
No move, since small at L:	67	64	42	47	13	53	22	39	L75	Hxx	84
Move large number up:	67	64	42	47	13	53	22	39	LHxx	75	84
Put pivot at empty spot:		64	42	47	13	53	22	39	67	75	84

Then call Quicksort (Data, 1, 7) and Quicksort (Data, 9, 10)

FIGURE 5. *Trace of Example 6.7A as it partitions 10 numbers in an array. L marks Item[Low]; H marks Item[High]; xx marks the "empty" spot.*

The procedure in Example 6.7A is the coding for this algorithm, and Figure 5 traces the action. We use a Boolean value to keep track of whether the empty space is in the low part or the high part of the array. This allows us to have just one loop instead of nested loops, which should make the logic clearer to the reader. Inside this loop, you take one of four actions depending first on the Boolean value and second on a comparison with the pivot value.

⮕ PROGRAMMING STYLE

Example 6.7A illustrates the use of a four-alternative IF statement instead of nested IF statements. Some people think that it is clearer and more natural to write the body of the REPEAT statement using IF LowComponentIsEmpty THEN... ELSE... END, with IF statements inside; I don't, even though it would execute a bit faster.

It is possible to write the REPEAT statement more compactly, using repetition statements within the REPEAT. This would execute a bit slower than the coding given; changing the REPEAT statement to a LOOP statement would make it execute a bit faster. Any of these alternatives would only make a negligible difference in the speed of execution.

The linked list implementation of Quicksort can be made stable without too much trouble, but the array implementation cannot be without heavy revision of the logic. By contrast, both implementations of the Merge Sort given in Section 6.5 are stable sorting methods.

Both the array and the linked list implementations of Quicksort can profit from using the Insertion Sort when the number of items to be sorted becomes small; under 20 is a reasonable criterion. This can be done more efficiently with Quicksort than with Merge Sort. The easiest way is simply to refuse to sort any sublist with less than 20 items until the algorithm terminates, then execute the Insertion Sort for the entire list.

Check Your Understanding

1. What changes would you make in Example 6.7A so that you never call a procedure only to return immediately because you find that you have less than two items to sort?

2. Revise the Quicksort procedure in Example 6.7A so that you always choose the value in the middle of the array as the pivot value.

3. Replace the REPEAT statement in Example 6.7A by a FOR statement.

4. In the first recursive call of Quicksort in Example 6.7A, replacing "Spot−1" by "Spot" merely slows execution speed slightly; recursion must eventually terminate. Show that this is true.

5. (NA) In the second recursive call of Quicksort in Example 6.7A, replacing "Spot+1" by "Spot" could cause recursion to never terminate. Show that this is true.

6. (NA) Rewrite the FindSpotWherePivotGoes procedure of Example 6.7A using looping statements within looping statements. The bodies of the inner loops should be one statement each: DEC(High) and INC(Low), respectively.

7. (NA) Some people think that, if the second use of Compare in Example 6.7A had < rather than <=, the Quicksort would be a stable algorithm. Show that this is not true.

8. (NA) Rewrite Example 6.7A to find the Kth smallest item on a given list, where K is passed as a value parameter to the procedure.

6.8 THE SHELL AND RADIX SORTS

This section describes two more sorting algorithms that are often used. The Shell Sort is named after its inventor, D. L. Shell. The Radix Sort was the basis of sorting machines used years ago in data processing.

The Shell Sort

Assume that a utility procedure in an array implementation of ListADT is given an array of 60 items to sort. The following algorithm will accomplish this task: Consider the array to be divided into 4 overlapping sublists of 15 items each. List

The following list of 20 numbers is split into 4 sublists:
a indicates the first sublist, b the second, c the third, d the fourth:

a	b	c	d	a	b	c	d	a	b	c	d	a	b	c	d	a	b	c	d
21	48	69	37	54	17	49	62	35	27	42	65	64	25	23	45	31	39	58	51

Sort each of the 4 sublists using the Insertion Sort. For example, sorting sublist a
(21   54   35   64   31) yields (21   31   35   54   64).

a	b	c	d	a	b	c	d	a	b	c	d	a	b	c	d	a	b	c	d
21	17	23	37	31	25	42	45	35	27	49	51	54	39	58	62	64	48	69	65

Now sort the whole list using the Insertion Sort.

FIGURE 6. The Shell Sort using 4 sublists of 5 numbers each.

1 consists of the values in components 1, 5, 9,..., 57; List 2 is in components 2, 6,..., 58; List 3 is in components 3, 7,..., 59; and List 4 is in components 4, 8,..., 60 (indices go by fours). Sort List 1 using the Insertion Sort, leaving the values in components 1, 5, 9,..., 57 (but rearranged). Sort each of Lists 2, 3, and 4 similarly. Finally, sort the entire list of 60 items using an Insertion Sort. Figure 6 shows this logic applied to 4 sublists of 5 items each (since 4 sublists of 15 is a bit much for an illustration).

This sorting method obviously works correctly, because the last step is to use the Insertion Sort on the entire array; whatever happened before that point, the final Insertion Sort will take care of it. The surprising thing is that all the preliminaries make it so that the final Insertion Sort has so little to do that the overall time is much less than if you had done a simple Insertion Sort in the first place.

For a larger number of items to sort, such as when Size is several hundred, we might first divide the list into 40 sublists and sort each one (using the Insertion Sort and leaving the items in the same components but rearranged). The first list would be in components numbered 1, 41, 81,...; the second would be in components 2, 42, 82,...; the last one would be in components 40, 80, 120,.... Then we divide the list into 13 sublists and sort each one: 1, 14, 27,...; 2, 15, 28,.... Then we divide the list into 4 sublists and sort each one. Finally, we sort the whole array. This algorithm can be expressed more precisely as:

1. Set Increment = 40;
2. Do the following repeatedly until time to stop:
    2.a. For each number X from 1 to Increment, do the following:
            Use Insertion Sort on components X, X + Increment,
            X + 2 * Increment, X + 3 * Increment,...;
    2.b. STOP if Increment = 1;
    2.c. Subtract 1 from Increment and then divide it by 3.

The general pattern of this choice of increments is 1, 4, 13, 40, 121, 364,...; that is, each one after 1 is obtained by tripling the one before and adding 1. The addition of 1 each time assures that the sublists on one iteration overlap those on the second iteration, which intermixes the sublists. This pattern has been recommended by Donald Knuth, an authority on sorting methods. The increment you use first should give 3 to 10 items on each sublist; in the first example with 60 items, execution time would be better if you first used 13 sublists and then used 4 sublists. The coding of the Shell Sort is left as an exercise.

Why Is the Shell Sort a Good Sort?

The Shell Sort ends with a full Insertion Sort, which executes in $O(N^2)$ sort. So it seems as though the Shell Sort would be even worse. However, the Insertion Sort is $O(N^2)$ because it has a loop within a loop, and the statement sequence of that inner loop executes about Index/2 times when the number of items already sorted is Index-1, if the items are in random order. That is, the average position of a randomly chosen item in an already sorted list is in the middle.

Assume that the list is "nearly" sorted. More concretely, assume that each item is only 5 positions out of order on the average. Then the inner loop executes an average of 5 times, so the sort executes in $O(5*N)$ time, which is the same as $O(N)$ time owing to the proportionality factor. In other words, the Insertion Sort is faster than the Quicksort or Merge Sort in such cases.

The philosophy behind the Shell Sort is that it works quickly in the beginning because the sublists are small, and it works quickly toward the end of the algorithm because the sublists are nearly sorted. Mathematical analysis indicates that this choice of increments makes the Shell Sort execute in $O(N*lg(N)*lg(N))$ time for random lists of information.

The Radix Sort

Years ago, a popular machine in institutions that had to do a lot of sorting was a mechanical sorter. This machine accepts as input a number of punched cards, one card per information value. A numeric ID for the information is punched in certain columns on the cards; for instance, the ID may be a 4-digit number punched in columns 77, 78, 79, and 80. The machine has an input hopper where cards to be sorted are piled, and 10 output hoppers into which the cards are distributed as they are processed. The output hoppers are numbered from 0 to 9. The method of operation for this machine is to do the following once for each of columns 80, 79, 78, and 77, in that order:

Algorithm for running a Radix Sort machine
  1. Put the pile of cards to be sorted in the input hopper;
  2. Push buttons to set the specified column number;
  3. Push the GO button;

4. Wait while the machine puts all the cards with a 0 in the specified column in bin 0, all the cards with 1 in bin 1,..., all the cards with 9 in bin 9;

5. Take the cards out of the 10 output hoppers and put them in a pile, being *very careful* to put the ones from the 0 bin on the bottom, the ones from the 1 bin on top of those,..., the ones from the 9 bin on the top.

The machine takes one card at a time from the bottom of the input hopper and drops it in one of the 10 bins, on top of the pile that is already in that bin. After the first run, bin 3 contains all IDs whose last digit (column 80) is 3; similarly for the other bins. On the second run, sorting is done on the tens digit (column 79) of the ID, so bin 3 (for example) contains all IDs whose tens digit is 3. Thus all IDs ending in 30 are on the bottom of bin 3, all IDs ending in 31 are just above those, all IDs ending in 32 are just above those, and so on. The third run puts all IDs whose hundreds digit is 3 in bin 3; owing to the previous two runs, the cards in bin 3 are now in the order 300, 301, 302,..., 398, 399. The fourth run sorts on the thousands digit while keeping the ordering on the last three digits, so the cards are completely sorted by ID.

This algorithm is called the **Radix Sort** with a radix of 10. If you are sorting names, you can use a radix of 27 (26 letters plus a blank; the blank is used as a filler for short names). Note that the input hopper and the output hoppers are queues, so you can use imports from QueueADT (Fig. 7). The standard linked list implementation is much better for this algorithm than is an array implementation. You can use an array of 10 queues (or 27 queues or whatever) in place of the bins, and one large queue for the input hopper. Thus you could declare VAR InputHopper: Queue; Bin: ARRAY [0..9] OF Queue. This algorithm is also called a **Bin Sort**.

It is reasonable to have a Key function exported from InfoADT that returns the ID (also known as the **key**) for a given information value. If you write a Digit

The original list (the same one used for Figure 6):

21 48 69 37   54 17 49 62   35 27 42 65   64 25 23 45   31 39 58 51

Working left to right, put each number in the queue for its second digit:

0	1	2	3	4	5	6	7	8	9
–	21 31 51	62 42	23	54 64	35 65 25 45	–	37 17 27	48 58	69 49 39

Working left to right, put each number in the queue for its first digit:

0	1	2	3	4	5	6	7
–	17	21 23 25 27	31 35 37 39	42 45 48 49	51 54 58	62 64 65 59	–

FIGURE 7. The Radix Sort using 20 numbers.

function that returns the digit 0 to 9 of a given cardinal in a given decimal place (1, 2, 3, or 4, counting from the right), one pass of the machine (for Pass=1..4) can be coded as:

```
WHILE NOT IsEmpty (InputHopper) DO
    Dequeue (TheInfo, InputHopper);
    K := Digit (Pass, Key (TheInfo));
    Enqueue (TheInfo, Bin [K]);
END;
```

You can then put the bins together in the input hopper as follows:

```
FOR K := 0 TO 9 DO
    WHILE NOT IsEmpty (Bin [K]) DO
        Dequeue (TheInfo, Bin [K]);
        Enqueue (TheInfo, InputHopper);
    END;
END;
```

Put these two code segments inside a FOR statement that executes for Pass being 1, 2, 3, and 4, and you have the heart of the coding. In practice, of course, you would use the utility Join procedure for the second code segment.

Execution time for this sort is big-oh of N. This is better than for any other sort discussed so far. The reason is that we are using information about the nature of the IDs. If the only information we have about the relative ordering of information values is the Compare function, big-oh of N*lg(N) is the best result that is possible.

To see that this is a big-oh of N sort, note that there are four passes through the data, with each pass executing a series of actions once for each card. Thus the time required is c*N*4+d, where c is the number of seconds to process one card on a pass and d is the overhead.

Check Your Understanding

1. Write the Digit function described for the Radix Sort, with two CARDINAL parameters and a CARDINAL result.

2. Discuss the stability of the Radix Sort.

3. Show the two stages in a Radix Sort of 47, 16, 85, 13, 43, 49, 61.

4. (NA) Discuss the stability of the Shell Sort.

5. (NA) Complete the coding for the Radix Sort for use in a module that imports from QueueADT. The procedure is to sort a given Queue. Assume that the Digit and Key functions are available.

6. (NA) Assume that you perform a Shell Sort on a list of 13 items that are already in increasing order, and that you use an increment of 3 followed by an increment of 1. List all pairs of indices of components whose values are compared during the sort, in the order in which the comparisons are made.

7. (NA) Write the coding for the Shell sort as described in the text.

6.9 THE HEAP SORT

An almost-complete binary tree is what remains after removing from a complete binary tree a number of nodes on the bottom level, working from right to left. For instance, consider the complete binary tree of 15 nodes; it has 4 levels, with 8 nodes on the bottom level. Number the nodes as shown on the left of Figure 8. To obtain the almost-complete binary tree of 14 nodes, you must remove the one numbered 15. To obtain the almost-complete binary tree of 11 nodes, you must remove the four numbered 12, 13, 14, and 15. To obtain the almost-complete binary tree of 7 nodes, you must remove the entire bottom level. In particular, every *complete* binary tree is an *almost-complete* binary tree. There is one and only one almost-complete binary tree for any given number of nodes. A complete binary tree can be defined as an almost-complete binary tree for which the number of nodes is 1 less than a power of 2.

A **heap** is an almost-complete binary tree with a restriction, namely, for any information value X in the tree, X is the smallest value in the subtree for which it is the root; that is, all values in the left and right subtrees of X are greater than or equal to X. This section presents some procedures for working with heaps and gives an application of heaps to sorting. The right side of Figure 8 illustrates a

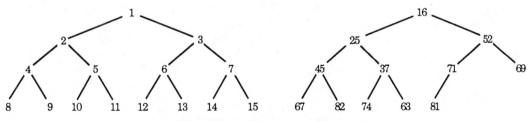

FIGURE 8. A complete tree and a heap.

heap; the numbers represent the IDs of the information values. *Note:* Some applications of heaps require that each information value be the *largest* in its subtree. In such a case, the results of this section apply mutatis mutandis.

Adding to a Heap

The context of this discussion is a module that imports from BinADT. This client module is to contain at least the two primary procedures for working with heaps: AddToHeap and DeleteMin. **AddToHeap** inserts one information value in a heap and then adjusts it so it remains a heap. **DeleteMin** removes the smallest information value from a heap and then adjusts it so it remains a heap. At any given time, the number of nodes in the tree is known. This number is used to keep the heap almost-complete.

The AddToHeap procedure has three parameters, one of type Information, one of type BinTree, and the third a cardinal variable that tells how many nodes are in the heap. AddToHeap adds one information value to the tree in such a way that it remains a heap if it was previously a heap and adds 1 to the Count accordingly. The basic idea is that the place where the new node is to go can be computed from the number of nodes in the heap. There is only one path from the root to that new node.

Visualize the algorithm this way: Pick up the information to be inserted. Follow the path determined by the Count. At each node you encounter, swap the information you are carrying for the information at that node if it is larger than the information you are carrying. When you get to where you are going, create a new node there and put in it the information you are carrying. Note that execution time for this procedure is big-oh of $\lg(N)$, since the number of levels is $\lg(N+1)$. Therefore, the entire heap for N values can be constructed in time big-oh of $N * \lg(N)$.

The hardest part of developing this algorithm is to calculate, for a given Count, what path you take through the tree to get to the node with that number. You should take some time studying Figure 8 to see if you can see what the algorithm is. It depends on the power of 2 just above Count; but the actual coding (Example 6.9A) is simplified by passing one fourth of that power as a parameter.

You have to spend quite a while staring at the complete binary tree in Figure 8 before you can figure out how you compute recursively where a node goes from the Count. The following explanation and example will take 5 to 10 minutes of thought to understand; if you want, you can skip to the next subsection. This algorithm clearly illustrates that, when you want speed without using excess space, you have to invest a large amount of programmer effort.

To add to an almost-complete 4-level tree in one of the positions numbered 8 to 15, the key number is 4 [one-fourth of $\lg(N+1)$]. You go left if Count is less than 12 (which is 3 times the key number) and you go right otherwise. Whichever way you go, you are in an almost-complete 3-level subtree and you want to insert at one of the positions that would be numbered 4 to 7 in that 3-level subtree. If

EXAMPLE 6.9A _____

```
PROCEDURE AddToHeap (TheInfo  : Information;
                     VAR Count : CARDINAL;
                     VAR Data  : BinTree);
   (* Insert TheInfo in the heap Data of size Count in
      such a way that it remains a heap; increment Count *)
   (* Context:  client of BinADT *)
VAR
    WhatsThere : Information;
   (*-----------------------------------------------------*)

    PROCEDURE PutInSubtree (Parent        : Location;
                            Power, Count  : CARDINAL);
       (* Put a new node at position number Count in the
          subheap of Data whose root is Parent.  Power is
          half of the position number of the first node on
          the bottom level of this subheap. *)
    BEGIN

        See (WhatsThere, Parent, Data);
        IF Compare (TheInfo, WhatsThere) < 0 THEN
            Swap (TheInfo, Parent, Data);
        END;
        IF Count = 2 THEN
            PutLeft (TheInfo, Parent, Data);
        ELSIF Count = 3 THEN
            PutRight (TheInfo, Parent, Data);
        ELSIF Count >= 3 * Power THEN          (* go right *)
            PutInSubtree (Right (Parent, Data),
                          Power DIV 2, Count - 2 * Power);
        ELSE                                   (* go left *)
            PutInSubtree (Left (Parent, Data),
                          Power DIV 2, Count - Power);
        END;

    END PutInSubtree;
   (*-----------------------------------------------------*)
VAR
    Power : CARDINAL;

BEGIN          (* AddToHeap *)

    INC (Count);
    IF Count = 1 THEN
        PutRoot (TheInfo, Data);
    ELSE
        Power := 1;
        WHILE Count >= 4 * Power DO
            Power := 2 * Power;
        END;    (*  now 2 * Power <= Count < 4 * Power  *)
                (*  example: Power=4 if Count is 8..15   *)
        PutInSubtree (Root (Data), Power, Count);
    END;

END AddToHeap;
```

Count is 8 to 11, you subtract 4 (the key number) from Count; if it is 12 to 15, you subtract 8 (twice the key); either way, you change Count to be in the range from 4 to 7.

Now Count is 4 to 7 and the key number is 2 (half of what it was before). You go left if Count is less than 6 (3 times the key), and you go right otherwise. Whichever way you go, you are in an almost-complete 2-level subtree and you want to insert at one of the positions that would be numbered 2 or 3 in that subtree. If Count is 4 or 5, subtract 2 (the key) from Count; if it is 6 or 7, subtract 4 (twice the key); either way, Count is 2 or 3, which tells you whether you are to insert as the left or right child of the node. Study Example 6.9A and try it out with a few numbers to see how it works.

SAMPLE RUN. Assume that you want to insert the number 30 in the heap in Figure 8. Count is 12, so the procedure changes Count to 13 and computes Power as 4 (since $2 \ast 4 <= 13 < 4 \ast 4$). PutInSubtree is called, passing the root of the tree and assigning 13 to Count:

1. Check to see if Parent contains a larger value than TheInfo; if it does, swap it for TheInfo. In this case, you do not swap 16 for 30.
2. You see that Count $>= 3 \ast 4$, so you call PutInSubtree again, changing Power to 2, Count to 5, and passing Right(Parent) as the new parent. Count=5 indicates you want to go to position number 5 in an almost-complete 3-level binary tree of which Parent is the root.
3. Check to see if Parent contains a larger value than TheInfo; if it does, you swap it for TheInfo. In this case, swap 52 for 30.
4. You see that Count $< 3 \ast 2$, so you call PutInSubtree again, changing Power to 1, Count to 3, and passing Left(Parent) as the new parent (this is at position number 6 in the original almost-complete 4-level tree). Count=3 indicates you want to go to position number 3 in an almost-complete 2-level tree of which Parent is the root.
5. Check to see if Parent contains a larger value than TheInfo; if it does, you swap it for TheInfo. In this case, swap 71 for 52.
6. You see that Count is 3, so you insert TheInfo as the new right child of Parent. Thus 71 ends up in position number 13.

The DeleteMin Procedure

Deleting the minimum is easy: Just take the value at the root. That works because each information value is less than or equal to each value in either of its subtrees. Next, you remove the node on the bottom level whose position number is the number of nodes currently in the tree. However, now the tree has a node with no information (at the root) and an information value with no node (from the removed leaf). The difficulty comes in shifting the information values around to maintain the heap property.

As a first approximation, consider this algorithm: There is only one path from the root of the tree to the node that is to be deleted. Shift each information value on that path (other than at the root) up to the node above it on the path. That leaves you free to delete the leaf node without losing any information values in the tree.

The problem is that, when you move a value up to its parent node, it may be larger than the other child of that node. Then you do not have a heap any more. For example, assume that you call DeleteMin when the heap is as shown on the right in Figure 8. Then you remove 16, move the 52 to where the 16 was, move the 71 to where the 52 was, and move the 81 to where the 71 was. Unfortunately, the 52 is larger than the 25, and the 71 is larger than the 69.

When this happens, you make an adjustment in the tree by "sifting" the offending value further down in the tree. This adjustment has to be made twice for this example, once for 52 and once for 71. To adjust for the 52, you swap it for the 25 and compare it with both of its children. Since 52 is larger than both 45 and 37, swap it with 37 (since 37 is the smaller of 37 and 45) and compare the 52 with its children again. Since 52 is smaller than both 74 and 63, you have finished the adjustment for 52. To adjust for the 71, you swap it for the 69 and compare the 71 with its children. However, it has no children, so you have finished the adjustment for 71.

The overall logic for the DeleteMin procedure is to return the value at the root of the tree and then look at each other value along the path to the node to be deleted (the rightmost node on the bottom level). If a value X at which you look is smaller than its sibling, move X up and go down one level. Otherwise move the sibling up and compare X with the smaller of the sibling's former children. If X is smaller, put X where the sibling was, otherwise move the smaller of the sibling's former children up and compare X with the smaller of its former children. Repeat until you can put X in the tree (which may be when you get to where there are no more children). Execution time for each call of DeleteMin is big-oh of lg(N), so the overall time required to obtain the sorted list from the original heap is big-oh of N*lg(N). The coding for this procedure is more complex than the coding for AddToHeap; I leave it as a programming problem.

A priority queue (defined in Section 3.9) that has a large number of elements is often implemented as either a heap or a binary search tree, using the priority numbers for the ordering. Execution time for both the deletion and the insertion procedures for a heap implementation of a priority queue is big-oh of lg(N).

Sifting can be avoided by moving up the smaller of the two children of an "empty" node, regardless of whether that maintains an almost-complete binary tree. Execution time is greatly improved this way. The only time when this is not a good idea is when you use an array implementation of a heap and you want to store the values back into the array as they are sorted, to save space (described next).

Summary of Array Sorting

A Heap Sort is easily adapted to the standard array implementation of binary trees, described in Section 5.7. Remember that the root of the tree is in Item[1], the left child of Item[K] is in Item[2*K], and the right child of Item[K] is in Item[2*K+1]. The tree is an almost-complete binary tree, so it is stored in Item[1]... Item[N] without any unused components in that range.

Assume that, instead of printing the values as they are removed from the heap, you want to store them in the array in increasing order. This can be done without any significant additional use of space if you make two adjustments to the algorithms described in this section:

1. Change the logic to put the larger values higher in the heap, rather than the smaller ones. This means that the logic produces the values in decreasing order. You would of course also change the name of the DeleteMin procedure to DeleteMax.

2. Store the sorted values in the array as follows: When the heap is first built, it is in Item[1]... Item[N], where N is the number of values to be sorted. After the first deletion and adjusting of the heap, the heap is in Item[1]... Item[N−1], so you can store the deleted value (the largest of all the values) in Item[N]. After the second deletion and adjusting of the heap, the heap is in Item[1]... Item[N−2], so you can store the second deleted value (the second largest of all the values) in Item[N−1]. Keep doing this for all the deletions, and you end up with the values stored in increasing order in Item[1]... Item[N].

The Heap Sort has the best worst-case execution time for sorting using Compare, namely big-oh of N*lg(N). It also has the minimum space requirements possible, namely just a few variables in addition to the array of N values. However, of all the sorting methods you have seen in this book, it takes the most programming effort.

The following summary permits a direct comparison of five methods for sorting values in an array on the basis of these three criteria. The list is in order of execution time and also in order of programmer effort:

Algorithm	Effort	Space	Execution Time
Insertion Sort:	Low	Low	High—N-squared
Shell Sort:	Medium	Low	Med—perhaps $N*lg(N)*lg(N)$
Quicksort:	Medium	Low	Low on average—$N*lg(N)$ High worst-case—N-squared
Merge Sort:	Medium	High	Low—$N*lg(N)$
Heap Sort:	High	Low	Low—$N*lg(N)$

Check Your Understanding

1. What happens if AddToHeap is called several times when the binary tree initially contains two values, 17 at the root and 10 as its left child (and thus is not actually a heap)?

2. Each time PutInSubtree is called with Power $>= 2$, the 4-alternative IF causes evaluation of three conditions. Rewrite it to execute faster by only evaluating two conditions in such cases.

3. In Example 6.9A, once Swap is called in PutInSubtree, Swap will be called in all further recursive calls of PutInSubtree (except in the rare case of a tie). Add a subprocedure whose first statement is Swap(TheInfo, Parent, Data) and use it to increase execution speed.

4. (NA) Trace the action of AddToHeap when 20 is added to the heap in Figure 8, assuming that 30 has just been added (thus you are adding to a 13-node tree).

5. (NA) What happens if AddToHeap is called when the binary tree is a heap but the Count is too big?

6. (NA) Rewrite Example 6.9A without using recursion.

6.10 EXTERNAL SORTING

Some applications require you to sort so large a number of information values that the memory of the computer is not large enough to hold all the values at once. For instance, the memory may be able to hold 1000 information records at one time when there are tens or hundreds of thousands of records. This situation requires that you keep most of the values in external storage during the sorting procedure. By contrast, the methods presented earlier in this chapter discussed only internal sorting. An algorithm known as **balanced merging** is an excellent method for managing external sorting.

Sequences

This discussion requires that we have procedures available for reading a record from external storage and for writing a record to external storage, and other procedures as well. The names used for these procedures vary greatly from system to system. I will therefore use names that are (I hope) clear enough that you will be able to make the translation for your system.

The procedure ReadOneRecord is assumed to read one information value from a specified file into a given Information VAR parameter. The procedure Write-OneRecord is assumed to write a given Information value to a specified file. I also assume that you cannot write to a file from which you are reading and you cannot read from a file to which you are writing. Thus there have to be two kinds of procedures that *open* (initiate access to) a file, analogous to OpenInput and OpenOutput: OpenForReading permits you to read (only) from a given file, and OpenForWriting permits you to write (only) to a given file. Once you have executed one of these procedures for a file, you cannot execute the other unless you first execute the procedure CloseTheFile. Finally, you need a way of telling whether there are any more values that can be read from a given file. The headings of these six procedures could be:

```
PROCEDURE  ReadOneRecord   (VAR F : Sequence;  VAR X : Information);
PROCEDURE  WriteOneRecord  (VAR F : Sequence;  X : Information);
PROCEDURE  OpenForReading  (VAR F : Sequence);
PROCEDURE  OpenForWriting  (VAR F : Sequence);
PROCEDURE  CloseTheFile    (VAR F : Sequence);
PROCEDURE  AttemptToReadFailed (F : Sequence) : BOOLEAN;
```

Note that this is a description of something like a queue, only more restricted. The usual term for such a data structure is a **sequence**. When you open a file for writing, it is like an empty queue for which you can only perform enqueue, never dequeue. You can then close the file and reopen it for reading, in which case it is like a queue for which you can only perform dequeue, never enqueue. The AttemptToReadFailed function corresponds to IsEmpty, though it returns true only after you attempt to read from an empty file. OpenForWriting corresponds to Create for queues; if anything was in the file, it is deleted when OpenForWriting is executed.

FOR PASCAL PROGRAMMERS. Reset is OpenForReading, Rewrite is OpenForWriting, EOF is more like IsEmpty than AttemptToReadFailed, and plain Read and Write are used for ReadOneRecord and WriteOneRecord, respectively. Standard Pascal performs CloseTheFile automatically as needed, although some dialects of Pascal require a close procedure.

Balanced Merging

It is best to keep in mind a concrete example for this discussion. So assume that you have 98,900 records to sort and you have a sorting algorithm that can sort no more than 1000 records at one time, owing to limitations of the size of memory. The internal sorting algorithm you use can be any of those given earlier in the chapter; I will refer to it as Sort. I also assume that A1, B1, A2, and B2 are four identifiers for sequences, and that B2 contains the 98,900 records to be sorted. The sorted records are to be placed in one of the four sequences.

You should do as much sorting in memory as possible, since that should execute much faster than external sorting. To begin with, you read 1000 records from B2, sort them, and write them to A1. Then you read 1000 more records from B2, sort them, and write them to B1. Then you read the third thousand from B2, sort them, and write them to A1. This keeps up, alternating between A1 and B1, until all the records have been read. The last group will have just 900 records.

STATUS AT THE END OF STAGE 1. There are 50 groups of records in A1 and 49 groups in B1; each group has 1000 records and is sorted, except the last group in A1 has 900 sorted records.

In the next stage, you act just as you did for the Merge Sort, except that you use sequences instead of queues. That is, you repeatedly merge two groups of 1000 records into one group of 2000 records. It might be helpful at this point to review Example 6.5A. The logic is greatly simplified if you have the counts from Stage 1 available. Thus assume that you have four variables with the following values: NumberOfFullGroups = 49; SizeOfFullGroup = 1000; AGroup = 900; BGroup = 0. These last two values tell how many records are in the last group in each sequence, after the 49 full groups.

Begin by reading one information value from each of A1 and B1; this simplifies the coding for the merging procedure. Then repeat the MergeTwo procedure in Example 6.10A 49 times, passing SizeOfFullGroup to both the ASize and BSize parameters. ASeq is A1 and BSeq is B1; but Dest is A2 on the first call, B2 on the

EXAMPLE 6.10A _____

```
PROCEDURE MergeTwo (VAR ASeq, BSeq, Dest : Sequence;
                        ASize, BSize      : CARDINAL;
                        VAR AInfo, BInfo  : Information);
    (* Read ASize records from ASeq and BSize records from
       BSeq and sort them into Dest.  But the first record
       of each has already been read, so do not sort the
       last record read from each; instead, return it to be
       used in the next call of this procedure *)
BEGIN

    REPEAT
        IF (BSize = 0) OR (ASize > 0) AND
                (Compare (AInfo, BInfo) < 0) THEN
            WriteOneRecord (Dest, AInfo);
            ReadOneRecord (ASeq, AInfo);
            DEC (ASize);
        ELSE
            WriteOneRecord (Dest, BInfo);
            ReadOneRecord (BSeq, BInfo);
            DEC (BSize);
        END;
    UNTIL (ASize = 0) AND (BSize = 0);

END MergeTwo;
```

second call, A2 on the third call, and so on. Finally, the MergeTwo procedure is called for the remaining 900 records. Thus the sequence of statements executed is:

```
ReadOneRecord (A1, AInfo);
ReadOneRecord (B1, BInfo);
MergeTwo (A1, B1, A2, 1000, 1000, AInfo, BInfo);
MergeTwo (A1, B1, B2, 1000, 1000, AInfo, BInfo);
MergeTwo (A1, B1, A2, 1000, 1000, AInfo, BInfo);
(* 44 more times, alternating third parameter between A2 and B2 *)
MergeTwo (A1, B1, B2, 1000, 1000, AInfo, BInfo);
MergeTwo (A1, B1, A2, 1000, 1000, AInfo, BInfo);
MergeTwo (A1, B1, B2, 900, 0, AInfo, BInfo);
```

STATUS AT THE END OF STAGE 2. There are 25 groups of records in A2 and 25 groups in B2; each group has 2000 records and is sorted, except the last group in B2 has 900 sorted records.

Stage 3 is just like Stage 2, except that you use MergeTwo to merge 2000 records from A2 with 2000 from B2 and put the groups of 4000 sorted records alternately in A1 and B1. That is, the sequence of procedure calls is:

```
ReadOneRecord (A2, AInfo);
ReadOneRecord (B2, BInfo);
MergeTwo (A2, B2, A1, 2000, 2000, AInfo, BInfo);
MergeTwo (A2, B2, B1, 2000, 2000, AInfo, BInfo);
MergeTwo (A2, B2, A1, 2000, 2000, AInfo, BInfo);
(* 20 more times, alternating third parameter between A1 and B1 *)
MergeTwo (A2, B2, B1, 2000, 2000, AInfo, BInfo);
MergeTwo (A2, B2, A1, 2000,  900, AInfo, BInfo);
```

STATUS AT THE END OF STAGE 3. There are 13 groups of records in A1 and 12 groups in B1; each group has 4000 records and is sorted, except the last group in A1 has 2900 sorted records.

By now you should be able to see what this is all leading to. Eventually all 98,900 records will be in A2 in sorted order. This version of the merge sort accomplishes its task efficiently except for the large number of times that information values have to be read from external storage. That number is $1+\lg(G)$, where G is the number of groups in the original division at Stage 1. That is, G is the total number of records divided by the number that are sorted internally as a group. Figure 9 illustrates the balanced merge for 7500 records.

After Stage 1:
A1 contains 4 sorted groups: 1-1000, 2001-3000, 4001-5000, 6001-7000
B1 contains 4 sorted groups: 1001-2000, 3001-4000, 5001-6000, 7001-7500
After Stage 2:
A2 contains 2 sorted groups: 1-2000, 4001-6000
B2 contains 2 sorted groups: 2001-4000, 6001-7500
After Stage 3:
A1 contains 1 sorted group: 1-4000
B1 contains 1 sorted group: 4001-7500
After Stage 4:
A2 contains all 7500 records in sorted order

FIGURE 9. *Balanced merge of 7500 records, sorting 1000 internally. Numbers shown refer to the original order of the records in B2.*

Radix Sorting Using External Files

The Radix Sort logic can be used to sort an arbitrary number of records if your system allows you to keep a large number of files open. For instance, assume the keys are cardinals and that you can keep 11 files open at one time. First you read the given file and write each record to one of 10 different files, depending on the least significant digit. Call those 10 files group A. Then you close those 10 files in group A for writing and open another 10 files (group B) for writing. You read from each of the group A files in order, writing each record to one of the group B files, depending on the next-to-least significant digit. You close each group A file before opening the next for reading. When you are done, you repeat with the roles of A and B reversed. This keeps up until the last pass, at which point you write everything to one file. All records will be sorted at that point.

External Sorting Done Internally

The heading of this section is self-contradictory. What I really mean is, it is often the case that, even when the internal memory is too small to contain all the records to be sorted, there are ways to do all the sorting in internal memory. An illustration should clarify this statement.

Assume that you have 2000 records to sort, each of which is 1024 bytes in size (1 K). The total storage space required is 2000 K, also known as 2 megabytes. It is usually the case that sorting is to be done based on a key field such as a 10-character ID. If this is the case, you can read the file of records and store for each record the 10-character ID and the position number (1..2000) in the file. This requires a total of $12 * 2000 = 24,000$ bytes of space, if cardinals require 2 bytes and characters require 1. You can then sort these 12-byte information values completely internally.

When you are done with the sorting, you can reorder the file of records accordingly. This is easy to do if your system allows you to access records in a file by position number, as most do.

Check Your Understanding

1. Describe the status at the end of Stages 4 and 5 for the 98,900 records, similar to the description given in the text for Stages 1, 2, and 3.

2. Tell how many times each information value is read and written throughout the sorting described for 98,900 records.

3. (NA) Show that the number of reads performed for the balanced merge is $1+\lg(G)$, where G is the total number of records divided by the number that are sorted internally as a group.

4. (NA) Write the procedure that accomplishes Stage 1 of the balanced merge, calling on a Sort procedure as needed.

5. (NA) Write the procedure that calls MergeTwo to accomplish everything after Stage 1 of the balanced merge.

6.11 TOPOLOGICAL SORTING

The task of building your own house can be divided up into many subtasks. For discussion purposes, assume you divide it up into the following five subtasks (real-life applications will have scores of subtasks):

1. Lay the foundation of the house.
2. Build the garage.
3. Buy the land.
4. Build the house.
5. Move in.

Obviously, these tasks are not numbered in the order in which they will be done. It is easy to reorder them properly, since there are so few. But in situations with scores of subtasks, or even hundreds of subtasks as in the construction of a jetliner, it is helpful to have a computer algorithm to reorder the subtasks properly. This kind of reordering, called a **topological sort**, is the subject of this section.

Context of the Algorithm

A computer algorithm for this situatiom requires information as to which tasks directly follow which other tasks in the order of performance. In the example just described, building the garage and laying the foundation come after buying the land; building the house comes after laying its foundation; and moving in comes after building the house and garage. These relations can be specified by giving a list of "come-afters" for each subtask (telling what comes after it):

		"COME-AFTER" LISTS
1.	Lay the foundation of the house	4
2.	Build the garage	5
3.	Buy the land	2, 1
4.	Build the house	5
5.	Move in	—

The actual phrases used to describe the subtasks are irrelevant to an algorithm for properly reordering the numbers. All you need for the algorithm are declarations as follows:

```
CONST Loval = {some simple value};
      Hival = {a larger simple value of the same type};
TYPE  Information = [Loval..Hival];
      ArrayOfLists = ARRAY Information OF List;
VAR   ComeAfter : ArrayOfLists;
      Result : List;
```

The constants Loval and Hival are usually integers, but they may be characters or elements of some enumeration type. The algorithm is to create the Result list and put on it the information values in the proper ordering. Most applications of topological sorts have ComeAfter lists whose average size is independent of the number of values to be sorted; typically, the average size of a list is between 2 and 5.

The algorithm cannot work properly if the situation is **cyclic**, which means that (1) there are two values each of which comes after the other; or (2) there are three values A, B, C such that A comes after B, which comes after C, which comes after A; or (3) the analogous condition holds for four, five, or any other positive number of values. It is preferable that the algorithm indicate when this happens by returning an empty Result list. Even if this is not convenient, the algorithm should not fall into an "infinite loop" if the situation is cyclic.

A Naive Algorithm

A straightforward way of solving this problem is:

1. Find a value for which nothing comes after it;
2. Put the value you found on the Result list;

3. Do the following until all values have been put on the Result list:

    3.a. Find a value for which nothing comes after it except values which are already on the Result list;

    3.b. Put the value you found at the front of the Result list.

Two things are wrong with this "algorithm." One is that no provision is made for when you cannot find a value with the specified property (i.e., the situation is cyclic); the other is that it executes slowly.

The first problem can be solved by adding the following qualification to both the steps that find a value: If there is no such value, make Result empty and terminate the algorithm. The second problem may or may not be solvable; further analysis is necessary.

Execution time for the algorithm as given can be computed as follows: The overall algorithm executes N = Hival − Loval + 1 times, putting one value on Result on each iteration. One iteration of the overall loop requires looking through all N information values until you find one with no followers other than those already in the Result list, which is a big-oh of N algorithm. Looking to see whether a particular value G has no already-used followers requires comparing each value on G's list of followers with each value on the Result list; so the execution time of one of those steps is big-oh of N ⋆ Avg, where Avg is the average size of a ComeAfter list. Thus the overall algorithm is big-oh of N-cubed, assuming that Avg is independent of N.

This can be reduced to a big-oh of N-squared algorithm by taking advantage of the fact that the information values are [Loval..Hival] instead of arbitrary values stored on a list. You can declare an array of Boolean values with [Loval..Hival] as the index type and use it to note which values are on the Result list. For instance, if the name of the array is Used, you can inspect Used[K] instead of searching the Result list.

A Recursive Algorithm

An even faster algorithm (big-oh of N) can be obtained by a proper use of recursion. Define a **successor** of a value G to be any value that is required to come later than G in Result. Thus the successors of G consist of all values on the Come-After[G] list plus all successors of those values. The overall algorithm is:

For each value K in [Loval..Hival], call a procedure that first puts all successors of K in Result and then puts K in Result.

The recursion in this algorithm is not immediately obvious. That is because it is in the algorithm for the procedure itself, which can be described as follows (It denotes the value for which the procedure was called):

Call this procedure for each value in ComeAfter[It] for which this procedure has not yet been called; then put It at the front of the Result list.

The procedure puts its parameter at the front of the Result list only *after* putting the direct successors of its parameter in the Result list, so the proper ordering is achieved for its parameter. The direct successors of its parameter are put at the front of the Result list only after their direct successors are put in the list, which happens only after *their* direct successors are put in the list, and so forth until you reach a value that has no direct successors (i.e., its ComeAfter list is empty).

For this algorithm to work correctly, you have to keep track of the values for which the recursive procedure has previously been called; a Boolean array with indices [Loval..Hival] does this easily. Since the procedure can only be called once for each value, you do not have to worry about "infinite" recursion happening. Each additional recursive call decreases the number of FALSE values in the Boolean array by 1, and there cannot be any further recursive call when there are no more FALSE values in the Boolean array.

What happens if the situation is cyclic? A direct successor that has been processed before is ignored, regardless of whether it is a predecessor of the value currently being processed. So the recursion terminates, but the Result list is incorrect; it gives an ordering that would be correct if a few of the values on the ComeAfter lists were removed to make the situation acyclic. One of the exercises gives a hint on how to improve the algorithm so that it returns an empty list whenever the situation is cyclic.

This algorithm is big-oh of N because the recursive procedure is called exactly N times altogether, and the statements in the recursive procedure are all big-oh of 1 except for the call to itself. This assumes, as before, that the average size of a list is independent of the total number of values in [Loval..Hival].

Some applications have a "base value" such that every other value is a successor of that base value. For the example of building a house, buying the land is a base value. In that case, the algorithm can be written to execute even faster, although it is still big-oh of N. This is left as an exercise.

Some applications have an array of ComeBefore lists instead of ComeAfter lists. That is, for each value, you are given a list of all values that come directly before it. A similar logic can be used to program such applications; this is also left as an exercise.

The ComeAfter lists imply what is called a **partial ordering** of the values in [Loval..Hival]. A special case of this is called **total ordering**: Each ComeAfter list has one value on it except that one list is empty; and no two lists have the same value. In such a case, the ComeAfter lists essentially specify links from one value to another, and what we really have is a single list that has lost its head. Then Example 6.11A translates easily to an algorithm for finding the first node on a standard linked list when you have all the nodes stored in an array.

EXAMPLE 6.11A _____

```
PROCEDURE TopSort (ComeAfter  : ArrayOfLists;
                   VAR Result : List);
    (* Create a List Result containing [Loval..Hival] in
       an order such that, for all values X and Y,
       if X is in ComeAfter[Y] then X comes after Y in
       the Result List.  If the ComeAfter Lists make this
       impossible, Result is indeterminate *)

VAR
    Used : ARRAY Information OF BOOLEAN;
  (*--------------------------------------------------------*)

    PROCEDURE AddToResult (It     : Information;
                           AfterIt : List);

    VAR
        Where   : Location;
        TheInfo : Information;

    BEGIN

        Used [It] := TRUE;
        Where := FirstLocation (AfterIt);
        WHILE InList (Where, AfterIt) DO
            LookAt (TheInfo, Where, AfterIt);
            IF NOT Used [TheInfo] THEN
                AddToResult (TheInfo, ComeAfter [TheInfo]);
            END;
            Where := NextLocation (Where, AfterIt);
        END;
        Insert (It, FirstLocation (Result), Result);

    END AddToResult;
  (*--------------------------------------------------------*)

VAR
    K : Information;

BEGIN           (* TopSort *)

    FOR K := Loval TO Hival DO
        Used [K] := FALSE;
    END;
    Create (Result);

    FOR K := Loval TO Hival DO
        IF NOT Used [K] THEN
            AddToResult (K, ComeAfter [K]);
        END;
    END;

END TopSort;
```

Check Your Understanding

1. In Example 6.11A, it could be disastrous to move the first statement of Add-ToResult down to just before the last statement of AddToResult. Explain why.

2. Assume that, instead of a ComeAfter array of Lists, you have a ComeBefore array of Lists that tells, for each Information value, which values come before it. What changes are required in Example 6.11A in addition to replacing "After" by "Before"? You may assume that ListADT exports the utility Enqueue procedure.

3. Modify the coding of Example 6.11A under the assumption that Loval is something like the root of a tree in the sense that (a) every other value is a successor of Loval and (b) the situation is not cyclic.

4. (NA) Write the procedure for the naive algorithm.

5. (NA) Revise Example 6.11A so that it returns an empty Result list whenever the situation is cyclic. *Hint:* Use a second Boolean array ToBeUsed; change the first statement of AddToResult to ToBeUsed [Given] := TRUE and assign a value to Used later in AddToResult.

CHAPTER REVIEW

It is often useful to have a stable sorting algorithm, which means that matching information values are left in the same order they had in the original list. In some situations, it is also useful to have an incremental sort, which puts the list in order after each information value is put in the list. The Insertion Sort has both these properties; the Selection Sort has neither.

The method of analysis of algorithms categorizes the execution time for an algorithm in terms of the number of items to be processed, independently of the machine and the compiler being used. Consequently, the results are stated in terms such as "it is a linear function of N" or "it is a quadratic function of N" or "it is a logarithmic function of N," where you are processing N items. The big-oh notation for these phrases is big-oh of N, big-oh of N-squared, and big-oh of lg(N), respectively. In this book, lg(N) means the exponent on the power of 2 just above N (or on N itself if N is a power of 2).

The Tree Sort consists of putting information in a binary search tree. Then inorder traversal of the tree produces the information in sorted order. The Tree Sort is a stable incremental sorting algorithm.

The Merge Sort consists of dividing a list into two parts with the same number of information values (plus or minus one), sorting each half recursively, and then carefully merging the two sorted lists together. Most of the work is done in the merging of the two sorted lists.

The Quicksort consists of dividing the list into two parts, one part containing all values smaller than a chosen value and the other part containing all other values. Then each part is sorted recursively and the two parts are put back together. Since the split is made with discrimination, very little work has to be done in putting the two parts together. The Quicksort can easily be modified to find the Kth smallest item in a list quickly.

The Merge Sort, Quicksort, and Tree Sort are all $N*\lg(N)$ sorts on the average. The Quicksort is about the fastest method of sorting values in arrays; the Merge Sort is about the fastest method of sorting values in linked lists. The Tree Sort and the Quicksort are big-oh of N-squared in the worst case and big-oh of $N*\lg(N)$ in the average case. The Merge Sort is big-oh of $N*\lg(N)$ even in the worst case.

The Shell Sort is intended only for sorting values in an array. It consists of dividing the list into "intertwined" sublists. For instance, four sublists would be obtained by using components 1,5,9,...; 2,6,10,...; 3,7,11,...; and 4,8,12,.... Each sublist is then sorted using an Insertion Sort. This continues for a number of iterations, with a fewer number of larger sublists on each iteration. The last iteration has only one sublist, namely the entire list.

To perform the Radix Sort, you have to know something about the nature of the key fields that Compare uses. By contrast, all the aforementioned sorts depend only on the value returned by Compare. The Radix Sort is faster than any of the other sorts, when the number of items to be sorted is large enough. When the key fields are cardinals, the Radix Sort requires you to sort items on the ones digit, then on the tens digit, and so forth until you have sorted them on the highest digit in the key.

A heap is an almost-complete binary tree in which the root of every subtree contains the smallest information value in that subtree. The Heap Sort consists of constructing a Heap from a list of values, then repeatedly deleting the root value and rearranging the tree to be a heap again, until you have removed all values from the tree.

Balanced merging is a way of sorting the records in a file, no matter how many there are, as long as you have three additional files to use. If N denotes the number of records you can sort in memory at one time, the algorithm is: Read N records at a time, sort them, and write them alternately to two files. Then repeatedly merge N records from each of those two files to form sequences of $2*N$ sorted records in two other files (including the one from which you read the records originally). Repeat forming sequences of $4*N$ sorted records, then $8*N$, and so forth until all the records are in one sequence.

PRACTICE TEST

1. Write the Insertion Sort as a utility in the simple array implementation of ListADT. [Example 6.1A]

2. Write the Insertion Sort for a client module of ListDT. [Example 6.4A]

3. Write the Tree Sort for a client module of StackADT. [Example 6.4B]

4. Write a code segment that merges two sorted lists named AList and BList into one larger sorted list named Data. Import from ListADT and assume the availability of Enqueue, Dequeue, and Peep. [Example 6.5A]

5. Write a code segment that splits a list named Data into two lists named AList and BList, with AList containing all information values smaller than PivotInfo and BList containing the rest. Import from ListADT and assume the availability of the Enqueue and Dequeue utilities. [Example 6.6A]

6. Write coding that accomplishes one pass of the Radix Sort, assuming imports from QueueADT and a function Digit that returns digit number Pass of the key field of a given information value. [end of Section 6.8]

PROGRAMMING PROBLEMS

1. Write the Selection Sort in the same context as Example 6.4A. Do not use an auxiliary List variable, nor recursion.

2. Write the Insertion Sort as a utility procedure for linked lists.

3. Write the Selection Sort as a utility procedure for linked lists.

4. Write the Merge Sort procedure (Example 6.5A) as a utility procedure in an implementation of ListADT using header nodes.

5. Write the faster form of the Merge Sort described at the end of Section 6.5 (a utility for the simple array implementation of ListADT), wherein an Insertion Sort is used when the number of values to be sorted is less than 20 and there have been an even number of recursive calls.

6. Rewrite the Merge Sort in Example 6.5B using circular lists.

7. Rewrite the Quicksort in Example 6.6B using circular lists.

8. Rewrite the Quicksort in Example 6.6B using header nodes.

9. Write the Shell Sort as a utility procedure in the simple array implementation of ListADT.

10. Write the Radix Sort as a utility procedure in a circular linked list implementation of ListADT. Use an InfoADT module that exports the Digit function and two constants LoDigit and HiDigit, which are the lowest and highest digits that Digit can return. InfoADT should also export a constant that tells the number of digits in one ID. Note that this means you can write the Radix

Sort without caring whether digits or characters or some other simple value is being used by InfoADT.

11. Write the Heap Sort as a utility procedure in the simple array implementation of ListADT, wherein the parent of component K is stored at component K DIV 2.

12. Complete the coding in Example 6.9A for the Heap Sort using imports from BinADT.

13. Write a program that repeatedly reads a file of information values into a list, sorts it, and reports the time required. Use several different Sort utilities in either the array or the linked list implementation of ListADT. Use a sufficient variety to test the timing assertions in this chapter.

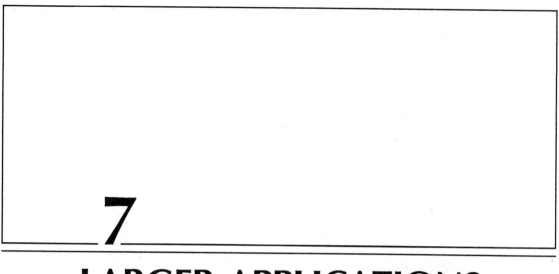

7
LARGER APPLICATIONS

This chapter is intended to achieve several goals:

- [ ] To present a number of different applications of the abstract data types you have seen in this book—StackADT, QueueADT, ListADT, TableADT, and BinADT.
- [ ] To increase greatly your experience with recursion.
- [ ] To illustrate the use of modularization in the construction of a large programming project.
- [ ] To deepen your understanding of syntax and operator precedence.

The first five sections of this chapter present five independent applications. Sections 7.6 through 7.10 present one large programming project. For all but Sections 7.2 through 7.5, you are expected to have read Section 1.11, since LOOP, CASE, and enumeration types are used wherever appropriate.

7.1 A TURING MACHINE PROGRAM

The kind of program discussed in this section can be called a **Turing program** because it acts like a **Turing machine**. Turing machines are important in the theory of computability because they are the simplest possible computerlike constructs. A Turing machine acts as follows:

1. It starts with a string of characters (the input).
2. It executes a number of actions as described below.
3. It leaves a revised string of characters (the output), which can be shorter or longer than the input string, with substantially different characters in it.

The set of characters with which a particular Turing machine can work is called its **alphabet**. At any given time during execution of the program, there is a special marker that is on one of the characters in the string. Initially, the marker is on the rightmost input character. The input string is considered to be on a "tape" that has an unlimited number of blanks to the left and right of the input string.

The easiest way to explain the kinds of actions permitted a Turing machine is to describe a special kind of procedure for a program that simulates a Turing machine: For purposes of this section, a **case-procedure** is a procedure that can be coded with just one statement, namely a CASE statement for which the control expression is the character currently marked and the case labels are all the characters of the machine's alphabet. Each statement sequence in the CASE statement is to cause the following sequence of three actions:

1. Change the currently marked character to a given value (which may be the same value it already has).
2. Move the marker one character to the left or right.
3. Execute a particular case-procedure, or quit.

A program that acts like a Turing machine should simply execute one case-procedure or its functional equivalent. Thus the actions that a Turing machine can carry out are extremely limited. However, it can be shown that, for any Modula-2 program that can be written without using files, there is a corresponding Turing machine that does precisely the same thing. The following AddOne procedure illustrates how these actions can be used to add 1 to any given input number, assuming it is written in base 3 (base 3 was chosen for the illustration because base 10 is analogous but a lot longer). The alphabet for this Turing machine has four characters: the digits '0', '1', and '2', plus a blank. I assume that c denotes the currently marked character (initially the rightmost).

```
PROCEDURE AddOne;
BEGIN
    CASE c OF
        '0': c := '1'; GoLeft; Quit;
      | '1': c := '2'; GoLeft; Quit;
      | '2': c := '0'; GoLeft; AddOne;     (* carry 1 to next place  *)
      | ' ': c := '1'; GoRight; Quit;      (* leftmost end of number *)
    END;
END AddOne;
```

SAMPLE RUNS. If this procedure is called with c the rightmost character of 221, it changes the 1 to a 2 and quits. If 22 is the input, it changes the rightmost 2 to a 0 and goes to the left, where it finds another 2; it changes that 2 to a 0 and goes to the left, where it finds a blank; it changes that blank to a 1 and quits; so the result is 100.

A Sample Turing Program

The next example is a Turing machine that tells whether a given base 3 number is even or odd. Specifically, the output is '2' if the input number is even, but the output is '1' if the input number is odd. I assume as before that c denotes the character that is currently marked (initially the rightmost character).

The key to this algorithm is that you only need see whether the number of 1's in the base 3 number is even or odd (if you think about it for a few minutes, you will see why that is true). So you inspect the characters one at a time, moving to the left after each one and erasing as you go (since the output must be a single digit). When you see a '1', you know that the number so far is even if it previously was odd, but odd if it previously was even. When you see a '0' or '2', that does not affect the decision as to evenness. When you see a blank, you know you have come to the leftmost end of the number, so you print '1' or '2' (as the case may be) and quit.

The program in Example 7.1A embodies this algorithm. ProcessEvenNumber is called whenever there is an even number of 1's to the right of the currently marked character. ProcessOddNumber is called whenever there is an odd number of 1's to the right of the currently marked character. Initially, there are no 1's to the right of the currently marked character, so it is reasonable to begin by calling ProcessEvenNumber. This program assumes there is a Turing library module that exports convenient identifiers.

Figure 1 is a diagram of this logic in a form that many find useful. You start with the box named "Even." The currently marked character determines which arrow you follow out of a box. The arrow shows the action to be taken (e.g., "b" means "write a blank" and "L" means "go left") and points to the box you are to go to next.

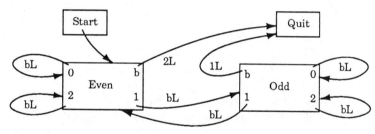

FIGURE 1. *Diagram for Example 7.1A, telling whether a given base 3 numeral is odd or even.*

EXAMPLE 7.1A _____

```
MODULE OddOrEven;
FROM Turing IMPORT c, GoLeft, GoRight, Quit,
                GetInput, GiveOutput;
    (* Turing machine to tell whether a given base 3
       numeral is even or odd.  2 is printed if it is
       even, 1 if it is odd.  *)
    (* Written by Dr. William C. Jones, Nov 19-- *)
(************************************************************)

PROCEDURE ProcessEvenNumber;
    (* there is an even number of 1's
       to the right of the marker *)
BEGIN
    CASE c OF
        '0': c := ' '; GoLeft; ProcessEvenNumber;
      | '1': c := ' '; GoLeft; ProcessOddNumber;
      | '2': c := ' '; GoLeft; ProcessEvenNumber;
      | ' ': c := '2'; GoLeft; Quit;
    END;
END ProcessEvenNumber;
(************************************************************)

PROCEDURE ProcessOddNumber;
    (* there is an odd number of 1's
       to the right of the marker *)
BEGIN
    CASE c OF
        '0': c := ' '; GoLeft; ProcessOddNumber;
      | '1': c := ' '; GoLeft; ProcessEvenNumber;
      | '2': c := ' '; GoLeft; ProcessOddNumber;
      | ' ': c := '1'; GoLeft; Quit;
    END;
END ProcessOddNumber;
(************************************************************)

BEGIN            (* program *)
    GetInput (15C);
    ProcessEvenNumber;
    GiveOutput;
END OddOrEven.
```

I have put the two case-procedures in a full program module of the type I would like to be able to write whenever I create a Turing program. Specifically, I would like to have a library module that lets me simply call a procedure to get the input, then call one of the case-procedures to carry out all the actions, and finally call a procedure to give the output to the user. And I would like to be able to call procedures to GoLeft, GoRight, and Quit as needed.

It is feasible to write such a library module, although a small compromise has to be made. You need some way of telling when the end of the input string occurs;

I used an end-of-line (character number 15 in octal notation) in Example 7.1A. You might think that an end-of-line would always suffice, but then what do you do if the input string has tens of thousands of characters? After all, you might be writing a Turing machine to compile a Modula-2 program. So it is necessary to supply the GetInput procedure with a character that can be used as a sentinel value.

The Turing Library Module

There are several reasonable approaches to developing the library module implicitly described in Example 7.1A; the one I like uses two stacks of characters. It has a LeftStack for all the characters to the left of the currently marked character c, with the ones closest to c on top of LeftStack. It has a RightStack for all characters to the right of the currently marked character c, with the ones closest to c on top of RightStack. So I import the stack declarations from StackADT, after changing the declaration of Information to TYPE Information=CHAR. This makes it so that StackADT does not have to import from any other module. I could, of course, have an InfoADT module, but that is going a bit far when the only declaration it exports is TYPE Information=CHAR.

c is a CHAR variable exported by this Turing library module. I begin by initializing the stacks as empty stacks before the client module can start execution. This makes the module work correctly for programs that have no input. Then, if the GetInput procedure is called, characters are read one at a time and put on the LeftStack. When the end of the input is signaled by the sentinel value, the most recently pushed character is popped off again, since that is the one currently marked.

Going to the left is a simple matter of pushing the current character onto the RightStack and popping a new current character off the LeftStack. A similar logic applies to going to the right. However, a problem arises when the stack is empty. In that case we just append as many blanks as needed. This applies whether we go to the left or the right.

The GiveOutput procedure should print the results from left to right. But we cannot access the character at the bottom of LeftStack until we have popped the ones above it. So we shift the characters one at a time from the LeftStack to the RightStack until the LeftStack is empty. Then we can repeatedly pop a character from the RightStack and write it, until the RightStack is empty.

The Quit procedure is provided as a notational convenience. The nature of the case-procedures is such that a simple return from Quit without making another procedure call will terminate all case-procedures, since Quit is the last statement executed in the whole case-procedure. So Quit does not need any statements at all. The implementation module for the Turing library module is in Example 7.1B; the definition module has the declaration VAR c: CHAR and the headings of the five procedures.

EXAMPLE 7.1B _____

```
IMPLEMENTATION MODULE Turing;
FROM StackADT IMPORT Stack, Push, Pop, IsEmpty, Create;
FROM Terminal IMPORT WriteString, Write, WriteLn, Read;
    (* Environment to simulate a Turing machine *)
    (* Export only VAR c : CHAR and the 5 procedures.  Quit
       is for convenience; it does nothing *)
    (* Written by William C. Jones, November 19-- *)

CONST
    nix = ' ';    (* used to extend the string as needed *)
VAR
    LeftStack  : Stack;    (* values left of the marker *)
    RightStack : Stack;    (* values right of the marker *)
(************************************************************)

PROCEDURE GetInput (Sentinel : CHAR);
    (* call this procedure first to get the initial
       values.  Sentinel is the value the user will use
       to indicate the end of the input string.
       Sentinel cannot be in the machine's alphabet *)
BEGIN

    (* describe program, initialize stacks *)
        WriteString ('Turing machine:  Give the input ');
        WriteString ('followed by the sentinel ');
        Write (Sentinel);
        WriteLn;

    (* read a string of characters into the left stack *)
        Read (c);
        IF c = Sentinel THEN
            c := nix;
        ELSE
            REPEAT
                Push (c, LeftStack);
                Read (c);
            UNTIL c = Sentinel;
            Pop (c, LeftStack);
        END;
        WriteLn;

END GetInput;
(************************************************************)

PROCEDURE GoLeft;
    (* move marker one character to the left *)
BEGIN
    Push (c, RightStack);
    IF IsEmpty (LeftStack) THEN
        c := nix;
    ELSE
        Pop (c, LeftStack);
    END;
END GoLeft;
(************************************************************)

(* continued on next page *)
```

```
(* EXAMPLE 7.1B continued *)


PROCEDURE Quit;
    (* no more calls, so we terminate the machine *)
END Quit;
(**************************************************************)

PROCEDURE GoRight;
    (* move marker one character to the right *)
BEGIN
    Push (c, LeftStack);
    IF IsEmpty (RightStack) THEN
        c := nix;
    ELSE
        Pop (c, RightStack);
    END;
END GoRight;
(**************************************************************)

PROCEDURE GiveOutput;
    (* call this procedure last to tell the user the
       results of executing the machine  *)
BEGIN

    (* move all characters into the right Stack *)
        Push (c, RightStack);
        WHILE NOT IsEmpty (LeftStack) DO
            Pop  (c, LeftStack);
            Push (c, RightStack);
        END;

    (* print all characters in the right Stack *)
        WHILE NOT IsEmpty (RightStack) DO
            Pop (c, RightStack);
            Write (c);
        END;
        WriteLn;

END GiveOutput;
(**************************************************************)

BEGIN          (* Turing automatic initialization *)
    c := nix;
    Create (RightStack);
    Create (LeftStack);
END Turing.
```

Quintuple Notation

People can be lazy. They do not like to do all the tedious writing required to produce a client module, so they often use a shorthand method of writing out a Turing machine. Consider, for instance, the AddOne procedure given at the beginning of this section. The "meat" of the procedure can be expressed by the following four sequences of five objects:

<AddOne,0,1,L,Quit>   <AddOne,1,2,L,Quit>
<AddOne,2,0,L,AddOne>   <AddOne, ,1,L,Quit>

In each of these **quintuples**, the first object is the name of the procedure to be constructed. The second is the current value of c, and the third is the value to which it is to be changed. The fourth is the direction to move (L or R), and the fifth is the procedure to be called. This notation can be used to specify any Turing machine, from which the client module can be written if wanted. The writing of the client module from a given set of quintuples is left as a programming problem.

The Double-Case Form

There is an equivalent form of a Turing program that uses just one procedure, with a CASE statement containing several CASE statements. This could be called the **double-case form**, as opposed to the case-procedure form. Example 7.1C illustrates this form. In place of five procedures each containing one CASE statement, you have a large CASE statement with five alternatives, each of which is like the CASE statement of the corresponding case-procedure. You use an enumeration type with five values, one for each case-procedure. A **state** variable of this enumeration type determines the current state of the machine. Instead of calling procedure X, you assign X to the state variable. The larger CASE statement is inside a LOOP statement; EXIT is used instead of Quit.

In addition, some obvious economies are instituted: (1) When two different cases have the same commands, they are combined into one; (2) When c or state is assigned the same value it already had, the assignment statement can be omitted (but does not have to be).

The main reason I include Example 7.1C is to illustrate the double-case form, but the task it accomplishes is also interesting. Starting with any positive number, you can apply the following algorithm until N becomes 1:

```
IF ODD (N) THEN
     N := 3 * N + 1;
ELSE
     N := N DIV 2;
END;
```

For instance, if you start with 7, you get the following sequence of numbers: 22, 11, 34, 17, 52, 26, 13, 40, 20, 10, 5, 16, 8, 4, 2, 1. The "fact" that you always eventually reach 1 has been verified for numbers well past one million, but no one knows for sure that it is true for every single number. The Turing program in Example 7.1C accepts as input one positive number in base 3 notation and applies this algorithm until it arrives at 1, if it ever does.

EXAMPLE 7.1C _____

```
MODULE Wondrous;
FROM Turing IMPORT c, GoLeft, GoRight,
                   GetInput, GiveOutput;
    (* Turing machine to do interesting things to a given
       base 3 numeral until the result is 1  *)
    (* Written by Dr. William C. Jones, Nov 19-- *)
(***********************************************************)

PROCEDURE Execute;
VAR
    state : (FarLeft, Divide, Rem1, DoneQ, AllZerosQ);
BEGIN
    state := DoneQ;
    LOOP
        CASE state OF
          DoneQ: CASE c OF (* see if number is 0...01 *)
                   '0','2': GoLeft;  state := FarLeft;
                 |    '1': GoLeft;  state := AllZerosQ;
                 |    ' ': GoLeft;  EXIT;(* no input *)
                 END;
        | AllZerosQ: CASE c OF
                      '0': GoLeft;
                 | '1','2': GoLeft;  state := FarLeft;
                 |    ' ': GoRight; EXIT;
                 END;
        | FarLeft: CASE c OF  (* go to leftmost character *)
                    '0','1','2':   GoLeft;
                 |        ' ':   GoRight; state := Divide;
                 END;
        | Divide: CASE c OF  (* divide by 2 *)
                    '0': c := '0'; GoRight;
                 | '1': c := '0'; GoRight; state := Rem1;
                 | '2': c := '1'; GoRight;
                 | ' ':           GoLeft;  state := DoneQ;
                 END;
        | Rem1: CASE c OF (* divide by 2 with remainder 1 *)
                    '0': c := '1'; GoRight;
                 | '1': c := '2'; GoRight; state := Divide;
                 | '2': c := '2'; GoRight;
                 | ' ': c := '2'; GoLeft;  state := FarLeft
                 END;
        END;  (* overall CASE *)
    END;  (* LOOP *)
END Execute;
(***********************************************************)

BEGIN          (* program *)

    GetInput (15C);
    Execute;
    GiveOutput;

END Wondrous.
```

The basic logic is: Go to the far left digit of the number, and as you go, see if the number is 1 with perhaps some leading 0s. If it is, you can stop. If not, divide the number by 2 in the usual way. However, if you come to the right end with a remainder of 1, it means you should have multiplied by 3 and added 1 before you did the division. But for a base 3 numeral, that simply requires appending a 1 to the right end of the numeral. So you do so and finish the division. Then repeat from the beginning of this paragraph.

You may find it interesting to spend some time checking the coding to see that this is in fact what this Turing program does. By the way, "DoneQ" is shorthand for "testing: are we done?" and "AllZerosQ" is shorthand for "testing: is it all zeros?"; in other words, a terminal Q represents a question mark.

Check Your Understanding

1. What simplifications could be made in Examples 7.1A and 7.1B if you always required that the sentinel value for input be an end-of-line?

2. What changes would have to be made in Examples 7.1A and 7.1B to permit the client module to have any character used in place of a blank (i.e., on the left and right of all input strings)?

3. Write a Turing program using the AddOne procedure to act as described except when there is no input (i.e., the user enters just the sentinel value), in which case there is no output (except blanks).

4. Write the four quintuples that describe ProcessEvenNumber in Example 7.1A. Use Odd and Even as abbreviations for the two procedures.

5. (NA) What changes should be made in Example 7.1B so that it can be assumed that the marker starts on the leftmost character of the input?

6. (NA) Rewrite Example 7.1A in the double-case form.

7. (NA) Trace the action in Example 7.1C for the input 10, which is 3 in base 3. Do not trace it for 1000 (27 in base 3), because it takes several thousand iterations of the LOOP statement before 1 is reached.

8. (NA) Draw the diagram of Example 7.1C similar to the one in Figure 1.

7.2 PERMUTATIONS

The problem considered in this section is the writing of all permutations of a given set of objects, using a stack and a queue. As an example, if the set of objects is the set of digits from 1 to 4, a permutation is a listing of those four digits in a certain order. There are 24 such permutations, as follows:

4321 3421 4231 2431 3241 2341
4312 3412 4132 1432 3142 1342
4213 2413 4123 1423 2143 1243
3214 2314 3124 1324 2134 1234

If the set of objects to be permuted is the set of three letters A, B, and C, there are six permutations, as follows: CBA, BCA, CAB, ACB, BAC, ABC. The general formula for the number of permutations of N objects is N * (N−1) * (N−2) *... * 3 * 2 * 1, the product of all the integers from N down to 1. The hard part is to find a way to list all the permutations without writing any one of them twice.

I start off with a queue of values to be permuted—call it ToPermute. If you look at the list of permutations of 1, 2, 3, 4 just given, you should see a pattern. First I listed all permutations that end with 1, then all that end with 2, then all that end with 3, then all that end with 4. Note that the permutations that end with 1 can be obtained by listing all permutations of 2, 3, 4, each followed by 1. Similarly, the permutations that end with 2 can be obtained by listing all permutations of the other three numbers, each followed by 2. Thus permutations of four values can be described in terms of permutations of three values. This gives us a basis for developing a recursive solution.

The solution that I present here imports from InfoADT, StackADT, and QueueADT. I assume that SizeOf and ReadAll are utility procedures in QueueADT, and WriteAll is a utility procedure in StackADT. Notice during the development how the availability of these procedures and the hiding of the Information type free your mind for concentrating on the hard part.

The fundamental algorithm for this problem is given a queue named ToPermute (which contains, for instance, 1, 2, 3, 4) and a stack of values that are to be printed at the end of each permutation of the values in the ToPermute queue. Call the stack EndPerm. Initially, EndPerm is empty, which means the algorithm is to print each permutation of the values 1, 2, 3, 4 with nothing at the end of each permutation.

The algorithm removes one value at a time from the queue, puts it on top of the stack, calls itself to work with the two revised structures, and then puts back on the queue the one it took off. On the first call of this recursive procedure, the EndPerm stack is empty. At each additional level of recursion, EndPerm has one more value and ToPermute has one less value. When the procedure receives an empty ToPermute queue, it simply prints all the values on the EndPerm stack. See Example 7.2A for the coding.

Sample Run

As a sample run, consider the permutations of the four digits from 1 to 4. I start with EndPerm empty. The overall sequence of actions is: (1) transfer 1 to End-Perm, (2) print out all permutations that end with 1, (3) take the 1 back and transfer 2 to EndPerm, (4) print out all permutations that end in 2, (5) take the 2

EXAMPLE 7.2A _____

```
MODULE Permutations;
FROM InOut    IMPORT WriteString, WriteLn;
FROM InfoADT  IMPORT Information;
FROM QueueADT IMPORT Queue, Create, Enqueue, Dequeue,
                     SizeOf, ReadAll, IsEmpty;
FROM StackADT IMPORT Stack, Push, Pop, WriteAll;
IMPORT StackADT;
(* Write all permutations of a given sequence of values *)
(* Written by William C. Jones, April 19-- *)
(**************************************************************)

PROCEDURE PrintPermutations (VAR EndPerm   : Stack;
                             VAR ToPermute : Queue);
    (* EndPerm and ToPermute together contain all values.
       Print all permutations for which the values
       on EndPerm come last, in the order they occur on
       EndPerm.  EndPerm and ToPermute are left as they
       were by this procedure *)
VAR
    K       : CARDINAL;
    TheInfo : Information;
BEGIN
    IF IsEmpty (ToPermute) THEN
        WriteAll (EndPerm);
    ELSE
        FOR K := 1 TO SizeOf (ToPermute) DO
            Dequeue (TheInfo, ToPermute);
            Push (TheInfo, EndPerm);
            PrintPermutations (EndPerm, ToPermute);
            Pop (TheInfo, EndPerm);
            Enqueue (TheInfo, ToPermute);
        END;
    END;
END PrintPermutations;
(**************************************************************)

VAR
    EndPerm   : Stack;
    ToPermute : Queue;

BEGIN           (* program *)

    WriteString ('This program prints all permutations ');
    WriteString ('of a number of values.');
    WriteLn;
    WriteString ('Now enter the values:');
    WriteLn;

    StackADT.Create (EndPerm);
    Create (ToPermute);
    ReadAll (ToPermute);
    PrintPermutations (EndPerm, ToPermute);

END Permutations.
```

back and transfer 3 to EndPerm, (6) print out all permutations that end with 3, (7) take the 3 back and transfer 4 to EndPerm, (8) print out all permutations that end with 4, (9) take the 4 back. This leaves EndPerm empty after each "taking back" operation.

In printing out all permutations that end with 1 (so just 1 is in the EndPerm stack), the following sequence of actions takes place: (1) push 2 onto the EndPerm stack, (2) print all permutations that end with 21, (3) pop the 2 and push 3 onto EndPerm, (4) print all permutations that end with 31, (5) pop the 3 and push 4 onto EndPerm, (6) print all permutations that end with 41, (7) pop the 4 off of EndPerm. Similarly, at the point when just 2 is in the EndPerm stack, I push the other three digits onto the EndPerm stack one at a time, print the permutations with the given two-digit ending, and pop the digits off again.

In printing out all permutations that end with 21, the following sequence of actions takes place: (1) push 3 onto the EndPerm stack, (2) print all permutations that end with 321, (3) pop the 3 and push 4 onto EndPerm, (4) print all permutations that end with 421, (5) pop the 4 off of EndPerm.

Eventually, the recursive procedure reaches the point where EndPerm has all the digits, at which point it does not call itself again; instead, it calls a procedure to write everything on the EndPerm list in order.

Warning

You might think that the use of VAR parameters in the procedure in Example 7.2A is unnecessary, since the stack and the queue have exactly the same values when the procedure is exited as they had when the procedure was entered. However, omission of VAR might cause the program to crash for some implementations. If a structure is implemented as a pointer to the first node on a linked list, the first node might change during execution of the procedure, although the information in the first node does not. In general, you should use a value parameter for a structure only if the structure is never altered within the procedure.

Check Your Understanding

1. Write all permutations of "abcde" that have the b to the left of the c. List them in alphabetic order.

2. What changes should be made in Example 7.2A so that SizeOf is called only once during execution of the program?

3. (NA) List all the permutations of "abcde" that have the c in the middle.

4. (NA) Describe the effect of replacing calls of Push and Pop by calls of Enqueue and Dequeue, respectively, in Example 7.2A.

5. (NA) Which variables mentioned in the recursive PrintPermutations procedure of Example 7.2A can be delocalized? Make the appropriate changes.

7.3 AN INDEX-CREATING PROGRAM

The task of constructing a program to create an index or concordance for a book illustrates the use of several different library modules. Assume that someone goes through a book typing all words or phrases that are to be entered in the index. If a phrase occurs on several pages, the phrase is typed once for each occurrence. Each time the end of a page in the book is reached, a special phrase is typed to mark that point; for instance, the character '/' on a line by itself might be used to indicate a page break.

You are to write a program that accepts such a file as input and produces an alphabetic listing of the phrases, one entry for each phrase. Next to each phrase, the program is to write the numbers of all pages on which that phrase occurred, in increasing order.

The kind of information value you use could be declared as a record with two fields: one field for the phrase and one field for a queue of page numbers. This information can be kept in a table. As you read the lines in the file, you keep track of the current page number. Each time a phrase is read (other than the page-break marker), you see if it is already in the table. If it is, you add the current page number to its queue; otherwise, you create a queue for it and add the current page number to that queue. This way, the page numbers are kept in order (Fig. 2). After the entire file has been read, you can print out the information from the table in alphabetic order.

The Library Modules

Apparently you need three library modules: QueueADT, InfoMan, and Dicti-ADT. Queues will contain page numbers instead of records of Information, so QueueADT should be revised by replacing the word "Information" by "CARDINAL" throughout. That is the only change needed in QueueADT from what is described in Section 3.4. DictiADT must be used since you need the additional WriteTable procedure to write the entries in the table in alphabetic order. Information can be declared as follows:

```
TYPE   Information = POINTER TO RECORD
                         Phrase : ARRAY [0..40] OF CHAR;
                         Pages  : Queue;
                     END;
```

list	Push	queue	stack	table
53,57,62	40	45	39,45	57

FIGURE 2. How the index could look at one point, assuming it is kept in an array in order.

Note that InfoMan imports from QueueADT rather than the other way around. InfoMan should export a constant PageBreak that can be compared to the current phrase. This can be implemented by declaring a variable named PageBreak and initializing it properly in the body of InfoMan. InputInfo should create one Information value, read the next line of the input file, and assign the string of characters to the Phrase field of Information. OutputInfo should print the Phrase and then all page numbers in the queue, with commas between them.

The only interesting algorithm required in this program is the one for putting the current phrase (the one just read) in the table. If you find the current phrase in the table, it means that the phrase has occurred earlier. So you add the current page number to the queue for that phrase, then dispose of the variable into which you read the phrase (since you do not need it for anything). If the attempted Find operation fails, it means that this is the first occurrence of the phrase; so you create the queue, put the current page number on that queue, and insert the information value in the table.

Example 7.3A presents the complete coding of this program. Note that there is not too much to it, and what is there is not too complex. That is because most of the work is done in the library modules. This is the advantage of using modules that have previously been written.

Check Your Understanding

1. What would be the effect of using Push instead of Enqueue in Example 7.3A (importing from StackADT instead of QueueADT)?

2. What would be the effect of omitting the call of DestroyInfo in the AddTo-Table procedure in Example 7.3A?

7.4 THE CNF-SATISFIABILITY PROBLEM

The problem discussed in this section is particularly interesting for the following reason: If you can find an efficient algorithm for solving this problem, then it is possible to derive from that algorithm an efficient algorithm to solve any interesting programming problem whatsoever. No one knows whether it is possible to find an efficient algorithm for solving this problem; it is one of the most famous unsolved questions in the theory of computability. If you can solve it, you will be famous too. The problem was the first one to be proven **NP-complete**—"complete" in the sense mentioned at the beginning of this paragraph.

Algorithms have been found to solve this problem, but they are all big-oh of 2-to-the-power-N or some other exponential function or worse. That means that the time required to work the problem for 1001 values is something like twice the time required for 1000 values.

EXAMPLE 7.3A

```
MODULE IndexWriter;
IMPORT QueueADT, DictiADT;
FROM InfoMan IMPORT Information, InputInfo, Okay, Compare,
                    PageBreak, DestroyInfo;
    (* Create an index or concordance for a book from a
       file of phrases.  Page breaks are indicated in the
       file by a special PageBreak value *)
    (* Written by William C. Jones, October 19-- *)
(**********************************************************)

PROCEDURE AddToTable (OneWord    : Information;
                      VAR Index  : DictiADT.Table;
                      PageNumber : CARDINAL);
    (* Add OneWord to the Index table with the given
       PageNumber.  But if OneWord has previously occurred,
       just add the PageNumber to its queue *)
BEGIN

    DictiADT.Find (OneWord, Index);
    IF NOT DictiADT.InTable (Index) THEN
        QueueADT.Create (OneWord^.Pages);
    ELSE
        DestroyInfo (OneWord);
        DictiADT.TakeOut (OneWord, Index);
    END;
    QueueADT.Enqueue (PageNumber, OneWord^.Pages);
    DictiADT.PutIn (OneWord, Index);

END AddToTable;
(**********************************************************)

VAR
    Index      : DictiADT.Table;
    PageNumber : CARDINAL;
    OneWord    : Information;

BEGIN           (* program *)

    DictiADT.Create (Index);
    PageNumber := 1;
    InputInfo (OneWord);
    WHILE Okay DO
        IF Compare (OneWord, PageBreak) = 0 THEN
            INC (PageNumber);
            DestroyInfo (OneWord);
        ELSE
            AddToTable (OneWord, Index, PageNumber);
        END;
        InputInfo (OneWord);
    END;
    DictiADT.WriteTable (Index);

END IndexWriter.
```

Description of the Problem

Assume that you have a Boolean expression formed using only AND, OR, NOT, parentheses, and some Boolean variables. Then some assignments of values to the variables will make the expression true, and other assignments of values will make the expression false. **The CNF-satisfiability problem** is to find at least one assignment of values that makes the expression true (if there is any such assignment). For example, the Boolean expression might be:

(A) (xr OR xg OR xb) AND (xr OR NOT yr) AND (NOT xr OR NOT zr) AND
      NOT (xg AND xr) AND NOT (yr OR NOT zr) AND (NOT NOT xg)

In expression A, there are five Boolean variables: xr, xg, xb, yr, and zr. Since each can be either true or false, there are 32 possible assignments of values to them (the fifth power of 2). You might take a few minutes now to see if you can find all assignments that make expression A true (the answer will be given shortly). Remember that NOT takes precedence over AND and AND takes precedence over OR in Boolean expressions.

Technically, the CNF-satisfiability problem is only concerned with a particular form of Boolean expression, a CNF-expression, defined by:

1. An **atomic expression** is either a Boolean variable or NOT followed by a Boolean variable.

2. A **special factor** is one or more atomic expressions connected using OR and enclosed in parentheses.

3. A **CNF-expression** is one or more special factors connected using AND. (CNF stands for **conjunctive normal form**, because AND is also known as the conjunctive operator).

By this definition, expression A is not a CNF-expression. But if you were to omit the two NOTs that come before parentheses, and if every parenthesized expression were a special factor, expression A would be a CNF-expression (take a few moments now to check that). When you check the six parenthesized expressions, you see that only the fourth and sixth ones are not special factors. If the fourth one had OR instead of AND, and if the sixth one left out one or both of its NOTs, all six parenthesized expressions would be special factors.

Equivalence of Boolean Expressions

Any Boolean expression can be rewritten as an equivalent CNF-expression. Two Boolean expressions are **equivalent** when every possible assignment of values to the Boolean variables makes both true or both false. There are five handy rules for rewriting a Boolean expression as an equivalent Boolean expression. I will illustrate the three of them concerning NOT using the following expression (B) and leave the other two rules until later in this section. In these rules, known as

DeMorgan's Rules, the capital letters P, Q, and R stand for any Boolean expression whatsoever.

(B) NOT (xg AND xr) AND NOT (yr OR NOT zr) AND (NOT NOT xg)

- ☐ *NOT-NOT Rule:* NOT NOT P is equivalent to P. Thus the last phrase of B can be rewritten as (xg), which is a special factor.
- ☐ *NOT-AND Rule:* NOT (P AND Q) is equivalent to (NOT P OR NOT Q). Thus the first phrase of B can be rewritten as (NOT xg OR NOT xr), which is a special factor.
- ☐ *NOT-OR Rule:* NOT (P OR Q) is equivalent to (NOT P AND NOT Q). Thus the middle phrase of B can be rewritten as (NOT yr AND NOT NOT zr). Then, by the NOT-NOT Rule, this can be further simplified as (NOT yr AND zr). This is obviously the same as writing (NOT yr) AND (zr), which means that the middle phrase is equivalent to two special factors connected by AND.

If you make such changes in A, you have a CNF-expression C that is equivalent to A and has seven special factors:

(C) (xr OR xg OR xb) AND (xr OR NOT yr) AND (NOT xr OR NOT zr) AND (NOT xg OR NOT xr) AND (NOT yr) AND (zr) AND (xg)

An Algorithm for the CNF-Satisfiability Problem

It is easy to find assignments of values that make a CNF-expression false—any assignment that makes any one special factor false will do. For instance, xr := FALSE, xg := FALSE, xb := FALSE makes the first special factor in C false, which makes C (and thus A) false. The second special factor in C tells you that xr := FALSE and yr := TRUE will do. The seventh special factor in C tells you that xg := FALSE will also do. But the hard problem is to find some assignment of values that makes a CNF-expression true.

One way of solving the problem is to use **brute force**: Try out all 32 possible combinations of values (since there are five variables). When you find one combination that makes the expression true, you are done. If you try them all and no combination makes the expression true, you have proven that there is no assignment of values that works, so you have also solved the problem. The only trouble with this straightforward approach is that it takes too long. If one more Boolean variable were involved, it would double the number of combinations; 10 more Boolean variables would make the number of combinations 1024 times as large. This brute-force algorithm is big-oh of 2-to-the-power-N.

Sometimes a heuristic approach works quickly. The last three special factors of expression C make it clear that zr and xg must both have the value TRUE and yr must have the value FALSE. Now you can see what the other special factors imply. (xr OR xg OR xb) must be true, since xg is. (xr OR NOT yr) must be true, since yr is false. For (NOT xr OR NOT zr) to be true, xr must have the value FALSE, since zr is true. (NOT xg OR NOT xr) is then true, since xr is false. Since those four assignments of values make expression C (and A) true regardless of the value of xb, xb can have either of the values TRUE and FALSE. Thus only two of the 32 possible combinations of values satisfy expression A. The two possibilities can be expressed as:

(D) zr AND xg AND NOT yr AND NOT xy AND xb   OR
     zr AND xg AND NOT yr AND NOT xr AND NOT xb

Logic programming provides a way of working on the CNF-satisfiability problem. For instance, in the Prolog language, a special factor can be written as a program statement: xr OR NOT yr would be written as xr :− yr; that is, the negated atomic expressions are listed on the right of the :− sign and the other atomic expressions are listed on the left of the :− sign. Making several such statements corresponds to joining the statements with AND. Thus each CNF expression is equivalent to a Prolog program. Then running the program provides a combination of values that satisfies the CNF expression.

Overall Logic of a Satisfiability Program

I can simplify the problem by insisting that the expression to be analyzed be in prefix notation rather than infix notation. This has the advantage of avoiding parentheses. A program to solve the CNF-satisfiability problem can be written to accept only prefix notation, or it can have an initial procedure that reads an expression in infix notation and converts it to prefix notation. Either way, the first stage of the satisfiability program reads the input and stores the expression in a queue in prefix notation. For maximum usefulness, assume that the program is to handle any prefix expression, not just a CNF-expression.

I assume that Information is a pointer value, probably a pointer to a string of characters (the details are unimportant to the overall logic). Initially, I create three information values named *and*, *or*, and *not*.

So you can have a concrete example to think about for this discussion, the following expression E is expression A written in prefix notation; I put spaces to separate six parts connected by ANDs:

(E) AND AND AND   OR OR xr xg xb   OR xr NOT yr   OR NOT xr NOT zr
         AND   NOT AND xg xr   AND   NOT OR yr NOT zr   NOT NOT xg

The second stage of the program simplifies the prefix expression using the three NOT-rules given previously. When that is completely done, every NOT will be directly followed by a variable, never by AND, OR, or another NOT.

The third stage of the program rewrites the expression as an equivalent expression that is a kind of reverse of a CNF-expression, called a DNF-expression (for

disjunctive normal form). A **DNF-expression** is one or more **special terms** connected using OR; a special term is one or more atomic expressions connected using AND. Parentheses are not necessary even in infix notation, owing to the order of precedence of operators that Modula-2 uses. In fact, a DNF-expression in infix form is any expression without parentheses and without two consecutive NOTs. For instance, expression D is a DNF-expression with two special terms, one for each assignment of values to the five Boolean variables that makes expression A true.

The fourth stage of the program inspects the DNF-expression and prints out an assignment of values to the Boolean variables that makes the expression true. It is easily modified to print all possible assignments, since the DNF form makes that easy. Specifically, any assignment of values that makes any one of the special terms true makes the whole expression true. Since a special term consists of atomic expressions joined by ANDs, there will be an obvious assignment of values that makes it true as long as there is no variable that appears both with and without NOT in front of it. In fact, an acceptable output from this program could be obtained by repeating the following algorithm for each special term:

1. Order the atomic expressions in the special term by variable name.
2. Omit duplicates (two identical atomic expressions).
3. If no contradiction arises (a variable that appears both with and without NOT in front of it), print the list of atomic expressions.

If no printout appears for any special term, there is no assignment of values that makes the original expression true. Otherwise, each printout specifies the values to be assigned (FALSE if the variable has NOT in front of it, TRUE otherwise).

This section does not develop the fourth stage any further. There are a few paragraphs at the end of this section on the third stage, sufficient to get you started on programming it. The next subsection develops the logic for the second stage.

Simplifying NOTs in a Boolean Expression

The task to be performed by the second stage of the program is to apply the three NOT-rules repeatedly until every NOT is directly followed by a variable. This makes the task of the third stage of the program much simpler, since it in effect ignores NOTs. The SimplifyNOT procedure to be developed next accepts a Queue representing any legal prefix expression and returns a revised Queue with every NOT directly followed by a variable.

A straightforward way of performing this "unnotting" task is to read values from the given queue and put them on another queue, making changes from time to time as needed. When the whole expression has been processed, the other queue is returned as the result.

The advantage of the prefix notation, as opposed to postfix notation, is that values can be repeatedly dequeued from the given queue and enqueued on the result queue until a NOT is seen. Only then must special action be taken. The special action depends on the nature of the expression that follows NOT. This reasoning leads naturally to the SimplifyNOT procedure in Example 7.4A; its NegateExpr subprocedure will be developed next.

The NegateExpr procedure is to take one expression from the Given queue and put its negation on the Data queue. The details of the action depend on the nature of the expression, as indicated by the next value on the queue:

- ☐ If it is a variable, we just put NOT and that variable on the Data queue.
- ☐ If it is AND, we apply the NOT-AND Rule, which means we put OR on Data and then negate the next two expressions (calling this NegateExpr procedure recursively).
- ☐ If it is OR, we apply the NOT-OR Rule, which means we put AND on Data and then negate the next two expressions (more recursion).
- ☐ If it is NOT, we apply the NOT-NOT Rule, which means we take the next expression from Given and pass its equivalent on to Data—in essence, the two NOTs cancel each other.

Only the last possibility listed requires more analysis. We need a procedure that takes one expression from Given and passes its equivalent to Data. A subprocedure FixOneExpr to accomplish this task is not difficult to develop, since it is a simplification of the logic for NegateExpr. We take one value off the Given queue. If it is a variable, we pass it on. If it is AND or OR, we pass it on and also the next two expressions (calling FixOneExpr recursively). If it is NOT, we sim-

EXAMPLE 7.4A _____

```
PROCEDURE SimplifyNOT (VAR Data : Queue);
    (* Simplify the prefix expression in Data so that NOT
        is always followed directly by a Boolean variable *)
    (* Context:  client of QueueADT *)
(* PROCEDURE NegateExpr goes here; see next example *)

VAR
    Given   : Queue;
    TheInfo : Information;
BEGIN
    Given := Data;
    Create (Data);
    REPEAT
        Dequeue (TheInfo, Given);
        IF Compare (TheInfo, not) = 0 THEN
            NegateExpr (Data, Given);
        ELSE
            Enqueue (TheInfo, Data);
        END;
    UNTIL IsEmpty (Given);
END SimplifyNOT;
```

ply call the NegateExpr procedure again to handle negating the expression that follows NOT. Example 7.4B contains the coding.

Simplifying ANDs and ORs in a Boolean Expression

The third stage of the program simplifies the prefix expression as a number of special terms connected using OR, with no other ORs in the expression. There are two useful rules for simplifying expressions, called the **distributive laws**. Each comes in two forms, owing to the fact that OR P Q is equivalent to OR Q P and also AND P Q is equivalent to AND Q P:

1. AND OR P Q R is equivalent to OR AND P R AND Q R.
   AND R OR P Q is equivalent to OR AND P R AND Q R.

2. OR AND P Q R is equivalent to AND OR P R OR Q R.
   OR R AND P Q is equivalent to AND OR P R OR Q R.

You will be convinced of the truth of these equivalences if you think about each one for a few minutes. For instance, AND OR P Q R means that OR P Q is true and also R is true. If P and R are both true, so are both of OR P Q and R. If Q and R are both true, so are both of OR P Q and R. Therefore, if either AND P R or AND Q R is true, so is AND OR P Q R. Thus OR AND P R AND Q R implies AND OR P Q R. Conversely, if OR P Q is true and also R is true, then either AND P R must be true or AND Q R must be true. Did you get lost in the middle of this paragraph? I said a few minutes, not 40 seconds. To help you remember the distributive laws, note that they have the same form as $X * (Y+Z) = (X*Y) + (X*Z)$, with AND for $*$ and OR for $+$ or vice versa.

The third stage of the program accepts a queue named Data and returns a queue that contains an equivalent prefix expression with no operand of AND being an OR-expression. The basic logic is to go through the given queue, dequeueing one value at a time and passing it on, until AND is seen. At that point you process the two operands of AND. If neither contains an OR-expression, you can go on. Otherwise you apply the first DeMorgan law to switch the AND-expression to an OR-expression with AND-expressions as its operands. This is left as a programming problem.

Check Your Understanding

1. Convert this prefix expression to a prefix CNF-expression:
   AND OR x NOT OR y z

2. Convert the prefix expression in Exercise 1 to a prefix DNF-expression.

3. Find all assignments of values for x, y, z that make the prefix expression in Exercise 1 true.

EXAMPLE 7.4B _____

```
PROCEDURE NegateExpr (VAR Data, Given : Queue);
    (* Take the next prefix expression in Given and put its
       negation in Data, wherein NOT is always followed
       directly by a Boolean variable  *)
    (* Context:  subprocedure of SimplifyNOT *)
  (*-----------------------------------------------------*)

    PROCEDURE FixOneExpr (VAR Data, Given : Queue);
    (* Take the next prefix expression in Given and put its
       equivalent in Data, wherein NOT is always followed
       directly by a Boolean variable  *)
    VAR
        TheInfo : Information;
    BEGIN
        Dequeue (TheInfo, Given);
        IF Compare (TheInfo, not) = 0 THEN
            NegateExpr (Data, Given);
        ELSIF (Compare (TheInfo, and) = 0) OR
              (Compare (TheInfo,  or) = 0) THEN
            Enqueue (TheInfo, Data);
            FixOneExpr (Data, Given);
            FixOneExpr (Data, Given);
        ELSE        (* it is a variable *)
            Enqueue (TheInfo, Data);
        END;
    END FixOneExpr;
  (*-----------------------------------------------------*)

VAR
    TheInfo : Information;

BEGIN          (* NegateExpr *)

    Dequeue (TheInfo, Given);
    IF Compare (TheInfo, not) = 0 THEN
        FixOneExpr (Data, Given);  (* ignore not not *)
    ELSIF Compare (TheInfo, and) = 0 THEN
        (* not and P Q --> or not P not Q *)
        Enqueue (or, Data);
        NegateExpr (Data, Given);
        NegateExpr (Data, Given);
    ELSIF Compare (TheInfo, or) = 0 THEN
        (* not or P Q --> and not P not Q *)
        Enqueue (and, Data);
        NegateExpr (Data, Given);
        NegateExpr (Data, Given);
    ELSE  (* okay if not is followed by a variable *)
        Enqueue (not, Data);
        Enqueue (TheInfo, Data);
    END;

END NegateExpr;
```

4. The REPEAT statement in Example 7.4A can be replaced by the single statement FixOneExpr(Data, Given). What other changes must be made in the examples of this section to allow this replacement? What is the advantage of not making these changes?

5. (NA) Write a procedure that accepts a queue that purports to contain a legal prefix Boolean expression and tells whether it really is. Return the queue unchanged. *Hint:* Make some minor modifications in the examples in this section.

6. (NA) A certain CNF-expression has 7 special factors, each with 5 atomic expressions. It is transformed into a DNF-expression using the first distributive law. How many special terms does the result have?

7. (NA) Write out a logical argument to show that the second distributive law is true. Make it as clear as you can.

7.5   HUFFMAN CODES

The situation is as follows: You are in charge of a group of spies working underground in an inimical country. Your spies have to radio messages to you from time to time. Every moment they are on the air endangers their cover, so it is essential to make the transmission time as short as possible.

All your spies have a code book with a list of 512 words from which they form their message. Each word has a special code that is 9 bits long. The number of different arrangements of 9 bits is 2 to the ninth power, which is 512, which is why the code book is limited to 512 words. Experience has shown that your spy operation cannot manage on much less than 512.

An average message is 100 words long. That means that 900 bits of information must be transmitted. It would be helpful if you could squeeze the information down to 800 bits or less, since that would cut the transmission time by more than 10%.

The solution is to use the **Huffman code**. The following illustration assumes the code book has just 8 words, to reduce the amount of computation that has to be made, but the principle applies to all similar situations. The first step is to find the frequency with which various words are used in messages. For instance, you might find that the frequencies are those shown in the following table, given in average number of occurrences per 100 words:

word:	is	spy	dead	war	infiltrating	radio	peace	secrets
freq:	40	30	10	6	4	5	2	3

With 8 possible words, the natural code to use is one arrangement of 3 bits for each word. This means that the average message of 100 words requires 300 bits.

The principle behind the Huffman code is that less than 3 bits are used for words that occur frequently (such as "is") and that more than 3 bits are used for words that occur rarely (such as "peace"). On balance, the total number of bits transmitted should be less.

Algorithm for Huffman Codes

The algorithm described here gives the minimum possible total number of bits; you will see that the answer is 234 bits, a savings of more than 20%. See if you can apply the algorithm to the 8 words in the table, then check your answer against the solution that follows. The overall algorithm is:

1. Start by constructing a list of eight binary trees, each with one node. Each tree is to contain one word. Associated with each tree in this list of eight trees is the frequency of that one word, taken from the table just given.

2. Do repeatedly until the list has just one binary tree:
   Choose the two trees with the smallest frequencies (in case of ties, any reasonable tie-breaker will do; you could, for instance, choose the least-recently created tree first). Create a new tree with those two trees as the subtrees. Leave the root of this new tree empty. Replace the two trees in the list by the new tree; thus the size of the list of trees has decreased by 1. The frequency for this new tree is considered to be the sum of the frequencies for its two subtrees.

3. At this point, the leaves of the one binary tree contain the words. The code for each word is found by tracing the path from the root to the corresponding leaf, writing 0 for a left branch and 1 for a right branch.

For the foregoing table of eight words and their frequencies, you first combine the "peace" and "secrets" trees to obtain a new tree with frequency 5. Now combine the "infiltrating" and "radio" trees to obtain a new tree with frequency 9 (you could have used the "peace/secrets" tree instead of the "radio" tree). Now combine the "peace/secrets" tree with the "war" tree to obtain a new tree with frequency 11. At this point, you have the five trees shown in Figure 3.

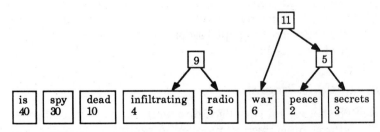

FIGURE 3. Five trees left during the Huffman algorithm.

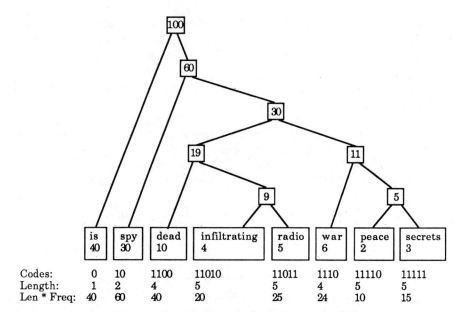

FIGURE 4. The final tree in the Huffman algorithm.

The two lowest frequencies are 10 and 9, so combine the "dead" tree with the "infiltrating/radio" tree to obtain a new tree with frequency 19. Then the two three-word trees are combined to form a new tree with frequency 30. That leaves three trees with frequencies 40, 30, and 30. So the two 30s are combined, then the resulting tree is combined with the "is" tree. The overall result is shown in Figure 4.

Figure 4 also shows the code assigned to each word by using 0 and 1 to indicate left and right branchings in the tree. The length of each code and the product of length times frequency is also given. The total of these products is 234, which is therefore the average number of bits per 100-word message. By comparison, the computation when using 3 bits for each word would multiply the frequency by 3 for each word to arrive at a sum of 300 for the average number of bits per 100-word message.

As an example of a message in this Huffman code, "spy is dead" is coded as 1001100. Note that there is no need to separate the bit groups; the first word cannot be anything but 10, the second must be 0, and the only possibility for the third word is 1100.

The Huffman Code Program

The coding for this algorithm would require several more pages, so most of it is left as a programming problem. A skeletal form of the program is developed next, to get you started on the problem.

Information type can be a word plus a frequency. If you call the information-handling module CodeADT, it should have not only the usual six procedures (CreateInfo, DestroyInfo, CopyInfo, InputInfo, OutputInfo, Compare) but also two procedures to permit storage and retrieval of a frequency. The frequency should be a real number from 0 to 1 instead of a cardinal, to allow for fractions such as 1/8 and 0.0281:

```
PROCEDURE SetFreq (VAR TheInfo : Information; Freq : REAL);
    (* Assign Freq as the frequency associated with TheInfo *)
PROCEDURE FreqOf (TheInfo : Information) : REAL;
    (* Return the frequency associated with TheInfo *)
```

The difficult part is that nothing presented in this book so far permits you to have a list of trees (or even better, a priority queue of trees) as an abstract data type. A general solution for this and similar situations is in Section 8.7; for now, you have no choice but to implement the list of trees directly. The most direct way is to declare a Node to have not only the usual Info, Left, and Right fields for the tree connections, but a Link field for the list connections:

```
TYPE    PointerToNode = POINTER TO Node;
        Node = RECORD
                    Info : Information;
                    Left, Right, Link : PointerToNode;
                END;
VAR     Data : PointerToNode;
```

You should begin by creating a standard linked list named Data, containing one node per information value read in. Reading an information value should include not only the code word but also the frequency. This procedure ignores the tree structure and puts the list in increasing order of frequency (because we want to be able to easily access the two information values with smallest frequency).

Next you make each node on the list a one-node binary tree by assigning NIL to its Left and Right fields. Third, you process the list so it has just one binary tree on it. Finally, you print the binary coding:

```
BEGIN            (* body of program *)
    Data := NIL;
    ReadInfoAndMakeSortedList (Data);
    MakeAOneNodeTreeOutOfEachNodeOnList (Data);
    TurnListIntoHuffmanTree (Data);
    PrintBinaryCodes (Data);
END Huffman.
```

The ReadInfoAndMakeSortedList procedure is much the same as the ReadAll procedure except for inserting a node into the list so the frequencies are in increasing order. Since Huffman problems usually involve a large number of values, it would be best to read the list completely and then use an efficient list-sorting method described in Chapter 6; your instructor will tell you whether you should do that. However, for testing purposes, you could simply insert each information value in order as it is read.

An InsertInOrder procedure that accomplishes this is easy to develop. You need it anyway when you turn the list into a binary tree, since at each stage you have to create a new tree node with the sum of two frequencies and insert that new node in increasing order of frequency. To give you a concrete idea of how the fields of a Node are used, I have coded the TurnListIntoHuffmanTree procedure in Example 7.5A in accordance with the algorithm described earlier; but the InsertInOrder procedure is left for you. Note that the information value in a created node is left indeterminate except for the frequency value, since that is all that is important.

Printing the Binary Codes

The final part of the Huffman algorithm could start with an empty list of characters and then search the entire binary tree recursively. At each nonleaf, you put 0 on the front of the list, go to the left, change the 0 to a 1, go to the right, then delete the top character as you back up to the parent. When you get to a leaf, you write the word at the leaf and its code (all the characters in the list in reverse order). When the whole tree has been traversed, you have printed all the words and their codes.

To implement this, I suggest you declare a new kind of node that has two fields, a character field and a link field.

EXAMPLE 7.5A _____

```
PROCEDURE TurnListIntoHuffmanTree
                    (VAR Data : PointerToNode);
VAR
    P : PointerToNode;
BEGIN
    WHILE Data^.Link # NIL DO
        NEW (P);
        CreateInfo (P^.Info);
        P^.Left := Data;
        P^.Right := Data^.Link;
        Data := Data^.Link^.Link;
        SetFreq (P^.Info, FreqOf (P^.Left^.Info) +
                          FreqOf (P^.Right^.Info));
        InsertInOrder (P, Data);
    END;
END TurnListIntoHuffmanTree;
```

```
TYPE   CharList = PointerToSmallNode;
       SmallNode = RECORD
                       Ch   : CHAR;
                       Link : PointerToSmallNode;
                   END;
```

The difficulty is going to be in printing the list in reverse order. I suggest you use recursion for this, at least at first, since it is easier. If speed of execution is vital, you can later replace the recursion by a more complex algorithm.

The frequency of an information value in the tree is an example of an abstract data type called a **mapping**. Notice that the capabilities we need are (1) the ability to assign a frequency to an information value, and (2) the ability to retrieve the frequency previously assigned to an information value. These two essential procedures are the hallmark of a mapping ADT.

Section 5.4 discussed an implementation of ListADT using a binary tree, in which each node has a Count field that can be assigned a value or from which a value can be retrieved. Thus that data structure was a combination of a mapping and a tree.

Using Imports from an Extended BinADT

The reason you cannot use BinADT for the Huffman problem is that you have to work with a list of binary trees, so you have to be able to insert and delete binary trees in a list. You can add some procedures to BinADT to permit this.

Assume that you want to construct a list of three binary trees named T1, T2, and T3. Consider a binary tree named Data with three nodes, in which each node has an empty left subtree. Then Data is essentially a standard linked list, using the Right pointers instead of Link pointers. Now make T1 the left subtree of the first node, T2 the left subtree of the second node, and T3 the left subtree of the third node. You now have a list of binary subtrees. The information in the nodes on the list is irrelevant, except that for the Huffman problem the frequency should be the sum of the frequencies of the words in the left subtree.

As an illustration, assume that you have four words "is," "spy," "war," and "dead," with frequencies of 40, 30, 20, and 10, respectively. The tree on the left of Figure 5 shows the list of binary trees after merging "war" and "dead"; the tree on the right shows the list after merging the first two binary trees on the list.

For this application, you need to add some procedures to BinADT to permit the manipulation of binary trees the way information can be manipulated. The following four procedures would do. TakeTreeLeft removes the subtree to the left of Where (if Where is not NoNode) and returns it in T; similarly for TakeTreeRight. PutTreeLeft inserts T as the new subtree to the left of Where if there is no subtree there already; similarly for PutTreeRight.

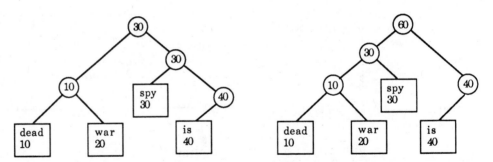

FIGURE 5. Huffman algorithm using one binary tree.

```
PROCEDURE TakeTreeLeft  (VAR T : BinTree;   Where : Location;
                                            VAR Data : BinTree);
PROCEDURE TakeTreeRight (VAR T : BinTree;   Where : Location;
                                            VAR Data : BinTree);
PROCEDURE PutTreeLeft   (T : BinTree;  Where : Location;
                                       VAR Data : BinTree);
PROCEDURE PutTreeRight  (T : BinTree;  Where : Location;
                                       VAR Data : BinTree);
```

Now the procedure in Example 7.5A can be coded as shown in Example 7.5B. The logic is that we create a new tree to be the combination of the first two trees in the list. We take the first information value from Data, along with its left

EXAMPLE 7.5B _____

```
(* Recoding of TurnListIntoHuffmanTree using BinADT *)
    WHILE Right (Root (Data), Data) # NoNode DO
        Create (NewTree);
        TakeTreeLeft (FirstTree, Root (Data), Data);
        TakeRoot (FirstInfo, Data);
        PutRoot (FirstInfo, NewTree);
        PutTreeLeft (FirstTree, Root (NewTree), NewTree);
        TakeTreeLeft (SecondTree, Root (Data), Data);
        PutTreeRight (SecondTree, Root (NewTree), NewTree);
        PutTreeLeft (NewTree, Root (Data), Data);
        See (SecondInfo, Root (Data), Data);
        SetFreq (SecondInfo, FreqOf (SecondInfo) +
                            FreqOf (FirstInfo));
        Swap (SecondInfo, Root (Data), Data);
        InsertInOrder (Data);
    END;
```

subtree. We put that information value at the root of the combined tree and put the subtree on its left. Next we take the left subtree of the second information value in Data and make it the right subtree of the combined tree. Finally, we put the sum of the two frequencies in the root of Data, we attach the combined tree on its left, and we call InsertInOrder. This procedure must move the first node of the tree, along with its left subtree, down the righthand branch of Data until the list is again in order of frequencies.

Check Your Understanding

1. Find the Huffman code for the four words "Kiss", "me", "I'm", "Welsh" when the frequencies are 50, 25, 15, and 10, respectively.

2. In constructing Figure 4, the rules allow you to combine the "infiltrating" tree with the "peace/secrets" tree rather than with the "radio" tree. Explain why this would not have changed the outcome of 234 bits per 100-word message.

3. For the five words Abel, Baker, Charlie, Dog, and Evelyn with frequencies 45, 30, 14, 6, 5, respectively, the Huffman codes are 0, 10, 110, 1110, and 1111, respectively. What is the average number of bits per 100-word message?

4. If Data is a circular linked list with header node, the InsertInOrder procedure can be made to execute significantly faster. However, the rest of the coding in Example 7.5A would execute a little slower. What changes would be required in Example 7.5A?

5. (NA) Draw the tree that would have resulted from making the alternate decision described in Exercise 2.

6. (NA) Discuss why a Huffman coded message can be decoded without ambiguity even without spaces between the groupings. *Hint:* The final binary tree can be reconstructed from the code book, so assume in your discussion that the decoder has the tree available.

7.6 INTRODUCTION TO THE SYNTAX CHECKER

The subject matter of the next few sections is the development of a complete working program, written in Modula-2, that checks the syntax of programs written in Modula-2. This is called **parsing** the program. This SynCheck program is useful even when you already have a Modula-2 compiler. For instance, you can include extensive messages to be displayed for the user when an error appears; this provides a much more congenial programming environment for a beginning student.

Uses of the SynCheck Program

One Modula-2 software development system has a syntax-directed editor, which can be a pain to use. You may want to avoid the irritations by writing your programs on an outside editor and bringing those programs into this system for compilation. But this system refuses to accept a program you have written using a different editor unless the syntax is flawless. If there is any syntax error, you have to exit the system, correct the error on the outside editor, and try again. The SynCheck program can eliminate this problem.

The problem is compounded when your programs worked fine on another compiler but the syntax rules in the target system are different. You can easily modify this SynCheck program to check the syntax according to the target system's rules; more modification would allow it to revise the program appropriately as it is processed. You could use what you consider improvements in Modula-2 syntax in your programs and have SynCheck preprocess them to the "official" syntax. For instance, you could have it enforce the rule that every comment must be terminated on the line where it began. When you forget to terminate a comment, it will warn you. I have known some students to spend hours looking for an error in a program when it turned out that they had only written *) as *(or otherwise mistyped the comment terminator.

The SynCheck program has a number of uses as the basis for other programs. Some moderate modifications would allow it to format a program according to specified formatting conventions. Different modifications would allow it to check for the use of a simple variable that has not been previously initialized or for an extraneous assignment to a variable. In fact, some extensive additions to the SynCheck program would make it a compiler; it so happens that I obtained this program by stripping down a compiler to have a program small enough for this book. The resulting compiler can be used to create a Modula-2 compiler for one machine when you already have a Modula-2 compiler for another machine; the method is described in Section 7.10.

Scope of the SynCheck Program

This chapter develops the entire program. However, I have greatly restricted the language in order to obtain a manageable undertaking; it comes to about 160 statements in the SynCheck program module, about 60 in the LexAnal library module. You can add to the program presented here to obtain a full syntax checker for Modula-2; several moderate additions are suggested as programming problems.

SynCheck has the following restrictions: TYPE and CONST sections are not allowed; every variable must be of INTEGER type, and even empty blocks must have their BEGINs. The only structured statements allowed are IF and WHILE; ELSIF is disallowed, although ELSE is accepted. Procedures within the program being checked cannot have parameters; there are no functions or internal modules. The only operators are +, −, *, =, #, >, <, >=, <=, AND, OR. Only procedures can be imported. String literals are not allowed (they are left for a programming problem).

There are few deviations from Modula-2 that can slip by SynCheck: IMPORT sections are not checked to be sure that the library declarations exist and are actually procedures, and the number of parameters for imported procedures is not checked. The second deviation is that mixing of integers with relational operators is not detected.

The Lexical Analyzer

The SynCheck program imports from five library modules, named LexAnal, Info-Man, TableMAR, Helpful, and SayStuff. One library module has the responsibility of reading the source program and separating it into tokens. Such a module is called a **lexical analyzer**, so I name it LexAnal. *Reminder:* A program consists of tokens and spacing. A token is the smallest unit of meaning in a program. There are three kinds of *tokens:* word tokens (reserved words and identifiers), literals (string and numeric), and special symbols (such as semicolons, plus signs, and :=). They can be distinguished as follows: A word token begins with a letter; a literal begins with an apostrophe, a quote, or a digit; and a special symbol begins with something else.

LexAnal exports four fundamental identifiers: **SymbolType** is an enumeration type, **Token** and **TokenSymbol** are variables, and **GetNextToken** is a procedure without parameters. Every token in the input file is assigned one of the following SymbolTypes:

```
TYPE  SymbolType = (begin, var, procedure, while, if, else,
                    do, then, module, from, import, end,
                assignment, semicolon, period, comma,
                colon, leftparen, rightparen,
                relop, addop, mulop, endfile,
            identifier, number, string, unknown);
```

The first 12 SymbolTypes are reserved words, the next 10 are special symbols, and the last five are the remaining categories of tokens. The relop value is used for all relational operators (>, =, etc.), the addop value for all addition-level operators (+, −, OR), and the mulop value is used for all multiplication-level operators (*, AND). The logic of LexAnal requires that all values representing reserved words be listed together in SymbolType, beginning with BEGIN and ending with END. However, AND and OR are categorized as special symbols, not reserved words.

TokenSymbol is a variable of type SymbolType. At the beginning of execution of SynCheck, a call of GetNextToken assigns the first token in the source program to Token and sets TokenSymbol correspondingly. Each additional call of

GetNextToken assigns the next token in the source program to Token and sets TokenSymbol correspondingly. When all tokens in the entire source program have been found and GetNextToken is called, a sentinel value called **endfile** is assigned to TokenSymbol.

Token is a string of characters. The definition and implementation modules for LexAnal are postponed until Section 7.10; the only part of them that is not straightforward is the coding of the GetNextToken procedure.

The InfoSYN Library Module

The InfoSYN module collects all type declarations needed relative to Information in one separate library module. This InfoSYN module, tailored to the syntax checker program, does not hide the inner structure of Information, since it must be accessed frequently. However, only SynCheck itself accesses that structure, and then only by using " ↑ ."; thus it would not be overly difficult to change the implementation used. In fact, the Information type could be made opaque by exporting several pairs of procedures such as GetName(ResultName, TheInfo) and SetName(GivenName, TheInfo).

In addition to Information, InfoSYN exports an enumeration type KindOfIdentifier=(TypeIdentifier, VariableIdentifier, ProcedureIdentifier). This value is also kept in one of the fields of Information. When SynCheck sees a declaration of an identifier, it assigns its KindOfIdentifier appropriately before it inserts it in the table of identifiers. When SynCheck sees a usage of an identifier, it inspects the table to make sure that the identifier has been previously declared and is used properly. The InfoSYN definition module is in Example 7.6A. Note that the procedures in the implementation module were all developed in Chapter 2 except for MakeInfo.

Information has one additional field named Level. This cardinal value tells how many layers deep the current procedure is. Level is 1 for the global declarations; identifiers local to a global procedure have Level 2, and so forth.

The MakeInfo procedure is useful for obtaining an Information variable for use with the Inspect procedure of TableMAR. The NoInfo declaration is only used by TableMAR.

The TableMAR Library Module

The SynCheck program uses a variant of the TableADT library module described in Section 3.7: The TakeOut procedure is replaced by two procedures named Mark and Release. Each of these has one Table parameter. Mark(Data) has no direct effect on the Table, but a note is made that all insertions after that point are considered to be in a new **subtable**. When Release(Data) is executed, all information values in the most recently created subtable are deleted. Thus a Table could be considered to be a stack of subtables, with the proviso that you are allowed to Inspect any information in a subtable in the stack (the most recently inserted information value is accessed). The names Mark and Release are derived from analogous procedures available with some forms of Pascal.

EXAMPLE 7.6A _____

```
DEFINITION MODULE InfoSYN;
EXPORT QUALIFIED Information, CreateInfo, CopyInfo,
                 DestroyInfo, Compare, MakeInfo, NoInfo,
                 KindOfIdentifier;
    (* Core Declarations needed for the SynCheck program *)
    (* Written by William C. Jones, July 19-- *)
CONST
    StrMax = 30;
    NoInfo = NIL;
TYPE
    KindOfIdentifier = (TypeIdentifier, VariableIdentifier,
                        ProcedureIdentifier);
    Information = POINTER TO
        RECORD
            Name  : ARRAY [0..StrMax] OF CHAR;
            Kind  : KindOfIdentifier;
            Level : CARDINAL;
        END;
(*********************************************************)

PROCEDURE CreateInfo  (VAR TheInfo : Information);
PROCEDURE CopyInfo    (VAR TheInfo : Information;
                           Source  : Information);
PROCEDURE DestroyInfo (VAR TheInfo : Information);
PROCEDURE Compare (First, Second : Information) : INTEGER;
PROCEDURE MakeInfo  (VAR TheInfo : Information;
                         Given : ARRAY OF CHAR);
    (* Create an Information variable and assign Given to
       the Name field.  Leave other fields empty.  *)

END InfoSYN.
```

The Mark procedure is called each time processing of a procedure begins. The Release procedure is called when the END of the procedure is processed, to remove all variables local to that procedure from the table. If TableMAR is the simple array implementation or a linked list implementation (either of which is feasible), with all insertions made at the same end of the structure, Mark can be implemented by putting a sentinel information value in the table using PutIn-(NoInfo, Data). Then Release for the reverse array implementation would be coded as follows (within WITH Data ↑ DO... END):

```
WHILE (Size > 0) AND (Item [Size] # NoInfo) DO
    InfoSYN.DestroyInfo (Item [Size]);
    DEC (Size);
END;
IF Size > 0 THEN
    DEC (Size);
END;
```

The SayStuff Library Module

When an error is seen by the program, it must give an error message to the user. This could be on the screen for immediate consumption or in a file to read at leisure. In some situations, such as a syntax checker for beginning programmers, the messages should be fulsome; in other situations they can be almost cryptic. Thus, for maximum flexibility, all communications to the user should be kept in a separate module. I name this library module **SayStuff**. This module exports just one enumeration type named **MessageType** and two procedures called **Say-WhatWasExpected** and **SayErrorMessage**. The SayWhatWasExpected procedure has a SymbolType value as its parameter; it will say that the token of that category was expected at that point in the program. It could be something like:

```
WriteString (Token);
WriteString (' is not acceptable here.  ');
CASE GivenSymbol OF
    then       : WriteString ('THEN expected for IF statement');
|   identifier : WriteString ('identifier expected here');
    ...
```

SayErrorMessage will give one of a fixed number of error messages. Since I do not want to know the exact language of the message, SayStuff exports an enumeration type naming the various error messages. The declaration of MessageType could be:

```
MessageType = (EndFileTooSoon, ExpectedVarProcBegin, ExtraTokens,
               IdentifierDeclaredTwice, IdentifierNotDeclared,
               ExpectedProcedureName, ExpectedTypeName,
               ExpectedStatement, BadIdentifierType,
               BadFactor, UnknownError);
```

The body of the SayErrorMessage procedure can just be a CASE statement that enumerates the various values the GivenMessageCode parameter can have and provides a reasonable error message for each, as in:

```
CASE GivenMessageCode OF
    EndFileTooSoon : WriteString
        ('end of file came before "END." of program');
|   ExpectedProcedureName : WriteString
        ('procedure name required after its END');
    ...
```

A good library module is one that hides a well-defined aspect of the program. Note that the SayStuff module hides communications to the user so well that you cannot even tell whether those messages are in English or German without reading its implementation module.

To review: The SynCheck program depends directly on the following five library modules (Figure 6). Note that LexAnal handles all input and SayStuff handles all output.

☐ InfoSYN contains the usual declarations relevant to Information; it must be compiled before TableMAR or SayStuff.

☐ Helpful (from Section 2.1) exports CompareStr, used in LexAnal, InfoSYN, and SynCheck.

☐ LexAnal contains the GetNextToken procedure and associated declarations; its job is to convert the input file to an orderly sequence of tokens, omitting comments and spacing.

☐ TableMAR handles the Table abstract data type, exporting Create, Destroy, PutIn, Inspect, Find, InTable, Mark, and Release. Mark and Release obviate the need for TakeOut.

☐ SayStuff exports two procedures for giving messages to the writer of the program. It must be compiled after LexAnal.

Check Your Understanding

1. Assume that Table is implemented with a standard linked list implementation in which each inserted value is put at the front of the linked list. Write the coding for Release(Data), assuming that Mark(Data) is essentially Push(NoInfo, Data).

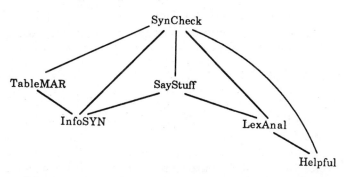

FIGURE 6. *Dependencies among the six compiled modules.*

2. Each of CreateInfo, CopyInfo, and DestroyInfo has one statement. Write those statements.

3. (NA) Give two more likely cases in the CASE statement of SayErrorMessage.

4. (NA) Write the implementation of the MakeInfo procedure for Example 7.6A.

7.7 THE OVERALL LOGIC OF THE SYNTAX ANALYZER

The fundamental algorithm for SynCheck consists of three steps: First, create a table in which to store all the identifiers used in the program; I call it IDTable. Second, put all the permissible built-in identifiers of this restricted form of Modula-2 in the table. Third, see if the input file conforms to the required syntax for a program in this stripped-down language. The required syntax for a program is that it be a sequence of five units: (1) the module-heading, (2) whatever import sections are used, (3) the block of the program, (4) the module-identifier, and (5) a period.

Each of the first three syntactical units will, of course, require a procedure of its own. I will name such procedures ProcessX, where X is replaced by the name of whatever unit is to be processed. For instance, one procedure will be Process-ModuleHeading. Some prior experience with programs of this type indicates that the easiest way to manage these ProcessX procedures is: (1) obtain the first token of unit X (and store it in the Token variable) before calling the ProcessX procedure; (2) be sure that the ProcessX procedure obtains the first token that follows unit X in the input file (and stores that token in Token). To parse the program, that means that you take the following actions:

1. Execute GetNextToken (which obtains the first token of the heading).
2. Call ProcessModuleHeading (which finishes by obtaining the first token of the import sections).
3. Call ProcessImportSections (which finishes by obtaining the first token of the block of the program).
4. Call ProcessBlock (which finishes by obtaining the module-identifier after the END of the block).
5. Verify that Token contains the identifier of this module.
6. Get the next token and verify that it is a period.

It should be clear that ProcessModuleHeading should return the module-identifier to the main program as a parameter so it can be used in step 5.

You should be able to see that there will be many times in this program that you will look at the current token to see if it is a particular symbol type (such as a period, for step 6). If it is the period (or whatever), you can go on to get the following token. If the current token is not what it is supposed to be, you should give an appropriate message; usually, you should *not* get the following token in such cases. For instance, if you expect THEN and find END, you should give an appropriate message but keep the END to match up with an earlier statement. This tactic is important for **error recovery**—finding a token to get us back on the track for further analysis after an error occurs. It is not really necessary with the final period at the end of the program, but it does not hurt to use it there.

The coding in Example 7.7A contains all the program except for the three ProcessX procedures just described. The PutBuiltinIdentifiersInTable procedure just allows INTEGER; it is easy (though tedious) to extend this procedure for any other built-in identifiers you might wish to have.

Throughout this program, a procedure that is to analyze a semantic construct is described by giving the EBNF notation for the construct it is to analyze. It may help to review the meaning of braces, brackets, and vertical bars (Section 1.2) at this time.

ProcessModuleHeading and ProcessImportSections

The ProcessModuleHeading procedure is straightforward, since a module heading consists of precisely three tokens: the word MODULE, then the module-identifier, then a semicolon. Three calls of GetNextTokenIfThisOneIs(T) for various T will work fine. The only other thing we have to do is pass the module-identifier back to the main program. Since this is given as an array of characters, it is converted to an information value by calling MakeInfo. See Example 7.7B for the coding.

The import sections consist of a number of phrases beginning with FROM. We cannot know how many such phrases there will be, so a WHILE loop is appropriate; each occurrence of FROM indicates we should process another import section. In general, a syntactic construct whose EBNF is enclosed in braces will be analyzed by a WHILE loop. This allows for 0 or 1 or 12 or whatever number of those constructs.

The word IMPORT is followed by an identifier-list. It is necessary to store these identifiers in the IDTable for later reference, which complicates the analysis of an identifier-list. Besides, there will be other times when an identifier-list must be analyzed. Therefore, it is best to develop a separate procedure Process-IdentifierList. When an identifier is put in the IDTable, it must be stored with its Level (which is 1 for the program module and more than 1 for all local identifiers) and the kind of identifier it is (procedure, variable, or type). That is why the procedure has 1 and ProcedureIdentifier as its parameters.

The tokens in a FROM phrase are completely determined except for the identifier-list. This means that the rest of the coding of ProcessImportSections consists primarily of calling GetNextTokenIfThisOneIs(T) for various T; the coding is in Example 7.7C. Note that each ProcessX procedure has a comment that gives the EBNF of the construct being processed; this serves as a clear and unambiguous statement of the task to be performed by the ProcessX procedure.

EXAMPLE 7.7A _____

```
MODULE SynCheck;
FROM Helpful  IMPORT CompareStr;
FROM InfoSYN  IMPORT Information, MakeInfo, CopyInfo,
                     DestroyInfo, KindOfIdentifier;
FROM LexAnal  IMPORT SymbolType, TokenSymbol,
                     Token, GetNextToken;
FROM TableMAR IMPORT Table, Create, PutIn, Find, Inspect,
                     InTable, Mark, Release;
FROM SayStuff IMPORT MessageType, SayWhatWasExpected,
                     SayErrorMessage;
(*********************************************************)

PROCEDURE PutBuiltinIdentifiersInTable
        (VAR IDTable : Table);
VAR
    TheInfo : Information;
BEGIN
    MakeInfo (TheInfo, 'INTEGER');
    TheInfo^.Kind := TypeIdentifier;
    TheInfo^.Level := 1;
    PutIn (TheInfo, IDTable);
END PutBuiltinIdentifiersInTable;
(*********************************************************)

PROCEDURE GetNextTokenIfThisOneIs (Desired : SymbolType);
BEGIN
    IF TokenSymbol = Desired THEN
        GetNextToken;
    ELSE
        SayWhatWasExpected (Desired);
    END;
END GetNextTokenIfThisOneIs;
(*********************************************************)

    (* $ program  =  module-heading  imports
                     block   identifier  '.'  .  *)
VAR
    IDTable : Table;   (* saves all declared identifiers *)
    Saved   : Information;   (* saves module identifier *)

BEGIN          (* program *)
    Create (IDTable);
    PutBuiltinIdentifiersInTable (IDTable);
    GetNextToken;

    ProcessModuleHeading (Saved);
    ProcessImportSections (IDTable);
    ProcessBlock (IDTable, 1);  (* 1 is the global level *)

    IF CompareStr (Saved^.Name, Token) # 0 THEN
        SayErrorMessage (ExpectedProcedureName);
    END;
    GetNextToken;
    GetNextTokenIfThisOneIs (period);
END SynCheck.
```

EXAMPLE 7.7B _____

```
PROCEDURE ProcessModuleHeading (VAR Saved : Information);
    (* $ module-heading = MODULE identifier ';' . *)
BEGIN
    GetNextTokenIfThisOneIs (module);
    MakeInfo (Saved, Token);
    GetNextTokenIfThisOneIs (identifier);
    GetNextTokenIfThisOneIs (semicolon);
END ProcessModuleHeading;
```

The ProcessIdentifierList Procedure

An identifier-list consists of one or more identifiers separated by commas. So after you process one identifier, you look at the next token; if it is a comma, there should be another identifier in the list to be processed, otherwise the list is terminated. This procedure can therefore be written as a WHILE statement that tests whether the current token is a comma. However, the LOOP construct cuts out a large amount of repetition of coding, so LOOP is used instead of WHILE. The main reason is that there are two conditions for terminating the loop, and one or two statements must be executed between testing for an identifier and testing for a comma.

When an identifier is declared, you must enter it in the IDTable. But first you have to check that it is not already declared with the same level (it is all right to have different declarations of the same identifier as long as they are at different levels of locality). If you find a duplicate declaration, you of course give an appropriate error message. For purposes of error recovery, however, you might as well go ahead and add the newly declared identifier to the table anyway; that is the simplest thing to do.

EXAMPLE 7.7C _____

```
PROCEDURE ProcessImportSections (VAR IDTable : Table);
    (* $ imports = { FROM any-identifier IMPORT
                          identifier-list ';' } . *)
BEGIN
    WHILE TokenSymbol = from DO
        GetNextToken;
        GetNextTokenIfThisOneIs (identifier);
        GetNextTokenIfThisOneIs (import);
        ProcessIdentifierList (ProcedureIdentifier,
                                 1, IDTable);
        GetNextTokenIfThisOneIs (semicolon);
    END;
END ProcessImportSections;
```

Notice that there is a separate global EnterNewIdentifier procedure in Example 7.7D. We will have other situations in which a single identifier must be entered in the IDTable, so this is not a subprocedure of ProcessIdentifierList.

The only part of the program left to develop is the ProcessBlock procedure. However, that will require considerable effort. The next section begins that development.

EXAMPLE 7.7D _____

```
PROCEDURE EnterNewIdentifier (GivenKind : KindOfIdentifier;
                              CurrentLevel : CARDINAL;
                              VAR IDTable  : Table);
VAR
    TheInfo, TempInfo : Information;
BEGIN
    MakeInfo (TheInfo, Token);
    Find (TheInfo, IDTable);
    Inspect (TempInfo, IDTable);
    IF InTable (IDTable) AND
            (TempInfo^.Level = CurrentLevel) THEN
        SayErrorMessage (IdentifierDeclaredTwice);
    END;

    TheInfo^.Level := CurrentLevel;
    TheInfo^.Kind := GivenKind;
    PutIn (TheInfo, IDTable);
END EnterNewIdentifier;
(************************************************************)

PROCEDURE ProcessIdentifierList (Given : KindOfIdentifier;
                                 CurrentLevel : CARDINAL;
                                 VAR IDTable  : Table);
    (* $ new-identifier-list = new-identifier
                       { ',' new-identifier } .   *)
BEGIN
    LOOP
        IF TokenSymbol # identifier THEN
            SayWhatWasExpected (identifier);
            EXIT;
        END;

        EnterNewIdentifier (Given, CurrentLevel, IDTable);
        GetNextToken;

        IF TokenSymbol # comma THEN
            EXIT;
        END;
        GetNextToken;
    END;
END ProcessIdentifierList;
```

Check Your Understanding

1. What do you add to Example 7.7A to put the built-in Modula-2 identifiers INC and DEC in the table of identifiers?

2. Rewrite the ProcessIdentifierList procedure to use WHILE instead of LOOP.

3. Which if any of the following tokens can be omitted from the import section of an otherwise correct program without causing more than one error message?

    (a) FROM   (b) IMPORT   (c) a comma   (d) the semicolon

4. The Saved variable declared in Example 7.7A is created (in ProcessModule-Heading) but never destroyed. Why not?

5. (NA) Give a detailed logical argument to show that it is impossible for this program to become stuck in an "infinite loop," on the assumption that it does not become stuck within ProcessBlock.

6. (NA) How would you change Example 7.7A so that it gives an appropriate error message when there are additional tokens following the period at the end of the program?

7.8 PARSING A BLOCK IN A PROGRAM

A block consists of any number of VAR declarations and PROCEDURE declarations in any order, followed by the statement part of the block. The statement part has to have a BEGIN, according to the restrictions given in Section 7.6. The words VAR, PROCEDURE, and BEGIN break up the block into manageable units.

You may have noticed that error recovery has been rather primitive up to this point; for instance, if there is an extra comma in the module-heading, the program could "spin its wheels" at that comma until the end of the program is reached, without analyzing any of the rest of the input file for errors. Error recovery is somewhat better in the ProcessBlock procedure. The basic concept is that the words VAR, PROCEDURE, and BEGIN dictate the construct to be analyzed next. If none of these appears, tokens are discarded until one of them is seen (unless the end of the input file is reached). This allows some intelligent analysis of material that comes after an error.

VAR, PROCEDURE, BEGIN, and end-of-file are considered to be the **major dividers** of the block. The analysis of a construct beginning with a major divider does not go past another instance of a major divider unless the syntax is correct (such as a block within a procedure declaration). The TokenIsMajorDivider function is in the next section.

This use of major dividers dictates the basic algorithm of the ProcessBlock procedure. It is essentially a three-alternative statement that is repeated over and over again until BEGIN or end-of-file is seen. At that point the appropriate action can be taken and the procedure exited.

When VAR is seen, we have to allow for the possibility that there are no variable declarations. The syntax of Modula-2 allows the sequence VAR BEGIN; you can have 0 or more variable declarations each with a semicolon after it. This implies a WHILE loop that calls ProcessVarSection as many times as necessary, verifying that there is a semicolon after each VAR declaration. You can tell whether there is another VAR declaration to be processed by seeing whether the current token is an identifier.

Processing a procedure declaration is a simple matter of calling ProcessProcedure and then checking that the token after the procedure is a semicolon. Processing a BEGIN is no harder: Just call the ProcessStatementSequence procedure and then check that the token after the sequence is the word END. All these procedures are to be subprocedures of ProcessBlock, to avoid having them call ProcessBlock from a point earlier in the program, which some Modula-2 compilers do not allow. See Example 7.8A.

ProcessVarSection and ProcessProcedure

A variable declaration consists of a list of identifiers, then a colon, then the type to be associated with each variable. The only type allowed is INTEGER, but this procedure is written so that any type-identifier is acceptable.

We already have a procedure, developed for use with IMPORT sections, that processes a list of identifiers to be entered in the IDTable, if we tell it the kind of identifier (VariableIdentifier in this case) and the level at which the identifier occurs; ProcessIdentifierList was written to accommodate this situation. After we check that the next token is a colon, we can go on to the token after that. It should be a type identifier, so we retrieve that entry from the IDTable. If we find that it is not a type identifier that has previously been entered in the table, we give an appropriate error message. We do not read another token from the input file unless we verify that this one is an identifier. That keeps us from passing up a major divider in the program. Example 7.8B has the coding.

A procedure declaration is more complex than a variable declaration. For one thing, it consists of five syntactic units:

```
( * $ proc-decl = PROCEDURE new-identifier ';'
                  block proc-identifier . *)
```

EXAMPLE 7.8A _____

```
PROCEDURE ProcessBlock (VAR IDTable  : Table;
                            CurrentLevel : CARDINAL);
     (* $ block = { declaration }  BEGIN
                    statement-seq  END . *)
     (* $ declaration = VAR  { var-decl ';' }
                    | proc-decl ';' . *)
(*============= all later procedures go here =============*)


BEGIN           (* ProcessBlock *)

    WHILE (TokenSymbol # begin) AND
          (TokenSymbol # endfile) DO
        IF TokenSymbol = var THEN
            GetNextToken;
            WHILE TokenSymbol = identifier DO
                ProcessVarSection (IDTable, CurrentLevel);
                GetNextTokenIfThisOneIs (semicolon);
            END;
        ELSIF TokenSymbol = procedure THEN
            ProcessProcedure (IDTable, CurrentLevel);
            GetNextTokenIfThisOneIs (semicolon);
        ELSE
            SayErrorMessage (ExpectedVarProcBegin);
            REPEAT
                GetNextToken;
            UNTIL TokenIsMajorDivider ();
        END; (* of IF *)
    END; (* of WHILE *)

    IF TokenSymbol = endfile THEN
        SayErrorMessage (EndFileTooSoon);
    ELSE  (* it is BEGIN *)
        GetNextToken;
        ProcessStatementSequence (IDTable);
        GetNextTokenIfThisOneIs (end);
    END;

END ProcessBlock;
```

What makes it even more complicated is that one of the syntactic units (the block) is itself made up of several units. However, we already have a procedure to process a block (Example 7.8A), so that will not require any extra development work. This and similar uses of recursion make the development of this program enormously simpler.

We begin analyzing a procedure declaration by getting the next token and making sure it is an identifier. If it is, we enter it in the IDTable as a new procedure identifier and also make a note of it for later use when the END of the procedure is seen. Then we advance past the semicolon at the end of the procedure heading.

EXAMPLE 7.8B _____

```
PROCEDURE ProcessVarSection (VAR IDTable  : Table;
                                 CurrentLevel : CARDINAL);
    (* $ var-decl =  identifier-list ':' type  . *)
VAR
    TheInfo : Information;
BEGIN
    ProcessIdentifierList (VariableIdentifier,
                           CurrentLevel, IDTable);
    GetNextTokenIfThisOneIs (colon);
    IF TokenSymbol # identifier THEN
        SayWhatWasExpected (identifier);
    ELSE
        MakeInfo (TheInfo, Token);
        Find (TheInfo, IDTable);
        DestroyInfo (TheInfo);
        Inspect (TheInfo, IDTable);
        IF NOT InTable (IDTable) OR
                (TheInfo^.Kind # TypeIdentifier) THEN
            SayErrorMessage (ExpectedTypeName);
        END;
        GetNextToken;  (* should be semicolon *)
    END;
END ProcessVarSection;
```

The block of the procedure is analyzed simply by calling ProcessBlock with a level 1 more than that of the procedure identifier. Thus, if it is a global procedure (level 1), all identifiers in its block will have level 2. If it is a subprocedure of a global procedure (thus level 2), all identifiers in its block will have level 3. Just before processing the block, we "mark" the current point in the IDTable. Immediately after processing the block of the procedure, we "release" all identifiers declared within that block (Example 7.8C). The block of the procedure ends with END, so we check that the procedure-identifier follows that END. Figure 7 shows the relation of ProcessBlock to its major subprograms.

This method of parsing a syntactic unit by a direct application of the recursive EBNF notation is called **recursive descent**. The method requires that the EBNF form be such that, at each point where a choice can be made, the next token is enough to tell which alternative is chosen.

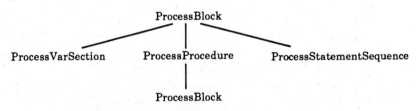

FIGURE 7. *Key procedure calls involving ProcessBlock.*

EXAMPLE 7.8C _____

```
PROCEDURE ProcessProcedure (VAR IDTable  : Table;
                                CurrentLevel : CARDINAL);
     (* $ proc-decl = PROCEDURE new-identifier ';'
                        block procedure-identifier . *)
VAR
     Saved : Information;
BEGIN

     (* process procedure heading *)
         GetNextToken;
         MakeInfo (Saved, Token);
         IF TokenSymbol # identifier THEN
             SayWhatWasExpected (identifier);
         ELSE
             EnterNewIdentifier (ProcedureIdentifier,
                                  CurrentLevel, IDTable);
             GetNextToken; (* should be semicolon *)
         END;
         GetNextTokenIfThisOneIs (semicolon);

     (* process body of procedure *)
         Mark (IDTable);
         ProcessBlock (IDTable, CurrentLevel + 1);
         Release (IDTable);
         IF CompareStr (Saved^.Name, Token) # 0 THEN
             SayErrorMessage (ExpectedProcedureName);
         ELSE
             GetNextToken;  (* should be semicolon *)
         END;
         DestroyInfo (Saved);

END ProcessProcedure;
```

Check Your Understanding

1. Why is GetNextToken called just before calling ProcessVarSection and ProcessStatementSequence in Example 7.8A, instead of calling it as the first statement in each of those two procedures?

2. What would have to be added to Example 7.8A if we allowed constant sections? Assume the existence of a ProcessConstSection procedure.

3. What happens if an otherwise correct program omits the procedure name after the END of a procedure or the following semicolon or both?

4. (NA) Write Example 7.8A as a CASE statement inside a LOOP statement. The CASE statement should have five alternatives including its ELSE clause.

7.9 PARSING STATEMENT SEQUENCES AND EXPRESSIONS

To review: The SynCheck program is now completely done except for the Boolean TokenIsMajorDivider function and the ProcessStatementSequence procedure, both of which are subprocedures of the global ProcessBlock procedure. The ProcessStatementSequence procedure has only the table of identifiers as a parameter; the table and the global Token and TokenSymbol variables contain all the information needed to process a sequence of statements. The IDTable is a value parameter, since it is not changed by statements.

The TokenIsMajorDivider function simply tells whether the current token is one of VAR, PROCEDURE, BEGIN, or end-of-file; it is used in error recovery. But if an error is seen when processing a statement sequence, it is wasteful to skip forward to the next major divider. It is more useful to have a procedure that skips forward to the next semicolon or END, because a new statement should start directly after one of those two tokens; they can be called **minor dividers**. To be safe, such a procedure should also not advance past a major divider. The two procedures are in Example 7.9A.

A statement sequence consists of one or more statements separated by semicolons. The obvious thing to do about this is to process one statement, then see if a semicolon follows; if so, process one statement, then see if a semicolon follows; and so forth. You do not have to call GetNextToken after returning from ProcessStatement, since (by agreement) every ProcessX procedure is to get the token following the semantic construct it processes.

There are five possibilities for a statement: IF, WHILE, assignment, procedure call, and empty statement. They are easily distinguished by the first token, except that an identifier could introduce either an assignment statement or a procedure call. Thus the basic logic should be a CASE statement with IF, WHILE, identifier, and "other" as the cases. If an identifier is not seen, you call the

EXAMPLE 7.9A _____

```
PROCEDURE TokenIsMajorDivider () : BOOLEAN;
BEGIN
    RETURN (TokenSymbol = var) OR (TokenSymbol = procedure)
      OR (TokenSymbol = begin) OR (TokenSymbol = endfile);
END TokenIsMajorDivider;
(*=========================================================*)

PROCEDURE SkipToMinorDivider;
BEGIN
    REPEAT
        GetNextToken;
    UNTIL TokenIsMajorDivider () OR (TokenSymbol = end)
          OR (TokenSymbol = semicolon);
END SkipToMinorDivider;
```

appropriate ProcessX statement, passing IDTable as the sole parameter. If an identifier is seen, you call a procedure to determine whether it is the beginning of an assignment statement or a procedure call.

In this restricted form of Modula-2, the only tokens allowed to directly follow a statement are END, ELSE, and a semicolon. Therefore, after returning from processing a statement, you should check for such a token; if not there, you should skip forward to the next minor divider.

The SeeWhatKindOfStatement procedure in Example 7.9B has the job of determining whether to call the ProcessAssignmentStatement procedure or the ProcessProcedureStatement procedure. The first token of the statement is known to be an identifier, so all that is needed is to look in the table of identifiers to see whether the identifier is a variable-identifier or a procedure-identifier, then call the appropriate procedure. Of course, if the identifier is not found in the table, an appropriate error message is issued. If it is the wrong kind of identifier (such as a type-identifier), the last part of the ProcessStatement procedure will take care of giving an appropriate error message.

Processing the Four Kinds of Statements

Part of processing a WHILE statement is the analysis of the Boolean expression that is between WHILE and DO. This requires a new procedure, ProcessExpression. Other than that, each semantic unit that makes up a WHILE statement can be processed by a single statement that has previously been discussed. An assignment statement is just as easily processed, since it is a variable-identifier, then an assignment symbol, then an expression. The coding for both of these is in Example 7.9C. If you want to verify that you understand what we have covered so far, look only at the coding for ProcessWhileStatement and then see if you can write the coding for ProcessAssignmentStatement.

Processing an IF statement is analogous to processing a WHILE statement except for the possibility that there is an ELSE clause. This simply requires an IF statement at the appropriate place, checking for the presence of ELSE and, if so, processing a second statement sequence.

A procedure statement has two optional parts (indicated by brackets in the EBNF), so there are two corresponding IF statements in the coding of ProcessProcedureStatement. If both IF conditions hold true, we process a number of expressions separated by commas, which as usual implies a WHILE statement in which the test for reiteration is whether the current token is a comma. The last expression should be followed by a right parenthesis. Example 7.4D shows how this is coded.

Note how closely the EBNF notation corresponds to the coding: Braces call for an IF statement without ELSE or ELSIF; brackets indicate a WHILE statement; and vertical bars call for a CASE statement or an IF statement with ELSE and ELSIF.

EXAMPLE 7.9B _____

```
PROCEDURE ProcessStatementSequence (IDTable : Table);
    (* all later procedures go here *)
  (*-----------------------------------------------------*)

    PROCEDURE SeeWhatKindOfStatement (IDTable : Table);
    VAR
        TheInfo : Information;
    BEGIN
        MakeInfo (TheInfo, Token);
        Find (TheInfo, IDTable);
        DestroyInfo (TheInfo);
        Inspect (TheInfo, IDTable);
        IF NOT InTable (IDTable) THEN
            SayErrorMessage (IdentifierNotDeclared);
            SkipToMinorDivider;
        ELSIF TheInfo^.Kind = VariableIdentifier THEN
            ProcessAssignmentStatement (IDTable);
        ELSIF TheInfo^.Kind = ProcedureIdentifier THEN
            ProcessProcedureStatement (IDTable);
        END;
    END SeeWhatKindOfStatement;
  (*-----------------------------------------------------*)

    PROCEDURE ProcessStatement (IDTable : Table);
        (* $ statement = if-statement
                       | while-statement
                       | assignment-statement
                       | procedure-statement |    .        *)
    BEGIN (* ProcessStatement *)
        CASE TokenSymbol OF
            if         : ProcessIfStatement (IDTable);
        |   while      : ProcessWhileStatement (IDTable);
        |   identifier : SeeWhatKindOfStatement (IDTable);
        ELSE
            (* do nothing; presumably empty statement *)
        END;

        IF NOT TokenIsMajorDivider () AND
                (TokenSymbol # end) AND
                (TokenSymbol # semicolon) AND
                (TokenSymbol # else) THEN
            SayErrorMessage (ExpectedStatement);
            SkipToMinorDivider;
        END;
    END ProcessStatement;
  (*-----------------------------------------------------*)

    (* $ statement-seq = statement { ';' statement } '.' *)
BEGIN          (* ProcessStatementSequence *)
    ProcessStatement (IDTable);
    WHILE TokenSymbol = semicolon DO
        GetNextToken;
        ProcessStatement (IDTable);
    END;
END ProcessStatementSequence;
```

EXAMPLE 7.9C _____

```
PROCEDURE ProcessWhileStatement (IDTable : Table);
    (* $ while-statement = WHILE expr DO
                           statement-seq END . *)
BEGIN
    GetNextToken;  (* discard WHILE *)
    ProcessExpression (IDTable);
    GetNextTokenIfThisOneIs (do);
    ProcessStatementSequence (IDTable);
    GetNextTokenIfThisOneIs (end);
END ProcessWhileStatement;
(*----------------------------------------------------------*)

PROCEDURE ProcessAssignmentStatement (IDTable : Table);
    (* $ assignment-statement = variable-identifier
                                ':=' expr  . *)
BEGIN
    GetNextToken;  (* discard variable-identifier *)
    GetNextTokenIfThisOneIs (assignment);
    ProcessExpression (IDTable);
END ProcessAssignmentStatement;
```

EXAMPLE 7.9D _____

```
PROCEDURE ProcessIfStatement (IDTable : Table);
    (* $ if-statement = IF expr THEN statement-seq
                        [ ELSE statement-seq ] END . *)
BEGIN
    GetNextToken;  (* discard IF *)
    ProcessExpression (IDTable);
    GetNextTokenIfThisOneIs (then);
    ProcessStatementSequence (IDTable);

    IF TokenSymbol = else THEN
        GetNextToken;  (* discard ELSE *)
        ProcessStatementSequence (IDTable);
    END;
    GetNextTokenIfThisOneIs (end);
END ProcessIfStatement;
(*----------------------------------------------------------*)

PROCEDURE ProcessProcedureStatement (IDTable : Table);
    (* $ procedure-statement = procedure-identifier
         [ '(' [ expr { ',' expr } ] ')' ] . *)
BEGIN
    GetNextToken;  (* discard procedure-identifier *)
    IF TokenSymbol = leftparen THEN
        GetNextToken; (* discard left parenthesis *)
        IF TokenSymbol # rightparen THEN
            ProcessExpression (IDTable);
            WHILE TokenSymbol = comma DO
                GetNextToken;
                ProcessExpression (IDTable);
            END;
            GetNextTokenIfThisOneIs (rightparen);
        END;
    END;
END ProcessProcedureStatement;
```

EXAMPLE 7.9E _____

```
PROCEDURE ProcessExpression (IDTable : Table);
  (* - - - - - - - - - - - - - - - - - - - - - - - - *)

    PROCEDURE ProcessFactor  (IDTable : Table);
        (* $ factor = number | variable-identifier
                    | '(' expression ')' .  *)
    VAR
        TheInfo : Information;
    BEGIN
        IF TokenSymbol = number THEN
            GetNextToken;
        ELSIF TokenSymbol = identifier THEN
            MakeInfo (TheInfo, Token);
            Find (TheInfo, IDTable);
            DestroyInfo (TheInfo);
            Inspect (TheInfo, IDTable);
            IF NOT InTable (IDTable) OR
                (TheInfo^.Kind # VariableIdentifier) THEN
                SayErrorMessage (BadFactor);
            END;
            GetNextToken;
        ELSIF TokenSymbol = leftparen THEN
            GetNextToken;
            ProcessExpression (IDTable);
            GetNextTokenIfThisOneIs (rightparen);
        ELSE
            SayErrorMessage (BadFactor);
        END;
    END ProcessFactor;
  (* - - - - - - - - - - - - - - - - - - - - - - - - *)

    PROCEDURE ProcessTerm (IDTable : Table);
        (* $ term = factor  { mulop  factor }  .  *)
    BEGIN
        ProcessFactor (IDTable);
        WHILE TokenSymbol = mulop DO
            GetNextToken;
            ProcessFactor (IDTable);
        END;
    END ProcessTerm;
  (* - - - - - - - - - - - - - - - - - - - - - - - - *)

    PROCEDURE ProcessSimpleExpression (IDTable : Table);
        (* $ simple-expr = [addop] term { addop term } . *)
    BEGIN
        IF TokenSymbol = addop THEN
            GetNextToken;
        END;

        ProcessTerm (IDTable);
        WHILE TokenSymbol = addop DO
            GetNextToken;
            ProcessTerm (IDTable);
        END;
    END ProcessSimpleExpression;
  (* - - - - - - - - - - - - - - - - - - - - - - - - *)
```

(* continued on next page *)

```
(* EXAMPLE 7.9E continued *)


    (* $ expr = simple-expr  [ relop simple-expr ]' .  *)
BEGIN           (* ProcessExpression *)
    ProcessSimpleExpression (IDTable);
    IF TokenSymbol = relop THEN
        GetNextToken;
        ProcessSimpleExpression (IDTable);
    END;
END ProcessExpression;
```

Processing an Expression

You will be happy to learn that we have only one SynCheck procedure left to discuss—ProcessExpression. It is a long one, however. An expression is defined to be either (1) what is called a **simple expression**, or (2) two simple expressions separated by a relational operator (such as < or =). A simple expression consists of one or more **terms** (defined shortly) separated by addition-level operators, possibly with an addition-level operator at the beginning of the simple expression. The addition-level operators are + − OR.

A term consists of one or more **factors** (defined shortly) separated by either * or / or AND. Finally, a factor is either a number, a variable-identifier, or an expression in parentheses. This all leads to the indirect recursion in Example 7.9E.

Check Your Understanding

1. What is the simplest way to modify Example 7.9D to allow for ELSIF clauses within IF statements?

2. What modifications would you have to make in Examples 7.9A and 7.9B to allow for a REPEAT statement-seq UNTIL condition? Assume the existence of a ProcessRepeatStatement procedure.

3. Write the ProcessRepeatStatement procedure referred to in the previous exercise.

4. (NA) Revise Example 7.9E on the assumption that another SymbolType value is notop, representing NOT. Expand the definition of a factor to include the fact that a factor can be NOT followed by a factor.

5. (NA) List all procedures in Example 7.9E that are called when parsing the following expression, in the order they are called:
(A <= B) AND (C + D > E) OR F OR (G * (H + K) = 5) AND L < M

7.10 THE LEXICAL ANALYZER

The LexAnal module exports the Token variable (the string of characters forming the next token), the SymbolType enumeration type (one value for each category of token), the TokenSymbol variable (the symbol value for the next token), and the GetNextToken procedure (which returns Token and TokenSymbol). The entire purpose of this module is to serve as the interface between the source program and the parsing program. The source program is a file of characters. The LexAnal library module (Example 7.10A) makes it so that the parsing program can treat the input as a file of tokens, with comments and spacing removed.

Side Effects

The implementation module declares some global variables that are used or modified by various procedures in the module without being passed to them as parameters. This is normally to be avoided. One of the most important principles for making a program understandable to a person reading it is: Every variable declared *outside* a procedure and referenced *inside* the procedure is to be passed as a *parameter* of that procedure.

Unfortunately, in this case that cannot be done. When you read a word token, you must keep reading characters until you come to one that is neither a letter

EXAMPLE 7.10A _____

```
DEFINITION MODULE LexAnal;
EXPORT QUALIFIED SymbolType, TokenSymbol,
                 Token, GetNextToken;
    (* Written by William C. Jones, Mar 19-- Rev July *)
TYPE
    SymbolType = (begin, var, procedure, while, if, else,
                    do, then, module, from, import, end,
                  assignment, semicolon, period, comma,
                     colon, leftparen, rightparen,
                     relop, addop, mulop, endfile,
                  identifier, number, string, unknown);
CONST
    StrMax = 30;
VAR
    Token      : ARRAY [0..StrMax] OF CHAR;
    TokenSymbol : SymbolType;

PROCEDURE GetNextToken;
    (* Obtain the next token from the source program
       Assign values to TokenSymbol and Token
       TokenSymbol := unknown if it is unrecognized
       TokenSymbol := endfile when no more tokens  *)

END LexAnal.
```

nor a digit; that is the only way to tell when you have reached the end of the word token. But if the character after it is a less-than character or some other such symbol, you have read part or all of the next token. That character must be saved until the next time the GetNextToken is called. That can only be done with a global variable. When a library module is accessed by a client module, the global variables belonging to the library module retain their values until the client module terminates execution. So I use the character variable Ch to retain this value. Ch is not exported from LexAnal.

What we have so far is, when you call GetNextToken, the first character of the token may be in Ch or it may not. However, uncertainty is anathema to computers. It would be possible to declare a Boolean variable that tells whether Ch contains a significant character, but it is simpler to design the algorithms so that Ch *always* contains the first character after the previous token. That is the reason for the otherwise unnecessary Read(Ch) several places in the implementation; in particular, in the initialization part (just before END LexAnal). *Reminder:* The statement sequence before the end of an implementation module is executed before the client module is executed.

Another global variable declared in the implementation module (Example 7.10B) is really a constant—Reserved is an array containing all reserved words as character strings; the index of each is the corresponding enumeration value in SymbolType.

The GetNextToken Procedure

A program is allowed to have any number of blanks, tabs, and ends-of-lines between two tokens, as long as there is something between any two tokens that begin with a letter or a digit (number and word tokens). We should allow for form-feeds and other control characters, whose ASCII codes are less than that of a blank. The easiest way to allow for this is to read until we see a character "greater than" a blank. That gives us the first character of the token, which can then be processed appropriately.

The only problem that arises with this algorithm is that we might reach the end of the file at any time (especially if the program is not syntactically correct). So we have to check Done after reading each character. If Done becomes false, we close the input file, assign endfile to TokenSymbol, and leave the Token (name) unchanged. On later calls of GetNextToken (if any), we check TokenSymbol; if it is endfile, we know not to execute CloseInput again (some systems may crash if you try to close a file that is not open).

We decide how to process a token by finding out what category it is in: word token, number token, or special symbol. The first character of the token tells us the category. Since we will in any case store that first character in Token, it is convenient to store it now and read the following character. It will tell us whether we have one of the 2-character special symbols. If that following character is not part of the token, we will have it ready for the next call of GetNext-Token. See Example 7.10C for the coding.

EXAMPLE 7.10B _____

```
IMPLEMENTATION MODULE LexAnal;
FROM Helpful IMPORT CompareStr;
FROM InOut   IMPORT Read, EOL, Done, OpenInput, CloseInput;
    (* Written by William C. Jones, Mar 19-- Rev July *)
CONST
    Blank = ' ';
    Null  = 0C;
VAR
    Ch : CHAR;   (* first character after previous token *)
    Reserved : ARRAY [begin..end] OF
               ARRAY [0..StrMax]  OF CHAR;
(*---------- procedure GetNextToken goes here ----------*)
(**********************************************************

PROCEDURE InitializeArray;  (* 12 reserved words *)
BEGIN
    Reserved [begin]     := 'BEGIN';
    Reserved [var]       := 'VAR';
    Reserved [procedure] := 'PROCEDURE';
    Reserved [while]     := 'WHILE';
    Reserved [if]        := 'IF';
    Reserved [else]      := 'ELSE';
    Reserved [do]        := 'DO';
    Reserved [then]      := 'THEN';
    Reserved [module]    := 'MODULE';
    Reserved [from]      := 'FROM';
    Reserved [import]    := 'IMPORT';
    Reserved [end]       := 'END';
END InitializeArray;
(**********************************************************)

BEGIN          (* initialization *)
    TokenSymbol := unknown;     (* in case of blank file *)
    OpenInput ('');
    Read (Ch);                  (* get first character *)
    InitializeArray;
END LexAnal.
```

Processing the Special Symbols

When ProcessSingleToken or ProcessDoubleToken is called, we have read all the characters that form that token. It is straightforward to assign the values of Token properly. Remember that the Null character is put at the end as a sentinel value. In Modula-2, the assignment of a string literal to a string variable automatically appends the Null value when the string literal is shorter.

The only thing left to do now is assign the proper value to TokenSymbol. Since we have the Token already, that can be a CASE or IF statement that lists all the alternatives and acts accordingly. You never can tell what might be accidentally typed in a program, so it is essential to have an ELSE clause for the CASE to catch

EXAMPLE 7.10C _____

```
PROCEDURE ProcessToken;
BEGIN
    Token [0] := Ch;
    Read (Ch);
    CASE Token [0] OF
        'A'..'Z#, 'a'..'z# : ProcessWordToken;
    |   '0'..'9'          : ProcessNumberToken;
    |   ':', '>', '<'     : IF Ch = '=' THEN
                                ProcessDoubleToken;
                            ELSE
                                ProcessSingleToken;
                            END;
    ELSE
        ProcessSingleToken;
    END;
END ProcessToken;
(*************************************************)

PROCEDURE GetNextToken;
    (* Obtain the next token from the source program
       Assign values to Token.Symbol and Token.Name
       TokenSymbol := unknown if it is unrecognized
       TokenSymbol := endfile when no more tokens   *)
BEGIN
    WHILE Done AND (Ch <= Blank) DO
        Read (Ch);
    END;
    IF Done THEN
        ProcessToken;
    ELSIF TokenSymbol # endfile THEN
        CloseInput;
        TokenSymbol := endfile;
    END;
END GetNextToken;
```

any illegal characters (Example 7.10D). As a general rule, you should always put an ELSE clause with each CASE unless you have listed every alternative.

Processing Words and Numbers

A word or number consists of one or more letters and digits. You tell the difference between them by the first character: An initial letter indicates a word token, an initial digit indicates a number token. Since the logic for reading the rest of the token without going too far is the same in either case, I wrote a ReadRestOfName procedure to take care of this situation. This procedure basically reads characters until something other than a letter or digit is seen. That last nonalphanumeric character is left in Ch for the next call of GetNextToken. All other characters are put in Token, up to the maximum that Token array can hold. Then the null

EXAMPLE 7.10D _____

```
PROCEDURE ProcessDoubleToken;
BEGIN
    Token [1] := Ch;
    Token [2] := Null;
    Read (Ch);                     (* char after this token *)
    IF Token [0] = ':' THEN
        TokenSymbol := assignment;
    ELSE
        TokenSymbol := relop;
    END;
END ProcessDoubleToken;
(**********************************************************)

PROCEDURE ProcessSingleToken;
BEGIN
    Token [1] := Null;
    CASE Token [0] OF
        '=', '#', '>', '<' :  TokenSymbol := relop;
    |            '+', '-' :  TokenSymbol := addop;
    |                 '*' :  TokenSymbol := mulop;
    |                 ';' :  TokenSymbol := semicolon;
    |                 '.' :  TokenSymbol := period;
    |                 ',' :  TokenSymbol := comma;
    |                 ':' :  TokenSymbol := colon;
    |                 '(' :  TokenSymbol := leftparen;
    |                 ')' :  TokenSymbol := rightparen;
    ELSE    TokenSymbol := unknown;
    END;
END ProcessSingleToken;
```

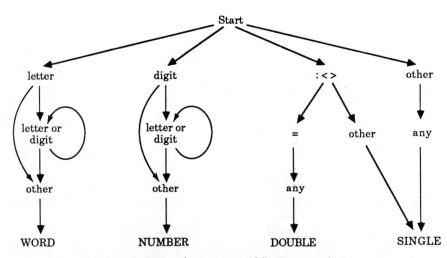

FIGURE 8. Characters read by ProcessToken.

EXAMPLE 7.10E _____

```
PROCEDURE ReadRestOfName;
    (* read letters and digits into Token *)
VAR
    K : CARDINAL;
BEGIN
    K := 1;
    WHILE Done AND ( (Ch >= '0') AND (Ch <= '9') OR
                     (Ch >= 'A') AND (Ch <= 'Z#) OR
                     (Ch >= 'a') AND (Ch <= 'z#)  )   DO
        IF K < StrMax THEN
            Token [K] := Ch;
            INC (K);
        END;
        Read (Ch);
    END;
    Token [K] := Null;
END ReadRestOfName;
(**********************************************************)

PROCEDURE ProcessNumberToken;
BEGIN
    TokenSymbol := number;
    ReadRestOfName;
END ProcessNumberToken;
```

character is put at the end of that array. Figure 8 shows how the various tokens are constructed.

The only other thing that has to be done for a number token is to assign TokenSymbol appropriately (Example 7.10E). More work is required for a word token, since you have to check whether it is a reserved word.

After you have read a word token, you compare it with each of the reserved words to see if it is one of those. If it is, you assign it the proper SymbolType value. Otherwise you assign it the value *identifier*. All the reserved words except AND and OR are in the Reserved array, so a FOR statement is appropriate to inspect each of those. If none of them match, you check AND and OR; if they do not match, you have an identifier. See Example 7.10F for the coding.

Something about Compilers

SynCheck is the foundation for a Modula-2 compiler. A reasonable question is: Why write a Modula-2 compiler in Modula-2? The compiler is no good unless you run it, which requires that you compile it, which means you already have a Modula-2 compiler, which means you do not need to write a Modula-2 compiler.

The answer is, the Modula-2 compiler you use compiles into the machine code for the machine with which you are working; but what if you want a Modula-2 compiler that works on a different machine? Assume that you already have a

EXAMPLE 7.10F _____

```
PROCEDURE ProcessWordToken;
VAR
    Sym : SymbolType;
BEGIN

    ReadRestOfName;
    FOR Sym := begin TO end DO              (* until RETURN *)
        IF CompareStr (Reserved [Sym], Token) = 0 THEN
            TokenSymbol := Sym;
            RETURN;
        END;
    END;

    IF CompareStr ('AND', Token) = 0 THEN
        TokenSymbol := mulop;
    ELSIF CompareStr ('OR', Token) = 0 THEN
        TokenSymbol := addop;
    ELSE
        TokenSymbol := identifier;
    END;

END ProcessWordToken;
```

compiler program that translates from Modula-2 to machine-code-A when running on machine A, and you want one that translates from Modula-2 to machine-code-B when running on machine B. Call the compiler you have MA/A, which is short for "Modula-2 to A in machine-code-A." You can then make an MB/B compiler (Modula-2 to B in machine-code-B) if you carry out the following plan:

1. Write the Modula-2-to-machine-code-B program in Modula-2; call it MB/M. SynCheck can serve as a basis for this MB/M program.

2. Compile your MB/M program on machine A using the MA/A compiler, producing a new program MB/A that is now expressed in machine-code-A and translates Modula-2 to machine-code-B.

3. Compile MB/M on machine A using MB/A, thereby producing a new program MB/B that is now expressed in machine-code-B and translates Modula-2 to machine-code-B.

4. Transfer that program MB/B to machine B, along with the text of a number of Modula-2 programs you have already written on machine A.

5. Use the MB/B compiler to compile the Modula-2 programs so they will run in machine-code-B on machine B.

The fascinating aspect of this is step 3, in which your program compiles itself.

1. Rewrite the body of GetNextToken to begin with IF TokenSymbol # endfile THEN.

2. Show that, even if the final period of the program is not followed by any character, not even an end-of-line, GetNextToken works okay.

3. (NA) Explain why the body of LexAnal assigns unknown to TokenSymbol. Could any other value have been assigned instead?

4. (NA) Explain how the execution time of ProcessWordToken can be improved by a proper choice of the order in the Reserved array and by a revision in the coding.

5. (NA) Some people do not like a RETURN from within a FOR statement (although they often do not mind it from within a WHILE statement). Rewrite Example 7.10F without a RETURN statement, but also without calling CompareStr twice for the same reserved word (since the CompareStr procedure takes a fair amount of execution time).

CHAPTER REVIEW

A Turing machine acts on a string of characters, each of which is in the alphabet of that machine. It has a marker at a certain character in that string, initially on the far right character (although some descriptions of Turing machines specify that the marker is on the far left character). A Turing machine takes a sequence of three actions of the following type, depending on the current "state" and the currently marked character: (1) Change the marked character if desired; (2) Move one character to the left or right; (3) Change to a different state if desired. One of the states causes termination of the program. The character string that remains at that point is called the output of the Turing machine. Although these rules are highly restrictive, it turns out that a Turing machine can do everything that any computer program can do. Thus it is a subject of study in the theory of computability. A Turing machine can be simulated by a Modula-2 program using two stacks.

A permutation of a number of objects is a listing of those objects in a certain order. Two permutations of the objects are considered different if they differ at any point in the list. The number of permutations of N objects is therefore N-factorial, the product of all the integers from N down to 1, inclusive. Section 7.2 presents a program to write all the permutations of some objects using a stack and a queue.

An index for a book is a list of all the key words and phrases that appear in the book, in alphabetic order, and for each one a list of the page numbers on which they occur. Section 7.3 presents a program for constructing an index using queues and tables.

The CNF-satisfiability problem is to find an assignment of values to the Boolean variables in a Boolean expression that makes the expression true, or to show that there is no such assignment, as the case may be. Section 7.4 describes a program to do that and presents the coding for a significant part of that program.

A Huffman code for a given set of words with their associated frequencies of occurrence is an assignment of a string of 0's and 1's to each word with the property that (1) a message in this code can be decoded unambiguously and (2) no other way of coding produces fewer 0's and 1's for the average message. The algorithm described in Section 7.5 creates a binary tree in which the leaves contain the words and the sequence of left and right turns taken in a path from the root to a leaf determines the sequence of 0's and 1's in the code for the word at that leaf.

SynCheck is a program that analyzes the syntax of a restricted subset of Modula-2. It can serve as the foundation for constructing a Modula-2 compiler. SynCheck imports from five library modules:

☐ InfoSYN contains the usual declarations relevant to Information; it must be compiled before TableMAR or SayStuff.

☐ Helpful (from Section 2.1) exports CompareStr, used in LexAnal, InfoSYN, and SynCheck.

☐ LexAnal contains the GetNextToken procedure and associated declarations; its job is to convert the input file to an orderly sequence of tokens, omitting comments and spacing.

☐ TableMAR handles the Table abstract data type, exporting Create, Destroy, PutIn, Inspect, Find, InTable, Mark, and Release. Mark and Release obviate the need for TakeOut.

☐ SayStuff exports two procedures for giving messages to the writer of the program. It must be compiled after LexAnal.

PRACTICE TEST

1. Write a Turing program to tell whether a given base 3 numeral is even or odd. [Example 7.1A]

2. Write the GoLeft procedure for the Turing environment, in which the currently marked character is exchanged for the one on its left, using the two stacks LeftStack and RightStack and the constant nix. [Example 7.1B]

3. Write the GiveOutput procedure for the Turing environment, in which all characters in the string are printed from left to right. Use the two stacks LeftStack and RightStack. [Example 7.1B]

4. Write the NegateExpr procedure, which takes a Boolean expression from a Given queue and puts the equivalent of its negation on another Data queue in such a way that NOT is always directly followed by a Boolean variable. Call on the FixExpr procedure as needed (which does the same as NegateExpr except it does not negate it). [Example 7.4B]

5. Write the ProcessImportSections procedure for SynCheck, which calls on the procedures GetNextTokenIfThisOneIs and ProcessIdentifierList in order to analyze a set of 0 or more import sections. [Example 7.7C]

6. Write a procedure that analyzes a simple expression. The syntax is given by $ simple-expr = [addop] term { addop term } . Call the ProcessTerm procedure as needed. [Example 7.9F]

7. Write the GetNextToken procedure, calling on the ProcessToken procedure as needed. The task to be accomplished is to get the first character greater than a blank (if any); if none, adjust for the end-of-file situation. [Example 7.10C]

PROGRAMMING PROBLEMS

1. Write a program that accepts quintuples such as <AddOne, 1, 2, L, Quit> and produces the appropriate client module. Assume that the alphabet does not include any comma or > and that end-of-line is the sentinel value. Make additional reasonable restrictions on the format of the quintuples.

2. Write a Turing program that reads two nonnegative numbers in base 3 notation and replaces them by their sum. Assume that there is exactly one blank between them and that they have the same number of digits.

3. Write a Turing program that doubles a given number written in base 10.

4. Revise Example 7.2A so that, when given abcd, it prints first all permutations that begin with a, then all that begin with b, and so on. Note that the example as given prints first all permutations that end in a, then all that end in b, and so on.

5. Write a program to generate test data for sorting algorithms. The program should accept as input two numbers SampleSize and NumSamples. The program should then write a file consisting of NumSamples permutations of the integers from 1 to SampleSize, by generating permutations and writing out say every fifth permutation. You might want to change from intervals of 5 to

intervals of some other number; part of this project is to find out whether some choices of interval sizes can avoid bias of the samples for some choices of SampleSize.

6. Write a program to accomplish the third stage of the CNF-program described in Section 7.4.

7. Write a program to accomplish the fourth stage of the CNF-program described in Section 7.4.

8. Complete the program described in Section 7.5 to read a list of words and their frequencies of occurrence, then write out the list with the Huffman code for each. The program should also compute the average bits per word. Assume that frequencies are decimal fractions that add up to 1. For instance, for the example of Section 7.5, the frequencies would be divided by 100, giving 0.40, 0.30, 0.10, 0.06, and so on.

9. Revise Example 7.9E to handle the order of precedence of operators used in languages such as BASIC, where all non-Boolean operators take precedence over all Boolean operators.

10. Revise the SynCheck program so that it prints the line number of each error for which an error message is printed.

11. Revise the SynCheck program so that it handles REAL, CHAR, and BOOLEAN types. Check all expressions and assignments for improper mixing of types.

12. Revise the SynCheck program so that it handles all control statements: REPEAT, FOR, LOOP, ELSIF, and (for extra credit) CASE.

13. Revise the SynCheck program so that it handles string literals and CONST sections.

8

ADDITIONAL DATA STRUCTURES

This chapter contains a number of independent topics. The most important of these topics is graphs, to which the first three sections are devoted. Both breadth-first search and depth-first search algorithms are presented. Other topics considered in this chapter are sparse matrices, strings, sets, and generalized lists.

8.1 GraphADT: BACKTRACKING ALGORITHMS

Your introduction to the graph data structure is via a famous programming problem called the **Traveling Salesman problem**. A salesman named Ed Lee has the job of visiting each of eight different cities once each week to call on customers. Each city is the capital of a different European country, and each city has an airport. Ed lives in one of the cities, so he flies from his home city to one of the other cities for which there is a flight connection (some cities cannot be reached directly from Ed's home city). Once Ed makes his sales calls in that second city, he flies to any one of the remaining six cities for which there is a flight connection. This continues until Ed has visited all eight cities, at which point Ed flies directly home (assuming there is a flight from the eighth city to his home city). The problem is to choose the order in which cities are visited so as to keep the total traveling time as small as possible. Thus we need to have a record of the

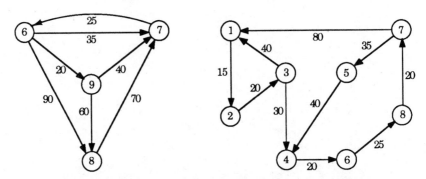

FIGURE 1. *Two Traveling Salesman situations, the left-hand one with four cities and the right-hand one with eight. An arrow indicates a flight connection, and the two-digit number by each arrow is the time required for the flight.*

time required for each flight connection. Figure 1 shows two sample Traveling Salesman situations.

The GraphADT Module

In the kind of data structure associated with problems of this type, each city is called a **vertex**, and each flight connection is called an **arc**. There is a flying time (a number of minutes) associated with each flight connection; the generic term for such a number is the **weight** of the arc connecting one city to another. For instance, in the 4-city diagram of Figure 1, the cities (vertices) are numbered from 6 to 9 and the flight from city 6 to city 9 takes 20 minutes, so we say the weight of the arc from 6 to 9 is 20. To keep this problem as generally applicable as possible, I make the following assumptions:

1. The cities are numbered from **Loval** to **Hival**, where Loval and Hival are integers. "Loval" is short for "lowest value" and "Hival" is short for "highest value" (of a vertex). In the 4-city diagram of Figure 1, Loval is 6 and Hival is 9; in the 8-city diagram, Loval is 1 and Hival is 8.

2. There is a Boolean function **Connecting** that tells whether there is a flight connection from the first given city to the second given city. Note that it may be the case that Connecting(C1, C2) is true but Connecting(C2, C1) is false; this is the case for cities 6 and 9 in the 4-city diagram of Figure 1.

3. There is an integer-valued function **Weight** that tells what the flight time is from one given city to another, assuming that there is a connection from the first to the second. For instance, Weight(6, 9) is 20 and Weight(8, 7) is 70 in the 4-city diagram of Figure 1. Many problems involving graphs do not use weights; an example is the Hamiltonian Circuit problem solved later in this section. When the weight is relevant to the problem, as for the Traveling Salesman problem, the graph is called a **weighted graph** or a **network**.

4. There is a procedure called **InitializeGraph** that reads values from a file or otherwise obtains the information necessary to work the problem. This includes whatever information is needed to calculate Connecting and Weight for various pairs of integers.

This sort of data structure is called a **graph**. In general, a graph consists of a certain number of vertices and a certain number of arcs. The arcs of a graph can be thought of as objects in themselves or as a Boolean function on ordered pairs of vertices. Example 8.1A is a definition module for such graph operations. Loval and Hival are declared as constants to allow the user to declare an array with vertices as indices.

This module has three additional procedures that I have not yet discussed. In programming problems of this type, you will often find it useful to be able to assign an integer to a vertex or to an arc so that a later part of the program can refer to the number previously assigned. For instance, in the Traveling Salesman problem, as you visit each city, you can mark the first city (vertex) visited with 1, mark the next one with 2, mark the next one with 3, and so on. If you first mark all cities 0, you can tell which cities have been visited so far by seeing whether the mark is 0, and you can tell the order in which they are visited by seeing what the mark is.

It is easy to declare an array with indices in the range [Loval..Hival] to store this numbering information for vertices; you will see an example of this later in this section. The **MarkArc** and **MarkOf** procedures have the analogous purpose for arcs instead of for vertices; there are applications in which numbering or "coloring" an arc makes sense. The MarkArc and MarkOf procedures are not used for the Traveling Salesman problem.

The **NextVertex** procedure is used to go through all the vertices connected to a given vertex, one at a time. The Noval vertex is used in conjunction with Next-Vertex as a sentinel value. For instance, in the 4-city diagram of Figure 2, an acceptable definition for NextVertex is indicated on the right. The idea is that

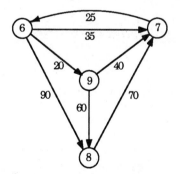

For 6: Noval, 7, 9, 8, Noval

For 7: Noval, 6, Noval

For 8: Noval, 7, Noval

For 9: Noval, 7, 8, Noval

FIGURE 2. *The four-city Traveling Salesman situation from Figure 1, with the sequence generated by NextVertex for each possible value of the first parameter.*

EXAMPLE 8.1A _____

```
DEFINITION MODULE GraphADT;
EXPORT QUALIFIED Vertex, Loval, Hival, Noval,
                 InitializeGraph, Connecting, NextVertex,
                 Weight, MarkArc, MarkOf;
        (* Module to permit working with the information
           in a single graph.  The vertices of the graph and
           the "arcs" (connections between vertices) are not
           modifiable by the client module *)
        (* Written by Dr. William C. Jones, October 19-- *)
CONST
    Loval = 1;
    Hival = 8;
    Noval = 0;
TYPE
    Vertex = INTEGER;

(* The values of Loval, Hival, and Noval will vary from
   one application to another, so no client module shoud
   make any assumptions about them other than
   Noval < Loval < Hival.  Noval is a sentinel like NIL;
   the actual vertices are in the range Loval..Hival *)
(*************************************************************)

PROCEDURE InitializeGraph;
        (* Do whatever is necessary (perhaps including reading
           information from a file) to obtain the information
           needed for computing Connecting and Weight *)

PROCEDURE Connecting (First, Second : Vertex) : BOOLEAN;
        (* Tell whether there is a connection from First to
           Second, if both are in the range Loval..Hival.
           Such a connection is call an "arc" *)

PROCEDURE NextVertex (First, Second : Vertex) : Vertex;
        (* If Second = Noval, return the first vertex V for
           which Connecting (First, V) is true.  Otherwise,
           return the next vertex V after Second for which
           Connecting (First, V) is true.  In either case,
           return Noval if there is no such vertex *)

PROCEDURE Weight (First, Second : Vertex) : INTEGER;
        (* Tell the "weight" assigned to the arc from First to
           Second, if there is such an arc  *)

PROCEDURE MarkArc (First, Second : Vertex;
                   Mark : INTEGER);
        (* Assign the given integer to the given arc, to be
           retrieved by the following function *)

PROCEDURE MarkOf (First, Second : Vertex) : INTEGER;
        (* Tell what integer has been assigned to this arc, if
           any; if none has yet been assigned, return 0 *)

END GraphADT.
```

NextVertex(6, Noval) = 7, NextVertex(6, 7) = 9, NextVertex(6, 9) = 8, and Next-Vertex(6, 8) = Noval. Noval might be 0, for instance. The exact value is irrelevant, as long as it is not in the range from Loval to Hival.

For a vertex Given, the following coding prints a list of all vertices for which there is an arc from Given to that vertex:

```
V := NextVertex (Given, Noval);
WHILE V # Noval DO
    WriteInt (V, 1);
    WriteLn;
    V := NextVertex (Given, V);
END;
```

Actually, the Connecting function is a utility function; it can be coded using NextVertex and Noval, as follows:

```
V := NextVertex (First, Noval);
WHILE V # Noval DO  (* UNTIL RETURN *)
    IF V = Second THEN
        RETURN TRUE;
    END;
    V := NextVertex (First, V);
END;
RETURN FALSE;
```

Note that the NextVertex procedure establishes an ordering of the vertices connected to a given vertex. That is, for a given vertex Given, we can talk about the "first" vertex connected to it (obtained by V := NextVertex(Given, Noval)), the "second" vertex connected to it (obtained by V := NextVertex(Given, V)), and so on. If you think of the vertices connected to the Given vertex as being on a list named Data, then:

☐ V := NextVertex(Given, Noval) is equivalent to:
  W := FirstLocation(Data); LookAt(V, W, Data).

☐ V := NextVertex(Given, V) is equivalent to:
  W := NextLocation(W, Data); LookAt(V, W, Data).

☐ V = Noval is equivalent to NOT InList(W, Data).

The simplest implementation of GraphADT is a two-dimensional matrix, indexed by the vertices, of records with three fields for the connections, weights, and marks. This is the most space-wasting of implementations when you have very few arcs per vertex. Space-saving implementations using a one-dimensional array of linked lists or an "irregular matrix" are implicit in Sections 8.4 and 8.5, if you study those sections.

The Hamiltonian Circuit Problem

First we consider a simpler problem than the Traveling Salesman problem. A **circuit** is a path that goes through each city once, except that it begins and ends at the same city. For now, I consider only the question of *whether* there is any circuit in the graph; this is known as the **Hamiltonian Circuit problem**. By contrast, the Traveling Salesman problem consists of finding the circuit with the shortest traveling time. In the 4-vertex graph of Figure 1, a Hamiltonian Circuit is 6 −> 9 −> 8 −> 7 −> 6. See if you can find a Hamiltonian Circuit for the 8-vertex graph in Figure 1.

Note that I can, without loss of generality, assume that the salesman lives in Loval city. For if I find a circuit Loval −> C2 −> C3 −> C4 −> C5 −> C6 −> C7 −> Loval, and if it turns out that the salesman lives in C4 instead of Loval, he can travel the circuit C4 −> C5 −> C6 −> C7 −> Loval −> C2 −> C3 −> C4.

The basic logic is to try out all the possible **paths** (sequences of arcs) that go from Loval city to another city to another city, and so on without going through the same city twice. When I find one that goes through all eight cities with an arc from the eighth one back to Loval city, I have a Hamiltonian circuit. I begin by labeling Loval city 1, since it is the city from which I start. Then I choose any unlabeled city connected to Loval city and label it 2. Then I choose any unlabeled city connected to it and label it 3, and so on. If I ever label a city 8, I check whether it is connected to Loval (if so, I have found a circuit and I can quit). Whenever I find I cannot label a city, because all connected cities are already labeled, I unlabel the city I just labeled and try another one instead.

Thus the overall algorithm is: (1) Label Loval city 1 and then (2) see if I can finish the labeling. I call a procedure that tells me whether I can travel all remaining cities beginning from Loval. It is advantageous to pass Loval as a value parameter to this TryToTravel procedure. I can then have the procedure tell me whether I can travel all remaining cities beginning from whatever the value parameter is, so the procedure can be used recursively. The coding of the body of the program could be as shown in Example 8.1B.

The WriteAllLabels procedure, called by the body of the program, simply writes each vertex number and the order it occurs in the circuit; the coding is in the next example. You may prefer that the vertices be written in the order in which they are chosen; this is left as an exercise.

The TryToTravel procedure has the job of telling whether the circuit-so-far (as recorded by the labels) can be completed; it gives its answer by assigning a value to Ok. When TryToTravel is first called, its vertex parameter is labeled 1. On each call of TryToTravel, the first thing to do is to see if the current spot (the vertex parameter) is labeled 8. If so, I have a path through all eight cities, so the

EXAMPLE 8.1B _____

```
MODULE BackTracker;
FROM InOut    IMPORT WriteString, WriteInt, WriteLn;
FROM GraphADT IMPORT Vertex, Loval, Hival, Noval,
                InitializeGraph, Connecting, NextVertex;
    (* Find a Hamiltonian Circuit of a graph *)
    (* Written by William C. Jones, October 19-- *)
TYPE
    LabelArray = ARRAY [Loval..Hival] OF INTEGER;
(*-- procedures TryToTravel and WriteAllLabels go here --*)
(*********************************************************)

VAR
    Labeled : LabelArray;
    K       : INTEGER;
    Ok      : BOOLEAN;

BEGIN          (* body of Hamiltonian Circuit program *)
    InitializeGraph;
    FOR K := Loval TO Hival DO
        Labeled [Loval] := 0;
    END;

    Labeled [Loval] := 1;
    TryToTravel (Loval, Labeled, Ok);

    IF Ok THEN
        WriteAllLabels (Labeled);
    ELSE
        WriteString ('cannot do it.');
        WriteLn;
    END;
END BackTracker.
```

only question is whether Loval is connected to the current spot. If the current spot is labeled anything from 1 to 7, I try out each of the cities connected to the current spot. For each one not yet labeled, I label it 1 higher than the current spot is labeled and see if I can complete this circuit-so-far. If so, TryToTravel returns TRUE. If I do not find any city that permits completion of the circuit-so-far, TryToTravel returns FALSE.

This algorithm is coded in Example 8.1C. Note that I use Hival−Loval+1 instead of 8, to allow for full generality. That way, no change has to be made if there are 6 or 20 cities. I have named certain statements in this procedure Part 1, Part 2, and Part 3; these names will be used later in this section to refer to these parts of the coding.

SAMPLE RUN. The application of this algorithm to the 4-city situation shown in Figure 2 labels city 6 with a 1 and calls TryToTravel(6) (with two other parameters, but I omit them to make this paragraph more readable). That procedure sets

EXAMPLE 8.1C _____

```
PROCEDURE TryToTravel (CurrentSpot : Vertex;
                       VAR Labeled : LabelArray;
                       VAR Ok      : BOOLEAN);
VAR
    V : Vertex;
BEGIN
    IF Labeled [CurrentSpot] = Hival - Loval + 1 THEN
        Ok := Connecting (CurrentSpot, Loval); (* Part 1 *)
    ELSE
        V := NextVertex (CurrentSpot, Noval);
        WHILE V # Noval DO    (* UNTIL RETURN *)
            IF Labeled [V] = 0 THEN
                Labeled [V] := Labeled [CurrentSpot] + 1;
                TryToTravel (V, Labeled, Ok);   (* Part 2 *)
                IF Ok THEN                       (* Part 2 *)
                    RETURN;                      (* Part 2 *)
                END;                             (* Part 2 *)
                Labeled [V] := 0;
            END;
            V := NextVertex (CurrentSpot, V);
        END;
        Ok := FALSE;                             (* Part 3 *)
    END;
END TryToTravel;
(*********************************************************)

PROCEDURE WriteAllLabels (Labeled : LabelArray);
VAR
    K : Vertex;
BEGIN
    FOR K := Loval TO Hival DO
        WriteInt (K, 1);
        WriteString (' is chosen at step number ');
        WriteInt (Labeled [K], 1);
        WriteLn;
    END;
END WriteAllLabels;
```

V to 7, labels city 7 with a 2, and calls TryToTravel(7). That second activation
of TryToTravel sets V to 6, sees that it is already labeled, sees that there are no
other cities connected to city 7, and thus returns FALSE to the first activation.
That first activation relabels city 7 with 0, sets V to 9, labels city 9 with a 2,
and calls TryToTravel(9). That second activation of TryToTravel sets V to 7,
labels it 3, and calls TryToTravel(7). That third activation cannot extend the
circuit further, so it returns FALSE. Then the second activation relabels city 7
with 0, sets V to 8, labels it 3, and calls TryToTravel(8). That third activation sets
V to 7, labels it 4, and calls TryToTravel(7). That fourth activation returns TRUE,

since the label is Hival−Loval+1 (9−6+1=4) and Connecting(7,6) is true. This terminates all activations, returning TRUE each time.

That completes the solution of the Hamiltonian Circuit problem. The key part of the algorithm is the method for trying out all the possible circuits without trying any one of them more than once. The method shown in the TryToTravel procedure is called a **backtracking** algorithm and is useful in many contexts. The context determines the exact coding used for Parts 1, 2, and 3.

Solution of the Traveling Salesman Problem

The original Traveling Salesman problem has much the same logic as the Hamiltonian Circuit problem, only a little more complicated. You can still check out all the possibilities in the same way, but now you cannot stop just because you find one. You have to total all the travel times for each circuit you find and then, if it is smaller than any total time recorded so far, you have to save it. Thus the modifications you make are analogous to the usual logic for finding the smallest of a set of numbers.

You can have a LabelArray named SaveLabels in which you save the labels for the circuit for the smallest total time. You can also have a variable SmallestTime (for the best circuit found so far). You do not have to change WriteAllLabels, as long as you fix the body of the program by replacing the two lines beginning IF with the following:

```
SmallestTime := 0;
TryToTravel (Loval, Labeled, SaveLabels, SmallestTime, 0);
IF SmallestTime > 0 THEN
    WriteAllLabels (SaveLabels)
```

The TryToTravel procedure has several more parameters in this application. The last parameter is TotalTime, the travel time required so far starting from Loval (which is why 0 is passed to it on the first activation). The Part 1 statement in that backtracking procedure, executed if and when a circuit is found, can be replaced by the following coding. The rest of the coding is left as an exercise.

```
IF Connecting (CurrentSpot, Loval) AND ((SmallestTime = 0) OR
        (TotalTime + Weight (CurrentSpot, Loval) < SmallestTime)) THEN
    SmallestTime := TotalTime + Weight (CurrentSpot, Loval);
    SaveLabels := Labeled;
END;
```

Check Your Understanding

1. What changes must be made in Examples 8.1B and 8.1C to tell whether there is a path through each vertex once, not necessarily a circuit?

2. Write out the full heading of TryToTravel for the Traveling Salesman problem, as indicated at the end of this section.

3. What changes must be made in Example 8.1C in addition to those described at the end of this section, to obtain a solution for the Traveling Salesman problem?

4. What variables can be delocalized in the recursive TryToTravel procedure of Example 8.1C? Make the appropriate changes.

5. (NA) Rewrite the TryToTravel procedure in Example 8.1C to avoid the use of RETURN by using WHILE (V # Noval) AND NOT Ok DO instead. *Careful:* This is tricky. Make sure Ok has been assigned a value before it is tested in the WHILE condition.

6. (NA) Revise the WriteAllLabels procedure in Example 8.1C to print the vertices in the order they are chosen. *Suggestion:* Use nested FOR statements with the outer loop starting from 1. This is reasonably efficient for less than 100 vertices.

8.2 MORE BACKTRACKING ALGORITHMS

The **Knight's Tour problem** is stated as follows: Put a knight on any square of an empty chessboard (an 8-by-8 board, so it has 64 squares). Is there any way to make 64 legal knight moves so that each square is "visited" (landed on) exactly once? If so, find that way. This section, which is independent of Section 8.3, discusses the solution of this classic problem and also the solution of the classic Eight Queens problem.

The fact is, the Hamiltonian Circuit program given in Section 8.1, the heart of which is in Example 8.1C, is a program that solves the Knight's Tour problem. The vertices are the 64 squares on the chessboard, and two vertices are connected if and only if it is legal for a knight to move from one of them to the other. Thus the only new coding that has to be done is in the implementation of GraphADT. The next two pages are devoted to developing that coding of GraphADT.

First we need to assign a number to each square on a chessboard. There is a standard numbering system for chessboards, shown on the left in Figure 3. The second digit of the number tells what column the square is in (counting from left to right), and the first digit tells what row the square is in (counting from bottom to top). Thus Loval is 11 and Hival is 88. The problem is that all the numbers in

81	82	83	84	85	86	87	88
71	72	73	74	75	76	77	78
61	62	63	64	65	66	67	68
51	52	53	54	55	56	57	58
41	42	43	44	45	46	47	48
31	32	33	34	35	36	37	38
21	22	23	24	25	26	27	28
11	12	13	14	15	16	17	18

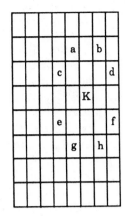

FIGURE 3. A numbering of a chessboard; legal knight moves.

the range Loval.. Hival are supposed to be vertices, which is not the case for numbers such as 39 and 60. However, we can pretend that we play chess on an 8-by-10 board for which the first and last columns are not allowed to have pieces on them. In other words, the vertices ending in 0 or 9 are not connected to any others. This has a great advantage over numbering the squares from 1 to 64, as you will see later. The small letters on the right of Figure 3 mark the squares to which a knight could legally move from the square marked K.

GraphADT could be implemented so that it simply reads the required information from a file. Then the Knight's Tour problem, as well as any other Hamiltonian Circuit problem, can be specified simply by changing the file to be read, leaving GraphADT unchanged except for the constants Loval, Hival, and Noval. However, it is more interesting to code the connections between vertices directly.

A legal knight's move is either 2 squares vertically and 1 square horizontally, or 1 square vertically and 2 squares horizontally. Thus there are up to 8 possible legal moves from a given square. There may be as few as 2 possible legal moves, since the square may be too close to the edge of the board. On the right of Figure 3, note that the difference between the numbers of the K square and the b square is 21 (77 − 56), and that this difference holds for any move 2 squares up and 1 square right.

The difference between the numbers of the K square and the g square is −21 (35 − 56); this difference holds for any move 2 squares down and 1 square left. The difference between the numbers of the K square and the c square is 8 (64 − 56); this difference holds for any move 1 square up and 2 squares left. From squares 51 and 52, adding 8 yields 59 and 60, which are not the numbers of squares on the board; so those moves are not legal. In general, we can use the following rule for finding all legal knight's moves from the numbering: Add to the number of the knight's square one of the following 8 numbers: +21, +19, +12,

+8, −8, −12, −19, −21; omit those for which the result is not the number of a square on the board.

If the squares had been numbered from 1 to 64, a similar rule would apply, except that it would be very difficult to specify which of the eight possibilities should be omitted. In fact, it would be easier to have InitializeGraph read in 64 lines that tell, for each square from 1 to 64, the squares to which a knight can move. This is why I chose to number the squares the way I did. Note that you can also pretend that there is an extra row at the top and bottom of the chessboard, on which it is illegal to put a piece. In general, algorithms for programs involving an N-by-N arrangement of values are often simplified by assuming that an (N+2)-by-(N+2) arrangement is used, with the outside edge off limits.

It is useful to have a private function in this GraphADT implementation module that tells the next arc after a given arc, without worrying about which values are to be omitted. This function could be called NextInSequence and coded as shown in Example 8.2A.

Now the Boolean Connecting function can be coded simply as:

```
RETURN NextInSequence (First, Second) # First;
```

The NextVertex function is also easy to code:

```
REPEAT
    Second := NextInSequence (First, Second);
UNTIL (Second = Noval) OR (Second = First) OR
      (Second >= Loval) AND (Second <= Hival) AND
      (Second MOD 10 # 0) AND (Second MOD 10 # 9);
RETURN Second;
```

EXAMPLE 8.2A _____

```
PROCEDURE NextInSequence (First, Second : Vertex) : Vertex;
BEGIN
    CASE Second - First OF   Noval : RETURN First + 21;
                         |    +21 : RETURN First + 19;
                         |    +19 : RETURN First + 12;
                         |    +12 : RETURN First + 8;
                         |     +8 : RETURN First - 8;
                         |     -8 : RETURN First - 12;
                         |    -12 : RETURN First - 19;
                         |    -19 : RETURN First - 21;
                         |    -21 : RETURN Noval;
                         ELSE        RETURN First;
    END;
END NextInSequence;
```

The other four procedures in GraphADT are not used for the Knight's Tour problem, so you can write them with no statements between BEGIN and END. You have to have a value for Noval that makes these procedures work correctly. If you are considering a move from square First=12, you want to see that First−12 is a border square instead of Noval; so 0 cannot be used for Noval. Noval= −999 solves this sort of problem.

Finding All Possible Knight's Tours

It may be that you want to find every possible Knight's Tour for the 8-by-8 chessboard. The backtracking program described in Section 8.1 can be modified to accomplish that. All you do is print out each solution as it is found and not terminate execution until all possibilities have been tested. To print out each solution as it is found, replace Part 1 of Example 8.1C by the following coding:

```
IF Connecting (CurrentSpot, Loval) THEN
    WriteAllLabels (Labeled);
END;
```

To continue execution until all possibilities have been tested, simply omit the BOOLEAN parameter Ok. That means that, in Example 8.1C, the IF statement in Part 2 and all of Part 3 should be omitted. You can also omit the IF...ELSE statement in the body of the program.

The Eight Queens Problem

In chess, a queen can move in any direction—horizontally, vertically, or diagonally. In 1850, Friedrich Gauss attempted to solve the problem of finding all ways to arrange eight queens on a chessboard so that no queen has any other queen under attack. That is, you put one queen in each column so that (1) they are all in different rows, (2) they are all in different "high diagonals" (the diagonals running from upper left to lower right), and (3) they are all in different "low diagonals" (the diagonals running from lower left to upper right). Gauss failed.

This is also a situation in which we can simply try all possibilities using the backtracking logic. Since we know that each of the queens must be in a separate column, we can let a vertex represent the row in which a queen is placed. First we choose any of the rows 1..8 in which to place the queen of column 1. Then we choose any of the rows 1..8 other than the one just chosen and place the queen of column 2 there. Then we choose any of the rows 1..8 other than the two just chosen and place the queen of column 3 there. This continues until we have placed all eight queens or until we cannot place another queen to avoid attack.

The graph therefore consists of eight vertices numbered 1 to 8, with an arc from each vertex to each of the other seven vertices. Noval can be 0, and the

NextVertex procedure can be coded as:

```
IF (Second = 8) OR (First = 8) AND (Second = 7) THEN
      RETURN Noval;
ELSIF Second + 1 = First THEN
      RETURN Second + 2;
ELSE
      RETURN Second + 1;
END;
```

The problem is now to find every **Hamiltonian path** (a path through all the vertices) in the graph that does not have two queens on the same diagonal.

Study the chessboard in Figure 4 until you can see that there are 15 "high diagonals" and 15 "low diagonals" (although some of those diagonals consist of just one square). We can use two Boolean arrays of 15 values each to note whether or not a given diagonal is already in use. Thus we can declare HighUsed, Low-Used: ARRAY [1..15] OF BOOLEAN. All squares on a given high diagonal have the sum of the two digits equal; the sum can range from 2 to 16. So we can make HighUsed[K] true when the sum of the two digits for the square where a queen is placed equals K + 1. All squares on a given low diagonal have the difference of the two digits equal; the difference can range from -7 to $+7$. So we can make LowUsed[K] true when the difference of the two digits for the square where a queen is placed equals K $-$ 8.

Now perhaps you can see how to modify the program in Examples 8.1B and 8.1C. You add to the main program coding that initializes the HighUsed and

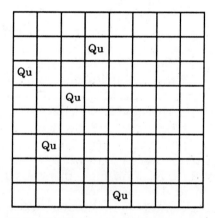

FIGURE 4. *A chessboard with five mutually nonattacking queens on it. Can you see where to place the other three queens?*

LowUsed arrays to FALSE, and you have the main program check out each of the numbers 1..8 as a starting point. Thus the body of the program could be:

```
FOR K := 1 TO 15 DO
    HighUsed [K] := FALSE;
    LowUsed [K] := FALSE;
END;
FOR K := Loval TO Hival DO
    Labeled [K] := 0;
END;
FOR K := Loval TO Hival DO
    Labeled [K] := 1;
    TryToTravel (K, Labeled, HighUsed, LowUsed);
    Labeled [K] := 0;
END;
```

The TryToTravel procedure begins by marking the diagonals for the choice just made. So you need to insert the following two statements just after the ELSE in Example 8.1C:

```
HighUsed [CurrentSpot MOD 10 + CurrentSpot DIV 10 - 1] := TRUE;
LowUsed  [CurrentSpot MOD 10 - CurrentSpot DIV 10 + 8] := TRUE;
```

Other than the insertion of those two statements, only the segments of Example 8.1C marked Part 1, Part 2, and Part 3 are changed; the basic backtracking logic is left intact. Part 3 can reset the Boolean values to their former values:

```
HighUsed [CurrentSpot MOD 10 + CurrentSpot DIV 10 - 1] := FALSE;
LowUsed  [CurrentSpot MOD 10 - CurrentSpot DIV 10 + 8] := FALSE;
```

Part 1 can simply call WriteAllLabels, since Part 1 is executed only if all eight queens were successfully placed on the board. In Part 2, you only need to omit the IF Ok... statement. The WriteAllLabels procedure need not be changed, although you might want to change the string of characters to "is the row number for column number".

The methods presented in this section can be used for other board sizes besides 8-by-8. For instance, if you wanted to see whether there is a knight's tour for a 14-

by-14 board, you would pretend that you have a 14-by-16 board for which you cannot use the first and last columns. This board would be numbered from 16 to 31 on the bottom row, 32 to 47 on the next-to-bottom row, up to 224 to 239 on the top row; however, the 14-by-14 part would have only 17 to 30, then 33 to 46, and so on. Other changes that would be made consist mainly of substituting 14 for 8 and 16 for 10 in the appropriate places. The sensible way to do this would be to have constants Size=14 and Outsize=Size+2. This also works for generalizing the Eight Queens problem.

Check Your Understanding

1. Assume that the chessboard is numbered from 1 to 8 in the bottom row, 9 to 16 in the second-to-bottom row, and so forth, with the numbers 57 to 64 in the top row. If each row is numbered left to right, what are the eight numbers that tell the difference between a knight's square and a square to which the knight could move?

2. (NA) What changes would be made in the Eight Queens program to have the Boolean arrays assigned values for a vertex before TryToTravel is called for that vertex?

3. (NA) With the 14-by-14 board numbered as described in the last paragraph of this section, what are the eight numbers that tell the difference between a knight's square and a square to which the knight could move? And what are the first two statements after ELSE in the TryToTravel procedure for the 14 queens problem?

8.3 ADVANCED ALGORITHMS FOR GRAPHS

A graph is a set of vertices and arcs. Vertices form a set of consecutive integers (in this book; this is not always the case). Arcs are connections from one vertex to another. Actually, the kind of graph usually discussed in this book is a **directed graph**, which means that an arc goes in a particular direction, that is, one vertex is its "head" and the other is its "tail." In drawing a directed graph, we usually put an arrowhead on the line representing an arc, to show its direction. There is no need for the arrowhead with trees, since by convention the direction is always down. A tree can be defined to be a directed graph with the following properties:

1. There is one particular vertex (the root) from which it is possible to get to any other vertex in the tree.

2. There is no cycle, that is, a way to travel from a vertex back to itself by following the arcs.

3. There is only one way to get from the root to a given vertex.

Breadth-first Search

The backtracking logic is an example of **depth-first searching**; you look at *all* the possibilities starting with a given arc from some given vertex V0, then you look at all the possibilities starting from another arc from V0, and so on until you have investigated each arc starting from V0. Another method of searching through a graph is **breadth-first searching**. The basic idea is that you first investigate each vertex connected to V0; if you do not find what you want, you look at each vertex connected to one of those vertices, and so on until you have investigated all the vertices in the graph.

As an example, there are several applications in which you want to find the shortest distance from Loval to each vertex in a graph. That is, for each vertex V in the graph, you want to mark V with the length of the shortest path from Loval to V. One way is to start off by marking Loval 0 (since it is 0 arcs away from itself). Then you mark all the vertices connected to Loval 1, since they are 1 arc away. Then, for each of those vertices marked 1, you mark any vertices connected to them 2, unless they have already been marked (with a lower number, of course). Then, for each vertex marked 2, you mark any vertices connected to them 3, unless they have already been marked with a lower number. This continues until you cannot find any unmarked vertices connected to any marked vertex. This algorithm can be expressed as:

Algorithm for finding the minimum distance of each vertex from Loval
1. Mark Loval 0;
2. Set NextMark to 1;
3. Repeat the following until time to stop:
    3.a. For each vertex marked NextMark−1, do the following:
        3.a.a. Find all as-yet-unmarked vertices for which there is an arc from the given vertex (marked NextMark−1) and mark them NextMark;
    3.b. STOP if no vertex was found in step 3.a;
    3.c. Add 1 to NextMark;
4. Report the marks for each vertex; those not marked cannot be reached from Loval.

It seems reasonable to declare an array to hold the marks for each vertex. You have to initialize it in some way to indicate that a vertex is not yet marked. Since the marks will be nonnegative integers, it makes sense to initialize the array with −1 in all components.

It is obvious that you could use a FOR statement for step 3.a of the algorithm, going through all the vertices to find those marked NextMark−1. You can initialize a Boolean variable Found to FALSE before step 3.a, to be changed to TRUE if any vertex marked NextMark−1 is found. You can then use this Boolean variable to determine when the larger loop should be terminated. However, there is a much faster-acting way of handling this situation. You can create a Queue and initialize it by putting Loval on the Queue. This Queue is to hold all vertices that have been marked but not yet had their connecting arcs inspected. This makes it unnecessary to keep track of NextMark. The initializing coding could be:

```
FOR K := Loval + 1 TO Hival DO
    Distance [K] := -1;
END;
Distance [Loval] := 0;
Create (Data);
Enqueue (Loval, Data);
```

The advantage of using a Queue is that you can retrieve vertices from it in the order they were marked. In particular, you begin by dequeueing Loval and enqueueing all vertices connected to Loval, after marking them 1. Then you dequeue a vertex and enqueue all vertices connected to it, after marking them 2 (Fig. 5). Those vertices marked 2 will not be dequeued and processed until after all vertices marked 1 have been dequeued and processed. This sort of thing continues until the Queue is empty:

```
REPEAT
  Dequeue (AlreadyVisited, Data);
  V := NextVertex (AlreadyVisited, Noval);
  WHILE V # Noval DO
      IF Distance [V] = -1 THEN
          Distance [V] := Distance [AlreadyVisited] + 1;
          Enqueue (V, Data);
      END;
      V := NextVertex (AlreadyVisited, V);
  END;
UNTIL IsEmpty (Data);
```

The final part of the algorithm is to print out the values in the Distance array or to pass it back as a VAR parameter if this algorithm is a procedure in a program. Note that a Distance value of −1 signifies that the vertex cannot be reached from Loval; in some applications, this is all the information you want.

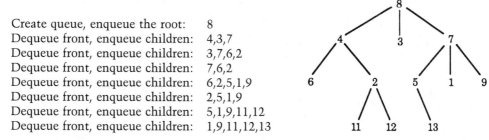

Create queue, enqueue the root: 8
Dequeue front, enqueue children: 4,3,7
Dequeue front, enqueue children: 3,7,6,2
Dequeue front, enqueue children: 7,6,2
Dequeue front, enqueue children: 6,2,5,1,9
Dequeue front, enqueue children: 2,5,1,9
Dequeue front, enqueue children: 5,1,9,11,12
Dequeue front, enqueue children: 1,9,11,12,13

FIGURE 5. *The breadth-first search using a queue, applied to a tree.*

Execution time for this algorithm is at worst roughly proportional to the total number of arcs, since no vertex can be placed on the queue more than once during the algorithm.

The algorithm just described uses breadth-first search. If you replace Enqueue by Push and Dequeue by Pop in this algorithm, you have depth-first search using a stack instead of recursion. Of course, this is not a good idea when you are trying to find the *shortest* path from Loval to each other vertex. But if the problem were to find *which* vertices can be reached from Loval, either depth-first or breadth-first search would do.

Floyd's and Warshall's Algorithms

Consider a situation in which you want to find the least cost involved in going from any one vertex to any other vertex in a graph. For instance, the Weight function might return either the airfare or the flying time between two given cities (assuming that vertices represent cities). For the following algorithms, all Weights are nonnegative.

The problem is to calculate components of a square array MC of values, in which MC[i,j] denotes the minimum cost of going from vertex i to vertex j. You can initialize MC[i,j] := Weight[i,j] for all vertices i and j, except initialize MC[i,j] to −1 if they are not connected, and initialize MC[i,i] to 0 for all vertices i (since it costs nothing to stand still). This initialization tells the minimum cost using only paths of length 1.

A plausible algorithm is simply to use brute force: Look at all possible sequences i,j,k of three vertices; calculate Sum := MC[i,j] + MC[j,k] and, if Sum is smaller than MC[i,k], execute MC[i,k] := Sum. That is, we use triply nested FOR statements. This way, we find all cases where the minimum-cost path is of length 1 or 2. However, it may be the case that the minimum-cost path requires going through three or four vertices on the way, so this algorithm misses those cases. For instance, the minimum-cost path on a standard linked list from the front to the rear requires going through all intermediate nodes. Obviously, an algorithm to compute MC will require much more work.

Some "obvious" truths are lies, however. R. W. Floyd showed that the afore-mentioned algorithm does in fact work, as long as the outermost of the three nested FOR statements has j as its control variable. The logic behind this surpris-ing conclusion is as follows (the coding is in Example 8.3A to help you follow the logic):

- [ ] Initially, each nonnegative MC[i,k] records the minimum cost of traveling from vertex i to vertex k without going through any other vertex along the way (i.e., directly from i to k).

- [ ] At the end of the first iteration of the FOR j loop, each nonnegative MC[i,k] records the minimum cost of traveling from vertex i to vertex k without going through any vertex numbered above Loval along the way [i.e., either by going (1) directly from i to k or (2) from i to Loval and then to k].

- [ ] At the end of the second iteration of the FOR j loop, each nonnegative MC[i,k] records the minimum cost of traveling from vertex i to vertex k

EXAMPLE 8.3A _____

```
PROCEDURE AllPairsShortestPath (VAR MC : Matrix);
(* Floyd's Algorithm to construct a square array giving
   the shortest path between any two vertices *)
VAR
    i, j, k : Vertex;
BEGIN

(* initialize *)
    FOR i := Loval TO Hival DO
        FOR k := Loval TO Hival DO
            IF Connecting (i, k) THEN
                MC [i, k] := Weight (i, k);
            ELSE
                MC [i, k] := -1;
            END;
        END;
        MC [i, i] := 0;
    END;

(* calculate minimum costs of nondirect paths *)
    FOR j := Loval TO Hival DO
        FOR i := Loval TO Hival DO
            FOR k := Loval TO Hival DO
                IF (MC [i,j] >= 0) AND (MC [j,k] >= 0) AND
                    (MC [i,j] + MC [j,k] < MC [i,k]) THEN
                    MC [i, k] := MC [i, j] + MC [j, k];
                END;
            END;
        END;
    END;

END AllPairsShortestPath;
```

without going through any vertex numbered above Loval+1 along the way (thus allowing i to Loval+1 to Loval+2 to k, for instance, using MC[i,Loval+2] + MC[Loval+2,k]).

☐ In general, at the end of each iteration of the FOR j loop, each nonnegative MC[i,k] records the minimum cost of traveling from vertex i to vertex k without going through any vertex numbered above j along the way.

☐ Therefore, when the FOR j loop terminates, each nonnegative MC[i,k] records the minimum cost of traveling from vertex i to vertex k without going through any vertex numbered above Hival along the way (which is of course the minimum cost of all paths).

Sometimes all you want to know for each pair of vertices i,k is whether there is any path from vertex i to vertex k. A straightforward simplification of the foregoing **Floyd's algorithm** can calculate this; it is called **Warshall's algorithm**. The following changes are made in Example 8.3A (remember that Connecting is a BOOLEAN function):

☐ Replace MC by a matrix ADJ of Booleans rather than of integers. ADJ[i,k] is to record *whether* you can travel from i to k.

☐ In the initialization part, replace everything inside both FOR statements by ADJ[i,k] := Connecting(i,k).

☐ Replace the second IF statement by the following coding:
ADJ [i, k] := ADJ [i, k] OR (ADJ [i, j] AND ADJ [j, k]).

ADJ is called the **adjacency matrix** for the graph at the point where it is initialized, since it tells which vertices are adjacent to which. At the end of execution of Warshall's algorithm, ADJ is the **transitive closure** of the adjacency matrix. The breadth-first search coding given earlier provides a way of finding the transitive closure of the adjacency matrix much faster, when the number of arcs is much less than the square of the number of vertices.

For Floyd's algorithm, you can print the vertices in the minimum-cost path found by declaring a square array Pr of vertices, initializing it to Noval in each component, and executing Pr[i,k] := j within the second IF. An exercise asks you to show how to use this matrix to print the shortest paths.

Warning

Several compilers cannot handle the coding given in Example 8.3A because the Boolean expression is too complex. If you encounter such a problem, you could change the second AND to THEN IF and insert another END with the other four, which will probably let the coding compile. The diagnostic message given by the VAX 780 is "Expression too complicated (branch too long)." Evidently, five pairs of subscripts in one condition is too much.

This is an example of an implementation (the compiler) failing to conform to its definition, similar to the situation of a simple array implementation of a list failing because you try to put too many items in a list. The diagnostic message should have added, "This is not your fault; it is a limitation of the compiler."

Minimum Cost Spanning Trees

Consider the following problem: A communications company wants to establish its own telephone lines connecting the group of eight cities shown on the right of Figure 1. The total cost of the lines should be as small as possible; the cost is recorded as the weight of an arc. The direction of the arc is irrelevant for this problem. Every city is to be able to communicate with every other city, even if calls have to be routed through several other cities in the network. Find the connections that have to be made.

For the cities on the right of Figure 1, the solution consists of seven arcs, namely all but the ones with weights of 40 and 80. The total cost is 165 units. These seven arcs form what is called the **minimum cost spanning tree** for the graph.

In general, a graph is **connected** when you can get from any one vertex to any other by following the arcs, ignoring directions of arcs if necessary. A **spanning tree** for a connected graph of N vertices consists of N − 1 arcs that connect the N vertices together. An exercise asks you to justify the following algorithm:

Prim's algorithm for finding a minimum cost spanning tree

1. Create a list L of vertices and put any one vertex on it;
2. Do the following N−1 times:
   2.a. Choose the arc of smallest weight that connects a vertex in L to a vertex not in L (if there are several arcs, any will do);
   2.b. Add to L the vertex for that arc that is not in L.

Scheduling Problems

The following are some situations in which a computer program would be useful in solving a problem. The nature of the problem in each case is such that the graph data structure is useful in **modeling** the situation (i.e., in representing the facts of the situation). It is beyond the scope of this book to discuss them thoroughly.

SITUATION 1. A high school offers a number of different courses. Each student registers for certain courses. After registration is completed, the problem is to find times to schedule the courses so that no student is signed up for two courses that meet at the same time, but the least possible number of meeting times is used.

MODEL 1. On a sheet of paper, draw a graph in which each vertex represents one course. Between any two vertices, draw an arc if some student is registered for both courses, otherwise do not have an arc connecting them. Using several different colors of crayons, color each vertex so that adjoining vertices are of different colors and the least possible number of colors are used. Then assign one meeting time to each color.

SITUATION 2. A football conference has 10 football teams. The rules of the conference dictate which teams are to play which other teams. Teams can play only on Saturdays and Tuesdays. The problem is to schedule play so that the entire set of games can be played in the least possible amount of time.

MODEL 2. On a sheet of paper, draw a graph in which each vertex represents one team. Between any two vertices, draw an arc if the teams are to play each other, otherwise do not have an arc connecting them. Using several different colors of crayons, color each arc so that, for every vertex, all arcs emanating from that vertex are of different colors. Use the least number of colors possible. Then assign one playing date to each color. Note that the MarkOf and MarkArc procedures are used here, with each color represented by an integer.

SITUATION 3. A large map has a number of countries drawn on it. Some of the countries have borders in common and some do not. A publishing company wants to color each country to make them all stand out. Bordering countries have to be different colors, but the same color can be used for two countries that have no border in common. Printing costs are highly dependent on the number of colors used. The problem is to find out whether three colors are sufficient for this map and, if so, what countries are to be colored which colors.

MODEL 3. On a sheet of paper, draw a graph in which each vertex represents one country. Between any two vertices, draw an arc if the countries have a border in common, otherwise do not have an arc connecting them. Using several different colors of crayons, color each vertex so that, for every arc, the vertices that it connects are of different colors. Use the least number of colors possible.

These situations are similar in a number of different respects. One significant respect is that no more efficient way is known to solve such problems than to try out all the possibilities. The map-coloring problem has been around for more than a hundred years. It is not too hard to show mathematically that five colors are *sufficient* for any map of countries, and it is easy to construct a map that *requires* four colors. But it was not until 1975 that someone proved that any map of countries can be colored with just four colors. The proof was done by dividing the problem into a very large number of cases, so many that they could only be completely checked out by a computer program.

SITUATION 4. A large aircraft-construction company has won a bid for constructing a large aircraft. Construction can be divided up into a large number of jobs that have to be accomplished, such as drawing up blueprints, putting the seats in, wind-tunnel testing, and ordering the engines. Certain jobs cannot be started until certain other jobs have been finished. The company has made a list of the hundreds of jobs involved, the time that each job will require for completion, and the jobs that other jobs require to have done first. The problem is to schedule the jobs so that the entire airplane can be completed in the least possible amount of time.

MODEL 4. On a sheet of paper, draw a graph in which each vertex represents one job. From any one job to any other job, draw an arc if the first must be completed before the second is started; otherwise, do not have such an arc. At each vertex, write in the amount of time required for that job.

This situation differs from the others in that no coloring (or its equivalent) is required. There is a straightforward, efficient algorithm for solving such problems. First add two additional vertices: a BEGIN vertex with an arc going to each vertex that has no arc already going into it, and an END vertex with an arc from each vertex that has no arc coming out of it. Write a time of 0 at each of these two special vertices. Now mark each arc of the graph with the total time that must elapse before the job that it exits from can be completed. To start with, you can mark all arcs exiting the BEGIN vertex with 0. For any vertex where all incoming arcs are marked with a total elapsed time, you can mark all its outgoing arcs with the sum of the time in the vertex and the largest total time on the incoming arcs. This process can continue until all arcs are marked. Then the least time required to complete the whole airplane is the largest total time on the incoming arcs at the END vertex.

Check Your Understanding

1. Find the minimum cost spanning tree for the graph on the left of Figure 1. Assume that Weight(6, 7) is 25.

2. What changes would be made in Example 8.3A to compute the length of the shortest path (least number of arcs) from any vertex to any other vertex in a graph? Use -1 if there is no path at all.

3. (NA) Write a procedure that uses recursion to print the minimum-cost path between any two given vertices using the Pr matrix described for Floyd's algorithm.

4. (NA) What changes would be made in the breadth-search coding to use a Boolean variable Found and FOR statements, as described in this section?

5. (NA) Discuss why it is that the use of a Queue for breadth-first searching is much faster than the method used for Exercise 4.

6. (NA) Revise Example 8.3A to implement Warshall's algorithm as described in the text, then use the concept of Exercise 3 to write a procedure that prints the shortest path (if any) between each and every pair of vertices of the graph.

7. (NA) Revise the coding of the initialization part of Example 8.3A so that there is only one assignment per MC component. Then discuss why this probably executes more slowly.

8. (NA) Write out a detailed argument that Prim's algorithm does in fact produce the spanning tree with the minimum possible cost.

9. (NA) Change the breadth-first coding to have it find the minimum cost of reaching any vertex from Givert, by adding Weight(AlreadyVisited,V) to Distance[AlreadyVisited] instead of adding 1. Then prove that this algorithm does not always give the right answer. Next, improve the coding further by also inserting the following just before the IF:

```
Dist := Distance [AlreadyVisited] + Weight (AlreadyVisited, V);
IF Distance [V] > Dist THEN
    Distance [V] := Dist ELSE
```

Now prove that this revised algorithm also does not work.

8.4 SPARSE MATRICES

A **sparse matrix** is one in which very few of the components have a value other than 0. An example is a matrix with 1000 rows and 1000 columns, in which there are only about 3000 nonzero entries. If such a matrix is declared as ARRAY [1..1000], [1..1000] OF REAL, it will require 4 million bytes of space (assuming that each REAL number takes up 4 bytes of space). But you could theoretically get by with 12,000 bytes of space for the information—3000 nonzero REALs times 4 bytes per REAL. The difference could be crucial.

As a more concrete example, consider the scheduling problem for courses and students at a school, discussed in Model 1 at the end of the previous section. The school might have several hundred courses and several thousand students, but the average number of arcs per vertex (course) might reasonably be only 50. Thus a savings of 98% of the space could be expected with the right choice of an array implementation.

Declaring a Sparse Rectangular Matrix

First you must consider what is needed in the definition module. Assume that there is only one matrix in use in the program, similar to what was done with graphs. This means that you do not have to worry about having Create or Destroy. This one matrix is hidden in the implementation module; it is not passed as a parameter between procedures (again, just as was done with graphs). In programs that need several sparse matrices, significant changes would have to be made in this definition module.

You only need to be able to do two things with a matrix, or with any other array: (1) Put a given value in a given component; (2) Retrieve the value stored in a given component. Example 8.4A gives the complete SparsADT definition module. The module has to refer to the type REAL and the value 0.0. By using the identifiers Numeric and Zero for these two objects, it is easy to convert the module to work with INTEGER or CARDINAL and with 0 by simply changing these two declarations. The IndexType is also easily modified by changing the values given to Loval and Hival.

Some Implementations of SparsADT

Now we come to the decision of what implementation to use. One possibility is to use an ARRAY [Loval..Hival], [Loval..Hival] OF Numeric; but that is only

EXAMPLE 8.4A _____

```
DEFINITION MODULE SparsADT;
EXPORT QUALIFIED IndexType, Loval, Hival, Zero, Numeric,
                 InitializeMatrix, SetValue, ValueOf;
     (* Module to permit working with the numbers in a
        single sparse matrix of REALS. To work with a matrix
        of INTEGERs, just change Zero and Numeric *)
     (* Written by William C. Jones, October 19-- *)
CONST
     Loval = 1;
     Hival = 1000;
     Zero  = 0.0;
TYPE
     IndexType = [Loval..Hival];
     Numeric   = REAL;
(* The values of Loval and Hival will vary from one
     application to another, so no client module should make
     any assumptions about them other than Loval < Hival *)
(*************************************************************)

PROCEDURE InitializeMatrix;
     (* Initialize the matrix to Zero in each component *)

PROCEDURE SetValue (Row, Col : IndexType; Given : Numeric);
     (* Assign the Given Numeric to component [Row, Col] *)

PROCEDURE ValueOf (Row, Col : IndexType) : Numeric;
     (* Tell what Numeric has been assigned to component
        [Row, Col]; return Zero if none has been assigned *)

END SparsADT.
```

feasible when the matrix is small. If that is the case, the program might as well declare its own array and dispense with SparsADT altogether.

Another possibility is to use a linked list of nodes. Each node would contain a nonzero Numeric value and the row and column numbers of its component, as well as the linking value. The total space requirements of such a node, under the assumptions of Section 1.9, would be 4 bytes for the REAL, 2 bytes for each of the two indices, and 2 bytes for the link, for a total of 10 bytes per node. Thus 1000 nonzero components would require 10,000 bytes of space. This implementation is developed in the exercises. The problem is that it takes a long time to search such a linked list for a value; most applications would require that you at least use a binary tree instead of a linked list.

A third possibility is suitable if the array size is somewhat smaller and the nonzero values are fairly evenly distributed over the rows. For instance, a 1000-by-1000 array with 3000 nonzero components averages three nonzero values per row; perhaps you can expect about 800 of the rows to have at least one nonzero component. The linked list of nodes just described would require 30,000 bytes of space (at 10 bytes per nonzero component). We can instead use a one-dimensional array of 1000 linked lists, one list per row (Fig. 6). Then each node need only contain a nonzero Numeric value (4 bytes) and the column number of its component (2 bytes), plus the link (2 bytes). That means a total of 24,000 bytes for the nodes, plus 2000 bytes for the array of 1000 addresses. This 26,000 bytes is not much improvement over 30,000 bytes. The primary advantage is that it permits very fast access to a given node, when the number of nodes per row is small. This is the implementation developed here. Some appropriate declarations are:

```
TYPE   PointerToNode = POINTER TO Node;
       Node = RECORD
                     Info : Numeric;
                     Colm : IndexType;
                     Link : PointerToNode;
              END;
VAR    Data : ARRAY IndexType OF PointerToNode;
```

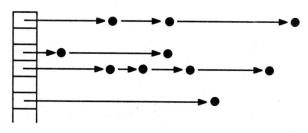

FIGURE 6. A sparse array implemented as an array of pointers to linked lists, one for each row.

EXAMPLE 8.4B _____

```
IMPLEMENTATION MODULE SparsADT;
    (* Module to permit working with the numbers in a
       single sparse matrix  *)
    (* Written by William C. Jones, October 19-- *)
(* Already defined:  Loval = 1;  Hival = 1000;  Zero = 0.0;
   IndexType = [Loval..Hival];   Numeric = REAL;  *)
TYPE
    PointerToNode = POINTER TO Node;
    Node = RECORD
                Info : Numeric;
                Colm : IndexType;
                Link : PointerToNode;
            END;
VAR
    Data : ARRAY [Loval..Hival] OF PointerToNode;
(***********************************************************)

PROCEDURE InitializeMatrix;
    (* Initialize the matrix to Zero in each component *)
VAR
    Row : IndexType;
BEGIN
    FOR Row := Loval TO Hival DO
        Data [Row] := NIL;
    END;
END InitializeMatrix;
(***********************************************************)

PROCEDURE Pointer (Row, Col : IndexType) : PointerToNode;
    (* return a pointer to the node indexed [Row, Col] *)
VAR
    P : PointerToNode;
BEGIN
    P := Data [Row];
    WHILE (P # NIL) AND (P^.Colm # Col) DO
        P := P^.Link;
    END;
    RETURN P;   (* NIL if no match was found *)
END Pointer;
(***********************************************************)

PROCEDURE ValueOf (Row, Col : IndexType) : Numeric;
    (* Tell what Numeric has been assigned to component
       [Row, Col]; return Zero if none has been assigned *)
VAR
    P : PointerToNode;
BEGIN
    P := Pointer (Row, Col);
    IF P # NIL THEN
        RETURN P^.Info;
    ELSE
        RETURN Zero;
    END;
END ValueOf;
(***********************************************************)
```

(* continued on next page *)

```
(* EXAMPLE 8.4B continued *)


PROCEDURE SetValue (Row, Col : IndexType; Given : Numeric);
    (* Assign the Given Numeric to component [Row, Col] *)
VAR
    P : PointerToNode;
BEGIN
    P := Pointer (Row, Col);
    IF P # NIL THEN  (* change the value there *)
        P^.Info := Given;
    ELSE  (* make a new node and push it on the Row list *)
        NEW (P);
        P^.Info := Given;
        P^.Colm := Col;
        P^.Link := Data [Row];
        Data [Row] := P;
    END;
END SetValue;
(* ************************************************************ *)

END SparsADT.
```

Initialization of the matrix is fairly straightforward—just assign NIL to each component of Data. The ValueOf function, which is supposed to return the value for a given row and column, need only look down the linked list Data[Row] until it finds the Node with the given column value or until it gets to the end of the list. If it finds a Node with the given column value, ValueOf returns the Numeric value in that Node; otherwise it returns Zero.

The SetValue procedure has to first look down the linked list Data[Row] to see if there is already a Node with the given column value. If there is, it should change the Info value there to the Given Numeric. Otherwise it should create a new Node and put it in that linked list. The easiest place to put a new Node in a linked list is at the front of the list, so I do that. An alternative is for SetValue to ignore the possibility that there is already a Node with the given column value and in any case create a new Node and put it on the list. However, that may well cost more execution time in calls of ValueOf than it saves in calls of SetValue.

Since both SetValue and ValueOf search the list for a Node with a given column value, it is worthwhile to write a (hidden) function to do the searching. This function is then called by both SetValue and ValueOf; the coding is given in Example 8.4B.

An implementation of GraphADT can be organized something along the lines of this implementation of SparsADT when the number of vertices is large. Each Node represents one arc, connecting from vertex Row to vertex Col. The Node contains fields for the weight and the mark on the corresponding arc. The Connecting function can be simply coded as RETURN Pointer(Row, Col)#NIL. Many applications of graphs have an average of three or four arcs per vertex, so it is appropriate to use such an implementation.

The Cross-linked Implementation of SparsADT

Some situations require you to process the sparse array by rows for some purposes and by columns for other purposes. If speed is particularly crucial and you can afford the extra space required, you can use the more complicated structure implied by the following declarations:

```
TYPE   PointerToNode = POINTER TO Node;
       Node = RECORD
                  Info : Numeric;
                  Colm, Row : IndexType;
                  NextColm, NextRow : PointerToNode;
              END;
VAR    DataColm, DataRow : ARRAY [Loval..Hival] OF PointerToNode;
```

In this implementation, DataRow[K] is a pointer to the Node with Row=K and the lowest column number (stored in Colm). The NextColm field points to the Node with Row=K and the next-lowest column number. Similarly, Data-Colm[K] is a pointer to the Node with Colm=K and the lowest row number (in Row), and the NextRow field points to the Node with Colm=K and the next-lowest row number (see Fig. 7). This **cross-linked implementation** of SparsADT can be messy to code, but processing the matrix by columns can be sped up by a factor of 100 or so.

Check Your Understanding

1. Assume that a single linked list is used to implement SparsADT, namely VAR Data: PointerToNode, where TYPE Node = RECORD Info: Numeric; Colm, Row: IndexType; Link: PointerToNode; END. How does that change the coding of the Pointer function given in Example 8.4B?

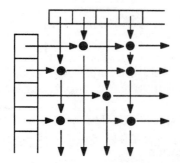

FIGURE 7.   A sparse array implemented as two arrays of pointers to linked lists, for rows and columns respectively.

2. Under the same assumptions as in Exercise 1, how does the coding of the ValueOf function in Example 8.4B change?

3. If you implemented SparsADT using VAR Data: ARRAY [Loval..Hival], [Loval..Hival] OF Numeric, what would be the coding for ValueOf and SetValue?

4. (NA) Under the same assumptions as in Exercise 1, code the SetValue procedure.

5. (NA) What revisions are necessary in the SparsADT implementation module of Example 8.4B if each component of Data represents a column instead of a row?

8.5 STRINGS THAT VARY IN LENGTH

A data type that occurs frequently in applications is that of a varying-length string of characters. One such string value is 'Hello', a string of 5 characters. Another is 'Virginia', a string of 8 characters. It is useful to have a type of variable that can have either of these two values or similar values. I will call the type Strng; by leaving out the 'i', I avoid a clash with the name String that is provided by some compilers as an extension of Modula-2. Thus a variable of **Strng** type can have a value that consists of 0 or more characters.

The StrngADT Library Module

You need several procedures that allow you to manipulate variables and values of Strng type. You need to be able to allocate and deallocate space for Strng variables, to assign character values to a given Strng variable, and to retrieve character values from a Strng variable. The StrngADT module in Example 8.5A describes a sufficient variety of procedures. For instance, the statement CreateStr(Result, 'Hello') creates a Strng variable with the value 'Hello'.

A Strng is a sequence of characters in which the location is given as a cardinal value. Length corresponds to SizeOf, GetChar corresponds to LookAt, and PutChar is something like Modify. DeleteSubStr is more powerful than ListADT.Delete, since it can be used to delete one or more characters from a Strng. Similarly, InsertSubStr is more powerful than ListADT.Insert, and CreateStr is more powerful than ListADT.Create (since CreateStr (X, '') creates an empty string).

If you want to make Result into a duplicate copy of Given, you can use this coding for a utility procedure CopyWholeStr:

```
CreateStr (Result, '');
InsertSubStr (Result, 1, Length (Given), Given, 1);
```

EXAMPLE 8.5A _____

```
DEFINITION MODULE StrngADT;
    (* basic operations on strings of characters *)
    (* Written by William C. Jones, Jr.  Jan 19--  *)
EXPORT QUALIFIED Strng, CreateStr, DestroyStr, Length,
      GetChar, PutChar, GetArray, InsertSubStr,
      DeleteSubStr, CompareStr, JoinStr, Position;
TYPE
    Strng;
(*************************************************************)

PROCEDURE CreateStr (VAR Result : Strng;
                         Given   : ARRAY OF CHAR);
    (* Create a Strng variable containing the characters
       of Given down to 0C or the end of the array *)

PROCEDURE DestroyStr (VAR Result : Strng);
    (* Deallocate the space used by the Strng variable *)

PROCEDURE Length (Given : Strng) : CARDINAL;
    (* Return the number of characters in Given *)

PROCEDURE GetChar (Given : Strng;  Pos : CARDINAL) : CHAR;
    (* Return the character at position Pos in Given;
       no effect unless 1 <= Pos <= Length(Given) *)

PROCEDURE PutChar (VAR Given : Strng;  Pos : CARDINAL;
                       NewCh : CHAR);
    (* Replace the character at position Pos by NewCh;
       indeterminate unless 1 <= Pos <= Length(Given)+1 *)
(*************************************************************)

PROCEDURE GetArray (VAR Result : ARRAY OF CHAR;
                        Given   : Strng);
    (* Give Result the string value denoted by Given,
       with.0C as a terminator; truncate if necessary *)

PROCEDURE InsertSubStr (VAR Result    : Strng;
                        Pos, HowMany : CARDINAL;
                        Given        : Strng;
                        Start        : CARDINAL);
    (* Insert HowMany characters from Given, beginning at
       character number Start of Given, into Result,
       beginning at character number Pos of Result.  But:
       No more than Length(Given) + 1 - Start are copied.
       Do nothing if Pos > Length(Result) + 1 *)

PROCEDURE DeleteSubStr (VAR Result    : Strng;
                        Pos, HowMany : CARDINAL);
    (* Delete HowMany characters from Result starting at
       character number Pos in Result. But just delete from
       that point on if Length(Result) < Pos + HowMany *)

PROCEDURE CompareStr (First, Second : Strng) : INTEGER;
    (* Return 0 if the values are equal; return a positive
       if First > Second, a negative if First < Second *)

(* continued on next page *)
```

```
(* EXAMPLE 8.5A continued *)


PROCEDURE JoinStr (VAR Result      : Strng;
                      First, Second : Strng);
    (* Create Result as the characters in First followed
       by the characters in Second, maintaining the
       relative order in First and in Second *)

PROCEDURE Position (Sought, Given : Strng;
                    Pos            : CARDINAL) : CARDINAL;
    (* Return the position of the first instance of Sought
       as a substring of the part of Given starting at Pos.
       Return 0 if not there, Pos if Length(Sought) = 0 *)

END StrngADT.
```

If you want to make Result the substring consisting of the sixth through tenth characters of Given, you can use this coding:

```
CreateStr (Result, '');
InsertSubStr (Result, 1, 5, Given, 6);
```

If you want to replace the sixth through tenth characters of Result by the first five characters of Given, assuming that both Result and Given have at least five characters, you can use this coding:

```
DeleteSubStr (Result, 6, 5);
InsertSubStr (Result, 6, 5, Given, 1);
```

The JoinStr procedure is actually a utility procedure. If you want to concatenate two strings to obtain a new string Result consisting of the characters in First followed by the characters in Second, keeping the relative order in First and Second, you can use this coding instead of calling JoinStr (Result, First, Second):

```
CreateStr (Result, '');
InsertSubStr (Result, 1, Length (First), First, 1);
InsertSubStr (Result, Length (First)+1, Length (Second),
                                        Second, 1);
```

The Position function is used to find out whether one Strng occurs as a substring of another and, if so, where it occurs. For instance, you can remove all blanks from a Given Strng using the following coding:

```
CreateStr (OneBlank, ' ');
Pos := Position (OneBlank, Given, 1);
WHILE Pos # 0 DO
    DeleteSubStr (Given, Pos, 1);
    Pos := Position (OneBlank, Given, Pos);
END;
```

Some Implementations of StrngADT

There are several candidates for implementations of Strngs. A commonly used method is to set an upper limit on the number of characters that can be in a Strng, such as 132. Then a counted array can be used. The appropriate declarations and the coding of CreateStr and CompareStr are given in Example 8.5B. The DestroyStr procedure has just one statement, namely DISPOSE(Result).

If Strngs are implemented as standard linked lists of characters, they are not as limited in size as with a counted array. Also, short Strngs take up much less room than they do using counted arrays. On the other hand, the space required is three times as much as the space for the actual characters, assuming that an address requires 2 bytes and a character only 1. The CompareStr function could be coded as follows:

```
(* body of CompareStr, standard linked list impl. of StrngADT *)
WHILE (First # NIL) AND (Second # NIL) DO
    IF First↑.Info # Second↑.Info THEN
        RETURN INTEGER (ORD (First↑.Info)) -
               INTEGER (ORD (Second↑.Info));
    END;
    First := First↑.Link;
    Second := Second↑.Link;
END;
RETURN INTEGER (ORD (First # NIL)) - INTEGER (ORD (Second # NIL));
```

Actually, I would not write that last RETURN statement in a program that I wanted to be able to read easily several months later. It works correctly, but it is far harder to understand than a simple IF statement that tests which of First and Second is NIL at that point. Therefore, this RETURN statement is an example of what you should not write in a program, as a matter of style. The appropriate IF statement is left as an exercise.

EXAMPLE 8.5B _____

```
(* Part of the simple array implementation of StrngADT *)
TYPE
    Strng = POINTER TO CountedArray;
    CountedArray = RECORD
                        Item : ARRAY [1..MaxSize] OF CHAR;
                        Size : CARDINAL;
                   END;
(***********************************************************)

PROCEDURE CreateStr (VAR Result : Strng;
                         Given  : ARRAY OF CHAR);
VAR
    K : CARDINAL;
BEGIN

    NEW (Result);
    K := 0;
    WHILE (Given [K] # 0C) AND (K <= HIGH (Given)) AND
                        AND (K < MaxSize) DO
        Result [K + 1] := Given [K];
        INC (K);
    END;
    Result^.Size := K;

END CreateStr;
(***********************************************************)

PROCEDURE CompareStr (First, Second : Strng) : INTEGER;
VAR
    SmallerSize, K : CARDINAL;
BEGIN

    IF First^.Size > Second^.Size THEN
        SmallerSize := Second^.Size;
    ELSE
        SmallerSize := First^.Size;
    END;

    FOR K := 1 TO SmallerSize DO
        IF First^.Item [K] # Second^.Item [K] THEN
            RETURN INTEGER (ORD (First^.Item [K])) -
                   INTEGER (ORD (Second^.Item [K]));
        END;
    END;

    RETURN INTEGER (First^.Size) - INTEGER (Second^.Size);

END CompareStr;
```

The Flexible Implementation of StrngADT

The following is an implementation of StrngADT that combines the advantages of both implementations just given. I call it the "flexible" implementation. The primary advantage of this implementation is that it minimizes the amount of space used. For instance, a file with 500 lines of type will require only 2000 bytes of space more than the space required for the characters themselves. I declare as before:

```
TYPE  Strng = POINTER TO CountedArray;
      CountedArray = RECORD
                        Size : CARDINAL;
                        Item : ARRAY [1..MaxSize] OF CHAR;
                     END;
```

However, I define MaxSize to be nearly the largest CARDINAL there is, perhaps 65,520 (some compilers accept 65,520 but not 65,535). This would require far too much space, except that I use a private procedure named MakeStr that allocates just as much space for a Strng as needed, rather than using NEW. The space required is the number of characters plus 2 for the cardinal Size and 2 for the pointer value, assuming that space is calculated in bytes and cardinals require 2 bytes of space:

```
PROCEDURE MakeStr (VAR Result : Strng;  Len : CARDINAL);
BEGIN
    ALLOCATE (Result, 2 + Len);
    Result↑.Size := Len;
END MakeStr;

PROCEDURE DestroyStr (VAR Result : Strng);
BEGIN
    DEALLOCATE (Result, 2 + Result↑.Size);
END DestroyStr;
```

Now CompareStr is the same as in Example 8.5B, and DeleteSubStr(Result, Pos, HowMany) could be coded as follows (guards to check for unreasonable parameters are left as an exercise):

```
(* body of DeleteSubStr, "flexible" implementation of StrngADT *)
Saved := Result;
MakeStr (Result, Saved↑.Size - HowMany);
```

```
FOR K := 1 TO Pos - 1 DO
    Result↑.Item [K] := Saved↑.Item [K];
END;
FOR K := Pos TO Result↑.Size DO
    Result↑.Item [K] := Saved↑.Item [K + HowMany];
END;
DestroyStr (Saved);
```

Some compilers use 4 bytes for an address value. This means that the flexible implementation of strings has an **overhead** of 6 bytes per string value—4 for the pointer value and 2 for the length value (besides 1 byte per character). There are two reasonable ways to reduce this overhead, each saving 1 byte of overhead per string value. One way is available if you know that no string will have more than 255 characters; then the size can be stored in a single byte rather than two. The other way is to note that, on most microcomputers, a 4-byte address value can be compressed to 3 bytes without losing any information. If you study the manual for your compiler and see how to do this, you can declare a Strng as a 3-byte value in the definition module and then make conversions between the address value and the 3-byte coded value.

Check Your Understanding

1. Write the body of the JoinStr procedure for the "flexible" implementation of StrngADT.

2. What changes must be made in your answer to the preceding exercise to have the coding for the simple array implementation of StrngADT?

3. Rewrite the odious RETURN statement in the coding of CompareStr for the standard linked list implementation as a longer but much clearer IF statement.

4. Revise the coding given for DeleteSubStr in the "flexible" implementation of StrngADT to make appropriate corrections for unreasonable parameters.

5. (NA) Write the DeleteSubStr procedure for the simple array implementation of StrngADT.

6. (NA) Write the DeleteSubStr procedure for the standard linked list implementation of StrngADT.

7. (NA) Write the GetArray procedure for the "flexible" implementation of StrngADT.

8. (NA) Show that the first five procedures listed in Example 8.5A (CreateStr, DestroyStr, Length, GetChar, and PutChar) form a complete set of primitives, by demonstrating how each of the other six procedures can be implemented using the first five, without reference to the underlying implementation.

8.6 SETS

One standard storage unit in the computer's memory is called a **word**. Each word is made up of a number of **bits**, which can be in either of two states (such as yes/no or on/off). The number of bits that make up a word depends on the processor used. For many microcomputers, the length of a word is either 8 bits or 16 bits. If it is 8 bits, the number of different values that can be stored in one word is 256, since that is the eighth power of 2. If the length of a word is 16 bits, the number of different values that can be stored in one word is 65,536, since that is the sixteenth power of 2.

Modula-2 provides a SET type to allow manipulation of the bits in a single word. The first part of this section discusses this SET type. The latter part discusses a library module for general sets of simple values.

Since the length of a word varies from one processor to another, I use the constant-identifier WordLength in this section to refer to that length. WordLength is not a built-in identifier; you must declare WordLength to have the appropriate value for your processor if you wish to use this constant-identifier in your programs.

Definition of a BITSET

Braces denote certain sets in Modula-2. The set of all cardinals less than WordLength is denoted by {0..WordLength−1}. **BITSET** is a built-in type-identifier for the sets of cardinals less than WordLength.

You can declare a variable to be of type BITSET. For example, the declaration VAR X, Y, Z: BITSET means that X and Y are sets whose **elements** are cardinals in the range from 0 to WordLength−1, inclusive.

To initialize X as the **empty set** (i.e., the set that contains no elements), you execute the statement X := { }. To initialize X to the set of the first four cardinals, you execute the statement X := {0,1,2,3}. To see if Y is that set, you test the condition Y = X or the condition Y = {0,1,2,3} or even Y = {0..3}. In general, any set of cardinals less than WordLength is indicated by listing the elements of the set between braces with the same notation that is used for the labels of a CASE statement. No element is listed more than once, and the order does not make a difference. For example, {1,2,3} is the same set as {3,2,1}. If all the elements listed are constant expressions, this is called a **set constant**.

Operators for Sets

The **union** of two given sets is the set that contains all the elements that *either* of the two sets contains. The operator that denotes union is the + symbol. For example, if X = {0..3} and Y = {1,3,5}, then Z := X + Y makes Z the set {0..3,5}. Similarly, {2,5} = {2} + {2,5} = { } + {2,5} = {2} + {5}.

The **intersection** of two given sets is the set that contains all the elements that *both* of the two sets contain. The operator for intersection is the * symbol. For example, if X = {0..3} and Y = {1,3,5}, then Z := X * Y makes Z the set {1,3}. Similarly, {2,5} = {2,5,7} * {2,5} and { } = {2,5} * {3,7}.

The **difference** of two given sets is the set that contains all the elements of the first set that are not in the second set; the operator is the − symbol. For example, if X = {0..3} and Y = {1,3,5}, then Z := X − Y makes Z the set {0,2}. Similarly, {2,5} = {2,3,5} − {3} = {2,5} − {7} = {2,5} − { }.

The **symmetric difference** of two given sets is the set that contains all the elements that are in *exactly one* of the two given sets; the operator is the / symbol. For example, if X = {0..3} and Y = {1,3,5}, then Z := X / Y makes Z the set {0,2,5}. Similarly, {2,5} = {2,3,5} / {3} = {2,5} / { }.

The four operators +, *, −, and /, illustrated in Figure 8, are the only Modula-2 operators that you can use to combine two sets to obtain a set. Three of these four operators are **commutative**. That is, for any two sets X and Y: X+Y = Y+X, X*Y = Y*X, and X/Y = Y/X, but X−Y is not necessarily the same as Y−X. In fact, X−Y equals Y−X only if X=Y, in which case X−Y = { } = Y−X. It is also interesting to observe that the empty set has some of the properties that zero has for numbers. That is, for any set X, X+{ } = X, X*{ } = { }, and X−{ } = X.

Relational Operators

Four of the six relational operators can be used between two sets. For any two given sets X and Y, the following are conditions (Boolean expressions): X = Y, X # Y, X <= Y, and X >= Y. The operators < and > cannot be used for sets.

X = Y means that X and Y have exactly the same elements. X # Y means that they do not; that is, X # Y is the same as NOT (X = Y). The <> symbol can be used in place of # for sets as well as for other types of values.

X <= Y means that every element of X is an element of Y. For example, {2,5} <= {2,5,7}. This is called **set inclusion**. X >= Y means that every element of

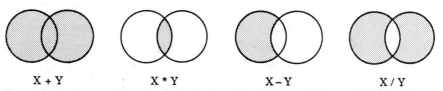

X + Y   X * Y   X − Y   X / Y

FIGURE 8. Operations on sets. In each pair shown, X is on the left, and Y is on the right.

Y is an element of X; that is, X >= Y is the same as Y <= X. Note that it is *not* true that {1} <= {2,3}.

The IN Operator; INCL and EXCL

IN is used to determine whether a given cardinal is an element of a given set. For example, 3 IN {2,5} is a FALSE condition and 2 IN {0..3} is a TRUE condition. IN is the only relational operator whose operands can be of different base types. IN can only be used if its second operand is a set and its first operand is an expression whose value is in the acceptable range of elements for that set.

You can add an element to a set or take one away using the built-in statement procedures INCL and EXCL. These identifiers are abbreviations for "include" and "exclude," respectively. **INCL(X,e)** causes the element e to be added to the set X (no effect if e was already in that set). **EXCL(X,e)** causes the element e to be removed from the set X (no effect if e was not in that set). Both require that the first parameter be a set variable and that the second parameter be an expression whose value is in the acceptable range of elements for that set.

You might think that INCL and EXCL are not needed, because you could use X := X + {e} in place of INCL(X,e) and X := X − {e} in place of EXCL(X,e). This is true if e is a constant expression. However, many implementations of Modula-2 will not allow an expression to be listed inside set braces when it involves variables or function calls. If you have such an implementation, you will sometimes need the INCL and EXCL procedures.

Other Types of Sets

You can define other types of sets. The syntax is illustrated by TYPE SetType = SET OF [2..9]. Then VAR U, V: SetType is a declaration of U and V as set variables of type SetType. However, U := {3} is not legal, since {3} is a BITSET and U is not. Each set constant is assumed to be a BITSET unless explicitly stated otherwise. This is done by using U := SetType{3}; that is, the left brace is preceded by the type of the set whenever its type is not BITSET.

In a set type-denoter, the phrase after SET OF must be a subrange of CARDINALs or an enumeration type or a subrange of an enumeration type. Most processors put a very low limit on the ordinal value of the highest possible element, often 15 or 31. But some processors may allow other types for the element type, such as CHAR or INTEGER.

A Definition Module for Large Sets

It is occasionally useful to be able to work with the set of all characters or a set of hundreds or thousands of integers. The following material discusses a library module for that purpose. Loval and Hival can be used as the names of the lowest and highest values allowed for elements of a set. The external module that provides the definitions for the data abstraction of a set of these values should include procedures that allow you to (1) *Create* a set (initialize it as the empty set), (2) *Destroy* a set (i.e., free its storage space for other uses), (3) *Include* a given element in a set, or (4) *Exclude* a given element from a set. The last two procedures are the analogs of the built-in INCL and EXCL procedures. You must also be able to find out whether a given element is a member of a given set. A BOOLEAN function *IsThere* is used in place of the IN operator. Note that these are a simplified form of the procedures for TableADT.

These are all the procedures you really have to have. For example, to assign to X the union of two sets A and B, you can execute the following statements:

```
Create (X);   (* makes X the null set *)
FOR E := Loval TO Hival DO
    IF IsThere (E, A) OR IsThere (E, B) THEN
        Include (E, X);
    END;
END;
```

It would be easier to have union and intersection available from the library module. The ability to compare two sets using *IsEqualSet* and *IsSubset* would also be handy. So these procedures are included in the library module. The definition module is shown in Example 8.6A. I postpone the declaration of Set until the implementation module, since that is not relevant to the data abstraction created by this module.

An Implementation Module for Large Sets

Now we have to choose a reasonable implementation of these large sets of numbers. We would use a linked list of elements if we knew nothing about the kinds of elements we have. But since we know that they are a subrange of ordinals, it is easier to use an array of BOOLEAN values, one for each element of the subrange; that is, Set = POINTER TO ARRAY ValueType OF BOOLEAN. We assign TRUE to a component to indicate the index is in the set and FALSE to indicate it is not.

The body of the Create procedure is a loop that assigns FALSE to every component, as follows:

```
NEW (Data);
FOR K := Loval TO Hival DO
    Data↑[K] := FALSE;
END;
```

EXAMPLE 8.6A _____

```
DEFINITION MODULE SetADT;
EXPORT QUALIFIED Loval, Hival,  ValueType, Set,    Create,
                Copy,  Destroy, Include,  Exclude, Unite,
          Intersect, IsThere, IsSubset,  IsEqualSet;
    (* Provide useful manipulations of sets of values *)
    (* Warning:  All sets must be Created before they are
       used in any other procedure except as the first
       parameter of Unite or Intersect *)
CONST
    Loval = 0C;    (* character number 0   *)
    Hival = 177C;  (* character number 127 *)
TYPE
    ValueType = [Loval..Hival];
    Set;
(*********************************************************)

(*                  THE PRIMITIVES                     *)

PROCEDURE Include (Elt : ValueType;  VAR Data : Set);
    (* Put Elt in Data (no change if already there) *)

PROCEDURE Exclude (Elt : ValueType;  VAR Data : Set);
    (* Take Elt out of Data (no change if not there) *)

PROCEDURE IsThere (Elt : ValueType; Data : Set) : BOOLEAN;
    (* Tell whether Elt is in Data *)

PROCEDURE Create (VAR Data : Set);
    (* Initialize Data as an empty Set *)

PROCEDURE Destroy (VAR Data : Set);
    (* Deallocate storage used by Data *)
(*********************************************************)

(*                  SOME UTILITIES                     *)

PROCEDURE Unite (VAR Data : Set;  First, Second : Set);
    (* Create Data and make it the union of First and
       Second *)

PROCEDURE Intersect (VAR Data : Set;  First, Second : Set);
    (* Create Data and make it the intersection of
       First and Second *)

PROCEDURE Copy (VAR Data : Set;  Source : Set);
    (* Make Data (initially empty) a duplicate copy
       of Source *)

PROCEDURE IsSubset (First, Second : Set) : BOOLEAN;
    (* Tell whether First is a subset of Second *)

PROCEDURE IsEqualSet (First, Second : Set) : BOOLEAN;
    (* Tell whether First equals Second *)

END SetADT.
```

You can include an element in a set by executing Data ↑ [Elt] := TRUE. You can form the union of two sets by assigning TRUE to a component if the corresponding component of either operand is TRUE and otherwise assigning FALSE; so the body of Unite could be:

```
FOR K := Loval TO Hival DO
    Data↑[K] := First↑[K] OR Second↑[K];
END;
```

You can find out whether First ↑ is a subset of Second ↑ by making sure that every Element in First ↑ is also in Second ↑. To check this, you can go through the components in order; if you find one that violates the condition, return FALSE; if you never find such a one, return TRUE. Thus the body of the IsSubset procedure could be:

```
FOR K := Loval TO Hival DO
    IF First↑[K] AND NOT Second↑[K] THEN
        RETURN FALSE;
    END;
END;
RETURN TRUE;
```

The rest of the algorithms are similar, so they are left as exercises.

Some processors store an array of BOOLEANs with one word of storage for each component. This limits us to only a few thousand values in the subrange, since otherwise we could easily run out of storage room. If you wished to deal with hundreds of thousands of elements, you would probably have to find some way of using only one bit of a word for each component. This can be done using SET, but it is messier than what is developed here.

Implementation of SetADT using Linked Lists

If an application requires that you have a very large number of sets, each with a small number of elements, but that the total number of elements is large, the standard linked list implementation would be appropriate. The following type declarations could be used:

```
TYPE   PointerToNode = POINTER TO Node;
       Set = PointerToNode;
       Node = RECORD
                     Info : ValueType;
                     Link : PointerToNode;
              END;
```

The elements of these sets do not have to be kept in any particular order, but it greatly increases the speed with which Unite, Intersect, and other operations can be performed if they are kept sorted. Therefore I will keep each set in increasing order of its elements. Thus the Create procedure simply executes Data := NIL. Example 8.6B shows how Intersect might be coded.

EXAMPLE 8.6B _____

```
PROCEDURE Intersect (VAR Data : Set;   First, Second : Set);
    (* Make Data the intersection of First and Second *)
    (* Context: standard linked list impl. of SetADT *)
VAR
    P : PointerToNode;
BEGIN

    (* create a header node for the Data list *)
        NEW (Data);
        P := Data;

    (* create a new node in P^.Link for each common info *)
        WHILE (First # NIL) AND (Second # NIL) DO
            IF First^.Info < Second^.Info THEN
                First := First^.Link;
            ELSIF First^.Info > Second^.Info THEN
                Second := Second^.Link;
            ELSE  (* they are equal *)
                NEW (P^.Link);
                P := P^.Link;
                P^.Info := First^.Info;
                First := First^.Link;
                Second := Second^.Link;
            END;
        END;

    (* tie off the list and get rid of the header node *)
        P^.Link := NIL;
        P := Data;
        Data := Data^.Link;
        DISPOSE (P);

END Intersect;
```

The algorithm for Intersect first creates the new Data list with a header node and then goes through the two given lists looking for two nodes with the same value. When such matching nodes are found, a new node is created with a copy of that information and put at the end of the Data list. When the list is completed, the header node (which was used solely for convenience in coding) is discarded. To see how convenient this is, you might try recoding the example without using a header node.

Check Your Understanding

1. Assume that X = {1,5,8..10} and Y = {3,5,9,10} at one point in a program. Write the following as set constants: X+Y, X∗Y, X−Y, Y−X, X∗{ }.

2. If X+Y = Y, what can you deduce about X and Y?

3. In the implementation of SetADT using an array of Booleans, the bodies of Delete, Destroy, and IsThere require one statement each. What are those statements?

4. Write the body of Intersect using the implementation of SetADT as an array of Booleans.

5. (NA) Write the body of IsEqualSet using the implementation of SetADT as an array of Booleans.

6. (NA) Write the body of Unite using the standard linked list implementation of SetADT.

8.7 GENERALIZED LISTS

Some programming problems require the use of a list that can have not just information values on it but also other lists. Such a list is called a **generalized list**. This section develops a library module named **GenADT** that provides these capabilities. The module includes a design for lists different from ListADT. Figure 9 displays a list with five values, some list values and others information values. For this figure, Information is assumed to be a single word.

This GenADT module uses functions almost exclusively, rather than statement procedures. There are two reasons for this: (1) It provides you with additional practice using functions; (2) It provides an introduction to LISP, a programming language used heavily in artificial intelligence.

An application of generalized lists is in constructing an **expert system**. The information values are **attributes** and their **values**. The basic data structure could be a list of structures each containing (1) an attribute, (2) its value if known, and

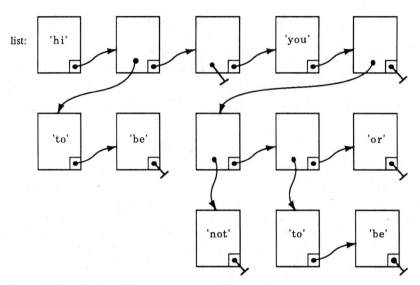

FIGURE 9. A list with five values, of which the first and fourth are information (a single word), the second is a list with two information values, the third is an empty list, and the fifth is a list with two list values and an information value.

(3) a list of several rules for deducing the attribute's value. Each rule is a list of phrases, each of which is a list of attribute-value pairs. For instance, the rule "IF temp=high AND spots-on-face=visible THEN diagnosis=measles" could be represented as a list of three two-element lists: (diagnosis, measles), (spots-on-face, visible), (temp, high). The basic data structure is therefore a list of lists each containing a list whose elements are lists that consist of lists of lists containing an attribute and a value.

Stack Operations in GenADT

The primary data structure exported by GenADT is named List. GenADT also declares Information as a WORD. This has the advantage that GenADT can be compiled independently of InfoADT and used with several different kinds of information. It has the disadvantage that the Information parameter must be a type that takes one word of storage, but this is normally the case for any pointer type.

```
(* The type-identifiers exported from GenADT *)
TYPE  List;
      Information = WORD;
```

GenADT contains six procedures that correspond to the six stack-handling procedures in StackADT. However, four of them are rewritten as functions instead of as statement procedures. The names have been changed to distinguish them from the statement procedures. Thus PushInfo returns the new list obtained by adding the given information value first on the given list, and Popped returns the new list obtained by removing the first value from a given list. EmptyList returns a valid empty list.

```
(* The stack-handlers in GenADT, presented as functions *)
PROCEDURE PushInfo (TheInfo : Information; Data : List) : List;
PROCEDURE Popped  (Data : List) : List;
PROCEDURE FirstInfo (Data : List) : Information;
PROCEDURE IsEmpty  (Data : List) : BOOLEAN;
PROCEDURE EmptyList () : List;    (* in place of Create *)
PROCEDURE Destroy (VAR Data : List);
```

The new aspect of GenADT is that the first value on a list may itself be a list. You can push or pop or look at that list as well as an information value. Of course, you have to know what kind of value is first on a list. The ContainsInfo function tells you that:

```
PROCEDURE PushList (TheList, Data : List) : List;
PROCEDURE FirstList (Data : List) : List;
PROCEDURE ContainsInfo (Data : List) : BOOLEAN;
```

As an example of how these functions can be used, the following coding removes and saves the first value on a list, no matter which kind it is:

```
IF ContainsInfo (Data) THEN
    SaveInfo := FirstInfo (Data);
ELSE
    SaveList := FirstList (Data);
END;
Data := Popped (Data);
```

Locations in GenADT

A big difference in design between GenADT and ListADT is that a location on a list is itself a list, namely the sublist consisting of all values from that point on.

Thus the first location on a list is the entire list. The essential function for moving one step down the list is called **RestOf**; it returns the sublist consisting of all but the first value on the given list. The given list is required to have at least one value on it, otherwise the program could crash. For instance, the following coding finds the size of a list named Data:

```
Count := 0;
P := Data;
WHILE NOT IsEmpty (P) DO
    INC (Count);
    P := RestOf (P);
END;
```

You often need to find the last location on a nonempty list, that is, the sublist containing only the last value. A utility function to find the "tail" of a given nonempty list can be written as:

```
(* body of TailOf function with imports from GenADT *)
P := Data;
WHILE NOT IsEmpty (RestOf (P)) DO
    P := RestOf (P);
END;
```

You might at first think that RestOf and Popped are the same. The difference between them is that RestOf does not change the values on any list, whereas Popped does. Popped subtracts one from the number of values on its parameter; RestOf merely accesses the sublist that Popped would return without changing the Data list. Popped deallocates a node if a dynamic implementation is used; RestOf does not.

The ReplaceRestOf Procedure

GenADT also offers a powerful procedure for making changes in the second value on a given list. The **ReplaceRestOf** procedure replaces everything after the first value on a list by another list.

```
PROCEDURE ReplaceRestOf (Data, NewSublist : List);
    (* Replace the rest of (all but the first value on)
    Data by NewSublist.  Data must be nonempty *)
```

If P is assigned the sublist of Data consisting of the last value on Data (perhaps by using P := TailOf(Data)), another list Second can be joined to the end of Data with this coding:

```
ReplaceRestOf (P, Second);
```

Deletion of a value from any place on a list except the front of the list is coded as follows, assuming P has been assigned the sublist beginning with the value before the one to be deleted:

```
ReplaceRestOf (P, Popped (RestOf (P)));
```

In other words, this coding deletes the second value on P, which affects any list of which P is a sublist. Similarly, an information value can be inserted as the second value on the nonempty list P as follows:

```
ReplaceRestOf (P, PushInfo (TheInfo, RestOf (P)));
```

A list can be split into two parts after P, leaving the value at P as the last value on the revised list, as follows:

```
LatterPart := RestOf (P);
ReplaceRestOf (P, EmptyList ());
```

CHALLENGE. Now that you have seen all 11 of the imports from GenADT, take a few minutes to see if you can think of a reasonably efficient implementation. Compare your conclusions with the implementation at the end of this section.

The procedure in Example 8.7A counts the number of information values at the **top level** of a list. In other words, it counts only those that are members of the list, not those that are within lists that are members of the list.

A small modification of the NumberOfInfos function allows you to perform a **deep count** of all the information values anywhere in a generalized list, including

EXAMPLE 8.7A _____

```
PROCEDURE NumberOfInfos (Data : List) : CARDINAL;
VAR
    Count   : CARDINAL;
    Sublist : List;
BEGIN
    Count := 0;
    Sublist := Data;
    WHILE NOT IsEmpty (Sublist) DO
        IF ContainsInfo (Sublist) THEN
            INC (Count);
        END;
        Sublist := RestOf (Sublist);
    END;
    RETURN Count;
END NumberOfInfos;
```

members of structures that are members of the list. After the INC(Count) statement of Example 8.7A, you simply insert the following coding:

```
ELSE
    INC (Count, NumberOfInfos (FirstList (SubList)));
```

Implementations of GenADT

An array implementation of GenADT is possible but unwieldly. The simplest way is to use pointers to nodes. The problem is that you cannot simply have a two-field node with a link field and a field that specifies the member of the list at that point. The reason is that: (1) The member could be either of two types, Information or List; (2) The ContainsInfo function must be able to determine which type is there.

The following solution is left as an exercise: Declare a List as a pointer to a node, and declare a node to have three fields—a member field, a link field, and a Boolean field that tells whether the member is an information value. The member field can be a variant of either Information type or List type. An alternative is to have the member field be of WORD type and use a type transfer to obtain a List value from a WORD value. This latter implementation means that FirstInfo and FirstList can be identical.

The implementation used for Example 8.7B has a node with three fields, Left, Right, and Info, as for binary trees. The Right pointer is the pointer to the next node on the list. If the member of a given list is an information value instead of a list value, the Left field is filled in with a special value named None to indicate

EXAMPLE 8.7B _____

```
IMPLEMENTATION MODULE GenADT;
    (* Binary tree implementation of generalized lists.
       Some procedures have been left as exercises.  *)
    (* Written by Dr. William C. Jones, April 19-- *)
 (* FUNCTIONS: PushInfo, FirstInfo, IsEmpty, Popped, RestOf,
               PushList, FirstList, EmptyList, ContainsInfo;
    STATEMENT PROCEDURES: ReplaceRestOf, Destroy;      *)
 (* Preconditions:  All list parameters of these procedures
        must have been initialized using EmptyList().
        The following require a nonempty list:  FirstInfo,
        FirstList, Popped, RestOf, ReplaceRestOf.  *)

TYPE
    List = POINTER TO Node;
    Node = RECORD
               Info : Information;
               Left, Right : List;
           END;
VAR
    None : List;
(*************************************************************)

PROCEDURE ContainsInfo (Data : List) : BOOLEAN;
    (* Tell whether the first value on Data is Information;
       returns FALSE if Data is empty *)
BEGIN
    RETURN (Data # NIL) AND (Data^.Left = None);
END ContainsInfo;
(*************************************************************)

PROCEDURE PushList (TheList, Data : List) : List;
    (* Add TheList as the first value on Data *)
VAR
    P : List;
BEGIN
    NEW (P);
    P^.Left := TheList;
    P^.Right := Data;
    RETURN P;
END PushList;
(*************************************************************)

PROCEDURE ReplaceRestOf (Data, NewSublist : List);
    (* Replace the rest of (all but the first value on)
       Data by NewSublist.  Data must be nonempty *)
BEGIN
    Data^.Right := NewSublist;
END ReplaceRestOf;
(*************************************************************)

BEGIN           (* GenADT initialization *)
    NEW (None);
END GenADT.
```

this. The Info field is used only when the Left field contains None. Some of the procedures are omitted from Example 8.7B so they can be used as exercises.

Many of the procedures in this implementation require only one statement. The following procedures can be coded as shown:

```
FirstInfo (Data) :      RETURN Data↑.Info;
FirstList (Data) :      RETURN Data↑.Left;
RestOf (Data) :         RETURN Data↑.Right;
IsEmpty  (Data) :       RETURN Data = NIL;
EmptyList () :          RETURN NIL;
Destroy (VAR Data);     (* do nothing *)
```

Another implementation of GenADT could use a header node for each list, but that may be more trouble than it is worth. In some applications, it is worthwhile to add two more procedures to GenADT that allow you to replace the value stored at a particular place on a list without disturbing any connections of other lists to that list:

```
ReplaceFirstInfo (TheInfo, Data);  (* replace first value on Data *)
ReplaceFirstList (TheList, Data);  (* replace first value on Data *)
```

You can implement queues as circular lists using GenADT. For instance, you could enqueue an information value on an empty queue Q using:

```
Q := PushInfo (TheInfo, Q);
ReplaceRestOf (Q, Q);
```

If the queue is not empty, you could enqueue an information value with the following coding:

```
ReplaceRestOf (Q, PushInfo (TheInfo, RestOf (Q)));
Q := RestOf (Q);
```

Check Your Understanding

1. Write the PushInfo function for Example 8.7B.

2. Write the Popped function for Example 8.7B.

3. Write a program segment that assigns to TheInfo the second value on a list Data using imports from GenADT. The segment should have no effect if Data does not have two values or if the second value is a list.

4. Write the ReplaceFirstInfo and ReplaceFirstList procedures described at the end of this section, as additions to Example 8.7B.

5. (NA) Write the Dequeue function for the implementation of queues described at the end of this section, using imports from GenADT.

6. (NA) Write a utility function for Example 8.7B that returns the result of reversing the pointers in a list so the order of its elements is reversed.

7. (NA) Write a function that tells whether two generalized lists are equal. Use imports from GenADT and Compare from InfoADT.

8. (NA) Write a recursive function DeepCopy that creates an exact duplicate of a given list. All lists on the given list are duplicated, as well as lists on those lists, and so forth.

CHAPTER REVIEW

A graph consists of a number of objects called nodes or vertices, together with things called arcs that connect one vertex to another vertex (or, in some cases, connect one vertex to itself). For purposes of implementing graphs in a program, the vertices are assumed to be numbered using a subrange of integers Loval..Hival.

The Hamiltonian Circuit problem is the problem of finding a path (following the connecting arcs) that goes through each vertex one and only one time, except the starting and ending vertices are the same. Such a path is called a circuit. In the Traveling Salesman problem, each arc has a value associated with it, called its weight; the problem is to find a circuit for which the sum of the weights of the arcs traveled is as small as possible.

The primary operations offered by the GraphADT library module are a Boolean function Connecting that tells whether there is an arc from a given vertex to another given vertex, and a NextVertex function such that NextVertex(F, S) gives the next vertex after S for which there is an arc from F. This function returns a special Noval vertex if there is actually no such vertex; if S is Noval, it returns the first of the vertices for which there is an arc from F. "First" and "next" are not necessarily related to the ordering Loval..Hival.

A backtracking solution to a problem has the following logic: Given a vertex V0, try out each vertex V1 for which Connecting(V0, V1) is true to see if the problem can be solved by starting with the arc from V0 to V1. Apply the same logic recursively to see if the problem can be solved by continuing with any arc from V1.

The Knight's Tour problem is the problem of finding a sequence of 64 moves by a knight on a chessboard so that it visits each of the 64 squares exactly once and then moves to its starting square. The Eight Queens problem is the problem of finding a way of placing eight queens on a chessboard so that no queen is attacking any other queen. Both these problems use the rules of chess in their definitions.

Backtracking is also known as depth-first search in a graph. In breadth-first searching starting from a vertex V0, you first investigate all the vertices for which there is a connection from V0, then you investigate all the vertices connected to those, and so forth. Queues are normally used for breadth-first searching; stacks (or equivalently, recursion) are used for depth-first searching. An example of a problem solvable using breadth-first searching is that of finding the minimum distance of various vertices from a given vertex. Floyd's algorithm provides a method of solving such problems and some generalizations of such problems. Warshall's algorithm can be used to find out whether there is a path from any given vertex to any other given vertex.

A sparse matrix is in effect a large 2-dimensional array in which very few components have values other than 0. Often the array is so large that the computer has insufficient space available to contain it as an array. But you can implement it as a linked list of nodes or as a one-dimensional array of linked lists, which can save most of the space that would otherwise be wasted on storing zeros. The two primitive operations required for an array, sparse or otherwise, are assigning a given value to a given component and retrieving the current value from a given component.

Some basic operations that should be provided by a library module for strings of varying length are (1) accessing or replacing a character at a given position in a string; (2) "adding" two strings together to get a new string; (3) inserting or deleting a specified substring of a given string; (4) comparing two strings for ordering. Some reasonable implementations of varying-length strings are as a counted array or as a linked list. In Modula-2, you can in effect declare the size of an array during execution of the program and change it from time to time during execution. However, this necessitates a fair amount of computational time for recopying values.

Modula-2 has a built-in SET type that is highly restricted; it only allows sets of up to 16 cardinals or the equivalent (though sometimes a higher limit than 16 is used). If you want to work with much larger sets, you have to write an appropriate library module. The primitive procedures in such a module, assuming e is an element and S is a set, should include the ability to insert e in S, to delete e from S, and to tell whether e is in S.

The GenADT library module provides general-purpose facilities for manipulating lists that can contain either list or information values as their members. Several pointer implementations of GenADT were described in the text.

PRACTICE TEST

---

1. Write the recursive TryToTravel procedure, which finds out whether it is possible to travel the rest of a graph from the current vertex, using a Label-Array of integers that gives the ordinal number of each vertex on the path constructed so far (0 if the vertex is not on the path). [Example 8.1C]

2. Write the Pointer procedure for the implementation of a sparse matrix using a one-dimensional array of standard linked lists, with each index representing a row: VAR Data: ARRAY [Loval..Hival] OF PointerToNode. The procedure returns a pointer to the node for a given index pair [Row, Col]. [Example 8.4B]

3. In the same context as for the previous problem, write the SetValue procedure that assigns a given Numeric value to a given index pair. Use Pointer as needed. [Example 8.4B]

4. Write the CompareStr function for the simple array implementation of StrngADT. [Example 8.5B]

5. For the implementation of a set as POINTER TO ARRAY [Loval..Hival] OF BOOLEAN, write the IsSubset procedure that tells whether a given set is a subset of another given set. [text of Section 8.6]

6. Write the PushList function for the binary tree implementation of generalized lists. [Example 8.7B]

PROGRAMMING PROBLEMS

---

1. Write a procedure to implement Prim's algorithm for finding a minimum cost spanning tree of a connected graph. Import from GraphADT and use an array of Boolean values to tell what vertices are in the list.

2. Write a program to solve the football scheduling problem (Model 2 at the end of Section 8.3).

3. Write a program to solve the map-coloring problem (Model 3 at the end of Section 8.3).

4. Write a program to solve the aircraft-construction problem (Model 4 at the end of Section 8.3).

5. Assume that you are writing an implementation for an application in which the matrix has very few rows with any nonzero components. For instance, a 1000-by-1000 array might have at most 10 rows with nonzero components. Revise SparsADT with Data being a linked list of row arrays instead of an array of linked lists (from Section 8.4).

6. Write a full implementation module for SparsADT using the cross-linked implementation described at the end of Section 8.4.

7. A matrix has a **saddle point** at a component if the value of the component is the largest in its column and the smallest in its row. Write a program using imports from SparsADT to read a matrix and find all its saddle points.

8. Write a full implementation module for StrngADT using the CountedArray implementation illustrated in Example 8.5B.

9. Write a full implementation module for StrngADT using the standard linked list implementation described in Section 8.5.

10. Write a full implementation module for StrngADT using the "flexible" implementation described in Section 8.5.

11. Write a full implementation module for SetADT using the array of Boolean implementation described in Section 8.6.

12. Write a full implementation module for SetADT using the standard linked list implementation used in Example 8.6B.

13. Write a full implementation module for SetADT using an array of BITSETs for each set, with each bit TRUE or FALSE depending on whether the corresponding element is in the set. For instance, a range of 1600 values requires an array of 100 BITSETs. Note that this generally cuts the space requirements by a factor of 8 to 32.

14. Write a full implementation module for QueueADT in the context of GenADT using a circular linked list, as described at the end of Section 8.7.

15. Write a full implementation module for GenADT using a node with a Boolean field to tell what kind of value is stored at a location.

ANSWERS TO CHECK YOUR UNDERSTANDING EXERCISES

Section 1.1   Exercise 3 is NA

1.
```
CONST
    PhraseToBeTyped = "Winter isn't far away.";  (* several errors*)
VAR
    N, M : CARDINAL;                    (* one error  *)
    X, Y : REAL;                        (* one error  *)
BEGIN
    X := 1.3 - FLOAT (M);               (* two errors *)
    N := TRUNC (47.0);                  (* two errors *)
    WriteReal (4.72 * 3.0, 1);          (* two errors *)
```

2.
```
BEGIN
    WriteString ('Enter two nonnegative integers: ');
    ReadCard (First);
    ReadCard (Second);
    WriteLn;
    WriteString ('Their product is ');
    WriteCard (First * Second, 1);
    WriteLn;
END Exercise1point2.
```

Section 1.2   Exercises 3–4 are NA

1. $ import-section = FROM identifier IMPORT new-identifier
                      { "," new-identifier } ";" .
2. $ assignment = variable-designator ":=" expression .
   $ procedure-call = procedure-designator
            ["(" [expression { "," expression }] ")"] .

Section 1.3   Exercises 4–5 are NA

1. FOR K := 30 TO 98 BY 6 DO
        WriteCard (K, 4);
   END.
2. Replace the line beginning WHILE by the word REPEAT.
   Replace the END of the WHILE by UNTIL Transaction = 0.
3. Condition := (X > 5) AND (U <= 7);
   Condition := (X > 5) OR TimeToStop;

Section 1.4   Exercises 3–4 are NA

1. Put OpenOutput('') before the last three statements.
   Put CloseOutput after the last three statements.
   Add OpenOutput and CloseOutput to the list of imports from InOut.
2. OpenInput ('');
   Sum := 0.0;
   ReadReal (Value);
   WHILE Done DO
        Sum := Sum + Value;
        ReadReal (Value);
   END;
   CloseInput;
   WriteString ('The sum is ');
   WriteReal (Sum, 1);

Section 1.5   Exercises 3–4 are NA

1. (a) 16 * 3 MOD 5 = 48 MOD 5 = 3
   (b) 16 * 3 DIV 5 = 48 DIV 5 = 9
   (c) 16 MOD 3 DIV 5 = 1 DIV 5 = 0
2. The segment would always say the LCM is the product of the two.

Section 1.6   Exercises 5–7 are NA

1. Global procedures: WriteString, WriteLn, WriteInt, ReadInt,
   GetInput, LCM. Global variables: Done, First, Second.
2. The parameters would be local variables whose values are read with
   no effect on the global variables, which therefore have
   indeterminate values. Any output could occur, or the program could
   crash.
3. The program would fail to compile at the next-to-last statement,
   since the actual parameters of LCM are not variables.
4. PROCEDURE CountNumbersOver50 () : CARDINAL;
   VAR Count : CARDINAL;
        Value : INTEGER;
   BEGIN
        Count := 0;
        ReadInt (Value);
        WHILE Done AND (Value # 0) DO
            IF Value > 50 THEN
                Count := Count + 1;
            END;
            ReadInt (Value);
        END;
        RETURN Count;
   END CountNumbersOver50;

Section 1.7   Exercises 4–9 are NA

1. TYPE Pair = ARRAY BOOLEAN OF REAL;
2. The values would be recorded in each array in reverse order, but
   the program results would be just the same.
3. Add 15 to each index of A to obtain the corresponding index of F.
   So HIGH (F) is 22, F [4] is A [−11], and F [10] is A [−5].

Section 1.8   Exercises 3–6 are NA

```
1. FOR Ch := 'A' TO 'Y' BY 2 DO
       Write (Ch);
   END;
2. PROCEDURE Capitalize (VAR Phrase : ARRAY OF CHAR);
   VAR
       K : CARDINAL;
   BEGIN
       FOR K := 0 TO HIGH (Phrase) DO
           Phrase [K] := CAP (Phrase [K]);
       END;
   END Capitalize;
```

Section 1.9   Exercises 6–7 are NA

```
1. TYPE StockRecord = RECORD
                          ID, NumberInStock : CARDINAL;
                          Description : ARRAY [0..40] OF CHAR;
                          Price, OriginalCost : REAL;
                      END;
2. VAR
       LotsOfStuff : ARRAY [0..999] OF StockRecord;
3. PROCEDURE TotalProfit (Given : StockRecord) : REAL;
   BEGIN
       RETURN (Given.Price - Given.OriginalCost) *
               FLOAT (Given.NumberInStock);
   END TotalProfit;
4. PROCEDURE TotalAmtOwed (VAR School : LotsOfInfo) : REAL;
   VAR
       Total : REAL;
       K : CARDINAL;
   BEGIN
       Total := 0.0;
       FOR K := 1 TO 500 DO
           Total := Total + School [K].AmtOwed;
       END;
       RETURN Total;
   END TotalAmtOwed;
```
5. Each real takes 4 bytes, so each array component takes 8 bytes. Thus X[13] is in 2024–2031, with X[13].B in 2028–2031. X[20] is in 2080–2087, so X[20].A is in 2080–2083.

Section 1.10   Exercise 3 is NA

1. Put WITH School [K] DO just after DO, put END just before the FOR's END, and omit "School[K]." directly after the IF.

```
2. PROCEDURE IsEarlier (First, Second : Date) : BOOLEAN;
   BEGIN
       WITH First DO
           IF Year # Second.Year THEN
               RETURN Year < Second.Year;
           ELSIF Month # Second.Month THEN
               RETURN Month < Second.Month;
           ELSE
               RETURN Day < Second.Day;
           END;
       END;
   END IsEarlier;
```

Section 1.11   Exercises 5–6 are NA

1. 53C is character 43, which is "+". 101C is character 65, which is "A". 141C is character 97, which is "a".

2. PROCEDURE TheKindItIs (Given : INTEGER) : WhatKind;
   ```
   BEGIN
       IF Given > 0 THEN
           RETURN Positive;
       ELSIF Given = 0 THEN
           RETURN Zero;
       ELSE
           RETURN Negative;
       END;
   END TheKindItIs;
   ```
3. Count := 0;
   ```
   FOR K := 1 TO NumberOfEmployees DO
       IF Emp [K].Person = Staff THEN
           INC (Count);
       END;
   END;
   ```
4. X requires 2 + 7*4 + 3 = 33 bytes; Information requires 2*2 + 4 + 21 + 1 = 30 bytes. A variant record with ID as the common field would require 33+1 bytes — the larger plus 1 for the BOOLEAN.

Section 2.1   Exercises 3–4 are NA
1. Put the procedure heading in with the others in Example 2.1A, and add ",ReadLine" to the export section, before the semicolon. In Example 2.1B, put the whole procedure in the implementation module and add ",Read" to the list of imports from Terminal, before the semicolon. Change the WHILE condition to Ch >= ' ' in the procedure.
2. There would be no difference in effect, because of the previous test for equality of the two components.

Section 2.2   Exercises 5–6 are NA
1. FOR K := 1 TO Data.Size BY 2 DO
       OutputInfo (Data.Item [K]);
   END;
2. Change >0 to <0 just before the DO.
3. Put the function heading among the others in Example 2.2A, and add ",DebtOf" to the export section, before the semicolon. In Example 2.2C, put the whole function in the implementation module; its only statement is RETURN Student.AmtOwed.
4. Change the IF condition to: DebtOf (School[K]) > DebtOf (Culprit)

Section 2.3   Exercises 3–4 are NA
1. Put in with the imports: FROM Storage IMPORT ALLOCATE, DEALLOCATE; Declare Transaction as follows: Transaction: POINTER TO REAL; Put NEW(Transaction) as the first statement, DISPOSE(Transaction) as the last statement. Replace Transaction by Transaction↑ in the four places it occurs in the other statements.
2. It creates P (owing to the local VAR section), creates storage for an integer, puts the address of that storage in P, then disposes of P (since the procedure ends). The net effect is totally negative: it makes less storage space available to the program.

Section 2.4   Exercises 5–10 are NA
1. Change ORD(Item[K]) to (ORD(Item[K])−28) in two places.
2. Insert the following IF statement just before the END of the FOR:
   IF (Size + 1 − K) MOD 20 = 0 THEN (* new line every 20 pairs *)
       WriteLn;
       Write ('   ');
   END;

3. Omit the first and second statements. Put a caret directly after each other reference to First or Second.
4. Replace HIGH(Data) by MaxSize, and replace the other two references to Data by TheInfot.

Section 2.5   Exercises 4–6 are NA

1. Bottom := 1;   Top := 8;   (* look in 1–8*)
   WHILE: 8 > 1, so: Middle := 4 ((8 + 1) DIV 2);
                        Item[4] >= 'fib', so Top := 4; (* look in 1–4*)
   WHILE: 4 > 1, so: Middle := 2 ((4 + 1) DIV 2);
                        Item[2] < 'fib', so Bottom := 3;(* look in 3–4*)
   WHILE: 4 > 3, so: Middle := 3 ((4 + 3) DIV 2);
                        Item[3] >= 'fib', so Top := 3; (* look in 3–3*)
   WHILE: Both Top and Bottom are 3, so the loop terminates;
   Item[3] is 'fib', so RETURN 3.
2. Put the following statement after the first THEN:
   IF Compare (TheInfo, Item [Middle]) = 0 THEN
        RETURN Middle;
   END;
   Also change Top := Middle to Top := Middle–1, since you do not have to look at Item[Middle] again.
3. 8 items require 3 iterations, 16 require 4, 32 require 5. 20 require either 4 or 5 iterations, and 400 require either 8 or 9 iterations.

Section 2.6   Exercises 6–9 are NA

1. Insert Write(Ch) as the second statement, after Read(Ch).
2. Change 10 to 8 in all three places.
3. Any number beginning "10" loses the 1, including 10, 107, and 1042.
4. F(1) = 1;   F(2) = 2;   F(3) = 2 * F(1) = 2;   F(4) = 2 * F(2) = 4;
   F(5) = 4;   F(6) = 4;   F(7) = 2 * F(3) = 4. In general, F(N) is the highest power of two that is not larger than the Given number.
5. Exchange the first two statements after the ELSE.

Section 2.7   Exercises 4–7 are NA

1. It only slows execution, since Hi=Lo causes a comparison of equals and then another recursive call, which returns TRUE.
2. When Hi–Lo is odd, recursion continues until the program crashes.
3. The entity is the parameter Levels, since it decreases on each additional activation of PrintTree and there are no additional activations when Levels is 1 or less (so 1 is "small enough").

Section 2.8   Exercises 4–7 are NA

1. Fib(8) = 34, Fib(9) = 55, and Fib(10) = 89.
2. AP(3,7) = 1021. Each number in row 3 is 3 less than a power of 2.
3. After 3, 4 come 7, 11, 18, 29, 47.

Section 2.9   Exercises 4–5 are NA

1. First activation with 21, 27: returns GCD (6, 21).
   Second activation with 6, 21: returns GCD (3, 6).
   Third activation with 3, 6: returns GCD (3, 0).
   Fourth activation with 3, 0: returns 3. So all return 3.
2. Fib(3) activates 1+1 more, a total of 3. Fib(4) activates 3+1 more, a total of 5. Fib(5) activates 5+3 more, a total of 9. Continuing to 12 gives the sequence 15,25,41,67,109,177,287; the answer is 287
3. Change "RETURN x" to "RETURN 1" in both functions.
   Put "+1" in the second RETURN statement of the recursive version.
   Assign 1 to TheFibBefore instead of 2, in the nonrecursive version.
   Put "+1" between "TheFibBefore" and the semicolon right after it.

Section 3.1   Exercises 4–11 are NA

1. The body of SwapTopTwo (VAR Data: Stack) could be:

```
IF NOT IsEmpty (Data) THEN
    Pop (TopOne, Data);
    IF IsEmpty (Data) THEN
        Push (TopOne, Data);
    ELSE
        Pop (NextOne, Data);
        Push (TopOne, Data);
        Push (NextOne, Data);
    END;
END;
```

2. The body of HasAtLeastTwo (Data: Stack): BOOLEAN could be as
follows (HasAtLeastTwo is also declared as a local variable):

```
IF IsEmpty (Data) THEN
    RETURN FALSE;
END;
Pop (TopOne, Data);
HasAtLeastTwo := NOT IsEmpty (Data);
Push (TopOne, Data);
RETURN HasAtLeastTwo;
```

3. The body of SplitOddsAndEvens (VAR Odds, Evens: Stack) could be:

```
Create (LocalStack);
WHILE NOT IsEmpty (Odds) DO
    Pop (TheInfo, Odds);
    Push (TheInfo, LocalStack);
    IF NOT IsEmpty (Odds) THEN
        Pop (TheInfo, Odds);
        Push (TheInfo, Evens);
    END;
END;
Destroy (Odds);
Odds := LocalStack;
```

Section 3.2   Exercise 4 is NA

1. (a) $20\ 3\ 2 - 5\ * / = 20 / ((3 - 2) * 5) = 4$
   (b) $4\ 2\ 4\ 2\ 4\ 2\ * + * + * = 4 * (2 + 4 * (2 + 4 * 2)) = 168$
2. (a) $* - 7 / 8\ 4\ 2 = (7 - (8 / 4)) * 2 = 10$
   (b) $- 1 - 2 - 3 - 4 - 5\ 6 = (1 - (2 - (3 - (4 - (5 - 6))))) = -3$
3. (a) $* - 7\ 4 + 6\ 3$ (b) $+ 2 * 3 + 4 * 5 + 6\ 7$

Section 3.3   Exercises 5–7 are NA

1. PROCEDURE SizeOf (Data: Stack): CARDINAL;
   ```
   BEGIN
       RETURN Datat.Size;
   END SizeOf;
   ```
2. The body of WriteAll (Data: Stack) could be:
   ```
   FOR K := 1 TO Datat.Size DO
       OutputInfo (Datat.Item [K]);
   END;
   ```
3. The body of DestroyAllInfo (VAR Data: Stack) could be:
   ```
   FOR K := 1 TO Datat.Size DO
       DestroyInfo (Datat.Item [K]);
   END;
   Datat.Size := 0;
   ```
4. Change Datat to Data in the five places where it occurs, and omit
   the NEW and DISPOSE statements. Now Destroy has no statements.
   It would be nice to also delete the line importing from Storage.

Section 3.4   Exercises 5–9 are NA

1. The body of Join (VAR First, Second: Queue) could be:
```
     WHILE NOT IsEmpty (Second) DO
         Dequeue (TheInfo, Second);
         Enqueue (TheInfo, First);
     END;
     Destroy (Second);
```
2. The body of WriteAll (Data: Queue) could be:
```
     IF Datat.Rear >= Datat.Front THEN
         FOR K := Datat.Front TO Datat.Rear DO
             OutputInfo (Datat.Item [K]);
         END;
     ELSIF Datat.Rear # 0 THEN
         FOR K := Datat.Front TO MaxSize DO
             OutputInfo (Datat.Item [K]);
         END;
         FOR K := 1 TO Datat.Rear DO
             OutputInfo (Datat.Item [K]);
         END;
     END;
```
3. The body of SizeOf (Data: Queue): CARDINAL could be:
```
     Create (LocalQueue);
     SizeOf := 0;
     WHILE NOT IsEmpty (Data) DO
         Dequeue (TheInfo, Data);
         Enqueue (TheInfo, LocalQueue);
         INC (SizeOf);
     END;
     Destroy (Data);
     Data := LocalQueue;
     RETURN SizeOf;
```
4. The body of ReadAll (VAR Data: Queue) could be:
```
     Create (Data);
     InputInfo (TheInfo);
     WHILE Okay DO
         Enqueue (TheInfo, Data);
         InputInfo (TheInfo);
     END;
     DestroyInfo (TheInfo);
```

Section 3.5   Exercises 5–12 are NA

1. It is testing to see whether Data has at least two values in it.
2. Where := FirstLocation (Data);
```
   WHILE InList (NextLocation (NextLocation (Where,
                            Data), Data), Data) DO
       Delete (TheInfo, Where, Data);
       DestroyInfo (TheInfo);
   END;
```
3. The body of Seek (Pos: CARDINAL; Data: List): Location could be:
```
     Where := FirstLocation (Data);
     FOR K := 1 TO Pos - 1 DO
         Where := NextLocation (Where, Data);
     END;
```
4. The body of SizeOf (Data: List): CARDINAL could be:
```
     SizeOfList := 0;
     Where := FirstLocation (Data);
     WHILE InList (Where, Data) DO
         INC (SizeOfList);
         Where := NextLocation (Where, Data);
     END;
     RETURN SizeOfList;
```

Section 3.6   Exercises 5–7 are NA

1. The body of SizeOf (Data: List): CARDINAL is: RETURN Datat.Size;
2. The body of LookAt (VAR TheInfo: Information; Where: Location;
                                    Data: List) could be:
```
    IF Where <= Datat.Size THEN
        TheInfo := Datat.Item [Where];
    END;
```
3. In Example 2.3B, TheInfo is an out parameter of CreateInfo,
   CopyInfo, and InputInfo. TheInfo is an in–out parameter of
   DestroyInfo and an in parameter of OutputInfo. Source, First,
   and Second are in parameters.
4. The body of Delete (VAR TheInfo: Information; Where: Location;
                                    Data: List) could be:
```
    WITH Datat DO  (* fields are Item, Size *)
        IF Where <= Size THEN
            TheInfo := Item [Where];
            FOR K := Where + 1 TO Size DO
                Item [K - 1] := Item [K];
            END;
            DEC (Size);
        END;
    END;
```

Section 3.7   Exercises 4–5 are NA

1.
```
    Find (TheInfo, Data);
    WHILE InTable (Data) DO
        TakeOut (TheInfo, Data);
        DestroyInfo (TheInfo);
    END;
```
2.
```
    Find (TheInfo, Data);
    IF NOT InTable (Data) THEN
        PutIn (TheInfo, Data);
    END;
```
3. Declare VAR LocalTable:Table in LookFurther and replace the body:
```
    REPEAT
        PutIn (TheInfo, LocalTable);
        TakeOut (TheInfo, Data);
    UNTIL NOT InTable (Data);
    REPEAT
        TakeOut (Saved, LocalTable);
        PutIn (Saved, Data);
    UNTIL NOT InTable (LocalTable);
```

Section 3.8   Exercises 6–9 are NA

1. Replace the call of Find in the body of TakeOut by a duplicate of
   Find except change the first statement to: Where := Datat.Loc;
2. The body of Count (TheInfo: Information; Data: List): CARDINAL
   could be:
```
    Saved := Datat.Loc;
    Count := 0;
    Where := FirstLocation (Data);
    WHILE InList (Where, Data) DO
        LookAt (WhatsThere, Where, Data);
        IF Compare (WhatsThere, TheInfo) = 0 THEN
            INC (Count);
        END;
        Where := NextLocation (Where, Data);
    END;
    Datat.Loc := Saved;
    RETURN Count;
```

3. Replace the line WITH Data DO by the following:

```
     WITH Dataꜜ DO
     IF (Compare (TheInfo, Item [Size]) > 0) THEN
          IsThere := FALSE;
          Loc := Size + 1;
     ELSE    (* find Top = index of the first greater—equal TheInfo*)
```

Replace the RETURN statement by the following:

```
          IsThere := Compare (TheInfo, Item [Top]) = 0;
          Loc := Top;
     END;
```

4. The first procedure called might be InTable, Inspect, or TakeOut.
5. The body of Create (VAR Data: Table) could be:

```
     NEW (Data);
     Dataꜜ.Size := 0;
     Dataꜜ.IsThere := FALSE;
     Dataꜜ.Loc := 1;   (* in case FindNextIn is called first *)
```

Section 3.9   Exercises 3–5 are NA

1. The body of DePriQ (VAR TheInfo: Information; VAR Data: List) is:

```
     SmallsLocation := FirstLocation (Data);
     LookAt (TheInfo, SmallsLocation, Data);
     Where := NextLocation (SmallsLocation, Data);
     WHILE InList (Where, Data) DO
         LookAt (WhatsThere, Where, Data);
         IF Compare (WhatsThere, TheInfo) <= 0 THEN
             SmallsLocation := Where;
             TheInfo := WhatsThere;
         END;
         Where := NextLocation (Where, Data);
     END;
     Delete (TheInfo, SmallsLocation, Data);
```

2. WITH Dataꜜ DO   (* fields are Item, Size, Front, Rear *)

```
     IF Spot < Front THEN   (* wrapped around *)
         FOR K := Spot TO 2 BY −1 DO
             Item [K] := Item [K − 1];
         END;
         Item [1] := Item [MaxSize];
         Spot := MaxSize;
     END;
     FOR K := Spot TO Front + 1 BY −1 DO
         Item [K] := Item [K − 1];
     END;
     IF Front = MaxSize THEN
         Front := 1;
     ELSE
         INC (Front);
     END;
END;
```

Section 3.10   Exercises 4–6 are NA

1. The body of Find (TheInfo: Information; VAR Data: Table) could be:

```
     Dataꜜ.Loc := Hash (TheInfo, MaxSize);
```

2. The body of InTable (Data: Table): BOOLEAN could be:

```
     RETURN (Dataꜜ.Loc # 0) AND Dataꜜ.InfoThere [Dataꜜ.Loc];
```

3. The body of Inspect (VAR TheInfo: Information; VAR Data: Table)
   could be:

```
         IF (Dataꜜ.Loc # 0) AND Dataꜜ.InfoThere [Dataꜜ.Loc] THEN
             TheInfo := Dataꜜ.Item [Dataꜜ.Loc];
             Dataꜜ.IsThere [Dataꜜ.Loc] := FALSE;
             Find (TheInfo, Data);
         END;
```

Section 3.11   Exercise 4 is NA

1. For the direct implementation, one list has 60 items each with 300 bytes, so each list needs 18,002 bytes (2 for the Size), so 40 lists need 720,080 bytes. For the cursor implementation, you need a StoreRoom of 300 items at 300 bytes each, a total of 90,000 bytes. One list has 60 cursors on it at 2 bytes each, so each list needs 122 bytes. Thus 40 lists need 4880 bytes and the total storage space needed is 94,880 bytes instead of 729,080.

2.
```
FOR K := 1 TO MaxInfos - 1 DO
    StoreRoom↑ [K].Link := K + 1;
END;
StoreRoom↑ [MaxInfos].Link := 0;
Available := 1;
```

3. `StoreRoom [TheInfo].Info := StoreRoom [Source].Info;`

Section 3.12   Exercises 4–5 are NA

1. In the body of ModifyListAsToldByUser, put the following just before ELSIF:
```
ELSIF Ch = 'e' THEN
    Where := FirstLocation (Data);
    WHILE InList (Where, Data) DO
        Where := NextLocation (Where, Data);
    END;
    WriteString ('Enter the information now: ');
    InputInfo (TheInfo);
    Insert (TheInfo, Where, Data);
END;
```
Also describe the 'e' option in the WriteString statements and add AND(Ch#'e') as part of the UNTIL condition.

2. If you do not deallocate the storage used for the information value, you may run out of space if the program runs for a long time. CreateInfo is not needed because InputInfo takes care of the allocation of storage.

3. Declare VAR Count: CARDINAL locally to WriteAll and insert Count:=0 as the first statement. Then put three statements directly after DO: INC (Count); WriteInt (Count); WriteString (' ');

Section 4.1   Exercises 5–6 are NA

1. Only NEW (P) is legal; NEW requires that the variable inside the parentheses be declared as POINTER TO something.

2. Only P := Head, P↑ := X, P↑ := Head↑, and X := Y are legal.

3.
```
IF (Data # NIL) AND (Data↑.Link # NIL) THEN
    TheInfo := Data↑.Link↑.Info;
END;
```

4.
```
Saved := Data.Info;    (* assuming VAR Saved: Information *)
Data↑.Info := Data↑.Link↑.Info;
Data↑.Link↑.Info := Saved;
```

Section 4.2   Exercises 6–8 are NA

1. The first information value would not be printed. The program would crash at the end when an attempt is made to print NIL↑.Info.

2. The body of Shift (VAR Data, Source: Stack) could be:
```
IF Source # NIL THEN
    P := Source;
    Source := P↑.Link;
    P↑.Link := Data;
    Data := P;
END;
```

3. The body of SizeOf (Data: Stack): CARDINAL could be:
```
        Count := 0;
        WHILE Data # NIL DO
            INC (Count);
            Data := Data↑.Link;
        END;
        RETURN Count;
```
4. The body of Inspect (VAR TheInfo: Information; Data: Table)
   could be:
```
        IF Data.Loc # NIL THEN
            TheInfo := Data.Loc↑.Info;
        END;
```
5. The body of Find (TheInfo: Information; VAR Data: Table)
   could be:
```
        P := Data.Head;
        WHILE (P # NIL) AND (Compare (P↑.Info, TheInfo) # 0) DO
            P := P↑.Link;
        END;
        Data.Loc := P;
```

Section 4.3   Exercises 5–8 are NA

1. AList has no nodes. BList has Beth. CList has Dawn. Anne is
   disposed of and Cathy is lost.
2. AList has no information. BList has Two. CList has One. Three is
   lost.
3. The body of LastLocation (Data: List): Location could be:
```
        IF Data = NIL THEN
            RETURN NIL;
        ELSE
            Where := Data;
            WHILE Where↑.Link # NIL DO
                Where := Where↑.Link;
            END;
            RETURN Where;
        END;
```
4. The body of Seek (Pos: CARDINAL; Data: List): Location could be:
```
        IF (Pos <= 1) OR (Data = NIL) THEN
            RETURN NIL;
        ELSE
            Seek := Data;    (* the second location *)
            Pos := Pos — 2;
            WHILE (Pos > 0) AND (Seek↑.Link # NIL) DO
                Seek := Seek↑.Link;
                DEC (Pos);
            END;
            RETURN Seek;
        END;
```

Section 4.4   Exercises 5–9 are NA

1. The body of Modify (VAR TheInfo: Information; Where: Location;
                        VAR Data: List) could be:
```
        Saved := TheInfo;
        IF (Where = NIL) AND (Data # NIL) THEN   (* first one *)
            TheInfo := Data↑.Info;
            Data↑.Info := Saved;
        ELSIF (Where # NIL) AND (Where↑.Link # NIL) THEN
            TheInfo := Where↑.Link↑.Info;
            Where↑.Link↑.Info := Saved;
        END;
```

```
2. PROCEDURE HasLastInfo (Where : Location; Data : List) : BOOLEAN;
   BEGIN
        IF Where = NIL THEN
            RETURN (Data # NIL) AND (Data↑.Link = NIL);
        ELSE
            RETURN (Where↑.Link # NIL) AND (Where↑.Link↑.Link = NIL);
        END;
   END HasLastInfo;
3. PROCEDURE Enqueue (TheInfo : Information;  VAR Data : List);
   BEGIN
        IF Data # NIL THEN
            Enqueue (TheInfo, Data↑.Link);
        ELSE
            NEW (Data);
            Data↑.Info := TheInfo;
            Data↑.Link := NIL;
        END;
   END Enqueue;
4. The body of  Join (VAR First, Second: List) could be:
        IF First = NIL THEN
            First := Second;
        ELSE
            P := First;
            WHILE P↑.Link # NIL DO
                P := P↑.Link;
            END;
            P↑.Link := Second;
        END;
```

Section 4.5   Exercises 6–8 are NA

```
1. The body of Join (VAR First, Second: List)  could be:
        Where := First;
        WHILE Where↑.Link # NIL DO
            Where := Where↑.Link;
        END;
        Where↑.Link := Second↑.Link;
        DISPOSE (Second);
2. PROCEDURE Seek (Pos : CARDINAL; Data : List) : Location;
   BEGIN
        WHILE (Data↑.Link # NIL) AND (Pos > 1) DO
            Data := Data↑.Link;
            DEC (Pos);
        END;
        RETURN Data;
   END Seek;
3. PROCEDURE TakeOut (VAR TheInfo : Information; VAR Data : Table);
   VAR
        P : PointerToNode;
   BEGIN
        IF Data↑.IsThere THEN
            P := Data↑.Loc↑.Link;
            TheInfo := P↑.Info;
            Data↑.Loc↑.Link := P↑.Link;
            DISPOSE (P);      (* add ",TRUE" if using variant records *)
            P := Data↑.Loc↑.Link;  (* the following info node *)
            Data↑.IsThere := (P # NIL) AND
                              (Compare (TheInfo, P↑.Info) = 0);
        END;
   END TakeOut;
4. For the trailer node implementation, just change (Data↑.Link # NIL)
   to (Data # NIL) in the WHILE condition of the answer to Exercise 2.
```

5. The body of NextLocation (Where: Location; Data: List): Location
   could be:
```
IF Where↑.Link # NIL THEN
    RETURN Where↑.Link;
ELSE
    RETURN Where;
END;
```

Section 4.6   Exercises 5–8 are NA

1. The body of LookAt (VAR TheInfo: Information; Where: Location;
                       Data: List) could be:
```
IF (Data # NIL) AND (Where = NIL) THEN  (* at the front *)
    TheInfo := Data↑.Link↑.Info;
ELSIF (Data # NIL) AND (Where # Data) THEN  (* not after end *)
    TheInfo := Where↑.Link↑.Info;
END;
```
2. The body of HasOneInfo (Data: List) could be:
```
P := FirstLocation (Data);
RETURN InList (P, Data) AND
        NOT InList (NextLocation (P, Data), Data);
```
3. The body of WriteAll (Data: List) could be:
```
IF Data # NIL THEN
    P := Data;
    REPEAT
        OutputInfo (P↑.Link↑.Info);
        P := P↑.Link;
    UNTIL P = Data;
END;
```
4. The body of Push (TheInfo: Information; VAR Data: List) could be:
```
NEW (P);
P↑.Info := TheInfo;
P↑.Link := Data↑.Link;
P↑.Prior := Data;
Data↑.Link := P;
P↑.Link↑.Prior := P;
```

Section 4.7   Exercise 3 is NA

1. For each nonnegative I that is less than K, First[I] is the same as
   Second[I] and neither is the null character.
2. CheckCount is the number of negative numbers that occur in the list
   of all values read so far other than the one in Transaction;
   moreover, TotalCount is the total number of numbers that occur in
   that same list (that is, excluding the one currently in
   Transaction).

Section 4.8   Exercises 3–4 are NA

1. The body of TakeOut (VAR TheInfo: Information; VAR Data: Table)
   could be:
```
IF Data.Index # 0 THEN
    Delete (TheInfo, Data.Loc, Data.Lst↑ [Data.Index]);
    WHILE InList (Data.Loc, Data.Lst↑ [Data.Index]) DO
        LookAt (WhatsThere, Data.Loc, Data.Lst↑ [Data.Index]);
        IF Compare (TheInfo, WhatsThere) = 0 THEN
            RETURN;
        END;
        Data.Loc := NextLocation (Data.Loc,
                                   Data.Lst↑ [Data.Index]);
    END;
    Data.Index := 0;
END;
```

2. The body of Destroy (VAR Data: Table) could be:
```
FOR K := 1 TO MaxSize DO
    ListADT.Destroy (Data.Lst↑ [K]);
END;
DISPOSE (Data.Lst);
```

Section 4.9   Exercise 4 is NA

1. Records number 8, 16, 24,..., 1800, are put in the index, for a total of 225 records. The average is 8 + (1+8)/2 = 12.5.
2. If NumValues is 0, you have a CARDINAL operation that yields a nonCARDINAL, which is illegal in Modula-2. A crash can occur only if GroupSize=0, which means NumValues=0, in which case the FOR statement does not execute its body (including the DIV operation).
3. The body of FindFirstIn (VAR Data: Table) could be:
```
Data↑.Loc := Data↑.Head;
Data↑.IsThere := Data↑.Loc↑.Link # NIL;
```

Section 4.10   Exercises 3–6 are NA

1. Declare another Information variable TheTerm and then replace the call to Insert by the following three statements:
```
CreateInfo (TheTerm);
CopyInfo (TheTerm, FirstTerm);
Insert (TheTerm, s, Sum);
```
2. Put a minus sign before CoefficientOf(SumTerm) and put the following statements before s := NextLocation(s, Sum):
```
SetCoefficient (SumTerm, -CoefficientOf(SumTerm));
Modify (SumTerm, s, Sum);
```
For clarity, change some identifiers and comments appropriately.

Section 4.11

1. The body of ProcessAllInfo (Process: InfoProcessor; Data: List) could be:
```
Where := Data;
WHILE Where # NIL DO
    Process (Where↑.Info);
    Where := Where↑.Link;
END;
```
2. Replace FROM InfoADT IMPORT Information by FROM SYSTEM IMPORT ADDRESS; TYPE Information = ADDRESS. Also declare CompareInfo as shown in the text for ListADT utilities, since it is needed.

Section 4.12   Exercises 3–5 are NA

1. Change the heading of FindBigEnoughBlock to the following:
PROCEDURE FindBigEnoughBlock (WordsNeeded:CARDINAL): PointerToNode;
Declare Parent locally to the function and insert RETURN Parent as its last statement. Change the procedure call to a function call:
Parent := FindBigEnoughBlock (WordsNeeded);
2. Declare P: PointerToNode in FindBigEnoughBlock and make its body:
```
Parent := NIL;
P := Avail;
WHILE P↑.Link # NIL DO
    IF (P↑.Link↑.Size >= WordsNeeded) AND ((Parent = NIL) OR
            (Parent↑.Link↑.Size > P↑.Link↑.Size)) THEN
        Parent := P;
    END;
    P := P↑.Link;
END;
IF Parent = NIL THEN
    HALT;
END;
```

Section 5.1
Exercises 7–9 are NA

1. The complete binary tree of height 4 has 16 leaves and 31 nodes altogether.
2. The tree in Figure 1 has 8 leaves.
3. The tree in Figure 1 has 8 paths of length 3: 6 starting from the root and 2 starting from "Is it a feline?"
4. Is it a mammal? Is it a feline? Is it tame? Is it striped?
5. One with 3 nodes; none with 4 nodes; 2 with 5 nodes.
6. 2, 2; 3, 3, 3, 3; 4.

Section 5.2
Exercises 5–13 are NA

1. Preorder traversal: A B C D E F G
   Inorder traversal: C B D A F G E
   Postorder traversal: C D B G F E A
2.
```
PROCEDURE MoreThanTwoNodes (Data : BinTree) : BOOLEAN;
    VAR
        R : BinTree;
    BEGIN
        R := Root (Data);
        RETURN (Left (R,Data) # NoNode) AND
                        (Right (R,Data) # NoNode)
            OR (Right (Right (R,Data), Data) # NoNode)
            OR (Left  (Right (R,Data), Data) # NoNode)
            OR (Right (Left  (R,Data), Data) # NoNode)
            OR (Left  (Left  (R,Data), Data) # NoNode);
    END MoreThanTwoNodes;
```
3.
```
PROCEDURE Leftmost (Data : BinTree) : Location;
    VAR
        R : Location;
    BEGIN
        R := Root (Data);
        WHILE Left (R, Data) # NoNode DO
            R := Left (R, Data);
        END;
        RETURN R;
    END Leftmost;
```
This procedure executes somewhat faster if you declare L locally, insert the statement L := Left (R, Data) after each assignment to R, and then replace "Left (R, Data)" by "L" in two places.
4.
```
PROCEDURE HasInfo (TheInfo : Information;
                    Data : BinTree) : BOOLEAN;
VAR
    WhatsThere : Information;
    PROCEDURE IsThere (Where : Location) : BOOLEAN;
        BEGIN
            IF Where = NoNode THEN
                RETURN FALSE;
            ELSE
                See (WhatsThere, Where, Data);
                IF Compare (WhatsThere, TheInfo) = 0 THEN
                    RETURN TRUE;
                ELSE
                    RETURN IsThere (Left (Where)) OR
                                IsThere (Right (Where));
                END;
            END;
        END IsThere;
    BEGIN          (* HasInfo *)
        RETURN IsThere (Root (Data));
    END HasInfo;
```

Section 5.3   Exercises 4–5 are NA

1. Omit StillLooking:BOOLEAN and StillLooking:=TRUE.
   Replace StillLooking:=FALSE by Ch:=Exit.
   Change IF StillLooking to IF Ch#Exit.
2. Pass M or F in Ch and change the procedure heading to:
   FindParent (VAR Parent : Information; Child : Information;
                      Ch : CHAR; Data : BinTree);
   Change the PutLeft statement to See (Parent, Left (Spot), Data).
   Change the PutRight statement to See (Parent, Right (Spot), Data).
   Guards are needed if the parent may not be in the tree.
3. PROCEDURE ReadLeftSubtree (Spot : Location; VAR Data : BinTree);
       BEGIN
           InputInfo (TheInfo);
           PutLeft (TheInfo, Spot, Data);
           IF IsOp (TheInfo) THEN
               ReadLeftSubtree (Left (Spot, Data), Data);
               ReadRightSubtree (Left (Spot, Data), Data);
           END;
       END ReadLeftSubtree;

Section 5.4   Exercises 6–11 are NA

1. PROCEDURE Transpose (First, Second : Location; VAR Data : BinTree);
       VAR
           Saved : Information;
       BEGIN
           IF (First # NoNode) AND (Second # NoNode) THEN
               Saved := First↑.Info;
               First↑.Info := Second↑.Info;
               Second↑.Info := Saved;
           END;
       END Transpose;
2. PROCEDURE PutRight (TheInfo : Information; Parent : Location;
                        VAR Data : BinTree);
       BEGIN
           IF Parent # NoNode THEN
               PutRoot (TheInfo, Parent↑.Right);
           END;
       END PutRight;
3. PROCEDURE Reflect (VAR Data : BinTree);
       VAR
           P : PointerToNode;
       BEGIN
           IF Data # NoNode THEN
               Reflect (Data↑.Left);
               Reflect (Data↑.Right);
               P := Data↑.Left;
               Data↑.Left := Data↑.Right;
               Data↑.Right := P;
           END;
       END Reflect;
4. WHILE (Data # NIL) AND (Where # Data↑.Count) DO
       IF Where < Data↑.Count THEN
           Data := Data↑.Left;
       ELSE
           Where := Where − Data↑.Count;
           Data := Data↑.Right;
       END;
   END;
   IF Data # NIL THEN
       TheInfo := Data↑.Info;
   END;

```
5. PROCEDURE PutRoot (TheInfo : Information;  VAR Data : BinTree);
       VAR
           Ins : PointerToNode;
       BEGIN
           NEW (Ins);
           Ins↑.Info := TheInfo;
           Ins↑.Left := NIL;
           Ins↑.Right := Data;
           Data := Ins;
       END PutRoot;
```

Section 5.5   Exercises 6–9 are NA

1. 63, 46, 47, 62, 48. 49 goes to the right of 48.
2.
```
PROCEDURE PrintInReverseOrder (Data : BinTree);
    BEGIN
        IF Data # NIL THEN
            PrintInReverseOrder (Data↑.Right);
            OutputInfo (Data↑.Info);
            PrintInReverseOrder (Data↑.Left);
        END;
    END PrintInReverseOrder;
```
3. Declare a local integer variable Comparison; make the statement after the first ELSE: Comparison := Compare (TheInfo, Spot↑.Info). Then you can use Comparison in both IF conditions.
4. The WITH Data↑ DO phrase requires that Data↑ exist at that point in the execution of the program.
5. In the declaration of Table, omit "Parent,". In Find, omit the Parent:=Child statement and replace Parent by Child in two places. In PutIn, omit the Data↑.Parent:=Spot statement.

Section 5.6   Exercises 5–11 are NA

1. The 47 moves up into the place of the 46; the left subtree of 47 is the former left subtree of 46, and the right subtree is unchanged.
2. In the DeleteLeftmost subprocedure, omit the second line that begins with IF and the END on the second line after that.
3. The difference is that the older of two matching Information values is found in the more recent one's left subtree instead of in its right subtree. Examples 5.5A and 5.5B are not changed. In PutIn, it suffices to change < to > and to swap Left with Right in the PutInSearchTree subprocedure. TakeOut can be fixed by swapping Left with Right throughout.
4. The only thing you can deduce is that the 2 must have been inserted before the 5.

Section 5.7   Exercises 5–9 are NA

1.
```
PROCEDURE Transpose (First, Second : Location;
                     VAR Data      : BinTree);
    VAR
        Saved : Information;
    BEGIN
        IF (First <= MaxSize) AND (Second <= MaxSize) AND
                (First >= 1) AND (Second >= 1) AND
                Data↑ [First].IsANode AND
                Data↑ [Second].IsANode THEN
            Saved := Data↑ [First].Info;
            Data↑ [First].Info := Data↑ [Second].Info;
            Data↑ [Second].Info := Saved;
        END;
    END Transpose;
```

2. The body of Swap (VAR TheInfo: Information; Where: Location;
                                VAR Data: BinTree) could be:
    IF (Where >= 1) AND (Where <= MaxSize)
                                AND Data↑ [Where].IsANode THEN
       Saved := Data↑ [Where].Info;
       Data↑ [Where].Info := TheInfo;
       TheInfo := Saved;
    END;

3. Reverse the sense of the IF condition as follows:
   IF (Where < 1) OR (Child > MaxSize) OR NOT Data [Where].IsANode OR
   NOT Data↑ [Child].IsANode THEN...

4. PROCEDURE Copy (VAR Data : BinTree; Source : BinTree);
    VAR
       K : CARDINAL;
    BEGIN
      FOR K := 1 TO MaxSize DO
        Data↑ [K].IsANode := Source↑ [K].IsANode;
        IF Data↑ [K].IsANode THEN
          CreateInfo (Data↑ [K].Info);
          CopyInfo (Data↑ [K].Info, Source↑ [K].Info);
        END;
      END;
    END Copy;

Section 5.8   Exercises 4–6 are NA

1. The first activation (Size=4) calls with Size=2 and Size=1. An
   activation with Size=1 calls twice with Size=0. An activation with
   Size=2 calls with Size=1 (calling twice with Size=0) and Size=0.
   In preorder, the 8 subcalls are with the Sizes 2,1,0,0,0,1,0,0.
2. TheInfo and Data have been delocalized.
3. In the statement part, omit the first three lines (through ELSE)
   and the last line (END;). Guard the first recursive call with IF
   SizeOnLeft > 0 and guard the second with IF SizeOnLeft < Size−1.

Section 5.9   Exercises 3–6 are NA

1. The Fibonacci tree with 7 levels has a left subtree with 12 nodes
   and a right subtree with 20 nodes (the middle and right trees in
   Figure 15), so it has 33 nodes altogether. Thus the Fibonacci tree
   with 8 levels has subtrees of 20 and 33 nodes, so it has 54 nodes
   altogether.
2. The 4 replaces the 2 and the 2 moves to the left of the 4.

Section 5.10   Exercises 4–11 are NA

1. Node 1 has degree 3 and level 0. Node 2 has degree 4 and level 1.
   Node 7 has degree 0 and level 1. Node 8 has degree 2 and level 1.
   Nodes 3, 4, 5, 6, 9, and 10 have degree 0 and level 2.
2. Children come before parents: 3 4 5 6 2 7 9 10 8 1.
3.

Section 5.11   Exercises 5–8 are NA

1. One 1024–byte block can hold a node with N addresses of child nodes (4 bytes each) plus N–1 IDs (4 bytes each) plus N–1 addresses of complete blocks of information (4 bytes each) plus the address of the parent (4 bytes) and NumInfos (2 bytes). This makes a total of 4∗N + 8∗(N–1) + 4 + 2 = 12∗N – 2 bytes. Since this quantity must be at most 1024, you solve 12∗N – 2 <= 1024 and find that N could be 85 and still allow a node to fit in one block. 4 accesses allow 85∗85∗85∗85 = 52,200,625 records, and a fifth access gives the record itself. It is worse if more than one block is used for a node, so a B-tree of order 85 should be used.

2. We need 12∗N – 2 <= 512, which allows a B-tree of order N = 42.

3. 1 with 3 nodes (the root has 2 children), 2 with 4 nodes (the root has 3 children, or it has 1 child and 2 grandchildren), and 1 with 5 nodes (the root has 1 child and 3 grandchildren).

4. If the root does not have just 1 child, the binary tree must have two subtrees for each nonleaf and all leaves on the same level; so it is a complete tree. Thus the number of nodes is one of 1, 3, 7, 15, 31, etc. If the root has just 1 child, its subtree must be a complete tree, so the number of nodes in the whole tree is one of 2, 4, 8, 16, 32, etc.

Section 5.12   Exercises 3–5 are NA

1. In FindLoc, declare VAR Top, Middle: CARDINAL and replace the WHILE loop by the following:

```
Top := NumIDs;
WHILE Top > K DO
    Middle := (K + Top) DIV 2;
    IF CompareID (TheID, ID [Middle]) > 0 THEN
        K := Middle + 1;
    ELSE
        Top := Middle;
    END;
END;
```

2. MaxSubtrees = 146, MinSubtrees = 73.

Section 5.13   Exercises 4–7 are NA

1. FindAdvantage calls itself only for a child (Where) of the node for which it was called. Thus the height of the subtree for which it is called decreases on each call, so it must eventually reach 0. At that point, OldestChild(Where, Tree) is NoNode, and the IF statement prevents an additional recursive call in that case.

2. You can control the game if you leave a multiple of 20 cents in the pot after each of your moves. This is because you can maintain this multiple–of–20 property once you have established it; you take 5 if your opponent takes 15, 10 if she takes 10, 15 if she takes 5. This means you take the last nickel, so you collect the extra 50 cents.
   This tactic requires you to go first and take 10, which leaves 140 in the pot. Thereafter, the best the opponent can do is take 15 each time, so you take 5 each time, so she gets 105 and you get 45. But when you collect the extra 50, you win 95 to 55. If she goes first and takes 5, you should take 5 and apply the multiple–of–20 tactic, which lets you win at least 90 to 60. If she goes first and takes 15, you should take 15 and apply the multiple–of–20 tactic, which lets you win at least 95 to 55. But if she goes first and takes 10, your best bet is to take 15 each time and hope she makes the mistake of taking more than 5 some time, in which case you switch to the multiple–of–20 tactic and win.

3. The only reason for having See(BestMove, Where, Tree) is to return a value from the first recursive call. So write an exact copy of the FindAdvantage procedure under a different name, omit these calls to See in the copy, and change the call to FindAdvantage to a call to the copy, in both FindAdvantage and in the copy. You can also omit BestMove as a parameter of the copy.

Section 6.1   Exercises 4–6 are NA

1. Change <0 to >0 and change >=0 to <=0 after the calls to Compare.
2. Omit WITH Datat DO and its END. Also, since the indices range from 0 to Size-1 within the procedure, the FOR statement has to be FOR Index := 1 TO Size-1 DO and (K = 1) must change to (K = 0).
3. Replace the REPEAT statement by the following:

```
    WHILE (K > 2) AND (Compare (Saved, Item [K - 1]) < 0) DO
        Item [K] := Item [K - 1];
        DEC (K);
    END;
    IF Compare (Saved, Item [1]) >= 0 THEN
        Item [K] := Saved;
    ELSE  (* K must be 2 *)
        Item [2] := Item [1];
        Item [1] := Saved;
    END;
```

Section 6.2   Exercises 4–7 are NA

1. Change <0 to >0.
2. Change the first line with FOR to FOR Index:=Size TO 2 BY -1 DO. Change the second line with FOR to FOR K := 1 TO Index - 1 DO. Change <0 to >0.
3. Index := 1; Position := 1;
The inner FOR loop sets Position to 5, the index of 1;
Switch Item[1] with Item[1], so the array becomes (1,6,2,3,2);
Index := 2; Position := 2;
The inner FOR loop sets Position to 3, the index of the first 2;
Switch Item[2] with Item[3], so the array becomes (1,2,6,3,2);
Index := 3; Position := 3;
The inner FOR loop sets Position to 5, the index of the second 2;
Switch Item[3] with Item[1], so the array becomes (1,2,2,3,6);
The remaining two iterations, for 4 and 5, do not change Position, so they also do not change the array.

Section 6.3   Exercises 4–6 are NA

1. Each of the two statements subordinate to WHILE is big-oh of 1; the loop executes N times (where N is the number of items on the list), so the procedure is big-oh of N.
2. Each of the statements subordinate to WHILE is big-oh of 1; the loop executes little more than lg(N) times (where N is the number of items on the list), so the procedure is big-oh of lg(N).
3.
```
    PROCEDURE Log (N : CARDINAL) : CARDINAL;
        VAR
            Log : CARDINAL;
        BEGIN
            Log := 0;  (* Log of 1 is 0 *)
            WHILE N > 1 DO
                N := N DIV 2;
                INC (Log);
            END;
            RETURN Log;
        END Log;
```
Note: If you used something like Power := 1; WHILE Power < N DO Power := Power * 2, that only works for half of the cardinals.

Section 6.4   Exercises 4-8 are NA

1. One answer is 2, 2, 1. When you swap the first 2 with 1, the 2's are not in the order they were in the original list.
2. Put the following just before the WHILE loop in the body of Sort, and put END; just after than WHILE loop:

```
IF NOT IsEmpty (Data) THEN
    Delete (TheInfo, Where, OriginalList);
    Insert (TheInfo, FirstLocation (Data), Data);
```

3. Replace Stack by Queue, Pop by Dequeue, and Push by Enqueue. Also swap Root↑.Right with Root↑.Left in the two recursive calls.

Section 6.5   Exercises 4-11 are NA

1. (a) 31 in the body of MergeSort, and 16+2*8+4*4+8*2 = 64 in the splitting-up part, for a total of 95 times.
   (b) 31+2*15+4*7+8*3+16*1 = 129 times.
   (c) A similar calculation for 64 yields 63+128 for the first answer; in general, it will be 3*N-1 for N being any power of 2.
2. You save a test each time the procedure is called with 2 items on a list. This happens almost N/2 times, where N is the number of items on the original list.
3. The easiest way is to replace the IF statement beginning IF Half>=2 by:

```
        IF Half >= 20 THEN
            MergeSort (AList, Half);
            MergeSort (BList, Total - Half);  (* might have 19 *)
        ELSE
            InsertionSort (AList);
            InsertionSort (BList);
        END;
```

Section 6.6   Exercises 5-9 are NA

1. If the original list was in increasing order, all ALists will be empty; if the original list was in decreasing order, all BLists will be empty. The algorithm is symmetric in terms of ALists and BLists except in the putting-together stage, which is omitted entirely if the AList is empty. So greater speed is obtained when the original list was in increasing order.
2. Just change >0 to <0.
3. If you replace the body of Sort by the following coding, you will sort the linked list with header node by working only with standard linked lists throughout Quicksort:

```
        IF (Data↑.Link # NIL) AND (Data↑.Link↑.Link # NIL) THEN
            QuickSort (Data↑.Link);
        END;
```

4. Spot and Saved can be declared in Sort rather than in QuickSort because neither has a value before the middle part (the recursive calls) that is referred to after the middle part.

Section 6.7   Exercises 5-8 are NA

1. Omit the IF Lo < Hi THEN part, and instead guard each call of Quicksort by an IF statement. In the body of Sort, use the test IF Data↑.Size > 1. In the body of Quicksort, use IF Lo < Spot - 1 and IF Spot + 1 < Hi.
2. Replace the first assignment statement in the body of Quicksort by:

```
        Pivot := Data↑.Item [(Lo + Hi) DIV 2];
        Data↑.Item [(Lo + Hi) DIV 2] := Data↑.Item [Lo];
```

3. Replace UNTIL High=Low by END and replace REPEAT by:
   FOR K := 1 TO High - Low + 1 DO. Also declare VAR K: CARDINAL.

4. Nonterminating recursion can occur only if one activation of Quicksort calls another with a part of the array of the same size. If you change "Spot-1" to "Spot", this could only happen for the lower half of the array (since Lo <= Spot <= Hi). That requires that High not be decremented within Quicksort. Careful study of the coding shows that that happens only when Item[Lo] > Item[Hi] and none of Item[Lo+1]..Item[Hi] is larger than Item[Lo]. In that case, Spot is assigned Hi and Item[Hi] becomes the pivot for the lower half of the array on the next call. Although that lower half is the same size, it will be smaller on the next deeper call, since the first pivot is left out of the lower half on that next call.

Section 6.8   Exercises 4–7 are NA

1. PROCEDURE Digit (N, Key : CARDINAL) : CARDINAL;
     BEGIN
          WHILE N > 1 DO
               Key := Key DIV 10;
               DEC (N);
          END;
          RETURN Key MOD 10;
     END Digit;
2. Because queues are used, equal values in the original queue will keep their original order in each pass, so the Radix Sort is stable.
3. The original list is 47, 16, 85, 13, 43, 49, 61.
   Sorting on the ones digit yields 61, 13, 43, 85, 16, 47, 49.
   Sorting on the tens digit yields 13, 16, 43, 47, 49, 61, 85.

Section 6.9   Exercises 4–6 are NA

1. If any of the numbers added later is less than 17, the tree will become a heap anyway. Otherwise it will not.
2. Insert IF Count<4 just before IF Count=2, insert END just before ELSIF Count >= 3*Power, and replace ELSIF Count=3 by ELSE.
3. Call the new subprocedure PutModified. It should be just like PutInSubtree except (a) omit the first, second, and fourth lines after the BEGIN, and (b) change the two calls of PutInSubtree to calls of PutModified. Then replace the call of Swap in PutInSubtree to a call of PutModified.

Section 6.10   Exercises 3–5 are NA

1. Status at the end of Stage 4: There are 7 groups in A2 and 6 groups in B2. Each group has 8000 records and is sorted, except the last group in A2 has 2900 sorted records.
   Status at the end of Stage 5: There are 4 groups in A1 and 3 groups in B1. Each group has 16000 records and is sorted, except the last group in A1 has 2900 sorted records.
2. Each stage reads and writes each record once. Stage 6 has groups of 32,000; Stage 7 has groups of 64,000; Stage 8 puts all records in one file, so there are 8 read/write pairs for each record.

Section 6.11   Exercises 4–5 are NA

1. The situation should not be cyclic, but if it is, infinite recursion can occur. This happens, for instance, if Loval connects to Loval+1 which connects to Loval.
2. Change the call of Insert to a call of Enqueue.
3. Replace "Loval" by "Loval+1" in two places in the body of TopSort and put Insert(Loval, FirstLocation(Result), Result) as the last statement of the body of TopSort.

Section 7.1 Exercises 5–8 are NA

1. In Example 7.1A, omit "(15C)". In Example 7.1B, make Sentinel a constant and omit "(Sentinel: CHAR)".
2. Example 7.1B should have a global CHAR variable named nix. Example 7.1A should pass ' ' to nix as an additional value parameter when calling GetInput, so Example 7.1B can initialize nix.
3. Write a case–procedure CheckBlank that is the same as AddOne except that c := ' ' for the case when a blank is seen. Copy Example 7.1A except the body calls CheckBlank, CheckBlank replaces ProcessEvenNumber, and AddOne replaces ProcessOddNumber.
4. <Even,0, ,L,Even>   <Even,1, ,L,Odd>   <Even,2, ,L,Even>
   <Even, ,2,L,Quit>

Section 7.2 Exercises 3–5 are NA

1. There are 120 permutations of "abcde", half of which have the b to the left of the c. In alphabetical order, they are:

```
abcde abced abdce abdec abecd abedc adbce adbec adebc aebcd
aebdc aedbc bacde baced badce badec baecd baedc bcade bcaed
bcdae bcdea bcead bceda bdace bdaec bdcae bdcea bdeac bdeca
beacd beadc becad becda bedac bedca dabce dabec daebc dbace
dbaec dbcae dbcea dbeac dbeca deabc debac debca eabcd eabdc
eadbc ebacd ebadc ebcad ebcda ebdac ebdca edabc edbac edbca
```

2. Add an extra CARDINAL value parameter to PrintPermutations; call it Size. The last statement of the body of the program passes SizeOf(ToPermute) to Size. The recursive call within PrintPermutations passes Size–1 as the value of the extra parameter. Change the FOR statement to have the phrase TO Size DO.

Section 7.3 There are no NA exercises

1. All the page numbers would be in reverse order.
2. A large amount of storage space would be made unavailable, which causes the program to crash unnecessarily.

Section 7.4 Exercises 5–7 are NA

1. AND OR x NOT OR y z   z becomes:
   AND OR x AND NOT y NOT z   z which becomes:
   AND AND OR x NOT y OR x NOT z z
2. AND OR x AND NOT y NOT z z (second line above) becomes:
   OR   AND x z   AND AND NOT y NOT z z which becomes:
   which is equivalent to AND x z, since AND NOT z z is always false.
3. x is TRUE, z is TRUE, and y is either TRUE or FALSE (2 cases).
4. You only need make FixOneExpr local to SimplifyNOT instead of local to NegateExpr. The disadvantage is the the number of procedure calls and the depth of recursion is greater, normally much greater. For instance, if the expression has no NOTs, the original coding never calls any other procedure in the program.

Section 7.5 Exercises 5–6 are NA

1. Combine "I'm" and "Welsh" for a total frequency of 25.
   Combine "me" and "I'm Welsh" for a total frequency of 50.
   Combine "Kiss" and "me I'm Welsh" for a total frequency of 100.
   Result: "Kiss" = 0; "me" = 10; "I'm" = 110; "Welsh" = 111.
2. If you combine "infiltrating" with "peace/secrets" instead of with "radio", the code for "radio" would have 1 less bit and the codes for "peace" and "secrets" would each have 1 more bit. "Radio" has the same frequency as do "peace" and "secrets" together, so that would not affect the average frequency of a 100–word message.
3. 45*1 + 30*2 + 14*3 + 11*4 = 191 bits per 100–word message.
4. Replace "Data" by "Data↑.Link" in all but the call of InsertInOrder. Also replace "NIL" by "Data".

Section 7.6   Exercises 3–4 are NA

1. PROCEDURE Release (VAR Data : Table);
       VAR
           TheInfo : Information;
       BEGIN
           REPEAT
               Pop (TheInfo, Data);
           UNTIL IsEmpty (Data) OR (Compare (TheInfo, NoInfo) = 0);
       END Release;

2. the one statement in CreateInfo : NEW (TheInfo);
   the one statement in CopyInfo   : TheInfo↑ := Source↑;
   the one statement in DestroyInfo: DISPOSE (TheInfo);

Section 7.7   Exercises 5–6 are NA

1. Add the following 4 statements to PutBuiltInIdentifiersInTable.
   Then add 4 more statements the same except change 'INC' to 'DEC':
       MakeInfo (TheInfo, 'INC');
       TheInfo↑.Kind := ProcedureIdentifier;
       TheInfo↑.Level := 1;
       PutIn (TheInfo, IdTable);

2. Put after the END of the LOOP: SayWhatWasExpected (identifier);
   Replace LOOP by WHILE TokenSymbol = Identifier DO
   Omit the IF statement that follows LOOP (4 lines)
   Change the other EXIT statement to a RETURN statement

3. Only IMPORT and the semicolon.

4. By the time you do not need it any more, the program just executes
   two simple procedure calls and terminates. You do not need the
   space used by Saved for those two procedure calls, and termination
   automatically deallocates all space used by the program.

Section 7.8   Exercise 4 is NA

1. It is easier to keep things straight if you consistently apply the
   principle that (a) on entry to any ProcessX procedure, Token is
   the first token of the construct being parsed, and (b) on exit
   from any ProcessX procedure, Token is the first token after the
   construct just parsed.

2. Insert the following coding before the first ELSE:
       ELSIF TokenSymbol = const THEN
           GetNextToken;
           WHILE TokenSymbol = identifier DO
               ProcessConstSection (IDTable, CurrentLevel);
               GetNextTokenIfThisOneIs (semicolon);
           END;

3. Just one error message is generated for each omission; everything
   else is processed correctly.

Section 7.9   Exercises 4–5 are NA

1. Put REPEAT after the BEGIN of ProcessIfStatement.
   Put UNTIL TokenSymbol # elsif before IF.

2. Insert OR (TokenSymbol=until) in the SkipToMinorDivider procedure
   of Example 7.8A. Insert AND (TokenSymbol # until) in the IF
   condition of ProcessStatement. Insert | repeat:
   ProcessRepeatStatement(IDTable) before the ELSE of Example 7.8B.

3. PROCEDURE ProcessRepeatStatement (IDTable : Table);
       BEGIN
           GetNextToken; (* discard REPEAT *)
           ProcessStatementSequence (IDTable);
           GetNextTokenIfThisOneIs (until);
           ProcessExpression (IDTable);
       END ProcessRepeatStatement;

Section 7.10   Exercises 3–5 are NA

1. Put IF TokenSymbol # endfile THEN after BEGIN, and END before END GetNextToken. Change ELSIF TokenSymbol # endfile THEN to ELSE. You could also replace the WHILE statement by IF Ch <= Blank THEN REPEAT Read(Ch) UNTIL NOT Done OR (Ch > Blank); END.

2. When GetNextToken reads the period token, ProcessToken will attempt to read the following character, which will simply make Done FALSE and Ch indeterminate. The next time GetNextToken is called, the FALSE value in Done prevents iteration of the WHILE and execution of ProcessToken; instead, the input file is closed and endfile as assigned to TokenSymbol.

Section 8.1   Exercises 5–6 are NA

1. Change Part 1 to read Ok := TRUE.

2. PROCEDURE TryToTravel (CurrentSpot : Vertex;
                          VAR Labeled, SaveLabels : LabelArray;
                          VAR SmallestTime : INTEGER;
                          TotalTime : INTEGER);

3. Omit the Part 3 statement and replace the Part 2 statements by:
   TryToTravel (V, Labeled, SaveLabels, SmallestTime,
                TotalTime + Weight (CurrentSpot, V));

4. Ok and Labeled can be delocalized, but not CurrentSpot or V.

Section 8.2   Exercises 2–3 is NA

1. +17, +15, +10, +8, and their negatives.

Section 8.3   Exercises 3–9 are NA

1. Use the arcs of weights 20 (6–9), 25 (6–7), and 60 (8–9).

2. Replace "Weight(i,k)" by "1".

Section 8.4   Exercises 4–5 are NA

1. The body of the Pointer function is only slightly different:
   ```
   P := Data;
   WHILE (P # NIL) AND ((Pt.Row # Row) OR (Pt.Colm # Col)) DO
       P := Pt.Link;
   END;
   RETURN P;
   ```

2. There is no change in the coding of the ValueOf function.

3. ValueOf would have the one statement RETURN Data [Row, Col];
   SetValue would have the one statement Data [Row, Col] := Given.

Section 8.5   Exercises 5–8 are NA

1. The body of JoinStr (VAR Result: Strng; First, Second: Strng):
   ```
   MakeStr (Result, Firstt.Size + Secondt.Size);
   FOR K := 1 TO Firstt.Size DO
       Resultt.Item [K] := Firstt.Item [K];
   END;
   FOR K := Firstt.Size + 1 TO Firstt.Size + Secondt.Size DO
       Resultt.Item [K] := Secondt.Item [K — Firstt.Size];
   END;
   ```

2. Replace the body of JoinStr by the following:
   ```
   IF Firstt.Size + Secondt.Size > MaxSize THEN
       Write ('Implementation fails');
       WriteLn;
   ELSE
       NEW (Result);
       Resultt.Size := Firstt.Size + Secondt.Size;
       ... the two FOR statements in the answer to Exercise 1
   END;
   ```

```
3. IF (First = NIL) AND (Second = NIL) THEN
       RETURN 0;
   ELSIF First = NIL THEN
       RETURN -1;
   ELSE
       RETURN 1;
   END;
4. Put the following statements at the beginning of the coding:
   IF (Pos = 0) OR (Pos > Result↑.Size) THEN
       RETURN;
   END;
   IF HowMany > Result↑.Size + 1 - Pos THEN
       HowMany := Result↑.Size + 1 - Pos;
   END;
```

Section 8.6   Exercises 5–6 are NA

1. X = {1,5,8,9,10} and Y = {3,5,9,10}, so X+Y = {1,3,5,8,9,10}, X∗Y = {5,9,10}, X–Y = {1,8}, Y–X = {3}, and X∗{ } = { }.
2. X must be a subset of Y.
3. The body of Delete is Data↑[Elt] := FALSE.
   The body of Destroy is DISPOSE (Data).
   The body of IsThere is RETURN Data↑[Elt].
4. FOR K := Loval TO Hival DO
       Data↑[K] := First↑[K] AND Second↑[K];
   END;

Section 8.7   Exercises 5–8 are NA

1. PROCEDURE PushInfo (TheInfo : Information; Data : List) : List;
          (∗ Return the result of pushing TheInfo on Data ∗)
       VAR
           P : List;
       BEGIN
           NEW (P);
           P↑.Info := TheInfo;
           P↑.Left := None;
           P↑.Right := Data;
           RETURN P;
       END PushInfo;
2. PROCEDURE Popped (Data : List) : List;
          (∗ Return the result of popping the first value
              from the nonempty Data ∗)
       VAR
           P : List;
       BEGIN
           P := Data↑.Right;
           DISPOSE (Data);
           RETURN P;
       END Popped;
3. IF NOT IsEmpty (Data) AND NOT IsEmpty (RestOf (Data)) AND
           ContainsInfo (RestOf (Data)) THEN
       TheInfo := FirstInfo (RestOf (Data));
   END;
4. The body of ReplaceFirstInfo could be:
       Data↑.Left := None;
       Data↑.Info := TheInfo;
   The body of ReplaceFirstList could be:
       Data↑.Left := TheList;
```
```

BIBLIOGRAPHY

Aho, A. V., J. E. Hopcroft, and J. D. Ullman: *Data Structures and Algorithms*, Addison–Wesley, Reading, Mass., 1983.

Brinch Hansen, P.: *Brinch Hansen on Pascal Compilers*, Prentice–Hall, Englewood Cliffs, N.J., 1985.

Dijkstra, E. W.: *A Discipline of Programming*, Prentice–Hall, Englewood Cliffs, N.J., 1976.

Folk, M. J., and B. Zoellick: *File Structures: A Conceptual Toolkit*, Addison–Wesley, Reading, Mass., 1987.

Ford, G. A., and R. S. Wiener: *Modula-2: A Software Development Approach*, Wiley, New York, 1985.

Hughes, J. K., and J. I. Michtom: *A Structured Approach to Programming*, Prentice–Hall, Englewood Cliffs, N.J., 1977.

Jones, W. C.: *Modula-2: Problem Solving and Programming with Style*, Wiley, New York, 1987.

Kernigan, B. W., and P. L. Plauger: *The Elements of Programming Style*, 2nd ed., McGraw–Hill, New York, 1974.

Knuth, D. E.: *The Art of Computer Programming. Volume 1: Fundamental Algorithms*, 2nd ed., Addison–Wesley, Reading, Mass., 1973.

Knuth, D. E.: *The Art of Computer Programming. Volume 3: Sorting and Searching*, Addison–Wesley, Reading, Mass., 1973.

Ledgard, H. F.: *Programming Proverbs*, Hayden, New York, 1975.

McNaughton, R.: *Elementary Computability, Formal Languages, and Automata*, Prentice–Hall, Englewood Cliffs, N.J., 1982.

Meek, B., and P. Heath (eds): *Guide to Good Programming Practice*, Horwood, New York, 1980.

Singh, B., and T. L. Naps: *Introduction to Data Structures*, West, St. Paul, Minn., 1984.

Tenebaum, A. M., and M. J. Augenstein: *Data Structures Using Pascal*, 2nd ed., Prentice–Hall, Englewood Cliffs, N.J., 1986.

Van Tassel, D.: *Program Style, Design, Efficiency, Debugging, and Testing*, 2nd ed., Prentice–Hall, Englewood Cliffs, N.J., 1978.

Wilensky, R.: *Common LISPcraft*, Norton, New York, 1986.

Wirth, N.: *Algorithms and Data Structures*, Prentice–Hall, Englewood Cliffs, N.J., 1986.

Wirth, N.: *Programming in Modula-2*, 3rd ed., Springer Verlag, New York, 1985.

Zelkowitz, M. V., A. C. Shaw, and J. D. Gannon: *Principles of Software Engineering and Design*, Prentice–Hall, Englewood Cliffs, N.J., 1979.

SUBJECT INDEX